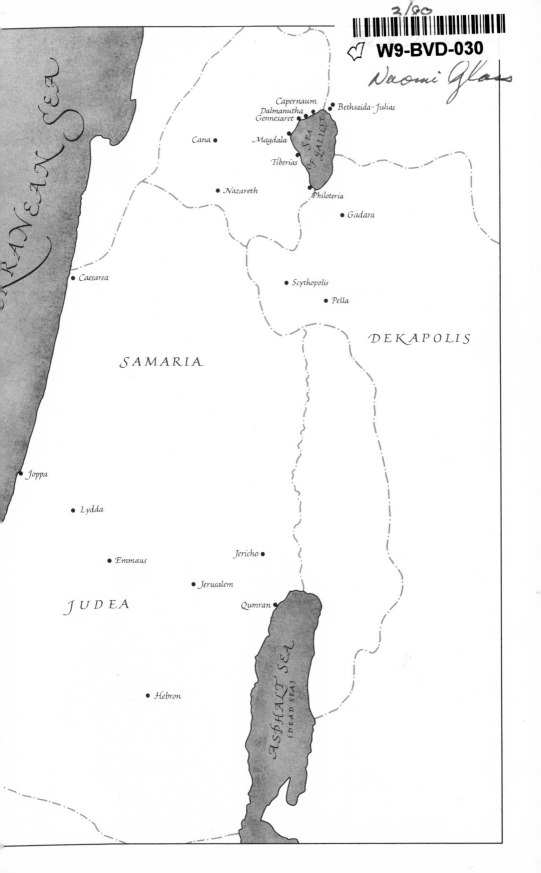

UPON
THIS
ROCK

ALSO BY WALTER F. MURPHY

The Vicar of Christ
The Roman Enigma

UPON THIS ROCK

THE LIFE OF ST. PETER

WALTER F. MURPHY

MACMILLAN PUBLISHING COMPANY | NEW YORK

Macmillan Publishing Company
866 Third Avenue, New York, N.Y. 10022
Collier Macmillan Canada, Inc.

The excerpts from Leviticus and Isaiah are taken from the
New American Bible, copyright © 1970 by the Confraternity of Christian
Doctrine, Washington, D.C. 20005. All rights reserved.

"Sing a New Song," words and music by Daniel L. Schutte,
S.J., copyright © 1972, 1974 by Daniel L. Schutte. Published
exclusively by North American Liturgy Resources,
Phoenix, Arizona. All rights reserved.

Library of Congress Cataloging-in-Publication Data
Murphy, Walter F., 1929–
Upon this rock.
1. Peter, the Apostle, Saint—Fiction.   2. Bible.
N.T. History of Biblical events—Fiction.   I. Title.
PS3563.U763.U6   1987   813'.54   87-15896
ISBN 0-02-588270-8

10 9 8 7 6 5 4 3 2 1

Designed by Jack Meserole

Endpaper maps:
Cartography by Lisa T. Davis
Calligraphy by Jerry Kelly

PRINTED IN THE UNITED STATES OF AMERICA

To my sister Jean

Contents

Note to the Reader

Writing about early Christianity is somewhat like walking blind-folded through a minefield. The age has been so strewn with popular mythology for which there is scant scriptural basis—Mary of Magdala was a prostitute, for example—that we inject those stories into the gospels and expect them to be repeated in what we read about the period.

Moreover, the gospels differ among themselves on details that are critical for understanding the early church. For instance, only the account ascribed to Luke in Acts of the Apostles says that, after the crucifixion, the apostles took up long residence in Jerusalem, where they often saw the risen Master; and Luke alone reports the miracle of Pentecost. Matthew has the apostles return more or less immediately to Galilee, where they see Jesus. John, the only gospel whose author explicitly claims to be an eyewitness to the events, reports the "disciples"—he never uses the word "apostle" or "apostles"—stayed at least eight days in Jerusalem. Then, in an appendix probably added by another writer, this gospel records a resurrection appearance at the Sea of Galilee. The early version of Mark, the gospel first written, reports no post-resurrection appearances at all. He says the young man at the tomb ordered the women to tell Peter and the others that Jesus had gone to Galilee and that they would see him there.

Paul, in his first letter to the Corinthians, written perhaps twenty years before Mark, offers a cryptic but somewhat different picture from those of the gospels and Acts.

These sorts of inconsistencies do not subvert the truth of the basic story, but they do make it difficult to weave a coherent narrative faithful to Christian tradition. For there is not one but at least five such traditions of the resurrection. Other happenings present similar, though less central, differences.

There is also the matter of chronology. The gospels and Acts were written long after the events they describe, Mark no earlier than 70 C.E. and John in its final form perhaps as late as 100 C.E. And all are much more theologies than histories. None has much regard for systematic, chronological arrangement. Even Acts, the book of the New Testament closest to a modern history, reports in consecutive sentences, as if they followed hard upon each other, events that must have been separated by months or even years.

Dating poses similar problems. John differs radically from the other three in setting the time of crucifixion. Because he is the most knowledgeable about Jewish ritual, I have followed his reckoning, and put the date at 30 C.E. Still, not even John's narration of the last week of Jesus' life perfectly fits Jewish Law and custom, which required two trials before a man could be sentenced to death and would not have allowed the Sanhedrin to meet on the eve of Passover (Friday of the year 30). Using the Essenes' calendar, which Jesus may well have done, makes the chronology more, but still not exactly, compatible with the gospels' varying accounts of the circumstances surrounding the crucifixion.

The time of Peter's death is easier to calculate. If he was killed in Nero's persecution that followed the great Roman fire (and we have only a pious tradition that this is so, no scriptural or other contemporary or near-contemporary sources), then his martyrdom occurred in the summer of 64 C.E. Discerning dates between the crucifixion and Peter's death involves much guesswork. To help the reader keep track of chronology, I have put approximate times at the beginning of each part of this book.

Language complicates matters. Although ordinary people in Galilee and Judea used Aramaic for daily discourse, the gospels, Acts, and Paul's epistles are written in Greek, the *lingua franca* of the Mediterranean world. Moreover, many people who speak English associate Scripture with the magisterial prose of the King James translation. In fact, however, much of the New Testament is quite colloquial in style. Indeed, Mark's rather bad Greek embarrassed educated Christians. In sum, the beauty of the King James version and more modern translations leads us to expect these people to have spoken like Semitic Shakespeares; but they probably talked more like uneducated people usually do, colorful in idiom, with minimal respect for nuanced phrasing and technical rules of grammar. I have retained some of the colloquial aspect of their language but with regard for proper grammatical usage.

The situation is no clearer when we come to measurements of weight and length. A cubit, for example, may have signified as many as six different lengths, depending on the context in which the word was used. Measurement of time is similarly confused. As indicated above, there was no standard calendar, even within Jewish society. Thus, to spare the reader the agonies of reading tedious footnotes to explain all these variations, I have used modern terminology, such as miles for distance, and pounds and tons for weights. I have also called the days of the week by our names and divided the year by seasons rather than months.

Cultural biases add to our difficulties in reading the literature of first-century Christianity. It is worth noting, for it is often skipped over, that Matthew, John, and the later version of Mark report the first resurrection appearances as being experienced by women. And early in the second century, Pliny the Younger writes to the emperor about torturing Christian ministers who are women. Later in that century, a large literature develops extolling the prominent role of women in the apostolic church and deploring their subsequent degrading. Mary of Magdala is one of the heroines of these writings, emerging as a woman of great moral strength.

As a scholar, I find such problems frustrating. As a novelist I find them fascinating and even useful, for only by creative imagination can we make sense of what really happened. I make no claim to having captured ultimate truth, to having finally discovered the "historical Peter" buried beneath the few paragraphs of the New Testament that allude to his life. I have tried to reconstruct what seems to me to be the best fit between what we "know" and what actually happened to those people, who, though suffering from all the weaknesses humans share, managed to spread a set of ideals across and beyond the Roman Empire.

Because of them, with all their flaws along with their wonders, large portions of this planet have never been quite the same again. They brought visions of a "new heaven and a new earth." It is, I think, worth suspending disbelief to try to reenter their world, to share their pain and glimpse their glory.

W. F. M.
Princeton, N.J.
June 28, 1987

Prologue
(Sixty-Four Years after
the Master's Crucifixion)

We stopped. We had to. We had been traveling since dusk of the previous night and now it was almost dusk again. Simon Peter could have trudged straight through the second night. Fear was pushing him like the huge wind of the storm at our backs, making his sweat reek and infusing him with energy that surpassed what we others could muster. I think he would have driven us until we dropped. It was Jephthania, Jephthania the Silent, who caused us to stop. Not that she complained. She could not, and she would not had she been able to speak. But the three brothers from Rome who were carrying her were completely exhausted. Simon Peter spelled them, despite his years, carrying his frail daughter on his thick, still heavily muscled shoulders. The brothers themselves took turns, two at a time; but our pace had been too fast, our rests too few.

The lightning was flicking at our heels like flashes of an angry asp's tongue, and black thunder was slapping closer and closer behind us. It was early August and Latium expected—and needed— the kind of deluge those thick clouds were pushing on top of us. Sensible people were snug in their homes or shops. Obviously, we were not sensible people, but we saw some hope of shelter several dozen paces off the road. It was wise to stop now, rather than to have the brothers faint from exhaustion or all of us sicken from exposure. The Romans might change their minds about letting us escape. If they did, they would expect us to be running for Ostia, trying to find a ship bound for the East or any ship sailing immediately, as the legate who engineered our escape had suggested. But, where escapes were concerned, Simon Peter had a shrewd instinct, an instinct that, no doubt, explained how he had survived as a guerrilla fighting in the hills of northeastern Galilee against the

Herodians, that awful Passover time in Jerusalem, the persecutions in Judea, the troubles in Antioch, and still later the missions to Asia and Greece. That instinct for survival was also why we were now southeast of Rome itself, running rather than being coated with tar and tied to crosses on Vatican Hill, impatiently waiting to provide light for Nero's night.

Simon Peter had decided that we would avoid Ostia. We started out that way, but once outside the city had swung around and were now on the Appian Way, intending to burrow ourselves into the mountains of south central Italy. The Romans would never think we would dare use a road so heavily trampled by imperial traffic from the Eternal City to Brundisium and the Eastern world.

We made it to the farm only moments before the storm smashed over our heads. It was easy to see why the house had been abandoned. The front wall was crumbling; the left side was a gaping wound that gave the wind license to flog us; and the roof sent water cascading down from a half dozen places. But it would serve. Anything would serve better than the open road. From one corner of the ruins, I could hear Naomi's words. From my other account, you recognize their source: "Foxes have dens, and the birds of the air have nests, but the friends of the Son of Man have nowhere to lay their heads."

The brothers gently placed Jephthania in a dry place and opened their knapsacks to share with us some heavy brown bread and vinegary yellow wine. I ate greedily, as did the women and the brothers; we were famished from the ordeal of escape.

Simon Peter ate nothing. He contented himself with huge swallows of sour wine. He was no longer the awkward, sometimes drunken Galilean peasant whose Greek was no more than pidgin and whose Aramaic was that of a country bumpkin. Now, thanks to my tutelage, his spoken Greek was fluent, at times even eloquent. He could not read much or write anything, of course. Wisely, he generally left those tasks to me—and less wisely, on occasion, to John Mark.

Simon Peter's hair was thinner, less tightly curled, and mostly white, yet still laced with strands of ebony, a far cry from that wild mass of disheveled black that I had first seen along the Jordan three dozen years earlier. Nor was his beard that earlier dense jungle of matted wire that had seldom felt a razor's edge. Our stint in prison had left him unkempt; but years before his arrest he had become carefully barbered (even lightly perfumed) in the Greek manner, or at least in the manner of those Jews who scattered along the Mediterranean and adopted our higher civilization. Even there in the Roman hill country, with the rain turning the dirt of prison and road into rivulets of mud running down his face and arms, one could sense the moral power in his massive frame. Now he had an aura about him—*gravitas*, the Romans would have called it—as well as an understanding of the world.

This was the man the Master had chosen to lead us. This was the man who had so often failed in that task, but also had so often succeeded. He had founded the community at Jerusalem, kept on good terms with that community even after James had ousted him from leadership, unified the communities at Antioch despite the quarrels of James and Paul and Barnabas, founded communities in Asia and Greece, nourished communities in Galilee and Corinth, and tried to unite the communities in Rome. It was in this last that he had failed so miserably. The penalty was betrayal, arrest, escape—at a fearful price—and once more being the terrified quarry of a ruthless government. At this moment the Master's living followers still looked to Simon Peter for leadership. When the news of the price he had paid for his escape spread, he would rival Judas in Christian infamy.

Simon Peter was bearing that burden with ill grace, but I do not suppose many men bear the brand of coward with pride. He stood in the open doorway, his back turned to us, watching the lightning slash at the murky sky that had shrouded us. The rain beat on his face, but he felt nothing. His eyes were open, but he saw nothing. He did not so much as twitch when a crackling axe of lightning splintered a tree not a hundred yards distant. I mis-speak. He was seeing something, but nothing in our world. His eyes were focused a thousand miles and thirty-four years away. He was reliving a spring afternoon outside of Jerusalem. He had run away that day, too; and then he had also halted to escape the rage of a storm.

*   *   *

I am Quintus: Greek through my mother's culture, Roman by my father's blood, would-be philosopher by my choice, Christian by the Holy Spirit's will. This is not my first book. Earlier I recorded the Master's life. As I recounted there, much of what I wrote was what I saw. Simon Peter gave me additional details, as did Mary of Magdala, Andrew, and the others, including John the son of Zebedee and the other John—John the priest, the disciple whom the Master loved. (I have heard that he grows old in Ephesus and prepares *his* account of the Master's life. And, like many old men, he no doubt remembers what he wishes had happened as much as what actually happened. I am grateful that is not among my faults.)

Never having had the gift of eloquence, I could not preach. Never having been strong, I could not offer physical support. But I was there, first as Quintus the doubting God Fearer, more curious than believing, then as Quintus the distant follower of the Master, later as Quintus the philosopher who wanted to believe more than he believed, and finally as Quintus the Greek who tried to make up for his dearth of faith through works. I was there: in Galilee, in Judea, and in Samaria, in Antioch and the rest of Asia, in Greece, and now in Italy.

I saw it happen, all of it. I have felt the Holy Spirit's fiery touch and the icy grasp of the Evil One. And I can remember it clearly, all of it. And I can write about it clearly—not elegantly, perhaps, but accurately in prose that intelligent readers can comprehend without suspicions about hidden meaning and refractions of imagery. That has been my contribution to spreading the good news of the kingdom of God: a lucid history of the Master's ministry. I do not write the decorated poems of my gentile cousins or the rhythmic prayers of Jewish psalmists, but an account that is as true to life as a Greek sculpture.

The *Book of Quintus*, or Q, as the communities call it, has been the means of spreading the Master's message throughout the civilized world, the source of his teachings. Where Greek is read, my words, *his words*, are also read. Others may edit those words and claim them for their own; but they are *his* words and, through me, the world's.

Having written of the Master, I turn to his servant, to Simon Peter, the quivering Rock, the affirming denier, the cowardly hero. If I am correct that the Master's return is not a single future event but a process that began shortly after the crucifixion and will never cease, then his work will have to be carried on not only by those who, like Paul, are zealously righteous or, like James, righteously zealous. That work must also be carried on—mainly must also be carried on—by those who, like Simon Peter, know how to survive, because they themselves are survivors; who sympathize with cowards because they themselves are cowards; who understand the terrors that shake the poor in spirit and paralyze the downtrodden because they themselves are poor in spirit, downtrodden, and shake with terror. If these people are heroes, it is as much because of what they suffer as because of what they achieve.

In his own way, quite different from that of Paul, Simon Peter was a leader and a creator. He was the great bridge builder, uniting the faith of Abraham, Isaac, and Moses with the fulfillment of their words among their own people as well as among the gentiles. Yet he was also, as Scripture has it, "an obstacle and a stumbling block to both the houses of Israel"—and also to many houses of gentiles. For his patience was short and heavily tinged with impetuousness, his steadfast faith tinted with fear, even panic, his love colored with resentful envy, his virtue corrupted by the flesh, his courage tainted by cowardice. Sometimes his judgment was rash, sometimes it was timid, often it was flatly bad. But always, no matter how often he failed, he could recapture his vision of the Master and the sense of his own mission. Always, always, that is, until now. Now he was once again running, fleeing martyrdom, denying the Master.

I
PASSOVER
(30–37 C.E.)

1

❖ I, too, could call up from that spring the ghosts who haunted Simon Peter. Those shades were simple and they were complex, dancing in a Jerusalem that now sometimes seems dreamlike and yet at other times more real than the warmth of today's sunshine.

The city and its surrounding area were jammed with pilgrims. All adult, male Jews are under moral obligation to make every reasonable effort to come to Jerusalem to celebrate the three great feasts; and Passover is the greatest of these. The influx of believers always at least triples, sometimes quadruples, the town's usual population of less than 50,000. People come from Arabia, Armenia, Asia, Greece, Italy, Persia, and Syria; from Babylon, Antioch, Ephesus, Tarsus, Alexandria, Athens, and even as far west as Cyrene and Rome itself.

The turmoil generated by the construction of a new aqueduct, the continuing work on Herod's temple, the babble of crowds pushing and shoving through the narrow streets, talking, joking, bargaining, disputing, and cursing in a dozen tongues, made Jerusalem a threatening city to a foreigner. The feast itself added to the hostile atmosphere, for Passover commemorates the liberation of Jews from Egyptian bondage. And on the city's walls as well as above the mighty Temple itself, fully armed Roman soldiers, all too tangible evidence of a new form of bondage, stared disdainfully down at the pilgrims.

The Jews were restless under Roman rule, though no more so that year than was usually the case. As a precautionary measure, Pontius Pilate, Prefect of Judea, had left his capital at Caesarea and come to Jerusalem with additional troops, ready to stamp out, with typical Roman ruthlessness and efficiency, even the slightest hint of sedition against Caesar.

Our week—it was to be our final week with the Master—began with a triumphal procession into the city. An hour before noon on

3

a magnificently bright, cool spring morning, the Master had arrived at the Essene Gate, which pierces the southern wall. A few
dozen followers were waiting for us. They had laid down palm
branches, some had even stretched out their cloaks to mark a
path. The Master entered the city riding sidesaddle on a dull
brown donkey. For a Roman that would have been a humble not a
regal arrival. To Jews, however, it had special significance, for the
prophet Zechariah had written:

> Rejoice in your heart, O daughter Zion, shout for joy,
>   O daughter Jerusalem!
> See, your king shall come to you; a just savior is he,
> Meek, and riding on an ass, on a colt, the foal of an
>   ass. . . . [And]
> His dominion shall be from sea to sea. . . .

At most other times of the year, the entry would have been
barely noticed, but at Passover any out-of-the-way happening attracts a huge audience. Soon several hundred people were gaping
at us. I heard names ripple through the crowd—"healer," "wonder
worker," "John the Baptizer," then the darkly ominous word "Messiah." Some of the pilgrims recognized the symbolism of the
donkey and began shouting, "Blessed is the King of Israel!" Others
along the narrow streets took up the chant: "Hail, Son of David!
Hail, King of Israel."

Hearing those words, the crowd quickly turned into a happy mob.
Soon, there was no street at all; what little space there was between
the buildings became a mass of shouting people, most of them trying
to embrace the Master or at least get close enough to touch him.
Simon Peter was leading the donkey by the bridle, his brother
Andrew was on his right. The two of them were good-naturedly pushing ahead against the tide of people, grinning as they accepted hugs
and congratulations. The rest of us closed around the Master to keep
him from being crushed. Despite all the shoving, the disciples were
enjoying themselves immensely. As sweet as honey, the anticipation
of princedom was in their mouths and running down their beards.

I was to the right rear of the donkey, next to John, the son of
Zebedee. "Now we will establish the kingdom!" he shouted in my

ear, trying to be heard above the din. "Do you think the Master
will lead the people to storm the Roman garrison or will he call on
a legion of angels?"

It was a stupid question, but one completely in keeping with
John's mentality—and that of his brother James and any of the
other Twelve, except perhaps Levi and Judas. Still, I was sufficiently unsure of the Master's reaction to the crowd's sudden and
volatile adulation that I looked at his unsmiling face before I
shook my head *no*.

I was deeply troubled. As a Roman citizen who was half Greek,
half Roman by blood and fully Greek by culture, I was not a
supporter of Jewish nationalism. Indeed, I had initially steered
well clear of the Master and his followers because I thought they
were just another group of Jewish revolutionaries, and I knew
enough recent history to understand that these movements tended
to impale themselves on Roman lances. I had learned better about
the Master's teaching, but many of the disciples had not. Nor had
the mob that was pushing on us.

It took us no less than fifteen minutes to make our way a
hundred yards to an open square. There the Master grabbed the
halter from Simon Peter, kicked the donkey, and trotted up the
hill. Simon Peter was surprised, but he realized the Master was
trying to escape and, running to the narrow exit from the square,
tried to hold the mob back. The rest of us rallied around him. We
were successful, though only for the few moments it took the
Master to lose himself in another maze of twisting streets.

Confused and disappointed by the Master's apparent spurning
of his royal role, the disciples tried to find our rendezvous at the
pool of Siloam in the Lower City. Our progress was slow, not only
because of the crowds that packed the streets but also because
Simon Peter insisted on leading us. He scarcely knew Jerusalem,
but that ignorance did not incline him to listen to my directions
or those of Judas. The result was an extended tour of the Upper
City that took us past the palace of Caiaphas, the High Priest, and
even to the edge of Herod's palace that the Romans were using as
a praetorium. When we arrived at the pool, the Master had long
been there and was impatient at our delay.

As the others slaked their thirst, I found myself next to him. He offered me a cup of water. I gulped it down, then tried to warn him of the danger of the mob's arousing the Romans by calling him king and son of David. He looked at me for a moment before making a strange reply: "If the crowds had been silent, the very stones would have cried out."

My life of the Master speaks in considerable detail about those next days. I shall only summarize them here. As you recall, the Master's first visit to the Temple sealed his fate far more tightly than his disputes with teachers of the Law, for Jews enjoy debate as much as we Greeks do. They tend to be both savage against arguments with which they disagree and tolerant of those, at least if they are also Jews, who espouse them. But the Master did more than debate.

He was anxious to go to the Temple to make his offering the very afternoon of the entry. I had a sense of foreboding, no doubt a residue from the morning's near riot. Nevertheless, I broke my usual rule and decided to accompany the group. We would, the Master said, go only to the Court of the Gentiles.

The pool was in the southeastern part of Jerusalem, the Temple in the east-central sector. To visualize the city, one should understand that it is built on a pair of hills, coming together at the top to form a V opening toward the south. They are separated by the Valley of the Cheesemakers, a cut on whose steep sides the poorer people had built homes.

The more westerly hill is the higher, and here the town is known as the Upper City. But the eastern hill is where David first built his settlement, and it is here that Solomon and then centuries later Herod the Great, the father of Herod Antipas, constructed their temples.

I must tell you in some detail about Herod's Temple, for it figured prominently in both the Master's and Simon Peter's lives. More than fifty years earlier, Herod had decided to build a Temple more magnificent than Solomon's, which the Babylonians had burned before taking the Jews into captivity. In a move saturated in irony, he imported Roman engineers to settle problems of technical design and execution.

The undertaking was stupendous. Engineers smoothed off the knob on which the old temple had been located. But Herod had not been content to build on a hill; he turned that hill into a mountain. He laid a foundation that was massive: One of the short sides is almost 800 feet in length, the other 900 feet; the longer sides, those that went generally north and south, run for almost 1,500 feet. At places on the northwestern side, the Temple walls and platform rise only sixty feet; but on the southeast, overlooking the Kidron Valley across to the Mount of Olives and the garden at Gethsemane, they soar more than 200 feet above the surrounding ground.

But, just as the Temple and its hill dominate the city to the south, west, and east, so the Fortress Antonia to the north dominates the Temple. It is, for that reason, always occupied by Roman troops; and, as usual at a feast, they were making themselves martially evident.

The Temple's foundation is constructed of huge stones. Most weigh four to six tons, but some as much as 400 tons. And these were not simply laid together. Each stone visible to the eye was carefully carved so that there is an aesthetically pleasing raised portion in the center; and every stone was chiseled on top and bottom so that each faces cleanly into the one above and below it. The joining is so close that even the Iscarii would have difficulty inserting knife blades between the stones. Of course, given the weight and closeness of fit, there was no need for mortar.

In his effort to outdo Solomon, Herod had spared neither his subjects' money nor their sweat and blood. His successors followed his example. Yet it was, as far as I could determine, a popular undertaking. The work was completely accomplished by free labor. No slaves were ever employed. Gifts from Jews around the world augmented what the Herodians and their chief priests could steal and squeeze from Judean and Galilean Jews as well as those on pilgrimage. Even the priests performed manual labor. Because it would have profaned the more sacred precincts to have been constructed by unclean hands, more than a thousand priests

learned the requisite trades and did much of the interior work
themselves.

The Temple itself is largely of stone because of its strength,
longevity, and availability. Jerusalem sits among limestone quarries. Indeed, the city's foundations are honeycombed by tunnels
and galleries from which rock has been stripped for walls and
buildings. The men, animals, and machinery that dragged huge
blocks—some of them more than sixty feet in length—through
and around the city not only jammed the narrow streets and
completely sealed off all traffic but also, in some cases, required
entire squares to be razed to clear a passage.

The top of the Temple mount covers thirty-five square acres.
Stairs link it to the Antonia and the city's northern sector. A
bridge over the Valley of the Cheesemakers connects the Temple
to the upper or western part of the city. Enclosing the entire
hilltop is a colonnade, some forty-five feet wide, supported by
double columns of pure white marble thirty-seven and one-half
feet high. Within is the huge Court of the Gentiles, where, as its
name indicates, non-Jews can enter, subject to the jurisdiction of
the Temple guards.

Almost at the center of the Court of Gentiles is the raised and
walled area of the inner courts, and within those the Temple
building itself. These are set off from the Gentiles by a stone
balustrade, four and a half feet high. An uncircumcised male who
crosses that barrier takes his life in his hands. The Romans,
always sensitive to matters religious, though in the case of the
Jews usually quite baffled, allow the chief priests to impose the
death penalty on trespassers. In all fairness, the risks are clear. At
various points on the balustrade warnings are carved in stone in
both Greek and in Latin:

> No foreigner is to enter within the balustrade and
> enclosure around the Temple area. Whoever is caught
> will have himself to blame for his death which will
> follow.

Of the Temple building itself I cannot speak from firsthand
knowledge, since I have never entered it. It stands 150 feet high

and measures thirty by ninety feet in area. Its outside façade of marble is trimmed with gold. Around its roof are pointed gratings of gold, the tops of all the columns in the inner court are faced with gold, and two completely gilded. Inside, John the priest told me, it is even more heavily adorned with gold and embroidered tapestries. The beams are of cedar, brought all the way from the Lebanon, as is the paneling in the ceilings of the colonnades. The building is divided into several storeys and chambers. One contains the altar on which the blood of sacrifices is poured, a slab twenty-two feet high, fashioned without the use of iron. The most sacred chamber is the Holy of Holies, a veiled room that no one except the High Priest can enter, and he only for a few minutes on the Day of Atonement. By law, John the priest, the disciple whom the Master loved best, said it is empty.

Near the southwestern corner of the Temple, a huge set of stairs runs down into the Valley of the Cheesemakers, allowing entrance into the lower levels of the mount. It is here, in the bowels of the Temple, that most of the merchants sell bread and small animals for the cultic sacrifices. It is also here that the money changers set up their tables. Roman coins are imprinted with images of Caesar or other notables or even pagan deities and thus violate the First Commandment. While under the Empire one has little choice but to use such money in everyday life, Jews cannot use it for holy purposes. For a price, the bankers exchange profane Roman money for unpolluted coins.

Pilgrims have to make the long climb up from the Valley of the Cheesemakers to go into that lower level, change their money, make their purchases, and then walk back down the stone stairs, trudge south around the corner of the Temple mount, and then reascend from the southern side to present their offerings to the priests.

On great feasts this arcane routing creates chaos, as thousands of people try to get in and out of the bankers' hall. Pushing, shoving, pickpocketing, and shortchanging by the bankers often cause tempers to flare. Violence is not uncommon, and consequently there is, whenever a great crowd is expected, a large contingent of Temple guards on duty in the area.

*   *   *

We set out for the Temple after only a brief rest. In all there were perhaps twenty of us. We made slow progress through the crowded streets to the Valley of the Cheesemakers, then pushed our way up the long flight of stairs into the hall of the merchants and bankers. It is a rectangular chamber, perhaps fifty feet wide and 200 feet long, lit by oil lamps suspended by iron hooks from its low ceiling.

Inside, the din was nerve-shattering. Thousands of other pilgrims were shuffling in and out, talking to one another, bargaining with—and sometimes cursing at—dozens of money changers and merchants. The clank of coins was incessant, as was the huckstering of merchants or bankers whose stalls were not busy. Several thousand doves were cooing and hundreds of lambs bleating pitifully for their mothers. Periodically, guards banged their staffs on the stone floor, vainly calling for order.

The smell added to the oppressiveness. The place must have always been heavy with the dank odor of mildew, for the hall gets no sunlight, and its walls, floor, and ceiling are all thick stone. But now the air was also rife with the acrid aroma of unwashed pilgrims and the urine and feces that the animals shamelessly and continuously deposited on the floor.

Just inside the entrance, the Master stopped abruptly. Suddenly, I saw a stranger born. His face turned crimson and his eyes seemed to shoot fiery darts of rage, first at the bankers whose benches were lined up along one side of the hall, then at the animal sellers lined up along the other. He snatched a rope from one of the merchants, knotted it several times, then leaped up onto the nearest banker's table.

"You swine!" he shouted, "this is a house of prayer, but you have turned it into a den of thieves!" With that he let out a long, blood-curdling yell that I can only describe as a battle cry, and, jumping from table to table with the agility of a mountain goat, began to flay away at the bankers. Those worthies shrieked in anger and shouted to the guards for help.

It was too late. Coins were spilling on the floor and people in the crowd raced to pick them up. Others tried to take advantage of the confusion to help themselves to what was on the bankers' tables. Still others preferred another sort of revenge for their annual fleecing and began turning over the tables and physically assaulting the money changers and animal sellers who they believed had robbed them.

The hall turned to mad chaos. People were shouting in glee, in anger, and in agony as they scooped up coins, wrestled with each other over coppers, tipped over tables, punched bankers, or tried to kick their way clear of the thick gravy of moving, biting, clawing bodies. Men carrying lambs on their shoulders were knocked down and lost the animals. Worse, several merchants panicked and lost control of their beasts, allowing dozens of lambs to try to butt and bleat their way to freedom, while fifty or more doves flew around the low-ceilinged hall, desperately seeking a fluttering escape as they screamed and excreted on the heads of the mob. Had those not been human bones that were being broken and human teeth smashed, the scene would have been comic. But in its suffering it was sad, in its ramifications, tragic.

The guards, though reinforced for the feast, were unable to handle the rioting mob. They were quickly pushed into the back of the hall, near the door that exited deeper into the Temple's recesses. The violence rapidly spread beyond the hall onto the outside steps, as pilgrims, bankers, and merchants trying to escape the melee ran head-on into fresh pilgrims, who, after their hard climb up from the Valley of the Cheesemakers, did not respond charitably to being shoved back down the long stone stairs.

Simon Peter grabbed the Master with one hand and me with the other and pushed us toward the door leading to the steps. We were making some progress until an enraged banker caught hold of the Master. "Guards!" the man screamed. "Guards! Help me! I've got the thieving Galilean whore's son! Guards!" A heavy thud from a big fist transmitted Simon Peter's instantaneous reaction, and the stunned Judean reeled backward, swallowed in the rampaging mob. Grinning, Simon Peter somehow steered us through the dense human tide and onto the steps, where we carefully picked our way down. At the bottom, we had to leap aside to make way for a company of guards jogging up the stairs in lock-step to end the disturbance swiftly before the Romans stepped in and contaminated the Temple.

We and all our brethren escaped the melee with only bruises and torn clothing. But the long-range price would be enormous. Obviously, the Master had been recognized as he stood on the table. Worse, he would long be remembered. People do not forget a man who costs them that much money. And, although the Temple guards stopped the brawl before the Romans intervened, Pilate would have a full report shortly after Caiaphas received his. If either or both of them also heard about the Master's tumultuous entry at the Essene Gate in the morning, he was doomed. A prophet, even a Galilean prophet, might be tolerated if he spoke quietly and went home promptly, but a "king of Israel" who set off a near-riot in a triumphal entry into Jerusalem and only hours later led a full-scale riot against the Temple would have to be executed. Or he would have to escape quickly.

When we were safely back outside the walls on the slopes of the Mount of Olives, where we had camped the previous evening, I said as much to the Master and urged that we slip out of Jerusalem at dusk, spend the night in Bethany, only a short distance away, with Lazarus and his sisters, Martha and Mary, then start back to Galilee in the morning. He looked away from me at the city: "Jerusalem has always stoned those sent to save it and murdered its prophets." He was silent for a moment, then added in a flat voice: "For this I was born, for this I came into the world."

I was upset, not simply worried for the Master's safety or for my own—though I freely admit I was badly frightened. Rather, what little faith I had was beset by grave doubts. I feared that it was I and not the disciples or the crowds who had misread the Master's message. I could not help asking myself if Jerusalem had not transformed him into another, though more subtle, Jewish revolutionary aiming to oust the Romans and restore the kingdom to Israel. Deeply troubled, I left. I needed time and quiet in which to think.

2

❖ I did not have far to go. My home was in Scythopolis, a city near the Jordan, not far from the southern edge of the Lake of Galilee, but my family owns a villa on the northwestern outskirts of Jerusalem. I went there, far enough away to think in peace, close enough to return to the Temple within half an hour.

On my mother's side, I was descended from a long line of merchants. We were not as wealthy as some, but we were more than comfortable; to the dirt-poor peasants of Galilee and Judea, we seemed rich beyond imagination. Like most people who lived in the region of the Dekapolis, abutting the Land of Israel on the east, we wanted peace, enjoyed peace, and profited from peace. Peace allowed my uncles and cousins to run their fat caravans across the great trade routes. Peace allowed my father to hunt animals and women. Peace allowed my mother to weep undisturbed. And peace allowed me to study, to travel, to reflect, and to write. I felt no need to tempt death by joining some lunatic Jewish political faction.

After all, I was only a God Fearer, one who believed in the God of Abraham, Isaac, and Moses. I was not a Hebrew by blood, and I was not and am not—may the Most High bless Paul for that—circumcised. For me, Judaism's sole attraction was the purity and steadfastness of its belief in one God. I did not find its elaborate cultic code of ritual purity appealing, and I certainly was not seeking some sort of mystical reunion with my ancestors. Indeed, one of the stumbling blocks to my full conversion was the provincialism—the tribalism—of Jews of Judea and Galilee. It was in Alexandria, where I studied under Philo, the great Greco-Jewish philosopher, that I had first been drawn to Judaism. From him I learned a version of this faith that was universal, transcending tribe and nation. Philo's Judaism was Jewish in its monotheism but Greek in its vision, though even his followers counted returning to Jerusalem for Passover as one of life's sweeter dreams.

Here, nearer to home, I had difficulty in remaining a Greek and still sharing with Jews the one, true God, the omnipotent, just, yet loving father of all men. As a citizen of Scythopolis, the largest, most prosperous, and most cultured of the cities of the Dekapolis, I looked down on the inhabitants of Galilee and Judea as barely civilized. Samaritans, of course, did not even rise to that level. In my other work, I have written how the Master had gazed directly at me when he told that parable about the Samaritan who had lovingly befriended a stranger.

My father was a retired Roman Praefectus Castrorum, an honorable rank for a soldier. Thus while my culture is Greek, my name is Roman. My father was a newcomer to the Dekapolis, but my mother's family had come there many centuries before, when Scythopolis was only a cluster of Semitic villages called Beth Shean. Thus my ancestors had been in place before Alexander and his Macedonian barbarians swept across Asia and, by force of arms, spread their vulgar version of Greek—or, as we prefer, Hellenic—culture across the Eastern world.

But even in Alexander's day, our city had been no mean town. Situated in the Valley of the Jezreel above the west bank of the Jordan south of the Sea of Galilee, it has always been an important stop on the caravan routes between Damascus to the north and, to the south, Egypt and the kingdoms of Arabia. It is also on the east-west route between Babylon and the Mediterranean port you know as Ptolemais. That strategic location at the throat of trade is why my maternal ancestors, who were merchants from Athens, settled there.

On a map, our valley seems part of southeastern Galilee, but the people are a hodgepodge of Jews, Syrians, Greeks, Persians, Arabs, remnants of ancient Semites such as Philistines, and only the Most High knows what—not, of course, that Galilee's population is exclusively Jewish, only largely.

Almost four centuries ago, Alexander's generals, when they were dividing up his empire, allowed Scythopolis the status of a Greek city-state. Although lacking full political independence, we gained many cultural and economic privileges in exchange for fealty to Egypt or to Coele-Syria, depending on which group of

Alexander's successors was at the moment the more powerful. Our becoming a city-state and later, at Pompey's "suggestion," aligning ourselves with cities on the east bank of the Jordan to form the confederation called the Dekapolis meant increased trade and prosperity and so was popular with all our people, except the Jews. They, as always, wanted to be part of an independent Hebrew nation and were willing to sacrifice prosperity for politics.

Among my family's lore were lurid tales of exile during the period when the Jews, under the cruel Hasmonean John Hyrcanus, had temporarily driven out the Syrian Greeks and occupied Scythopolis. Thus I inherited only antipathy toward Jewish nationalism. Prudence reinforced that prejudice. For even in my lifetime several Jewish leaders have tried to organize resistance to Rome. Their careers have been short, their deaths long and painful.

I had come to believe that the Master's message was of a different order. That it was seditious was evident, but its sedition ran not only against Rome, perhaps not even principally against Rome, but against the ethics the world practiced. The Master preached loyalties and ethics that transcend self, family, tribe, city, nation, or empire; and he had set his face against all forms of violence—which made his outburst in the bankers' hall completely out of character.

Or had he taken on a new personality? That question was sorely troubling me. True, the Master had escaped the crowd that was proclaiming him king. That had been prudent. That rabble would have deserted him at the first encounter with a Roman patrol. But had his rejection been motivated only by prudence? His remark about the stones crying out was as bothersome as it was strange. His assault on the bankers—as much as they deserved whipping—was even more disturbing. I could not help wondering if it was a sign of his shifting from the role of peaceful prophet to militant messiah. For the leader of a riot against the money changers would be as popular with the crowds of pilgrims as he would be feared by the High Priest and his coterie.

Equally disquieting was the Master's last remark to me about Jerusalem's murdering its prophets and his apparent acceptance of such a violent end as his own destiny. That comment hinted at a deranged quest for death. The thought of his courting his own murder alarmed me as much as the possibility of the Master as a political messiah.

In retrospect, these concerns may seem foolish; but, lacking knowledge of the future, I found them frightening then. I needed solitude to think through them. The villa was empty except for guards and servants; its shady atrium and walled gardens provided a near-perfect place for meditation.

Sunday night I ate dinner, drank a bit too much wine, and went to bed. I spent Monday morning in our salon, the noontime in the garden, and the afternoon walking about. That night I again drank too much wine. By then I needed to stop thinking, at least for a few hours. I followed the same cycle on Tuesday.

Wednesday I awoke at dawn. My head was hurting, but not as much as my conscience. Guilt at deserting the Master had drowned both my intellectual doubts and, for the time being, my fear for his—and my own—safety. I was still troubled, but my guilt persuaded me that my earlier analysis of the peacefulness of the Master's message had been correct. At the same time, my mind insisted that something strange was happening to him—and so to us.

The Master had planned to go frequently to the Temple to speak to the pilgrims. Before Sunday's "events," that had seemed an ideal means of reaching thousands of people. Now, however, it would lead straight to disaster. Anyone who entered the Temple gates, even into the Court of the Gentiles, put himself under the jurisdiction of the chief priests. By Roman dispensation, they could administer their own justice and could even impose the death penalty.

My two uncles had told me something of the mentality of Caiaphas, the current High Priest; Annas, his father-in-law and former high priest; and their allies. Mostly Sadducees, these men were from wealthy, noble families who judged collaborating with Rome the lesser evil for Israel. If they knew about either of Sunday's events, Caiaphas and his friends would most probably arrest the Master when he was inside the Temple and "dispose" of him. Or, if they thought he was too popular with the people, help the Romans do their own dirty work—but outside the Temple.

I wanted to rejoin the Master but was not sure how to do so. On Friday evening before sundown we had camped on the Mount of Olives with several thousand other pilgrims. On the Sabbath we had taken the short walk, more or less within the permitted distance, to Bethany and visited Lazarus and his family. In the evening we had returned to the Mount of Olives, but had broken camp before entering Jerusalem on Sunday. Thus even if I managed to find the exact site again, the group might not still be there.

I decided to go to Lazarus's house and find out what he knew. His sisters Martha and Mary were there, along with Mary of Magdala and the Master's mother. The Master and the Twelve had celebrated the Passover meal with them the previous evening. (He, like Lazarus's family, followed the Essenes' calendar, which calculated Passover as always beginning at sundown on Tuesday rather than as a movable feast, like the Temple's calendar.) Lazarus's report of the evening was sparse, but it confirmed the mood of calm acceptance of violent death I had sensed.

Shortly after I arrived, John the priest came to the house looking for the Master. He had still more bad news. The chief priests had learned about both episodes on Sunday and had determined that the Master was a menace to peace. "It is better for one man to die for the people," John quoted Caiaphas, "than for the whole nation to be destroyed."

The Master's brazenness, however, had taken the chief priests aback. In the company of the Twelve and a few others, he had been spending his days in the Temple, preaching the Way to the pilgrims. And they were very receptive to his message, treating him like a hero for attacking the bankers. Thus, John reported, Caiaphas was proceeding very carefully, wary that arresting the Master in the Temple, where the priests had jurisdiction, might provoke yet another riot. And a disturbance in full view of the Roman sentries on the Antonia's walls could trigger swift pagan intervention and pollution of the Temple.

Although John disclaimed knowledge of Caiaphas's specific plans or even the extent to which the Romans would be directly involved, he was certain that unless the Master quickly left Judea, he would be arrested, imprisoned, and executed. I wanted to go to

Jerusalem immediately and warn him, and Mary of Magdala—always quick to decide and always as quick to defend her decisions— urged me to do so. The Master's mother, however, sat silent; and Lazarus said I should not go. His tone was resigned: "The Master knows the risks; I warned him last night. This is not the first time we've had such news."

"We're not talking about risks," I protested. "We're talking about a certainty."

"The Master knows that, too."

"Is he mad, then?" I blurted out, forgetting for the moment that his mother was there.

She cut me off before I could apologize: "I once thought that, Quintus, and went with several of his brothers to have him put away. By the Lord's standards, my son is quite sane, though he may be mad by man's standards."

Hers was a gentle, but not a particularly helpful, response. She was speaking from emotion, like a woman, not from evidence and reason, like a man. Yet my own three days of meditation had yielded nothing more substantial than an emotionally based belief that I had earlier read the Master's message correctly. I could not even pretend to understand what was happening now. I looked at John for guidance, even reflection; but he looked away and said nothing.

Lazarus answered my next question before I could ask it: "There is nothing you can do to help. If you went into the city and found the Master, you would only make the Romans think the 'conspiracy' had spread to the gentiles. Go back to your uncles' house. I'll send a messenger if I get news."

I went back to the villa and waited the rest of the day. Lazarus had said that on that night, Wednesday, the beginning of the second day of Passover according to the Essenes' calendar, the Master planned to celebrate that meal with his followers. But neither Lazarus nor the others knew where, other than that it would be some place in the Essene Quarter. Frustrated, I read some philosophy, wrote a letter to my sister, walked in the garden, and once again drank too much wine.

After midnight, in the small hours of Thursday, I was awakened by a banging at the gate. My head was fuzzy from wine and sleep, and, as I heard the guards talking, I started to slip back into unconsciousness. Then I vaguely realized they were trying to speak Aramaic. They were Syrian—they claimed, of course, to be Greek—and could get by in Aramaic, but the visitor's clotted Galilean accent was confusing them. Suddenly I recognized the voice and leaped out of bed. I had moved too fast and dizzily fell back again. After a few minutes I arose more slowly and went down into the garden, where the guards were still trying to decipher the man's patois.

It was Thaddaeus, one of the Twelve, a small man noticeable for his weakness even among the weak. His character provided a lovely touch of irony, for his name signifies "man of courage." His tunic was even more stained than usual. He was gasping for breath; whether because of too much running or too much fright, it was difficult to tell. But that rapid breathing did nothing to improve the quality of his usually slurred speech. As soon as he saw me, he blurted out, "They've taken the Master, Quintus! They attacked our camp and captured him!"

I quickly dismissed the guards and led Thaddaeus inside the house. There was always a lamp burning in the salon and a flagon of wine on the table. I motioned for him to help himself, while I stirred the fire to take some of the chill out of the air. He sat down heavily on the divan, his hand still trembling enough to spill some of the wine—fortunately it was white—on the silk cushions.

"All right, who took the Master?"

"Roman soldiers—and Temple guards," he added quickly. "I saw both. There were dozens of them. We had no chance. Judas led them to us. Our Judas!"

Perhaps *his* Judas, I thought, not mine; and "dozens" of guards probably meant six. But I curbed my tongue. "When did it happen?" I asked.

"Perhaps two or three hours ago, maybe four. I'm not sure. I ran, then I hid for a while, then I walked around the city. I wanted to go to Bethany, but I must have run the wrong way. When I got my bearings I was closer to your house."

"What did the guards do with the Master?"

"I don't know. He was off by himself with Simon Peter and John ben Zebedee. I saw Judas come up and kiss the Master, then the guards went straight for him. Simon Peter pulled out that sword he carries in his pack and cut one of the guards. He was going after another when the Master shouted something, and Simon Peter dropped the sword and ran away."

"And the Master?"

"He just stood there. They grabbed him and put ropes around him and began to drag him off. I ran before they could come after me."

"Who grabbed him, the Romans or the Temple guards?"

"I don't know. I couldn't tell. They were a distance away from me, and it all happened too fast."

"And the rest of the disciples?"

"They ran, too." He showed no shame but spoke as if deserting a friend was the most natural thing in the world. My father would have agreed. He always argued that it was precisely because courage was rare that soldiers needed harsh training and severe discipline.

"Did the guards get anyone else?"

"I don't think so—I don't know. Quintus . . ." Thaddaeus's voice broke into sobs. "What am I going to do?"

I felt superior, but only for a few seconds. I, too, feared violent death, and I would do my best to avoid it. "You can stay here for the time being." I did not want to make even that limited commitment, lest I compromise my uncles with the Jews or the Romans; but I could not turn that whimpering, shaking man out.

"Just for the night," Thaddaeus said. "Tomorrow I'll be on my way back to Galilee."

"I'm not sure that's wise. It might be smarter to wait another day or two. If they are after disciples, they'll be watching the roads tomorrow." I was careful not to say who "they" were.

I got Thaddaeus settled down in one of the guest cottages and called for two of the guards to saddle horses to ride to Bethany again. Lazarus and his family and guests would have to be warned. I disliked taking the guards for the same reason that I hesitated to let Thaddaeus stay in my uncles' villa. But, it was Passover; and with so many pilgrims camping out around the city, there would undoubtedly be robbers at work.

Even in the dark, we reached Bethany in half an hour and found Lazarus's household awake. Bartholomew and Simon the Zealot had made up in good sense what they lacked in courage and had run to Bethany to bring the news. Both men had filled skins with water, accepted some food, and had started immediately for Galilee. They had been, Lazarus gently noted, frightened. Mary of Magdala was sitting in the shadows, wrapped in a shawl that enhanced rather than hid her beauty. Her words were harsher, but she was never tolerant of weakness.

By the time I arrived, Mary of Magdala and the Master's mother were preparing to go to Jerusalem. I argued against it, and Lazarus was even more opposed. He and I, however, were merely talking to each other. The two women went on with their preparations, as oblivious to our reasoning as to the supposed Jewish custom of women obeying men. Having argued and lost, I had no choice but to accompany them. I confess I volunteered mostly out of shame—and fear lest I seem less than worthy in Mary's eyes.

The sky was clear but cold. Jerusalem is 2,500 feet above the level of the sea, and, though spring days are gorgeous, nights can be uncomfortable. The weather gave me an excuse to wrap my burnoose tightly around me with the hood up and close about my head. I wanted to stay warm, but even more I wanted to stay unnoticed. A blond Greek would attract attention in Jerusalem.

Just as dawn was lighting the sky, we arrived at the Essene Gate. Our entry was more humble than the Master's triumph a few days earlier, but that was not bad. At the great feasts—unlike "normal" times—the Romans kept the gates open all day and night to allow pilgrims free entry to the holy city. The sentries did not give us a second look as we went through. I dismissed my uncles' guards and would have been at a loss about what to do next had not Lazarus told us the Master would probably be taken to Caiaphas's palace for a hearing of some sort.

The walk was short, for the palace—and it was indeed a magnificent building, second only to Herod the Great's in size and beauty—was snuggled against the western wall of the city, 300 or 400 yards from the Essene Gate. It was quite light when we got there. The gates to the outer courtyard were open, but they were attended by a servant woman, with guards—all Jewish, I noted—patrolling just inside. Farther in we could see other guards stationed at the doors to the palace itself and around the porticos leading to two side courtyards. Several dozen people had been allowed to enter and were clustered in gossiping groups, stamping their feet and blowing on their hands to fight the early morning chill.

I looked around the courtyard for a familiar face. At first I recognized no one. Then, I saw John the priest, standing not far off with several of his colleagues. I coughed and caught his attention. He came over, spoke to the servant, and she allowed us to enter. "Simon Peter's here," John whispered. "I let him in. Don't speak to him. It might be dangerous." I followed John's glance and, off in the corner by a small door that led into the palace, I saw Simon Peter warming his hands over a charcoal fire while chatting with a pair of guards and a serving girl. I nodded to the women and, as unobtrusively as possible, we made our way slowly toward him.

We stopped when we were still twenty feet distant and stood silently in place. Within a few minutes, one of the smaller palace doors opened and another maid came out. She took a long look at Simon Peter and said loudly in Aramaic: "Listen to that accent. This big oaf is a Galilean too. Aren't you one of this false prophet's disciples?"

"I am a Galilean," Simon Peter replied in his stentorian voice, "but I am not a follower of this man—or any other man. And I don't like sluts who make stupid charges."

"Wait," one of the other spectators said as he strolled over to the fire. "I know you. I saw you on Sunday with this false prophet."

"You're a fool or a liar," Simon Peter snapped. "I don't know the man."

Another guard walked over and grabbed Simon Peter by the shoulder. "Now, I recognize you. I helped make the arrest. You're the bastard who cut my cousin last night."

Simon Peter threw the guard's arm off his shoulder. "You're out of your pig-eating mind. I told you I don't know the man. And if I'd tried to cut your cousin up, he'd already be in his tomb." With that, he turned and stalked out of the courtyard.

I stood there in shocked silence, but Mary of Magdala had quicker reflexes. "Satan!" she hissed as Simon Peter neared us, eyes straight ahead. As he came abreast of us she spat in his face. He continued to walk, the spittle lost in the tangled forest of his beard.

I heard the Master's mother begin to sob, but before I could try to comfort her, there was a commotion in the side courtyard on our right. Caiaphas and a cluster of other robed men appeared in one of the palace doors. These were members of a sanhedrin, or ruling council. This was not the Great Sanhedrin, which was composed of seventy-one people and met in the Temple. It judged religious disputes, though it could impose penalities as well as answer difficult questions.

What we were seeing was a smaller group, a political sanhedrin. (That word, of course, was Greek, but the Jews themselves had come to use it in place of the Hebrew *Bet Din*, a sensible recognition of the superiority of our language.) This sanhedrin was headed by the High Priest, and its jurisdiction was basically limited to secular issues. It was, however, little more than a sham ruling council. The Romans allowed it to pick up only a few droppings of power from the wake of the imperial army.

Evidently, this was to be a rump session, for nine of the twenty-three seats were empty. The councillors were sauntering, not marching as Romans would have, into the side courtyard. They took seats on camp stools arranged in a semicircle, with Caiaphas at the center. For a few minutes nothing happened, then Annas came hurrying out to take his place. Only then did our guards lead the Master out and stand him in the middle of the semicircle, two guards on each side, his hands bound in front of him. There was a halter around his neck. After a few more minutes the guards allowed the people in the outer courtyard to enter the second court, where we could view the proceedings.

"Are you Joshua, the Nazarene, the son of Josef the carpenter?" Caiaphas asked. His expression was bored, and his voice was flat, without an overtone of either enmity or sympathy.

"You know I am."

"You know with what you are charged?"

"I do not."

Caiaphas did not change his expression or his tone. "You are charged with blasphemy against the Temple and against the Most High, blessed be His name. You are also charged with acts against the peace. You have fomented revolution. How do you plead to these charges?"

"They are false. I have taught in the Temple and in the synagogues of Galilee and Judea. Nothing I have said is secret. Your people have questioned me in public and have found neither blasphemy nor sedition in my teaching. Nor has the Great Sanhedrin, the only court with authority to try cases of blasphemy, accused me of such a crime."

Caiaphas's thin lips curled in what he must have meant as a smile. "You are a lawyer then?"

"No, only a Jew who knows the Law, as all Jews should."

The faint facsimile of a smile vanished from the High Priest's face. He snapped his fingers and the guards pulled the Master twenty feet or so feet farther back into the courtyard, while the councillors conferred in whispers. After a few minutes Caiaphas signaled the guards to push the Master forward again. "We have heard your plea and we know something of the evidence against you. Were you to be tried under our holy Law by the Great Sanhedrin, you would undoubtedly be found guilty of blasphemy. But because some of your crimes are also offenses against Rome, it is our decision to turn you over to the Roman authorities for their disposition."

Caiaphas banged his staff on the stone floor of the courtyard; at that signal the Sanhedrin rose and walked back into the palace. An ugly piece of business had been disposed of with tact and diplomacy. The guards jerked the Master's halter and half-led, half-dragged him into the palace through a different door from that which the councillors had used. "It's over. Everybody out!" one of the guards in the courtyard yelled. "Everybody out!"

As I was following the women back into the street, I felt a hand on my shoulder. I turned. It was John the priest. I hadn't noticed at our brief encounter at the gate, but, in contrast to his usual handsome, carefully groomed appearance, he looked worn. Heavy black bags puffed up under his eyes, indicating he had slept little in recent nights. He exuded, however, a faint aroma of perfume, an indication that he had not completely ignored his toilette. "You saw?" I asked.

He nodded but said nothing. When we were clear of the palace area, he indicated a narrow street twisting off to the left. We took it. John moved us fifty yards along in an arching path to a gate in a wall at least eight feet high. We found ourselves in the garden of a small but attractive house.

Before I could ask the important questions, Mary of Magdala had begun to speak in a hoarse whisper whose harshness conveyed her outrage as sharply as her words: "Did you hear Simon Peter? He denied knowing the Master! Not Simon Peter the Rock or even Simon bar Jonah; but Simon the filthy coward or Simon bar Satan! He ran away, then he came back. Why did he come to Caiaphas's palace if he didn't have the courage to speak out?"

"And be killed?" John asked.

"Yes. At least he could have died in honor; now he has to live in shame—unless his 'manly' mind can justify his evil to himself, and it probably can. How did he get in the courtyard?"

"He wanted to see the Master again," John said. "His conscience was troubling him about running away. He came to my house before first light, told me everything, and I got him in the palace."

"You always did the Master wonderful service," Mary sneered.

"What now?" I asked.

John sighed. "What you just saw was a hearing, not a formal trial. The Master was correct. Had he been formally accused of blasphemy, he would have to have been tried by the Great Sanhedrin. It's controlled by Pharisees and its president is a Pharasaic scribe. Caiaphas is not a popular man in that circle. This group, however, is his. He and Annas chose most of the members. It has enough diversity to seem to be representative, but it's dominated by Sadducees. Sectarian rivalries aside, I don't think Caiaphas could make a charge of blasphemy stick. He's been working on it for several days. For conviction, two or three witnesses to the act must agree in their testimony and the accused must repeat his blasphemy before the court. The Master wouldn't blaspheme, and the witnesses Caiaphas collected disagreed with each other. And an acquittal would have made the Master more popular than ever."

"Why then the talk about blasphemy?" I asked.

"It provided an excuse for the Temple guards to go with the Roman soldiers to make the arrest."

I confessed to some confusion about the maneuvering. "Why not let the Romans do their own dirty work?"

John looked at me curiously. "You think like a Greek, not an Oriental. That would be too straightforward. Caiaphas wants the Romans to think he's helping them even while he's making them, as you put it, 'do their own dirty work.' "

"And now?"

"And now, Caiaphas turns defeat into a triple victory: By handing the Master over to the Romans, he puts the onus on Pilate for any punishment inflicted on a popular prophet, shows the Romans that his little packed Sanhedrin is collaborating in good faith, and accomplishes his main purpose, getting rid of a man who he fears would provoke the Romans into further oppression."

"When are the guards going to take the Master to Pilate?"

"Tomorrow."

"Not until tomorrow? Not until Friday?"

"Yes. That's complicated, too. Giving him to the Romans is the equivalent of a sentence of death, at least that's the purpose behind it. And some scribes claim that the Law does not allow a sentence of death on only one verdict. There must be two, at least twenty-four hours apart. And Caiaphas is a stickler for the Law. He might not believe the two-verdict rule is valid—many writers do not—and, even if it were valid, it's unclear whether it would apply to a hearing rather than a trial. So Caiaphas has devised what he thinks is a clever stratagem. He'll hold the Master for twenty-four hours and if a majority of his Sanhedrin ask for it, have a second hearing."

"Is that likely?"

John smiled in anger. "Not with this group. Besides, even if they do it's doubtful they could meet on Friday. This year, according to the Temple's calendar, Passover begins on the Sabbath, and many scribes hold that neither sanhedrin should meet on the day before a feast."

"So?"

"So, they'll hold the Master in the palace dungeon for twenty-four hours, then bring him to Pilate."

"Then?"

"We all know what Pilate will do. He was in on the arrest. There were Roman soldiers along with the Temple guards in the garden last night. Simon Peter told me that, and I heard it from one of the guards in the courtyard. Pilate learned all about that foolish entry into the city and the riot in the bankers' hall. He was willing to let Caiaphas handle it, maybe even look the other way if a mob stoned the Master, but the Law and politics got in the way of a Jewish solution. Pilate will take over—Rome will take over. The evil thing is done."

John looked at the Master's mother. "Forgive me, but I think it's more cruel to hold out false hope. Pilate hates us, and he fears us. He thinks brute force is the only way to keep us quiet. Ten days ago, he caught up with a band of guerrillas in Galilee and wiped them out. He let his barbarian Celtic legionnaires drain blood from some of our wounded and offer it as sacrifice to their gods. Then he had his troops run through all the prisoners except two. He brought these poor devils to Jerusalem with him and will help us celebrate Passover by crucifying them tomorrow. There's no hope in dealing with an animal like Pilate—or any Roman."

"There is," Mary of Magdala cut in before I could take offense, "one hope. You." Alas, she looked at me, not John. "You," she went on. "You're a Roman citizen from a rich and famous family. You've visited Rome and even met Caesar. You could go to Pilate and tell him the truth about the Master."

All of this was true, including my audience with the imperially morose Tiberius himself, but it was also largely irrelevant. I tried to explain: "When I sailed to Rome a few years ago, we were becalmed for two days. The sailors joked about 'whistling up a wind.' I'd have a better chance of doing that than persuading Pilate or any other Roman governor who sniffs sedition in the air."

"And let the Master die because you wouldn't take the chance?"

3

❖ Not being able to think of a response to Mary's question, I left John with the women and rode back to the villa, bathed, put on fresh clothes, chose my uncles' four best horses, and, with an entourage of three guards, rode to the Praetorium.

As I have mentioned, the Romans had taken over Herod the Great's palace. It was the only set of buildings in Jerusalem more elaborate and more elegant than Caiaphas's palace—save the Temple, of course. Herod had followed his usual grand style of architecture. The complex extended for more than 750 feet and was separated on three sides from the rest of the city by its own huge wall, with the city's outer wall providing coverage on the fourth. Inside the walls, the buildings were surrounded by a moat.

At the northern end of the compound were barracks for the troops. The palace proper consisted of two large villas facing each other. Each not only had its own reception and banquet rooms that could hold hundreds of people, but also its own Roman baths. The two buildings were separated by a huge courtyard. Parts of it were marble-floored, with bronze-fountained ponds; other parts were covered with thick clay and planted with flowers, shrubs, and even small trees. Caesar himself would have been envious, for it was more grandiose than any of the villas I had seen on the Palatine Hill in Rome.

I left the guards and horses inside the gates to the wall and, escorted by a middle-aged *optio spei* (one awaiting promotion to centurion), walked to the villa closer to the barracks. The soldier, speaking Greek as abominable in syntax as it was scatological in vocabulary, presented me to Pilate's secretary. It was noon and the man was not optimistic about my gaining an audience with the prefect that day and certainly not the next because of trials and executions already scheduled. I stressed the importance of seeing Pilate immediately. The secretary was very solicitous, as much out of hope for some reward from my uncles as out of respect for my father, I am sure.

After a half-hour wait, he returned and ushered me through a maze of rooms within the villa. We climbed several flights of stairs and eventually found ourselves in an apartment with a covered terrace arranged as a dining chamber with heavily cushioned sofas. Pilate and his wife, Procla, were still reclining as they completed their midday meal. The panorama was magnificent. At their feet were the palace grounds, the white marble and gold of the Temple, and much of the city and the Kidron Valley. In the bright sun, Jerusalem's houses were yellow, tan, and ochre, colors reflected by the surrounding hills and wadis.

Pilate motioned for me to take the couch across from the two of them, and a servant poured me a cup of wine while another deftly set a dish with meat and cheese on the table before me.

The prefect made an impressive appearance. He looked like a model imperial officer. He was a tall, muscular man who, though in his late forties, exercised twice a day in the gymnasium. It showed, for his body seemed as hard as that of a young legionnaire. His thinning hair evidenced aging, though it was thicker than mine; and, after six years in Judea, his naturally fair skin was developing some of the leathery wrinkles that the Oriental sun creases into human flesh.

His manner was bluff, reminding me of my father's. He was the type of person who tried to convey the impression that his exterior layer of sternness was only a mask required by the heavy authority of his office, and deep down there was a warmhearted human being who would make a true friend. In fact, however, beneath his hard exterior were alternating strata of pride, slyness, and ruthlessness. He lacked great intelligence, but he was shrewd and calculating in that unpredictable manner that characterizes men of limited intellect and vast ego. Most dangerously, his pride filled him with driving ambition. He took himself and Rome very seriously and thoroughly blurred distinctions between the interests of the two.

His eyes provided the only clue to his real nature. Had it not been for them, he would have been handsome. But they constantly flickered about like insects' antennae testing the air for signs of danger.

I had no chance for reflection on Pilate's character, for as soon as I entered the chamber, he called out to me in a gruff but not unfriendly voice: "Welcome, Quintus. Come visit with us. Procla and I have been taking advantage of this marvelous weather to dine in the open air. Caesar's affairs do not leave us much time for such leisure in this pestilent sinkhole. How are your noble father and your very rich uncles?" He winked as he spoke the last few words.

"Quite well, sir. They would have all sent their most respectful regards had they known I would see you." I saw, though only for an instant, his eyes flick so close together at this information as to seem almost to touch. Obviously, he was carefully storing this datum away for later use. I knew that this indirect confession would lessen the weight of my argument, but I wanted it clear that my family had nothing to do with my enterprise.

"What brings you to us? I hope these Jew brigands haven't been attacking your uncles' caravans. I've brought two of them back to crucify tomorrow."

"There's a lot of talk in Jerusalem about that."

"Yes." He ran his hand over his smooth chin and smiled. "A lot of angry talk, too. Well, we've taken precautions. Jews are always bellyaching about something. Even Antipas is cross with me." Pilate affected a mock half-frown, half-wounded grimace to accompany the pretense of a hurt tone. "He says I offended him by invading Galilee, his tetrarchy, to capture those outlaws. But. . ." he paused and nodded his head several times, "but deep down he's sympathetic to the scum. He's part-Jew himself, you know. I'll make up to him by inviting him to the execution and letting him drive the first spike into their hands."

"Don't be cruel," Procla said. "Antipas is a friend of Rome."

"Antipas is a friend of Antipas and of no one else. He has the blood of the Herods in his veins; they're a sly, murderous lot. But enough of these petty problems. How can Rome serve the son of one of her noblest officers?"

"Let the lad eat," Procla protested. She was ten years younger than Pilate, but overweight and dowdy, dependent on hairdressers, dressmakers, and jewelers to impart a modicum of grace to her appearance. I had twice been with her before: Once, on their way to see Antipas at Tiberias, she and Pilate had visited my father at Scythopolis; and once at Caesarea I had accompanied my uncles to a reception Pilate had given. On those occasions, Procla had struck me as a shallow, whiny, spoiled child.

I pushed the plate away and took a sip of wine. "It's about the trial, sir."

"What about the trial?" Pilate's eyes blinked rapidly.

The truth, that the Master was innocent, would be of no avail,
I knew. There was strong evidence against him; and Pilate, like
most Roman administrators, would prefer to execute a hundred
innocent provincials to prevent the escape of a single guilty one.
"The man, this Joshua, the Galilean prophet. He's no enemy of
Rome," I began. "It's all an internal dispute among Jewish sects.
The Sadducees who run the Temple are trying to get you to kill
one of their critics, do their dirty work for them."

Pilate said nothing, but rubbed his chin again.

"This Joshua talks of a next life," I continued, "and the Sadducees
deny that there is a next life. And he publicly upbraids them for
being hypocrites."

"He's got a point; all Jews are hypocrites, as far as I'm concerned," Pilate chuckled. "But how do you know these things?" I
was finding his blinking distracting.

I decided to admit what Pilate might already know. "I know
one of the priests; and, as part of my study of Jewish philosophy,
I've been following this Joshua around. He seems perfectly harm-
less to me. In fact, most of the time he sounds like a pacifist."

Pilate stood up and walked to the railing. "Quintus, I am a
Roman and I hate this dry, dusty land, but in the spring it can be
beautiful." He gestured toward the hills to the west of us. Then he
spun around. "And I hate these dry, dusty people, and at no time
of year is there beauty in them or their atheism, except perhaps in
their hypocrisy. If Caesar had let me, I would have ground them
into submission. . . ." His voice trailed off.

*He was alluding to a pair of incidents. Soon after his arrival
in Judea, he had tried to plant the imperial standards in Jerusalem. These "graven images" had grossly offended the Jews as
blasphemous violations of the First Commandment, and thousands of Jews had staged a peaceful demonstration before Pilate
at his capital in Caesarea. For several days they had camped in
front of his praetorium until he finally agreed that he'd meet with
them in the stadium; and when the crowds entered the arena
they found themselves surrounded by legionnaires who had been*

waiting in the stadium's seats. At Pilate's signal, they drew their swords and began to move toward the protesters; but the Jews, instead of panicking, prostrated themselves on the ground and bared their necks, as their leaders shouted that they would all die rather than survive the pollution of their holy city with the "abomination of desolation."

Pilate's initial reaction, according to what one of the officers had told my father, was to order his troops to oblige the Jews by cutting off their heads—deeds most of the officers and men would have been happy to perform. But two of Pilate's senior advisers had been more prudent and had suggested that Tiberius Caesar, who was a friend of the Herod family, would be displeased. Faced with that possibility, Pilate backed down. He stalked out of the stadium and left it to one of his subordinates to tell the Jews that the standards would be removed.

The prefect, however, was a very stubborn man, and he was determined to rule the Jews, not merely preside over puppet governments. His next step, taken about a year later at Pentecost, was to set up gilded shields here on the ramparts of Herod the Great's palace. Unlike the Roman standards, these shields bore no images of men or gods, merely the name of the person to whom they were dedicated and the name of the dedicator. Technically, there was no violation of the Law, but the Jews were outraged. They knew Pilate was trying to infect their holy city with pagan symbols. The chief priests and the Herod family barely managed to prevent rioting. They persuaded the leaders of various groups to appeal to Caesar instead. And, in a letter joined by four of the Herodian princes, they wrote a long and bitter protest to Tiberius.

Caesar's response was immediate and positive. He ordered Pilate to remove the shields forthwith and take them to Caesarea and dedicate them to the temple of Augustus there. The tone of the letter was sharp, for Pilate had crassly violated the imperial policy of respecting local religious customs.

I heard about the severity of this criticism of Pilate's administration from both my father and my uncles and later from John the priest. In effect, then, the reprimand was public and only whetted Pilate's hatred of the Jews and his appetite for revenge. Soon he seized the opportunity. As an efficient administrator, he realized Jerusalem needed its system of aqueducts repaired. On a visit to the city, he drew up a careful plan to obtain the necessary funds: Very simply, his troops raided the Temple, seized the Corban—a sacred treasure—and brought it back to the Praetorium. Pilate had his money, but he also soon had a riotous mob at the gates of Herod's palace. He came out on the wall to explain to the crowd the necessity of repairing the aqueduct but was shouted down, as I suspect he knew he would be.

He had learned something about tactics if nothing about diplomacy from his earlier defeats. This time he was prepared either for violent or passive resistance. He had divided his troops into small units and scattered them among the mob. They wore burnooses over their armor so they would look like people from the area; and instead of the usual swords, they were armed with cudgels. At Pilate's signal, the legionnaires tore off their cloaks and assaulted the Jews. Totally surprised, the mob panicked and stampeded. The soldiers broke dozens of skulls as well as arms and legs, but most of those killed were trampled to death in the panic.

Pilate ripped me away from my memories: "I've heard he's a magician, casts spells and works all sorts of amazing tricks. He terrified Antipas once by feeding thousands of people out of a couple of baskets. Did you see him do that sort of thing?"

I nodded. "I saw, but he's no magician. I've seen him heal the sick by touching them and praying over them. And I saw the feeding you're talking about. There was a miracle but not the magic Antipas imagined. He didn't make fish and bread mysteriously multiply or hypnotize his listeners into thinking they'd been fed."

"What kind of miracle was it then?" Procla interrupted.

"He worked a miracle in people's hearts," I explained. "Most of the people had walked miles to hear him talk. It was early spring and they had traveled in the Eastern fashion, carrying food in their cloaks or in small baskets. Each meant to feed only himself, but this man's message of love, of sharing, and his own willingness to share what he had turned, at least for the moment, these tight-fisted peasants into generous human beings. They offered their neighbors what they had to eat. It wasn't exactly a feast, but all the people had enough to eat—and they all benefited from caring about one another."

Pilate coughed as if politely concealing incredulity. I recognized his boredom and my mistake. A magician might have attracted him, not a saint. "What you say is interesting, very interesting; but this Joshua calls himself 'king of the Jews.' We can't have that. We let old Herod call himself a king, but that was Caesar's decision."

"No, sir," I interrupted. "This man does not call himself a king. Others—others who do not understand his message—have called him king or messiah, but that is not how he . . ."

"Quintus," Pilate cut in, "when you've been engaged in politics as long as I, you'll realize that most of the world's real problems come from misunderstandings. It's only how others understand us that counts. If people think this yokel is king of the Jews then he's creating a revolutionary movement, whether he means to or not. And believe me, no man can withstand the temptations of power. If he lives to see what he's made, he'll use the instrument he's created."

"I don't like it," Procla suddenly said. "I've been having dreams about all this killing and crucifying. Most Jews are animals, but I heard this man speak and . . ."

"You heard this Jew speak?" Pilate's eyes were racing back and forth and his lids blinking faster than I could keep count. "When? Where?"

"Here in Jerusalem, a few days ago. He was talking to a small group near the Essene Quarter. He spoke mostly in Aramaic—only some Greek at the end—so I couldn't be sure about his words. But his voice was gentle. He did not sound like a revolutionary or a fanatic."

Pilate was silent, but he continued to blink. He walked back to his couch and sat down, carefully examined a bowl of fruit, and selected an apple. "Quintus, we thank you for coming. You are Caesar's friend, just as your father was his faithful servant. We wish we could indulge ourselves the pleasure of listening to your argument at greater length, but. . . ." Indicating the scope of his burdens, he swept his arm toward the city and the hills beyond. "Rest assured that we shall keep in mind what you have told us. Your Joshua sounds interesting, probably a better sort of Jew than that pompous peacock, Caiaphas."

I accepted my dismissal, told my guards to return to the villa with my horse, and walked about the city for some time, trying to lose myself and my thoughts in the crowds. Eventually, I reached the house of John the priest and rapped on the door in the wall. A servant swiftly let me in and seated me in the garden. I felt very cold, though the day was still warm. John and Mary of Magdala joined me in the garden. As a priest, John would not contaminate himself by inviting a non-Jew, even a God Fearer, into his house. Even association with me caused him some difficulty, but it would have been more awkward for him to refuse to associate with one whom the Master accepted.

I told them what had happened. John nodded sadly. Neither of us had expected anything positive. "At least," I said more to console myself than the other two, "I have planted a seed of doubt in Pilate's mind."

"It was little enough," Mary of Magdala snapped. "Why didn't you insist? Your family is rich; you've met Caesar himself. You could have demanded that Pilate release the Master. He would have listened to you, if you'd had the courage. Like all bullies, Pilate can be bullied. But you, like a philosopher [in her mouth it became a sorry profession] tried reason. You don't reason with animals, you command them."

I left. I seldom wanted to argue with Mary and certainly not on this issue. I needed her sympathy, not her scorn. Her reaction was simplistic, but not altogether wrong. In my walk around the city, I had thought of at least twenty more effective tactics than those I had used. And I could have been forceful. . . . Perhaps I had not because I had been afraid that I might end up next to the Master on a tree.

The next morning, I entered the city well before dawn. Pilate's working day started before first light, and I wanted to be in his courtyard before the proceedings began. As it was, I was not very early. An hour after dawn, Caiaphas and a troop of Temple guards moved swiftly up the street. The troops pushed the Master along at a half trot. Clearly they wanted to get him to the Romans before a crowd could gather to interfere. As it was, already about thirty people were there, and more were straggling up every minute.

The Jewish contingent stopped outside the gates. They would not contaminate themselves by entering a pagan house, especially at Passover. In a play that had no doubt been rehearsed, a unit of legionnaires came outside the walls of Herod's palace to accept custody of the Master. The Temple guards pushed the Master roughly toward the Romans, who grabbed the halter around his neck and pulled him quickly inside the walls.

Earlier, the sentries, having recognized me from the previous day as a moderately important person, had allowed me to step inside the gates. I had seen Pilate and tried to approach him to renew my argument, but I stopped when I recognized his curt nod as denying me an audience. When they took the Master inside the gates, I tried to catch his eye; but the legionnaires, also alerted to the dangers from the crowd, pulled him along so swiftly that he had to devote his full attention to keeping his balance.

At that point Pilate, flanked by his adjutant and the secretary I had met the previous day, strutted outside the gates and faced Caiaphas. Despite my fear for the Master, I found myself mesmerized by the confrontation between the representatives of Caesar and God. Pilate wore the uniform of a Roman soldier—heavy sandals, with thongs running up almost to his knees, short trousers, his white tunic covered by a leather breastplate, a burnished, plumed helmet on his head, and a scarlet cape draped over his left shoulder. At his waist was a short Roman broadsword. His aide carried a staff mounted by the imperial eagle.

Caiaphas was, in terms of physique, intellect, and possibly ego, larger than Pilate, standing several inches taller and having perhaps fifty pounds more weight. The High Priest was not dressed in ceremonial regalia, but more simply: Persian-style breeches and a shirt of sorts under a leather breastplate. The only signs of his office were a beautiful blue robe edged in gold bells and pomegranates of red cloth. On his head he wore a plain turban. He was unarmed, of course, though his Levite soldiers carried swords.

Despite his bulk, Caiaphas was as handsome a man as Pilate. In other ways, however, the two contrasted sharply: Pilate was lean and muscular, Caiaphas was fleshy, even flabby. Pilate was clean-shaven, Caiaphas, densely—though very neatly—bearded. Pilate was tanned, Caiaphas, almost pale, no doubt from excessive praying within the shade of the Temple.

If one was caught by the furtiveness in Pilate's eyes, it was pride that Caiaphas's demeanor transmitted, a pride beyond arrogance that can only be affected by those supremely certain that God, displaying the good sense for which He is noted, has taken them into His confidence. Caiaphas's aura was not that of a suppliant, but of a moral superior dealing with an accident: Rome ruled Israel now, but only because the Lord God wished to test His people, or punish them, or both; Rome's being morally unentitled to rule Jews, now or ever, was a fact, not a question.

Caiaphas's demeanor conveyed the same message to Pilate as to me, for as soon as he saw the High Priest, the Prefect began to blink rapidly. Then he jutted out his chin and looked directly at Caiaphas. "What charges do you bring against this prisoner?"

"Do you think that if he were not a criminal, we would have brought him to you?" There was no trace of humility in Caiaphas's voice.

"If he's a criminal, try him by your own law," Pilate rejoined. "Didn't his offenses take place inside the Temple where you have plenary jurisdiction?" I thought the seed I had planted had taken root; Pilate knew all the answers to these questions since he had sent soldiers to help arrest the Master.

"Is sedition against Caesar not your concern?" The High Priest let his words dance on the morning air for a few moments, then finished his thought: "Should we not give a seditionist to Caesar's agent?"

"What is the nature of his sedition against Caesar?"

"Do you not recall that he calls himself the king of the Jews?

Do you not understand that to mean he is trying to set himself up in Caesar's place?"

"That is a serious charge," Pilate said. "We shall talk to the man. Be good enough to wait." He spun on his heel, strode a few paces inside the gates, and motioned for the soldiers to bring the Master forward. He stood before Pilate, erect but with eyes cast down. He was dirty from a night in a dungeon, but though haggard did not seem to have been subjected to torture. Pilate looked him over slowly and thoroughly, much like an Arab examines a horse he might buy—or steal. Finally, when the Prefect spoke, he came straight to the point: "Are you a king?"

"Do you ask this on your own, or have others told you about me?" The Master's voice was soft but firm.

Pilate glanced at me and asked, "Why is it Jews always answer a question with a question?"

The Master did not look up and so probably did not see me. I wanted him to know that a friend was present, but I also worried that, seeing me in the Praetorium, he might think that I was the one who had betrayed the location of the camp.

Pilate turned back toward the Master. "Do I look like a Jew? Your own High Priest has just turned you over to me. He says you're a king. Why? Are you a king?"

"My kingdom is not of this world."

"So," Pilate hissed, "you are a king!"

"It is you who say this, not I." The Master stopped and sighed deeply, lifted his head, and for the first time looked straight into Pilate's eyes. "Yes, I am a king. For this was I born, for this I came into the world: to bear witness to the truth. All who are on the side of truth will hear my message."

"Truth?" Pilate feigned surprise. "What is truth?"

The Master made no answer but continued to look directly at Pilate. After a few moments the Roman's blinking increased to the point that even he was aware of it. He spun and marched back outside the gates, accompanied by his adjutant and secretary, and addressed Caiaphas in a voice that was barely a rasping whisper. Had I not walked behind the three Romans, I could have heard nothing. "We do not like it, Caiaphas. This man does not speak like a revolutionary and he does not act like a revolutionary. We are willing to admit he is your enemy; but it's not clear he's Caesar's enemy."

Caiaphas shrugged his shoulders and affected a slight, mocking bow. "If he were only my enemy, would I not try him myself?"

"Not if you could get someone else to do the job for you and take all the blame."

Caiaphas nodded. "That would indeed be clever, but only by half. Would you soon not find me out and depose me as High Priest? After all, you appointed me High Priest; can you not remove me? What profit is there in bringing down an enemy if I also bring myself down? But you are right about that man's being my enemy: Are not all Caesar's enemies my enemies?" Caiaphas smiled condescendingly and added: "And are not we all Caesar's good friends?"

"Some of us are his friends," Pilate snarled. "And some are slick, devious bastards." Then he broke off the conversation and returned inside the gates to address the Master in a rapid, clipped tone. "Directing your attention to several years ago, were you not a follower of John the Baptizer, whom Herod Antipas executed for sedition?"

"Antipas murdered John for convicting him of incest and adultery," the Master corrected.

Pilate ignored the response. "Directing your attention to the same general time frame, did you not perform some sort of magic in Galilee and gather huge crowds who called you king? Did not Herod Antipas send troops to arrest you? Did you not flee and hide somewhere?"

Before the Master could respond, Pilate snapped his fingers at the officer in charge of the troop that had taken custody of the prisoner from the Jews. "Take this man to Herod Antipas. Let him conduct the trial. He is Tetrarch of Galilee and these crimes were committed within his jurisdiction." Then after a slight pause: "And tell Caiaphas to wait until we have breakfasted."

With that Pilate strode back into the villa where we had lunched the previous day. I started to leave, but Pilate pointed a stubby finger at me. "Stay, Quintus. We need you." I accompanied him back to his office in the villa and up to the penthouse where we had dined yesterday. The day showed signs of being as clear as yesterday, but at that hour it was still quite chilly. I kept my burnoose wrapped tightly about me, but Pilate wore only a short Roman cloak.

"Sit down," he said to me, then clapped his hands, and two servants appeared with food. I noticed there was nothing for the secretary and assumed that I was about to eat his breakfast. If I could have thought of a polite way of transferring the plate, I would have used it, for food was the last thing I wanted. "Tell us all you can about this man," he ordered, "all, that is, you can tell in the next hour."

I would have preferred to have been alone or at least to share my grief and fear with one of the other followers, but I did as I was told, hoping that somehow it might help the Master. My only consolation was that Caiaphas and his entourage would be standing outside the gates in the morning chill while I sat and ate in a warm room. The thought that they might have hunger pangs almost gave me some appetite.

I had not been surprised by the High Priest's outmaneuvering Pilate—disappointed but not surprised. I had had a slim hope that the seed I had planted would arouse his suspicions. It had, but Caiaphas, alas, was smarter and more agile and had easily been able to snare Pilate in his trap. What did surprise me was Pilate's cleverness in sending the Master to Antipas. For Antipas had been one of the Jewish princes who had written the letter to Tiberius about the second incident with the shields in Jerusalem, the letter that had brought about Pilate's reprimand. I had underestimated the man. He was shunting off on an enemy the onus that Caiaphas had passed to him. Pilate's mind was neither quick nor subtle, but it was geared for survival.

Because Antipas proclaimed his Jewish heritage when it suited him, each year he came to Jerusalem for the three solemn feasts, though usually he held court in Tiberias, Jericho, or Caesarea. Since the Romans had taken over his father's great palace, when in Jerusalem he stayed, along with any other Herods who chose to be Jewish for the occasion, at the older and smaller Hasmonean palace on the edge of the Valley of the Cheesemakers straight across from the Temple, but still in the Upper City. It was to that palace that Pilate had sent the Master.

Pilate gave me somewhat more than an hour, though not without a half dozen interruptions, to tell him about the Master. I presented the information as simply as I could, stressing the essence of the message of peace, justice, love, and disdain for the things, including power, of this world. I carefully avoided the phrase "the kingdom of God."

I could not read Pilate's reaction. Most of the time he seemed to be attentive, and he asked several questions that showed some understanding. Still, with people of his mentality, one can never be sure what they are hearing. Certainly it was not the Holy Spirit.

Our conversation ended when we heard a commotion in the courtyard below. It was the legionnaires returning, dragging the Master with them. Someone had stuck a crown of thorns on his head. As we approached, one of the troops put a reed in the Master's hand and called out, "Hail, king of the Jews!" The others thought it amusing, but all laughter ceased when Pilate appeared. He accepted the salute of the centurion in charge. "Well? Why have you brought this man back?"

"Prince Herod sends his respects, sir, and says that the most serious of this man's crimes were committed here in Jerusalem, and his actions in Galilee are now old and best forgotten. Thus he defers to the jurisdiction of Rome."

"These scurvy Jews want independence, but they can't even accept responsibility for wiping their own rear ends. Well, when a Roman sees his duty, he does it, and the sly bastards know that and take advantage of it." Pilate's voice betrayed his frustration. He had used up half a year's ration of subtlety, and still two Jews had outmaneuvered him in one morning. "We'll remember this, and some day we'll make Antipas remember it. For now, we'll show them that Romans are men. Bring the prisoner!"

As soon as the Master was brought back in, Pilate began speaking in rapid, clipped Greek: "Directing your attention to the immediate present, you are called the Nazarene, are you not? Are you of the royal family of David?"

The Master said nothing. He stared at the ground in front of the prefect's feet.

Pilate waited for a few moments in heavy silence, then continued: "Have you not said that it is unlawful for a Jew to pay tribute to Caesar?"

A full minute passed. It was as if the Master had not heard the question.

"Directing your attention to the first day of this week, did you not enter Jerusalem, riding on a donkey like your Jewish writers predict their messiah will do, and did your followers not proclaim you king?"

Again Pilate waited, but the Master remained silent.

"Maintaining your attention on that same day, did you and your followers not attack the Temple, try to seize its bank, and take over the building as a base for insurrection?"

The Master still held his tongue.

Pilate's patience broke. "Look at me, man! Don't you realize I have the power to free you or to crucify you?"

The Master raised his head and gazed straight at the prefect, but he still did not speak.

Pilate lowered his voice; his tone became less harsh. "Tell me, do you really preach that a man should turn the other cheek when he is struck? Do you teach that we should love our enemies?"

The Master broke his silence: "This is the only truth you have spoken."

Pilate stepped back as if he had been slapped. "You are, indeed, a dangerous man and your teaching is a threat to the empire. No one loyal to Rome can love Caesar's enemies." There was a hint of sadness in Pilate's voice, but only for a fraction of a second. He turned to the officer in command of the detachment of legionnaires. "Scourge him and crucify him with the other two seditionists!"

"What shall I write on the *titulus* for his cross?" the secretary asked. The Roman custom was to write out a placard giving the victim's name and reason for execution. It would be carried in front of him on the march to the place of execution and then hammered to the top of the cross.

"Joshua, the Nazarene, King of the Jews."

"Caiaphas won't like that, nor will Antipas," his secretary noted.

"Why do you think I'm doing it?" Pilate snapped. Then he turned to me. "You believe we're wrong, Quintus. You don't see this man as a threat to Caesar. If we were in your place, we might not either. But we are in our place, not yours."

4

❧ I stood in the courtyard, transfixed, immobile, while the soldiers dragged the Master to the barracks, where they would give him and the other two condemned men thirty-nine lashes with a bullwhip studded with pieces of bone and metal. I do not know how long I was there. At the first sound of a scream I came out of my trance and hurried out the gates. It was all I could do to keep from running. I stopped at the nearest tavern and drained two cups of cheap wine as quickly as a Galilean. Then I sat and wept and waited.

Shortly after midday, the soldiers led the three prisoners out of the gates. Each carried the crossbar for his stake—troops would have already put a trio of posts in place. The guard was heavy, an obvious indication that the Romans expected trouble. In command was a centurion, mounted, as were two of his noncommissioned officers, on big horses. A squad of legionnaires marched ahead of the prisoners, a squad marched on each side, and yet a fourth followed close behind. All the troops were in full armor, half had lances in addition to their swords, half had cudgels—left over, perhaps, from Pilate's last affair with a Jewish mob.

The soldiers could well have been concerned about an effort to free the guerrillas. Today, people calling themselves Zealots have

been stridently preaching strict adherence to the Law and disobedience to Rome. They are always brooding, conspiring, organizing,
as they wait for the moment to strike. In the Master's time, they
were not so well organized, there were fewer of them, and they did
not always take the name Zealot for themselves. Still, whatever
the name groups adopted, there were enough conspiracies and
counterconspiracies blowing around the Land of Israel to confuse
natives as well Romans.

With his usual sardonic touch, Pilate had ordered that the
titulus of each of the two men would read "Brigand." It was the
Roman's code word for revolutionary, a term, after all, not to
be used in public when it could be both punished and covered
over.

Straggling after the execution detail was a ragtag collection of
Arabs, Syrians, Idumeans, and Jews from Judea, Galilee, and the
Greek-speaking world. We followed the Roman soldiers out from
Jerusalem to a small hill near a stone quarry, northwest of the
second, outer wall of the city. Just below was a cemetery. That
location or the fact that the hill had long been used as a place for
public executions explains its name, Golgotha, "the place of the
skull."

Violent death always attracts crowds, and the opening stages of
crucifixions can be cruelly dramatic, especially when the executioners use spikes instead of ropes to fix the victims in place. The
shrieks of agony and pleas for mercy usually bring cheers of appreciation from the crowd. They did that day. To the mob's applauding
delight, both guerrillas screeched like wounded camels, first in
pain, then in terror, and finally in despairing rage, as their newfound
height on the gibbet allowed them to see that their succumbing to
slow, asphyxiating death had meaning only as a fleeting source of
amusement for the rabble they had thought to liberate from Roman bondage.

Even the Master groaned. I could hear that sound then as
distinctly across a hundred paces as I can hear now across the
years the sound of the hammer driving iron through the flesh and
bone of his wrist, into soft wood.

After an hour, the crowd thinned out. A few people stayed on to jeer, but not many. Some had come hoping to witness a miracle; some had come expecting to see a rescue attempt or the beginnings of a popular uprising, either from the followers of the two guerrillas or from us. Most had come merely to revel in the smell of blood and the sound of anguish. There were enough of each of the latter, but no miracles and no gallant efforts at rescue. Our people were as scattered as the guerrillas' bands, far fewer in number, and much less competent in war.

The Master's followers were too unsophisticated to plan a revolution. They might have dreamed of a miracle, but in the Jewish apocalyptic tradition: Men would only be witnesses, not actors. Any miracle would come in the form of the Lord's sending legions of angels to throw the Romans out and restore the rule of Israel from Syria to Egypt.

During that fateful Passover week, the brothers would have made a pitiful revolution. Simon Peter and Judas were the only two of the Twelve who had had any experience in matters of blood, and I doubt if Simon Peter had done much more than march around the hills northeast of the Lake of Galilee with a few other restless young men, shaking swords to make the Herodians feel nervous and themselves manly.

I must add, however, that I never doubted that in a fit of rage, especially when he was drinking, Simon Peter could have killed a man. Perhaps he once did. I sometimes suspected so. When we traveled, he carried a short sword, as did Judas. Simon Peter's excuse was that, to make camp, we often had to clear underbrush or cut down a small tree and besides, there was always danger from snakes. Judas offered neither an explanation nor an excuse.

It is true the other Simon was called a Zealot, but he did not practice violence; he did not even preach it; he merely mumbled it on rare occasions. The only threat he posed was to himself and his friends, if he were overheard by a Roman soldier who could decipher what a Galilean tongue did to Aramaic or Greek.

Judas was a cloak of a different weave. He had been an Essene, a full-fledged monk, not like the Master, one who had spent time with them and respected their ways. For some reason, Judas had left the Essenes and joined a group who would later be called the

Sicarii, dagger men, assassins who are the most zealous of the insurgents. Their targets have been Jews who do business, economic or political, with the Romans. The day of the Sicarii is coming in blood, but even then, in Pilate's time, they existed. I never dared to ask, but I suspected that Judas's blade was no virgin. He carried his sword openly but his razor-sharp dagger was concealed under his colobium, the long, one-piece tunic most Jews wear. His weapon was nine inches long with a slight curve at the end of the blade. I once watched him pare and core an apple. In his hands a knife was a fearful, loving instrument that raced around the apple with such dexterity that the skin came off as one long, curled layer. The core fell out almost as neatly.

The Master said he had come to save sinners, not the just, to return the lost sheep of Israel to the fold. Judas fit in both those categories.

When one is gripped by the shock of sudden agony, one can often detach oneself from the events that are producing that anguish to become, in effect, a disinterested spectator of one's own suffering. I found myself in a dreamlike state that terrible afternoon outside Jerusalem. It was as if my mind had clasped my emotions in irons, lest they explode.

As I have noted, the crowd soon began to get bored after the two guerrillas quieted, their voices hoarse from cursing. A crucifixion can go on for a long time. My father claimed that if the victim wiggles his hands and tosses his head about—and if he is in good physical condition to begin with—he can last for several days. Most die in a day or so, less when it is very hot or very cold. None of these three was likely to set records for endurance.

The rebels were young men, but they had been wounded and captured in the hills of Galilee, then half-marched, half-dragged eighty miles back to Jerusalem. I doubt if any legionnaire had tended their wounds or shared food and water with them. The Master had, as far as I know, always been strong and in good health. Nevertheless, in the last few weeks he had eaten and slept little, and the previous two days must have sapped his energy.

Indeed, Judas's betrayal and the desertion of the others might have affected his will to live.

All three victims now hung motionless. The Master, I knew, was praying—for us and those who were murdering him, as well as for himself. None of the three was even responding to the pellets of donkey dung that some of the bored remnants of the rabble occasionally threw at them. My own state of shock was so deep that I felt no anger at this superfluous cruelty.

I looked around and caught a glimpse of Simon Peter on the far side of the hill, next to a clump of Idumean bumpkins who were starting back into the city, eating fruit, tossing jokes, and sharing a skin of wine as they walked. On the near side of the hill, I recognized John the priest. With him were several women. Because they had covered themselves with the traditional headdress of Jerusalem, I could not see their faces; but I was sure the Master's mother and Mary of Magdala were in the group. They were inching closer to the cross, even as Simon Peter was edging away, pathetically trying to conceal his bulk behind a pair of withered olive trees.

I looked around for Josef, the merchant from Arimathea, the little town northwest of Jerusalem. My mother's family had done business with his family as long as the memory of either side ran. He, too, followed the Master, though, until now, even less openly than I. He was a member of the smaller, political version of the Sanhedrin headed by the High Priest.

As dapper and lively a man as he was rich, Josef loved the trappings and prestige that position gave him. His justification for keeping his belief in the Master a secret had been that we might some day need a friend in court, and surely he would lose his place were it known that he was fraternizing with a radical teacher. The irony was that, at the moment his influence was most needed, Caiaphas, a Sadducee, had artfully neglected to notify Josef—who as a Pharisee was likely to oppose Caiaphas on anything—of the Master's hearing the previous morning.

I had met Josef as I walked—let me be honest, sneaked—behind the soldiers as they pushed and pulled the Master and the "brigands" from Herod's palace to Golgotha. Josef had been at the brink of madness. His usually bright, dark eyes were fixed in an open-pupiled stare. I had taken him aside and tried to calm him. It had been no easy task; and I was not completely successful. And what success I achieved was due more to force than to reason. I had to use physical restraint. Fortunately, he was an elderly man, for I was never strong.

I had feared he was either going to throw himself bodily against the soldiers or fall into some kind of fit. He was torn with grief, I knew, not only because of the Master's impending execution, but also because of the guilt of his own silence. Then suddenly he calmed, though not in a rational manner. An idea had lodged in his disturbed brain: He would go to Pilate and plead for the right to bury the Master's body.

I thought it foolish, no more than a temporary escape from guilt or from the responsibility to do something useful. Still, I had offered to go along and reinforce his request for an audience. As a Jew, Josef could only beg or buy what was mine by right. He said it was something he had to do on his own. Even at that age, I was enough of a philosopher not to stand between a man and his penance.

After a few hours, heavy thunderheads began darkening the sky, and the soldiers stopped their dice games and began talking nervously among themselves. Their orders were to let the bodies hang about three more hours until they heard the trumpeting of the great Ram's horn from the Temple mount, signaling sundown and marking the official beginning of the first day of Passover as well as the Sabbath. Caiaphas had sent a messenger to Pilate to ask him to cut the bodies down before the double feast began. Naked bodies hanging in front of the Holy City would be a double blemish. The Romans were quite willing to comply—they had had enough trouble with Jews that week—as long as the prisoners were thoroughly dead.

I have provided the details in my other chronicle. I remind the reader that, when the lightning from the storm crept near, the centurion wisely ordered the soldiers to move early and break the legs of the two rebels. It was an act of mercy. Humors collect in the feet and legs of a man being crucified, swelling the limbs like goats' bladders filled with new wine. Shattering the bones causes blood to burst forth, and the victim dies in a few minutes.

When the soldiers reached the Master, they were unsure if he were still alive. One stuck his spear in the Master's side. There was no gushing of blood, only a thin, red trickle. He gave a great sigh as the spirit fled from his ravaged body.

Then the darkened sky spat its lightning and roared its thunder directly at us gathered on that hill. A bolt of lightning struck near where Simon Peter stood and rain began dumping on us like a tidal wave. Most of us ran. I did. Only the Roman soldiers, John the priest, and the women stood their ground.

Up ahead, I saw Simon Peter, racing away from the city wall. Without thinking, I followed him. Even in the half darkness and slashing rain, it was not difficult to keep him in sight. His clothes, like his speech, were those of a peasant from Galilee. He was a large man; my head reached only to his shoulder. His hands were rough and calloused, the big instruments of a fisherman who spent his days pulling ropes or oars and his nights mending nets. His matted beard was then rough and full, only occasionally trimmed by Naomi when it grew too long. The Galilean sun had burned its black wires red at the tips, just as it had darkened his already swarthy skin.

After a few minutes, the rain turned from cold talons clawing at our bodies to pelting missiles that threatened to crush our skulls. Rocks of frozen water burst around us. Several hit me on the back and shoulders, painful reminders of the Lord God's wrath. My breath was coming in burning gasps, but I was driven on by panic beyond panic.

Golgotha was well behind us now, but Simon Peter's pace seemed to increase. Perhaps my own had as well, but I knew it would soon turn to exhaustion. Reading and writing do not make for physical endurance. Then, as I should have known he would, Simon Peter stumbled and half fell. He partially regained his footing and tried, too rashly, to resume full stride immediately. He stumbled a second time and rolled headlong into a depression.

When I reached him, he was pulling himself up with one arm while trying to shield his face from the hail with the other. I saw a small cave off to the right and pushed him toward it. He allowed that shove to direct him to shelter. I let him go first and clear a path through the branches and vines that partially covered the entrance.

It took several minutes for the burning in my chest to subside so I could get my full breath. Simon Peter's breathing was much easier, but his fear, I sensed, ran much deeper than mine. He stood at the mouth of the cave, just as decades later he would on the Appian Way, staring out into the exploding blackness, saying nothing.

I gathered the olive branches and dry grape vines from the mouth of the cave, rifled through the pocket of my burnoose, and found the materials to start a fire. It took some doing, but I soon had a small blaze going. Grape vines throw off marvelous heat. I took off my soaked clothes, spread them around the fire, and sat shivering as close to the flames as I dared. Simon Peter must have heard the crackling; certainly he felt me move the branches and vines from around him; and the fire must have warmed him. Yet he did not turn or acknowledge my presence.

I did not try to start a conversation. I was weary—not only from the frustration of being unable to persuade Pilate, the hard labor of our panicked escape, and the horrible strain of the Master's trial and execution, but also of having had to cope with Josef's guilt, Simon Peter's cowardice, and my own full share of both. I was not certain I had enough inner reserves to soothe Simon Peter. Nor, in my heart, was I sure I could bring myself to forgive him, despite all the Master had said. I knew I would never forget his uttering those awful words, "I don't know the man." And as the shock of the day was ebbing, the throbbing pain in my own soul was welling up.

The storm and cold were the least of my problems. I was suffering something far more profound than physical pain. In pleading with Pilate—even with Mary—and in attending the hearing in Caiaphas's courtyard and the trial in the palace my mind had been fully engaged, though frightened.

Now, however, I had nothing to think about but my failure—and my loss. My grief, my despair, were growing like the huge

wave that often follows an earthquake. Its dark green volume
swelled the more I thought about it. It was not merely that
the Master was lost, but that the purpose I had found in life
—and beyond—was also lost, as finally as a map scribbled on
the desert floor is sacrificed to the swirling wind. Worse, there
was no hope of replacing that purpose. No substitute could serve.
My Greek soul, culturally attuned to respond to the chords of
tragedy, recognized that fact. For the first time, but hardly the
last, the thought of throwing myself into the black pit of suicide brought a measure of relief. To leap beyond the inane
emptiness of this life into another world, whether only of dream-
less sleep or fierce suffering, seemed better than living without
purpose.

I must have dozed off. When I awoke the rain had stopped and
the stars were out. Simon Peter was shaking me. "Wake up,
Quintus, wake up!"

I returned to consciousness slowly, like a diver who has made
it to the bottom of his lake and then, his chest still full of air,
lazily climbs circling watery stairs to the light above. I thought I
spoke, but probably only a moan escaped. Simon Peter shook me
again. "Wake up, Quintus."

By now I was breaking the surface of light—a few embers from
the remains of the fire. I was naked and cold again. I felt for my
robe. It was dry. I pulled it on.

"Where are we?" Simon Peter asked.

"In a cave outside Jerusalem, as far away as your legs could
propel you before you fell. Don't you remember?"

"I remember eating the Passover meal on Wednesday, like
those Essene friends of the Master. And I remember walking back
across the valley to Gethsemane, where we'd camped. I got sleepy.
I must've eaten too much lamb. You know the rule about not
serving the leftovers the next day. Then I'm here."

"You probably drank too much wine."

"Too much lamb, too much wine," Simon Peter agreed. "But
how did we get in this place? Where is the Master?"

"You don't remember?" I was young then and felt only a
contempt that was untouched by pity and certainly not yet by
empathy.

"Between the camp and now only demons run through my head. I don't recognize them. They form no pattern, and I'm afraid to try to make them. I don't know who or what they are, but I know they're evil. Where's the Master and what time of day is it?"

"It's night. Can't you see the stars?"

"I can see nothing."

"What do you mean nothing?" I doubt that my tone was kindly. I was still physically and emotionally exhausted.

"I'm blind, Quintus. How did I become blind?" Simon Peter spoke matter-of-factly, as one who had accepted the inevitable because he expected the inevitable and, in some perverse fashion, wanted the inevitable despite, or perhaps because of, its harm. He was playing more the role of the Greek who accepted his fate than of the Jew who thought that with the Lord's help he was master of his own destiny.

I hesitated. Simon Peter had a crude sense of humor; but not tonight, not after what had happened since that Passover meal. I passed my hand in front of his face. As far as I could tell in the semidarkness, he did not blink. "If you can't see now or remember anything that happened today, how did you know where to find me and who I was before I spoke?"

"You stink, Quintus. Everybody knows that. You Greeks use perfumed oil. You never smell of good fish or a farmer's honest sweat. You stink like a whore."

There was no point in asking him how he had learned about the odors of whores or in telling him how long it had taken me to accustom myself to the body odors of Galileans, how many times I had come close to suffocating at their proximity. Instead, I asked, "Are you cold? Hungry?"

"I feel nothing."

"Well," I said, "I am hungry and I'm also cold. Here, hold onto my arm. I'll guide you to my family's house outside Jerusalem. They'll feed us and give us shelter."

He groped and found my arm. His grip was powerful. "I'm afraid, Quintus, terribly afraid." He spoke those words in that same flat, accepting tone of voice. "What am I afraid of?"

"I don't know." It was a lie, but even my anger could not bring itself to destroy the man.

5

❧ The walk back to the city was long and slow. Simon Peter's terrorized legs had lacked the good sense to follow a path, so we stumbled south across the gnarled countryside for about a mile until we came close to the city's second, outer northern wall. My family's villa was more than a quarter mile northwest of the western gate at the junction of the inner and outer northern walls. Thus we still had a fair distance to travel. My footing was unsure; and, with Simon Peter tugging on my arm, I fell several times, taking him down with me onto the hard, rocky ground.

My landmarks were the huge shadows of the beautifully ornate triple towers, Phasael, Hippicus, and Mariamme, which Herod the Great had built to guard the northwest entrance to Jerusalem. As we passed near the quarry and Golgotha, I envied Simon Peter his blindness. I tried not to look, but I could not help myself, The three thick posts were bare. The bodies and the crossbars had been removed, leaving the trunks to stand like the masts of a great ship that had gone down in shallow seas.

Once we found the road to Emmaus, the way became relatively easy. A few years later, Herod Agrippa would build yet a third wall to protect the northern approaches to Jerusalem, and the scattered houses—mostly spacious villas of foreigners like my family—would become the nucleus of what would be called "the New City." But at that time the third wall did not exist.

Not wanting to compromise my relatives, I had never before invited the Master or any of his followers here—except Mary of Magdala. (Thaddaeus had arrived uninvited.) Because of Mary's social class, she was, from my family's point of view, acceptable as a guest. Her own status as a Jew was compromised, of course. For an unmarried woman to be seen outside her parents' home in the company of a male not of her immediate family was abundant cause for scandal, even severe punishment.

When the people with whom the Jewish woman came into

contact were gentiles, the taint was even more severe. To those who strictly observed the Law, she was treated as a harlot. Obviously, Mary's behavior caused heads to shake and tongues to wag; but, since she was neither married nor, alas, seemed to have any intention of marrying, offending a husband or potential suitors concerned her no more than matters of ritual purity. And because she had the arrogant contempt for public opinion that the wealthy often evidence, her "reputation" was not something she thought about.

I took Simon Peter to our villa rather than to John the priest's house. The city's gates were open but still guarded, and Simon Peter had already been recognized once. Our villa was also safer than John's. He was well known among the ruling circles in Jerusalem, and many people must have recognized him at the execution. If Pilate and the chief priests were to decide to eliminate the whole movement, none of us was safe. But—and this was more likely—if they decided only to act against those who were able to lead what was left of the Master's followers, then three of the brethren were especially vulnerable: Simon Peter, because the Master had singled him out (even the servant girl had recognized him in Caiaphas's courtyard); Levi, because he was literate and as a minor tax collector probably knew who was stealing how much from whom; and, then, John the priest. Because of his great intelligence, energy, and reputation as a man of blood, Judas would also have been vulnerable had he not gone over to the other side.

Of the group, John was both the most visible and potentially the most dangerous. He was not only a priest but also a scholar, studying under the noted scribe, Gamaliel. Thus he was well versed in cultic ritual as well as in the written and oral Law of Israel. When he finished his apprenticeship under Gamaliel, John would become a scribe in his own right, and the great prestige Jews bestowed on such people would immediately accrue to him.

There was another important factor. Like all priests he was of pure Israelite blood and before ordination had had to prove that purity for centuries past by very elaborate if not always rational rules. And John's family was of the priestly nobility, not one of the poorer, far more numerous clans of clerics. Now most of these people were related to each other somehow, since, to ensure racial purity, priests tended to marry daughters of other priests. And John was of the family of Annas, the former High Priest, and thus Caiaphas, who was Annas's son-in-law, was also John's in-law. A movement led by a scribe from a noble priestly family would by that very fact have legitimacy with many pious Jews. (The Master's descent from the royal family of David had heightened his appeal to many disciples, just as it had excited the fears of Caiaphas and Pilate.)

Moreover, in his own person John bridged a great gap in Jewish society. On his mother's side, his family was Sadducee—Annas was his grand-uncle. On the other hand, John's father and John himself were Pharisees as, of course, was Rab' Gamaliel. In contrast to the open contempt that Sadducees and Pharisees so often displayed toward one another, John had always been able to maintain close, even warm relations with Annas. Neither man was without a certain charm, and, I suspect, each recognized and respected the other's talents.

Whether at the moment John's family connections would insulate him from a purge or make him more vulnerable I could not be sure, but the negative effects of blood were apparent: John's adhering to the Galilean rabble might appear to his "cousin" Caiaphas as a betrayal of family loyalty as well as of religious orthodoxy. Further, he might see punishing a relative as a way to remind the poorer priests, who resented—and envied—him and his wealthy clique, that no man was safe from his wrath. It might serve the additional purpose of ridding the Temple of a potential leader of the Pharisees' faction.

Because I was a foreigner, the chief priests would probably not regard me as a threat. A blond youth whose first language was Greek and whose Aramaic was heavily accented was not likely to stir Hebrews to revolution. Besides, since I was not a Jew, only a God Fearer, I could not be charged with blasphemy—at least as long as I stayed outside the Temple, and that past Sunday had seen my sole venture into the Temple area since I had begun to follow the Master.

So, too, my own status as a Roman citizen by birth and my family's political connections made it improbable that any pru-

dent Jew would think that he could, with impunity, label me as
Caesar's enemy. Tiberius's friendship with my family was no
secret, and given Caesar's recent reprimand, Pilate would be wary
of punishing me. The worst I would suffer would be official lec-
tures about youthful indiscretions and the necessity of maturing
and taking my rightful, responsible, Roman place in society.

The servants let us in my uncles' villa, washed my feet, and
brought us fresh clothes, wine, and food. I asked about Thaddaeus.
The servants said he had left shortly after I had at midday. It was a
stupid decision, but I had other problems to worry about.

I bathed Simon Peter myself, though he objected—I was unsure
whether to my solicitude or to the thought of parting with the
layers of dried dirt and sweat that he cherished as mementos of his
childhood. He ate little but drank almost a full liter of wine. I put
the food in his hand; he found the goblet without my aid. When
he was done, he slept without moving from the couch.

The Sabbath dawn was streaking the sky when I lay down.
What sleep I got was fitful. The buzzing flies did not help; far
worse were the shapeless nightmares, always accompanied by the
awful sound of that hammer driving iron through flesh. Every
hour, at least, I came half awake with the emptiness of grief rather
than the stimulation of fear. I was grateful when a servant woke
me in mid-afternoon to say Simon Peter was stirring. With help,
he relieved himself and was led back to the main room. The
servants brought more food and wine. Again I put the food in his
hands. He took only a few dates to punctuate his rapid but steady
consumption of wine.

"Would you like to talk?" I asked while he quaffed his third
large goblet. Fortunately, a good portion of it ran down his beard.
He didn't bother to wipe it. Perhaps he enjoyed its aroma.

"No."

"What can I get you?"

"Nothing. I want nothing, not a damned thing, only to forget. . . .
And I don't even know what it is I want to forget." He was
still speaking in that abstract, matter-of-fact way, as if he were
reporting the emotions of a stranger. He clumsily groped for the
fresh flagon of wine the servants had imprudently brought and
refilled his goblet, managing to spill no more than went into the

cup. He swallowed it in one great gulp. "I think I'll sleep now," he said, "but just in case, leave the wine."

I did as he asked. He touched the flagon so that he could find it again, stretched out on the couch, and within minutes was snoring in an open-eyed sleep.

Because it was the Sabbath, the city was quiet. Jerusalem was the spiritual capital of the Jews; and the Romans, by and large, respected local gods and local customs. Even the other foreigners were usually careful not to give religious offense, less out of respect than fear—and of a mob rather than a deity.

Following the Jewish custom of bringing a bereaved family food, I filled a basket with several loaves of bread, some fruit, and a large flagon of wine, for Jews understand that the senses of mourners need numbing. So as not to attract attention, I borrowed one of the servants' plain burnooses and walked to the city. Entering by the western gate, protected by its three towers, I turned right into the Upper City, past Herod's palace, then after a few hundred yards turned left before the ground sloped down toward the Essene Quarter, walked by Caiaphas's palace and veered onto a small street where the cobblestones arced in a graceful U. At the middle of the arc I pushed on a small door on the right-hand wall, leading to the house of John the priest. The gate should not have been locked on Sabbath; but, after the events of the last two days, he may have allowed prudence to triumph over the letter of the Law. Fortunately for me, he had not. I slipped inside, strode down the short, narrow path, and pushed open the other gate that opened directly into the garden.

Mary of Magdala was there along with the Master's mother. The garden should have been filled with sympathetic friends and relatives and piled high with food and wine. But the two women were alone, consoling each other in silence. In the Land of Israel, the first seven days of mourning were intense. And, as custom prescribed, the two were sitting on the damp ground with their heads covered, their feet bare, their sorrow leaving them oblivious to the chill of the shaded garden. Not until the third day would they visit the tomb. Some people followed a tradition of rolling the rock back to make sure that the person inside was truly dead; in this case I hoped the women would dispense with that ritual.

The Master's mother was glad to see me, and Mary offered no reproach, at least not immediately. They bared their heads, as was proper, but neither stood. Mary accepted my basket, but did not offer to share its contents. At very minimum she should have offered me wine in a white glass cup. She did, however, share her staccato news: The Master had died when the soldier had pierced his side with a lance. Josef had received Pilate's permission to bury the body. He had taken it to a cave he had intended to use as his own family's tomb, located north of the city in the garden where he operated a perfume press. Judas was dead, found hanged from the walls of Caiaphas's palace.

That news troubled me. I wondered if he had killed himself, been murdered by one of the enraged brothers—Simon Peter would have been my prime suspect had I not seen his pitiful condition—or "executed" by Caiaphas. John the priest had gone to the Temple to pray this morning, even though all the priests must now know of his affiliation with the Master.

The women had no fresh news of the other disciples. There were, however, rumors, the women said, that Judas had obtained an audience with Caiaphas on Thursday afternoon.

I told them about Thaddaeus and his report of Judas's leading the soldiers to the camp. From their lack of surprise, I inferred they already knew. "Simon Peter is at my family's villa," I added. "He's blind."

The two women exchanged glances whose meaning I could not read.

"It is the hand of the Lord, blessed be His name," Mary of Magdala said after a few moments of silence. "He is ever just. From the beginning, Simon Peter was jealous of John and any other whom the Master loved, even of me. He was always quibbling with his own brother Andrew or the sons of Zebedee about who would be the first in the kingdom. He was like the rest of them, wanting only pomp and power and hearing only what he wanted to hear. He never grasped the Master's message of love and justice, of living the kingdom now. That was his blindness, not whatever is afflicting him. The Master put his trust in Simon Peter's brawn; he should have considered his brain as well."

"He is not a stupid man," I protested. "Blunt and uneducated, to be sure; but he is honest and he loved the Master as much as any of us. He has blinded himself out of sorrow as surely as if he had rammed a forked stick into his eyes."

"Sorrow?" Mary of Magdala looked at me scornfully. "He has cause for sorrow, truly he has. You saw and heard what happened in Caiaphas's courtyard. For those denials he shall suffer all his days."

"He has suffered enough already. The Master could forgive him; that means we must also." I felt only slightly hypocritical; hearing the rancor in Mary's voice made it easier to understand that my own anger toward Simon Peter had been intensified by anger at myself.

"The Master would forgive him. His mother probably already has." She nodded at the other woman, whose dark eyes reflected the grief I felt. "I cannot. I cannot because he did not sin against me, but against the Master and the Master's Father."

"If we cannot forgive Simon Peter, then the Master lived in vain. And don't forget that the Master chose him to lead us. 'You are Peter,' he said when he gave Simon the name of Peter, the Rock, 'and upon this rock I shall build my community.' It gave Simon Peter a special place among us."

"Yes," Mary conceded, "it gave Simon Peter a special place among us. But by denying the Master he threw that place away. 'The last shall be first and the first shall be last,' as the Master also reminded Simon Peter during one of those jealous disputes about who would be greatest in the kingdom. At the first test, Simon Peter's courage and his claim to lead us scattered like seed in the wind."

"We all ran."

"No!" she hissed and stood up to emphasize her words. "We did not *all* run away. The Master endured his trials and execution without the support of a single one of the Twelve. His chosen deputy had run away and was skulking around the courtyard, flirting with servant girls, and lying about his faith. Some of us stayed until the first trial was over. You at least were with us then. The next day we stood with John outside Herod's palace and saw you talking to Pilate while he condemned the Master."

"But you urged me to plead with Pilate, and when I failed once you berated me for failing. When I went back to try again, you imply I betrayed the Master. What did you expect me to do?"

"To act like a man, to win! To bully Pilate, order him to release the Master." Mary sat down again and covered her head with her shawl so that only her eyes were visible, a signal that I was dismissed.

But the Master's mother put in kindly: "None of us can bully the Romans. Quintus did what he could."

"What he could?" Mary's tone became less shrill, but her words were hardly soft. "He failed, that's what he could. And after he failed he went to a tavern to drown his conscience in wine. We waited and walked behind the Master to Golgotha, stayed with him until the very end, watched while they pulled his body down, walked behind Josef of Arimathea while his servants carried it to the garden, and helped lay it in the tomb. We were a few women, a priest, and an old man. Simon Peter, 'the Rock,' was not with us; Quintus the philosopher was not with us. We saw them hiding, then running for their lives when the sky began to roar against murder."

Mary could be hard, but she was seldom so harshly angry, at least at me. Still, there was enough truth in her words to discourage response, and I could not endure the grief in his mother's eyes. I stared at the small fig tree in the center of the courtyard. When his mother spoke, her voice was filled with pain, not rancor. "My son died alone, Quintus, abandoned by the Twelve and most of his other followers. Many years ago, at his presentation in the Temple, a saintly old man warned me that my son was destined for the rise and fall of many in Israel and that my own heart a sword would pierce. I knew then his years would be few and would end in sorrow, but not this way ... like a criminal, deserted by his friends. He died alone, crying out to reproach the Lord, the Lord whom he had always called Father, for abandoning him."

I continued to stare at the fig tree. After a long silence I looked up; both women were gazing at me, expecting some sort of response, whether of excuse or consolation, I was not sure. But what was there to say? Any excuse would be self-serving and I knew no words of comfort. The Master's mother had spoken the truth.

"You are right," I finally whispered. "I am ashamed, but you are right. Only a few had courage, and neither Simon Peter nor I was among them. Yet if Simon Peter acted the coward, he had much company. And he was the only one of the Twelve who dared to go to Caiaphas's courtyard—or to go to Golgotha."

"That is true," Mary of Magdala said, "and that is why we need a new leader, a shepherd for this flock of sheep who think themselves men, not a hireling who flees at the first sight of the wolf."

"My child," the Master's mother put in, "have faith. He said he would return. We have no need to replace him."

"No one can replace the Master," Mary agreed, "but someone has to keep us together until he comes again."

"And that man would be John the priest?" I asked. I avoided the business of the Master's return. Frankly, I had never been certain what he had meant by those few elliptical remarks about his "return"; he spoke so often in riddles that I was not convinced that he wanted those words to be taken literally.

"The choice will be that of the Most High. He might choose John—or some other, and not necessarily one of the twelve cowards or any of the other men who called themselves disciples. 'Who knows the mind of the Lord? Who has been His counsellor?' "

"Who indeed? Surely not a simple Greek."

I did not then grasp what Mary was hinting at, nor did I understand what the conversation was doing other than stirring acrimony between us. She and I had always been friendly—indeed, on my part there was more than friendship. She was only two or three years older than I. We were both of the same social class. Her family were the patrons of Magdala, a small town on the fertile western shore of the Sea of Galilee, north of Tiberias. They owned vineyards, olive groves, wheat fields, several large flocks of sheep, and a small estate farther north along the lake beyond Gennesaret. They also operated Magdala's largest wine press and one for olives as well. Moreover, they owned a stonecutting business in Capernaum that made such presses and sold them all over Galilee.

By eighteen, Mary had become the ruler of the family's property. It was shortly after her parents and eldest brother had been killed by a rampaging guerrilla band. One of Mary's two living brothers was a mystic who had joined a monastery of the Essenes near the Asphalt Sea; the other was a libertine who practically lived in the taverns and whorehouses of Tiberias, sins that some of the pious thought reflected on his family, including his sister.

Managing those estates required sober temperament, good judgment, and an iron will. Mary had all three. Her brothers accepted those facts as completely as did she.

I recognized and respected her quick mind and stony will; and she, unlike most of the others, appreciated my learning, though one would not have guessed it from her anger at that Passover.

I confess to having been romantically attracted to her. Perhaps she was not beautiful to others, but I found her so. She was tall and full bosomed, as so many Jewish women are, but not heavy. She worked hard, and, I suspect, her body was as muscled as those of a peasant woman. She wore her black hair long and, despite seldom bothering to put on a veil, had a fairer complexion than most women of Galilee. Her dark eyes were large and intense; their flash usually gave a split second's warning of her temper. Her thin lips were, perhaps, too wide for her mouth, her cheekbones a bit too high.

Most males were put off by her personality. But, though I, too, could fear her tongue, I found her independence attractive; and I understood how hard she had to fight to maintain it. Living with her would at times have been explosive, but it would always have been interesting, especially if one could touch the warm, ripe woman who, I believed, lived beneath that armor. Several times I tried to court her, dropping clear hints that we might marry. Economically, it would have made sense, and religion would have posed only small difficulties. She took Judaism far less seriously than I took philosophy, and I was, after all, a God Fearer. But she had shown interest in only two things, her estates and the Master. The former supported her obsession for the latter.

As I was about to leave, John the priest entered. He was a handsome man, taller even than Simon Peter but more slender and also younger by a half dozen years. Had he been fair and clean-shaven, he would have been a prototypical Greek athlete. Indeed, I had wondered if he did not indulge in the gymnastic exercises of the sort we love and so many pious Jews despise as pagan rituals. As I have explained, John was learned in the Scriptures and educated in other disciplines. His spoken Greek was excellent, possibly because of the pilgrimages to Jerusalem of so many Greek-speaking Jews from around the Mediterranean. And he could read it as well as he could speak it. His writing, however, was stilted, his vocabulary too limited. His style might have been adequate for Aramaic or even Hebrew, but it was too primitive for the nuances the written word of such a rich language can convey.

In our infrequent contacts, John's attitude toward me had been correct but distant, reminding me by its polite formality that I was only a God Fearer. As a foreigner in culture as well as looks and political allegiance, I was to be encouraged but not fully trusted. In turn, I admired John; his catholicity of outlook was difficult to match among the provincial priestly caste. Still, I found it difficult to get close to him.

Perhaps there was more envy in me than I could admit. Until yesterday, John had kept his association with the Master a secret. Nevertheless, he was the one whom the Master loved best. It did not seem fair to the others, who gave up everything and risked everything to follow him, that the Master should love John the most. Yet he did, and we all knew it. Simon Peter had the place of honor, but John had the place of love.

The three of us were relieved to see him and anxious to know of his reception in the Temple. As soon as he had washed his hands and feet, he told us in terms bare of detail that he had been treated as if all were normal. He had sensed, however, that he was being carefully watched, an intuition, he conceded, that might have been due to his own nervousness. I doubted that, for, as I have noted, John would appear to the authorities to be the most dangerous of us all.

I told him of Thaddaeus's sudden coming and going and then of Simon Peter's affliction. John nodded and replied, sincerely enough, "We must pray that He who dwells in the Holy Temple will be merciful."

I kept my eyes away from the two women because I feared Mary of Madgala would launch another assault on Simon Peter. I would have liked to hear John's response to her arguments, but I was too emotionally spent to listen to more vitriol. John must also have known Mary's animus and felt the same as I, for his weariness was evident and he did not encourage me to continue the discourse.

I used our mutual fatigue as my excuse to leave. At the villa, the servants reported that only moments before my arrival Simon Peter had roused again, with the help of two servants relieved himself, and then, after swallowing four more goblets of wine, one directly after the other, had literally fallen back onto his couch and into sleep. I hoped he would stay that way through the night, for I was still exhausted.

I went to my own quarters and tried by lamplight to write a letter to my younger sister in Scythopolis. She had long been interested in the Master and his teachings and, when I could, I wrote her about him. (She preserved those letters, incidentally, and they form the basis of much of what I wrote in my other account.) But I was too tired, too confused, and I admit it, wallowing too deeply in self-pitying sorrow to do more than scribble the date and salutation on the parchment. After a few arid moments, I put down my pen, took some supper and, like Simon Peter, drank too much wine.

6

❧ I heard the wild banging on the garden door before the servant came to waken me. The sun was up, its light thin but bright enough for it to be almost an hour past dawn. I got to my feet, slowly, very slowly, for the room was swaying. I pulled my robe over my head, careful to minimize the contact between my hair and the cloth, rinsed my mouth several times with cinnamon-flavored water, and then took a long, full drink of plain water. Neither helped. My mouth and throat remained less damp than the Judean desert and tasted like a much-frequented camels' privy in whose ammoniated soil someone had planted a small cinnamon tree.

I walked shakily into the atrium, passing Simon Peter on the way. The flagon of wine on the table was empty. He was half sitting, half lying on the couch, holding his head as if it were a treasured but damaged piece of fruit. My own felt tender enough, and he had drunk many times more than I. I signaled a servant to watch him. Even in my youth, I could cope with only one self-induced illness at a time.

Mary of Magdala was waiting—a different Mary from yesterday's shrew. The shawl of mourning was pushed back on her shoulders, its top covered by her long black hair. She pushed aside the servant who was trying to wash her feet and ran to embrace me. "The tomb is empty, Quintus, empty! He has been raised, just as he said he would be!" Her normally full, deep voice was high pitched—and exquisitely painful to my swollen brain, the more so because her mouth was only inches from my poor ear. Even the wet kisses she planted on my cheeks were sources of agony.

"Sit, please sit," I said as I eased my dizziness by reclining on a bench. "Start from the beginning."

"The Master's mother and I went out at dawn—you know our custom. When we reached the tomb it was empty. The stone was rolled back. The only things inside were the linen cloths I had wrapped around the body on Friday afternoon."

"And?"

"And I ran all the way back to find John and show him. The Master has been raised, Quintus! Raised! Now he will establish his kingdom!"

"Slowly, slowly," I cautioned, careful to breathe away from her. "An empty tomb may mean only that Caiaphas and his friends have been at work. They may have hidden the body and plan to produce it as soon as one of us claims that the Master has risen. We must be careful not to let him trick us."

"No, no, this is no trick. I am sure of it. He has been raised, just as he said he would be."

There is no point in arguing with certitude, even when it is only weakly supported by facts. I reached for the ceramic jar of water we kept in the atrium for guests' refreshment, dipped the gourd in, and drank it as greedily as Simon Peter had quaffed wine yesterday. "And what did John say when he saw the tomb?" I asked as soon as I could speak again.

"He won't go to the tomb unless Simon Peter goes with him." Her tone was ironic. I tried—but not very hard—to decide if she were more disappointed in John or contemptuous of Simon Peter.

"Prudent," I nodded, "very prudent. Where is he now?"

"Outside your gate, waiting. Now hurry, Quintus. Tell Simon Peter and the three of us can return to the tomb before the others find out."

Despite my pain, I noted that I was excluded from the group. I was annoyed but not angered. I had grown accustomed to being treated as a foreigner. I knew that, as a Pharisee and as a priest, John could not enter the house of one who was uncircumcised, even if he were a God Fearer. Still, he could have accepted from me the hospitality I accepted from him: He could have come into the courtyard.

"It will take a few minutes. Simon Peter is not in very good condition. Come, I'll show you."

Mary followed me into the banquet room and looked at Simon Peter's bulk. He was fully sitting up now—an encouraging sign, but his dark brown skin had a greenish hue.

"Who is it?" he asked. His tone indicated he really didn't care what the specific answer might be; he only wanted to be reassured he was not in danger.

Mary would not reply, so I began, without thinking, to relay the factual part of her news: "Mary of Magdala has just come from the tomb. It is empty."

"What tomb? Whose tomb? Damn it, man, tell me!" The reverberation of his voice off the walls was excruciatingly painful but at least Simon Peter was showing some emotional reaction. Something was prodding his brain even more cruelly than were the dregs of yesterday's wine.

Mary looked at me quizzically. I had neglected to tell her about his loss of memory. I gestured toward Simon Peter. "I forgot to explain yesterday," I said.

I sat on the couch next to him. The aroma of that wine at stale second hand was too much for my queasy stomach, and I quickly moved to the opposite couch. "Simon Peter, do you remember anything between returning to camp Wednesday night and Friday evening in the cave?"

He shook his head, very slowly and very carefully.

Mary looked perplexed, but not so much as to hold her tongue: "Blind and dumb. This is the Simon Peter we've always known."

"I didn't tell you," I explained. "He's lost his memory."

"Convenient. When it returns he'll probably remember himself as a hero."

Simon Peter groaned and waved his hand at us. "Wait, no more talk for a few minutes. Help me outside; I've got to take a leak—and probably throw up."

"No need to go outside. This is Jerusalem, not Capernaum. We have indoor privies and running water. You've been using these facilities since you came here."

I took his arm and the two of us went to the privy together. Just as I thought he was done relieving himself, he reached a pair of thick, hairy fingers down his throat and vomited loudly. My stomach responded automatically to the sound and smell. At the eruption and its echo, two servants came bounding to our assistance, wiped the bile from our faces with cool, damp cloths, and helped us back to our couches.

Mary watched us scornfully. Undoubtedly, she had heard the noises—Herod Antipas himself would have heard them if he were still in Jerusalem. "Let us go, now, this instant," she insisted.

"Is that you, Mary?" Simon Peter asked. "Fetch me some wine like a good girl."

She ignored him. "*Now*, Quintus, now!"

"Give him a moment, just a moment," I pleaded. "He's not up to walking yet. Just a few more minutes. He deserves answers. He honestly remembers nothing since Wednesday night."

"Damn you, Quintus, what're you talking about? Tell me about this tomb. And fetch me some wine, someone!" he shouted.

The servants looked at me, but I shook my head. "No wine now, maybe later." Then as gently and succinctly as I could, I explained the events of Wednesday, Thursday, and Friday. As I talked, Mary paced impatiently, suspicious and disdainful of both of us weaklings. Simon Peter listened in intense silence, great tears of disbelieving grief rolling down his cheeks.

When I was done, he whispered, "He's dead—murdered—and I ran away. I was the one, above all, who should have died at his side. My blindness is not punishment enough. I've got to live with this memory. It was yours, Quintus, but now it's mine. The Master once cursed me as 'Satan.' He knew me better than I knew myself; I'm worse than Satan." His voice, even in a hoarse whisper, had once more become flat, describing a person outside of himself.

"But the tomb is empty," I said, affecting an optimism I did not feel. "John and Mary will take you there to see it." The word slipped out; I was unused to dealing with a blind man.

"You must be my eyes, Quintus; we will see it."

Before leaving, I instructed two of my family's guards to follow us at a discreet distance. One had to be cautious in dealing with Caiaphas, and the cause of Judas's death—not the event, I confess—was sorely troubling me. As pagans, our guards would not be impressed by appeals to Jewish priestly authority, though they might be overwhelmed by physical force.

*   *   *

John the priest was waiting for us outside the house. He offered me a sign of peace but said nothing to Simon Peter, not even a greeting. Simon Peter accepted without comment the justice of the silent rebuke, for his own estimation of his character was now far lower than John's.

The way to Josef's garden was familiar to us. The Master had camped there several times. The trip, however, was slow. As the crow flies or even as the sighted could scramble, the distance to Josef's garden was less than a mile. But there was no direct road. Indeed, Simon Peter's flight had taken us somewhere near there Friday night, and I did not relish stumbling with him again over that rocky terrain, even in daylight. So we decided to go into the western gate of the city, at the triple towers, and accept the delay of Jerusalem's morning traffic.

Simon Peter stumbled frequently, and he would have fallen several times had we been rushing. It was the beginning of the second hour after dawn, and life was proceeding at full pace. Wealthy Greeks and Romans, able to afford lamps and servants, do not understand how poor people must regulate their lives by the sun. No moment of its light can be wasted. Oil is expensive; the poor need it to cook; they cannot afford it for illumination except under rare and urgent circumstances.

As we hobbled along, farmers were unloading their produce from carts or directly from the backs of donkeys, creating additional hazards of traffic and increasing the piles of dung around which I had to shepherd Simon Peter. Shops were open and women and men were crowding the street for their morning shopping and gossiping, forcing us sometimes to push our way through, at other times simply to wait for a group to disperse.

As we reached the edge of the garden, John suddenly broke into an unpriestly gallop and raced the last hundred yards, then halted just as abruptly and waited for us to catch up. As a priest, he could not contaminate himself by entering a tomb if a dead body were present. The tomb itself was a traditional Jewish burial site, a cave Josef had enlarged for his family's eventual use. The entrance was at ground level, about three feet square, so that one had to kneel down and crawl in. In front was a large wheel-shaped stone that, with some strength, could be rolled back and forth to block the entrance and open it later, either to remove bones for reburial elsewhere after the flesh had rotted away or to allow fresh corpses to be interred.

The scene was precisely as Mary had described: The circular stone at the mouth of the cave was rolled so that one could enter. Without speaking, John, still breathing heavily from his dash—he was not as athletic as I had thought—took Simon Peter's hand and led him to the mouth of the cave and guided his hand so he could feel the entrance. I followed him inside, into a tall room about nine by twelve feet, with niches for bodies carved in the walls. The entrance allowed small light, but enough to discern Simon Peter touching everything in that style the blind affect, reading the world through his fingertips. He felt the empty niche, where obviously a body had recently lain, picked up the blood-stained shroud that must have been wrapped around the Master's head, held it for a moment against his own cheek, then kissed it. After we crawled back out, he handed it to me to fold.

Only then, after my reassurance, did John enter the cave. He came back out quickly, able to shake the dirt from his clothes but not the puzzled scowl from his face.

For several minutes, the three of us stood outside the cave, feeling the bright sun on our faces. Even Simon Peter said nothing. Finally, he took a few tentative steps toward the city. John grasped his arm, so I took advantage of the opportunity to go back into the tomb. I had not been carried away by hysteria. It was, indeed, empty, except for pieces of burial cloth lying on the ground. I saw that with my own eyes; and, like Simon Peter, I ran my fingers over the niche where the body had lain. Both senses reported the same message. I closed my eyes and inhaled deeply. The air was heavy with the aroma of the myrrh that Josef must have packed around the body; there was no stench of death.

Still silent, we walked slowly away. Near the edge of the garden, Mary was sitting on one of the stone benches Josef had put up for his own enjoyment. Her face was now calm. The rancor of the previous evening, the impatience of the morning, even the grief she had shared with us had all been replaced by a serene radiance.

"I have seen the Master," she said very softly.

John looked at me sadly, his eyes full of pity. I shrugged my shoulders. Mary had loved the Master with an obsession that transcended sexual attraction—we call it fanaticism in those we dislike, devotion in those we admire. Nevertheless, she was not a woman given to hysterics, and surely she was not a mystic whose religiosity created visions. Still. . . .

"Tell us." It was Simon Peter who spoke.

"While you were at the tomb, I sat here, and for the first time I began weeping. Thursday, Friday, Sabbath, and this morning, I had to comfort the Master's mother; I couldn't give way to the sorrow that was festering in me like a huge boil. When I saw the empty tomb, I thought that he had risen, and my soul's dirge became a hymn of gladness. Then, Quintus, what you said about Caiaphas—how it might all be a trick—threatened my world again. I led you to the tomb and sat down here and began to weep. I could not help myself. Then I looked up. Two young men in white robes were standing where you are; they asked why I was crying. 'They have killed my Master,' I said, 'and now his body is gone.' "

"And what did they say?" Simon Peter asked.

"Nothing. Nothing at all. They smiled, very gently, to comfort me, I am sure, then walked away. I'm afraid I went on weeping for a few more minutes. Then another man came up. 'Woman,' he asked me, 'why are you weeping? Who are you looking for?' I thought he was the gardener and might have helped move the body; so I said, 'Sir, if you have taken him away, tell me where you have put him, and I will go and remove him.'"

"Then?"

Her face became even more rapt. "Then he spoke one word, 'Mary.' I knew it was he. 'Master!' I said and threw myself on the ground. I meant to close the few feet between us, to hug his knees; but he told me not to touch him because he had not yet gone to the Father."

"His exact words, Mary!" If Simon Peter's tone lacked its usual snap, neither did it have the flat, abstract quality of the past day and a half.

"His exact words: 'Go and tell Simon Peter and the others that I am ascending to my Father. I shall see them in Galilee.' "

"Was there anything else?"

"No. Then he was gone, simply gone." She paused and looked at John and me. Her tone became more emphatic, even as her voice became more quiet. "You don't believe me, do you? He was here, I tell you. I saw him with my own eyes and I could have touched him with my own hands. I know the Master. I am not an hysterical woman. I am not like Martha. He was real—flesh and blood. He has been raised."

John the priest gave me the same pitying look, took Simon Peter's arm, and began the slow trudge back to my family's villa.

This time John came inside the gate. I understood the cost to him in that gesture. So that we would not have to enter the house itself, I ordered the servants to wash our feet, bring cushions for the benches in the atrium, and serve us refreshments there—nonalcoholic, both out of respect for the ban on John's drinking and for Simon Peter's and my own head. John accepted no food, only water, as was allowed.

"We've got to find the others and tell them the good news," Simon Peter began.

"Is that wise?" I asked. "Even if we could find them—and I wouldn't know where to begin to look—it might not be prudent for the Master's followers to be together in one place, not now, not in Jerusalem."

"I know where to find some of them," Simon Peter claimed, ignoring most of what I had said. "Some'll be at Matthias's inn in the Essene Quarter, where we celebrated Passover, or in the Galileans' tavern in the Valley of the Cheesemakers. They'll be scared and looking for company—and for somebody to tell them what to do."

John, though ill at ease in the courtyard of a gentile household, repeated my principal point: "Do we want to claim a resurrection yet? The empty tomb may be one of Caiaphas's tricks. That would fit with his polite treatment of me yesterday at the Temple."

"I knew you didn't believe me." Mary spoke in contempt rather than anger.

"I believe you told us exactly what you experienced; but," John added, "it is not uncommon to have 'visions' of those we deeply love shortly after their deaths. We all loved the Master, and each of us feels great guilt at our inability to save his gentle soul from that brutal end."

"I understand all of that, but I still believe that he has been raised."

"Did you touch him?" John asked.

"I told you I didn't. I tried to, but he said I shouldn't. Why can't you believe?"

John's voice was soothing rather than arguing. "Mary, you were not out of our sight for more than a few moments; yet we saw no one."

At that point, the two guards came into the atrium. "I instructed these men," I explained to my guests, "to follow us to the tomb, in case there was trouble."

Mary looked at me angrily. "Those are the two men who spoke to me," she said before I could ask. "But that doesn't mean I didn't see the Master."

"What did you see?" I asked the older guard.

"We saw you and the other men going in and out of a cave—I assume it was the tomb you spoke of. We could not be sure of what was happening; you seemed excited. Then we saw the lady about twenty yards away, sitting on a bench weeping. We went to her and asked what was wrong. When she explained why she was weeping, we moved away to where we could continue to watch all of you."

"All of us?" I repeated. "Did you see another man—not one of us—come up and talk to the lady or to us?"

"No, sir; only the four of you."

"Was the lady always in your sight?"

"Not every instant. You three were a fair distance apart, but we kept a close watch. If a fifth person had come up, it's likely we would have seen him."

"Likely," Mary repeated, "but not absolutely certain."

"No," the guard said, "only probable."

I thanked the guards and dismissed them. I turned to my guests. It was not necessary to say anything more, I thought, but Simon Peter spoke: "He has been raised."

"How can you say that?" I asked. "The guards saw nothing, John and I saw nothing, and you can't see anything."

John nodded in agreement. "We can all understand Mary's vision and respect it. We can even envy it and share in its blessing. But let us not confuse a private vision, as holy and wonderful as it may be, with a resurrection of the body—a miracle of a very different order."

Simon Peter scrunched his face in what, had he been able to see, I would have described as an annoyed look. "I do not understand 'a miracle of a different order.' That's garbage. If Mary saw him, he's been raised." He turned toward me. "Your guards were in the garden with us, but John and you didn't see them either."

Before I could respond, he went on: "Quintus, you're always bragging about your Greek logic. Well, doesn't this all fit? Four people were in the garden, near the tomb. One—you, Quintus—never fully believed. He saw nothing. The second—you, John—never publicly admitted loving the Master until it was too late. He saw nothing. The third—me—was the worst of all. When it was safe, he shouted how much he loved the Master; but when it was dangerous, he denied the Master and ran away like an Egyptian eunuch. He, too, could see nothing. The fourth openly declared her love for the Master from the first day she heard his word, and she stayed with him to the last moment as he died on the cross. She saw everything. To her, the faithful one, the Master came back as he promised he would. 'I am the good shepherd,' he told us. 'I know mine and mine know me.' He knew his own—not John, not Quintus, and as sure as camels spit, not Simon Peter. It fits; it aches like a sore tooth, but it fits."

I could only shake my head. Simon Peter's logic was the logic of faith; mine, despite all my efforts, was only the logic of philosophy. He would go—or be led—to find what others of the brethren were still in Jerusalem and bring them Mary's good news.

7

❧ In my other work, I spoke of the Master's complicated relations with the Essenes, for those people played an important part in his life, not merely in his last days. Here I shall only summarize.

Early in his adult life, the Master had lived for some months at an Essene monastery above the Asphalt Sea, but had taken no vows, at least none I ever heard about. It may have been there that he first met Judas. I am not sure. When the Master left the monastery, he remained on good terms with the movement. John the Baptizer had been an Essene, and the Master followed him for a time. There was a small community of a dozen or so monks who lived in the caves above the Valley of the Doves that wound down from the plains of the western part of Galilee to the lake. I believe that when the Master slipped away from us for a few days—as he would do on occasion—he went up to join those monks in prayer.

This sort of loose relationship was not as strange as it may seem to a Greek or Roman, who would look on the Essenes as religious fanatics. But then, to most Greeks and Romans, Jews are all fanatics; and there is more than a trace of truth in such a view. Essene monks, or "men of perfect holiness," as they call themselves, are few in number. These professional ascetics live apart from the world in their desert or mountain communes, like those on the cliffs above the Asphalt Sea. They accept a harshly detailed regulation of their lives, surrender all their property to the group, accept in fact if not in name perpetual celibacy, eat at common table, perform hard manual labor, and spend the rest of their time in prayer, awaiting the Messiah, who will both drive foreigners out of Israel and destroy the priestly usurpers who control the Temple.

There are many other people who identified themselves as Essenes, as full "members of the community," but who do not become monks. They live in towns or around the countryside, teaching by the example of holy lives as they, too, await the blessed day of deliverance. They swear to abide by rules that are somewhat less severe than the monks', but still rigorously detailed. Members do not, however, give up their property, though they assume an obligation to contribute a minimum of two days' wages each month to feed the poor and help the monasteries.

On occasion, members of the lay communities undertake special obligations, frequently to celibacy. (The Essenes oppose vows, except for the oath of membership.) Members of a community are supposed to live apart from other Jews as well as gentiles and are governed by a "Guardian." All relations with outsiders, with "men of the Pit," are formal, with exchanges of goods and services paid for so as to minimize the likelihood of friendly as well as contaminating contact.

Yet an even wider circle has formed around these monastic and lay Essenes, sympathizers who share the Essenes' general apocalyptic hopes but who do not wish to regiment their lives. These people provide financial support and a buffer of public support that is critical to the Essenes, a small minority whose outspoken condemnations of the priestly oligarchy in Jerusalem would otherwise make them vulnerable to political reprisal.

The Master, I would judge, fell in the third group. His colobium, the long, close-fitting tunic common in the Orient, was always white, and white is the only color that Essenes wear. Moreover, he did not care for matters of dress and would wear clothes until they hung in rags about him—a trait Essenes share. To be sure, dress alone is not conclusive evidence. Lacking money for dyes, the poor typically wear garments of varying shades of white, though dust and grime soon impart their own hues.

More importantly, it was the Master's ascetic style and moral teachings that linked him to the Essenes. He may even have taken an obligation of celibacy. As an adult male Jew, he had a duty, at least under usual circumstances, to marry and beget children in accord with the command of the Lord God as given in Genesis. But the Master had no wife. I do not pretend to know the answer. Not even the closest of his disciples dared question him about such matters.

The Essenes' belief in an immortal soul destined for eternal

reward or punishment is close to what the Master, like the Pharisees and many Greeks, taught. And much that he preached about
love and justice is commonplace among the Essenes, but many of
them think such rules apply only to relations with other Essenes.
It is permissible to hate wicked men; and they are quite prepared
to kill, not only in self-defense but also to assist the Messiah
when he comes.

The Master, of course, preached the duty to love all mankind
as well as the evil of resisting evil with evil. He was also always
easy about ritual purity, while the Essenes almost obsessively
identify holiness with cleanliness, bathing after every possible
contact with any of a long list of items they consider polluting,
even insisting that one should wash after defecating.

In any event, the Master and his followers were always welcome in any Essene community. Like most small brotherhoods,
they either know one another or have common friends; a fellow
member or a sympathizer is welcomed like a lost brother.

Matthias, the innkeeper who had provided the meal, was the
Guardian of the Essene community in Jerusalem. Later, I would
come to know him well, but even before we were introduced I
would have recognized him from the descriptions I'd heard: tall,
swarthy, with almost no hair on his head but the rest of his body
covered with a pelt more like the skin of a bear than a man.
Simon Peter said it seemed as if Matthias's thick black beard
continued to erupt from every pore of his body below his neck. He
had taken an obligation of celibacy, as had his wife; and, my father
would have judged from their tempers, both kept their word.

I did not know exactly where Matthias's inn was located and,
given the Essenes' hostility toward foreigners, I would probably
have gotten little help had I asked. John knew Jerusalem far more
intimately than I, but he was almost equally ignorant of the
Essene Quarter. Only a few of the disciples had known he was one
of us, and the Essenes would distrust him, a priest of the Temple,
even more than they would me. Moreover, if Caiaphas heard of
John's being there, he might think John was flouting the High
Priest's authority and would strike out savagely.

Simon Peter agreed with my analysis, but he could not travel
by himself. That left only Mary to guide him, and she was un-

happy with the task. She would have preferred to have gone alone, as foolish as that sounds. Despite the fact that Simon Peter was the only one of us who believed her vision had been real, she was not about to forgive him for denying the Master. Her scales of justice have always been finely calibrated.

I tried to persuade my three guests to take a midday meal with me. Mary was willing, but John, of course, could not; and Simon Peter was anxious to find the other Galileans. I remained behind. Thus the episode I shall presently relate is not from my own observations, but from what Mary and Simon Peter—and the others—later recounted to me.

John tarried a few moments to tell me the details of what he had heard from other priests about Judas. The death had been self-inflicted. He spoke in Greek, though what secrets that would protect in my family's house, I do not know. The story he told is the one that I narrated in my other account.

"I confess I never understood Judas," I said. "He seemed the strongest and shrewdest of the Twelve. Of course, he was the most troubled by the way the Master would sometimes talk. He was especially upset when the Master told us that, unless we ate of his body and drank of his blood, we would not gain life."

"Did that bother you or the others?" John asked.

I smiled. "Yes, all of us. But our peasant friends easily brush aside unwelcome ideas, and I'm accustomed to living with concepts I do not fully comprehend."

John nodded in agreement. "I, too." He paused. "But I never became fully accustomed to the Master. I could not completely understand him or his message."

"Well, it bothered you less than it did Judas," I noted.

"Judas understood the Master," John replied. "At the beginning he thought, like some of the others did right up until the end, the Master was going to lead a revolt against Rome and the Temple. He'd probably been brooding about his mistake for some time, but last week it became clear the Master had no intention of leading a rebellion—at least of the sort Judas wanted."

"It's ironic." I mused. "The same actions that convinced Caiaphas and Pilate that the Master was a revolutionary convinced Judas that he was not, and led him to betray the Master to those who thought him dangerous."

John raised his eyebrows. "There may be no irony. I would not be surprised if Judas betrayed the location of the camp in the hope that the disciples would start a fight and kindle a revolt among the pilgrims around the city and then across the whole nation. I've heard Simon Peter boast of his prowess as a guerrilla in the Golan. Judas may have read Simon Peter's bravado as reality. It is a mistake the Master may have also made."

I passed the opportunity to defend Simon Peter. "And Judas took money from Caiaphas to betray the Master because Caiaphas would not have trusted Judas otherwise?"

"It's plausible," John said, "but not certain. From what I saw of Judas he was venal. Perhaps he couldn't miss the chance to pick up extra money."

"And he took his own life when his plot failed? Why?"

"Who knows? Perhaps an attack of conscience, I don't know. I find it all strange. And speaking of things strange, what do you think of Mary's 'vision'?"

I am afraid I responded with an elaborate circumlocution. John listened for several minutes before interrupting. "I agree, these past few days have put her under a heavy strain. Let us pray that the Most High, blessed be His name, will restore her strength of mind and body."

When Mary and Simon Peter arrived at Matthias's inn, Mary recognized Bartholomew and Thomas, called the Twin, skulking, hungry and frightened, around the alley. They had heard rumors of Simon Peter's denial, but only rumors, since they had been hiding most of the time since the soldiers had swept into the garden to arrest the Master. Whatever they might have thought of Simon Peter's lack of courage, the cloud of heel dust they themselves had raised estopped them from criticizing him openly.

Needless to say, they greeted the report of Mary's vision with derision. At their laughter, Simon Peter's temper flared; had he had his sight, bones might have been broken. There was, however, little he could do except curse them as blood-drinking sons of pig-eating prostitutes. After he had spilled several stanzas of such venom, he calmed down. "Mary's seen the Master. I know it."

"How can you possibly *know* it?" Thomas asked. "You can see nothing and you didn't hear him speak."

"I've seen him with the eyes of my soul. I know he's been raised."

"Simon," Bartholomew, the kinder of the two, said, "we also followed the Master. We thought he was the one who'd gather Israel around him and found a new kingdom. We expected to become princes. But he was too eloquent, and we were too foolish. You can't rouse a nation with love. It takes hate. We should've seen that, but we're simpleminded men. We fish and we farm and we beget children. We, too, had visions—of glory, not ghosts. We were foolish men. We knew nothing of the ways of governors and priests. Only Judas and Levi and the priest have education, and we saw Judas's betrayal. We should go back to our lake and the simple life we know."

" 'I shall make you fishers of men,' he promised us. Didn't we preach his word in Israel?"

"Yes, and we didn't do it well, either. But what does that matter? He's dead now. What point is there in preaching his word? We'd only be killed, too. We're going home."

"Wait! He lives. He's been raised."

"Simon, Simon," Bartholomew spoke less softly now, "he once told us to leave the dead to bury the dead. Let's take that advice. We have wives and children to feed."

"Not yet. Wait, for the love of the Master, wait."

"Wait?" Thomas asked. "It's easy for you to wait. You can make a better living begging in the Temple than fishing in the lake. A blind fisherman can only drown. We've got families. We want to bed with our wives, dump our seed in their bellies, and make children to support us in our old age. We can't live off women's foolish dreams."

Mary started to say something that undoubtedly would have scathed their skin off, but Simon Peter squeezed her arm for silence. A few days before, he would have smashed their heads together until sense had come in or brains had come out. Now, however, his words were meek: "I've got a little money. Matthias the innkeeper loved the Master; he'll feed us and give us the same room we used for the Passover meal. He'll even let us sleep there. We've got to stay in Jerusalem one more night."

"Why?"

"Why? I don't know why. I only know we must. It might be safer to wait until tomorrow anyway. No one'll be looking for us here, but Caiaphas and his Roman friends might be watching the roads today—especially the road to Galilee."

After a bit more cajoling, Thomas and Bartholomew agreed, though still reluctantly. Mary told me it was the offer of a free meal and a night's lodging out of the damp that persuaded them or else fear that the road might be watched, not Simon Peter's pleading for the love of the Master. I prefer to think it was guilt at their words to Simon Peter, all the more terrible for being true.

Later in the afternoon, another of the brethren, James, the son of Alpheus, showed up—like the others, frightened, hungry, and penniless. Because she was Simon Peter's eyes, Mary remained with the men.

As the group went into the upper room, Philip and Cleopas, two Galilean Jews with good Greek names, joined them. The two had fled the city that morning, and, at first, they gave no explanation for their return. As soon, however, as Matthias's servant had served the food, distributed several skins of wine—as an Essene, Matthias did not drink; but as an innkeeper he sold wine—and departed, Philip went to the door and made sure it was securely closed and no one was outside. Then he whispered to the group: "We've seen the Master."

The others said nothing—a response that puzzled him. After a few moments, he repeated: "We've seen the Master."

Still there was silence.

Finally, Simon Peter spoke in a carefully controlled voice: "Where and when?"

"At midday," Philip said. "Wednesday night we ran to one of the other camps on the hillside and stayed there all Thursday. Friday we came back into the city with a group of pilgrims and

heard the Romans were going to crucify the Master with the two
rebels. We saw the soldiers take them from the big palace. We've
been hiding and wandering since, from the tavern of the Galileans
to this place and out again to the camps. This morning, with our
few pennies spent, we set out for Emmaus. My wife has cousins
there."

"You were frightened," Mary cut in, "so you hid, then you ran.
We could guess that much. Tell us what happened."

"A stranger joined us outside the gate," Cleopas said, "and
asked us what we were talking about. I told him he must be the
only person in Jerusalem who didn't know what'd happened in the
last few days."

"The exact words, the exact words," Simon Peter insisted.

—" 'What things?' the stranger asked.

—" 'All about Jesus the Nazarene,' I answered. 'He showed he
was a great prophet by all he said and did in the sight of God and
the people. But the chief priests handed him over to the Romans as
a revolutionary, to be crucified. We'd hoped that he'd be the one to
set Israel free.' Then he looked at us and said—"

"His exact words!"

"I'm trying! If you'd stop interrupting it'd be less difficult. This
isn't easy to tell."

"Tell it, then. It gets no easier as time passes."

—"He said, 'You are foolish! You are slow to understand what
the prophets foretold. Did not Isaiah say that the Anointed One
would suffer and so enter his glory?' Then I can't remember all his
words, for, beginning with Moses, he explained the Scripture to us
as we walked. There was something about his teaching that almost hypnotized us. As we came near a small cistern in a clump
of trees, he suggested we refresh ourselves. We stopped and sat
down. He took a loaf of bread from his cloak, blessed it, broke it
apart, and gave us each a chunk. 'Take this and eat of it,' he said,
and we knew it was him."

"Then?"

"Then he was gone," Philip said simply.

"Gone?" Simon Peter inhaled the word.

"There was no one with us," Cleopas added. "Just the two of

us, each holding a chunk of bread, sitting in the shade by the cistern. We came back here as fast as we could walk."

"And we should believe that this, this stranger was the Master?" Thomas asked. "Why not Isaiah? Or Moses? Or maybe some friendly farmer who let you sample his new wine?"

"It was the Master," Philip said.

"But you didn't recognize him while he walked and talked with you."

"No."

"Then why do you think it was the Master now?"

"It was he," Philip insisted.

Cleopas nodded his head in agreement. "We knew it when he blessed the bread."

"Damn it, tell us his exact words!" Simon Peter broke in.

"I told you."

"You only said he blessed the bread. Tell us the words he used!"

Philip looked around, confused by the cynicism. "He started with the traditional blessing. You know it as well as I do: 'Blessed are you, Lord Our God, King of the Universe; through your goodness we have this bread, fruit of the earth and human labor.' Then he added, 'Take this and eat of it, for this is my body.' Those were the same strange words he said at the Passover meal that upset us so, the words that sent Judas running from this very room."

"It was the Master," Simon Peter said, but several of the others laughed.

"It was fear mixed with too much wine," Thomas jeered. "What was in that cistern, red water? An hysterical woman and two scared jackanapes running for cover have visions. Did you see the spike holes in his wrists or the wound from the spear that Simon Peter says the Romans stuck in his side?"

"No," Cleopas admitted. "I can barely remember what he looked like. He had a face but he had no face. I cannot even tell you how tall he was or what color robe he wore."

Thomas laughed. "When I can stick my fingers in those wounds and feel the torn flesh and watch the blood seep out, then I'll believe the three of you have not been dreaming—or drinking. In the meantime, let's eat and drink some wine ourselves; who knows who we'll see? Maybe Elijah or maybe Judas Maccabeus come back to reclaim his land from the Romans like he did from the Greeks. Well, he'll have to do it without me. I've had enough of visions and kingdoms in this world and the next. Pass me that skin of wine. I'll drink to a real body—my wife's. Ghosts and visions I leave to the rest of you."

"To ghosts and visions!" Bartholomew joined in and expertly squirted a long, thin stream of bright red wine into his mouth, then tossed the skin to Thomas.

Simon Peter, Mary, Cleopas, and Philip reclined on one set of couches, the others on another. There was little conversation within the two groups and none at all between them. Even had no cruel words been uttered, none of them could forget that only four nights earlier thirteen of them had eaten in this very room.

Then it happened, or so they believed: A faint scent of myrrh, a hushing sound like a mother comforting her child or a soft spring breeze pushing life-giving clouds toward farm land, and they felt a presence in their midst. "Peace be with you," they heard a voice say.

There was silence. Then Mary threw herself at the Vision's knees and clung to them, as she had tried to do in Josef's orchard. The others saw the Vision gently touch her hair and say: "As the Father sent me, so I send you."

Then he seemed to gaze directly at Thomas. "Put your finger here in my wounds, feel the torn flesh, watch the blood seep out."

But Thomas could only hang his head in shame. "Master," he muttered.

The Vision smiled compassionately. "Because you have seen, you have believed; blessed are they who have not seen, yet have believed." Then he appeared to touch Mary's hair a second time and looked at the rest of the disciples. "Peace be with you," they heard, and the Vision was gone. Only the soft sound of the breeze and the slight odor of myrrh remained

No one moved. No one spoke. They could not tell me how long they sat. Simon Peter, Mary, and Philip each reported having lost all sense of time. At some point, Cleopas asked, "What do we do now?"

There was no answer.

"What do we do now, Simon?" Cleopas repeated.

"I don't know. I don't know what we should do. He sends us but I don't know where or why. I am truly blind. I didn't see him. He spoke to Thomas and forgave him his disbelief. But he didn't speak to me or forgive me for my denial or give me back my sight. Ask someone who's seen the Master."

His words hung in the air for several minutes, then Mary spoke out. "We leave for Galilee at dawn. It is what the Master told me this morning: 'Go and tell Simon Peter and the others that I am ascending to my Father. I shall see them in Galilee.' "

The others nodded. They were accustomed to obeying orders.

8

✣ Not two hours after dawn on Monday, a servant summoned me to the house of John the priest. When I arrived, Mary of Magdala and the Master's mother were also there. I sat in the courtyard while the three made hurried preparations to leave for Galilee. Perhaps as an afterthought, Mary invited me to join them. Curiosity drove me to accept, as did the chance of visiting my family at Scythopolis, located two-thirds of the way between Jerusalem and Magdala.

Mary waited until I had agreed before telling me what had happened at the inn the previous evening. I was shaken; not convinced, but shaken. The story Cleopas and Philip had recited I could dismiss out of hand, but what the seven—or six of them— had seen together in the upper room was of a different order. I was aware, of course, that far larger groups could experience collective hallucinations; but that someone as cynical as Thomas would be convinced shook my disbelief. I very badly wanted to ask John about his reaction but could not with the two women present. Their eyes showed not only that they themselves believed but that they also desperately wanted us to believe. It was an assurance I could not offer. Instead, I asked John if it were not dangerous for him to leave Jerusalem now.

"Not as dangerous as to stay. I'm sure that Caiaphas, my good 'cousin,' now knows all about my relationship with the Master. He also caters to Annas, his father-in-law and my grand-uncle, and knows that the old man is very fond of me. He allowed me to keep this house even after he learned I was studying under Rab' Gamaliel. Annas for my sake and Caiaphas for his own would like to see me escape scandal."

John halted rather than stopped. I waited a moment, then asked: "And?"

He frowned and was silent for a few more seconds, then he answered, his words coming out slowly, reluctantly: "And there is a more compelling reason why I must go. At very long last, I must make my choice an open one. I can no longer carry my love for the Master as a guilty secret. I have written both Caiaphas and Annas letters explaining what I am doing. I think they'll ignore me, providing I do not resume my priestly duties. Annas will be deeply hurt, but he may understand—eventually. Caiaphas will be relieved. Like the Romans, he's had enough trouble these past few days."

The Master's mother made no comment at all, not even about the prospect of an eighty-mile walk that would mean six days and nights in the open, swallowing pounds of dust from the roads. I decided to lessen her discomfort and cut a day from the journey by borrowing a string of donkeys from my uncles. We could leave them at Scythopolis on the way up or I could bring them back from Magdala. (I could have offered camels; but with Galileans those beasts would have been more trouble than they were worth— and would have attracted robbers.)

We packed lightly, easier for Mary and the Master's mother than for me. Having come on a brief pilgrimage, they had brought little with them, but I had to take some goods to my family. Despite the bustle that always accompanies the beginning of a journey, John and I remained in a subdued mood, impervious to the clatter around us. The women, however, exuded an air of expectant joy, not of funereal grief. Happily, we moved with sufficient speed and quiet that few people outside of my household and John's took any notice of our departure. After all, 100,000 pilgrims were streaming out of the city that day.

Although it was nearly noon when we left, by dusk we reached Bethel, a full eleven miles north of Jerusalem. To be sure, it was not a pace we could expect to maintain, but it's always satisfying to make excellent progress when beginning a journey. The village was an ideal stopping place. My family did business with a merchant there, and he offered the hospitality of his house—which, because the man was a Jew, even John could accept, though I knew and cared more for the Law of Moses than our host.

That night I managed a few moments alone with John. I have already indicated that we had never been close. Personal difficulties aside, I distrust priests, an attitude I cannot ascribe to my Hellenism. I have met few Jews, even observant Jews, who have much good to say about priests. Most are only somewhat less poor than the people they serve, but the High Priest and his entourage are rich—ostentatiously so—and that creates a widespread belief that all priests are wealthy in a land driven into poverty by taxes, secular and religious.

For his part, John found it difficult to confide in a layman, more so in a foreign layman. Even a full convert to Judaism can never become the equal of a man whose mother was Jewish, and a God Fearer is only a step above a pagan—when, indeed, he is that. On the other hand, John and I were both more educated than any of our companions, more attuned to urban demands and values, and, most important, we shared a love for the Master. There, John did not look on me as a rival, as he did Simon Peter. Nevertheless, John knew that were he to try to wrest leadership of what was left of the Master's flock from Simon Peter, I would oppose him, for whatever that was worth.

Mary's personal and shared visions of the previous day had brought John and me closer together, though in doubt rather than in faith; just as those experiences had partially—but only partially—closed the gap between Mary and Simon Peter. I was not then aware of precisely how vast and complicated that gap was. I grossly underestimated her audacity. The concern about the "visions" John and I shared and the journey by which we both intended to reaffirm our dedication to the Master enabled us to strike an unspoken, if incomplete, alliance. The glue may have been our mutual need to discuss recent events with another sympathetic and reflective person.

"What does your Greek philosophy make of this second vision?" John asked me before I could ask him.

"My philosophic heritage is at war with my Mosaic adoption," I parried, happy to thrust a reminder of my status as a God Fearer into John's forgetful ear. "Philosophy says it is foolishness—at best love and guilt having their final play—but my fear of the Lord says it is possible. Scripture warns us that a generation shall see visions."

John looked annoyed at my verbal fencing, but his words might have been my own, had I spoken candidly: "I am troubled, Quintus, sorely troubled by all that has happened. The pain, the anguish I suffered at the Master's trial and death I shall never be able to comprehend, much less explain. I walked along the edge of suicide, may the Most High forgive my thoughts. The Master had warned us that he must die, yet I could not accept that, not when he told us, not even when I saw the Romans killing him. I have only slowly come to understand that our task is to continue his work, his message, to bring about the kingdom of God."

"To understand is not to act," I put in.

"Exactly. I have lacked the will to fire my understanding. Worse, I don't know what it is I should do, assuming I have the will to do it."

"Nor do I," I admitted.

"Perhaps it is too soon after the shock of his death to do more than mourn. Mary is playing the fool, as are those Galilean peasants. But she is leading them, keeping them together—for the moment at least. I doubt if that will last. Still, I envy her capacity to decide and to act. I don't know how to separate my grief from my reasoning. All my thoughts are shadows. I find myself not caring."

"He did promise to return."

John looked directly at me. His eyes flashed a message I could not decode. "Then Mary's . . . vision. Next this . . . this shared thing, this group hallucination. To cast my lot with the Master was difficult enough, as you yourself understand. To cast it now with these simple, superstitious peasants raises the hairs on the back of my neck."

"And yet."

He nodded. "And yet."

As Mary had planned, we overtook Simon Peter and the others the next afternoon. In fact, they had spent the night just outside of Bethel, but in a field rather than in a comfortable home. Simon Peter had slowed them down, as he now would us. Cleopas had cut a cane for him, but he had to be led part of the time. We tried to get him on a donkey—no easy task—but once he was seated the beast refused to budge. In that stubborn way donkeys have when they feel overburdened, the animal stared coldly at us as we vainly pushed and pulled. The most he would offer were some fresh droppings for the road. Simon Peter walked with the rest of the men, groping awkwardly and sometimes stumbling.

At least we met with no serious mishaps. Even with the four donkeys, we probably looked too poor to tempt robbers. Most of the horde of other returning pilgrims must have seemed far better off than we. Moreover, to their credit, the Herodians had waged vigorous campaigns against raiding Bedouin bands, and the Romans had carried on that work even more systematically. But the general safety of the roads did not mean there was no danger at all. My uncles always hired a large force of private guards for a caravan, lest greed tempt brigands' prudence; even so, at each night's stop they suffered losses from pilferage by sneak thieves.

For groups like ours, the danger from petty thievery and unorganized robbers was far more serious than from professional raiders. Furthermore, when Jews and Samaritans meet, the possibility of trouble is always high. And several times as we crossed Samaria I was concerned. The inhabitants, though passive, made no effort to conceal their sullen hostility toward their Jewish relatives. What they felt toward a Greek I did not care to discover.

Just past noon of the fourth day, we passed around the western slopes of Mount Gilboa, where the Philistines had smashed King Saul's army a thousand years ago. From the high ground, I could glimpse the rich Valley of Jezreel and its river flowing into the Jordan. Ahead and to the east, on its commanding hill, was the white acropolis of my city, surrounded by smaller villages lower in the valley. It is a lovely site, an oasis of culture in a hard land that, for political not ecological reasons, must give first and almost total priority to bare existence.

The earth itself is rich. Lower Galilee—of which geographically, though not politically, ethnically, or culturally, Scythopolis is really a part—is among the most fertile areas of the Orient. Almost everything grows here: wheat, olives, figs, pomegranates, almonds, grapes, even exotic balsam trees. Barley and dates would flourish, would it not have been wasteful to put them where the earth is so good and rain so plentiful.

One might expect a new Eden in Galilee. It could be a land flowing with milk and honey. And it is, but only for a small minority. Much of the rich earth is owned by a few families who appropriate most of the earth's wealth. Many, like Mary of Magdala's people, are Jewish, with claims going back beyond the memory of man. Others, whether Jewish, Greek, or Syrian, base their ownership on grants from the Ptolemys or Seleucids, when those rival successors of Alexander the Great alternated in controlling the lands between Egypt and Syria, from the Maccabees, from Pompey and his successors, or from Herod the Great and his descendants like our contemporary, Herod Antipas.

Peasants work these estates for a small share of what their sweat produces when mixed with the thick, black soil. Others own their own tracts; in fact, many do—but, typically, only small farms of a few acres. Even so, if left alone, these people could make the land yield a comfortable living. The farmers voluntarily pay taxes to the Temple in Jerusalem—if not, as the priests so often complain, the first and second tithes, still more than men would give except from their hearts. Alas, these sacrifices do not reduce the burdens of the government's levies.

The Romans take a full quarter of the produce every other year. That may seem a large sum, but it represents a marked reduction from the one-third each year that Jewish rulers had sometimes exacted to support their armies, ambitions, and luxuries before Pompey came to the Promised Land some sixty years before the Master was born. Even during the Master's lifetime, the Herodians sometimes laid special levies on their people's backs. During the time about which I write, the region had been enjoying many years of peace, if one does not count occasional guerrilla attacks or bloodlettings within the Herodian family. But there were other expensive enterprises afoot. Herod Antipas, for instance, had erected a magnificent new city at Tiberias, "persuaded" people to move there, and maintained himself and his entourage in splendor, allowing the peasant and tenant farmers the privilege of paying for his magnificence.

Moreover, when these farmers take their goods to market, they are subject to special "tolls"—another name for taxes—when they cross certain borders, like the one between Philip's tetrarchy and that of Antipas. Before the Master called him, Levi had collected such duties for Herod near the Jordan, between Bethsaida and Capernaum. He had been only one of the minor hirelings to whom the Romans and the Herodians leased the task of gathering revenue. The collectors, of course, kept a share; and, while they may have given the government its proper amount, what they kept was usually larger than what their contracts specified—in effect, a tax on top of a tax, both extracted from the peasants.

To the northeast, the Lake of Galilee is filled with fish. Although fishing is not such a profitable occupation, most fishermen are much better off than either tenant farmers or small landholders. The water is common property and even without a boat one can eke out a living. But here, too, huge inequities abound. Modern discoveries in the use of salt as a preservative have made it possible to send some of the catch all around Galilee, Judea, Syria, and even Babylon and Egypt. When the Ptolemys ruled the area, they stocked the lake with the freshwater fish the Egyptians prefer; thus Galilee can now compete for the market at Alexandria. This advantage, however, seldom helps the small fishermen, only people who, like my uncles, can hire laborers to cure the fish and finance transporting them beyond the region of the lake itself.

In Sepphoris, the central city of Galilee, and in Scythopolis, it is not popular in the better circles to speak candidly of the way the peasants and fishermen are systematically robbed. To voice such sentiments in the capital city of Tiberias is to risk one's life.

I had taken no notice of such injustices until I heard the Master. His own family was moderately well off by the standards of Galilee. They were, in fact as well as claim, of the Jewish royal family, of a branch that had come back to the Promised Land less than 250 years before, long after most Jews who were to return at all had come back from Babylon. Josef, his father, had been an independent craftsman, well enough off to set up his sons by his earlier marriage in their own businesses and to see that the Master received the training in sacred Scriptures that he wanted.

Affluence is a relative concept, and the Master understood the plight of the poor on the estates, the small farms, in villages, and fishing settlements. It was to them he directed his message about the kingdom of God. He drew most of his followers from the oppressed—the ignorant, the downtrodden, and the alienated; people who could not speak proper Aramaic or Greek, or read or write any language; people with rotting teeth and bodies vulnerable to every kind of disease; women who would die early from hemorrhaging complications of childbirth, men who would die early from too much labor in the hot sun and whose infants would not even see childhood because of inadequate nourishment.

On the other hand, the Master also attracted followers who were not destitute. Judas had private resources about which I knew little—and dared not try to discover more. Simon Peter teased Levi that some of his tax collections had stuck to his fingers, probably a daily happening. Simon Peter himself owned a small boat, and his mother-in-law, a widow, had a pleasant house, adequate if not commodious for herself, Simon Peter, his wife and daughter, as well as for Andrew, his wife, and three surviving children. Zebedee, the father of James and John, did well enough to hire several men to help him work the two boats he owned.

But by the standards of the civilized world, even these people were poor. That they were middle class at the lake testifies to the poverty of Galilee. Further, only Judas and Levi could read and write. Even John the priest, poor by the standards of Caiaphas and his family, was by those of Simon Peter a man of considerable means; and John's education, though considerably less than mine, so far surpassed that of most of the other disciples that they had no concept of either his knowledge or their own ignorance.

Political influence had been beyond their ken, at least until they heard the magic words, *"The kingdom of God is at hand."* It is no wonder that a people to whom government was no more than a rapacious thief would so often and so badly misunderstand the Master's message. To most of the disciples, the centurion from the Roman post at Capernaum was a man of boundless power, though from my own father's military career I knew a centurion was not an important official.

The Master also, of course, attracted followers who had real wealth and some power. Mary of Magdala and Lazarus accrued large incomes from their estates, and Josef of Arimathea's buying and selling made him rich even by the standards of Rome itself. Others, including priests and merchants like Nicodemus, had stood on the edges of the crowds to hear the Master's words and talked to him at night in the shadows that flickered around our camps. And, I must add, there was Quintus, whose family's indulgent largesse allowed him to pursue a restless curiosity.

Of this last group, however, only Mary and Lazarus and his family made no secret of their loyalty during the Master's lifetime. The rest of us—and I include myself—were not only wary of the political and social costs of openly following such a radical teacher; we were also embarrassed to be seen in the company of such shabbily clad, rough-spoken, unlettered men. Like most country people, the disciples, even those more or less middle class, like Simon Peter and Levi, were dirty, reeking of sweat from unwashed clothes and unwashed bodies. Naturally the Pharisees, with their obsession for ritual cleanliness, would find these people uncouth.

What was surprising was that the Essenes, with their even greater obsession for purity, would welcome the Master and his followers. Worse, some of them, like Andrew and Judas, had also been followers of that wild man, John the Baptizer—even, we hesitated to concede, as had the Master himself for a short time.

Because Scythopolis was in the territory of the loose confederation of the Ten Cities—the Dekapolis—its citizens and the residents of the surrounding villages and farms suffered less onerous burdens of taxation than did the people of Galilee, Samaria, or Judea. Although I cannot claim that our peasants received justice, they were treated no worse than in the rest of the world—certainly no worse than at Alexandria, Antioch, Athens, or, the city of the one true God, Jerusalem itself. And Scythopolis was my own. Distinguishing between one's own and the good may be the beginning of philosophy, but it is not the end of humanity. By right of birth, I was a citizen of Rome, but I was also a citizen of Scythopolis.

The city is as old as it is famous. Located near the junction of the valleys of the Jezreel and the Jordan, it straddles caravan routes from Damascus to Egypt and others that eventually reach from the coast to Babylon. The ancient King's Highway, linkinq Damascus to the Gulf of Aqaba, runs twenty-five miles to the east, across the Jordan. We also sit at a climatic divide. To the west and northwest, Galilee receives ample rainfall, thirty to thirty-five inches in an average year, the lake about two-thirds that amount. The region to the south along the Jordan, however, is arid. We receive scarcely more than ten inches annually; and near the southern outskirts of the city, rain virtually stops. Only a few miles below us, hardly five inches will fall in a year.

Scythopolis was originally a cluster of villages, as, in many respects, it still is. The ancient Semites called it Beth Shean long before Israelites came to their Promised Land. Centuries later, after the Philistines defeated King Saul, they cut off his head and impaled his body and those of his three sons on our city's walls. Hearing the news of the death of his beloved Jonathan, David laid the curse of drought on our valley and, according to legend, marched against the Philistines. By some means—legends seldom provide satisfactory details—he captured what had been deemed an impregnable fortress atop our central hill and burned it. If it was not David who sacked the city, it was someone who was truly enraged. To this day, you can see the mud bricks of the Philistines' buildings baked red by a terrible heat—probably from oil poured over them.

Still more centuries later, according to another legend, wild Scythian warriors swept down from the northern shores of the Black Sea and founded a new settlement on our hill, the City of the Scythians. Yet another legend has the city named after the Scythians who accompanied Iphigenia on her wanderings after the goddess Artemis had miraculously saved her from Agamemnon's sacrifice before he set out to conquer Troy.

One takes legends as one finds them. There may well have been Scythians in our valley, just as there were—and still are descendants of—Amalekites, Arabs, Assyrians, Canaanites, Edomites, Egyptians, Gibeonites, Greeks, Hittites, Idumeans, Jews, Macedonians, Mesopotamians, Moabites, Parthians, Persians, Philistines, Phoenicians, Syrians, and riff-raff without pedigree whose ancestors' seed spilled from centuries of caravans. If it pleases a man to believe his city is named for one of those groups, he is welcome to that belief. It harms no one else.

Our pace from Jerusalem to Galilee had been slowed by Simon Peter. But even the prospect of the hospitality my family would lavish could not persuade the disciples to spend the night in Scythopolis. Time provided the excuse. Mary of Magdala and Simon Peter were anxious to return to Galilee to await the Master; indeed, a swift return had become an obsession with them. A night, they argued, would become a night and a day, and then we would have to spend Sabbath there as well.

For James, the son of Alpheus, and Bartholomew, however, time was only a lame excuse. Dust from the road soon obscured Sunday night's vision. During the last few days, they walked by themselves, talking in low voices. I suspected they were planning to desert and only wanted to do the deed nearer home.

John had religious reasons for avoiding my city. Even from a distance of three miles, we could see the graceful white temple of

Dionysius crowning the acropolis. In the plaza that opened before it stood a statue, more than twenty-five feet tall, of the god himself, Scythopolis's special deity. To John, any city that so ornamented itself was an abomination.

He could not conceive of the temple and statue as art. To him they were flagrant violations of the First Commandment, just as the reveling rites of the Dionysian cult were obscene transgressions of most of the other nine. He was unmoved by the fact that in and around Scythopolis thousands of Jews live quite happily and, as far as I can judge, quite religiously.

So we plodded on and camped north of the river and trod another fifteen miles the next day, stopping well within the historic boundaries of Galilee. We spent the Sabbath there, along the southern edge of the lake. We pushed on all through the first day of the week, avoiding Tiberias even more carefully than Scythopolis. The disciples feared Herod Antipas might kill them if he knew who they were. And, I confess, I feared that petty tyrant would not respect my Roman citizenship. Sober, he certainly would have; but one could not be sure he would act only when sober. After all, when in his cups he had murdered John the Baptizer.

It was past dark when we reached Mary's estates at Magdala on the northwest shore of the lake. The manor house was modest, given the size of her family's holdings. It was a set of three buildings with a high wall forming the fourth side of a square and allowing a small atrium in the center. The wall was made of black basalt, the houses of tan colored stone and purplish-red clay. Straw and several pieces of farm equipment were scattered around the rough stone floor of the atrium, and our arrival caused a half dozen sleepy chickens to scamper noisily around until they lit in a wheelbarrow.

I detected a distinctive aroma, a mixture of smoke from olive wood, manure from the nearby fields, and chicken droppings in the atrium itself. But, after our nights on the road, I was not critical. Indeed, I soon became very grateful for a roof over my head, for shortly after we arrived it began to rain, a boon to farmers but a bane to travelers camping in the fields.

We awoke the next day to find that, as I had suspected, Bartholomew and James had slipped away before dawn. One could anticipate that they would not be the last. Visions have a habit of rapidly fading from memory when viewers are tempted by flesh. Mary was angry but she said very little. Instead she wisely moved ahead, sending a servant by boat to Capernaum, seven miles away, to fetch Andrew. Shortly after noon, he arrived with the other James and his brother John, the sons of Zebedee. All eleven of us—the three newcomers, Mary of Magdala, the Master's mother, Simon Peter, Thomas, Philip, Cleopas, John the priest, and I—sat in Mary's garden, ate her food, drank her wine, and, like good Jews, argued.

Andrew, of course, was upset about Simon Peter's blindness, but Simon Peter brushed the matter aside. "Tell them the good news, Mary," he insisted. She leaped at the invitation, but the three greeted her story with guffaws. Not even Thomas could persuade them. Mary tried. She reasoned, then cajoled, then flayed them with her heaviest sarcasm. By all the rules of rhetoric, she won a smashing victory; nevertheless, she failed to persuade them. She turned—with obvious distaste—to Simon Peter and commanded: "Tell them what you think."

He spoke softly—for Simon Peter, very softly. "The Master's been raised. He showed himself first to Mary, then to Philip and Cleopas, then to six of the seven in the upper room of the inn at Jerusalem."

"Six of the seven? Why not all seven?" Andrew asked.

"I was the seventh. I could see nothing, but I could hear him. I couldn't make out the words, but I know it was him."

"You heard something; I don't doubt that," Andrew mused. "But how can you be sure it was the Master you heard?"

"How can *I* be sure? How can *I* be sure? Do I have a fool for a brother? Do you think I'd mistake that voice? He was there, I tell you. Listen to Mary. The rest of us have."

"I saw and I heard," Thomas said simply, "and I believe." Andrew winced at Thomas's words, but he was not convinced.

"The rest of you? Mary said there were seven in the upper room. Where're the other two?" Andrew asked.

"They've gone home," Mary responded.

"Gone home? Gone home? 'They've gone home.' " Andrew had raised his voice several octaves, to mock Mary's tone. "Yes, men who've just seen a vision of a man raised from the dead would do that. Had John the Baptizer's disciples seen him resurrected after Herod executed him, they'd have 'gone home,' too."

"We're all weak," Simon Peter said. "I sat closest to the Master for three years; but I 'went home' when he was before me in the flesh. Listen to what Mary's saying."

"Listen to a *woman*?" John, the son of Zebedee, protested.

"Who are you to question her?" Simon Peter asked. "You ran away in the garden and you didn't stop, except to hide, until you were in Galilee."

"All right," Andrew cut back in. "He ran away; I ran away. That proves nothing. So did we all."

"*You*, all the Twelve, all the men close to him, ran away," Mary cut in, echoing what had become and would remain a familiar refrain. "I did not. His mother did not. The only male who stood at the cross was John the priest, and he was not one of the Twelve. I was last at the Master's death at the cross and last at his grave. Was it not fitting that I should be first at his resurrection?"

Andrew was silent, Mary was relentless. "He could have come to any of you or to any of those others who ran away. But he came not to the weak, not to the cowards, but to the strong. Does that not tell you anything?"

"It tells me," Andrew said, "that you're claiming the role of shepherdess. You're claiming to replace my brother, whom the Master chose."

"Your brother rejected that choice first by deserting the Master and then by denying him. Even Simon Peter now concedes he has forfeited his gift."

Andrew nudged his brother. "Speak up, man. Don't let a woman nag you out of your place."

Simon Peter's quiet eloquence surprised me: "By a woman, our mother Eve, first came death. By a woman, our sister Mary, first came news of life. Both came in a garden, one of paradise, the other of sadness. He's been raised and has chosen Mary as his instrument."

For a moment Andrew was silent again. There was little he could say, but that did not necessarily mean defeat. There were other ways to challenge. "What, then, O Highest of Priestesses and Kindliest of Shepherdesses," he asked, "do you order your humble flock to do now?"

"What do you mean?"

"I mean what do we do now, woman? If you want to lead, lead!" Andrew seemed pleased with himself.

Mary did not hesitate. "The Master said to me, 'Go and tell Simon Peter and the others that I am ascending to my Father. They will see me in Galilee.' "

"Well, we're in Galilee. I don't see the Master—unless you claim that he's changed sex and you are he."

"Do not blaspheme, you ignorant peasant!" Mary snapped.

"I am an ignorant peasant," Andrew sneered, "and so are we all except for you, your perfumed Greek friend, and this Judean priest whose soft hands've never known calluses. But that doesn't answer my question. What do we do?"

"We wait."

"How? Where?" Andrew asked.

"Where did you first meet the Master?"

"Simon Peter and I were casting our nets, catching fish among the reeds along the shore, south of Capernaum at that little harbor we came to call Dalmanutha."

"Then we go to Dalmanutha and wait there."

It was quickly settled. Mary's first attempt at leadership had been a success, in large part because she gave the order her potential followers most wanted to hear, to return to their families at Capernaum. Only John the priest was disappointed. He would have much preferred staying in Mary's villa to sleeping in the open or in a tent. He could always help the others fish, I chuckled to myself. A few blisters on his hands might be good for his soul. (I recognized the hypocrisy in that thought but enjoyed it nevertheless.)

It is interesting to speculate what would have happened had Mary ordered the group to wait at Magdala. Perhaps she had learned something from the desertion of Bartholomew and James; if so and if she learned other lessons as quickly, she might make a formidable leader despite her sex. But, like John, I doubted her authority would last long.

I decided to go back to Scythopolis immediately rather than to accompany the group to Dalmanutha. I felt a great need to be alone and in familiar surroundings. The necessity of returning the donkeys provided the excuse to visit my family and to escape, perhaps permanently, the seething struggle for leadership. I had no further concern about the Master's mother. John the priest or Mary of Magdala would take care of her. If they could not, the Master's half brothers might help, though they had always thought him mad.

9

❧ That night, along with John the priest, the Master's mother, Simon Peter, Andrew, and the disciples who had not deserted us, I stayed with Mary's household in Magdala. The next morning, I rose long before dawn to start back to Scythopolis. I immediately went out to the servants' quarters and roused my guards.

As I was returning to my own apartment, I noticed a light flickering in the center building and walked over to that room. Through the half open door I saw Mary, fully unclothed, bathing herself. For several moments I watched without breathing, then tried to back silently away, only to bump loudly against a water jar. Somehow, even in the thick shadows, Mary knew it was I. She hesitated for a second then pulled a jellaba in front of her body and said without fright or anger, "No, Quintus."

"I'm . . . I'm sorry, I didn't mean . . ." I stammered as I quickly retreated.

That I had not intended to invade her privacy was entirely true, but sorry I was not. I still carry that sweet but unattainable image in my memory, for her full body was every bit as desirable as my salacious mind had imagined. Nevertheless, I did feel heavy shame, not for what I had seen but because in the midst of my overpowering grief I could still be so erotically moved. I was, after all, still very young.

A few minutes later Mary, now fully dressed, joined me in the atrium. Neither of us spoke about the intrusive incident, then or ever.

She insisted on preparing breakfast for me and later for the guards—figs, hard green olives, goat cheese, and bread, washed down with mugs of well watered, sweet white wine. "I could not sleep," she explained. "The Master's death, his reappearances, the move, these people. . . ." I detected a slight catch in her voice. But she asked for no advice and I, stupidly, ate in silence, confused by my role in her life and despondent about the worth of my role in anyone's life.

With only the guards and the donkeys, the journey back to Scythopolis was not arduous. We were on the road by dawn and, not being troubled by Jewish scruples, went straight through Tiberias. We reached my family's villa at dark, footsore but glad to be home.

That is not correct. I was relieved, but there was no gladness in my soul. Occasional recurrences of the picture of Mary's body incited additional shame. I was encapsulated in a melancholia whose darkness was occasionally penetrated by lights that flashed and spun the way they had when as a child I had fallen from my horse and struck my head. And there was physical pain as well— not the sharp stab that comes when bone abruptly meets rock but a gnawing ache more like hunger after a day without food.

I could not make these lights burn steadily nor discern any pattern in their pulsings. Like all of us, I could remember the Master's promise to return, though my interpretation of those promises differed from the others'. Like Simon Peter, though not so urgently, I needed to believe in the visions that first Mary, next Philip and Cleopas, and then the others thought they had experienced. On the other hand, like John, my mind told me that we were confronting no more than the reactions of a grief-stricken woman and of superstitious, uneducated men to a tragic death, for which they, as well as John and I, justifiably felt some responsibility.

This period was, as I have said, the nadir of my life. On the trek from Jerusalem to Galilee, the faith that glowed from Mary and the Master's mother had warmed me. It was, I concede, not rational to enjoy a faith I could not fully share. But, as Simon Peter would try to teach me, human feelings do not obey the rules of Greek logic. In any event, I left that warmth behind in Magdala.

As I walked through the Galilean countryside toward Scytho-polis, I amused myself with variations on an intricate fantasy of how news of my own death might be received. My family would, to be sure, be badly hurt; but, even armed with the ego of youth and its equal delight in self-congratulation and self-pity, I could not imagine how the world would be one iota the worse for my departure. Perhaps it was that understanding and my own self-love and a desire to be "missed" beyond the circle of parents and siblings that kept me from more serious consideration of suicide. For, make no mistake about it, despair made it a tempting thought. I walked with shoulders stooped, spoke to no one, and took no notice of either birds or flowers, objects that usually fascinate me and abound along the lake's spring shore. During that season, the banks and hillsides are madcap splashes of red, purple, blue, yellow, and white, all against the rich green of the grass that the wonderful rains coax from the earth.

By the time I arrived at my parents' villa in my uncles' larger complex of buildings, my family was taking their evening meal. In Galilee and Jerusalem and even in Athens, women seldom ate with the men; but in my family, perhaps because of Roman, perhaps because of Stoic, influence, we usually took dinner together, reclined on couches in the Greek fashion.

My father soon retired, taking with him a large cup of sweet red wine, thickened in the Roman fashion with a kind of jam that had been simmered in a lead pot. We embraced—his grip was still that of a Roman officer, his body thick with muscles, though marbled with more fat than his vanity could admit—and exchanged promises to have a good talk in the morning. We each knew, however, we would spend much of my visit avoiding serious conversation with each other.

We had long ago arrived at an uneasy truce. He accepted, if he did not approve, my devotion to philosophy as a deviation he should have expected for mating with a Greek. For my part, I could neither accept nor approve his obsessive hunting—for animals to kill and women to bed, and I wondered if there were any connection between the two activities. Still, I realized I could no more change his ways than he mine. At least I could admire the symmetry of his sense of justice. "I live off my rich in-laws," he had once admitted at the close of one of our more lengthy and less bitter arguments, "why should I deny my son that pleasure? Roman blood buys the peace that lets these Greeks reap their profits."

My mother and sister were very much awake. Our embraces were warmer, and serious communication began as soon as I had reclined on a couch. I confess, however, that I spoke very little that night. But then I didn't need to; these two could understand what I said as well as what I didn't say.

My mother was clearly aging, but her beauty was still apparent, along with graying hurt. My two uncles, my mother's elder brothers, were decent men and, when they were not away on business, supportive of my mother. My father's readiness to accept my uncles' largesse to live in playful indolence far beyond his own income did not increase my family's regard for her marriage. From the very start, I gathered, they had looked down on him. They knew enough about the imperial army to realize that a Roman from Rome, son of a moderately well-to-do, equestrian family, who had risen to the rank of camp prefect, must have committed some serious error to be finishing his career in a distant province, commanding barbarian Celts of an auxiliary legion. The reason for his coming down I never heard discussed; that it involved the wife or daughter—or both—of an officer or civilian official with stronger political connections was not a wild guess.

His callous womanizing was a source of embarrassment as well as potentially costly trouble to my uncles. I do not imply that they idealized faithful monogamy. They would not have been concerned had he taken a mistress or two or merely preyed on slave women. But the thrill of the hunt, conquering, excited my father more than sexual indulgence. And his amorous adventures with free servant girls threatened the peace of the household, and, more seriously, his romantic advances toward several of the wives and daughters of local merchants and town notables endangered the peace of the city as well as the stability of a delicate web of relationships that sustained our prosperity.

If my uncles were quietly disdainful of my father, intervening only to prevent violence or economic upheaval, my aunts were openly scornful, though never to his face. They feared his muscular temper, as did several irate husbands. My mother, "poor, poor Daphne," received the bulk of their contemptuous patronizing, which was why we had our own villa in the family's complex. My uncles were, after all, kindly men, at least where their relatives were concerned.

Theodora, my sister, was now nineteen and happy to be unwed. She was no beauty—thin, wiry, almost gaunt with a nose that might have fit a fuller face or even her own had she fleshed out. Her hair was a pale brown like my father's must have been when there was enough of it to tell; her eyes, like mine and our parents', were bright blue. What was to me her greatest attraction was a razor wit. She was a gentle soul, but the usual kind of suitor felt only the cutting edge of her humor. Moreover, it was obvious that my father, though he doted on Theodora, could not muster much of a dowry. Two years ago, out of consideration for my mother, my uncles had let it be known they would handsomely supplement whatever my father would provide. We were all aware, however, that the offer had come too late for a suitable match.

I slept a great deal the first few days I was home. The price, which I willingly paid, was refusing my father's invitations. I must give him credit: Every day he asked me to hunt with him, though I think he was relieved by my refusals. He took a servant or two and occasionally a Syrian acquaintance or even more occasionally another old Roman soldier. The party would ride out across the

Jordan just east of town and hunt in the rugged hills around Pella. The typical victim was a wild boar. Once or twice he brought back that rare beast, a deer.

As a result of his forays, we ate even better than people of our station normally would. (As merely a God Fearer and not a Prose-lyte of Righteousness, that is, one who through baptism and circumcision was formally admitted to Judaism, I never felt any obligation to follow the dietary laws; when I observe them I do so only out of politeness to Jewish friends who might be present.)

Slowly I began to return the confidences of my mother and sister. It was easier with my sister. She may not have been intrinsically more intelligent than my mother, but her mind was more inquiring and she had a flair for languages. Her Greek was perfect—as good as mine—and she was good in Aramaic, could read Hebrew, and could converse with peasants in several of the local Semitic dialects.

As I have mentioned, Theodora had showed an interest in the Master from the first time I had mentioned him to her. In fact, she had confided to me that she had once chanced to listen to John the Baptizer. I, too, had seen him, and Theodora agreed that his sulphurous presence burned as fiercely as his reputation.

About a week after my return, she invited me to walk with her into the city. We strolled down the small hill that our family's cluster of buildings topped and on to the edges of the city. The smells were stronger here—of food markets and donkey dung, but mostly of people. The large seaport towns I had visited were built on elevations so that gravity would flush the water that ran through the trough in the center of the streets downhill and into the sea or river. Jerusalem also took advantage of its location atop two hills to carry its sewage into the Valley of the Cheesemakers and then into the Kidron.

Scythopolis, however, was at a disadvantage. Much of the city was built in low, rather swampy land that had been filled in as dams were built to redirect rivulets from the hills into the Jezreel River. Thus sewerage was among the city's most serious problems, and those who were jealous of our city liked to joke that Scythopolis's affluence was matched by its effluence.

That particular morning, Theodora and I moved as quickly as we could through the jostling crowds toward the Temple of Dionysus. It was a magnificent building, modeled on that of Artemis at Ephesus. I've seen both. Ours is by far the more impressive, not only because of its location on a hill dominating flat terrain and so focusing attention on itself, but also because of the giant statue in the plaza, executed with such artistry as to complement the temple's grandeur without competing with it. Together the pair form a monument—a monument, John the priest would argue, to pagan revelry and uncleanliness. To a point he would be absolutely correct. But the two also form a monument to man's efforts to transcend himself and his dingy, tangible world, to reach out his creative might toward a reality beyond his understanding.

We spent a full ten minutes absorbing the beauty of the scene before Theodora spoke. "Your letters fascinated me, but I was never clear about what they were really saying. This Master of yours sounded like several different men. Was he an Essene?"

"As a monk, no; on the fringes, yes, to an extent, but not really. In some ways he was more like one of those Pharisaic rabbis with a small school of disciples who pass through the valley."

She nodded, half out of politeness, half out of understanding. After a few moments of silence, she asked: "He was a follower of John the Baptizer, was he not?"

"For a time, a short time." She was rubbing a bruise in my memory.

Theodora was silent again.

"Well, yes," I continued. "There was always something of John the Baptizer in the Master. Perhaps I should have said that occasionally he seemed like John the Baptizer come back to life—very angry, very righteous. Both were Jews, and you know how righteous Jewish prophets were."

"I know. I read some of the Greek translations of the Jewish Scriptures you brought back from Alexandria."

She had; I was aware of it, just as I was aware that she had read many of my philosophers and, as I did, inclined toward Stoicism. Theodora was a true Hellene, intellectually inquisitive, open-minded, and tolerant, much more so than I. It is too bad she was a woman, for, although she was neither as broadly traveled nor as disciplined in close analysis as I, she was more creative. Alas, even in this advanced, modern age, there is yet no place for women as professional philosophers.

As a Stoic, she was a believer in one god over all the universe. But, whereas monotheism had made Judaism attractive, indeed irresistible, to me, Theodora's reaction was more tolerant—more Greek. Just as she was not offended by the variety of cults and local deities who populated our valley, so she looked on Judaism as merely a more intelligent groping toward the ultimate deity than the cults of Zeus or Osiris, though she also thought the Jewish God was the most ill-tempered of the lot.

Her detachment was what I needed at the time. Cynical analysis might have destroyed what was left of my sanity as thoroughly as would have mindless sympathy for ideas not understood.

"Yes, you've seen something. My letters must have been more accurate than I realized," I muttered. "He was several different people. He could be as reclusive as an Essene monk, as puritanical as a Pharisee, and as damning of sin as the Baptizer. Yet he was also full of gentleness and compassion—not out of weakness, but strength. He once said 'I am meek and humble of heart.' That was not wrong, only partially correct. Except at the end, he was neither meek nor humble in the usual sense of the those words. It was more that he felt no need to boast or to push himself forward. He took his own worth, his authority, for granted; his interest was in helping others, not publicizing himself. He was simply as he was. He was."

"A Jewish Stoic?"

"Yes, but more."

"What more?"

"I can't explain it. Simon Peter said he was the Messiah."

"Another Jewish revolutionary?"

"Yes, but in a different way. And more."

"A miracle worker, a magician?"

"Perhaps, but more."

Watching Dionysius's shadow suddenly became more important than talking. I could almost see it shorten, millimeter by millimeter.

I noticed Theodora was staring at me. She cleared her throat, a sure sign she was going to say something she had carefully rehearsed. "Quintus, you're not married or betrothed, you don't own a concubine, and, according to the gossip, you don't visit the local prostitutes or even chase the servant girls, like Father does."

I blushed, thinking of my reaction to seeing Mary bathing.

"Does that mean you prefer men?"

"Well . . ." I started to explain.

"No, I don't mean like occasionally wanting to make love to a beautiful young boy or a handsome athlete. I mean do you *always* prefer to bed with men rather than women?"

"No," I laughed, much more embarrassed than she was. "I much prefer girls to boys. In fact, I can't imagine the circumstances in which I'd go to bed with a man."

"Then your attraction to the Master was not homosexual?"

"You mean homoerotic?"

She shrugged her shoulders, mistaking my annoyance for pedantry.

"How could you have thought such a thing?" I asked.

"One hears rumors, gossip."

She was right. My initial reaction had been petty. "Yes, some Jewish leaders were concerned that we were a group of male lovers. The Master used the term 'love' very freely, and he exchanged kisses on the mouth with his disciples. Some of his words might have also been misleading. He was always speaking in parables and allegory. We both know what an abomination Jews consider homosexuality. Curiously, some other Jewish leaders were concerned about the opposite. They accused him of associating with prostitutes—and he did, though not for the reasons his accusers imagined. Those were sinners, he said, and it was sinners who needed to be saved, not saints."

Theodora was silent for a few more moments, then she put the critical question: "Did your Master come back from the dead?"

"Mary of Magdala insists she saw him twice; and she's not given to hysterics. Philip and Cleopas also claim to have seen him twice; they're less dependable. Three others say they saw him once. Thomas is reliable; the other two less so. Simon Peter is the most certain of all, but he does not claim to have seen the Master, only to have heard him speak. On the other hand, John the priest, the most intelligent of the disciples except Judas, thinks they've all deluded themselves."

"But Quintus, what about him? What does Quintus believe?"

"Quintus thinks. As usual, he only thinks; he does not believe."

"And what does he think?"

"With all his God Fearer's heart he wants to believe Mary of Magdala is right. But he thinks with all his Greek soul that John is right."

"And does that thinking disturb his belief in the truth of his Master's teaching?"

"Not a bit. What the Master taught is either true or not true. His death only provides evidence that *he* believed in its truth. Belief in a resurrection only provides evidence about the mental state of his disciples. Neither has anything to do with the truth or falsity of his teaching."

"Unless he was raised from the dead."

"I said '*belief* in his resurrection'; the *fact* of his resurrection would be something else. I'm not prepared to cope with such a 'fact.' I'll wait to face that one until I have to, if I ever do."

"But meanwhile, even if this *belief* is false, you aren't shaken?"

"Why should I be?"

Theodora got up and began to walk slowly back toward our villa. I fell in step beside her, not knowing what else to say. After a few hundred paces, she found the words, words that startled me: "I'm glad and I envy you."

"Why? Why me of all people in the world?"

"I envy you because you've found something to believe in with your whole heart and mind."

"But I don't—I didn't. I never acknowledged him. I was always curious but never committed, always on the edges, watching, analyzing, making notes, writing you reports. And I guess that's what my letters really were, reports. All my training pushes me toward detachment; belief demands commitment."

She nodded. "You describe all the things you do so well. Are they not your form of commitment?"

I didn't respond.

"And now, you fall into a black depression that has us all frantic, even poor Father, who never notices anything except horses and whores. We're afraid of what's happening to you."

I looked away so she could not see my eyes, then spoke very slowly. "My understanding came too late."

"Too late for what? If your description of your Master is accurate, he understood you. So your commitment wasn't too late for him. If it came too late, it was only too late for your vanity. A philosopher should be above pettiness."

I smiled at her stratagem. "I wish it were that easy. It's not my vanity—well, not *only* my vanity—but my integrity. Why didn't *I* wash his feet? Why didn't *I* incorporate myself into his inner circle? He never asked me, but I knew I was welcome. I walked behind him, but I did not follow him. I only observed him, as I would have an exotic bird or a strange animal. I did not embrace him. Instead, I analyzed his words just as I would have Zeno's prose, not as the teachings of a man from the one true God."

"That is your commitment, Quintus, the commitment of the questioning scholar, not of the credulous peasant."

"The scholar and the peasant. Now we get to the core; now we get to vanity . . . and to snobbery. I knew I was better than his followers. I was more educated, more intelligent, more cosmopolitan, more refined, and cleaner and richer, a philosopher rather than a fisherman or farmer, a Greek rather than a Galilean or any other kind of Jew. If all the disciples had been like John the priest I might have made a full and open commitment. And perhaps the Master would still be alive."

"*Now* we get to the real core: foolishness, absolute foolishness. What more could you have done? You tried to persuade Pilate and failed. Do you think violence would have done any good? Those Celtic legionnaires would have eaten you alive. They hate Greeks even more than Jews, and the only athletic games you were ever good at were races. When we were children even I could beat you at wrestling."

"That angered Father more than anything else." We both laughed at memories of our fights and the whippings I got afterwards—not for beating my little sister but for being beaten by her. "Well, maybe I could have made them chase me."

"You couldn't outrun a lance, much less an arrow. Quintus, stop being a fool. You made the kind of commitment that you could make. Mourn for your friend. He seems to have been a truly wise man. You've lost him and you should mourn that loss. But don't mourn for being what you are."

"Perhaps I should be something else now and should have been something else then."

"I haven't read so much of your philosophy to lose all my belief in fate. If the gods—or the one God—wanted you to be someone besides Quintus, he wouldn't have made you Quintus. As I read those tragic plays you used to give me before you got so fascinated with Jews, hubris can be a fatal failing."

"That's not hubris; that was the Master's promise, to have a new life in which death will have no meaning."

"Death is all that matters if you strangle your soul in a mood of depression or kill your body in a fit of despair."

"To think I taught you all you know."

She smiled. "At least you taught me all *you* know."

"Well, then, what should I do, O wise and gracious Oracle of Scythopolis, besides suddenly stop being sad?"

"You're not sad, you're despondent; you're in mourning. And you can't stop being despondent, not suddenly, but you can realize what is afflicting you. Mourn, but understand why you're mourning. Someone you love is dead, lost to you forever. Weep for that loss; it's real and it hurts. Admit what you've lost and accept the pain you suffer. That way the process can have an ending as well as a beginning." She paused for several seconds. "Then show your commitment."

"Show my commitment? Now? How is that possible?"

"Why not write a life of the Master? Why shouldn't the world know about him? You found in him answers to your questions. Perhaps your role is to teach others what he taught."

My mind and my feet stopped. It was an intriguing idea, one I had toyed with but discarded. "You may be right." I paused and thought about it. Immediately objections popped up. "But I know almost nothing about him before I met him two years ago."

"Well, I've kept all your letters, so you have a detailed record of that period. For the rest, rejoin the others. His mother will remember his childhood and youth. You say this man Simon Peter was with him from the first. If he's blind, he'll have little to do other than talk to you. Our uncles would give him some sort of work that won't tire him at our salting factory in Magdala.

"And there's something else," she continued. "Most of the disciples, you say, have gone back to their old lives. Why should they? You could help this Mary of Magdala persuade them to live the new life your Master taught. You envy their commitment; but, aside from the two women none of them showed any more commitment than you. In fact, most have shown far less."

"Perhaps I could write an account of the Master's life and teaching. But what could I do to help Mary keep those people together? A woman as a leader is foolishness."

"What about Hippolyte, who ruled the Amazons? Theseus loved her and married her. She died in his arms after helping him defeat his enemies."

"But she led other women. Besides, that was Greece and this is the Orient; and it's all legend anyway, not reality. In that grubby world just north of us, I doubt if anyone but John the priest and the Master's mother have stayed with Mary. The others have probably gone back to their wives and their fish. And they'll never be able to tell them apart by smell."

"Help Mary find them and organize them."

"Even if a woman could lead them, what would she have them do?"

"Quintus, how do I know?" She suddenly sounded weary. "Whatever it is they would have done had your Master lived."

"I'm not sure I know what that is."

"And you won't know until you go back to Galilee and look for the answer. You can search for it while you talk to people for your book."

* * *

I went. Not immediately, not even the next day, but soon. And I didn't know what I would do. But then I didn't need to know—another lesson I had not yet learned.

10

✣ I made my way to Dalmanutha slowly and indirectly, walking alone, going first northwest to Nain, where the Master was said to have raised from the dead the only son of a poor widow. Then I went farther north near Sepphoris, the largest city in Galilee, to the hill town of Nazareth, where the Master had grown up. Two of his half-brothers, Joses and Simon, still lived there, running their father's carpentry business. I found their shop easily. More than a year earlier I had seen them with their brother James try to have the Master put away as insane, but they did not recognize me. I introduced myself merely as my uncles' nephew, a name that immediately caught their attention. They offered me a cup of sweet wine and some bread as we exchanged gossip and enjoyed the cool afternoon breezes.

As soon, however, as I managed to turn the conversation to the Master, their reaction hardened. "We know what happened at Passover," Joses said, intoning what seemed a carefully rehearsed speech. "We have talked to Herod's soldiers, the Roman centurion from Caesarea, and the priest from Jerusalem. We have assured them, just as we assure you, that we were concerned about him for many years. Even as a child he was strange. Later we thought he was merely another religious fanatic. We understand that peculiarity. James, our eldest brother, has been close to the Essenes all his life, though he's become more of a Pharisee. But our stepbrother, this Joshua, he was a different basket of fruit; he was mad or possessed by a demon."

"By a demon or an evil and very arrogant spirit of some sort," Simon agreed.

Joses, however, was not to be distracted from saying the lines he had prepared. "Joshua was convinced he had a special calling. He believed he knew the mind of the Lord, blessed be His name. In his teens, he used to go off for a week or more and stay with those crazy Essenes who live in the caves above the Valley of the Doves. Later, he went for several months to one of those monasteries in the cliffs over the Asphalt Sea. When he returned, he was a total fool. It was ridiculous to hear him order people around, to command them to change their lives and 'follow' him. Who did he think he was? Who was he to talk to us like that? He was our younger half-brother, not a prophet. Even James, when he heard the reports, lowered himself to visit us; and he came with us to try to have Joshua put away. We even persuaded our stepmother to cooperate. But those disciples of his were always protecting him. One of them, Judas, was an assassin. We were not strong enough to face him. Eventually his mother turned soft and joined the lunatic rabble who wandered around Galilee and Judea with him."

"I hear they even went to Samaria, to the gentile side of the lake, and north into Phoenicia," Simon added. "May the Holy One protect us from pagan contamination."

I took no notice of the insult. I knew it was thoughtless rather than deliberate.

"After that," Joses went on as if his brother had not spoken, "we had no more contact with him. We knew he would be killed. Our only question was who would do the merciful deed and when."

At the end of the speech, I left that oasis of brotherly love as quickly as Oriental courtesy allowed, and moved northeast to Cana, where the Master was rumored to have changed water into wine at the wedding of one of the area's leading sons. It was an attractive place, set in rich farming land; but the people were wary of strangers and I learned little, except that the memory of the Master was still alive. I was not optimistic, however, that it would long survive if not refreshed. Already there were new "prophets" talking of "last days" and wonder workers who would deliver Israel from Roman bondage.

The next morning I set out almost due east. For a time the walk was easy. I meandered through wheat fields that were being harvested. (Foreigners often do not realize our growing season for grain is in the winter; we harvest in spring, before summer turns the earth to rock.) Later, I found myself among vineyards and olive groves. People were working hard and seeming to enjoy it. Some of them were singing. The real rains were done, but they had been plentiful that year and crops bountiful. Even after the tax collectors' stealing and the landlords' gouging, there would be plenty to eat for another season. Seeing life bubbling and people sharing, however fleetingly, in its yield made me feel much much more cheerful than when I left Scythopolis for Nazareth. True, I had gathered little material for my book beyond an appreciation of the Master's family, but I had gained a finer sense of the countryside and its people.

I walked across the gently bumping plateau of western Galilee to the Valley of the Doves, which slices down and down until it meets the lake at Magdala, almost 700 feet below the level of the sea. The town's name comes from the Semitic word for tower; but, if a tower ever stood there, it has long disappeared. The only building of note is a hippodrome, one of the many signs of Greek civilization even in Galilee.

Magdala is a town of some size. It spills out from the valley and runs along the shore. Then, it had more than 5,000 inhabitants; now it has half again as many. Several hundred people work for the local government that controls the northern lake region and perhaps a hundred more are employed in my family's fish-salting operations. (The Greeks and Romans call the town Taricheae, "the salting place," but Jews know it only as Magdala or Migdal.)

Mary's villa was located on a small hill about a mile north of the town. Her family's estates were large, running for several more miles to the north-northeast, almost to Capernaum. She did not own the shore at Dalmanutha, but her property began less than hundred yards inland. I thought it wise to stop at her house to make sure she had not abandoned the project—or been abandoned by her "followers." I need not have asked. Her estates shouted her absence. The wine and olive presses were idle, which was to be expected for this time of year, for the grapes would not be harvested until September and the olives not until two months later. Still, no one was looking after these expensive machines. Worse, her hired men were lounging in the shade while ripened wheat stood tall in the fields.

I tarried at Mary's house a full two days, talking to the people who should have been bringing in her crops or repairing her presses, barns, and houses. I doubt they were completely open with me, but they had seen me often enough and knew I was close enough to their mistress for them to put some trust in me, at least as much as Galilean peasants dare put in a Greek.

These people had seen and heard the Master. All had watched him when he stopped at Mary's house; some had been in the crowds who walked to Simon Peter's house in Capernaum and followed the Master around the lake. They recounted things he had said and done—or that they had heard he had said and done. Even in their tales of miracles they had not deliberately meant to deceive me, and some may have offered accurate reports. I took notes, not while they were speaking, of course, but later, when I was resting during the afternoon's heat or in the evening after dinner.

They professed to know nothing of his final days, though they had heard many rumors: Antipas had beheaded him; the Romans had crucified him; the High Priest had had him stoned; he had fled to Egypt. Without going into detail, I told them what I had witnessed in Jerusalem. No one expressed doubt about my story. Most were saddened by it, but no one showed surprise or anger. As one old man said, "They could not allow him to live and to teach." I had no need to ask who "they" were nor to probe for reasons behind acceptance of the inevitability of butcherous injustice. My ancestors, after all, murdered Socrates.

It was I who was surprised by one of their reactions. Several times, after I had related my account of that terrible Passover, someone put—and on each occasion quite matter-of-factly—the crucial issue: "Has he been raised from the dead?" No one had asked that question in Nain, Cana, or Nazareth. Its source could have been house servants who had overheard the argument among Mary, Andrew, and Simon Peter; or it could have been recollections of the Master's promise to return. I replied that I did not know but several people were sure they had seen the risen Master. What is more odd is that my questioners never went further; there was, at least within my earshot, no additional comment.

I might have stayed longer at Mary's house and even tried writing a bit had not a servant given me—or, rather allowed me to draw from him—a further piece of intelligence: Mary was trying to sell her family estates. She and her younger brother, who lived at Tiberias, had had an angry discussion, and she had sent a messenger to her elder brother with the Essenes near the Asphalt Sea. According to the servant, the reason for her decision was to obtain money for the community at Dalmanutha. At that point, his information, or understanding, became very vague.

I decided to leave for Dalmanutha immediately. It was only a short walk of five miles along the arc of the lake. I chose the beach and soon regretted it. As I should have remembered, the shore was heavily pebbled; some of the rocks were small, some as large as a foot across, some smooth, some jagged, and all hard. Most were basalt, solidified lava. I watched the fishermen and their families walk barefoot across those rocks to tend their boats and nets, while my own sandaled feet ached from contact with protruding edges.

Dalmanutha surrounded a small harbor about a mile south of Capernaum. Poorer people who could not afford boats still followed the ancient ways of reed fishing. It was near here that the Master first encountered Simon Peter and Andrew, wading in the lake casting their nets outside the reeds as their wives thrashed those reeds from the shore side to frighten the fish out.

Travelers stopped here to refresh themselves from its seven springs. The water from some is warm, from others cool; some are slightly sour, others wonderfully sweet. For some reason, no village has grown up at this spot. Perhaps that was why the Master had loved it so. He came here often; hence the disciples named it Dalmanutha, "the place where he dwells." Back from the beach a half mile away was the hill from which he had delivered the Beatitudes. Below that gentle hill was a cave where he had several times slept when he had needed to spend a night alone, away from the din of Simon Peter's house.

I paused and rested beneath a willow on the bank. It was a day to enjoy, warm and bright, with only a few clouds scudding down from the Golan. I watched two lizards, one of them almost eight inches long come out of the shadows to sun themselves; they quickly scampered away when I moved my foot. In the reeds a frog was croaking loudly. Overhead a covey of laughing gulls circled patiently, watching the poorer fishermen work the reeds and waiting for someone to become careless and let them pounce on his catch. The scene brought back happy memories. I thought of Capernaum and Simon Peter's house—or rather his mother-in-law's house—and of the lovely synagogue not thirty paces away. A hundred yards north, physically separate so as not to pollute the Jews, was the camp of the small Roman garrison, permanent enough to have a bath, equipped with a boiler to make steam, for its officers.

Capernaum, standing on a knuckle of land into the lake, had no harbor. Nearby, however, were several dents in the shoreline that allowed fishermen to beach their craft. It was a small village, even by the standards of Galilee; less than a thousand people lived here. Fishing and farming were the main occupations, but, as I have mentioned, Mary's family owned a stonecutting establishment. Its workers used the hard, black basalt to make presses for olives or wheels to grind wheat. As one would expect where such craftsmen live, pottery making flourished.

For several years most of the people here had been hospitable to the Master. He preached and taught here with no real interference. Then Antipas began to get nervous. He heard of the Master's "miracles" and, fearing that it was John the Baptizer risen from the dead or some similar prophet who would publicly accuse him of crimes against God and man, Antipas made plans to arrest the Master.

Undoubtedly the Tetrarch had spies in Capernaum. While it is unlikely that Pharisees would have worked for a Herod, especially the founder of Tiberias, any of the other people might well have agreed to spy. For the poor, the temptation of a few denarii would have been powerful. Besides, some people deeply resented the Master, not only because he treated women as if they were as important as men, but even more because he accepted Levi into his inner circle. For that roly-poly little man had for years sat in the tool booth on Antipas's side of the Jordan between Capernaum and Bethsaida, at the throat of the lake's life, and gouged taxes from those who crossed the river from his brother Philip's jurisdiction.

The crisis, our first of many, came when the Master fed the multitudes on the hill above Dalmanutha. Stories spread that he had caused bread and fishes to multiply. And the people of Galilee, so often pushed to the edge of starvation by tax after tax piled on their backs, wanted to make the Master their king. It was a move, I suspect, that Simon Peter and the sons of Zebedee fomented. It was the sort of foolish idea that would have appealed to Simon Peter, and its promise of pomp and power would have severely tempted the two brothers. None of the three would have calculated the risks to themselves—or to the Master and the rest of us.

As I had tried to explain to Pilate, the Master's real "miracle" in the feeding of the multitude was of a different sort from that which spread around the country. But Rumor, as Virgil says, "is a terrifying enormous monster" who "holds fast to falsehood and distortion as often as to messages of truth." What better man for overburdened peasants to make king than a magician who could cause fish and bread to multiply like fleas? What more dangerous man to hated rulers like Antipas and his Roman masters? What is more to be feared than an army that does not need to be fed?

The Master understood. At dusk the crowd descended on us at Dalmanutha. When they were yet a half mile away, we could hear the cries and feel the demand rippling ahead like a huge, undulating snake. The Master pushed the disciples into their boats and told them to go quickly to the other side, to the tetrarchy of Philip, who, though a Herod, was a just ruler. The Master stayed behind, as did Mary of Magdala and I.

The two of us lost him in the dark and spent the night with a family of one of Mary's caretakers near Dalmanutha. It was then that I recognized my real feelings toward her; and, as we wandered about in the blackness, I had prayed, may the Most High forgive me, that we would be forced to find shelter in a cave, ourselves alone.

The Master had intended to escape to the Essene monks above the Valley of the Doves, but could not get around the crowd. Later that night a violent storm arose; its easterly winds beat the boats back toward the western shore. From my other account, you know what really happened—the storm, the sudden appearance of the Master as if he were on the water, and Simon Peter's renewed foolishness.

In the morning, Mary and I saw the boats beached at Gennesaret, south of Dalmanutha. We walked down to join the disciples, but others were as observant as we. Several hundred people also saw the Master and chased after him, still determined to make him king. Antipas's soldiers could not be far behind. The Master reacted promptly, ordering the disciples to beach the boats and flee. Simon Peter and the sons of Zebedee hesitated. The boats were their treasure—or in the case of James and John, their father's. With those craft, these men were by Galilee's standards middle class, and their families could eat well; without them they might starve.

The Master shook his head sadly and strode on. "Where a man's treasure is, there also is his heart," was all he said. We moved rapidly, heading northwest, not stopping until we neared Tyre in ancient Phoenicia, beyond Antipas's jurisdiction. I need not rehearse those travels. It was there the Master cured the daughter of the Syrophoenician woman, who, understandably, fancied herself as Greek. When she shouted "Son of David, take pity on my child," he pretended not to hear. Her response was to run after us, screaming more and more loudly that he must help her. After a few minutes, Simon Peter took up her case.

The Master stopped. "I was sent only to the lost sheep of Israel."

The woman fell on her knees in front of him. She ignored his words and looked straight into his eyes. "Help my child, Teacher."

"It is not right to take the children's food and throw it to dogs."

"Yes," she replied, "you are right, but even dogs can eat the scraps that fall from the table."

The Master reached out his hand and touched her cheek. "You have great faith, woman. Bring the child to me."

This was the only debate I ever heard him lose. As a gentile, I like to think of this incident as persuading the Master that his mission was to all people. It is an event—and a mission—that many of the brothers in Jerusalem have never accepted.

When, several months later, we returned to the lake, we went down the eastern side, through Philip's tetrarchy into the region of the Dekapolis. We camped directly opposite Capernaum for several days, until two disciples went across and returned with the news that Antipas had found other enemies to frighten him.

While we were on the eastern bank, the Master performed his second "miraculous" feeding of a multitude. Even pagans succumbed to his message of sharing love, reinforcing the message we learned in Syria. I think he was happy during those short days.

Antipas's fresh enemies notwithstanding, we did not stay long in any one place in his jurisdiction again. I was always footsore and weary from the constant moving about, but the crowds seemed to invigorate rather than tire the Master. He now talked more and more of his impending death, not in a tone of fear or even concern for Antipas, except for the possibility that "the Fox" would upset the timing—something none of us pretended to comprehend.

I would only remind you that it was during our return from exile in the north, when we were outside of Caesarea Philippi, that the Master asked me who people said he was. "Some say Elijah," I responded, "others John the Baptizer; a few say Jeremiah." It was a scholar's answer, concise, accurate, comprehensive, and coldly factual. It was not the one the Master sought.

He turned to Simon Peter: "And who do you say I am?"

"You are the Messiah," Simon Peter blurted out without a thought, "the anointed one."

"Blessed are you, Simon. It was not human intellect that revealed this truth to you, but the Father. So I now tell you: You are *cepha* and upon this rock I shall build my community, and the gates of hell shall not prevail against you. I shall give you the keys to the kingdom of heaven. Whatsoever you bind on earth shall be bound in heaven; whatsoever you loose on earth shall be loosed in heaven."

The Aramaic word for rock is *cepha*, thus the pun in the name Cephas. (The play on words works even better in Greek with "Peter.") This incident formed the basis of the claim of Simon—since that moment Simon Peter—to leadership. Or rather it had been until his triple denial, the empty tomb, and Mary's claim to have seen the risen Master.

I have repeated this much of my earlier book so that the reader will recall Simon Peter's special status and also keep in mind the centrality of the lake for the Master and his disciples. All of the Twelve except Judas and Nathaniel were born near here, grew up here, and worked here fishing and farming. Simon Peter and Andrew were born at Bethsaida —the Bethsaida on the hill about a half mile back from the lake, not the Bethsaida on the lagoon at the edge of the lake—and lived their married lives in Capernaum, only a few miles south. The Master had shared Simon Peter's house, and it was along the lake and its environs that he had spent much of his last few years.

Dalmanutha is a lovely place, except during the last of summer when it is encased in a wall of heat. Much of the rocky beach is fringed by reeds that run a dozen or so yards into shallow water, allowing the sort of fishing I have described. Where there are no reeds, graceful willows often lean over the water. Only a few yards inland, the earth is soft, black, and fertile in late fall, winter, and spring; brown and rock-hard in the summer and early fall, as the area bakes from May until October without rain.

Mary's olive groves begin 200 yards from the shore, with grape vines scattered between the trees. On higher ground, across the narrow dirt road that runs from Magdala to Gennesaret, Capernaum, Bethsaida, and beyond into the Upper Jordan Valley, is a large field of wheat encompassing the hill from which the Master had delivered the Beatitudes. This grain, unlike that on the part of the estates near Magdala, was being harvested as I approached.

On common land between Mary's estates and the lake are the seven springs, the Waters of Gad some people called them, probably incorrectly. When first I was there, the area was a huge mud patch, even in summer, as the waters erupted from the earth. In the interim, the Roman garrison at Capernaum had done the region a service by laying huge stones around the mouth of the springs, providing paving that enabled users to get water without taking a mud bath.

On the near side of the road, set among olive trees, was a barnlike structure and a smaller cottage surrounded by tents. I correctly assumed that the community was housed here. As it turned out, some of the members, like Andrew and Simon Peter, lived in their own homes in Gennesaret or Capernaum; but obviously a cluster of people, including a dozen or so small children whom I could see gamboling about, resided on the estate. The lake—three fishing boats were beached at the small harbor—would enable the community to survive. The vineyards, olive trees, and wheat fields would enable the community to prosper.

As I walked up from the beach toward the tents, I met John the priest. He seemed glad to see me, perhaps a tribute to the blessings of manual labor in reinforcing the Master's message of love toward all men. I suspect, however, that the absence of anyone with whom to engage in intellectual conversation was the real reason for his unaccustomed warmth.

We wandered around the camp until the evening meal. It was, as I expected, simple: figs, bread, fish, a few lentils, and some watered wine. I counted the Eleven, their wives, John, Mary of Magdala, the Master's mother, and twenty-six other adults. There were nearly that many children. Because neither the two buildings nor any of the tents could have held a third of those people, we reclined on the earth under the trees outside the barn, which Mary had converted into an office and a residence for herself and the Master's mother. This sort of open-air dining is quite pleasant in warm weather, but winters around the lake can be damp and cold. For those months the community would either have to construct some sort of large refectory or else divide into much smaller units for common meals.

The women took turns in teams serving the meals, but each family did its own cooking and contributed the prepared food to the common larder because there were no facilities large enough to cook for so many mouths. The children were supposed to help clean up after; but, if that night were typical, it would have been easier for the women had their offspring gone off to bicker elsewhere. Certainly I would have had greater peace had they done so.

At the beginning of the meal, Mary stood up and asked John to invoke the blessing. His prayer, delivered in a singsong chant as he rocked to and fro, was traditional:

Hear, O Israel: The Lord our God, the Lord is one.

To which the people responded:

Blessed be the name of His glorious kingdom forever and ever. The Eternal One, He is God.

Then John continued:

Blessed art Thou, Lord God of the universe: Through Thy goodness we have this bread, fruit of the earth and of the work of human hands.

The response came:

Blessed be God forever.

John intoned again:

Blessed art Thou, Lord God of the universe. Through Thy goodness we have this wine, fruit of the vine and of human labor.

The people repeated the response:

Blessed be God forever.

Toward the end of the meal, Mary rose again. Taking a piece of bread in one hand and a cup of wine in the other, she held up both toward the people and said in a loud voice:

In this cup of blessing we share in the blood of the Master. In this breaking of the bread we share in his body. As the loaf is one and the wine is one, so are we one with each other, one with him, and he one with us.

The response was:

Amen.

Then Mary went on:

We do this, as he commanded us, in remembrance of him. The Master has died, the Master has been raised, the Master will come again.

The final response was *"Maranatha!"*—an Aramaic idiom that John translated as "Come, Lord!"

I did not have an opportunity to meet Simon Peter until after the meal. When I touched his shoulder, he reached out his big arms and grasped me in a breath-shattering embrace. "Ah, my Greek friend, I don't need eyes to recognize you, you still smell like a whore." He laughed loudly but without joy. Thus I did not make the obvious response. Our conversation was brief. It was dusk and Naomi his wife, with their beautiful young daughter in tow, wanted to start back to Capernaum. There would be other times, we assured each other.

I tried to greet the rest of the Eleven, but none seemed especially anxious for the fellowship of a Greek. I did talk to several, but I cannot recall which. In half-light Galilean men tend to look pretty much alike, all swarthy and heavily bearded. Even in daylight I sometimes confused them. One could tell them apart more by size and shape than by the usual distinguishing features such as color of hair and eyes, complexion, and the presence of a beard. To make matters more difficult, all seemed to have gone equally long without bathing, proof absolute they were neither Pharisees nor Essenes.

Mary came up as John was inviting me to share his tent. "Welcome, Quintus." Her tone warmed her words. She extended her hand in a masculine greeting. "You will be joining us for some time, I hope."

"If I may. I can make a contribution." I took out a purse from my belt and handed it to her.

"This, too, is welcome," she said—it should have been, it contained twelve gold pieces, minted perhaps two centuries earlier in Babylon—"but not as welcome as Quintus himself. Where are your goods?"

"I didn't bring much, only a blanket roll and a pack."

"Who needs more? Life here is simple. Come, bring what you have into the house." She gestured toward the one-room cottage. "I'll move into the barn with the Master's mother."

John's mouth opened in anger. He was sleeping in a tent with three other people; but a priest should have been enough of a man of the world to realize he had not brought a purse full of gold coins. In fact, however, the cottage's thatched roof leaked and in dry weather housed all sorts of chirping insects. Inside the barn, incidentally, Mary's workmen had constructed rather comfortable living quarters.

I stayed longer than I had planned. In fact, except for several short visits to Scythopolis, I remained at Dalmanutha for almost two years.

During the winters, we were all cold, and during the summers we were all miserably hot. The food was primitive but edible; still, on my visits home I ate only red meat and no fish at all. My most severe discomfort was the absence of an indoor privy and of servants to empty a chamber pot. One simply had to use outhouses, a crude way of existing that well-to-do Greeks had transcended more than 2,000 years ago. (I confess, however, that we learned the technology from the Cretans at Knossos.)

The rules of the community were uncomplicated. Essentially, they lived, as did all Jews, by the Law of Moses. In addition, they ate together the two meals that peasants took, prayed together in the morning and the evening, and shared with one another whatever they produced. Almost all, John the priest told me, had sold all their goods, which had been pitifully few, and contributed those coppers to the community's treasury.

Mary had not gone that far, nor had Andrew and Simon Peter. Indeed, as a woman Mary could not have done so on her own. But, it was apparent, her generosity had channeled much of her family's assets into the community. Simon Peter and Andrew lived in the house of Simon Peter's mother-in-law. Whatever the technicalities of the Law, they could not morally sell it. Their only other asset of any value was Simon Peter's boat. And he could not bring himself to part with it, though he did share its catch.

The last rule of the community was the most important and the most difficult: The members agreed to respect and to love one another, to treat each other not only as the Law required, but by the additional principle of familial love the Master had laid down.

Except for the common meals and their attendant rituals, the brothers and sisters, as they referred to themselves, did not set themselves apart from other peasants in the region. They dressed as most Galileans always had, which is to say plainly, shabbily, and pretty much alike in undyed colobiums. When the weather was cold, each also wore a hooded cloak, much like a burnoose, which some males adorned with the tassels prescribed by the Law. Even though the community prayed together twice daily, on Sabbath the brothers also walked to the small synagogue in Capernaum to hear the Scriptures read and commented on and to join in the prayers of the villagers. In keeping with the practical nature of Galileans, they did not measure the distance to determine if it was with the limits of a "Sabbath's walk."

Had the brothers and sisters strictly adhered to rules of ritual purity, a casual observer might have easily mistaken them for a community of poor Pharisees, until he realized that they shared their goods; then he might have concluded that he had stumbled on a colony of Essenes. There would have been something to both observations.

During those years, I was able to do a great deal of research and even writing. After a short time, most of the disciples were willing to talk almost as freely to me as Simon Peter and Mary always had been. Further, I had the leisure to set down my own recollections and test them against the memories of others. I was able to complete more than two-thirds of my first book.

Mary recognized the importance of my writing and never insisted I do other work, or even asked if I were actually writing rather than thinking. I thought it would be good for me and my relations with the others to help a bit. I broke myself in slowly; once the wheat was in there was little to do until September, when we picked the grapes. In the fall I helped harvest the olives and plant, but not plough.

I warned Mary about conditions at her estate in Magdala, and she took measures which, though not fully effective, improved matters somewhat. She would have preferred to sell off all except the land the community needed, but her brother in Tiberias refused permission. Since he was unwilling to help, I kept the accounts for her. In that way, I contributed more, I believe, than did the sweat of any of the others.

Those were good days. I felt a closeness to Mary, which was both a source of joy and pain. I also grew closer to Simon Peter, John, and several of the other disciples. Mary was tense, uneasy in her position of leadership. On the other hand, we were steadily growing accustomed to her role. She knew how to run an estate, and the community was, in a sense, a religious estate. We kept most of the original people and new converts dribbled in, especially in the fall, when the improvident had gone through their store of food and pennies. By mid-winter, we numbered a hundred and twenty.

I particularly remember a day in early September. The night had been unbearably hot, and I had taken my pallet to the beach in an effort, only partially successful, to catch some movement of air. At this depth, the ground clutches the day's heat in a bear hug. I'm not sure if I was awakened by the first bands of light refracted from the back of the mountains on the eastern shore, the hoarse shouts of fishermen out on the lake, or the slow heavy sound of footsteps interspersed with the click of Simon Peter's cane against the stones.

"I smell something queer—a male Greek or a female whore, if they're different. It's got to be Quintus."

I smiled. "It is Quintus."

"Yes, the heat'd be hard on someone used to a villa with servants to fan him." There was more bite in his voice than he perhaps realized. "Let me sit down."

He felt for me with the cane. I took it and guided him down beside me. We sat there for a long time without talking. Simon Peter stared blankly ahead, and I watched the shadows turn from black to gray, then transform into solid objects. Not until the sun was streaming fully into our faces did Simon Peter break the silence: "There's a haze on the lake this morning."

"How can you tell?"

My voice must have sounded surprised because he laughed. "No, Quintus, I can't see. I can only remember. After nights like these, there's always haze on the lake at dawn. It'll clear off in an hour."

We had another few minutes of silence. When he spoke again, it was half-apologetically. "I wish I were at your villa, too, Quintus."

"Why?" I was genuinely curious.

"Why? Because I need a cup of wine—better, a flagon of wine; or even better a dozen flagons of good, strong red wine, maybe thickened with syrup the way the Romans take it. I need strong gentile wine to numb my weak Jewish mind."

I said nothing.

"These last few months, I've had time to think. I can help work the boat, but there're many things I can't do. So I think, and I remember. Things've come back to me, things I'd rather forget."

"Like what?" I was uncertain that was a proper question, but I did not want to seem uncaring.

He ignored me and once more lapsed into silence. He leaned over and felt for small, smooth pebbles, then threw them sidearm so they would skip across the lake. He did what would have been remarkably well even for a sighted man. Then with no warning he asked: "Do you know why I denied the Master? Everybody thinks it was because I'm a coward."

"Everyone ran away; it's hard to single out any one person as a coward."

"No, not all of us, as Mary keeps reminding us with her mouth and the Master's mother with her eyes."

"How do you know what's in her eyes?"

"Quintus, you Greeks're so smart when it comes to logic"—he pronounced the word with contempt—"but most people don't live by logic. You understand nothing about people like us. We don't have to *see* eyes; we feel them."

"I have seen no hatred or even accusation in her eyes."

"That'd be easier to bear," Simon Peter said. "I feel pity and forgiveness."

"Is that bad?"

"It doesn't help to be forgiven for the wrong sin. There was more, Quintus, much more."

"To what?"

"To my denial. What do you think, the haze?"

Once again silence, this time sullen silence. I was embarrassed and torn. I was seeing a corner of Simon Peter's soul I had not known existed and should have remained totally private. Yet, as a writer, I felt a necessity to learn more.

"I was hurt, hurt and angry," he blurted out.

"At what?"

"At the Master, at John the priest. The Master loved him more than me. He loved Mary more than me, but that I could understand and accept. A man can love a woman, even where no sex's involved, with a tenderness he can never feel for another man. But he loved John best. John didn't take him into his house, feed him, and follow him around for years. John didn't run with him from Antipas's soldiers, or stand beside him when he debated the Sadducees, or help him lead the crowd that tore up the money changers' tables in the Temple. John didn't even openly acknowledge him. But he loved John best."

He was half-sobbing as he went on. "I was the buffoon. I said what a rough Galilean peasant thought, not what a smooth Judean priest would say. My words were honest, from my heart, even if they were sometimes foolish. I was his loyal follower, his faithful servant, his slave. I left my house, my wife, my child—even my boat—and followed him. John risked nothing. At that Passover meal, John got the couch of honor. The Master knew the end was near—I didn't realize that until later—and he chose to spend his time with John. I drank too much that night. I wanted to get drunk and I got drunk. It wasn't fair.

"In the garden," he continued, "the others started to run when the Temple guards and soldiers came at us. But drunk as I was, I drew my sword. I was still ready to fight for the Master and die beside him. I cut down the first man who tried to grab him, but the Master ordered me to put up my sword. He was angry at me—at me, the only one who stood by him. When I heard his anger, I threw down my sword and ran after the others. You know what I thought?"

He didn't give me an opportunity to ask. "I thought 'To hell with you. Let John defend you.' That's what I thought, 'To hell with you. To hell with you.' "

"Where was John?"

Simon Peter grunted something and picked up a handful of pebbles from the beach, then dropped them. "John? John? Our beloved John? Why, the good priest was at his house. When we left the inn, the Master told him to go to his house and wait for a message. John was safe—and secret."

"I see. It wasn't so much that John didn't run away as that he didn't have to make the choice."

Simon smiled at the thought, but only for a fleeting second. " 'Lead us not into temptation.' Even there he protected John." Then abruptly: "Judas felt it, too."

"I never understood Judas." I really meant that I always feared him, but it was prudent to keep that to myself.

"He was strange," Simon Peter agreed. "None of us except the Master fully understood him. Sometimes I came close. When I was young, up in the Golan, I met a few men like him. They had his heat when they spoke about the Law and his coldness when they talked about other human beings. But I never saw one who was as able. And he loved the Master as much as I did."

"Then why?"

"Why? Why? I don't know. I'm an ignorant peasant who sounds like a fool in Aramaic and an idiot in Greek. Maybe he thought about things too much. Like you, Quintus, he asked questions, tested the Master about things the rest of us accepted. We didn't understand them, but we accepted them. Rabbis always speak in riddles, everybody who's intelligent speaks in riddles. If you're an ignorant peasant, you don't expect to understand. Judas did. And he felt it, too."

"Felt what?"

"Anger. No, that's not the word. You know all the words, Quintus. What's a man feel when he's been hurt by one he loves with all his soul?"

"Resentment, bitter resentment?"

"Bitter resentment and envy, too. He knew the Master didn't love him like he did John. I understand his envy and his resentment, even though the envy was directed as much against me as John."

"Why you?"

"Because the Master made me first among the disciples. Judas should've been first. He deserved it. He knew it. I knew it. We all knew it. It would've been fair and I would've accepted it. No, I would've offered it, willingly, gladly . . . if the Master had loved me more. I can forgive Judas; we suffered together."

"But you didn't betray the Master."

"Didn't I?" It was a sneer, not a question. "Help me up."

I noticed tears running down his cheeks. I gave him my hand and he walked toward the water, tapping his cane to avoid the bigger rocks. He stopped when he was standing in ankle-deep water. "That morning in Caiaphas's courtyard—it was cold."

"I know," I said. "I was there."

"Were you? I didn't see much. I saw only the Master and the guards; John the priest was there—safe. He let me in. That morning, in the cold, when that stupid girl said I was one of his followers, I was scared. I admit it, I was scared, damned scared. But fear didn't make me deny the Master. No, it was envy, resentment, anger. 'To hell with you,' I remember thinking again. 'If you love John so much let that bastard acknowledge you. Why should I?'"

I grunted something unintelligible. Simon Peter took a few tentative steps farther out into the lake. "I'd like to end it, to let these waters that've fed me ease my pain."

"That's not the way."

"If I thought it was, I would've taken it months ago. But still, like Job, I curse the night I was conceived and the day I was born:

Why did I not die in the womb?
Why did I not perish when I came out of the belly?
Why were there knees to receive me
And breasts to give me suck?

[I always marvel at how illiterate Jews could quote from their Scriptures. Of course, it is the only literature they ever heard, and it's read to them from earliest childhood. Still, the world of the illiterate is as unfathomable to us as ours is to them.]

"I may be a coward in not ending it all," Simon Peter went on, "but I was far worse than a coward in the courtyard. It'd be easy to forgive a coward. We're all cowards some time. I can't remember any man who wasn't a coward on some days. My pride'd be hurt—when you're a peasant like me, strength and courage and maybe a dozen children is all that make you a man. But I wasn't a coward, I was taking revenge. Maybe that's not the word you Greek philosophers'd use, but I was spiting the Master, not trying to save my own skin."

"We can never fully understand our own motives."

He spat out an obscenity. "I knew what I was doing. That's why I forgot everything when you found me after the execution. It's all only slowly come back to me. I remembered nothing in Jerusalem, nothing on the walk back. Then here at the lake, I saw flashes, just flashes like I was watching a parade of those paintings the Romans have. After a time, in my darkness, the flashes began to fit together. One day I remembered. That's when I began to dream of making the lake my savior."

"But you didn't."

"I didn't—and there I probably was a coward."

"Don't say that." I felt like a hypocrite. For far less reason, I had almost plunged into the same despair.

"Why not? My sin, whatever it was, was unforgivable; I'm sorry I did it; but worse, much worse, I'd probably do it again tomorrow. Still, I'd have taken his place on the cross if only he'd said, 'Simon Peter, you're closest to my heart.' "

I hesitated. Simon Peter's soul was in torment. How do you tell such an agonized man who has been feeding on his wrongdoing like an animal eating its own leg to free itself from a trap, how do you tell such a man that his sin was indeed unworthy, even nasty, but at root only petty? Spite is one of the more common and least remarkable of human failings. "You're trying to say that you love God, as you saw Him reflected in the Master. You're also trying to say you're a human being who sees himself as the most important thing in the universe and cannot understand why the Holy One sees things differently. You don't think it's fair the Lord should not recognize the beauty of His works."

He cursed again. "Speak plainly, Greek. Tell me why the Master didn't love me the most. Tell me why I'm blinded for denying him, when the priest, who never acknowledged him at all, can still see. Why, Quintus, why? I've prayed, I've begged for an answer. I cry to the Father, but I get no answer, nothing, except scorn from my own people. Like Job, 'I am the jackal's brother.' "

"That's not true. The community treats you with respect, Simon Peter."

"You don't know my people, Quintus. Outwardly they show respect, but inside I'm Job. 'To them I am loathsome, they stand aloof from me, do not scruple to spit in my face'—in their hearts if not in their actions."

I decided to play his game: "And the Lord answered Job: 'Where were you when I laid the earth's foundations? . . . Who decided the dimensions of it? . . . Who pent up the sea behind closed doors?' "

"Those're questions, Quintus, not answers. We Jews don't take Scripture like you gentile converts. The Lord gave it to us, and it's ours to interpret and use, not to worship. I find no comfort in those words."

I said nothing.

But Simon Peter was not yet done. "At first, when I could remember nothing, I accepted Mary's leadership. I had no choice. Later, when I could remember, I accepted her not only because I was blind. That had something to do with it, but it wasn't all. I agreed because I'm not sure of my faith or myself. Quintus, I'll tell you something: I don't know if it was the Master's voice I heard that Sunday afternoon in the inn at Jerusalem. I'm not sure but I guess it was."

He paused for a moment, but I said nothing.

"Well, it seemed right," he continued. "If the Master did return, he'd show himself to someone who stood by him. That's why I said I believed Mary at the tomb and said I heard his voice at the inn. I can accept it, but do I believe it in my heart? I'm not sure. Like Thomas, I haven't seen, so I don't fully believe. That's one more sin. The Master said, 'If the light inside you is darkness, what a darkness that will be!' I can't see inside the darkness of my soul, or outside the darkness of the world. I'm doubly blind."

"If doubting is a sin, it is a sin I share." I almost added, "And so does John," but caught myself. "We can doubt and still believe."

Simon Peter spat into the water. "That garbage is for gentiles. I'm a Jew. How can I doubt and still believe?" He turned and took two more steps into the lake. "I need wine, Quintus, hard wine, not soft words. If you don't have wine, leave me alone."

11

❦ At none of the great feasts did any of the members of the community at Dalmanutha make the pilgrimage to Jerusalem. Prudence, not lack of devotion, stopped them. But, during the second year, I visited my family at Scythopolis just after Passover, as soon as the roads were clear of pilgrims. I had planned to stay only a few days. My father, however, was not well and, having so often failed in my filial duties, I felt obliged to remain until he recovered. By then it was little more than ten days before Pentecost, but that particular date meant nothing to me, for I assumed that the people at the community would remain prudent—and alive.

I was, however, concerned about my long absence and hired a boat at Philoteria, where the Lower Jordan River leaves the Lake of Galilee to run to the Asphalt Sea. I found a captain of a fishing boat who, for a reasonably exorbitant fee—how often can a Galilean bargain from a position of advantage with a Greek?—would take me to Dalmanutha. Two hours before dawn found us well into the lake. The captain wanted to put me ashore in time to cast his nets before full daylight.

It was damp and cold at that hour, but the trip itself was easy. There was a gentle breeze from the southeast to push us along. We arrived off Dalmanutha as the first rays of light bent over the mountains on the eastern side of the lake. A sailor furled the sail about 150 yards out and let the boat drift slowly. Between us and the land, there were several other craft of about the same size and vintage. They had dropped anchor close together, and, hoping the fish would use the boats as a protective barrier behind which to feed, the fishermen were throwing their nets off to port, to lee-ward. From their curses I gathered their luck was no better than ours. Even across the distance, I recognized the loudest voice as Simon Peter's.

On the rock-strewn beach to the north of us, a small fire began to flicker. The morning's chill made me anticipate the fire's warmth—and the food that would be cooking there. We were drifting closer into shore and I could dimly make out a figure by the fire. I heard him call out to Simon Peter's boat, but the words were lost. The voice was familiar though indistinct. I would know soon enough, when the captain put me ashore.

Simon Peter responded, but I could not decode his message either. Then his crew—there was brightening enough for me to recognize Andrew and Thomas, and, I thought, no less than John the priest—hauled in their nets and threw them to windward. A few moments later, their boat began listing precipitously to star-board as they pulled back on their nets, apparently packed full of fish. I could hear Andrew scream an obscenity at John for his incompetence.

My own captain almost knocked me overboard as he rushed forward to join his crew in hauling in our nets and then throwing them out again toward Simon Peter's boat. "They're running! They're running!" he shouted.

I got up slowly, thankful I wasn't trying to swim—actually, I didn't know how—in the cold, green water. I heard John cry out. At first I thought he was protesting Andrew's injustice in expecting him, a priest of the temple, to perform like an experienced fisherman. Then I caught his words above the chaos on my own boat: "It is the Master!" Simon Peter was standing stark naked in the bow. Without an instant's hesitation he pulled the cloak right off Andrew's back, dove into the water, and began swimming toward shore.

I grabbed my captain by the shoulder and shouted, "Forget the fish! Put into shore now!"

He pushed me away roughly. "Forget your ass, boy. This sea is alive. It's a fisherman's dream." Then he turned back to his crew. "Haul in those nets slowly! Careful there, don't capsize us."

He was right on both counts. The sea was alive and we were listing even more than Simon Peter's boat had been. But I didn't care about fish or boats. "Forget the fish!" I screamed. "I'll pay you double what the catch is worth."

I may as well have spoken to the fish for all the captain heard. But I was too frantic to be ignored. I leaped into the middle of the ship and began climbing the short mast. "Put into shore now and I'll pay you double. If you don't, I'll break off your mast."

Like a big cat, the captain sprung after me and caught enough of my leg to send us both thudding onto the deck, next to the crewmen. There was no weight on the other side to balance us and the heavily laden nets. With a loud groan, the small boat turned turtle, throwing us into the sea. I went under the cold water, slapped in the face by thousands of struggling fish. I must have swallowed a liter of the slimy green liquid before a rough hand grabbed me by the neck and jerked me back up to precious air, where I spouted water like a surfacing porpoise.

To my surprise, the captain and his crew were laughing —hysterically, I thought—but I was too frightened to be concerned about their mental states, and too happy to be alive. I clung to the upturned hull with a grasp far beyond my usual strength. "Double, it will be, Greek," the captain roared. "And double again to repair my ship."

Within a few minutes, two of the other fishing boats came alongside, pulled me out of the water, and then helped the captain and his crew right their boat. I dried off as best I could, too cold and frightened to do more than shiver. When I regained a measure of self-control, we had drifted several hundred yards north of the beach, and I could make out nothing that was going on around the fire other than that a group of people were huddled together.

A full half hour elapsed before I was ashore and hobbling as fast as I could over the rocks toward the fire. When I arrived, John, Simon Peter, Andrew, and Thomas were sitting on the sand. There was an aura of peace in the air as tangible and as soft as a woman's caress. Three of them had the same look of serenity I had seen on Mary's face in the orchard on the morning of the anointing. John, however, seemed pensive, even troubled.

"Welcome, Quintus. You look like a fish someone threw back because it was too small." Simon Peter laughed, but his tone was gentler than his words.

"Can you see?" I asked. For some reason, I had known he would be able to, even before I had reached shore.

"I can see." It was a statement of fact, devoid of the ebullience one would have expected from a blind man who had suddenly regained his vision.

"When did it happen?" I asked, though I also knew the answer to that question. I may have been trying to postpone confronting information I could not accommodate.

"When John said 'It is the Master.' I saw him on the beach. I *saw*. At that very instant I *saw*; I saw him, standing here by the fire. I had heard him call to us to throw the nets over the starboard side, but I had not recognized his voice. It was John who did that."

I looked at John.

He avoided my eyes, but he nodded his head slowly.

"He has forgiven me, Quintus," Simon Peter continued. "He has forgiven me."

I was talking to a child, a happy child at peace with himself and the cosmos, but a child nevertheless. There was another question about forgiveness I wanted to ask, but this was neither the time nor the place.

"Three times he asked me, 'Simon Peter, do you love me?' Three times I replied, 'Yes.' Each time he then said, 'Feed my sheep.'" Simon Peter smiled at me. "Had you been there, you would've told me each question and answer wiped out one of my denials, redeemed me. But first he gave me back my sight as a free gift, not in exchange for my love."

I looked at John again. He continued to avoid my eyes. "And now?" I asked.

"And now," Simon Peter responded, "we return to Jerusalem for the feast of Pentecost, to spread the Master's teaching that the kingdom of God is at hand."

At that point, I felt rather than heard another person come up behind us. "What about our community here? And what about Mary of Magdala? Does she have a voice in this decision?" We turned. It was Mary herself who ground out the question.

Simon Peter stood up. "I can see, Mary. I saw the Master. He appeared to us here on the beach this morning. He has truly been raised."

"I know you can see. Everyone knew you were blind only because you couldn't face the sin you committed against the Master. And I know the Master has been raised. I knew it before anyone else. He appeared first to me, while you were still blind." Her anger was strangling what should have been her joy at the confirmation of her own visions. "I asked," she went on in the same tone, "what about Mary of Magdala?"

"You are one of us, Mary. You can come with us now or join us later, as can the Master's mother."

"Did the Master tell you to go to Jerusalem?"

"No, but I know what we are to do."

"You know? *You* know? You know nothing except how to run from danger. The Master told me we were to come here to Galilee and wait for him."

Simon Peter took no notice of the insult. Indeed, there was no plausible rebuttal. "But he has come to us. Now we must renew his work."

"For two years we've been renewing his work. Here at Dalmanutha, we work together and pray together, as the Master taught us, and we share our food in remembrance of him. We speak to other people here in Galilee each day. We accept new members and we encourage those who heard the Master but are not strong enough to join us. We have followers in Capernaum, in both Bethsaidas, and Chorazin."

"We must go to Jerusalem," Simon Peter insisted. "I tell you that, Mary, and I tell the rest of you that."

"No, Simon Peter, we must not go to Jerusalem. We must stay here in Galilee to reap the harvest the Master planted. What would you country bumpkins do in Jerusalem this time? When you were last there at Passover all you could do was cower in corners and hide from the Romans and the High Priest. They're still there and you're not any smarter—or braver. If you go back now, they'll stone you or crucify you—or, if you're lucky, chase you back here."

"I don't know what we'll do in Jerusalem," Simon Peter admitted. "I only know we must go."

Mary looked at me and said scornfully "He only knows we must go." Then to Simon Peter: "What about our community here?"

"They are firm in the Lord, Mary. We'll leave Cleopas to take care of them. He has seen the risen Master and can confirm their faith. All the rest of who wish to can go on to Jerusalem to teach others."

"Teach others? Teach others? How will you ignorant peasants teach the scribes of Jerusalem?"

"I don't know. All I know now is that we must go there. That is all we need to know."

"You do not know why you go or what you'll do? Madness! I forbid it!"

"Forbid it, woman?" Andrew cut in. "You challenge my brother's authority?"

"Authority? Your brother's authority? What authority? Who organized our community? Who provided the money to buy the tents and build the houses our people sleep in? Whose seed have they sown, whose fields have they tilled, whose food have they eaten? Who has taught these people about the Master and baptized them? Not Simon Peter—Simon Peter the denier. He fishes as best he can and walks the beaches dreaming that what happened never happened. I'm the one who organized this community and I'm the who has led it."

Andrew tried to speak but anger tied his tongue. Mary gave him no opportunity to proceed. "Authority! Your brother forfeited whatever authority he had when he ran away in the garden after that Passover meal. In Caiaphas's courtyard, he forfeited it three times more. And for good measure he forfeited it again when he ran away from that awful hill outside the city. Authority? He has no authority. Leadership passed to me when the Master appeared to me in Josef's orchard, before appearing to any of the rest of you. Simon Peter himself confirmed that transfer in the presence of seven of us in the Essenes' inn in Jerusalem and again at my house the night we got back. All of us here heard him; so did the Master's mother and the son of Alpheus. I memorized those words:

> By a woman, our mother Eve, first came death. By a woman, our sister Mary, first came news of life. Both came in a garden: one of paradise, the other of sadness. He was raised and has chosen Mary as his instrument.

"Those were your words, were they not, Simon Peter?"

"They were," he admitted. "But the Master's stewardship is not mine to give away. It's the Master's. He was here and told me three separate times to feed his sheep. All of us except you and Quintus heard him with our own ears. Didn't Job say, 'The Lord gives and the Lord takes away; blessed be the name of the Lord'?"

"It is the Lord who gave but it is not the Lord who is trying to take away. It is a mere man: a jealous, devious, stupid, and cowardly man."

For the first time John spoke: "Mary, I saw the Master. I heard him call to us when we were in the boat and then here on shore I saw and heard him speak to Simon Peter, exactly as he says. The Master has passed leadership back to Simon Peter."

Mary spun and faced the priest. She had been scoldingly contemptuous of Simon Peter, but at John she was enraged. "Now even you! Your masculine pride overcomes your good sense. The thought of being led by a woman, even if it is the Master's wish, has stuck in your throat like a giant fish bone; and you haven't got the courage to do the leading yourself. So you're ready to follow this overgrown fool. Only people like you and me can keep the Master's message alive. These peasants can barely lead themselves to a privy. They'll scatter in terror the first time Pilate sneezes. They mean well, but they're ignorant fools."

"The Master spoke clearly to my brother," Andrew broke in again. "He did it in front of witnesses, just as he did the first time when he called Simon the Rock—and those witnesses include your own Judean priest. We've only got *your* word, woman, that the Master appeared to you first. We know he's appeared to Simon Peter and said 'Feed my sheep.' We go to Jerusalem with him. You can stay here and run your community off what your family's stolen from the peasants. For years you've squeezed sweat out of them. Give it back bit by bit while you can. When we set up the kingdom, we'll take all your estates and give everything to the poor."

Simon Peter put his hand on Andrew's shoulder. "Enough. No harsh words we'll all regret. It's settled. Today we gather the rest of the Eleven. At dawn tomorrow, we set out for Jerusalem. As for you, Mary, there'll always be a place for you with us."

She ignored Simon Peter and looked at me. "Quintus?"

I shook my head.

"Another traitor," she said softly. "But the Master's work will go on. I swear it." She turned and strode toward the settlement.

The Galileans went off to search for other disciples, tell their wives, and prepare for the journey. John the priest made no move to leave. I sat down on a smooth rock by the remains of the fire. He joined me. Neither of us said anything until all the others were out of sight. "Well?" John finally asked, as he poked the ashes with a small stick.

"Well, indeed."

He stared at me for another moment or two, then flipped the

stick into the lake. "These few years have been good. Mary is right. She has organized the Master's followers and brought in new ones. We talk about the Master and what he said about the kingdom of God being at hand. We try to live out his commandments by loving one another and by sharing our blessings and burdens." He looked at his hands, feeling the large calluses. "It has been good, very good, even the physical labor. I miss Jerusalem—badly; but the Master would have approved of this life. Now this . . . this vision."

"Another hallucination?"

"I saw him, Quintus. My heart believes he has been raised." He spoke quietly but his voice was quivering with emotion. "I saw him!"

"Then why do you look so troubled?" It was not a fair question, but I had to ask it, for his sake as well as my own.

"You know the answer as well as I. Would you trust your senses?"

"I'm not sure I would if what my senses told me was so at war with everything I think I know."

"That's not precisely my problem—or yours. But it's close."

"Let's start with your senses." I saw what I was doing but could not help myself. After wallowing in guilt because of my noncommitment during the Master's life, I was once again playing philosopher, collecting evidence to analyze in the same dispassionate manner that Aristotle put on when he sought to explain why the Nile periodically flooded. I hated myself for it, but I also couldn't help myself. I was frightened—terrified—by this thing that I could not understand. "Do you believe you were participating in a group hallucination?"

"That's always possible, especially when dealing with superstitious peasants. Mary has a point, you know. They will probably scatter. They lack the brains and stomach to keep an organization going against the sort of opposition they will meet. I could be infected by their simplemindedness. But it *was* the Master, Quintus."

"Did you touch him?"

"No, but I saw and heard him. . . . I know, I know, that's what everybody says who claims visions. I've heard dozens of such people 'prophesy' in the temple. I checked the usual indicia of false visions. We were not asleep; we were very much awake and working hard. We were not in a state of ecstasy; we were tired but not exhausted. We did not see a disembodied spirit performing supernatural acts; we saw a human being cooking a meal for us."

"Was anything else said?"

"Yes—unpleasant. Another jealous wrangle."

"Tell me about it."

"When he forgave Simon Peter and told him to feed his sheep, there was joy. Then the Master looked at Simon Peter and spoke very gravely: 'When you were young, you fastened your belt and went about as you pleased; but, when you are older, you will stretch out your hands and someone will tie them tight and drag you where you do not wish to go. Even so, I tell you, follow me.' This upset Simon Peter."

"I can see that it would."

"The Master took a few steps back from the fire and I went toward him. Simon Peter turned angrily on us and asked: 'What about *him*?' The Master looked at Simon Peter with that look of gentle reprimand and said, 'Suppose I want him to stay until I come? What business is that of yours? Your task is to follow me.'"

"Now these people will think you're immortal."

"Who knows what they'll think? But that unpleasantness provides additional evidence I was not participating in some kind of group hallucination. There was no idealized behavior. Everyone acted exactly as he had a dozen times in the past. Simon Peter was effusive and jealous; the Master was gentle, forgiving, and enigmatic. The rest of us were silent. It was all real, absolutely real."

"Perhaps too real; you each played a well worn part, one you could have repeated in a dream."

"I realize that. I'm not one of these peasants." Then more softly: "But there was more, not altogether new but sufficiently different not to fit the mold of memory. At the end, just before he vanished, he spoke of a mission beyond Israel. He had hinted of it before, without ever speaking openly."

"What did he say? Exactly, I mean."

John closed his eyes as if to recapture the scene in his mind. "Exactly, he said: 'Go to all the nations and make disciples of them. Teach them all that I have taught you. And remember that I am with you all days, even to the end of time.' That was a frightening charge."

"The whole thing is frightening. What did Simon Peter say to those words?"

"He didn't respond. I don't think he understood. I did not understand it; and if I did not, certainly Simon Peter could not. It makes no sense."

"It makes sense," I said. "If the Master's message of love is valid at all, it is valid for all men at all times. I saw the Master speak to pagans, offer them his physical help and his message. You've heard us talk about the Samaritan woman at Jacob's Well? He offered her 'living water' and promised that no one whoever drank of that water would thirst again. You know what that metaphor means."

" 'Living water'? I wouldn't know what that metaphor means if I had heard it firsthand," John protested. "And I certainly don't know what it means when I hear it secondhand. More important, what does that direction to go to all nations do to the notion of the Messiah and the redemption of Israel? You and I, students of Isaiah, might be able to cope with the concept of a spiritual messiah, but do you think these peasants would work for 'the kingdom' if they thought that kingdom didn't mean overthrowing the Romans and reestablishing Jewish government in Israel? You've heard them bicker about who was going to be first in the Israelite kingdom. They weren't quarreling over 'living water' or suffering. They were arguing about pomp and power."

"And they were wrong. They misunderstood all that the Master was saying."

"Yes," John agreed. "I'm not sure I understood what he was saying, but I am sure they misunderstood. Where does that leave us?"

I shook my head. I was too confused in my own mind to be able to imagine—or to criticize—what others might think or do. I could only reach for the straw that this "vision" was only one of several hallucinations that I had not shared. "And yet you did not touch him all that time."

"No, I did not touch him. But that doesn't change the part of me that is convinced what I saw was no dream, no wish wished for so strongly as to appear real. But it only riles that part of me that says I have imagined the vision to solve my problems. Yet I can't accept that either, for whatever problems this episode has solved, it has created fresh ones that terrify me. If the Master has been raised, what does that mean? What have we been following? What is our mission if it is not to reform Israel? Where are we going? Whom are we following?"

"To Jerusalem. A Judean priest and a Greek philosopher are going to Jerusalem with ignorant Galilean peasants, following a man who reeks of fish and rashness and who intends to preach to persons unknown the good news, if his news indeed be good, that the kingdom of God, whatever that is, is at hand, whatever that means. And, may philosophy forgive me, the only response I can think of is 'amen.' "

My irony—or mild blasphemy—did not appeal to John. But his questions were my own. I had refused to confront them since the empty tomb; I saw no reason to confront them now. I had not seen the Master. Surely, I reasoned in my youthful humility, if he had in fact been raised, he would have included me in the group to whom he had revealed himself. The alternatives, which might have been the root causes of my earlier depression, were that my approach to understanding the Master was inadequate or that I myself was unworthy. Neither was acceptable.

II
JERUSALEM
(32–38 C.E.)

1

❧ The entire community assembled for the usual evening meal. Most of the people were subdued, and with excellent reason. They were chagrined by their behavior that day as well as physically exhausted. The news of the vision on the lake had spread within minutes. Peasants seem to know what happens as it happens, even if they seldom understand what it is that happens. As soon as they heard, the people went berserk—dancing, shouting, and singing. Children ran wildly about, screaming raucously at the top of their little lungs. Several people went into ecstatic trances and, when they emerged, asserted that they, too, had seen the Master. At least a half dozen men and women rolled around on the grass, babbling incoherently, claiming to speak ancient, magical languages. All the while, most of the community kept looking up at the sky, confident the Master would momentarily appear at the head of a vast army of heavily armed angels.

Mary, John the priest, and even I did the best we could, reassuring people that whatever vision had been seen on the beach did not portend the redemption of Israel. It was of little use. The community paid scant attention to us, even to John, although they knew he had been a witness to the "appearance." After all, he was a priest and I a Greek; neither came from a trustworthy class of people. The only break in these forms of madness came when some idiot reported great war chariots crossing the sky. For a few minutes that report stopped the babbling and set everyone to craning his neck in a vain effort to witness the opening stages of God's wrath against the pagans.

Then a little after midday, a thin, middle-aged man, one of the least intelligent in the community, proclaimed his own vision: "I feel him coming!" he shouted, with a certain primitive eloquence that belied his lack of reason. "I see the Master, on a cloud, riding a great white stallion, and wearing a cloak soaked red in blood. A sword spurts from his mouth to strike down the gentiles. Behind him, an army of avenging angels marches to attack the Romans, first at Capernaum, then Caesarea, and all of Israel, then in Rome itself! Arm yourselves!" he cried. "Arm yourselves! We join the heavenly host at the Master's mountain!" (He meant the hill where the Master had given the Beatitudes.)

Quickly, this new form of lunacy swept the community. Men grabbed scythes, pitchforks, pruning hooks, fish knives, and staves; women snatched up kitchen knives; children pulled up reeds from the water. At least a hundred people from the community ran, like the mindless, salivating mob they were, the half mile to the hill.

Fortunately, just at that time, Andrew and Simon Peter were coming down the road, returning from Capernaum. They broke into a trot to find out what was going on. As soon as they understood, Simon Peter raced ahead and got uphill from the mob. He held out his arms. "What are you doing?"

For a time, he was drowned out by choruses of "The Master is coming! The Master is coming to drive out the Romans and the Herods! Look up in the sky!" But such a small mob had little hope of long outshouting Simon Peter. "You fruit of seed spilled in whores!" he screamed back. "How dare you carry arms here! The Master made his place holy by teaching peace and patience. What've you learned in your time among us? Is this how you show love? How can you believe every man is your brother and still want to stick a pitchfork into a Roman's belly?"

"If the Lord didn't mean for us to stick pitchforks into Romans," some rural wag heckled, "why did he give them such fat bellies?"

Simon Peter fought to control his temper. He lowered his voice. "You're right, my brother. Our sweat has fattened Roman bellies, and every just man may want to stick a pitchfork into those bellies. But we follow the Master, not Judas Maccabee or Judas the Zealot. And the Master says [I noted the present tense, as well as the irony of Simon Peter's instant pacifism] we must love all men as we love ourselves, even those who oppress us."

"But he is coming to destroy the Romans. We have heard he promised it at the lake this morning!" another shouted.

"Garbage! What lying sheep fornicator told you that? I was there. He made no such promise. No, he said the opposite, as he always has. He told us to teach the whole world his message of love—a message you've forgotten."

"We heard different," someone called out. "How do we know you speak the truth?"

Simon Peter's eyes bulged, his chest expanded, his feet moved farther apart, and his voice grew even louder: "I am Simon Peter, Simon Peter who was blind and now sees. And these new eyes have seen the risen Master. He's spoken to me. Who dares to question my authority?"

There was silence. It was just as well that Mary was still at the settlement.

After a few moments, Simon Peter went on. "No one questions my authority because it comes from the Master. It came from him when he was alive, it came from him when he returned this morning. My renewed sight is the sign of his anointing." Again, he lowered his voice. "I am a sinner, my brothers and sisters. Just as you've denied the Master by this pagan madness, I've denied him in my own way. But if he taught us anything, it is that the Eternal One, blessed be His Name, is a loving Father who forgives us our sins. Put down your weapons. There'll be no killing in the Master's name."

"What do we do then?" someone asked.

"We do what we've been doing. We follow his teachings: We wait and we pray and we love all people. Some of us must also go out and preach his word to others. You, you holy Jews who have seen the Master's light, you return to our community to pray and wait. When he comes you won't have to arm yourselves. If the Master wishes to destroy the Romans, he has legions of angels. He has no need of your pitchforks."

There were mutterings, even a few shouted protests, but the crowd began to disperse, slowly walking back down the hill to the settlement. I was surprised— and gratified—by Simon Peter's firmness and by his articulateness. He had not been eloquent, but he had been clear—and, much more important, commanding. I was also pleased by his words. A few years ago I had, like the mob this morning, thought the Master's message was little different from the nationalism of the Zealots, which today threatens us with revolt against Rome. Later I had come to understand that he was not speaking of politics in the usual sense—though his message remained profoundly political— but of a way of life, of standards of conduct toward our fellow man and thus also toward our Creator. It seemed that Simon Peter had moved a long way toward that understanding.

Because the weather was seasonably mild that night, we ate outside rather than, as we were sometimes forced to do, splitting up into several of the frame buildings that, with Mary's money to pay the bills and her workmen to guide us, we had built. At the meal, Mary blessed the bread and wine, repeating what had become our traditional prayer:

> In this cup of blessing we share in the blood of the Master. In breaking this bread we share in his body. As the loaf is one and the wine is one, so are we one with each other, one with him, and he one with us.

> Amen.

> We do this, as he commanded us, in remembrance of him. The Master has died, the Master has been raised, the Master will come again.

> "Maranatha."

I was sitting next to John, and as the meal was nearing its end I could sense his becoming more and more tense, undoubtedly fearing what Mary would do or say. She, however, was quite cool. After an interval for meditation, she spoke to the people again: "Brothers and sisters, you have all heard the good news. The Master appeared this morning on the shore. He was seen by Simon Peter, whose sight he restored, by Andrew, Thomas, and John the priest of Jerusalem."

There was a penitential air in the community, as the group waited for a tongue-lashing. But, for once, she did not take advantage of an opportunity to raise welts of guilt on her charges' backs. John and I were also expecting her to launch an attack on Simon

Peter and those who planned to go with him to Jerusalem. But again she disappointed.

Mary continued to speak very calmly: "Some of our members are going up to Jerusalem, to preach the word of the Master there. Simon Peter, the rest of the Eleven, and John the priest leave tomorrow. Their journey will be long and their mission difficult in the city that crucified him. We shall pray for their safety and success. Meanwhile, our own work here will go on until all Israel has heard his words."

Simon Peter started to rise to make his own speech; but Andrew and Thomas, showing more wisdom than I had given them credit for, each put a hand on his shoulders and fixed him in place. No man is capable of two winning speeches in a single day. We sang several psalms, and then the community broke up into family groups, still quietly nursing wounded egos.

I left the gathering without making my private peace with Mary. I bravely reasoned that she had probably forgiven herself out for one evening, or at least controlled her temper to her limit. I did not care to be the one on whom she vented her wrath. Furthermore, I was miffed at her not mentioning that I was among those leaving for Jerusalem. I had been with the community for almost two years, helping both physically and financially. Simple courtesy required acknowledging my presence and absence.

I walked with Simon Peter to his house in Capernaum, where I was to spend the night. It was hardly a palatial villa, but it seemed no worse than most other homes in the community—in fact, a bit better than most. It was built around a small courtyard in the typical style of the Orient. Andrew's family lived in one section, Simon Peter's in a second, and his mother-in-law in the third. Only her quarters were spatially adequate. Three people crowded Simon Peter's section; and Andrew's were even more cramped, with himself, his wife, and four children.

Sheva, Simon Peter's mother-in-law, washed our feet when we entered. There were no servants and his wife, Naomi, was preparing food and his few belongings for the journey. I assumed, as apparently everyone else did, that I would provide whatever hard money we needed.

Naomi was a sturdy, handsome woman, with a certain appeal

to the carnal senses. She was a decade younger than her husband, making her twenty-two or -three, typically Semitic in looks: stocky, deep-bosomed, with dark eyes, hair, and smooth skin, except on her callused hands. She wore neither make-up nor jewelry of any sort, as Greek women or Jewish women from Jerusalem would have. Neither did she or any other woman in the community wear the covering for head and face formally required outside the home. Like most peasants, she saw it as a precious affectation, totally impractical for work.

And work was the lot of a Galilean wife. With her mother's assistance, Naomi ground the meal, baked the bread, cooked the other food they shared with the community, walked to Dalmanutha carrying the food; at the settlement, she took her turn serving that food and cleaning up after the meals, then walked back carrying empty pots. At home, she wove her family's new clothing, mended their old, did their laundry, cleaned their house, tended a small garden plot behind it, and, of course, washed Simon Peter's feet whenever he entered their home. In the rest of her time, I assume, she catered to his sexual needs and helped mend the nets, clean, dry, and sell the fish, and repair the boat, all while taking care of their child.

Their child—I must pause. Jephthania, already strikingly beautiful at six, was a child whom adults could not resist touching. It was apparent that she was going to be a tall woman, and she was proportionately much more delicate in bone structure than either Naomi or Simon Peter. Her skin was more finely textured and had a different tint, a dusky ivory rather than olive; her eyes, though brown, were also lighter in shade. It was her hair that first attracted one's attention. It was short and curled in soft ringlets that were dark auburn rather than the glossy ebony one is accustomed to see in Judea and Galilee.

Had the chastity of Galilean women not been legendary, I would have suspected a Celtic legionnaire had strayed from the Roman camp outside Capernaum when Simon Peter was on his boat. As it was, the cause of Jephthania's exotic beauty probably lay in the dalliance of an ancestor with a barbarian during the Babylonian captivity, centuries earlier.

＊　　＊　　＊

Simon Peter's house that evening held a mixture of moods. On the one hand, the three females, most obviously Jephthania, were full of joy at the return of his sight. I surmised that Sheva was not altogether surprised; she may have shared Mary's diagnosis of her son-in-law's affliction. On the other hand, Naomi made no secret of her distrust of the "visions" of the Master; and, of course, Jephthania could not comprehend what the adults were talking about, though, I noticed, they allowed her to be present during their discussions. Furthermore, Naomi and Jephthania were adamantly opposed to Simon Peter's returning to Jerusalem, the child tearfully so and Naomi not far behind.

At one point, the discussion turned bitter. Naomi began asking if it were wise for all the Eleven to leave the community. Simon Peter said he saw no harm in it. Most of the people had heard the Master's words from his own lips. Mary and Cleopas could strengthen the faith of the weak. There would be enough food. The harvest had been good and the fish plentiful. If other problems arose, Mary could provide money and leadership.

"And who will lead the house of Rab' Simon the fisherman? Who will take care of his family?"

"I must go, woman. He has spoken to me."

"Yes, the Master has called. The Master has spoken. I know how he has spoken. I recall what he told the crowd near the lake," Naomi retorted, utilizing that cruelly accurate memory for intricate detail that comes to many women as a special grace of marriage: "'He who does not turn his back on his mother and father, his wife and children, his brothers and sisters, even his very self, cannot be my disciple.' And that, Rab' Simon, is the choice you are making—again. You are turning your back on your wife and child, breaking your marriage vow to cleave only to your wife, just as if you were going off with another woman." Her voice had become quieter and had taken on a formal tone I was to learn to recognize. Only when angry did Naomi use the term "Rab'," the proper form of address from a dutiful Jewish wife to her husband.

It was then that Sheva spoke for the first and only time. "Who can hear a call from the Lord and pretend he is deaf? You know as well as Rab' Simon the Master is a messenger of the Lord. He said he would return, and he has returned and called Rab' Simon to him once again. I do not understand what it means, but we in this house learned to trust him. The Rab' must answer, even as Elisha answered the call of Elijah. The Master has thrown his cloak over your husband's shoulders. The call of the Lord should bring pride, not pain. He must follow and you must accept."

Neither Simon's following nor Naomi's acceptance was to come easily, but for the moment Sheva's speech had helped the crisis pass. The next morning we started out, retracing our steps, but this time without the donkeys to carry our goods. What we brought—and it was not much—we carried on our backs. The entire Eleven were with us, though not all were evidencing equal enthusiasm. With John and me in the group, we were thirteen, not an auspicious number. Nor were we an impressive assembly otherwise, but we fit in well with the other Galilean pilgrims.

Pentecost, sometimes called Weeks, Harvest, or First Fruits, is one of the three great pilgrimage feasts of Judaism on which male Jews, no matter where they live, are supposed to come to Jerusalem to offer sacrifice to the Lord at His holy Temple. Those who must travel vast distances are excused, but the moral burden to undertake the journey is a heavy one that most Jews feel deep in their hearts. The result is that at Passover in the spring, at Pentecost in early summer, and then in late summer at Booths, a huge influx of visitors descends on a relatively small and awkwardly located city.

The ostensible purpose of Pentecost is to offer to the Lord the first fruits of the recent harvest. The Book of Leviticus prescribes the time and form of the ritual:

> Beginning with the day after the sabbath . . . you shall count seven full weeks, and then on the day after the seventh week, the fiftieth day, you shall present the new cereal offering to the LORD. For the wave offering of your first fruits to the LORD, you shall bring with you from wherever you live two loaves of bread made of two-tenths of an ephah of fine flour and baked with

leaven. Besides the bread, you shall offer to the LORD a holocaust of seven unblemished yearling lambs, one young bull, and two rams, along with their cereal offering and libations, as a sweet-smelling oblation to the LORD. One male goat shall be sacrificed as a sin offering, and two yearling lambs as a peace offering. The priest shall wave the bread of the first fruits and the two lambs as a wave offering before the LORD; these shall be sacred to the LORD and shall belong to the priest. On this same day you shall by proclamation have a sacred assembly, and no sort of work may be done. This shall be a perpetual statute for you and your descendants, wherever you dwell.

Related to the three pilgrimage feasts and encouraging people to participate in them was a "second tithe" owed to the Temple. A believer could either donate that additional tenth of his income directly or spend that money in Jerusalem—an easy task, given the city's high cost of living and the skill of its merchants and inn-keepers in separating a pilgrim from the contents of his purse.

At Pentecost the hardy saved the cost of an inn by bringing or renting tents. The rainy season had ended and summer was beginning. Thus camping was not uncomfortable, though the city's altitude produced cool nights, even at this time of year. Food, however, is another matter. The nearby area grows little other than olives and roses. Rainfall is adequate, but the soil is a thin skin of clay stretched tight over clumps of limestone. Stone quarries flourish, but grain, fruit, and vegetables do not. The necessity of importing food inflates prices even during the seasons when pilgrims are not pumping up demand.

No doubt before the Jews drove out the ancient Semitic tribes, Jerusalem had been a city on a hill; but the modern town occupied two hills. The site is ideal for a fortress, as David and now the Romans have appreciated. Its location, however, is unpromising for commerce. It is not on any of the main north-south caravan routes. More than thirty miles distant from the sea on the one side, it sits astride no pass between the coast and Jericho, the Jordan, and Mesopotamia. To the west, toward the sea, a traveler has to bump along a road whose rocky twists through the Judean hills even the Romans have not been able to smooth.

Still, a traveler recalls that road as a marvel of comfort when he ventures east of Jerusalem. There the country quickly becomes a strange wilderness, zigzagging crags carved by swirling winds and equally zigzagging wadis scooped by winter flooding, then fried to near stone by summer heat. Over a distance of twenty miles, the central plateau on which Jerusalem is located tumbles almost 4,000 feet in altitude to the mouth of the Jordan where it enters the Asphalt Lake, 1,300 feet below the level of the sea.

Caravans go to Jerusalem despite, not because of, its location. Merchants come to sell, seldom to buy, though its tradesmen make jewelry that women admire. The city is rich solely because it is the cultic center of Judaism and, when Jews had military power, the center of their political universe as well. As such, it attracts prophets, priests, and princes, some real, some false. Taxes and tithes also bring massive contributions to its Temple and lure the sorts of people who hope to gain by the sacrifices that the pious make to their gods.

Toward evening on the first day of our journey, we again camped in the Valley of the Jezreel, this time on the south side of the river, on the slopes of Mt. Gilboa. After we had eaten our plain supper, Simon Peter took me aside and we walked a few dozen paces, stopping near a point where we could see lights faintly flickering in the homes of the wealthy, atop the hills of Scythopolis. "You're homesick for those lights, aren't you, Quintus?"

I nodded.

"You've lived in villas, with servants all around you. You don't even have to go outside to relieve yourself. You snap your fingers and someone brings you food and wine, clean clothes. Dawn is something you hear other people talking about; night is only the time when servants light lamps for you to read by—or roll around a soft bed with a beautiful woman. Now that you've lived with us, you've seen how real people exist, close to the earth, close to the bone. Andrew and me're better off than most, but we barely manage to scrape our living from the lake by the muscles on our backs. My wife'll soon be an old woman; by the time she's thirty, she'll be withered and ugly. She knows it, and she mourns it. My daughter'll be a beautiful woman, but only for a few years. She doesn't yet know it, but soon she will. What little is beautiful in my life will quickly fade. Can you understand that I'll miss my house and family just as much as you miss your finery?"

I grunted something I tried to make sound affirmative yet annoyed. I was not in the mood for one of those impassioned Jewish tirades about social injustice, the hunger of the poor, and the greed of the rich. I had long ago come to recognize those injustices, but I did not feel any personal responsibility for a situation I neither created nor exploited. Besides, I had been living with the poor, sharing their lot, for almost two years, not to mention the time I spent following the Master.

But Simon Peter went off in a different direction from what I had feared: "Naomi was right. He asks us to give up everything for him—our homes, our friends, our wives, children, what little goods we've gotten, even the comfort of familiar wrongs. In place of the joy of wishing evil on our oppressors, he commands us to wrench forgiveness from our bleeding hearts. That mob at the lake—I've felt what they felt. I understood them. I gave them the Master's message, but it was hard, Quintus, hard as goat turds in the desert. I wanted to find a sword and join them—lead them. If I hadn't known the odds, I probably would've."

He stopped. "I'm rambling. I know it. I know, you needn't remind me, Mary and John the priest do that—I'm ignorant. But am I also mad to do these things?"

"What things?" I was honestly having some difficulty following his words. Like most peasants, he had neither knowledge of nor concern for rules of logical discourse.

"Whatever it is that I am doing, what it is that I will do. Is that madness?"

"Probably. Certainly most people would so label it."

"And you, Quintus? By what name does Quintus the God-Fearing Greek call it?"

"I would not name it, Simon Peter. After all, I am here beside you. I only try to share it as best I can."

"As best you can, as best you can." His voice became louder.

"No one can share it and its pain as I do, no one. Not you, not Mary, not any of the others, and certainly not our beloved John the priest can feel that pain ripping through his guts, not the way I do."

I almost tried to explain that it was impossible to make inter-personal comparisons of utility, pain, or pleasure. But knowing that arrow would miss its mark, I said nothing.

"Will you help me, Quintus?"

Now I was thoroughly confused. "Help? How?"

"I am ignorant, but I've heard you say that because someone is ignorant doesn't mean they're stupid. I don't know if that's right. I know I'm not as smart as a lot of people—Judas, for instance—but I can learn. Will you teach me to speak Greek so it doesn't sound like it comes from the mouth of an idiot?"

"You want me to be your teacher?" I used the Aramaic term for rabbi, half in jest.

Simon Peter guffawed. "My rabbi, my Greek rabbi. Teach me, Quintus; teach me to speak properly. I'll work hard. Just don't humiliate me in front of the others."

It was a fascinating challenge, but prudence dictated I move cautiously. "I need to ask you a question, first. Do you remember that summer morning when you and I talked on the shore of the lake? You were still blind then." He nodded, but he also took a half step back. "Have you forgiven him?"

Simon Peter stared at the distant lights, half-turned away from me so that I could not read even the shadows on his face. "I don't know. I try not to think about it."

"You must have thought about it when you had that...," I groped for the word that would offend neither Simon Peter's nor my own integrity, "that vision on the lake shore."

He turned and looked at me with a rueful smile. "You've been talking to John, listening to him gloat about rubbing Simon Peter's nose in the dirt again."

"He didn't gloat. He was concerned and confused."

"Good, he should be." He paused for a few moments. "Yes, Rab' Quintus, I did think about it then. It angered me all over again. Simon Peter'll suffer, John'll prosper. I'm the Master's slave, John's the Master's beloved son. I'm Ishmael, he's Isaac. It tears my heart, drags on my faith like a heavy anchor. I try to keep it out of my mind, but when I get very tired or when things go bad. . . ."

"But have you forgiven him?" I prodded.

"John or the Master?"

"Either, both."

"I don't know. In my mind I've forgiven them both—at least a hundred times apiece. But in my heart? In my heart I don't know. Perhaps I have, perhaps I never will. But the scars'll be with me all my life. Maybe that's what he meant when he said 'I shall be with you all days.' As long as Simon Peter lives those scars will live—and burn."

"I don't understand," I said. "You resent what you think is the Master's love of John. You're jealous, even envious. You resent leaving your family and your life."

"Is that not natural?"

"Of course it's natural." I am afraid my tone was sharp. "What's unnatural is that you're going to Jerusalem anyway. Why? That's what I can't understand. Why?"

Simon Peter shrugged. "Why? You *think* like a Greek, Quintus; you don't *feel* like a Jew. Because he touched me. Because he touched me. It is enough."

He put his hands on my shoulders and with his face not a foot from mine looked into my eyes. "That's the best answer I can offer you, Quintus, the truth. I don't know if I forgive him, just as I don't know how much I believe that he's right, that we can persuade the world to love. I'm not sure this isn't a mad scheme that'll kill us all, orphan our children, and do no good except amuse the crowd at our execution. I don't even know why I follow the Master or why I love him; but, when he reached out his hand and touched me, it was all very clear. I know I love him—whether or not I forgive him or understand him. I love him with all the power in my soul. Now how will you answer me?"

"Shall we start tonight?"

2

✤ We made decent time in our walk and some progress in our tutorials. We covered as much as twenty miles miles between dawn and sunset, and every night Simon Peter and I spent an hour on Greek. At dusk on the fourth day, we approached Jerusalem from the north. Despite our fatigue, Simon Peter showed enough prudence to skirt around the walls to the northeast, near Mount Scopus, and cross the Kidron Valley on a gradual slope. He planned to camp on the Mount of Olives, east of Jerusalem. I had suggested we avoid Gethsemane, lest the double association with the Master alert those hostile to our return. Simon Peter, however, ignored my advice and led us to the area where we had camped several times earlier. Fortunately, the Lord was with us.

The garden where the Master had been arrested is directly opposite the Temple; and, though the valley is quite steep at that point, thousands of other pilgrims had decided to camp there. We could not find a place that offered sufficient privacy until our weary feet had trudged almost to the village of Bethpage.

In less than a mile we would have been in Bethany and the comfort of Lazarus's house. But Simon Peter knew that as well as I and chose not even to mention it. I accepted his decision without complaint, just as I had decided, for the time being, to camp with the brethren and not stay at my family's villa outside of Jerusalem. I had vowed to myself to do my best to keep my place as a fully participating member of the brotherhood. In a day or so I could yield to the temptations of a warm bath, freshly laundered clothes, and well prepared food.

When we finally found a good spot, we slept in the open, too tired to pitch our small tents. The next day, we awoke at dawn and watched the morning sun reflect off the gold and marble of the Temple across the valley. To a believing Jew no sight is more glorious than the Temple of Jerusalem. Indeed, as I have noted, to anyone with an interest in architecture or an appreciation of beauty, it is a majestic work, surpassing in imagination, design, and execution the Acropolis of Athens itself. Once I could become fully absorbed in its grandeur. At that time, however, my emotions were very mixed, for its noble, even heroic, design was marred in my mind by what its rulers had helped the Romans do to the Master.

We ate a bit of fruit and cheese before setting off for the city. For Simon Peter the first stop was to be the inn in the Essene Quarter where the Master and the Twelve had celebrated Passover. He hoped the innkeeper, an Essene named Matthias, whom I mentioned earlier, would feed and house us for a few days at least and perhaps more or less permanently. I hoped so, too. My uncles were generous, but there were limits to the demands I could make on them. Feeding and billeting thirteen adults is expensive under the best of circumstances, and Jerusalem during a pilgrimage feast did not qualify as the best of circumstances.

The inn was located in the middle of the Essene Quarter, at the southwest corner of the lower city, near the Essene Gate and the Serpent Pool. The immediate vicinity was poor; yet scarcely three or four hundred paces north in the upper city was Caiaphas's palace, and closer still the modest but elegant house of John the priest.

After the stop at Matthias's inn, the group—except for John and me—was going to the synagogue Galileans frequented. Because of the city's character as the center of Judaism, some synagogues, like some inns, have become known as places where Jews from particular regions gather. A synagogue's functions differ from those of the Temple, which is fundamentally a site of cultic sacrifice, a symbol of a people's dedication to the One True God, and for many pious Jews the actual physical location in which the Lord God Himself dwells.

Synagogues are places of private prayer and meditation as well as of communal reading of the Scriptures. The word designates a community rather than a building, a gathering of friends to talk, commiserate, gossip, and pray. For a transient Jew, a synagogue in Jerusalem provides a place in which he can see familiar faces and hear his native language spoken with the "correct" accent.

At the Galileans' synagogue, Simon Peter hoped to learn the news of Jerusalem from both locals and Galileans who had stayed over since Passover. If enough hours were left, the Eleven would then go to the Temple itself and offer the prescribed sacrifice of bread made from the new crop. As poor people, they were not expected to buy lambs or other animals. Bread baked in Cyrenica or Galilee would not have been fit even for priests' consumption when it arrived at Jerusalem, and transporting animals was out of the question for most pilgrims. Thus bread and smaller animals, like doves and lambs, were on sale in the lower level of the Temple, in the bankers' hall, where we had once made such a dramatic appearance. Just outside the city in the Kidron Valley, the rich can purchase bullocks and other large beasts for sacrifice.

Since our last visit, John's friends had sent messages via the priests of Judea and Galilee that Caiaphas and his colleagues had evidenced no desire to pursue a vendetta against the Master's followers. They knew about our community at Dalmanutha, of course. One kept few secrets in Antipas's domain. Such tolerance made a great deal of sense for the chief priests and the Romans as long as the brethren stayed quietly in Galilee, living like a colony of Essenes or Pharisees. Whether such an easy attitude would seem wise when it became known we had returned to the Holy City itself was a different matter.

Under the circumstances, we had all agreed it would be imprudent, just yet, for John to go to the Temple. Instead, he set out for Bethpage to visit an uncle, also a priest, and learn more about the Temple's mood from a firsthand source. For my part, I planned to accompany the brethren to the inn to allow them to assure Matthias and his friends that I was a follower, and then stroll around the city and talk to my family's servants as well as to several merchants whom I knew. I was not willing to put my foot inside the Court of the Gentiles and the jurisdiction of Caiaphas's guards until I had a sense of the reception awaiting us once we were recognized—and I had little doubt Simon Peter would do something that would soon get us recognized.

As we waded across the small rivulet in Kidron Valley, I fell in step beside Simon Peter and took up once more a topic I had several times tried to press during the trek from Galilee. I had been unable to secure a satisfactory, or even a coherent, response; and, for obvious reasons, I had hesitated to push him very hard. "Now that we are here, what do you intend to do?"

"Continue the Master's work."

"How?"

"I'm not sure."

"Are you going to speak to the crowds?"

Simon Peter looked at me, as if searching my face for a hint about the correct answer. "I've thought about it," he finally said, "but I don't know what to say. I know what I want to say, what I want to tell people, but I don't know how. The Master said not to worry, the words'd come, but I do worry. I could never talk like the Master. Words've never come easily to me except when I'm angry; and then people say I'm crude. I'm not angry now, only afraid the Judeans'll laugh at my accent if I speak Aramaic and the Greek-speaking Jews'll laugh at me if I use my poor Greek. I'm a fisherman, not a scholar. I should've asked your help months ago."

He was right, of course, on all counts. I was happy only that Mary of Magdala was not with us to complete the destruction of his self-confidence. After several dozen paces, Simon Peter spoke again. "I told you outside of Scythopolis, my ignorance is as plain to me as to everyone else. But even with all my ignorance and doubts, something inside me says I must speak out. Am I just an ignorant bumpkin like Mary says, one who's gone mad, or has the Holy Spirit truly come upon me?"

"I do not know, I honestly do not know." I didn't; but the fact that Simon Peter had to ask did not indicate the Holy Spirit was on him.

At the inn, I immediately recognized the big, hairy Matthias from the descriptions I had heard. He was glad to see Simon Peter and the others and was anxious to know what had happened to the rest of the disciples. The news of the latest "appearance" of the Master elated him, so much so he not only shook my hand but also gave me a welcoming embrace, an extraordinary outburst for an Essene toward a foreigner. His exuberance carried over into an insistence that we all live in the Essene Quarter. A few of us could move into his inn this week. After the feast when he had more space, all of us could live with him. Meanwhile, other Essenes would put the rest of us up in their homes, such as they were. I volunteered to ease problems by living in my family's villa.

I left the group in close discussion and went wandering about the city. The overwhelming impression on first entering Jerusalem is one of noise and turmoil at a level of cacophony that threatens sanity. Actually, Pentecost does not increase the chaos nearly as much as Passover. True, the narrow, hilly streets are packed with citizens and far too many pilgrims, all laughing, talking, shouting, enjoying the excitement. But not only are there far fewer pilgrims than at Passover, but at both feasts they replace as well as add to commotion, for Jerusalem is always being built or rebuilt (it took eighty years to finish the Temple), and the High Priest insists that all construction halt during the week-long celebrations of the great feasts.

I pushed my way through the noise and crowds of the city to the western gate by the three lovely towers, Phaesael, Hippicus, and Mariamme. From that gate I walked to my uncles' villa. There—I resisted the temptation to eat a meal, contenting myself with some fruit, fresh bread, and wine—I talked to the servants as I reveled in a hot bath. Being Syrians, they could tell me only that the taverns and *suqs* of both the Upper and Lower City had carried no rumors that Romans or the chief priests were still interested in the brethren. The servants, as I have mentioned, liked to call themselves Greeks and always spoke Greek to us, but they used the Semitic word for market, *suq*, rather than the Greek *agora*.

Clad in fresh clothes and much refreshed by the bath, I sought out two Jewish merchants whom I knew well. Both were wealthy Sadducees who worshiped regularly at Temple. They, too, had heard nothing. Their conclusion was the same as John's friends: Caiaphas and his entourage were content, as they grotesquely put it, to let dead dogs rest in peace.

After those conversations, I spent an hour at a tavern, but even at this time of year, when the city was crowded with Jews from all over the world, my blondness too obviously stamped me a foreigner to win any confidences. And the conversations I overheard mostly centered on the usual topics, dangers of travel and exorbitant prices in Jerusalem. In sum, I learned little except that one could truthfully repeat the prophet Isaiah's eight-hundred-year-old accusation, "Jerusalem, you water your wine."

Yet learning little was comforting, for the only positive intelligence I could have gathered was that the city was unsafe for us. Certainly that news would have sent some of the Eleven scampering back to Galilee. But now I was not at all sure how John and Simon Peter would have reacted. Somewhat cheered, I decided to return to my uncles' house and enjoy a siesta in a real bed before joining the others at the inn later that evening.

3

❧ Every year, soon after Pentecost, Jerusalem begins to be emptied of its hordes of visitors. The exodus is even more apparent than after Passover, for many of the Passover pilgrims who come from abroad stay on for Pentecost. But there is no other great Jewish feast until Booths in the fall—with a simmering Judean summer between. I welcomed the change, for it meant the streets would become less clogged with traffic and—what had never been important before—prices would drop. Both changes were evident that year, as I walked toward the Essene Quarter on the day after the Sabbath following Pentecost.

After I had left Simon Peter and the others on Friday, I returned to my uncles' villa and luxuriated in hot baths, massages, soft towels, clean clothes, cold water, fine wine, and excellent food, all attended by trained servants. The Master had never urged suffering for its own sake, only for some noble goal. Thus I saw no need to deny myself a day of real rest. Like the Lord God, the Jews enjoyed Sabbath; why shouldn't I?

Shortly after dawn on the first day of the week, I rejoined the brethren at Matthias's inn. Thinking it wise to share some of his burden, I was accompanied by a servant who carried several baskets of fruit, lamb, salted fish, and even some honey. Only John the priest would be concerned about dietary rules, and he no longer very much, not after two years at Mary's community.

The scene at the inn was strange. Simon Peter and John the priest were not there, but the others were, though most of them were still asleep. Even those who were up looked like they were not quite awake. These people should have been moving about at least as long as I had. I told the servant to put the food down and leave. There was no point in his knowing more about the group.

Within a few minutes Simon Peter and John the priest returned. Then I understood what had happened the night before. Simon Peter's face glowed like a live ember in a campfire bed, and John looked as worried as I had ever seen him. "When?" I asked.

"Last night," Simon Peter replied, controlling his voice with obvious effort. "At supper, John the priest, Matthias, our friend Barsabbas from the days of John the Baptizer, and the Eleven—we were all here together. As I broke the bread, suddenly he was in the room with us."

"What did he do?"

"Do? Do? He breathed on us, then he spoke to us."

"What did he say? Can you recall his exact words?"

"Could I forget them? He said: 'Peace be with you. As the Father sent me, so I send you. Receive the Holy Spirit. Whose sins you shall forgive are forgiven; those whose sins you do not forgive are not forgiven.' "

"Did you have any conversation?"

"No. I tried, but I couldn't think of anything to say. Then he was gone."

Later, when Simon Peter was distributing the food I had brought, I took John the priest aside. "What happened?"

"I don't know. Something. I heard a voice—*his* voice. The words were exactly as Simon Peter reported them."

"Did you see anything?"

"No. . . . I'm not sure. Some of the others say they saw the Master. I don't know whether I did or not. At the lake I saw him.

Here, I honestly don't know. But I do know I heard his voice and felt a warm wave of peace come over my body, as if he were breathing on me. I could have sensed his presence even if I had not heard his voice. He was here, with us. You recall his words at the lake: 'Behold, I am with you all days. . . .' "

"I recall your telling me those words. I didn't hear them myself."

"Quintus, I believe not only in the justice of the Master's message but that it is the true word from the Father, the Eternal One, blessed be His name, for He has raised the Master from the dead." He put up his hand. "I know, I know all the objections. I share them. But I cannot deny what my senses report."

Actually, I had reservations, not objections. It was not that I denied, only that I could not affirm. I wanted to pursue the matter further, but our discussion was cut short by Simon Peter's call for the morning meal. Then began an event I could have hardly anticipated. We reclined on the couches. I noted with interest how these Galilean peasants, who before Passover two years earlier had never seen a Hellenistic dining room, took so readily to the ease of the Greco-Roman style of eating.

Simon Peter recited the blessing Mary had composed for the community at Dalmanutha. As we responded *"Maranatha,"* the earth began shaking. The building trembled for an instant. I immediately recognized the phenomenon, one of the earth tremors so common around the Mediterranean. This one was minor and was over in seconds. I started to say something to reassure the others. A bit of science, I thought, might allay their irrational, peasant fears.

But as I rose, I saw on the others' faces neither fear nor panic, not even anxiety. Rather what I saw was closely akin to ecstasy. Indeed, I felt warm and a bit giddy myself. The two sons of Zebedee began talking in a tongue I did not understand—it sounded like the gibberish those fools at the lake had babbled after "the appearance" there. Whatever they spoke, it was not Greek, Latin, Hebrew, Aramaic, or any of the Semitic dialects with which I was familiar. Levi and Matthias responded in the same babble, as if they understood each other. They seemed to be speaking a part-prayer, with responses and counter responses. I was sure it was merely gibberish, but somehow I was not offended, as I had been at the lake.

After a lapse of some time—I believe the interval was short, but I cannot be certain—Simon Peter rose. First, he used the alien tongue, apparently to bring order to the gathering. Then he spoke in Aramaic: "My brothers, the Master's promise has again come to pass. We've received the Holy Spirit. Our faith's been confirmed. What was unclear is now clear. We shall found our community here, where he took his final meal with us. Matthias's house will be our place of assembly."

I glanced at Matthias; I was relieved that he looked delighted.

"We shall go out," Simon Peter continued, "and preach to the people—in the city, in the Temple, and perhaps elsewhere—of the Master's words and works, spreading the good news that the kingdom of God is at hand."

There was a murmur of assent. John the priest stood up next to Simon Peter and said, "Let us go out to the synagogues in the Lower City and proclaim the Master's good news."

Out we marched, or they marched. I straggled behind, more observer than participant, as was my style. The first synagogue we came to was less than a hundred yards away. As I have explained, Jerusalem abounds in synagogues, not only as places in which the local inhabitants meet and pray, but also for pilgrims. This particular synagogue was largely composed—so John the priest later told me—of Jews from Persia, Mesopotamia, and Babylon itself. There were no more than ten people there, all merchants dressed in the garb of the distant East, and looking more like Babylonian princes than Jews.

As we entered the small building, James and John, the two sons of Zebedee, began their strange language again, and once more Levi responded. "They're drunk," one of the Babylonians said in excellent Greek as he whipped his prayer shawl from his head and shoulders. "They should be ashamed, profaning our meeting place like Roman pigs."

"No, no, my fellow sons of God," Simon Peter responded. I was pleased that his Greek, while still flawed, was already somewhat better; and, whatever else it was, it was reasonably clear. The man had an ear and a memory; whether he had a mind, we would have to wait and see, but an ear and a memory, yes. "How could these men be drunk? It isn't yet much beyond the morning meal. This is what the prophet spoke of, when he said, 'In the days to come—it is the Lord who speaks—I shall pour out my spirit on all mankind. Their sons and daughters will prophesy, young men will see visions, and old men will dream dreams. In those days shall I pour out my spirit even on my slaves, men and women.' "

This long quotation from Scripture did not impress the Babylonians. "Why do you invade our sanctuary and disturb our prayers?" one of them asked.

"We don't come to disturb your prayers," Simon Peter replied, "but to bring you good news. We live in end times, last days. The kingdom of God is at hand. We shall soon have a new heaven and a new earth made by the Most High for a holy people. Repent your sins, throw off your old self; ask forgiveness from your brother even as you forgive him. The good news is that the Lord has visited his people. He has raised Jesus the Nazarene from the dead, as Jesus said he would." (Since Simon Peter was speaking in Greek, he used the word 'Jesus' rather than 'Joshua.')

"Jesus the what?" one of the Persians sneered.

"I didn't even know he was dead," another guffawed. "What are you talking about, man? Get out of here with your other rubes and let us pray in peace."

Simon Peter's Greek was good enough to understand the insult, but he wanted the rejection explicit. "You do not wish to hear about the kingdom of God and why the Romans crucified our Master for preaching it?"

"Any man the Romans crucified must have done some good," one of the merchants said, but the others shouted him down. "Get out of here or we'll call the soldiers. The Romans would love to catch followers of a man they crucified."

Simon Peter drew himself up to his full height. "Very well, I shake the dust of this house from my sandals." Then in Aramaic to the others: "Let's go, brothers. Our seed's fallen on stony ground."

Off we went farther around the nose of the hill toward the

Valley of the Cheesemakers. One part of me couldn't believe what I was doing. The rest of me seemed as taken with the enterprise as the brethren. Next we stopped outside a synagogue frequented by Greek-speaking Jews from Cyprus and Antioch. This time Simon Peter did not enter the building. Rather he stood on the steps that opened onto a small square and began to preach. "Men of Israel," he called out. "Listen to what I'm going to say."

There were still quite a few people milling around in the streets, though not like the throngs of the previous week. A crowd quickly gathered. Several men came out of the synagogue, still wearing their phylacteries and prayer shawls. They seemed more curious than the Babylonians. "We are living in last days. The Most High has visited his people. His messenger, Jesus the Nazarene. . . ."

"What would a member of the royal family have to do with yokels like you?" The voice was unfriendly, yet it was not so hostile as the heckler at the first synagogue. And this questioner, though a Greek-speaker, knew Semitic languages, for the word "Nazarene" means "of the royal family." It was a title that had frightened Antipas, Caiaphas, and Pilate alike.

"Who was Jesus the Nazarene? The Jew who the chief priests and the Romans crucified. It was he who drove the bankers from the Temple three Passovers ago."

I admired Simon Peter's shrewdness. The quickest way to grab the ear of Greek-speaking Jews is to link the chief priests, who treated the Jews of the Diaspora badly, with the bankers, who cheated all pilgrims, and with the Romans, who oppressed everyone without regard to religion or nationality.

Simon Peter went on: "This man, this Nazarene, taught of the love that the Most High, may His name be eternally blessed, bears for each of us. Jesus worked signs, curing the sick, healing the lame, giving sight to the blind, but most of all teaching us we must love each other as the Father loves us. For those sins, he was crucified. But . . . but. . . ." Simon Peter paused for dramatic effect. Not for nothing had he listened to the storytellers who wandered around Galilee, entertaining illiterate peasants with recitations of Jewish folk myths in exchange for a bit of food and wine and a few coppers. Simon Peter had the style down perfectly, and his first failure had led him to fall back on this ancient technique. That quickness to learn provided another favorable omen.

"But, my friends, the Eternal One, blessed be His name, raised this Jesus up from the dead. He died, Jesus rose, he'll come again! And his kingdom'll last for a thousand years. It's the kingdom of God, and it's at hand."

"When will this kingdom come about?" a man asked. There was genuine curiosity in his voice.

"I don't know, my friend, I don't know," Simon Peter replied. "It may come tomorrow, it may come next week, or next year—or the year after. But it'll come, and it'll come when we least expect it."

"How?" the questioner persisted.

"Again I don't know. I only know it'll come when the Most High decides and how He decides."

"How can we be part of this kingdom?" another asked.

"Repent, for this kingdom won't be a kingdom of soldiers, but of saints. You must repent your sins, you must be baptized, and you must receive the Holy Spirit to strengthen you to lead a holy life. For to love is more difficult than to hate, to accept wrong more difficult than to inflict it."

"What do you mean by 'holy life?' Was this Nazarene some kind of Pharisee or Essene?"

"No, he was a friend of the Essenes and wanted to be a friend of the Pharisees, but he was neither. A holy life doesn't mean ritual purity or living in the desert. It means treating your neighbor as you'd like him to treat you. It means asking not only forgiveness from the Eternal One when we sin, but also forgiveness from our fellow man we've offended. We must love the Most High with all our hearts and minds, and our neighbor as ourselves."

"What good Jew would not agree?" asked one of the men who was still wearing his phylacteries and prayer shawl.

"No good Jew would disagree, and probably few good gentiles," Simon Peter conceded. "But how many of us practice what the prophets've told us is the will of the Lord? And so we tell you as the Master told us, love your neighbor as yourself."

"And who is my neighbor?" It was a question that we had heard before.

"A certain man went down to Jericho. . . ." Simon Peter began to repeat the Master's response to the same question. At the end of the story, he asked, "Who is my neighbor? Every man, every Jew in the world, even a Samaritan. We are all brothers, sons of the loving Father. If you wish to hear more of our Master's teaching, we're staying at the inn of Matthias in the Essene Quarter. We're a community of brothers and sisters sharing a common life, as we wait for his triumphant return."

At the end of the talk, as good as it was, only one person, a young man, spoke up: "I would learn more."

"Then come with us," Simon Peter answered. "How are you called?"

"Josef. My family is from Cyprus. My father died at Passover a year ago when he was here on a pilgrimage. My mother and I bought a small house in the Lower City, and we have been living there since."

"Welcome, Josef. We'll call you Barnabas, Son of Encouragement, for you're the first person today to receive the gift of faith in Jerusalem. That gift is a sign of encouragement to you and to us also."

As the crowd dispersed, talking among themselves, two young men remained on the little square, arguing with one another in sharp, clipped tones. One was handsome, the other short, with a remarkably ugly face. From the way their Greek was accented, I guessed they were from Asia or Cilicia. I took an instant dislike to both. They had that supercilious half sneer the bright but immature affect because they think it makes them appear worldly. It was an expression I knew well, having seen it in my own mirror often enough.

The younger of the two, the handsome one, spoke to Simon Peter as he was preparing to lead us down the Street of the Steps to one of the poorer synagogues. "Sir," the young man said in Aramaic. Use of the word "sir" was polite, but the intonation let the listener understand that the speaker felt it was Simon Peter who should be addressing him as "sir." And his switching to Aramaic tacitly acknowledged Simon Peter's awkwardness in Greek. "Sir, my friend and I would have a word with you. I am called Stephen and he is Saul. We are from Tarsus [I was right about the accents], students of Rab' Gamaliel ben Hillel here in Jerusalem."

"An eminent man," Simon Peter said, though I doubted the name of that famous scholar meant anything more to Simon Peter than the name of Pontius Pilate's horse.

"You follow this Joshua," the young man named Saul began. "It is said you worship him as some sort of deity."

" 'Hear, O Israel, the Lord our God, the Lord is one,' " Simon Peter responded.

"Then what was he?" The orthodoxy of the reply had not taken the edge from Saul's voice. It was a bit high pitched, with an occasional slight whistle, probably caused by the gap between his upper front teeth, but anyone as ugly as this man was would naturally have a scarred character.

"He came to redeem Israel, to lead her to repentance, redemption, and loving service. He *is* the anointed one, the Messiah." (He used the Greek word, "christos.")

"*Is?*" Saul's eyebrows made an arch as pointed as an arrow tip. "You said the Romans crucified him."

"They did, but he has been raised."

"Where?" Saul looked around in mock search.

"We have seen him, not once but several times—here in Jerusalem as well as in Galilee."

"In Galilee one can see anything," Stephen noted. He affected what he undoubtedly thought was a droll tone.

Saul ignored his friend. "He would destroy the Law?"

"He said, 'I have come to fulfill the Law, not to destroy it.' "

"But he threatened to destroy the Temple, did he not?" And before Simon Peter could begin to answer, Saul added in a voice that ascended yet another octave: "Do not try to lie to us. Witnesses heard him make the threat."

"He made no such threat," Simon Peter said quietly. "I heard the Master; your witnesses must have lied to you."

"So you say; and you are an impartial observer."

Stephen cut in again, speaking more to Saul than to the rest of us: "It seems to me that what this man says sums up the Law of Moses. Remember when Rab' Gamaliel was asked the essence of the Law, he quoted his father and mentor: 'That which is hateful to you, do not do to your brother. That is the entire Torah. All the rest is commentary.' "

"You keep out of this," Saul snapped. "You waste our time quarreling with the rabbi; don't quote him now to support these revolutionaries. They would revolt against the Romans, the priests, and even the Eternal One Himself, blessed be His name, by assaulting His holy Temple."

Stephen's ears pricked up at his companion's retort. A smile flickered across his face like that of a naughty child who was entertaining a sinful thought.

"The Master didn't preach revolt against anyone or anything except sin," Simon Peter countered. "He said that if the Romans destroyed the temple of his body, the Father'd raise him again in three days. That was not a threat to the Temple. He was trying to tell us—though only now have we come to understand—that death had no power over him."

"He said nothing about the holy Temple?" Saul asked. "Did he not lead a riot against it?"

"He didn't lead a riot against the Temple, only against the money changers who were stealing from poor pilgrims. He did predict that some day the Temple'd be destroyed, but he didn't threaten to do it himself or urge others to do so. And it was a prophecy made in sadness."

I saw that look flash across Stephen's face again.

"It was still blasphemy," Saul insisted.

"No. One can blaspheme only against the Most High, not against a temple, no matter how holy. The Temple Solomon built was destroyed because our fathers hardened their hearts against the Eternal One. They wouldn't listen to the prophets who spoke the word of the Lord. And this generation's also hardened its heart against the anointed one."

"When he comes again," Saul persisted, "he will destroy the Temple because our hearts are hard?"

"I don't know what he'll do when he comes again. I only know that he'll come and we must be ready for him."

"I have heard enough blasphemous tripe for one day," Saul snorted. He turned and began walking away. "Are you coming, Stephen? This fool has given you enough arrows to disrupt our sessions with the rabbi for at least a month."

"I think I shall stay a bit longer. I want to hear more of this Joshua and his prophecy about the Temple."

And so Stephen joined Barnabas, the second "brother" gathered that day. He did not become a full-fledged member of the community for many months, but he visited us regularly—too regularly to suit some of us—and regularly argued with us.

Then we went down the Street of the Steps and along the Valley of the Cheesemakers. Several times we stopped while Simon Peter gave, with slight variations, the same talk as in the little square. By nightfall, we had collected a total of five new followers.

We were hungry and tired as we climbed back to Matthias's inn, and I, for one, was troubled. Like the Master, Simon Peter had spoken of the kingdom of God's being at hand. But I feared Simon Peter was backing down from the position he had taken to the mob at the lake and was implying the kingdom would be a physical one. More important, I was groping for an explanation to fit what the Master had said to what had happened since his death. But I was still confused. I was as yet unsure what to conclude about the "visions" of the risen Master so many of the disciples had reported. Despite John's assurances, I was not yet certain these were more than shared hallucinations.

I was half, only half, convinced the Master had meant to be taken literally when he said that the kingdom of God was within us. And, if the "visions" were real appearances, did they constitute his "return"? My training in philosophy, I thought, put me in a better position than these illiterate peasants to understand the complexity of the ideas here. But Simon Peter seemed so sure. I was very conscious of the possibility that, as foreigner, I had missed subtleties in—or perhaps read nonexistent subtleties into—the Master's message.

4

❧ We spent that day and so many months of others going from synagogue to synagogue that long ago I lost any ability to separate one day—or synagogue—from another. Our results were never spectacular. A few people were interested, but most walked away and some chased us away. Still, we made progress, small yet real over the long haul. In the short run, however, our defeats sometimes seemed huge and even more real. In all of this, Simon Peter was our leader. Usually he turned our defeats aside and pushed on to preach at still another place. Yet he, too, had dark days, when defeat dragged him down into its black pit.

As the community at Jerusalem first began after Pentecost, it bore marked similarities to Mary's at Dalmanutha. Some reasons were obvious, not least of which was that the Essenes provided the model for both. The members shared their tangible goods. For the Galileans that meant little; they had only the clothes on their backs and the Master's good news.

We prayed together in the early morning—I had to be up long before dawn to walk from the villa to the Essene Quarter. Then the women helped Matthias or their Essene hosts perform housekeeping chores and the men did some repairs or lounged about gossiping. An hour or so later, we took a common meal with the breaking of the bread. At mid-morning, some of the Galileans— and occasionally John the priest and, once in a while, I—instructed newcomers in the Master's message. Women were allowed to listen as well as men, though, it goes without saying, all the women could not attend every day. There were children to be minded, food to be bought and cooked, water to be hauled, clothes to be mended, and houses to be cleaned, things that most men could not—or would not—do. Still most of the women attended some sessions and some even found time to participate in discussions.

Most mornings, Simon Peter and several of the other Galileans would go around the city, preaching as they had at Pentecost. They would return home in the early afternoon, some days with no followers, some days with one; once they brought home three.

We lost followers, too. After a few days or weeks in the community, some people packed up quietly and left. Once or twice I caught glimpses of these people in other parts of the city, but only glimpses. They would quickly lose themselves in the crowds or shops.

In the evening, we again had prayers both before and after the other meal. At that meal we would once more have the breaking of the bread. After, we would talk informally about the Master. Almost invariably people would speculate about when he would return.

Matthias, as he had promised, put the inn largely at our disposal. The Galileans slept in the half dozen rooms he usually rented and ate in the dining room the Master had used to celebrate that fateful Passover. Matthias continued to operate a tavern on the first floor, from which he sold wine and some food—and gave both to our community.

Barnabas's mother owned a modest house in the Lower City, and, when she joined us, sold it, and gave the proceeds to Simon Peter. When finally he was baptized, Stephen brought some cash and a letter of credit on the Temple's treasury. He contributed the letter and most of the coins. I provided additional cash. More important, Josef of Arimathea visited us every few weeks when he was in Jerusalem and always left a purse full of coins. A few of the new followers brought something with them, usually not money but such items as an animal, tools, or skills like carpentry to help Matthias keep his inn and the Essenes their homes in decent repair.

The Essenes, both monks and peripherals, were generous. Some, perhaps as many as ten of the latter, eventually joined our community. Others were liberal with gifts of food and occasionally clothing.

We had begun with thirteen—the Eleven, John the priest, and me. Matthias was the fourteenth, and Barnabas and three others whom Simon Peter collected the first day brought us to eighteen males. With Barnabas's mother and the wives and children of two of three converts, we were quickly a good number. Several families from Bethany, who had known the Master when he visited Lazarus, heard of our existence; most days they made the journey, two miles each way. And we were often joined by either Martha or Mary, Lazarus's sisters from Bethany. Our size generated problems as well as encouragement.

Fortunately, the Essenes' kindness did not stop with food. During the early days, they sheltered some of the new families as they joined us. Other newcomers chose—or were forced by lack of space in the Essene Quarter—to remain in their homes in Jerusalem, usually in the poorest section, along the Valley of the Cheesemakers; but they shared both our meals and prayers as well as the instructions one or more of our group gave each day except the Sabbath.

Even with all the help we received, we soon had financial problems. Feeding, housing, and clothing those people and their children—after three weeks the community included nine children—required a steady flow of cash. There was no lake into which we could dip nets or rich farm land whose soil, if properly tended, would yield a plentiful harvest. The pilgrims' exodus after Pentecost made more space available and also reduced prices, but our gains were marginal. It was good to spend less, but we needed a steady flow of money to spend anything at all.

I was much more worried about these matters than were the Galileans. Indeed, they evidenced no concern at all, not being accustomed to an economy that regulated itself almost totally by money. Naïvely, they looked to me, Josef of Arimathea, and Matthias to provide what was necessary. I could do that for a short time, but my personal resources were limited; and I knew my good pagan uncles were not about to subsidize a colony of Jewish religious reformers. Matthias had no real capital, only the income from his inn; and by taking up his space the community was decreasing his capacity to earn.

After two months, when our numbers had more than doubled again and I had detected rumblings among the Essenes, who continued taking new followers into their already crowded homes, I

insisted that several of us talk about these matters. Simon Peter
had given them no thought, as he freely—proudly would be more
accurate—admitted. "You remember what the Master said, we
shouldn't be concerned about what we eat or wear. 'Behold the
lilies of the fields. . . .' "

"Lilies are beautiful in Galilee," I interrupted, "but in Jerusalem you need money to eat."

"We need faith, not money," he repeated. "The only important
thing's that the Master'll return soon."

"But what if he doesn't come soon? You yourself tell people
you don't know whether it will be tomorrow or next week or next
year. What do we do in the meantime?"

"We're all weak. We preach the return of the Master to found a
kingdom that will last a thousand years. If we start buying buildings and hoarding money, we'll be showing not only a lack of faith
ourselves, we'll shake the faith of others. We'd destroy ourselves."

"Have you considered," I asked, "that you've misunderstood?
The Master may not be coming at all in the way you imagine."

"How will he come then?" Simon Peter looked astonished.

"I don't know. I don't pretend to understand any of it." And I
didn't. In fact this was the first time, other than an occasional hint
to John the priest, I had been able to come close to articulating an
alternative theory of the Master's return; and I was less sure of
myself than my words might have indicated. "Perhaps he has
already come. That may have been what those 'appearances' were
all about."

Simon Peter was genuinely perplexed. "No. . . . No, I don't
think so. He will come again and found his kingdom. It will last
for a thousand years." His tone was authoritative, his voice loud,
two indicia, I had learned, that Simon Peter was beset by doubt.

"Quintus may have a point," John the priest put in. "Perhaps
the Master *has* come again. But even if he is coming as Simon
Peter thinks, we do not know when. Until the Master returns, our
work must go on. And it may have to go on for several more
years."

Simon Peter was angry—more, frustrated. There were issues
beyond money to which he had given no thought, and he suddenly

realized his failure. He threw up his hands. "All right, what then? What if we have to wait ten years? So what? I'm a fisherman, not a forager for an army. I teach people the Master's message, and he said don't worry about such things."

"Didn't he mean," I offered, "not to let those things be our reason for existence? He didn't urge us to starve to death. He went hungry like the rest of us when we had nothing; but he also ate well when we had food, and enjoyed wine when we had it."

"What then? What do we do?" Simon Peter was almost pleading for an answer to a puzzle he could not comprehend.

"There has to be a way," I said. "We can find it by careful planning."

"I would say use my house," John the priest noted, "but it is very close to Caiaphas's palace, and he is much more likely to tolerate a small community here in the Essene Quarter—he looks on Essenes as crazy anyway—than in his own neighborhood."

"Could you sell your house?" I asked.

"I could," he replied, drawing out the "could" for several full seconds. "I suppose I could," drawing out the "could" once more. "It was my father's home and his father's before him. It is mine by right. But then I would need to be housed here and so would my wife. And we have four children. Would there be room for them here?"

This news of a family came as a complete surprise to me. John had never mentioned a wife or children during the years at the lake, even during our most frank discussions. Yet I should have realized. Every Jew feels a divinely imposed duty to "be fruitful and multiply." This news also drove home to me once again how much I was an outsider, even to the person with whom I was intellectually closest. I was hurt more than angry.

The answer to John's question about space in the Quarter was obvious, as he knew. I thought it best not to offer that answer—yet.

"I also have money on deposit in the Temple," John continued. "Perhaps I could draw some of it out."

Simon Peter looked at him quizzically. I doubt if he knew what "on deposit" meant. There was much he had to learn. I shuddered at the work that lay ahead.

"Some of it?" I asked.

"Well, all of it, if we need it so badly."

"Yes, we do, and it is for the Master." I was annoyed at John for not telling me about his family and now only offering part of his money. After all his remorse for not acknowledging the Master during his lifetime, he was still reluctant to make a total commitment. Immediately, however, I felt like a hypocrite. I could hardly set myself up a model of total commitment. I tried to give John a way out: "Would it be dangerous to withdraw all your funds at once? Would your relatives suspect something?"

"Probably not. Annas still has great influence. The nobles respect him even more than they do Caiaphas. Annas wants peace among the Jewish factions. He despises the rebels and, like Caiaphas, is sure the Essenes are mad. And as a good Sadducee, he detests Pharisees. But he doesn't want a civil war any more than he wants the wrath of Rome on our heads. He'll make his influence felt. I doubt that he or any of the others care much about us, as long as we don't challenge them or the Romans."

"Or move into their neighborhood," I added.

"That, too," John smiled. "You can be sure Caiaphas knew all about us at the lake. If he didn't strike, it's because he bears us no ill will."

Simon Peter frowned. "He crucifies the Master and he bears us no ill will. I'm glad I'm a simple peasant."

"The Romans crucified the Master," John said sharply.

"Well, Caiaphas encouraged them."

"Since when does a Roman need encouragement to murder a Jew?" John asked.

"Let's try," I cut in, "to settle the problems at hand—how to feed and house and sooner or later clothe our community. The first thing we have to do is make some other living arrangements. The Essenes have been putting us up too long. They aren't rich, and our people are a burden. I propose we take the money from Barnabas's house, add it to John's money, and buy a couple of houses here in the Essene Quarter or in the Lower City. Then I think we're going to have to 'encourage' the brethren to find work."

"We have work!" Simon Peter snapped. "Our task, our only task, is to preach the Master's word to prepare for his return."

"But . . ." I began.

"No buts. My decision's final. When the Master told us the parable of the servants waiting for the bridegroom he was instructing us on how to act now, while we wait for his return in glory. We can try to buy the houses, but our work is to spread the good news."

Simon Peter spoke with authority if not logic. I was content to have moved us forward one step at a time. Later, I asked Matthias to find us houses to buy. He was not only intimately familiar with the city, but he had an incentive the Galileans lacked.

I remember one night in particular, perhaps a dozen weeks after Pentecost. The day had been very warm, but in early evening a breeze had picked up and, at its altitude, Jerusalem cools quickly. Matthias was inside tending to his few customers. (I thought it better not to point out to Simon Peter that he didn't want the Galileans to work but did not object to Matthias's continuing part of his old business.) Simon Peter and I had just finished our daily session of Greek and were sitting outside in the small square in front of the inn. He had brought a large skin of wine to our tutorial and was still nursing it. I wasn't pleased, but there was nothing I could do without creating a scene that would, at best, undermine his leadership.

John the priest had joined us, as had James and John, the sons of Zebedee, and Stephen from Tarsus, the student of Gamaliel. He was tall and lithe, an athlete by build. It was evident that he had spent some of his few years in a good Greek gymnasium. Earlier I described his face as handsome. He had a neatly trimmed mustache and a brief but thick black beard covering his chin. His cheeks were clean shaven, his clothes well cut, marks of breeding if not wealth. But he was the sort of person who is an alien in every community, always ready to quarrel, always delighting in antagonizing people. There was no humor in his provocations, only malice.

Many Jews of the Diaspora had ambivalent feelings toward the cult of the Temple. On the one hand, like good Jews they believed the Lord focused His activities in the Land of Israel. Jerusalem was His capital, a place, therefore, beloved by all true believers. The Temple is the uniting symbol of their faith. On the other hand, the arrogance and at times corruption of the High Priests, the way in which they demand money from Jews in the Diaspora yet treat them as less worthy because they choose to live in pagan lands, create bitter resentment. Often among "foreign" Jews—as in Galilee—deep religious devotion and rancorous anticlericalism coexist.

Stephen shared this ambivalence. His anger—it was not resentment, but live anger that must have sprung from some traumatic incident about which he never talked in our community—against the priests and everything about the Temple overwhelmed his devotion to what the Temple represented. As a result, he viewed John the priest as an enemy, and on occasion the two exchanged barbed words.

More than the priesthood bothered Stephen, however. He would sometimes attack other members of the community, and once or twice even the Master's message itself. Usually there was no contest. He was very smart and knew Scripture as well as some Greek philosophy and Jewish history. At times I wondered how much he loved the Master's message and how much he hated the Judean priests and saw our community as a way of hitting back at them.

That night, Simon Peter was Stephen's target. "What will the Master do about the Romans when he comes to establish his kingdom?" Stephen asked.

"Do?"

"Yes, do. The Romans aren't likely to fall down and swear oaths of allegiance to him. They'll try to crucify him again. He won't be able to establish a kingdom hanging from a cross. So what does he do about them? Will he order us to rise up and destroy them?"

"I don't know," Simon Peter responded. "You're talking about the work of the Holy One, blessed be His name. I don't think the Master wants us to rise up against anyone. When I cut a guard that was arresting the Master, he told me to put away my sword. 'He who takes up the sword shall perish by the sword.' "

"Yet you tell us," Stephen said, as if he were thinking about the matter for the first time, "he also told the crowds, 'I have not come to bring peace but the sword.' So he brings us a sword; if we pick it up, we shall die; if we don't then we are not his followers. I see a difficulty."

"Those were his words," John the priest put in, "but not his meaning. He spoke allegorically."

"He spoke what?" Simon Peter asked.

Even in the half light I could see the sneer form on Stephen's face at Simon Peter's question. "As in a parable," I explained before Stephen could say something hurtful.

"The Master meant," John the priest continued, "that loving him might cut his followers off from their normal lives and divide families, as he divided his own."

"And mine," Simon Peter muttered. I hoped I was the only one who had caught his words. Then he spoke more loudly. "I don't know the answers to your questions. The Master was an educated man; he didn't teach us like the scribes teach their students, chopping words and tossing scriptural sentences around like children's toys. I only know that he'll come again and found his kingdom and it'll last for a thousand years."

"He told you he would come and establish a kingdom and didn't explain what he was going to do about the Romans?" Stephen persisted. "I don't remember your telling us he said anything about a kingdom when you saw him at the lake."

"He didn't; he said it long before. He was always talking about the kingdom of God."

"Oh."

Simon Peter was fuming at this last bit of sarcasm; and, after taking a long swallow of the wine, he struck back, but not at Stephen. "Most of us do not even know if we'll be alive on that great day. Only John here has the promise that he'll never taste death."

"Those were not quite the Master's words." John was smiling, pretending to treat the matter as a joke. I knew he was troubled by Simon Peter's jealousy, but I doubted that he realized how deeply it ran.

"No," Simon Peter agreed, "those weren't his exact words. His words weren't always his message. But when he comes . . ." He gulped down more wine and wiped his beard on his sleeve. His voice became a hoarse, harsh whisper: "When he comes, don't you forget, any of you, that I'll be first; and I'll be first until he comes, too."

We were all uneasy, all except Stephen, that is. He seemed to enjoy the scene. I was especially concerned. I knew, as perhaps only Andrew and one or two of the other Galileans did, of Simon Peter's black moods—and that the smooth outer layers of unquestioning faith covered a mass of gnawing doubts. My principal worry was about the newcomers. Only Stephen was with us in the square, but in such a small community news travels almost instantaneously. Their faith was tender, and for them Simon Peter was the virtuous statesman, the font of wisdom about the Master's teaching and his impending return. A clear look into his troubled soul could wreck the community.

"I think," John the priest suggested, "we should say a prayer for the success of our work and then go to bed. We have another long day ahead tomorrow."

"Let's pray," Simon Peter agreed, "but let's also drink." He took yet another swallow from the wineskin. The glazed look in his eyes left no doubt he was now quite drunk.

"Pray?" Stephen asked. "Why pray? You say that the Holy One is all knowing, all good, all loving, and all powerful. If so, why pray? If He is all knowing, He doesn't need us to tell Him anything; if He is all good and all loving, He will do for us what He knows—and not what we think—is best for us; if He is all powerful He can and will do what He wants when He wants, without our suggestions. Don't we insult the Eternal One by praying for His intervention in our lives? Aren't we being as silly as those priests in the Temple who offer sacrifice as if the smell of burning flesh could 'please' an eternal being?"

"We pray," Simon Peter half shouted in a thick voice, "because the Master said we should. If he'd said we should get down on all fours and push stones around with our noses, we'd be on our hands and knees all day long. And we offer sacrifice in the Temple because the Holy One, blessed be His name, said we should. And there's an end to it. And tomorrow we go to the Temple to offer sacrifice and to pray." With that he put the wineskin to his mouth again and squeezed it, trying to get a few last drops out. When it was empty, he threw it over his shoulder and lurched away.

John the priest led the others in prayer while I followed Simon Peter to make sure he did not get into trouble. Fortunately he went no farther than the first inn in the Lower City that was still open, and with a few pennies bought another small skin of wine. Within ten minutes he consumed that and fell peacefully—if loudly—asleep. I paid the innkeeper to allow Simon Peter to spend the night where he sprawled, then returned home.

5

✤ It was late when I arrived at my uncles' villa and, fatigued, slept past dawn the next morning and had to hurry back to the inn. I needn't have rushed. Simon Peter was nursing a very tender skull and was at least an hour from a functioning condition. "What are you planning for today?" I asked, hoping his statement of the previous evening had evaporated into an alcoholic haze.

He held his head in both hands. "You know damned well what—and for the love of the Holy One, don't shout so. Matthias must've bought some bad wine."

"Or you drank too much good wine." I had seen Simon Peter in this condition too often to be sympathetic.

"That's a possibility." Then in a half whisper: "At times—you know it, the others don't—my faith falters, anger wells up inside me. I miss Naomi and I miss Jephthania. I miss my lake and my boat and my fish, sunrise above the mountains at the lake. I

miss simple people who speak simple Aramaic. I pray, Quintus,
I pray and I pray, but I get no answer. I cry out for help, and all
I hear is the hollow echo of my own voice. I feel that the Lord has
forsaken me."

"But you have seen the risen Master," I said feebly.

"You don't believe that. You and John never believed Mary or
the others. John believes now, even though he doesn't want to;
you don't believe even though you want to. And sometimes I'm
not sure myself. Was it a stupid peasant hoping so hard that he
dreamed it?"

"Well, you can see now. That's evidence of something."

"Yes, evidence of something, but of what? I don't know, Quintus,
I just don't know. Sometimes I've either got to get drunk or go
crazy. Maybe I've got a demon."

"Your only demon comes out of a wineskin," I said. I was curt
because I didn't know what to say. He needed comfort, but he had
come to the wrong person. For every doubt he had, I had ten. Yet,
curiously, we were both as committed as our temperaments would
allow. I knew that, but talk about demons annoyed me. These
peasants were always claiming that the Lord their God was One,
but that didn't stop them from believing in all sorts of minor
spirits who bedeviled mankind. Simon Peter's doubts caused me
pain because they were my own; his superstition angered me
because it denied the only thing of which I was absolutely sure,
human reason.

"No," he corrected me, "I try to drown my demon in a wineskin. Try not to be too hard on me, Quintus. We can't all be as
strong as you."

That was a puzzling remark. I always considered myself among
the weakest—more intelligent, more cultured than most, but certainly not strong in either physical strength or religious faith. I
changed the subject: "Why do you want to go to the Temple?"

"Why not?" He groaned and motioned for me to pass him the
bucket of water. He drank a huge swallow. "Where better to
proclaim the Master's message than in his Father's house? And
where better to fulfill his prophecy that I'd be bound and taken
where I would not go? . . . I don't know why I must go to the

Temple. It's like coming to Jerusalem: I've told you before: You always want reasons. Sometimes there aren't any. Maybe it's loneliness; maybe it's the dregs from wine a stupid fisherman drank while sailing a strange sea; maybe it's a demon; or maybe it's the Holy Spirit."

Then he smiled and added, "Whatever the reason, I have to go now. Give me enough time to think about it and I'll run all the way back to Galilee."

His voice dropped to a whisper that I could barely hear: " 'I am with you all days,' he told us at the lake; but where the hell is he when you come after me for money, when the Essenes complain about new followers crowding them out, when people like that sneering snob Stephen ask me questions I can't answer, and when strangers who I try to share the Master's message with spit at me?"

To the Temple we went, down into the Valley of the Cheesemakers, across through the Lower City, and then to the approaches to the Temple itself. I came along. My rational self found all sorts of excuses, some of them quite plausible; but my Muse urged me to go along to see what would happen so I could write about it with authenticity.

Six of us made the sortie. Simon Peter wanted a small group rather than a crowd, enough people for mutual protection, yet not so many as to pose the threat of a mob. We still agreed John the priest shouldn't go, and from the others Simon Peter chose James and John, the sons of Zebedee, Thomas, Levi, and me. I could only enter the Court of the Gentiles, but that, Simon Peter said, was as far as they intended to go.

The day itself was magnificent, though a bit on the warm side if one has to mingle closely with peasants. By the time Simon Peter's head had cleared, the sun had burned away the morning mists, and the white, gold tipped marble of the Temple stood above us as one of the wonders of the world. As architecture it was magnificent; as art it was inspired; and as a feat of engineering, it was truly a miracle. I had never "gone up," not all the way up, into the Temple itself before, though I had admired it from every possible outside viewpoint, including that of the Antonia, the fortress that towered above its northwest corner. Of course, I had gone with the Master and gotten as far as the bankers' hall, but, as you recall, we didn't make it to the Temple itself that day.

Today, with Pentecost well past, there were no crowds, only a few hundred people, most of whom were going to the Temple to gossip, gawk, and pray, not offer sacrifice or pay their tithes. We went straight to the double Hulda Gates at the south wall of the mount. A priest stood at each portal, nodding and speaking to every person who entered. He stared menacingly at me, an obvious Greek, until Simon Peter assured him I was a God Fearer. Still scowling, the priest welcomed me, "Go no farther than the Court of the Gentiles, Greek, or your life is forfeit."

Once on the Temple mount in the immense, stone-floored Court of the Gentiles, we turned right and went through the traditional ritual of walking around the inner courts and the Temple building itself, raised fourteen steps up and surrounded by a balustrade, before coming back to the front of the Temple and prostrating ourselves thirteen times in front of the Beautiful Gate. (I confess I was more a gawking tourist than a reverent pilgrim.) Lest any gentile have misunderstood the priest's threat at the Hulda Gates, the signs I described earlier warned in Latin, Greek, and Hebrew that foreigners, i.e., gentiles, who crossed the balustrade that marked the inner threshold would be killed.

From the top of the mount, the view of Jerusalem and its surrounding hills was spectacular. We were a hundred feet above the city's highest natural elevation. In August the open marble courtyard might be unbearably hot, but today it was only a bit warm in the sun; in the shade provided by the large porticos that went around the mount, it was delightfully cool. We walked in Solomon's Portico, which runs north and south along the eastern edge of the mount, looking out across the Kidron Valley, the Mount of Olives, and farther east, the village of Bethany.

Perhaps twenty people were clumped in a large group inside the portico. Their chatter quieted as we approached. Not unnaturally, they stared at the five yokels and one Greek who approached them. Simon Peter seemed unperturbed by their hostile stares. "Peace be to you," he said as he raised his hand in greeting. There was no return salutation, but Simon Peter began to address them in Aramaic: "Men of Israel, we come to tell you about Joshua the Nazarene, whom the Romans crucified."

Immediately, five or six of the group wandered off. Several others seemed embarrassed. But at least there was no heckling as Simon Peter continued, with minor variations, what had become his set speech. We gathered no followers that day but provoked enough interest among several of the group (all of them, I noted with pleasure, spoke Aramaic with Greek accents as heavy as mine) that they asked us to return the next day and continue the discussion. We were all relieved when we nodded good-bye to the scowling priest at the gate, but none was as relieved as I. I felt like some modern Jonah, poised in the mouth of a whale, then spat out before being swallowed.

In all, despite the calmness of the discussion, the visit to the Temple was not a pleasant experience. The menace of Caiaphas hung in the air. I did not look forward to repeating it; and in fact I remained at the inn when Simon Peter and the others returned to Solomon's Portico the next day and yet again the day after.

At the evening meal after the third visit to the Temple, Simon Peter (who took only a single cup of wine with his food) explained to the gathering about the results of the discussions. On the second afternoon, five people had returned to hear more of his message; on the third day they were joined by five more; and all had asked that Simon Peter come back the following afternoon at the time of the evening sacrifice. It was, everyone concluded, a good omen, but I argued that we should continue to send only a few people to these meetings. It was not wise to put many people into a heavily guarded area over which Caiaphas wielded the power of life and death. Simon Peter agreed.

With that much said, I accompanied the group, again in defer- ence to my muse rather than my good sense. And then it hap- pened. I had feared it would, dreaded it would. I knew in my very bones it would happen sooner or later. Given the Master's remark- able capacity to heal and the superstitious nature of the uneducated, a "miracle" was inevitable. I had only hoped it would come later rather than sooner.

On the broad steps that led up to the Hulda Gates, beggars—many blind or crippled or pretending to be—importuned worshippers, competing with one another for the honor of being the most afflicted. One of these people, who affected to be unable to use his legs, half dragged, half rolled himself, moaning and groaning, toward Simon Peter. He stretched out his palm and, eyes looking down, cried, "Help me, for the love of the Most High, help me."

"Look at me!" Simon Peter commanded. The man raised his eyes. "I don't have gold or silver," Simon Peter said, "but what I have, I give you." He took the beggar's outstretched hand and with a steady, powerful pull lifted him upright. "In the name of Joshua the Nazarene, walk!"

The man took a tentative step and started to topple, but Simon Peter steadied him. "Walk, I tell you. In the name of Joshua the Nazarene, walk!" The man took a second tentative step, then another; on the third he stumbled but caught himself; then walked, unsteadily but palpably.

Fortunately, no more than ten outsiders witnessed the happening, but unfortunately two of them were the priests at the Hulda Gates. Everyone, we as well as the outsiders, was astonished. So was Simon Peter. Two of the witnesses, Egyptian Jews, began chanting "Alleluia! The Lord has visited His people." Several others ran into the Temple to spread the news. The two priests disappeared. The "cured" beggar walked more and more steadily, then began running down the steps. He did not bother to thank Simon Peter. I had seen that behavior before.

"I must sit and rest," Simon Peter said as soon as we reached the shade of Solomon's Portico. "I'm weak. A power has gone out of me." Indeed, his usually dark olive skin was pale, almost ashen, and his hands were trembling.

The men who had been expecting him gathered around, impatient for him to regain his strength. Someone brought a gourd of water; by that time the news had spread and a crowd of perhaps fifty people came pushing and shoving to see "the miracle worker." None of them, I feared, would be touched by his message.

Simon Peter must have thought along similar lines, for his tone was sharp and his words harsh: "Why're you so surprised at what happened? Why're you staring at me as if I made that beggar walk by my own power? As Jews, you know better. The Holy One, the God of Abraham, of Isaac and Jacob, has shown Himself to you once again, as He showed Himself through his servant Joshua, the just one, that the Romans, with your help and the help of our leaders, crucified, as our people have time and again through history killed the messengers of God."

Several of the people in the front rank stepped back in surprise, and the babble from the others stopped. They had come to gape at a magician, not to be accused of conspiring with the Romans to murder a prophet. Simon Peter, who was becoming adept at reading a crowd's shifting moods, quickly softened his tone. "Now I know, brothers, no Jew understood what he was doing by helping the Romans. You were blinded by sin so you didn't recognize this Joshua as a holy one sent from the Most High Himself, may His name be blessed forever. But even the hardness of your hearts couldn't destroy the Eternal One's love for His people. He raised this Joshua from the dead. We have seen him, here in Jerusalem as well as in Galilee. He was crucified, he has been raised, and he'll come again to found his kingdom."

There was no heckling, no walking away. Simon Peter had the complete attention of the crowd. "Repent, turn back to the Holy One, so that your sins may be washed away. He's sent you His anointed one. You rejected the prince of life, but you can still follow his words, his Way. Listen to those words, to his message of love, so you can be ready when he comes again. For you're the rightful heirs to that kingdom."

"What is his Way?" someone asked, and Simon Peter began to explain the Master's message of love.

Before he could finish, the inevitable result of the inevitable "miracle" occurred. The two priests from the Hulda Gates came stalking into the portico along with the captain of the Temple guard and a squad of his police. These guards were always Levites, priests but also efficient soldiers. Simon Peter made no effort to resist. Indeed, he smiled as they grabbed him and pinned his arms behind his back. Fortunately, since only Simon Peter had worked the "miracle" and only he was speaking, only he was arrested.

But as the soldiers were shoving him along, John called out: "Captain, I am John ben Zebedee." Clearly that datum did not interest the captain. John continued, half running alongside the troop of priest-soldiers, trying to keep pace with their brisk marching step. "I'm also a follower of Joshua, the anointed. If preaching his word, the word of the Eternal One Himself, is a crime in this sacred place, then I, too, am a criminal."

The captain signaled his troops to halt. He looked at the two accusing priests for instructions, but they were taken by surprise. John spoke again as he moved toward the officer: "My Levite brother, I follow Joshua the Nazarene, whom the Romans, with your help, crucified. He has died, he has been raised from the dead, he will come again."

Anger replaced surprise. The priests, like most of the Temple establishment, were Sadducees. Not only were their policies those of peace and cooperation with the Romans, but they denied the resurrection of the body and life after death. "Silence that Pharisee and take him away," the older priest snapped. The captain motioned to three of his men, who grabbed John and pushed him along with Simon Peter.

The crowd broke up slowly. Some were disappointed and confused, others angry. Several of the latter shouted curses and threats at the soldiers, but only after they were sufficiently distant so as not to be able to tell who had been shouting. The other disciples, practiced in the art of indecision, did nothing except return to the inn and give the others the news. Matthias's reaction was the quickest: "It was a mistake to go to that place. The Eternal One, blessed be His holy name, does not dwell in buildings, only in human hearts."

Stephen, for once, agreed with someone. "Matthias is right. The Temple is a huge example of idolatry—or worse, of selling the things of the Lord when they are His free gifts to all His people. No good Jew should go near the place. Those self-righteous hypocrites who control Herod's idol will kill John and Simon Peter."

"They can't do that," James, the other son of Zebedee said. "The Romans don't let our courts impose death."

Before I could set James right, Levi, the chubby man who had been a tax collector, spoke up: "No, on the Temple mount, the Romans allow the priests power over life and death."

"We all know that," Stephen said, stomping on poor James's faint hope for his brother. "I say we gather all the community, go to the 'foreign' synagogues, and muster people who detest the priests as much as we."

"And then?" Andrew asked.

"And then we march to the Temple gates and demand that the priests release John and Simon Peter."

"Even if we could muster more than a few dozen people, do you think we'd be a match for the Temple guards?" I inquired. "Or if we were that the Romans wouldn't swarm down from the Antonia and nail us to crosses?"

"I would rather live an hour as a free man than a lifetime as a slave," Stephen said. "But I wouldn't expect a gentile to understand that."

"Foolishness, boy," Matthias said, "plain foolishness. If violence was the answer, we Essenes would have torn the Temple down before it was half done."

"This talk is worse than foolishness," John the priest put it. "It is blasphemy. The Temple is the house of the Eternal One. No pious Jew would disturb a stone of its magnificence. Only one who is a pagan at heart would even think such thoughts."

"Or an arrogant, bloodsucking priest who lives off the sacrifices of his people and then spits on them as inferior foreigners," Stephen retorted.

"Brothers," Andrew interrupted, "the Temple's not our problem, nor is where the Eternal One, blessed be His name, lives; He lives where He chooses to live, and all our feelings can't affect that. Let us plan how to help John and Simon Peter."

"That's what we're trying to do," Stephen said. "And I say we can get them out alive only by force."

"And I say that's stupid," Andrew countered.

"You would," Stephen shouted. "You ran away the last time

you saw the Temple guards. Old men are only good for talking and running away." Andrew, I noted, was younger than Simon Peter and only slightly older than I; but to children even the young seem old.

Andrew lunged for Stephen's throat. "We're not much for suicide, but you must be!" The Galilean was not as large or strong as his brother, and in a contest in the gymnasium I would have backed Stephen; but here in close quarters, with no holds barred, Andrew might have crushed the youngster.

Levi got his bulk between them and pushed Andrew back. "Peace, brothers, peace. We are followers of the Master's Way, not drunken brawlers. Let's talk sense."

And so, after two people held Andrew, and Matthias put an arm around Stephen's shoulder in a friendly but arresting fashion, we did talk sense as well as nonsense. Leaderless, we were reduced to the status of a debating society without rules. We talked and shouted and talked and whispered and talked and cursed and finally talked and prayed. In the end, of course, we did nothing, much to Stephen's disgust. It was a policy in which we excelled.

Yet it was a wise policy, for that evening, after we had exhausted ourselves in angry debate, four of the men with whom Simon Peter had been meeting in the Temple—all of them Greek-speaking, as I indicated—found Matthias's inn and asked if they might join us in talk about the Master's message. We were up late that night and put, I am afraid, a hole in Matthias's supply of wine. The talk was as fulfilling as the earlier debate had been frustrating.

I had expected that John the priest and I would carry the burden of explanation, especially since we were the only ones who spoke Greek fluently. But such was not the case. The four men understood Aramaic, and the Galileans made do with that language plus their awkward Greek. I was pleasantly surprised to find that Levi, Thomas, James, and even Andrew were able to express much of the essence (not the subtleties, of course) of the Master's message of a God who was a loving Father, Who required that we, in turn, love and care for one another as tender brothers. The Galileans erred, I thought, in talking about the kingdom that was about to materialize as if it were to be something like a theocratized version of the Roman Empire, but, happily, they did not dwell on the point; and our visitors were as interested, at least then, in the substance of the message as in its political implications.

6

✣ The trial of Simon Peter and John the son of Zebedee came the following day. I, of course, could not attend since the proceeding was held in an inner court of the Temple, beyond that triple-tongued menace to non-Jews caught trespassing. Stephen wanted to attend, all the more because of Andrew and Matthias's argument against, but Levi was able to persuade the brash youngster that his presence might make it worse for the two prisoners. Thus my account is necessarily somewhat biased here, because I depend largely on what John and Simon Peter told us, though I was able to verify some details with several priests who later embraced the Way, one of whom actually sat in the judgment.

Because the offense was disturbing the peace of the Temple and not some form of blasphemy or heresy, it was the smaller sanhedrin, the body with political jurisdiction, not the Great Sanhedrin, that held the trial. To avoid the necessity of moving the prisoners across the city and risking a disturbance of some sort, Caiaphas set the proceedings in the meeting place of the Great Sanhedrin, the Hall of Gazit in the Temple, rather than at his palace. Annas was present as was his son, Jonathan, who a few years later would succeed Caiaphas. Twenty of the twenty-three councillors were in attendance. Fifteen were priests arrayed in their tall-hatted, robed, sacerdotal splendor, the rest prominent lay people. Once again when we needed him, Josef of Arimathea was away. Also absent was Gamaliel, the great Pharisaic scribe whom Caiaphas had reluctantly appointed to the council.

The High Priest must have been annoyed to confront this troublesome sect once more, especially since it had seemed to go to earth so quietly in Galilee after the Romans had executed its founder. Still, his demeanor was, as usual, flat. The prisoners were led—"yanked" was the word Simon Peter used—into the hall by ropes looped around their necks. Their hands were tied behind their backs. There was a Levite guard on either side of each and two stationed behind the Galileans. To the side, about ten feet away, were six other guards and their captain. Nearby was the beggar who testified first about the miraculous "cure" of his paralysis. Then the two priests described the disturbance that had occurred on the Temple's steps and later within the Portico of Solomon. Next the captain testified about the loud crowd that was pushing and shoving around the two Galileans when he arrived on the scene. He said he feared a riot. Last, it was the prisoners' turn to speak.

"Who are you?" Caiaphas asked.

"I am called Simon Peter," he reported himself as speaking in a loud, clear voice. "I am a fisherman, born at Bethsaida Julias on the Lake of Galilee, where Philip, the son of Herod and brother of Antipas, rules; I live now in Capernaum in Galilee. This is John, the son of Zebedee, also a fisherman, born in Kinnereth in Galilee."

"What are you doing here in Jerusalem, disturbing the peace of this holy Temple?" Caiaphas asked.

"We didn't break the peace," Simon Peter replied, "but those two priests and your own guards did. We were talking quietly to friends in the Portico of Solomon, when these people arrested us like common criminals. Why? Is it because we've done this man"—he nodded toward the beggar—"a kindness?"

Caiaphas was taken aback at Simon Peter's brazenness, so much so that he made no immediate reply. According to my priestly sources, the two Pharisees on the tribunal snickered. It was Annas who spoke up: "How dare you, an ignorant peasant, question the acts of the Sanhedrin? Change your tone or you will be whipped before we proceed."

"I'm a Jew," Simon Peter said, "the son of a Jew, the grandson of a Jew. My ancestors've been Jews as far as memory runs. My Master, Joshua the Nazarene, is also a Jew; he traces his lineage to David himself. We have a right as well as a duty to use the Temple to worship the Holy One, blessed be His name. That's why I dare to question anyone's authority to imprison us for performing our duties as Jews."

Caiaphas motioned to the soldiers holding Simon Peter. One of them cracked him across the shoulders with the butt end of his spear. The force of the blow dropped Simon Peter to his knees. He struggled to get up. It was difficult with his hands tied behind his back. The two soldiers grabbed the rope that bound his hands and jerked him to his feet. "You know well," Caiaphas said, "that you were arrested for disturbing the peace of the Temple, not for performing your religious duties, do you not?"

"I know no such thing. I was only the instrument of an act of mercy to that man"—he nodded again toward the beggar—"and I was explaining to my fellow worshipers I had acted not through any power of my own but by that given to Joshua the Nazarene, the son of David, the Messiah, anointed by the Eternal One Himself to save Israel, who you surrendered to the Romans to be crucified and the Holy One raised from the dead."

Caiaphas spoke to the captain of the guards again. As at the Master's hearing, his tone was devoid of emotion, as if he were describing something rather than prescribing a punishment to be inflicted on a human being. "That man is treading near the edges of blasphemy, is he not? Would it not be an act of charity to teach him the straight path?"

The soldiers pushed Simon Peter to his knees again, and one of them laid five slow stripes across the Galilean's back with a thin rod. While this lesson was in progress, Jonathan leaned over and whispered something to Caiaphas: "I do not recall any such incident. When did we help the Romans crucify a Jew?"

Caiaphas whispered back: "It was a minor event several Passovers ago. As best I recall, the man was also a Galilean radical, connected with the Essenes in some fashion. He led that riot against the bankers. His followers had staged a parade at Passover hailing him as the son of David. The air was rife with revolution, Pilate thought, but Romans always think that. There wasn't much to it. Every Galilean boy thinks he'll grow up to be a new Judas Maccabee. I was able to keep Pilate off this Joshua, or whatever his name was, for a time; but as soon as he started that riot and then threatened to destroy the Temple, we had to act. In fact, Pilate almost sent a detachment into the Temple to put down the riot in the bankers' hall. There was some violence, and a great deal of money lost. To a few Galileans this character was a prophet turned messiah, to the Romans he was just another seditionist."

"But we did help?" The point troubled Jonathan.

"Yes, but not much. The only live question was whether Pilate would kill him with our cooperation or without. Your father and I thought it more prudent to help them. We earned some goodwill from Pilate, though he pretended to be reluctant to punish the man. He's the real fox, not Antipas. I didn't appreciate that until I heard about his performance at the trial. In a brilliant display of hypocrisy, he pretended to be sympathetic to the Galilean. Then he tacked this new Maccabee to a tree between two 'brigands' with a sign labeling him 'King of the Jews.' It was, I admit, a wonderfully sardonic touch. Never underestimate these Romans. They rule an empire because they know how to use and abuse men."

"What's this talk of 'resurrection'?" Jonathan asked.

"More Pharisaical claptrap. The man claimed he would rise from the dead. It makes a wonderful story. These Galilean peasants are more clever than you might think from the way they butcher our language."

At that point, the guards jerked Simon Peter back up to his feet once more. He was shaky from the two beatings, but still able to stand and speak.

"You are now prepared to testify truthfully, are you not?" Caiaphas asked smoothly. "The captain of the guard and these other holy priests charge you with disturbing the peace of the Temple. You gathered a large and noisy crowd about you and made threatening remarks against the holy priests who rule Israel according to the Law of Moses."

"I said nothing about priests. Besides," Simon Peter retorted, "pagans rule the Land of Israel. The 'holy priests' lick Roman spittle from the floor."

The captain of the guard reached out and slapped Simon Peter across the face. Once again he dropped to the floor. Two guards kicked him then pulled him up again. His nose and mouth were bloody.

"This is distasteful business, fisherman," Caiaphas said. "Can you not see that your slander gives weight to the charges? I fear for the peace of this holy house. Do you wish to say anything more before we impose sentence?"

"We caused no disturbance." Simon Peter paused to spit some blood from his mouth. He tried to wipe his face on his colobium, but could not because of his bonds. Caiaphas motioned to the captain and one of the guards wiped Simon Peter's face with a towel. He started to speak again: "It isn't a crime to carry out the word of the Lord and do a kindness to a fellow Jew."

Caiaphas ignored the rhetoric. "Now is that all?"

"No. Joshua our Master has died, he's been raised, he'll come again."

"Take the prisoners out," Caiaphas ordered. "We shall consider the punishment."

When the judges were alone, one of the two Pharisees on the Sanhedrin spoke first. "How extensive was this Galilean conspiracy?"

"How extensive is this threat now?" Jonathan asked.

"There is a small colony of believers living near Capernaum in Galilee," Caiaphas said, "a hundred or so. Their leader is a woman." He paused to allow his colleagues to chuckle. "Some of the men have come to Jerusalem. They're living in the Essene Quarter. You heard the fisherman. Their creed centers on this What's-his-name and the claim that he was raised from the dead."

"What do they intend to do about that miraculous 'fact'?" Jonathan put the question to Caiaphas.

"Nothing, at least nothing much. They're trying to make converts."

"To do what?"

"To await the return of their master who will found a kingdom that will last a thousand years."

"And while they're waiting, are they arming?"

"No. No, I don't think so." Caiaphas spoke slowly, as if stressing his lack of complete certainty. "The conduct they advocate is unexceptional—love one's neighbor as oneself, just like Leviticus and Deuteronomy command."

"I wish them luck," Jonathan said, smiling, "more luck than men have had since Moses in securing compliance with that rule. So, are they dangerous?"

"Well, some influential men are followers," Caiaphas noted. "Josef of Arimathea, who graces this very body, is a follower of the Galilean. He doesn't live with them, but he provides money; he even gave his own burial plot to the man after the Romans crucified him. There's a young Greek, a God Fearer, who hangs around the edges. [Alas, it was not an unfair description.] And at least one of our priests, my own 'cousin' John, has taken up with them. And," Caiaphas looked benignly around the room, "I hear rumors that several other priests are sympathetic."

"Hmmm," Jonathan mused. "What do you suggest we do?"

"Are they anything but trouble?" Caiaphas asked. "Two years ago a riot and threats; now another incident. Sooner or later are the Romans not going to hear that this messianic foolishness is still alive and step down hard, even violate the Temple? Don't you think it would be wisest for us to take them out and stone them—we all heard the bigger one come near to blasphemy—then tell the Romans about their community in the Essene Quarter and suggest they send spies to find out what these fools are preaching? As soon as they hear these people are still talking about a leader coming to establish a new kingdom, they'll take care of the rest right then and there—and away from the Temple."

"Let us not be precipitant," Annas put in. "Execution may be too heavy. The Romans disposed of their leader, but the movement seems no weaker now than then. Only with deep regret did I agree to hand this What's-his-name over to the Romans. I bitterly dislike turning over any Jew, however dangerous, to gentiles. I suggest a good whipping to teach these buffoons some manners and then ban them from the Temple. If the Romans decide to move against them. . . . Well, that's their business, as long as they don't defile the Temple's sacred precincts."

"We have a responsibility," the other Pharisee on the council noted, "to keep the Romans as much off the backs of our people as we can, but we're not Roman agents. Rebels, Essenes, and this new group may think we are, but they're wrong. Frankly, I don't care what the Romans think. I am concerned about how we treat Jews. I see no evidence to support the charge that these people broke the peace of the Temple. The big man is an arrogant, disrespectful hothead, but I could make the same charge—with stronger evidence—against some members of this body. I say let them go with a warning to watch their tongues. After all, the loud-mouth got beaten three times while he was before us."

"And you think he learned from that?" Caiaphas asked.

"I don't care whether he learned or not. As far as I can tell, until he was arrested and brought before us, he had done nothing wrong. His behavior before us was intemperate, but he was pun-ished for that. I don't think we should bar any Jew from worship-ing at the Temple—or anywhere else. And I can't help won-dering"—the Pharisee's tone took on an edge—"whether some of us are not anxious to kill these people or ban them from the Temple because they believe that our bodies will rise again at the Last Judgment rather than because of anything they did in the Temple."

Annas tried to smooth over the division between Sadducees and Pharisees. "His beliefs about the Last Judgment are irrelevant. He follows a criminal executed for sedition and talks—loudly—about a new kingdom. That sort makes the Romans anxious, and they react swiftly and ruthlessly. I don't want them coming into the Temple after these people. That's why I say beat them and bar them from the Temple."

The discussion went on for another half an hour. In the end, because of the argument of the two Pharisees and one younger priest, and because of Annas's wish not to worsen relations be-tween Sadducees and Pharisees, the decision was merely to ban the Galileans from further preaching about Joshua in the Temple.

When agreement was reached, Caiaphas called for the prisoners to be brought back in. (One of the guards had washed the blood from Simon Peter's face.) "You men of Galilee," Caiaphas ad-dressed them, "this tribunal finds that you have disturbed the peace of the Temple. First, insofar as you did so by 'curing' the beggar, who probably could walk as well yesterday as today, you meant an act of kindness. You acted without evil intent. Any disturbance resulting from that act was not due to your malice, and for that we impose no punishment. We only caution you to be aware of the fact that most of the beggars outside the Temple gates suffer from the same disease—laziness."

Caiaphas continued: "Second and more serious is your urging people to listen to the message of this man the Romans executed as a seditionist. We cannot be seditionists here, can we? Nor can we give aid and comfort to seditionists and their friends. We may not like Roman rule, but it is a reality, one that you can only make worse by spreading pipe dreams about a messiah coming to found a new kingdom. We live in a modern age, not the world of Judas Maccabee, do we not? We confront a militant, vigorous empire, not the decaying, corrupt regime our ancestors did."

"Our God is the Lord of History," Simon Peter replied, giving a perfect demonstration that, if he was learning courage along with Greek, he had yet absorbed nothing of prudence. "What can it matter to Him that His people's oppressors are Romans rather than Greeks?"

"Silence. Silence," Caiaphas repeated, "or you will be beaten again." He waited a few seconds, then went on: "You may speak all you wish in private or in synagogues of our obligation to love one another. Is that not, after all, the Law of Moses? But you may not preach in this Temple about anything again, not about any idea, person, or thing at all. You may enter these sacred precincts only to perform your duties to the Holy One, may His name be blessed, as the Law requires of all Jews; you may not teach or preach in any fashion whatsoever. Have I made myself clear?"

Simon Peter nodded. "You are very clear. But we must decide whether we should obey you or the Eternal One, blessed be His name."

"Must we not always obey the Eternal One? And in this holy place we and only we speak in His holy name. You may go in peace now. But if we ever again find you here for any purpose other than to offer sacrifice, it will go hard with you, very hard. That I promise you by the sacred Torah itself. Guards, take them away and release them outside the Temple gates."

7

✤ Simon Peter and John ben Zebedee returned as heroes. It was, many of the brethren declared, a miracle the two had escaped punishment, though Simon Peter's bruises showed his own escape had been less than full. I saw several miracles, but of a different sort. Simon Peter had tried neither to resist nor to run away when the guards approached, and John had volunteered to be arrested. Moreover, the two had proclaimed their faith before Caiaphas and his sanhedrin. Every stage of the affair contrasted dramatically with their behavior two years earlier.

Thus the incident formed another benchmark for the movement. Simon Peter had demonstrated both courage and leadership and had done so without the Master—or with him in a way we could not yet grasp. Yet the incident also demonstrated our vulnerability and fragility. It was fortunate that Simon Peter had escaped death, long imprisonment, or exile, for I doubt that any of the others in Jerusalem could have exercised leadership, at least beyond leading us in a frenzied exodus to Galilee. "Strike the shepherd and the sheep scatter," the Master had said.

When he learned of the arrest on that first night, John the priest made no move to take command, even temporarily. He was—is—a strange man. He has his own set of resentments against Simon Peter and perhaps even against the Master himself for not making him leader. There is something about being a philosopher that makes leadership especially difficult. Plato's ideal state ruled by philosopher kings would generate disaster. For a philosopher sees many sides to every problem and understands that several solutions are almost equally promising—and equally perilous. A peasant like Simon Peter may be unsure, but because of ignorance, which may be overcome, not because of sophistication, which can never be put aside.

John the priest seemed to understand that Simon Peter, far less sophisticated and educated, was the natural leader. That acceptance may have mitigated, but it did not remove, his resentment.

The others accepted Simon Peter because the Master had singled him out. Mary of Magdala had her own and very different opinions, of course.

In any event, during the hours of Simon Peter's arrest, we were an assortment of people who happened to live together, not a cohesive group and certainly not a movement. I read fear, even panic, in the brethren's eyes. They were planning how to scatter safely. I was concerned less about the Galileans—Mary would have taken care of them—than about the Judeans and even more the Greek-speakers we had gathered. Few of them had holes in which to go to earth.

But the Lord of History wanted our community to grow, and grow it did, not overnight but still steadily. Each week brought a few more people into the Essene Quarter: poor laborers from Judea out of work because the pilgrims would not return for several months; tenant farmers who could no longer support their families, landlords, Herod Antipas, and the Roman Empire; and Greek-speaking Jews who had settled in Jerusalem or its environs. There were also, to be sure, layabouts who seized a chance to be supported by others. By the end of the summer, we had 135 people, including wives, children, and eight widows.

Simon Peter also recognized that the movement needed someone who could take charge if he were disabled. At the next morning's meal, he told the group: "Brothers, we all know the fate of Judas. As the Book of Psalms says, we should let someone else take his place."

"Who?" James ben Zebedee asked. It was not a sophisticated question, but it did get to the nub of the problem.

"It should be someone who knew the Master, and knew him from the beginning, and also has been a witness to his resurrection," Simon Peter replied.

Everyone present thought that narrowed the choice to two people: Matthias and Barsabbas. Both had been with John the Baptizer and had begun to follow the Master from his days in John's ranks. They had not moved to Galilee, though they had visited on several occasions. In addition, the two had been witnesses to the "appearance" at Pentecost.

There was, however, a third person who fit the criteria and did so perhaps more closely than any of the Eleven themselves: Mary of Magdala. I waited to see if her name would be mentioned. It was not.

Simon Peter ordered us to pray for the guidance of the Holy Spirit and, while we were doing so, put two stones in a cup, a light colored one for Barsabbas and, appropriately enough, a dark one for Matthias. Then he shook the cup and told John the priest to close his eyes and remove one. John chose the darker one, a demonstration of the Holy Spirit's wisdom. Matthias was not a man of intellect, but he had practical sense and ability to lead—as well as some money. Barsabbas, while a holy man, was best at chanting prayers in that swaying, singsong manner Jews affect. Furthermore, despite his owning a beautiful woolen prayer shawl and an elaborate set of phylacteries, he did not have a drachma to his name when he followed the Baptizer, and his wealth had not increased since.

Binding Matthias more firmly to the movement did not end our economic problems. Indeed, they grew as our numbers grew. As a rule, only Greek-speaking Jews brought fungible assets to the community, and not all of them were able to do so. Moreover, what they brought was seldom enough to maintain them for very long. Matthias, who shared with me the burden of economic planning, was especially ardent in his prayers for the Master's speedy return. I once explained to him my theory about that return, but he wished to hear nothing about it. The second coming was to be a specific event, not a continuing process already begun.

We managed with difficulty, but we managed. Josef of Arimathea continued to be generous, and several times I traveled to Joppa and Jericho to solicit assistance from Nicodemus. John the priest did not sell his house, but he did withdraw—gradually—all of his deposits from the Temple treasury. Added to the proceeds from the sale of Barnabas's house, those sums gave us a bit of capital. We kept almost all of that with my uncles' offices in Jerusalem in my name. It would have been more convenient had I been the group's treasurer, but the ethnic bar never lifted. Trusting a foreigner comes hard to tribal people. As the only Galilean who could read and write, Levi became our official treasurer. He, after all, was accustomed to keeping accounts.

Simon Peter did not want to reconsider his decision against the brothers' working, but Levi and Matthias joined me in warning not only about the expense of feeding and housing an ever-growing community but also the impending costs of clothing our people when what they brought with them began to wear out. And in some cases that process had been well along before they joined us. Simon Peter would not budge for the eleven Galileans. They must, he insisted, devote full time to preaching the Master's message. I had started to ask why Matthias was an exception, but since Simon Peter was willing to compromise I restrained myself. He agreed that any of the others who wished to could work in or near Jerusalem, with the absolute condition that they still live within the community and join us at the morning and evening meals and accompanying prayer and ritual.

I would have preferred requiring rather than allowing work, for I knew some of the brethren were with us only to avoid all forms of labor. But at least we had taken a small step. As my father used to say, "Everything makes soup." In this case the Roman proverb fit nicely, for we ate a great deal of soup, much of it thin; but poor people were strangers to meat and much other food I considered ordinary.

For yet another two years we lived as I have described, only now at least half the brethren went out to work in shops, to haul garbage, or to do manual labor in the final stages of construction of Herod's Temple. I was able to complete the writing of a full draft of my account of the Master's life and also to take some notes about our daily life in Jerusalem.

Our routine was simple. We arose, ate, and prayed together. Those who had work usually left immediately and did not return until evening. Meanwhile, the Galileans, Matthias, and I took turns instructing the community, and, incidentally, with fewer men in attendance it was easier to persuade the Galileans to encourage greater participation among the women. No one likes to talk to an empty room. Those of us not engaged in that sort of instruction made daily visits to synagogues. I never spoke in such places, though I often went along.

In the evening, we again ate and prayed together. It was not an exciting life, nor was it always easy: Sometimes we were hot, sometimes cold, sometimes angry at each other, and often, very often, hungry. Yet I remember those days as both peaceful and fulfilling. By and large we lived as the Master had taught us, without realizing we were thereby in the kingdom. Most days Simon Peter and the two brothers went up to Solomon's Portico in the Temple and spoke to whoever would listen.

For several weeks after "the miracle," there had been a crowd of howling beggars at the Hulda Gates every time the trio appeared on the long steps. A few dozen Jews would follow them into the Court of Gentiles, and their walk home became a churning trail of people pitifully beseeching or merely curiously awaiting a new miracle. Fortunately, there were no more miracles at the Temple and interest soon faded.

Over the months, four of the original audience were baptized into our community, but most of the others drifted away. They were replaced, however, by fresh faces. The continued presence of the three disciples in the Temple was obvious. They came there, quietly spoke of the Master's message, and, even more quietly, left. It was as if Simon Peter and Caiaphas had worked out a tacit truce. That was John the priest's interpretation.

John and I recognized, though most of the other disciples could not, that the High Priest and his sanhedrin, were in an exquisitely delicate position. Were they not to collaborate with the Romans, Pilate would rule Judea directly in fact, as by imperial decree he was supposedly doing now, and the Jews' lot would become even harsher. The Temple oligarchy thus acted as a buffer between the talons of the Roman eagle and the bare backs of the Jewish people.

Most important in the minds of Annas and Caiaphas, John believed, was preserving the sanctity of the Temple. It was bad enough that Roman soldiers occupied the Antonia and thus commanded a view of the entire Temple mount. But if they thought the Jewish leaders could not keep order, they would invade the sacred precincts. And the chief priests could never forget Pilate's itch to set up in the Temple itself Roman standards, painted with images of false gods, and so profane all that was holy.

As all dilemmas must, this one had a second horn: Tithes, Temple taxes, and required sacrifices fell heavily on peasants. The

Temple oligarchy was set apart from them—even from Jeru-salemites—by birth, wealth, acceptance of Greek culture, and as-sociation with Roman oppressors. For all of these reasons, many Jews despised the priests and their associates both as collaborators with gentiles and as themselves oppressors of the nation.

Caiaphas was thus caught between the Romans and the mass of Jews. And he could put only limited trust in his associates. The Pharisees were his enemies, and the Sadducees were not a cohe-sive bloc. Indeed, some were his rivals for the position of high priest. Thus Caiaphas wanted peace as much as did the Romans and was unlikely to take unnecessary action to anger them or the Jewish people, or to do anything that might strengthen his rivals within the Temple.

But "unnecessary" is a flexible word. As the events of that awful Passover had demonstrated, there were few limits to what he would do to preserve peace or to keep alive in Roman minds the belief he could preserve it. His handling of Pilate also demon-strated considerable manipulative skill.

These were the sorts of things John the priest and I discussed when we were alone or when only Simon Peter was with us. John and I viewed such discussions as much a part of Simon Peter's education as my daily instructions in Greek. In the evenings, conversations among the rest of the community were usually dull. Some of these people were shrewd; but, with few exceptions, they were not given to reflection. Stephen was among the exceptions, but his sarcasm was a high price to pay for his intelligence.

During the first year, speculation about the Master's coming was rife. Had a thief showed up at night he would have been welcomed as the returning Master. During those discussions, Si-mon Peter was usually silent. Some days I believed he was coming over to the sort of theory I had suggested—incoherently, I admit—but, when pressed, he would merely repeat his old lines: "I don't know when the Master returns, perhaps tomorrow, maybe next week, perhaps next year. I only know that he'll come again."

Logically, this position accommodated a very long wait, but psychologically its limits were close and tenuous. Neither rural nor urban peasants are noted for intellectual discipline. They live in the immediate present, recall the past as better, and look to the future with fear. For most of them the delay had already been too long. By the summer of the second year in Jerusalem—the fourth after the crucifixion—concern within the community was approaching a crisis. A few people left us, saying we were living a hoax. Even among the most faithful, the return's delay became a source of difficulty, even embarrassment. Gradually discussion of this earlier obsessive subject of conversation became taboo.

The Galileans suffered in another and painful fashion. If they were married, the Judeans, including John the priest, and most of the Greek speakers had their families with them. A dozen children were born in those years and several new marriages celebrated. But the Galileans were separated from their wives and children. At the first Passover several families made the pilgrimage and several more at Pentecost, the rest at Booths in the fall. But these were only brief visits.

Not being Essenes, these people looked on celibacy as not only an unnatural but also a painful state, as their conversation and occasionally flaring tempers evidenced. Even I found it difficult not to enjoy the comfort of a woman, and my father used to remark that my sex drive was hardly that of a healthy male. Only when I was much older did I come to associate virtue with the ascetic standards of the Essenes about sexual abstinence.

In partial recognition of the likelihood of a long period of waiting, toward the end of the first year Simon Peter initiated a program of furloughs for the Galileans. Each month three went back to the lake and stayed there two weeks. With the trek back and forth, they were gone somewhat less than four weeks, returning just in time to allow the next group to leave. Simon Peter himself never took advantage of his own program. Intuitively, he understood that to remain the leader, he had to endure more than his followers.

At some unconscious level, he may at his trial have been goading Caiaphas to whip him so he could both suffer and seem to suffer more than the others. But I knew his tortured soul well enough to understand he had a compelling need for much penance. The simple Galilean fisherman, I began to realize, was becoming a very complex man.

Naomi did not feel the same restraints as Simon Peter. At both Passovers she and Jephthania came up to Jerusalem, and at the second she stayed until after Pentecost. Naomi was showing the signs of aging that Simon Peter had spoken of, but the child had become even more beautiful.

Despite or because of the crisis in expectations, Bartholomew and Simon, that mousey little man who had somehow once been a Zealot, dreamed up the possibility that the Master would come again in the fall, at the Feast of Booths, the third and least solemn of the three great Jewish feasts. Their reasoning was straightforward, if simpleminded: The Master had died and been raised at Passover in Jerusalem and made a set of appearances immediately thereafter; two years later he had appeared to his disciples at Pentecost in Jerusalem; thus he would return to Jerusalem at Booths, two years after the Pentecostal appearance. Not surprisingly, given the ability of hope to drown reason, many of the community accepted this forecast.

One evening in early September of that second year, after we had finished our meal and prayer, Simon Peter asked if John the priest, Andrew, Matthias, the two sons of Zebedee, and I would join him for a walk. We left the city via the Essene Gate, then turned left and walked in silence until we reached the Mount of Olives. The night's cool was welcome after the day's heat, and the view of Jerusalem, sitting astraddle its pair of hills, was magnificent. The Lower City was almost totally dark: The poor can seldom afford light. The Upper City, however, was a sea of flickering lamps, providing a glow that outlined the Temple's bulk and beauty and softened the squalor of the Lower City into spiraling shadows.

For me, the Mount of Olives brought back melancholy memories. I had not been at that Passover meal, but that made it worse, for my imagination created images that were probably more gruesome than the actual events. Either the area did not affect Simon Peter that way or he had found a strange way of doing penance, for this was the second time he had brought us here. The first had been just before Pentecost, more than two years earlier.

We propped ourselves against some rocks amid an olive grove—there would be little grass until the rains next month—and enjoyed the view. After a few restless minutes Simon Peter began to ramble. "Bartholomew and Simon have convinced many of the others the Master'll return at Booths. What faith can one put in that sort of prophecy?"

"It may be the Holy Spirit speaking to us," James said.

"Or my wine," Matthias suggested. As an Essene, he did not drink and was self-righteous about his own abstinence, though he sold wine to others and gave it to us.

"The Holy Spirit or holy wine," Simon Peter conceded. "How do we know which?"

"I think the whole idea of founding an earthly kingdom is all wrong," I put in.

Simon Peter waved his hand in dismissal. A Greek did not rate more. "John?" He looked at John the priest.

"I think it's foolishness. Like the Holy Spirit, the Master goes where and when he will, not where or when we wish him. He said nothing to support such a prophecy; no one claims a revelation; and, as Stephen says, though a bit viciously, the logic is faulty."

"If," Simon Peter added, "we say we believe this prophecy and the Master doesn't come, the movement'll scatter. The Master's delay's causing enough problems already. If we're silent, people'll say we're afraid to speak out. We'll seem like cowards. If we say we don't believe and the Master does return, he'll be furious."

"And disinherit us," James added.

Apparently Simon Peter could think of no appropriate response to that remark, for he ignored it. "What do we do? What should we say?"

"We should do nothing," Andrew suggested. "But you should go on saying what you have been saying: You do not know when the Master will return, only that he will come back to found his kingdom."

John the son of Zebedee grunted an assent, as did James, but John the priest cleared his throat, making it evident he had reservations. "Well?" Simon Peter asked. "You said you didn't believe in the Booths thing. What's wrong with that answer?"

The priest thought for a few moments before replying. "Nothing is wrong; it just does not seem right. We say the Holy Spirit speaks within us. We say it and we believe it. Yet we refuse to take a stand."

"But that is a stand," Andrew snapped. "We don't know. Neither the Master nor the Holy Spirit has told us anything. That's the honest answer."

"I guess. . . ." John the priest mused.

"Why not hedge our bet?" I asked. Even then I was not proud of myself for my suggestion. "Say what Andrew has suggested. To make sure everyone hears it, say it at morning and evening prayers tomorrow. But do something: Invite Mary to come up from Galilee to celebrate Booths with us. If the Master returns, we would be prepared. If he does not—and I doubt he will—Mary would have an excuse to see how we have progressed. It might also," I added, "soothe her feelings. She was deeply hurt when we left."

"She was as cold as a winter's swim when I saw her two months ago," John ben Zebedee agreed.

"We don't need a woman. And if we do," Andrew guffawed, "it's one who does what she doesn't do. Leave her in Galilee. We owe her nothing."

"She stayed with the Master until the very end," Simon Peter said. "After he was raised, he came to her first. Then for two years she kept our faith alive. We owe her a great deal, for his sake and our own. I like the idea. It has a nice Greek touch. And if the Master does come, then. . . . Quintus, could you go down to the lake and invite her and the Master's mother to join us for Booths?"

I hesitated. I had only recently visited Scythopolis and the thought of another eighty-mile trip each way was not appealing. If I went, I resolved to go with one of my uncles' caravans or borrow some pack animals and guards. In no case would I walk it again, not in September when the temperature on the road would stay at a boil all day long.

"Who else can go?" Simon Peter prodded. "Mary respects you. Even if she doesn't come back with you, you'll learn more about the community there and be able to tell her more about ours here than any of the rest."

I knew that wasn't quite true. John the priest would have made a better ambassador, but it would be easier—I gained respect for Simon Peter's shrewdness—to disavow a Greek than a priest. Reluctantly, I agreed.

8

✢ I went down to Galilee. Usually one says "went up" to describe a trip from the south to the north, but in the Land of Israel one always "goes up" to Jerusalem and "down" from Jerusalem to anywhere else. Although part of the explanation is topographical—Jerusalem is high up—the basic reason is religious. Spiritually, one must ascend to enter the House of the Lord.

Happily for me, one of my uncles, Theophilus, the elder and my favorite of the two, was taking a small caravan back to Scythopolis and then, after some reloading, a larger caravan on to Damascus. We left Jerusalem with a dozen pack camels plus mounts for the guards, the packmaster, and my uncle. He was delighted to add another animal for what he termed "my comfort."

I would never have associated comfort with camels. They are big, awkward, hideously ugly, foul-smelling, evil-tempered beasts. They spit like sailors and bite like wild dogs. They also make me sneeze, and their loping, swaying gait makes me nauseated for the first day or so that I ride them, just as did the ship I took from Caesarea to Alexandria, when I went to study with Philo. For all their vileness, however, they can bump across desert tracks at a remarkable pace, enduring days without water.

Except in winter, the best walking route between Jerusalem and the lake runs through the hill country of eastern Samaria and north-central Judea. With camels, the best route is northeast, down the mountains across the Judean desert to Jericho, 850 feet below the level of the sea, and then straight north along the Lower Jordan. Scythopolis is only a few miles west of the river, near its exit from the southern end of the lake.

The Judean desert is a wild place. It is not a sea of sand like the Arabian desert, but desolate hills and wadis, mountains and gorges, cut by the wind's razor and the occasional rush of water when a winter storm slashes the sides of the hills. Those scatterings of rain cause hundreds of flowers to burst into red, purple, yellow, and white flames. Somehow, these plants or their seeds survive the long dry months to bloom again the next year; but now, in September, after six months without a drop of water, the ground was only rock and clay baked so hard as to be barely distinguishable.

On a map, the distance between Jerusalem and Jericho is only twenty miles, yet it takes camels almost five hours to traverse those hills; and five hours in the desert can shrivel a man into a dried fig. Thus we left Jerusalem at midnight. The sky was clear at that time of year; indeed, it is at most times of the year. The moon was a sliver of lemon, and Polaris was beckoning brightly to the north. Traveling minstrels have likened the desert sky to a pail of diamonds tossed upon an ermine rug. As poetry it is lacking, but as description, close to perfect.

When we left Jerusalem, the air was already cooling, but as we lurched down the temperature rose. At lower altitudes, as all scientists know, the earth's capacity to retain heat increases. Soon we were covering terrain that formed a giant clay oven during the day.

We lost altitude, gained a bit, then lost even more as the ground fell off toward the Jordan. As I rode beside Theophilus, I could not help wondering why my uncle did not take his name seriously—Lover of God. Such had been my own self-centeredness that I had never had a real conversation with any of my uncles, indeed, with any of my family except my mother and my sister; and our talk had always focused on me, not them or their dreams.

Theophilus was much darker than I, due, no doubt, to his having spent much of life on caravan routes and in suqs of cities from Caesarea to Babylon and from Ephesus down to Sheba and across to Alexandria. He was swathed in a white burnoose, its hood thrown back over his shoulder. Around his head, he wore a kaffiyeh, bound close to his scalp by a thin, braided cord, interwoven with strands of gold. One might have mistaken him for an Arab chieftain until one got close enough to see the bright blue of his eyes.

I recognized a physical resemblance between us and was not displeased. He was fifty-six, an age I then considered to verge on the decrepit, but he had weathered handsomely, without the soft protrusion that bulged around my father's once hard middle. In only one respect did I disapprove of my uncle's appearance. Beneath the kaffiyeh his scalp was devoid of hair, an affliction shared by his brother. My vanity prayed that my bloodline did not include baldness in its gifts. It was a prayer the Most High did not deign to take seriously.

To keep my mind off the waves of nausea that sometimes swept over me, I tried to make conversation. It was neither difficult nor unpleasant. Unlike my father, both my uncles were pleased at my doing philosophy, but both were also concerned about my attraction to the Master and the group that continued his teaching. From their contacts in Jerusalem and their interest in all gossip that might affect trade, they were remarkably well informed about the Master and the movement. I also suspected they had engaged my sister in debate and obtained some accurate information.

Theophilus's opposition had nothing to do with religion; he had none and cared for none. Nor was his opposition based on philosophical grounds. What he had heard of the Master's teaching, he said, was admirable, "good, sound Stoicism, the only philosophy for the long haul." But he was, as I had been, wary of Jewish nationalism. "These Jews are always ripe for revolt," he noted. "And with all due respect to your father, Roman swords are always thirsty for blood. The Jews are a tough people, but they're no match for Roman discipline. They'll be butchered one day— probably during my lifetime, certainly during yours. That's why your uncle and I built our villa outside the walls of Jerusalem. It's their theological capital. Every Jew who wants to make a public pronouncement goes to Jerusalem to do it, in front of his people and his god. That's where they'll make their stand; and that's where the Romans will slaughter them. My advice, Quintus, my considered advice, is to stay well clear of these people and their messiahs. Your man met the only end possible when he proclaimed himself king."

"I share your fears; that's why I stayed away for so long. But the Master was different. The kingdom he talked about is not of this world. And he didn't claim to be a king. Some of the people in Jerusalem called him that."

"That may be true, but to the Romans it's irrelevant. Their tolerance for uncertainty is quite limited. And they're uncertain about men who call themselves kings or other men call kings, unless they are first and foremost vassals of Rome. Your Master was a philosopher. He was interested in the cosmos, but most men are only interested in this very real earth—how much of it they can control and how much they can squeeze out of it. If your friends are successful in converting many people to their beliefs, the Romans will wipe them out."

"Even if it's clear they pose no threat to the empire?"

"Eternal paranoia is the price of empire. And it is one the Romans have—until now—gladly paid. And in this case the investment may well have been wise. From what I've heard, these teachings pose a subtle but profound threat to Rome. This notion of loving my neighbor and every man is my neighbor, if everyone believed it, would destroy both business and politics."

"Pilate said something like that."

"It fits, both Romans in general and Pilate in particular. He's shrewd, not smart but shrewd—and a mean bastard." After a pause while our camels negotiated a break in the road, my uncle went on: "Well, there is one hope. If the Romans come to understand this Jesus movement, they may tolerate it in the provinces. After all, it would be useful to them if the conquered believed they should turn the other cheek. But if Romans themselves start accepting that philosophy, you'll be in trouble."

"What chance is there of that?"

"I don't know much about such things," Theophilus said sadly. "I wanted to do philosophy, but my father wanted his two sons to join him in business." I had never known that, an indication of how little I had really understood my own family.

"But I can tell you," he went on, "the Empire has seen its greatest day. You must have sensed that when you were in Rome. Nothing corrupts like success. Oh, there's still a conquering spirit there, but more and more people want others to do the conquering while they sop up the spoils. Many of the educated and more of the uneducated are eager for change, perhaps for a new religion. So far, they've mostly produced dogs of war, few men of thought. They don't yet understand philosophy, and they've aped our mythology about gods and goddesses. But, give them a new set of ideas and who knows what will happen?"

My uncle was much more perceptive than I had ever given him credit for. Supposedly I was the philosopher and also half-Roman by blood, yet this aspect of Roman culture had escaped me. I took it in for a few minutes before I answered. "Yes, I hadn't thought about it that way. I think you're right but I can't leave these people, at least not now. Does that sound foolish?"

"Foolish, yes, but also very human. Just be careful, and not only for your own sake. Your mother's life has not been easy. It would kill her if her only son were nailed to a cross." He stopped his camel and looked directly at me. "You know there's little love between your father and the rest of us. But it would be a horribly cruel thing for him to suffer. He is before all else a Roman soldier." Then his voice became warmer: "Besides, I don't want that fate for my favorite nephew."

When dawn began to break we were at the junction near Jericho. We stopped and rested the camels and our own bottoms for a few minutes. For a short time after riding camels, I always find it difficult to walk. I keep expecting the ground to take on the beast's pitching and rolling. Below us to the right, we could make out the road that led down to the Asphalt Sea, only a few miles distant.

To our left and slightly beyond the junction an oasis exploded out of the desert dawn—Jericho, probably the oldest city in the world. Layers and layers of buildings were there, tall thick walls built on top of earlier tall, thick walls that had become mere coping above the swirling dust and vegetation. Here the sound waves from Joshua's trumpets had supposedly cracked one set of walls.

It was obvious why men always settled in Jericho—water, not the Jordan's thin stream running along the oasis's eastern edge, but deep, cool springs that turned sand into loam and produced a crazy quilt of color from bright green grass, soft white, almost pink orange blossoms, gaudy red and purple of flamboyant trees, with white and lavender mimosa, jasmine, and bougainvillea. Fruit abounded: oranges, pomegranates, figs, dates, and even mangoes.

The Herods also recognized Jericho's beauty. Herod the Great had built a palace there that Antipas occupied during the cold months. Fortunately, our noble prince was at the coast now, at Caesarea, where sea breezes would cool him.

We spent the day up in the newer Jewish city. The green of the oasis stretches up the hillside like a man's beard uniting his chin to his temples, and Herod had taken advantage of that reach to build on a more defensible site. It was a thriving community, bigger than most towns in Galilee.

As in most places he traveled, my uncle knew a merchant who welcomed him as a guest. He slept much of the day, but I was up by mid-afternoon so I could have a few hours to find some of the Master's friends. Actually, I knew of no disciples of our movement here, but I did know some of John the Baptizer's followers were sympathetic to, though not uncritical of, our cause.

The first, and as it turned out the only, person I found was Neriah, a poor country priest whose contacts with the Temple oligarchy were infrequent and whose opinions of that group like those of the people of the land. After all, he shared the hardness of their life. He was in his early fifties, a man as lean and stringy as his wife. Years of desert sun had left their skin dark and cracked, like old saddles. We sat outside under a date palm, enjoying the shade, listening to the buzz of insects, and hoping, vainly as it turned out, to catch a wisp of moving air. His wife brought us cool water, dates, and figs.

I told Neriah about Mary's community at the lake and what we were doing at Jerusalem. He listened quietly. I suspect he knew a great deal about each but said nothing, perhaps out of politeness. When I was done, he put the crucial question: "Was your Joshua raised from the dead?"

"Mary of Magdala says she saw him, Simon Peter says he saw him, John the priest says he saw him, so do another half dozen of the disciples."

Neriah nodded and looked off toward the oasis. "Has Quintus seen him?"

"No."

We were both silent for several minutes. Neriah handed me another cup of water. "We heard many stories that John our Master had been raised from the dead, even," he smiled gently, "that Joshua your Master was the risen John."

"Herod Antipas apparently heard that story, too."

"Half Jew, half swine, and all drunken coward, he hears many voices, all of them evil spirits." Neriah put his cup down and sighed heavily. "Israel has always been harsh on her prophets. The patience of the Most High, blessed be His name forever, with His people is truly ineffable."

"Are many of John's followers still here in Jericho?"

"There never were very many. Large numbers came to hear him when he was baptizing in the Jordan. They submitted to his baptism, said they were cleansing themselves of sin, but his words were too hard for them to live by. A few of us remain close to his words—the Essenes who share their meager tract in the valley, possibly some of the monks who live around the Asphalt Sea. I don't know. I never see them. But here in Jericho? A dozen of us, perhaps twenty. We do not meet regularly like your communities. We shared his baptism; we pray for the redemption of Israel; and we repent our sins. That last is a lifetime's work. We seem able to commit sins as fast as we can repent them."

"Did you not think of joining my Master's group after John was murdered?"

"A few of us, not many. Perhaps with time we all would have, but our first contacts were not always easy. Some of your people looked on John as a rival to their Master, and in a way they were right. Many of us were not yet ready to be treated as less than equal, even in the kingdom of God."

"I can't speak for all the disciples; at times they exasperated even the Master. But I know he likened John to Elijah and said no man born of woman was greater than he."

"Yes, but Elijah to your Master's messiah. That was the rub. Your Josuha followed John for a brief time, then he thought he should be the first. It is not an uncommon thing. He was younger, smarter, and better educated than John, and more personable, too. John had a single message, repentance. His job was to purify Israel from within. He never claimed or implied he was the Messiah. Joshua's message was more positive. He said. . . ."

"No," I insisted, "he never said he was the Messiah."

"You're right," Neriah admitted. "He never claimed to be the Messiah, but he never denied it either. Besides, his message was more complex and subtle than John's. How many of his disciples really understood what he was saying?"

I often wondered the same thing, but I was not about to admit it right then. I merely shrugged my shoulders.

"There was more," Neriah continued. "It might not seem important to you, but it was important to us. For us repentance must include rejection of the flesh. John had lived in the Essenes' monastery at the Asphalt Sea, and in some central ways he remained an Essene. His call meant renouncing the pleasures and corruption of the flesh. Joshua, on the other hand, did not fast; he ate red meat and drank sweet wine and slept in fine beds when he visited the homes of the rich. In the eyes of some of John's people, he accommodated himself to wealth and power."

"Yet he usually lived with the poor. And he did not accommodate himself to power. After all, it was the Romans, with the cooperation of the High Priest, who killed him."

I am afraid my voice must have been taking on an edge, for Neriah laid his hand on my shoulder. "Let us not quarrel, my young friend. You asked for an explanation of why my friends and

I did not follow your Master. We may have been wrong, who knows? At least we know we all want the same things: Love of the Most High, repentance of sin, obedience to the Law of Moses, and restoration of the kingdom. For those noble goals, both our masters were murdered. They were holy men; we have been fortunate to have known and followed them."

I returned to say my good-byes to the merchant and took something to eat. Two hours later Theophilus and I walked down to the oasis, climbed aboard our camels, and turned due north up the Jordan. West of the road, the hills rose up, almost as barren as the Judean desert—in fact, these hills marked the desert's edge. Just to the east of us, the Jordan pushed its shallow waters sluggishly down toward the Asphalt Sea, its course marked by a thin, wavy line of bright green through the valley's drab floor. Across the river ran the wide Plain of Moab, then high hills. From the east, the west bank also seemed broad and its hills high.

On neither side of the Jordan was rainfall plentiful, but winter would bring precious drops of moisture. With ingenious use of irrigation, the valley could support some crops, not in the lushness of Galilee or the lavishness of Jericho but enough for a scattering of farmers to claw a living from the clay and shepherds to feed their mangy sheep. Life here was rock-hard, barely possible in winter and spring, painful in the fall, and searingly threatening during the long summer.

On that trip, I saw little of that cruel land, for night began to fall an hour after our departure, just as we were passing the place where I had first seen John the Baptizer preaching his strident call for repentance. He had been a living vision of a prophet: tall, so thin it made you ache to look at him. His beard was wild and untrimmed, his uncombed hair even wilder; both were dark, blood red. His sole garment was a goat skin wrapped about his middle. His long, bony finger pointed at the crowd, focusing the black fire leaping from his eyes so that each listener felt the hot wrath of the Almighty aimed directly at him.

Now, that part of the river was quiet in the last shadows of twilight. Whatever spirits played here would wait until full dark.

We stopped every hour to rest. Sometime after midnight we left the road and led the camels down to the river. They did not seem interested in drinking, but most of them took a few gnaws at the scraggly grass along the bank. We stopped there for a full half hour and ate some bread, cheese, and fruit and drank long gulps of water. Even with these delays, we passed Pella to the east at dawn, and soon we could see the high, flat acropolis of Scythopolis. We rested for another few minutes, then pushed on. The sun was beginning to beat down on us, but there was scant shade between us and the city and thus no point in pitching camp so close to home.

My family encouraged me to sleep most of the day, but I was awake by noon. To avoid conversation, I stayed in bed until late afternoon. After dinner, when my father had retired to his quarters and my mother to hers, I felt able to talk to my sister. I told her about the way the community in Jerusalem was functioning and malfunctioning, the number of people who were joining us, Simon Peter's maturing, my hopes for his becoming a leader, and even the way his Greek was improving. I also told her about the dark side of his soul, his problems with faith and with wine, the petty bickering within the community, and the difficulties we were having in making ends meet. I must have sounded pessimistic, because at that point she interrupted: "Yet you say the movement is growing."

"Yes, faster than our resources, I fear."

"But is providing for you not your God's task?"

I was not sure how serious she was, so my response was only half serious: "You sound like Simon Peter."

"Well, maybe he's right." She dismissed that part of my problem with a wave of her hand and aimed at the center of the difficulties. "If your Master doesn't come soon, will Simon Peter be able to hold the group together? From what you've said he's promised a great deal, and if he cannot make good on his promises, he might be among the first to fall away."

"That's one of my fears. I don't know how long he can hold out. To the community he talks as if he's absolutely certain; but he needs frequent reassurance, at times total support."

"Yet he's far stronger now than he was two years ago."

"He's not the same man. But there are other problems. The more I think about it the more sure I am that he and the others have misunderstood what the Master meant by 'coming again.' They believe in some sort of divine intervention, an invasion led by legions of angels blowing trumpets and hurling fire at Herod Antipas and the Romans and perhaps the High Priest as well. They think the Master will come on a great white stallion, galloping down a celestial staircase, a combination of King David, Judas Maccabee, Herod the Great, and Augustus Caesar, slaughtering all the people who've oppressed the Jews. When that gory work is done, they think he'll establish a kingdom, set them up as princes, and they'll rule together for a thousand years."

"And after that?"

"After that who knows? A thousand years is pretty far ahead for a peasant to think."

"Father might make a good disciple. Have you explained any of this to him?"

I smiled. "He'd become a disciple if he could bring himself to believe that even angels could defeat his beloved Roman legions."

"And you don't share this belief about a kingdom?"

"Of course not. It doesn't fit with the rest of the Master's message. 'The kingdom of God is within you,' he used to say; and he'd warn the disciples against thinking in secular terms, like 'princes of this world.' They didn't understand then, and they haven't quite understood yet."

"Then why do you stay with them?"

It was a fair question. "Partly . . . well, partly because I've been caricaturing their expectations. They do believe in some apocalyptic event in the very near future that will do all the things I've said. At the same time, they also believe in his message of love and justice and decency. They just haven't put it all together yet."

"And you have?"

"No, I haven't. That's a second part of it. I'm still working out what I believe, or if I believe anything. Talking to John the priest sometimes helps, though he's a strange, cold fish. Simon Peter helps, too, though you might think that's an odd thing to say. His bouts of faith are what I want; his bouts of doubt are what I usually have. And his combination of shrewdness and innocence—no, naïveté—is refreshing. His black moods are frightening; but, when we are alone in discussion, I sometimes see things from a different perspective. And perhaps his faith may become contagious, at least more infectious than his disbelief."

"And what is Quintus's faith?"

I smiled. "You've asked me that before, and I've asked it of myself a hundred times: I don't know. Part of me believes the Most High has raised the Master, part of me rejects that as not just implausible but impossible. Part of me believes he has come again, that they, not I, have seen the second coming; his kingdom develops within us in the way we treat one another and all men. And part of me says it's all mystic swill, a peculiar form of Jewish nationalism the Romans will drown in its own blood."

"And the return of Simon Peter's sight?"

"Since I don't know why he was blind, I don't know how he was cured. That he believes he saw the Master I have no doubt. Even John the priest believes he saw the Master, and at one time he was as skeptical of Mary and the others as I was. But John's a Jew and a priest at that. He got Jewish mysticism with his mother's milk."

"And Quintus got Greek logic?"

"Yes, Quintus got Greek logic, and for the first time in my life I'm not sure whether it's a gift or a curse."

"Mmmm. Now the philosopher questions philosophy. That's a healthy sign." Then completely without warning: "Will you take me with you when you go to the lake?"

The ability of women to leap from one subject to another is truly amazing. In my surprise I stammered rather than reasoned. "Don't be foolish. Those people barely tolerate me even though I'm a God Fearer. You're a full-fledged pagan and a woman besides."

"A woman, just like Mary of Magdala. Yes, that would disqualify me."

"Anyway, our parents would never let you go."

"I'll handle Father. He'll shout no at first, but he'll give in quickly. You work on Mother. She's tougher."

"You don't really want to live with ignorant Jewish peasants who'll despise you as a gentile. It sounds like a lark now, but not when you have to live without servants, eat what these peasants consider food, sleep in a hut or out-of-doors, and share a privy with fifty others."

"Why not? You survived, and we both know I'm much stronger than you. And what do I have to lose except a few weeks of my life? I doubt if any suitors will be calling while I'm gone."

"Or after you return, if word gets around you've been camping out with a group of fanatical Jews."

"That's my problem, if it happens. And if it does, we both know it won't make any difference."

9

✤ Theodora came along. My mother's consent had come with surprising ease, my father's with surprising difficulty. He and I rode down to the Jordan in the late afternoon and had one of our few man-to-man talks of my adult life. We tethered the horses, took off our clothes, and sat in the shallow stream bed, letting the slow moving waters keep us cool. I'd forgotten the scars on his body. As a child, before I had so bitterly disappointed this Roman knight, I used to run my fingers over those military stigmata, fascinated by the way the dark red lumps of keloid tissue rose up from his taut, bronzed skin. Now they had faded into the paleness of his body but, curiously, had become more ugly—the star-shaped knot on his left shoulder from a German arrow, a long curving arc from a Parthian's sword, plus a half dozen smaller mementos of skirmishes along the Rhine and the Danube.

He was concerned and that fact touched me, though it was plain—and natural—that he was more worried about my sister than me. His consent came slowly and only at the price of my having to listen (again) to several war stories whose moral was responsibility toward one's family and, even more important, toward the Empire. There was also a condition: He would accompany us to Dalmanutha. Since there was no danger this close to Tiberias, it was evident he wanted an excuse to make sure he could take his daughter away if the place did not suit her—or him. And, it pleased me to think, he may have been curious about the sort of life his strange son was living.

The escort meant we would have horses, for my father hated camels even more than I did. As she had since childhood, Theodora rode a horse like a man; and, as always, she rode better than I. Because of the heat, we again traveled at night, stopping the first day at an inn a few miles south of Tiberias. We rested most of that day and rode on to the city in the afternoon so that my father could dine with some of the Roman officers stationed in Antipas's capital.

Tiberias was not a city pious Jews liked to enter. Antipas had built it to honor Tiberius Caesar. An old village had to be razed, but Antipas considered that a small cost. The place was, the Jews thought, a nest of sin, full of whorehouses, taverns, and gambling places, along with palaces, baths, and gymnasia, all constructed and maintained by taxes extorted from the sweat of Galileans. There was much truth in this characterization, evidenced by the fact that our father left us to spend the evening with his cohorts—at some den of iniquity, we had no doubt. He returned at midnight, too drunk to ride, so, with a delicious touch of irony, we spent the night in Antipas's palace.

I had us up at dawn, much to Theodora's delight and my father's painful dismay. The ride to Dalmanutha from Tiberias takes less than two hours under normal conditions, but out of respect for my father's condition we rode slowly along the edge of the lake. There was a haze on the water, as Simon Peter had remembered even in his blindness. The green hills that in May had been spackled with bright flowers were now as dull a reddish brown as the Judean desert.

It had not rained here since I had left, and the grass was an equally dull tan. The lake itself added little color; it was a drab gray. The only contrasts were provided by palm trees and a few thin strips of green created by energetic farmers who had diverted water from the lake to nourish land nestled near the shore.

It was difficult to believe that within a month the rains would turn these parched fields into a soft breadbasket. But soon that annual miracle would reoccur. And it was to celebrate the coming gift of the Most High that the Israelites held the Feast of Booths.

We arrived at Dalmanutha well before midday. Theodora and I were more hot than tired. Our father had his own problems, with which Simon Peter would have sympathized far more than I. The place had changed a great deal in the intervening years. Two more buildings had sprung up, one a long hall in which, I correctly assumed, the brothers and sisters took their common meals. The second was smaller; I could not guess what special purpose, if any, it served. Although the barn and my small house were intact, the number of tents had doubled, a sign that Mary's work had progressed—or that many of the local peasants had not saved enough from the spring harvest to survive the year.

Except in Tiberias, the arrival of men on horseback was a great occasion anywhere in Galilee. Almost everyone here walked, and only the wealthy had a donkey to share the burden of carrying goods. Only the superwealthy, Antipas's officers, and Roman soldiers had horses.

Mary greeted us cooly but politely, offering us the hospitality of the community. Summer work had darkened her skin and roughened her hands. Yet, even standing there wearing a peasant's long gown, gathered at the waist by a rope, she was tall, pretty, and as obviously patrician as she was deep-bosomed—anatomical data, I noted, that did not escape my father's eye. Her Greek, while moderately accented, was syntactically and grammatically correct—data, again I noticed, that did not escape my father's ear.

Theodora was properly demure. Had I not known her so well, I would have thought she was the shy, dimwitted daughter of a rich man. I wanted to talk to Mary alone, but my father immediately began waging his own campaign, and a mere philosopher would have been ground up in his maneuverings. As a Roman officer, he would not let a little thing like parenthood come between him and his objective.

As soon as we were ushered into Mary's small house and were seated on reasonably comfortable cushions spread around the floor, my father took command. "I have heard many things about this Joshua." He used the Aramaic form rather than the Greek, Jesus, whether as a ploy to win favor by showing he knew her language or a piece of condescension, I was not sure. Perhaps there was a bit of both involved. As my life shows, I never understood the psychological warfare called courting.

"This Joshua," he went on, "whom you and my son call 'the Master' also fascinates my daughter."

Theodora, continuing to play her demure role, looked down at the floor. At that point Mary interrupted to ask a direct question: "Did you ever see or hear him?"

"No, I heard John the Baptizer once; but Quintus has told me much about the Master—and about you." Theodora did not raise her eyes. I was getting concerned. Mary was anything but stupid and it wouldn't take her long to figure out that Theodora was also very bright.

Before Mary could probe further, my father was once more at full marching stride. "She wants to come here for a time and live in your . . . your community. Naturally, I am concerned about the sort of life that a genteel young Roman woman would live here."

"Among the savage Jews?" Mary asked. Her voice was bland, almost sweet.

"It is Roman policy to respect the culture and gods of every nation. Personally, I do not share the religious superstitions of Jews or Greeks—or Romans, for that matter. We are born, we exist, we enjoy, we suffer, we die, and most of us are forgotten before our ashes blow away. I believe we control our own destinies, not spirits, evil or benign." It was a neat speech; I had heard it a dozen times before.

"Life is simple then," Mary said, her voice as thick as honey.

"No, life is complicated; but we don't need spirits to explain it."

"But *how* to live it remains a problem, with or without spirits, does it not?" I sensed that Mary was gaining the upper hand. My father was simultaneously waging two campaigns and she only one. Generals, I believe, speak of the desirability of concentrating one's forces.

"That is precisely why I am here, to learn how my daughter will spend her immediate future." He was annoyed, and it showed. For the moment, he was forced to abandon his wooing campaign. "I must make certain she would not be sating her curiosity about this Joshua person at the price of her honor as a Roman woman."

Mary looked at him for a moment. I knew her well enough to know she was resisting the temptation to say that she had not understood Roman women to be concerned with honor. Then she smiled before speaking. "We share the work, we share the return from the fields and the lake. We eat together and we pray together. We live simply as the Master taught us, with love and respect for one another and the commandments of the Lord."

"Love?" My father again moved to the attack on both fronts. "I've heard of the love cults of the Orient. . . ." He let his voice trail off for a few seconds, then asked: "Do you indulge in such practices here?"

Mary looked straight at him. "Those cults are gentile, at home in the Roman Empire, not in the Land of Israel. Our God is a holy God, not a satyr or a whore. 'Thou shalt not commit adultery,' the Most High, blessed be His name, has commanded us. And the Master taught that a man who looks at a woman with lust in his eye has already committed adultery with her in his heart. Do you require further information?"

My father was befuddled. He was not accustomed to women who could argue him down, and he didn't seem to like it. Before he could react, two women of the community brought in a plate of fruit and a pair of small stone pitchers of water. "Refresh yourselves," Mary invited. "The fruit is poor, but the water is good. It comes from the seven springs here. The pitcher on the left has artesian water, the one on the right sweet water."

Theodora took nothing, but I had a few sips and my father a very long drink. Excitement makes one thirsty, and last night's revelry had probably left him dry to begin with. He had undoubtedly hoped for something more potent to soothe his head, but he was not in a position to request it. "I expect to pay," he said, when he regained his composure. What he meant, of course, was that my uncles would pay.

"We accept contributions with gratitude, but we do not ask to be paid. We share our life and our work with all who are willing to share with us."

My father took out a purse and placed it in Theodora's hand. "She will share this with you, if and as she wishes."

"I wish," Theodora said and handed the purse to Mary.

"Thank you, but let us put it aside until we have decided other things." Mary laid the purse on a cushion, then looked at Theodora. "Why do you wish to join us?"

"I'm not sure I want to 'join' you, but Quintus has spoken so much about 'the Way' that I must understand what you're all about. When I learn more, I may want to leave." Theodora was still looking innocently at the cushions.

"No one is compelled to come here, except by the call of the Lord; and no one is obliged to stay except by that same call. But our life is not easy. Mere curiosity will not carry you through many hot days in the fields."

"There's no need for her to work in the fields," my father broke in. "She's a woman of nobility and education, not some peasant brood mare, born to pull a plough and whelp some yokel's brats. I have paid you for her keep."

"We work here as we are needed: to repair a net, pull a plough, take care of one another's children, or even"—she glanced at me—"write a book. You may reclaim your money." She glanced at the cushion on which the purse lay.

"I don't like that," my father said, but he made no move to pick up the purse. "I have paid you enough for her not to have to work at all or to work only as she sees fit."

"As _I_ see fit," Theodora—the Theodora I knew—broke in. "As _I_ see fit, you said. If the work gets oppressive, I shall leave, but I understand Mary's point."

Mary's eyes darted at me; Theodora's veil had been stripped away. A demure, naïve young girl does not so adroitly dispute her father or address the head of a community without a title.

Theodora went on: "I must make as honest a commitment to the life here as I can, not indulge in some dilettantish whim. I want to understand, perhaps even to believe. But I do not believe now and there's a good chance I never shall."

"Very well," my father conceded, "you work as *you* see fit, not as these people want. And I doubt if any intelligent Roman—even a woman—would ever believe the sort of twaddle about a seditious messiah that Quintus reports."

"Who reports?" I asked.

"That you've written to Theodora about," he said, clearly embarrassed by his comment.

"I read your letters to Father," Theodora said. "I assumed you wouldn't mind."

My anger turned to pleasure. I had never realized he would care enough to listen.

Mary was not interested in our domestic relations. "We are not seditionists, sir, and to love one's neighbor as oneself is hardly twaddle. It is the essence of the Law of Moses, by which the Jewish nation lives." Like Theodora, Mary had dropped her own veil.

My father should have found a graceful way to retreat, but that was a word he could not abide. Indeed, after too many cups of wine, I once heard him joke with old cronies that when he had to retreat he had entered in his log that the unit had "retrograded its advance." So, instead of a polite good-bye, we heard: "Pontius Pilate thought otherwise. He hanged your Joshua on a tree as a revolutionary, a self-proclaimed king of the Jews. As for twaddle, you people think this man was raised from the dead and is coming back to lead a rebellion against Rome."

If he had paid attention to my letters, he would not have thought that. I was always careful when writing to deny, even at the expense of accuracy, that the movement foresaw any harm to the Roman Empire. Evidently he had other sources of information; and that, too, was touching in its own way.

"I have seen the risen Master," Mary said calmly. "I saw him, I heard him. He will come again. How or when I do not know, but we are not revolutionaries. Whatever the Most High wishes to do, He will do. He is the Lord of History. There is nothing you or I or the whole Roman Empire need do or can do to change His will. We are not seditionists, we are not revolutionaries, unless to love and serve mankind are signs of rebellion."

"I see no point in continuing this conversation." My father rose, and we all got up. "I shall go to Tiberias for a brief stay and perhaps a few conversations with Antipas's officers before I return to Scythopolis." He embraced Theodora tenderly. "You know my friends in Tiberias if you need anything." Then he grasped my hand in the double Roman grip. "Quintus will report to me when he leaves; and he will help you leave any time you wish."

I was chagrined at my father's maneuvering toward Mary and her effective parries. Perhaps if I had not entertained similar desires myself, I would have been less resentful. But knowing my father, the affair had gone as well as could have been reasonably expected. Indeed, in later years, I wondered how much my father had been trying to goad me by making verbal advances toward Mary and to trap her into very clear and specific denials of hostile intentions toward Rome. And I do not know what he did and said when he returned to Tiberias. At the time, I believed he would spend a few days womanizing and drinking, but I may have done him an injustice, for neither the Herodians nor the Romans have yet made any overt effort to interfere with our work in Galilee.

It was not until after the evening meal that I had an opportunity to talk with Mary alone. She was still carrying a grudge; about that there could be no doubt. Despite the Master's message, forgiveness did not come any easier to her than to Simon Peter, and she had much to forgive where he and I were concerned. My sin was lack of loyalty, first to the Master and then to her; Simon Peter's included disloyalty, pigheadedness, and arrogant usurpation of her rightful position. John the priest, of course, shared in my sin, but he was in Jerusalem with Simon Peter and I was in Galilee, a handier target.

She gave me what she treated as an audience. I tried to start off on a neutral topic by noting I had not seen the Master's mother in the community. Her reply was fully responsive but terse: "Six months ago her stepson James came and persuaded her to live with him in Hebron."

"I had not heard. They did not stop at the community in Jerusalem."

She said nothing, though I knew her well enough to translate her stare into "Why should they?" I waited a few moments; as soon as it became apparent she was not going to volunteer any additional information about the Master's family or the community at the lake, I began to tell her about Jerusalem. She said nothing, but I felt she was impressed, at least by what happened with Simon Peter and John ben Zebedee in the Temple. The "miracle" she dismissed with the sort of shrug patricians reserve for peasants. When I was done, she said nothing for a few minutes. I became a bit nervous. "Do you wish to know more?"

She ignored my question. "So! For once they did not run away," she said, more to herself than to me.

"This time they looked death in the face."

She shrugged again.

I told her about the rumor—I did not mention Bartholomew and Simon as the originators—that the Master would return at Booths, and I explained that Simon Peter, John the priest, and I thought it was foolishness, yet we also thought she should know about it. Then I delivered Simon Peter's invitation to visit the community.

"Only an invitation, no apology? No acceptance of my leadership?"

"Mary," I probably sounded exasperated, for I truly was, "don't you remember what the Master said about the last being first and the first last, that places of honor are things pagans quarrel about?"

"I remember, Quintus, and I remember how Simon Peter ran away, and how sheep need a shepherd, not a hireling who is also a coward."

"I think you misjudge Simon Peter. Besides, this time he didn't run away."

"Give him time, Quintus; give him time and he'll run again."
She stood up and began walking away from her house toward the
narrow road that led up to Capernaum and Bethsaida. "He lived
here." Her voice was distant, almost faint. "When he wanted to be
alone, he sometimes came here to that cave." She pointed in the
darkness. I didn't need light or even directions; I knew the spot.
"Sometimes he went up to the Essenes above the Valley of the
Doves. *This* is his land, Quintus, not Jerusalem or any other city.
His message must be carried by simple people."

"Simple like you and me and John the priest? Not by Simon
Peter and the others?"

She sighed. "In our own way, we are simple people, Quintus,
very simple people."

I started to debate her, then grasped her point and shared her
silence.

"Very well," she said finally. "I shall go up to Jerusalem. You
are right, we must love one another. It is not an easy commandment to keep. Now," her tone changed abruptly, "what about this
sister of yours? She's not simple. What is it she really wants?"

I was happy Mary didn't ask about my father, so I answered
candidly: "What she says she wants. She knows a great deal about
the Master and his teaching. She wants to know more."

"To become a follower?"

"Perhaps. Or to walk away."

Mary stopped walking. I noticed we were at the edge of the
stones the Romans had placed around the springs. There was a half
moon that night and the lake was plainly visible through the
willows. "You gentiles are strange."

"Unlike you Jews?"

"Yes, unlike us. Whatever our problems, we have a purpose
and an identity. You Greeks always have difficulty deciding who
you are and what your purpose is, or even if you have a purpose.
We Jews know all those things. We may sin, but not through
ignorance or indecision. All right. She can stay as long as she
wants, and as long as she shares in the work. But it won't be easy
on her or on me. My people aren't likely to accept a gentile as a
sister."

I smiled. "I hadn't realized that."

Mary laughed softly. "The brothers and sisters have tolerated Quintus—"

"Barely," I put in.

She ignored me. "Because the Master tolerated Quintus. But Theodora carries no passport from the Master. She'll have problems finding friends."

"Even in a community based on love, on the notion that every human is our neighbor?"

"Even in a community based on love. To hear is not to obey—with the mind perhaps, but not with the heart. The Master tolerated Quintus for his own reasons, and I suspect they involved Quintus's ability to write good Greek and spread the message. How is your book going?"

"I've finished a full draft, now I'm rewriting. It moves."

"When will it be ready?"

"I don't know, honestly I don't. If I had six months of leisure I could finish it, but as it is. . . ."

"Why don't you take the time and finish it?"

"Do you think it would be important?"

"If his words were written down, especially in Greek, his message could spread throughout the entire Diaspora."

"And spread to gentiles? There aren't many Jews out there, Mary. Some in the big cities all around the Mediterranean, but they're a tiny minority. Most people in the world are idol-worshiping, pig-eating, blood-drinking, uncircumcised pagans. And you talk about Theodora causing problems."

Mary moved on toward the lake. The gushing noise of the seven springs slowly faded, masked less by distance than by a welcome breeze rustling the willows and rippling the surface of the lake. "I haven't thought it all through yet," she said as we reached the stony beach. "I am a Jew; the Master was a Jew; and he said he came to fulfill the Law, not to destroy it. Yet he let you follow him, but at least you're a God Fearer, or so you keep telling us."

"And," I added, "he took care of the servant of the centurion from that camp outside Capernaum; and he went to the other side of the lake and preached there and to the north into Syria as well."

"I haven't thought it out, Quintus; and if I haven't, then certainly Simon Peter has not."

I could have assured her on that point but I saw no reason to do so. Instead I asked: "Then why do you want me to finish this work?"

"You should," she responded in the female fashion. "Why not soon?"

"Because I have a part in the real world. When I write I see things and ask kinds of questions I would never think of if I were simply coping with the world. But the reverse is also true. This way, I have a double perspective. I share the problems that you, Simon Peter, and the others endure. I share not just in my imagination, but in my soul, Greek though it is. Perhaps I can help you and Simon Peter think things through, put some order in what the Master said and did."

"You might help me, but I doubt if Simon Peter would hear. The ears of peasants are usually painted on their heads. You know something else, my Greek Quintus? I think you're afraid of finishing this work, because you haven't thought it through either. And you're frightened by what you're thinking."

She was right, of course, but I was not about to admit it. Indeed, at that point I was not about to admit anything, except that I found her a compelling woman—an equal, not a simpering female of mere physical beauty, though images of that morning at her farm as she stood there in the lamplight bathing caused erotic emotions to erupt. I envied my father his sexual drive and lack of inhibition. He would have taken her in his arms, laid her in the soft ground beneath the willows, and made love to her through the entire night. I turned away not because of virtue or the spirituality I should have felt at that proximity to the Master's work, but because I lacked courage—and skill. And I ached with loneliness in a camp filled with people.

10

❖ We returned in time for Booths, the happiest of the great feasts. Most of the pilgrims take full advantage of the option of spending their offerings in Jerusalem rather than donating it to the priests. The city is crowded but less so than at Passover or even Pentecost. The weather is still warm and dry so that sleeping in tents is not an undue hardship, especially if one wants to save money for more joyful things. Still, the Galileans vacated Matthias's inn so he might earn money to help support us.

The Essenes' houses were already overcrowded so I arranged for Mary and her servant to stay at my uncles' villa. Theophilus was in Jerusalem and was flattered to have such a prominent Galilean Jew accept his pagan hospitality. I reminded him of her connections with the movement, which did not seem to bother him; but I didn't mention she was among the more unobservant Jews I had met.

Mary seemed genuinely impressed with the community, though I saw her eyebrows arch on several occasions. By Galilean standards, Simon Peter treated her with the utmost courtesy. I mean no slur, only that the ways of Galilean peasants could never be described as elegant. But within that tradition, his behavior was exemplary.

Matthias gave us the upper room for the first evening, and Mary joined the Galileans, John the priest, and several of the other disciples, including me, for the evening meal. Simon Peter asked her to perform the ritual of the sharing of the bread and wine. Given the male dominance of Jewish society and even that of the Jerusalem community, this invitation was radical, as several disciples sourly noted.

Afterwards, Simon Peter asked her for all the news of the community at the lake. She gave a brief but complete report that fit with all I had seen. She added an item some disciples found jarring: For a few weeks, the community had been visited by three gentiles from Pella, in the Dekapolis, across the Jordan from Scythopolis. They had asked to be instructed in the Way. "They left," Mary said, "accepting the Master's message. Now we have another gentile living with us, a young woman from Scythopolis, who also asks for instruction."

"Who were these gentiles?" Andrew asked. His shaggy eyebrows came together as he spoke.

"How do I know? All gentiles look alike." She looked directly at me when she said that, but I did not rise to the bait. "They said they had heard the Master when he preached on the east side of the lake and persuaded the people to share their food with one another."

"I remember that well," Andrew guffawed, "because before then we all thought the only things gentiles shared were their wives and daughters. You didn't baptize them, did you?"

"No, but we may have to decide that question."

"Deciding it is easy. It's a simple no," Andrew insisted. "I wouldn't even let gentiles make our people unclean by eating with them."

"They slept in separate tents, of course, but they ate with us."

"I do not like that, not at all," Andrew said gravely.

"Is that relevant?" Mary asked. "The Master ate with sinners, tax collectors, whores, and even cowards. Why not gentiles? Are they worse?" I saw Levi wince. All the Galileans should have, but they didn't.

"And we've all lived off Quintus's charity," Simon Peter put in firmly. "He is a God Fearer, but still a gentile, not a Jew. Mary has presented us with a problem we'll have to face at some time: what to do about foreigners who've heard the Master's message."

"And who may be Roman spies," Andrew added. "If they say they're serious, let them be circumcised, then baptized."

"You shouldn't do that," John the priest said, "unless they first convert to Judaism."

"Well," Andrew replied, "if they're going to follow the Master, they'll have to become Jews."

"Like Quintus?" Mary asked.

Before anyone could respond, Simon Peter spoke in his heaviest voice: "I said at some time we'll have to face this problem, but not now. We should pray over it and ask the Holy Spirit's guidance before we do anything. Now I think we should tell Mary about our work."

It was a good tactic, defusing for the moment what would become, as some readers may painfully recall, the most divisive issue the movement faced in Simon Peter's lifetime. His report about our community took almost a half hour; then John the priest added his news. For several months now, and two or three times a week, he had been seriously—and very quietly—talking about the Master's message to ten priests. He was sure four would soon join us and reasonably certain the others would follow.

I took this news with some fear. The defection of so many priests would both alarm and anger Caiaphas and his colleagues. They would be sorely tempted to strike back, either directly when Simon Peter and the others were in the Temple or indirectly through the Romans. Having crucified the Master as a revolutionary "King of the Jews," Pilate would not be kindly disposed to people who followed in his Way. I said as much, but the others thought my fears groundless. Even John the priest saw no real problem. James ben Zebedee made his usual intelligent contribution: "If the Romans arrest us, will that not be a sign the Master is about to join us again?"

I wanted to reply that Roman intervention would be a clearer sign we were about to join the Master, but there were limits to what these people would tolerate from a Greek. Simon Peter put an end to that part of the discussion with his usual statement of faith: "The Master'll come again, but we don't know when. It doesn't help to argue about what we can't know."

As is obvious, Booths came and went with no mark of the Master's return. Most of the brothers were disappointed, a few disheartened. Outwardly, Simon Peter seemed undaunted, as did John the priest and Mary. My disappointment lay in the desertion of two Essene monks and three Greek-speaking families. Four

Judean families also left us, but did so, I suspect, because they had made enough money at Booths to think they could survive financially without us. I wished a few more families felt that way. Simon Peter had shrugged off at the news. "Some seed falls on stony ground," he commented, echoing the Master's words, as he had at the first synagogue we visited at Pentecost.

As frequently happens, appearances were deceiving. On Mary's final evening—Theophilus had agreed to take her with him the next night as far as Scythopolis and then obtain an escort back to Dalmanutha—Simon Peter was absent from the common meal. I asked several of the brethren where he was, but no one had seen him since he and the two sons of Zebedee had left the Temple. I was concerned, as was Andrew, but there was nothing we could do.

I suggested to Andrew that Mary preside at the ritual of the bread and wine. He snorted at the suggestion. He had not been alone in disapproving her presiding the first evening, indeed, even her joining the men. It took some effort to persuade him that anything else would set off a volcano. Mary was both a force and a presence. All males appreciated her feminine attractiveness, but the disciples had also learned to respect her aristocratic haughtiness, iron will, and quick tongue. Against his better judgment, Andrew gave in, a decison we were both to regret.

When Mary had led us in the ceremony the Master had prescribed, she did not sit down. Instead, she paused for a few seconds to paragraph her remarks, then began a short sermon: "When I came, I brought the blessings of the community at Dalmanutha to you here in Jerusalem. I leave, I hope, with your blessing for those people. We are both following the Way—'I am the Way,' he told us—to Our Father, the Most High, blessed be His name. Together we await the Master's return."

So far, so good, I thought; but I was still fearful, for she was twisting a lock of her hair around her right fingers, a trait I associated with controlled anger.

"I have seen much here to applaud," she went on, "your common sacrifice, your courage in living the Master's Way under the very nose of the High Priest and the Romans, and your success in bringing the word to others. These things would have made—will make—the Master rejoice. But. . . ."

The inevitable "but," and from Mary it was not a quiet word. As usual, when she wanted to stress a point, she raised her pitch as well as her volume.

"I was disappointed that you treat women even as gentiles treat women and as Jewish men who have not received the Master's message treat women. With him we were all disciples, brothers and sisters, children of the same loving Father. I followed the Master as an equal of the men, as did other women. Here you treat women as menials. You must keep in mind that he said all of us should be servants; our role was not to be served but to serve. He came to serve all of Israel, not merely men."

There was muttering and even a few soft hisses as she sat down. For once, John the priest took command. He got up as she was sitting and led us in reciting psalms, first in Aramaic, then reprising in Greek. He managed to postpone a confrontation, but he had not even begun to resolve it, as it has not been resolved even to this day. I noted to myself that tonight two dangerous issues had surfaced. They could tear us apart if someone did not soon deal with them.

More pressing, however, was the problem of Mary herself. I wanted her back at the villa before she further engaged (or enraged) the disciples. John the priest's instincts were the same as mine; and, as soon as manners permitted, we both swiftly guided her out to the street where Matthias waited for us. He took her hand and bade her peace, then added: "You spoke the Master's words tonight." She nodded, not in thanks but as one does when another acknowledges the truth. It was interesting that an Essene who had taken a vow of celibacy would be among her few male supporters. What effect her words would have on the women, had any of them overheard her, I hesitated to think.

Two of my family's guards were waiting to escort us back. Booths was still going on, and pilgrims at this feast tend to be boisterous. I did not want to walk unguarded across the city with a lovely, if haughty, young woman. We moved from the Essene Quarter past the High Priest's palace and through the Upper City between Herod's palace and the Upper Agora and then out the gate guarded by the beautiful triple towers. As we turned toward the villa, the moonlight outlined Golgotha's shadow against the city's high walls. Mary stopped for a few moments, but neither of us spoke.

Having arranged for her to sleep in the wing of the villa farthest from my apartment, I had urged her to stay in bed as late as she could the next morning because she would get no rest that night atop a swaying camel. Nevertheless, she was up before dawn. I had decided to stay at home and spend the day with her. Certainly returning with her to Matthias's inn was out of the question. The brethren were probably still fuming, and Mary was also angry. She took Simon Peter's absence as a studied insult. I had two other interpretations: Either he was suffering one of his fits of black depression or he had been arrested.

As soon as I awoke I sent a messenger to Matthias's inn with instructions to see Simon Peter himself and tell him I would be at the villa; if Simon Peter were not there, the messenger was to wait for his return. The man came back as we were breakfasting, saying that he had delivered the message as I requested. That cryptic news meant my first hypothesis was probably correct.

Like most Galileans, Mary was no more a Pharisee at table than away from it. To be sure, she would not eat forbidden things like pork, but otherwise she paid little attention to dietary regulations. "Most of them are for priests, not people," she claimed. Thus she was completely at ease, unlike John the priest, whose sacerdotal conscience pricked him every time he faced food that had not been tithed or when he himself had not engaged in all the prescribed purifications.

While she and I were alone at breakfast, I tried to explain about Simon Peter's harrowed soul. I may have violated his confidence in speaking so candidly; my excuse was that Mary was vital to the movement, and the two communities would have to live together in harmony or cause great scandal.

She listened to all I had to say, even to the part where I spoke of the "appearance" at the lake, when Simon Peter regained his sight. "I hated that day," she said softly in an almost dreamlike tone. "That 'appearance,' or whatever it was, restored much of Simon Peter's right to rule. And I hated him for it."

"Why hate Simon Peter? He had nothing to do with it. If the vision was real, it was the Master's choice."

"I did not mean Simon Peter." Her voice dropped to a whisper. "Why did he do that? He lifted me up only to let me fall. I loved him more than life. I stood by him until the very end. He came first to me, gave me a mission, then as I was successfully performing that mission let me fall. Why? Why did he repay my love in such a cruel way?" She began to sob, then to weep. I had often seen tears of anger in her eyes and occasionally tears of joy, but never, except at the empty tomb, had I seen her weeping like an ordinary woman. And I hadn't seen that; she had told me about it. As usual, when I did not know what to do, I did nothing.

After a few minutes, she dried her face with a kerchief and rearranged her hair. The red around her eyes left her less lovely, but she quickly composed herself and became once more the Mary we all knew—tough and in command of her life and perhaps others' as well, certainly mine in a real way. When she spoke again her voice was still very soft. "Simon Peter sins out of weakness; I sin out of strength. I have the principal virtues and I commit the principal sins—pride, covetousness, envy, anger."

I tried to coax a smile from her. "But never sloth." Then I artlessly added: "And never lust."

For several long moments she looked at me strangly—not with anger or resentment or even hurt. "Never lust," she repeated slowly, but as a description not an affirmation. There was a trace of self-pity in her voice. It set off a sympathetic reaction in me. For the first time, I, too, felt anger against the Master, for, if he had not come into our lives, she and I might have joined lust into love—or perhaps the other way around.

"I'm a proud person, Quintus, and ambitious in my pride, and often angry. I'm ambitious for the Master. I want all Israel to accept his message. And I'm angry at all those people who ignored him, who were too weak to join him, who betrayed him, murdered him, denied him, and abandoned him, then would not believe when he rose from the dead as he promised he would."

"We all are angry, Mary," I said, though no one except possibly Stephen was as angry as she. "Even those who abandoned him hate themselves for it. But the Master spoke of forgiveness."

I need not have tried; she was in a mood to speak, not listen. "And I'm ambitious for myself and full of pride. I know that. I'm intelligent and strong and handsome by the standards males impose on us. Why shouldn't I know those things? Anyone with eyesight and half a brain can see them. But I'm also ambitious for women. You males treat us as breeding pits to sate your lust and bear your children. We serve your pleasure, cook your food, clean your miserable huts, and till your fields so you can fill your bellies with wine and your beds with joy. The Master understood my ambition. I think he shared it. For him justice was not a masculine word."

I nodded. She was right. The Master treated everyone with equal respect—or scorn when confronting hypocrites. His message was about love and justice; but, unlike Mary, he seldom tried to convince others by the sheer force of righteous indignation.

"Then why did he appear to Simon Peter at the lake and take my gift back? Why did he take my rightful place not only from me but from women?"

"Did he do that by restoring Simon Peter?" I asked. It was not a question she was then willing to confront.

We were sitting in the garden near midday when a servant ushered Simon Peter in. He moved toward the deep shade and sat down. "Mary," he began after a bit of hemming and even stuttering, "I am deeply sorry for my absence last night."

"It was nothing," she said. "I'm sure it was something you could not control."

"I went back to the Mount of Olives, not to a tavern. I spent the hours praying I could live that night over again. I can't help being weak, Mary. You're strong, I realize that. I know you have so many of the talents I lack. I try, I try, but. . . ." His voice trailed off into self-pity, the third of us in the villa so to indulge himself that morning. I got up and poured him a goblet of water from a stone ewer. He took only a sip, convincing evidence he was telling the truth about the night before.

He sounded a bit hoarse when he spoke again. "You're strong, Mary, but here in Jerusalem, you could not lead. In Galilee you're a freak." We could both tell that, while his choice of words was brutal, he was striving for accuracy not offense.

He went on: "You're a woman who commands and is obeyed, an institution in Magdala. You've been playing a man's part, and playing it better than most men, since you became a woman. At the lake, your family's wealth gives you freedom. Here you'd be ground under. You don't keep your head covered when you go out of doors. In Galilee that makes you sensible; here it brands you a loose woman, even a whore, a judgment you confirm in talking, even arguing, with men outside your family. You give direct orders to men, and you don't show the respect a woman owes to a man. Even some of the Galilean brothers've been scandalized."

"Is there a purpose to this blather?" she asked.

"You know the purpose, to explain why you can't lead the community here."

"And you can."

"I don't know, I don't know if I can. Sometimes I think I can, but then. . . ."

"When will the Master come again?"

"When? I don't know. Ask John the priest. The Master loved him more than me, maybe he told him. Ask yourself. He loved you better than me. Or ask Quintus here. He thinks the Master has already come again."

"I want Simon Peter's ideas," she insisted, showing no more interest in what I thought than had most of the others.

"I don't have ideas. Ideas're for the rich and educated, for priests and Greeks. Simon Peter only knows the Master said he'll come again; therefore he will come again."

Mary stood up and walked over to him and placed her hands on his shoulders. "You have more faith than you realize, Simon Peter, and more strength. The Holy Spirit is with you." She leaned over and kissed him first on each cheek and then on the mouth, as the Master did, and left us to help her servant prepare for the return to Dalmanutha.

That evening, as I was walking her to the caravansary behind the villa, she remarked it was strange that Simon Peter had such great faith in the Master and so little in himself, even though the Master chose him to lead the rest.

"That's one part of his problem."

She nodded. "Yes, only one part. After this morning, I understand much of the rest. I feel less hostility toward him now."

I wanted to ask, "And less rivalry?" but did not.

I took her hand to help her on a camel. She had never ridden one before, but as usual she showed no fear. "This meeting was not all you hoped for," she said, "but it was more than you had any right to expect."

We were close and I looked straight into her eyes. She made no gesture of affection toward me, no kiss, not even an embrace, only a smile. Yet that small flicker of her lips stirred me, and I sensed a similar stirring in her.

I remained at the villa that evening. The long walk back to the Essene Quarter was too much for me to face. I was very tired. More important, my nerves were on edge. My attraction to Mary was powerful, and, like a spoiled, rich young man, I did not handle frustration easily.

Perhaps because of the pain of that frustration, I felt a more generalized need for the warm intimacy of a woman. Having repeated Simon Peter's and Mary's confessions, I make my own of a liaison I had that night with one of the serving girls, a free woman not a slave, an Edomite who was young but well on the far side of virginity. I prayed for forgiveness, though not until the next morning. The Lord God had specifically forbidden only adultery and we were both unmarried; but the Master had made no distinction between adultery and illicit fornication.

11

❖ When I returned to Matthias's inn the next morning, I had expected to find the troublesome seed that Mary had planted among the women sprouting, and perhaps it was. My attention, however, was immediately focused on the eruption of a long festering set of grievances among the Greek-speaking Jews, those who had been born and reared in the Diaspora but had heard of the Master's message when they were in Jerusalem.

As I have mentioned, the Greek speakers were better educated and, though never wealthy, better off financially than the Judeans and Galileans. After all, they had had enough resources to finance the long pilgrimage from Alexandria, Antioch, Athens, Babylon, Corinth, Crete, Cyrene, or even Rome. Some of these people had come to Jerusalem for one of the great feasts; some were widows of Jews who had come to die in the holy city and be buried nearby.

On the other hand, the leaders of the community, the people who accepted contributions and made payments in food, lodging, and money, were Galileans. Galileans gave all the instructions and always in Aramaic; Galileans led all the prayers; and Galileans presided at the sharing of bread and wine. The only two exceptions were Matthias and John the priest, both Judeans, who, along with Levi, were the only three of the ruling elite who were fully literate. As merely a God Fearer, I, of course, did not fit into this hierarchy.

John and, as he became more fluent, Simon Peter had the good sense to offer some teaching and praying in Greek. Levi could do reasonably well, though with an embarrassing number of errors, some of them amusing.

In sum, the functions of the Greek speakers was, as one of them put it, "to pray, pay, and obey," all while deciphering bad Aramaic. Such a situation is unhealthy in a community supposedly based on love and justice and in which those doing the paying and obeying are better educated and more cultured than those claiming the right to rule.

I was sympathetic to these people of the Diaspora, possibly because of our shared language, possibly, too, because I had studied in the Jewish community in Alexandria and found it so much more intellectually open and advanced than similar circles in Jerusalem, if, in fact, there were similar circles there. The Greek speakers accepted Simon Peter's leadership and listened with respect to what the other Galileans had to say—the force of the message overcame the messengers' ignorance—but the Hellenistic Jews wanted a full role in the community. They were not children and resented being treated like children.

These people met and chose two men to present their case to Simon Peter. Alas, one of their spokesmen was Stephen. There were, to be sure, strong reasons to choose him. He was the brightest of the group, and he was certainly articulate. Nevertheless, his sneering style did not fit him to carry on diplomatic negotiations. The other representative was Philip of Ephesus. He lacked Stephen's fine intellectual edge but his disposition was pleasant, though he had a stubborn streak that was all the harder to deal with because of his good temper.

Simon Peter agreed to meet informally with them before the evening meal, when the women would be preparing the food or fetching the water and many of the men would be at work. Knowing something of the specifics of the grievances, he brought Levi and Matthias along as well as John the priest. Shrewdly, Simon Peter also asked if I would join them, and at the meeting he began speaking in Greek. How can one accuse a man of anti-Hellenism if he counts a Greek among his closest friends and speaks the language?

Simon Peter began with a prayer: "In this room, holy for its memory of the Master's final Passover and the coming of the Holy Spirit upon us, let us ask for divine wisdom."

"We'll settle for justice," Stephen broke in. "You speak of the Master's message to love others as we love ourselves. Yet we Hellenes [I could not help smiling] are treated as children. We are not full citizens. Our families and widows have to sleep in rooms your innkeeper can't rent and get only what your fat tax collector thinks is unfit for Galilean or Judean stomachs."

Levi sat bolt upright. His Greek was good enough to decode an insult. "That's a filthy lie!"

Simon Peter put his hand on Levi's shoulder and began what was, for him, a remarkable display of diplomacy. "The Holy Spirit moves like a dove, my brothers, not like a hawk. Anger drives away love. I'm sure Levi and Matthias have always acted fairly. Our money's limited, housing's crowded, and food's dear. We've all eaten more soup than we'd like and we've all gone to sleep some nights with growling stomachs. But these're not important things. What matters is that we've come together in love for the Master, his message, and one another."

The group listened silently—somewhat sullenly but silently nevertheless—to an irenical Simon Peter. It was a new experience for most of us.

"Does anyone have any suggestions how we can make the distributions seem more fair?" Simon Peter's question was general, but he was looking at Philip rather than Stephen.

"Yes," Philip replied. "I agree that Matthias and Levi have tried to be fair, probably they have been fair. But when people from only one group determine the share of all groups, there's bound to be concern."

"And cheating," Stephen put in.

I intervened quickly: "There is also the matter of instructions, when the newer people may begin themselves to spread the Master's message."

"What do you mean?" Matthias asked. "Only those who heard the Master can spread his message."

"But what if he does not come soon?" I rejoined.

"The Master will come in our lifetimes," Levi insisted. "He is the Messiah who will deliver Israel from her oppressors and establish his kingdom."

John the priest broke in with what had become "our" theory: "Did he ever claim to be the Messiah? I heard him ask 'Who do men say that I am?' I never heard him assert that he was the Messiah, though that was sometimes a fair inference from his tone. What if he is a messiah, but a different kind of messiah from what you have in mind, a spiritual messiah come to free us all from the oppression of selfish, sinful lives? What if he has already come again as he promised? What if he meant what he so often told us, that the kingdom of God is within us? What if that is the message we are to spread to the whole world?"

"Your questions are ones a priest would ask," Levi replied.

Before he could continue, Matthias took up his refrain: "When he returns in his glory as Messiah, the Master will be a man of iron and blood as well as love. The Land of Israel is holy land. It was given to us by the Most High Himself, blessed be His name. For a gentile to rule here is an abomination in His sight, a stench in His nostrils. Our Messiah—His Messiah—will root out that sacrilege."

If John missed the mark with Levi and Matthias, he may have touched Simon Peter. "Whatever the answers to John's questions, he has it right that the Master did tell me to 'teach all nations,' and we don't know he'll come in our lifetimes. He only promised to return. We must consider training the newcomers to spread his word."

"Never!" Matthias injected. "How could we let people who did not know and hear him spread his word? What would happen to the purity of his message?"

"The Holy Spirit blows where She will," John the priest put in. "None of us can demand She withhold Her wisdom from others."

"No," Matthias persisted, not seeing the irony of his arguing, as one chosen by the other disciples, not the Master, for restricting the right to teach. "Levi is right. We must maintain the purity of the message. Only we who sat with him can preach his word."

Philip tried to say something but Stephen was too quick. "We have a word for all this in Greek—monopoly. You Galileans and Judeans are keeping for yourselves the roles of princes in the kingdom before it has even come. Yet you tell us the Master said not to be concerned about such things."

"You've made a good point," Simon Peter admitted.

"A good point?" Levi half-shouted. "He insults us, we who followed the Master, slept in the cold rain, looked in the angry eyes of the rich and their armed guards, and ran for dear life from Herod Antipas in hot chase."

"Or ran for dear life away from the Master and his fate," Simon Peter added softly. "The newcomers've not shown our courage—or our cowardice. But they've shared our lives and learned the Master's truth from us. We must allow them to preach that word."

"Who knows what they will teach?" Levi asked. "How can we protect ourselves from corruption?"

"We find those answers in faith," Simon Peter responded, "in faith that the Holy Spirit will guide them as She guides us. We've instructed these people. We must have faith the Holy Spirit will also be with those we appoint to teach in his name."

"Let us think about faith for a moment," John the priest put in. "We believe because we knew the Master before his death and because we have shared visions of the risen Master since. But these Greeks have not seen, yet they have believed. Which of us believed before he had seen? Mary of Magdala and the Master's mother, but which others? Not you, Levi, and most certainly not I. The Holy Spirit has blessed them with a stronger faith than ours."

"I still don't like it," Levi replied, "not at all."

Simon Peter's patience snapped as sharply as a twig dried by the desert wind. "Like it? You don't like it? Of what importance is it what you don't like? I don't like living in Jerusalem in fear of my life. I don't like being away from my wife and my daughter, my village and my lake and my boat. I don't like sitting here listening to childish squabbles over food and glory. Most of all I don't like it that, despite all the Master told us, I still have the same worries as you about my own welfare and my place in the kingdom. I'm as petty and vain and selfish as the rest of you. I loathe it in myself just as I despise it in you." He lowered his voice several ranges down the scale of decibels. "We do what we must because the Master said we must and the Holy Spirit guides us. Let that be an end to it."

Simon Peter turned to Philip. "What is it you call the ruling council of Jews in Ephesus?"

"The seven good men of the city."

"Very well, we'll ask the Hellenes to choose seven of their number to help Matthias and Levi decide about buying and distributing food and rooms. And, if we're satisfied they understand the Master's message, we'll lay hands on them and command them to preach that message to others."

"The other brothers won't stand for it," Levi warned.

"What?" Simon Peter shouted. " 'You are Peter,' the Master said to me, 'and upon this rock I shall build my community.' He didn't say those words to Levi or to any of the others. He said them to Simon, Simon the Rock. Now Simon Peter rules that our Greek-speaking brothers shall do as I have explained."

"I will bring it up before all the Eleven," Levi said.

The muscles in Simon Peter's neck and temples bulged. "You can bring it up to the High Priest for all I care. Nothing'll change what I have said." He stalked out of the room, his face as florid as I had seen it in several years.

After the evening meal, there was a meeting of the Eleven, from which all others were excluded. The next morning, after the breaking of the bread and the blessing of the wine, Simon Peter announced that the Greek-speaking brethren would choose seven of their number to assist the Eleven in running the community and preaching the Master's word. I glanced at Levi and Matthias: They were glowering. I also looked over at Stephen. He was smirking broadly. He was insufferable.

Stephen's victory quickly increased. Two weeks later, he, Philip, and the other five chosen by the Hellenistic Jews (one of them was Nicolaus of Antioch, a God Fearer, and more recently a full convert to Judaism) presented themselves to Simon Peter and the Galileans and asked for permission to teach. I was with Simon Peter when the request came and, though not invited to stay, saw no reason to leave. Some of the previous argument was rehearsed, but Simon Peter cut it short and conducted an examination much like a school master.

The results were both pleasing and troubling. They could repeat the Master's teaching on almost every point Simon Peter or any of the others raised. But I did not get an inkling about how much they internalized the Master's message; and previous conversations had left grave doubts about Stephen on that score. In all, I left with somewhat more respect for the position of Levi and Matthias. My only comfort, such as it was, was that I also had grave doubts about how much the Galileans understood the Master.

*   *   *

Another year passed, hardly uneventfully, but it passed. Mary's attack on the community's leaders for their treatment of women softened few male hearts, but it did bring some results. Some of the women who had been serving that evening heard her remarks and reported them to the others. We soon had another confrontation. Simon Peter tried to handle the matter much as he had the ethnic conflict. This time he had allies in John the priest and Matthias, but his ability to effect change was more limited.

This was the more serious dispute. For, although Jews in the Land of Israel tended to treat Greek speakers as less than equals, they always claimed not to, recognizing such treatment as wrong in principle. Still, not only did men treat women as subordinates, they admitted they did and defended it as just, indeed, as divinely ordained. That the Galileans could have spent three years with the Master and so little of his teaching on this issue have been understood testified to how thick were the roots of male supremacy.

Thus the changes Simon Peter could make were less sweeping than for the Greek speakers. Outside the community, in Jerusalem itself, as Simon Peter had explained to Mary, relations could neither change nor seem to change. The city's culture simply would not allow women to attend synagogue much less tolerate their speaking there or anywhere in public. Further, most of the brothers could not take over some of the women's chores so that they would be free to attend more instructions or to give them themselves. For an adult male to perform such tasks as hauling water would invite ridicule and possibly provoke retaliatory violence.

The Essene monks were helpful. As celibates, they were accustomed to doing all work for themselves, and the Judeans tolerated this strange behavior. After all, most of them suspected Essenes of being mad anyway. In any event, the three monks who were with us took over several such tasks. The physical difference was small but the psychological benefit was large.

Women also assumed some of the teaching duties, at first only to other women but, as we grew, to new members of both sexes. Here the opposition was bitter, with Andrew his brother's principal opponent. "Putting aside the question of whether women can understand," he began his argument, "if we let them teach men, it will drive them away."

"If they can't accept that we're all equal children of the Father," Simon Peter replied, "can they accept the Way?"

"Perhaps not, but with time and patient instruction, they might become ready."

"Like you, who followed the Master for three years, lived two years as a member of Mary's community, and here for two more years? You're saying after all that you can't accept the Master's teaching that we're all equal."

"I don't agree that was the Master's teaching, and if you weren't afraid of Mary and didn't still feel so damned guilty about running away, you wouldn't either."

"You're part right. I do still feel guilty about running away and so should you. And I am afraid of Mary, but only when she's right. And she's right on this. The Master treated her as equal to us, more than equal in fact. He appeared first to her. Ask John the priest and Quintus; they were there."

Andrew looked at me. "Who gives a damn what a priest and a Greek think? They're all fairies."

"Enough!" Simon Peter shouted. "We'll do what we can do."

And what we could do was not much, but men shared some of the serving and cleaning within the houses, and women shared some of the teaching. We gained something in morale among the women. We also lost some families whose male heads would not submit to such degrading rules. And, I suspect, we also failed to recruit some others.

Questions about the timing of the Master's return continued to plague us during these years. Simon Peter stuck to his declaration of faith in the event coupled with ignorance about its time. During this period, I did not approach him again about my own views, but I continued to discuss them with John the priest.

Some members of the community worked out their concern and disappointment in another way. We had a good deal of "speak-

ing in tongues," babbling, I thought it. We had seen some of it in
the frenzied enthusiasm at the lake after the Master's "appearance" there, and on the Sunday after Pentecost, the sons of Zebedee
and several others had seemed to communicate with each other by
means of disconnected yet rhythmic syllables that had no relation
to Greek, Aramaic, Hebrew, Latin, or any dialect with which I was
familiar.

Most often these seizures came at evening prayers. Our growth
had forced us to change our ritual. There were too many of us to
eat at the same place and time. But we still came together in the
upper room—jammed together—to join in sharing a few bites of
bread and drops of wine, while Simon Peter or one of the other
original disciples declared our faith. After that ceremony, we would
adjourn to our various eating places.

After some weeks, however, Simon Peter decided the gathering
was too brief to keep alive a sense of community and had suggested that after the sharing of the bread and wine one of the
Galileans, John the priest, or Matthias recall for us something he
had witnessed during the Master's life. Then we would finish with
a prayer, which Simon Peter asked one of the new followers—
usually, I noted with appreciation, a Greek speaker and every
week or so a woman—to offer.

One evening, as Barnabas's mother completed her prayer, James
ben Alpheus and Bartholomew, those two weak sisters from the
first Passover, stood up and, swaying as Jews do at prayer, began
chanting: "Praise the Master! Praise the Master! The Master loves
us! The Master loves us! Praise the Master!" A half dozen people
in the crowd took up the chant, clapping their hands to keep time;
then the two disciples, their eyes glazed as if in a trance, began
groaning as if in time to music and soon broke into strange
babbling. The words—I'm not sure they were more than sounds—
came out as rhythmic monosyllables, something like:

> Mah zum um tay; say ray tee kee tay!
> Mah zum du say; rim rim kee tay tay!

The response was equally incoherent:

Tee kee, un se, un se, no.
Tee kee loo kay, za za ah!

James and Bartholomew claimed to have no specific recollection beyond the chanting of intelligible praises to the Master.
Then, they said, they felt possessed, as if something or someone
had taken over their bodies. All they could report was being
shrouded in a mood of ecstatic enthusiasm, and when they came
out of their strange state, a feeling of great and peaceful joy. Some
of the people claimed this behavior was a sign the Holy Spirit was
with us and that the Master had not forgotten us or his promise to
return. Some of them claimed to be able to decode the words,
though, when pressed, they disagreed among themselves about
what had been said.

Many of us were less certain what it meant beyond some form
of hysteria. For once, Stephen and I were in full agreement. But
cold analysis was not something in which most of these people
cared to indulge. Night after night, we went through a similar
ritual. Sometimes it was the original two who achieved this state,
but often others did so as well as, or instead of, James and
Bartholomew. On occasion, no one could reach this state of ecstasy,
and many people would leave depressed, others relieved.

Simon Peter never engaged in the practice himself, nor was he
pleased by it. He discussed the matter several times with John the
priest and me. I was baffled but John demonstrated both knowledge and wisdom. "This babbling is unusual, but it's not unknown," he said.

I agreed. At certain shrines in Greece, oracles or priestesses
would often speak incoherently, claiming to bring messages directly from some deity or other. More specifically, John said, the
phenomenon usually occurred in the Land of Israel among poorer,
less educated people. That much fit our situation closely. King
Saul, for instance, had babbled with these "prophets"—and had
suffered some loss of face for having "lowered" himself. Samuel,
however, had instructed him to cooperate: "The spirit of the Lord
will come upon you . . . and you will be changed into another man."

John's advice was to do nothing. "I think it will fade if you tolerate it. It does no real harm. Many people in the community were desperate when they came to us. The delay in what they expected to be the Master's return has been hardest on them. They need some sort of mystic experience to confirm what faith they have."

John's prediction turned out to be largely correct. Speaking in tongues gradually slackened until it became an unusual rather than a daily occurrence. Yet the practice never stopped. Especially at baptism some members expected the new follower to babble. Indeed, some of the disciples instructed people on how to achieve the ecstatic state. "In my Father's house, there are many mansions," the Master had said. I took comfort in that report.

12

✨ At mid-afternoon, some months after the first bout of speaking in tongues, during the winter of the fifth year after the crucifixion, one of the priests who was sympathetic to the Way but had not yet joined us came to the inn with a warning: Caiaphas and his associates were enraged at the rumor that more priests were planning to join the community. The Temple guards had special instructions to watch Simon Peter and the others closely when they entered the sacred precincts and to arrest them at the slightest hint of a violation of the rules. The priest's advice was to avoid the Temple and even consider leaving Jerusalem for a few months. It was advice I immediately took to heart and tried by gesture to communicate to Simon Peter.

He, however, ignored me. He looked at the two Galileans who were with us, Andrew and James ben Zebedee, reading the fear in their eyes as he would have read in mine had he bothered to look. "Never before have I been in Jerusalem at this time of year," he remarked. "It is truly good. The air is clear, the days are crisp, and at night one appreciates a good woolen cloak."

John the priest intervened. "This man knows what he is talking about. Caiaphas is not vicious, but if he sees this defection as a threat to his authority or the capacity of the Temple to keep order in the city and the Romans out of the sacred precincts, he'll do whatever he thinks is necessary to preserve order."

"The Master commanded us to preach his word."

"But not to seek death when death does not seek us," I put in.

"Who knows who death seeks? It sought John the Baptizer when he preached repentance; it sought the Master when he preached the kingdom; if it seeks us for following the Way, we should be satisfied."

"And the community?" John asked. "What will become of the community? Who will be waiting for his return?"

"That's the Master's problem," Simon Peter replied, "and the Holy Spirit's problem, not ours. We've been given a command; our job is to obey it." He motioned to James. "Fetch your brother. It's time for us to go to the Temple." James turned ashen, but he got his brother.

As they left, John the priest turned to me. Anger was still in his eyes. "I can never decide whether that man is more stubborn or more stupid."

"Simon Peter has a great need to prove his courage."

"I wonder if it is more important to prove it to us or himself," John mused. "If he is only proving it to himself, it is not courage at all but bravado, an excuse to avoid the responsibilities of leadership."

What the priest said was partially right. Simon Peter and the sons of Zebedee went to the Temple earlier than customary. Thus when they reached Solomon's Portico, their usual group had not yet gathered. Instead, they began talking to a cluster of strangers and soon were engaged in debate. At one point, one of the strangers, as it turned out a Sadducee from the Upper City, began shouting. The priest-guards moved swiftly. A dozen of them, with drawn swords, surrounded the three Galileans and roughly herded them into a room deep in the stone bowels of the Temple mount.

The soldiers attached shackles to the disciples' hands and feet and ran the chains through rings set in the floor. As long as the door was open, light flickered from a torch in the passageway. None of the three could make out any furniture in the room except a single slop bucket.

"What're we charged with?" Simon Peter demanded. (He gave me only a few details; James and John were my principal sources, and, as will become evident, their accounts are trustworthy.)

"You will know when it pleases the High Priest to tell you. If it doesn't please him to tell you, then you'll drown down here in your own stink."

The guards left. Once the bolt on the heavy metal door went home, the cell was left in pitch blackness. James—I have it from his own lips—began to sob, and John, who had been so brave at the first arrest, was barely fighting back tears. Simon Peter spoke sharply: "Are you men or sniveling women?" The question must have been rhetorical for the answer was painfully obvious, even in the dark.

"What will happen to us?" James asked.

"How do I know? There'll be a trial. You know enough of the Law to know they can't hold us long without a trial."

"Then what?"

"Then it is in the hands of the Most High, our Father, blessed be His name."

"The Master's loving Father will not let us die," John said. It was more a prayer than an assertion.

"He let the Master die," James whined. "How can he be a loving Father if he let the Master die such a disgraceful death and leaves us to rot in chains?"

"Enough!" Simon Peter shouted. "You know the answer to that question: 'Where were you when I made the earth and set the stars in the heavens?' "

"Since Quintus has taught him Greek, Simon Peter has become a scribe who can quote Scripture," James sneered. Actually, it had not been an exact quote from Job, but it was close enough in its acceptance of divine providence, something Simon Peter himself had bitterly rejected in his blindness at the lake.

"I listened to Scripture read in our synagogue at Capernaum, and so could you if you'd ever paid attention to anything but women."

"Women?" James said, "I haven't lain with my wife for so many months I've forgotten how. We've worked like animals and prayed like priests to end up like criminals. I curse myself for listening to him when he said, 'Come, follow me.' The guard is right, we could rot here."

"But you won't," Simon Peter responded. "You won't. He has touched you. It's enough. We're the chosen ones, the salt of the earth. We'll lead our people to a new Israel."

"Or drown in our own stink," James retorted.

"Only if that leads us to a new Israel. And if it does, we drown fulfilled."

"I wish I had your faith," James said.

"No, you don't. My faith is weak," Simon Peter argued. "You both know that. But it's easier to look trouble in the eye than to feel its breath on your neck."

Hours passed. In the complete blackness, the three were not certain how many. They tried to sleep, but the cold, damp stone of the floor and the heavy chains bonding them to the wall made it difficult to get comfortable. Finally the heavy iron door creaked open and, although there was only a quick flicker of light, they felt the presence of another human being. "Who're you?" Simon Peter asked.

"Never mind my name. I am one of you—a priest here in the Temple," the intruder whispered. "Consider me an angel of the Lord. Two of the guards on this watch are with us. I have the key for your shackles." He fumbled around in the dark for the disciples' legs. When they were free, he snapped the shackles back into a locked position. "I'll guide you through the maze to an opening that leads to the Kidron Valley. You can be in Bethany in less than an hour. Do not return to Jerusalem. Your very lives are in danger."

Simon Peter rubbed his leg where the chains had chafed the skin. "The Father will bless you for this kindness."

"It is not my work alone. You can thank John."

"John—'God is bountiful,' the name means. We share in that bounty. But we won't run away to Bethany or anywhere else. You'll see us teaching in the Temple again."

"That would be foolish, very foolish."

"John has probably told you that we're foolish men. The Holy Spirit has told us to stand in the Temple and tell the people about the Way. We must obey the Holy Spirit, whatever the cost."

"You must do what you must do, but we can't help you again. Caiaphas is fretful. If he sees you in the Temple, he might have you stoned—not out of malice, but caution. And cautious stones kill as finally as malicious ones."

"I know."

"Now, if you're going to escape," the priest said, "you'll have to move swiftly and quietly. We control only guards in this section. Turn left as we leave the cell, then left again at the end of the hall and follow the passage to the end. You'll see an opening."

In mid-morning, Caiaphas's political sanhedrin assembled in the Hall of Gazit inside the Temple. As at the previous incident involving Simon Peter, Caiaphas had decided to hold the hearing within the Temple rather than at his palace because he wanted to avoid risking a public disturbance by moving the prisoners through the city.

All twenty-three members were present, six were Pharisees, including Josef of Arimathea, the source for most of what I relate about the trial. They might be able to embarrass Caiaphas, but they could not outvote him if he could keep his majority of Sadducees united. After disposing of a few other items of business, the High Priest ordered the Galileans brought before the tribunal. The captain of the guard returned almost immediately, his agitation obvious. "Sir, sir," he stammered, "the prisoners are gone."

"Gone." As usual Caiaphas's voice betrayed no emotion beyond a trace of boredom. "The prisoners are gone. Do you not find that droll, my dear captain?"

"Yes, sir. I mean, no, sir. The, the door was securely fastened and the manacles were locked. Guards were on duty. I cannot explain what happened."

"You *will* explain what has happened, or you will resign, won't you?" Caiaphas asked in his flat tone.

The captain bowed and started to withdraw, but just then another guard came in and whispered something in his ear. "Sir," the captain addressed the High Priest, "the prisoners are in the Court of Gentiles, by Solomon's Portico, talking to people."

"Why not arrest them and bring them here? You can do that for us, can't you, Captain?"

Five minutes later the captain and his men returned with Simon Peter and the sons of Zebedee in custody. Caiaphas asked for no explanation of their escape but began with the charges against them. "Several years ago, after you created a disturbance, did we not give you a formal warning not to use this holy Temple to preach about that executed seditionist? Have you not ignored that warning all during this time? Because there was no further breach of the peace, we have, out of compassion, tolerated this disobedience. But yesterday did you not again provoke other Jews who came here to worship? Have you not once more disturbed the peace of this holy place? How do you explain your disobedience?"

"Obedience to God comes before obedience to men," Simon Peter answered. His voice was calm, but Josef said there was defiance in his eyes. "And our Master, the messenger of the Lord, has told us to preach his words to all peoples."

"How did you escape from the prison?" The questioner was Rabbi Gamaliel ben Hillel, the great Pharisaic teacher.

"An angel of the Lord freed us during the night," Simon Peter replied.

"He blasphemes!" one of the Sadducees hissed. "Stone him! Stone him!"

Rabbi Gamaliel quickly stood up. "May I ask the High Priest to take these prisoners away so that we can discuss the issue with more reason and less emotion?"

Gamaliel's request for discussion within the Sanhedrin was perfectly proper. Caiaphas motioned to the guards, who quickly pushed and shoved the Galileans out of the hall. "Men of Israel," Gamaliel began, "let us be careful in dealing with these people. They are simple, ignorant peasants, which does not mean they pose no danger, only that we must act cautiously. Our history of opposition to Roman rule begins with Roman rule itself. We have seen many such groups come and go, usually in their own blood."

"I would carefully and cautiously stone them," injected the Sadducee who had spoken earlier.

"It may come to that," Gamaliel nodded, "but it has not yet. And if we force it now, we may have a broad scale popular disturbance."

"Broad scale?" Caiaphas cut in. "I can tell you to the man how many followers they have in the Essene Quarter and at the lake. Less than two hundred males, some of them old, all cowards."

"Be that as it may," Gamaliel smiled. "I have heard that many more people in Jerusalem are sympathetic to their teaching. And, I note, we are meeting in the Temple rather than taking the prisoners across town. I suspect security had something to do with that decision."

"I don't want to excite the Romans," Caiaphas replied.

"Yes, that is understandable. They are an excitable people. We, too, are excitable; and alas, we have a history of opposing the true prophets. This movement may come from the Eternal One, blessed be His name forever. In recent decades, after much bloodshed among ourselves, we have developed a tradition of toleration for differences among ourselves. We insist only that one proclaim that the Lord our God, the Lord is one and accept the Law of Moses. From what I have heard of these people they meet both qualifications. I concede they are lax in matters of ritual purity and their interpretations of the Law can be strange. But, if we were to stone all who were lax or had strange interpretations, we would have to execute the entire population of Galilee and no small part of this holy city as well. My caution is that we should be certain we are not making war against the Holy One."

Annas coughed several times as if he wished to speak. Out of courtesy to the former High Priest's age, Gamaliel stopped and offered Annas the floor. But he waved for the rabbi to continue. "The matter of their escape—and it was an escape—I find especially troublesome."

"Could one of their rich friends not have bribed the guards?" Caiaphas asked, looking at Josef of Arimathea.

"Perhaps," Gamaliel admitted, "perhaps. But that, we have understood from the High Priest on other occasions, is impossible. Priests of this holy Temple, subordinates of the High Priest himself, taking bribes? No, I think not."

"Could it not have been the work of sympathizers among the priests? Several of our number have joined these Galileans and others are sympathetic."

"And perhaps," Gamaliel smiled, "just perhaps, it could be the work of the Most High, acting in His always benign and usually inscrutable fashion."

"Is it not interesting," Josef of Arimathea noted, "that, once these men escaped, they did not run but went back to teach in the Temple like good Jews?"

Caiaphas shook his head but said nothing. Sitting as he was at the center of the semicircle, he could probably see from the faces of the other councillors, even the Sadducees, that Gamaliel's doubts had taken root. The rabbi's reputation was based on fairness and dispassion in argument as much as on immense learning. The High Priest waited a few moments for others to speak, but no one cared to debate the great scribe. Caiaphas clapped his hands and when a guard appeared told him to bring the prisoners back into the hall.

The three Galileans faced the Sanhedrin. "You heard but did not heed our first warning. You have heard that some members of this body would stone you now for your disobedience and for what they consider blasphemy. We issue a second and final warning. You are not to speak in the name of this criminal in public again. If you come before us again, we shall not be merciful." Then he spoke to the captain. "Take these men out and give them the forty lashes less one to remind them of our words, then release them."

The guards dragged the three out of the hall and down into the lower levels of the Temple where they would not be seen by worshipers. They navigated the maze of tunnels and rooms and emerged in the Kidron Valley through a small gate, then trotted north for about a hundred yards to the edge of an abandoned stone quarry. There was an iron post set deep in the ground with a large ring connected to it. Simon Peter went first—out of fear, he later joked. The guards pushed him into a kneeling position, tied his hands to the ring, and stripped his colobium off, leaving him naked.

A big man, almost as round as he was tall, came up. He was carrying a stave an inch in diameter and wrapped in leather for all of its six feet. He paused near Simon Peter, looked up at the captain of the guard, then with a sudden, powerful motion sent the whip cutting into Simon Peter's bare back. After twenty lashes, that back was raw meat. After ten more Simon Peter fainted. Mercifully the executioner shifted his target to the buttocks.

The guards threw a bucket of water on Simon Peter as he lay on the ground, then cut him free from the iron ring and jerked him to his feet. He spun sharply, taking the two guards by surprise and causing them to lose their balance on the rocky, uneven ground. He confronted his torturer at a range of three feet. The man stepped back, either out of fear or an effort to get more room to use his weapon. But Simon Peter merely smiled and extended his bound hands. "Bless you, my brother, you've done your duty nobly."

The two guards got back up quickly, shoved Simon Peter down again, and kicked him several times. After, they cut the ropes from his hands and threw the remains of his colobium over him and grabbed John for his turn at the post. James soon followed. They moaned, Simon Peter reported, but neither man cried for mercy.

Josef of Arimathea's servants carried the three men back to Matthias's inn. They did not make a pretty sight. Matthias had them placed in bed, face down. He looked disdainfully at the medicines that Josef's men had brought and sent someone to the house of the Essene monks. Within a few minutes, four of the monks were at the inn. They looked at Matthias, who had been preparing his own potions, and without a word grabbed Simon Peter's arms and legs and pinned him to the bed. Matthias then poured a ewer of his concoction—it smelled heavily of wine—onto his back. The man who had refused to whimper during the scourging now bellowed like a wounded bull as the red liquid rolled over his skinless flesh.

Matthias and the monks then moved to James, who was trying to get up and run, but was too weak to move more than a few inches on the bed. Poor John could only moan as he saw the pain of the remedy. After all three had been cleansed, the Essenes began applying a thick unguent directly to the flesh. Then Matthias insisted that each man drink three cups of water. "We have seen this many times. It has often been our fate. You won't walk for a week and you'll ache for a month. But if we keep your backs clean and you drink a great deal of water, you'll live. If not. . . ."

Simon Peter's wounds had great ramifications for our community. The first concerned Stephen, the other Hellenistic Jews who had joined us, and, indirectly, most of the world. As I have mentioned, Jewish life has been heavily influenced by Greek culture, as attested in Jerusalem itself by the agora of the Upper or Lower City, various gymnasia, though these are anathema to pious Jews, the architectural style of palaces, and the language spoken by the better classes. Some of that influence, as shown by the philosopher Philo, is subtle, sophisticated, and uplifting. But some of it is also cheap, gaudy, and debasing as well as debased. The Herods, who, when not indulging their architectural ambitions, seemed to spend half their lives in one another's beds and the other half trying to murder each other, provide the most appalling examples.

Naturally, Greek influence on Jews in the Diaspora runs even deeper than in the Land of Israel. Jews who live in the Diaspora tend to be less concerned with ritualistic aspects of the Law and more with fundamental tenets of belief. Pharisaism can exist there, as Stephen and Saul demonstrated, but it cannot multiply. On the whole, these Jews are more universalistic than their cousins, less tribal in thought if not associations. Philo and his Judaic-Hellenism flourish in Alexandria; he would have been shunned in Jerusalem. Living in cities crowded with pagan temples also makes Greek Jews wary of the notion of Jerusalem's Temple as the place where the One True God lived. They can admire the building itself as a symbolic home of Judaism, while fearing many Judeans teeter on the brink of idolatry in the reverence they accord it.

As I related earlier, snobbery is also involved, exacerbated by Judeans' habit of treating Hellenistic Jews as less than full sharers in the Covenant. The Hellenes know they are more cosmopolitan, educated, and affluent than Judeans. And something in human nature makes those who have greater wealth believe themselves more worthy than those who have less.

When feelings of cultural superiority and resentment against exploitation are combined within a personality like Stephen's, the stage is set for tragedy. And the play went off as if the lines had been well rehearsed.

Before they joined our movement, Stephen and Philip had been attending the Synagogue of the Freedmen in the Lower City, across the Valley of the Cheesemakers from Matthias's inn. This synagogue was frequented mostly by pilgrims and émigrés from the cities of northern Africa, especially Alexandria and Cyrene, and a few, like Stephen and Saul, from the Asian provinces. The Sabbath after Simon Peter and the others had laid hands on him and pronounced that he could preach the good news, Stephen had engaged his fellows at this synagogue in debate. I was not there, but I can readily guess he antagonized as much as he enlightened.

That risk, however, was clear and Simon Peter, if not the others, had accepted it when they commissioned Stephen. I do not mean to belittle the man. His speech could be both elegant and graceful, and he was a person of real intellect. But when crossed, his charm could easily curdle into venom. Within the confines of a synagogue, especially a synagogue of Greek speakers, this problem would not be trivial but neither was it likely to be fatal.

When Simon Peter was bedridden, Stephen and Philip decided

to visit the Temple. They went in the late afternoon to Solomon's Portico and looked for a group fitting the description of those who met with Simon Peter and the sons of Zebedee. Alas, their judgment was poor. Apparently, Simon Peter's debaters had heard of the whipping and were not gathering for their regular discussion, though some of them were present for the evening sacrifice. They were conversing with a group of Judeans and several pious men from Asia and Cilicia, including Saul, Stephen's sometime companion and fellow student of Rab' Gamaliel.

Those two were a well-matched pair. Both were extraordinarily intelligent, both had been educated in the Greek-speaking world, both were Pharisees, and both had been trained by Judaism's leading scribe. There were, however, stark contrasts in physical appearance as well as religious commitment. I have said that Stephen was handsome—tall, slender, with features a sculptor would have loved to carve.

I also said that Saul was homely. His face looked like its parts had been thrown together at random. None of his features was ugly, but they did not fit together. His ears were as jug-handled as those of a Celtic legionnaire and protruded at right angles from his head. His hair was a bright, brassy mop of tightly curled red, his complexion light olive instead of fair. His beard was thin and scraggly, more that of a teenager than of a man almost thirty. It, too, was red, but several shades paler than his hair. If his Roman nose was too long for his face, his mouth was too wide. His teeth were irregular and there was a space between the upper two in front that sometimes forced a half-whistle to punctuate his sentences.

The rest of Saul's body followed the same random pattern. His upper torso, with its long, thick chest and broad shoulders, was that of a tall man, but his legs were made for a short person. They were thin, too thin for his weight, and were covered with thick fuzz the same shade as his hair. Had his beard been so rich, it would have better served him. In later years rumors abounded that Saul had once competed as a runner in Greek games held in Asia, well away from Tarsus so he would not bring scandal on his house. I doubt those stories. As a young man, he was obsessively pious and would not have even watched such games, much less participated. When older, he never had time. But even had I misjudged his character, I have watched enough games to know those legs could never have carried his body very far very fast.

Stephen's voice was deep and even. The honey of its flow could provide balm for the sting of his words. Saul's voice was slightly high-pitched, not effeminate in any way, just a half-tone too high to resonate as an orator's should. And, when he became excited, it raised even higher in pitch and took on a shrewish tone. The occasional whistle did not lend dignity to his demeanor.

Only Saul's eyes were attractive, or at least fascinating. They could change color from hazel to green to brown-flecked yellow, reminding me of nothing so much as one of the big lions on display in cages in Alexandria and Rome. The restlessness, pride, ambition, intensity, even ferocity were almost identical.

"Fellow sons of Abraham." Stephen's smooth baritone caught the group's attention as he spoke in Greek. "I have come to continue the work of the Galilean Simon Peter while he and his friends recover from the High Priest's whip."

"If you're a Jew," one of the Judeans said sharply, "speak our language. We are Jews not Greeks. Who are you?"

"I am Stephen, a Jew from Tarsus, where we speak Greek in our synagogues just as I have heard it spoken here in the Temple," he replied, switching to accented Aramaic.

"Why then do you speak for Galileans?"

"Because they have seen the Messiah, Joshua, whom the Romans crucified but who rose from the dead."

At that point Saul wandered over. "Stephen," he began, "my old friend Stephen, you must have drunk too much cheap wine to prattle so. What foolishness is this about a crucified man risen from the dead?"

"It is not prattle, Saul, but truth. His message. . . ."

"You have seen this risen man?" Saul interrupted.

"No, but I know many who have."

"Galileans all, no doubt."

"Not all. One is a priest from this Temple." Stephen tried to continue his message: "My task is to preach the good news that the kingdom of the one, true God is at hand."

"Is it God's kingdom or the Galileans'?" Saul asked.

"Joshua the Galilean, of the royal family of David, whom the Romans crucified after the people of Jerusalem proclaimed him king, has delivered this message. It is a message not only for Galileans or for the Land of Israel, but for the *people* of Israel, wherever they might be."

Saul would not let up. "What will happen to the Law in this . . . this kingdom of yours?"

"It is not mine but God's. And the Master's coming has fulfilled the Law. Once the Messiah has come, we no longer need the Law in the sense you understand it." His talk was drowned out by angry shouts of "Blasphemer!" Stephen waited, then tried to resume his speech: "The first part of the Master's message is like that of John the Baptizer: repentance of our sins."

"Did he repent his?" Saul cut in once more.

"Sin was something that did not touch the Master."

"No? Then he must have thought the Law of Moses did not bind him." Saul's pitch had risen to that harsh screech of which I spoke earlier, and the last words were accompanied by a slight whistle.

"I have told you that his coming fulfilled all that has been written in the Law and the prophets."

Shouts of "Blasphemer!" came again.

"Is that why he violated the sanctity of the Sabbath, allowed his followers to pick grain on that day, criticized the Law of Moses on divorce, preached cannibalism or homosexuality when he told his followers to eat his body and drink his blood?" Saul spat out the last phrase. The notion of drinking blood is so abhorrent to Jews that it was difficult for him to pronounce the words.

"You misstate his position on all these issues."

By now a large crowd had gathered, including several priests. They formed a circle in which Stephen and Saul faced each other like gladiators in the arena. Caiaphas himself stood a bare fifty paces away, with the captain of the Temple guard and a dozen of his priest-soldiers.

"Do I? Do I misstate?" Saul asked. "It is no small sin to try to lead the people away from the Law. Did your false prophet of a Master not say that Moses was wrong because divorce turns the divorced woman into an adulteress? Did he not eat in the houses of men who collected taxes for the Romans, apostate Jews, and even pagans? Did he not consort with prostitutes? Tell us what he meant by that obscenity 'Drink my blood.' "

Most of the crowd applauded Saul's rapid-fire interrogation. "I can answer all of those questions and more." Stephen no doubt realized he was in danger. "For, I, too, was once a skeptic, as you well remember. Where would you like me to start?"

"What about his threat to tear down this Temple?" one of the priests called out. "Tell us about that blasphemy against the Lord's holy house!"

"It is you who blaspheme!" Stephen had restrained himself remarkably in his exchanges with Saul, but now he began shouting angrily. "To blaspheme is to revile or ridicule the Holy One, exactly what many of you do. What do you come here to worship, an idol who lives in a man-made building? The Most High is a spirit, He does not live in tents or temples. Heaven is His throne, as the Prophet Isaiah has written, and the earth His footstool. What house could mere men build for Him? To think He lives here is idolatry. You have become little better than pagans!"

"Shut up, you blathering fool!" an enraged Judean shouted. "Who are you to liken us to pagans?" Another cried out: "Don't you dare call us pagans, boy! Do it again and you'll pay!" His audience would have agreed about the Lord God's being a spirit, but Stephen's accusing them of idolatry was viciously insulting.

The Greek's voice rang out just as loudly: "I call you pagans and worse! We Jews have always persecuted the messengers of the Most High. And we helped the Romans shed the innocent blood of Joshua, the son of David, whom the Eternal One has raised from the dead."

Saul tried to get back into the debate: "Did this Galilean make the blasphemous claim to forgive sins?"

"Yes, he made it; and he had that power and still has it. The all-loving Father gave it to him; and he, in turn, gave it to us. But don't you see, we all have it? Real sin only consists in injuring other human beings. When we forgive those who offend us, we forgive sins."

"We have the Law," Saul snorted, "the Law of Moses. To violate that Law is to offend not merely man but the Most High Himself. Answer my questions about the Law. I say your 'prophet' opposed the Law of Moses."

"When the Messiah has come, he supersedes the Law, not the principles of divine justice behind the Law, but the specific precepts. The essence of the Law of Moses, as Rab' Gamaliel insists, does not lie in dozens of precepts but in basic principles requiring us to treat one another with justice. The Master did not slavishly follow all specific provisions because, as Messiah, he was not bound by them. He went beyond the individual duties they impose to the higher perfection of love."

"Blasphemy! Blasphemy! He claims this Joshua was above the Law of Moses and so must be equal to the Most High Himself!" The priest who shouted these words tore his clothing as a sign of outrage against sin.

"Blasphemer!" a dozen people bellowed. "Stone the blasphemer!" Some one picked up a broken chunk of marble from the pavement and threw it at Stephen. It struck a glancing blow on his shoulder and ricocheted off, hitting one of the audience in the face and causing a bloody cut and a stream of curses. Other people began closing in on Stephen, cursing and kicking at him. What had been a curious, if hostile, gathering had turned into an enraged lynch mob. "Kill him! Kill him!" people in the rear of the group were yelling, as those in the front pressed in to assault the man.

At that point, Caiaphas and the guards trotted over to the melee. "Stop," the High Priest called out. "Stop! You are defiling the holy Temple! You know the Law! You can stone a blasphemer, but you cannot do it in a camp or a city, much less in the Temple!"

"Outside the walls with him then!" one of the Judeans yelled, and with the help of a half dozen friends picked Stephen up from where he had fallen from the blows and dragged him toward the passage that led down from Solomon's Portico to the Sushan Gate and then out into the Kidron Valley, far below.

By the time the lynchers had dragged Stephen outside the gate to the edge of the quarry that Simon Peter and the others had traversed in their escape, he was more dead than alive. His head was gashed in several places and blood was streaming out of his nose and mouth. The Lord God alone would know what damage the kicks had done to his internal organs.

Saul trailed behind. Part of him, he later said, was infected by the contagious madness of the mob, but part of him was also appalled by the impending death of his former friend. Philip, meanwhile, had also been trailing the mob, and as they stopped at the edge of the quarry and were stripping Stephen's clothes off, he ran forward, shouting, "Stop! Stop, you cannot kill a man without a trial."

"Not true," a Judean priest shouted. "This criminal is guilty of more than blasphemy. He tried to lead us away from the one true Lord, His sacred Law, and His holy Temple to follow some Galilean fraud. The Torah says if anyone tries to entice you away from the Lord your God, you must not spare him, even if he is your own son. 'You must show him no pity, you must not spare him nor conceal his guilt. You must kill him.' There is no mention of a trial. And the first hand to be raised will be that of a witness, then all the people will share in the stoning."

"But you must give him a trial," Philip pleaded. The only response he got was a heavy fist in his face that knocked him almost senseless.

One of the mob's leaders called for Saul to come forward. He did so and confronted Stephen's once handsome face, contorted out of shape by blows and kicks. "You, Greek," the Judean barked, "you know the Law provides that the witness casts the first stone. Your debate revealed his blasphemy. You have the duty to begin the execution."

A priest picked up a large rock and handed it to Saul. He let it drop onto the ground. "I know what the Law says, but I cannot do it," he whispered hoarsely.

"Here," the man who had called Saul forward said, "if you aren't man enough to do your duty, I'll do it for you. Hold my cloak." He tossed the garment to Saul, then turned toward Stephen and gave him a hard shove that sent him tumbling backward into the quarry.

Philip pulled himself up on all fours and cried out: "How can you call yourselves Jews if you do not have pity? The Law you claim to love requires a trial!" The Judean kicked Philip in the ribs and sent him sprawling again, then picked up the stone that Saul had dropped and threw it down at Stephen. It missed; that was not a mercy for it was heavy and might have done the deed in one blow. Someone else picked up another big rock and with better aim caught Stephen on the hip, probably shattering the joint. Stephen rolled over and looked up at his executioners. "Father, forgive them," he cried out. Those were his last words, as a volley of stones rained down to crush his skull.

I had small affection for Stephen during his life, and I believe he helped turn that crowd into a murdering mob. Yet, with that much said, I must confess he died a heroic death, forgiving others as he had never been able to do before that moment. When I heard the story from Philip and again years later from Saul, I realized the Master's message lived even in many of those who seemed not to grasp it.

13

❖ Bruised, frightened, and disconsolate, Philip returned to Matthias's inn to tell the story of Stephen's lynching. Immediately, Simon Peter ordered four men, all Jerusalemites, to recover Stephen's body. By the time they returned it was getting dark, but the community felt an obligation to follow tradition and bury Stephen that very evening. Matthias quickly consulted with several of the Essene monks and secured permission to use their cemetery in the Valley of Gehenna, southwest of the city.

Leaving the city posed no problem, but getting back late at night did. Fortunately, the sentries recognized me as a member of the burial party and let us reenter; otherwise we would have spent the night sleeping on cold, hard ground.

At the inn, John the priest was waiting for us with more bad news. His friends in the Temple had told him that Caiaphas had belatedly decided to charge Philip as a blasphemer as well. The strategy, the priests explained, was to eliminate the Hellenistic Jews, the people who the High Priest thought were more danger-ous not only because of the usual bias against Hellenes, but also because, if Stephen were typical, they were more radical in their religious beliefs and posed a threat not only to the peace but to the Temple's rulers as well.

We were reluctant to discuss the matter with Simon Peter, since he had already had one trauma today and was still weak and in considerable pain. But we needed an authoritative decision and went upstairs to waken him. He was lying naked on his stomach so that we got a full view of his back. Through the thick salve the Essenes were using, one could see a spackling of gray, which Matthias proudly identified as new skin. Simon Peter listened to us, his face twisted in a gnarled frown.

"The seven men of the city'll have to leave Jerusalem," he said.

"All of us?" Philip asked.

"All—and every other able-bodied Greek-speaking male."

John the priest nodded. "Caiaphas is angry, very angry. He agreed only to whip you. He was offering a bargain: Your lives in exchange for our keeping away from the Temple. Then a few days later, Stephen and Philip return to the Temple. He sees that as a rejection of his bargain and a challenge to his authority."

"Can he arrest me?" Philip asked.

"Yes," John said. "He can arrest you and try you for blasphemy or trap you inside the Temple and have you lynched. I heard you argue that Stephen had a right to a trial. Most scribes read the Law that way; but it is also possible to read it to allow instant punishment for blasphemy. That Caiaphas ran the risk of Roman intervention by not stopping the lynching is powerful evidence of how determined he is. Another Roman intervention in the Temple is an obsession with him; and Caiaphas is usually a stickler for legal niceties. Typically, he follows the most conservative course, observing every trivial technicality."

"I don't know much about the Law," Simon Peter put in, "but I do know something about guerrilla fighting. If the soldiers try to hunt the Hellenes down, we haven't a chance unless the people are with us. The big feasts're over, the city's population's shrunk, and Hellenes aren't popular. That means we can count only on ourselves and the Essenes, and we can't ask the Essenes for more help. So, you've got to go, all of you—now."

"Tonight?"

"Get ready tonight. Leave in the morning, but not at first light. Wait until there're crowds in the streets. That way you won't be noticed. A few of you should use each gate, but not the Essene Gate. If Caiaphas wants to stop you, that's where he'll be looking."

"Where can we go?"

Simon Peter groaned as he got his weight up on his elbows. "Where? Levi, go with Philip to the Hellenes' houses and distribute all the money we have." Then he looked at Philip. "Wherever you'll be safe, wherever you have friends or family. You'll have to decide. Mary of Magdala'll shelter you at the lake. One of the Galileans can go along and guide any that want to go there. You'll have to decide quickly."

"What about the widows and our wives and children?"

Simon Peter groaned again. "What about them? How do I know? John, are they safe here?"

The priest thought for a moment. "Yes, I think so, yes. Caiaphas is angry, but he's not likely to arrest women and children. He won't see women as important."

"There's your answer," Simon Peter said. "Mary wouldn't like it, but it helps us. All right, are we done?" Without waiting for an answer he lay flat in the bed again. As we started to file out of the door, Simon Peter yelled: "Matthias! Matthias, you stingy hypocrite, I need some of your rot-gut wine so I can sleep in peace."

Matthias smiled. "You need more water and red meat to recover. The only wine you get goes on your back."

Simon Peter winced at the thought. "I need more water like the desert needs more camel dung!" Suddenly he jerked himself back up on his elbows. "Philip, you've heard us talk about the times the Master sent us on those two missionary trips around Galilee?"

"Yes."

"Why shouldn't we send you to spread the good news?"

"Will these people listen to Greek Jews?" It was a fair question.

"In the countryside, probably not," John said. "But in the cities, who knows? In places where Jews speak Greek, like Joppa or Caesarea or even in the Diaspora, in Antioch, Damascus, Tarsus, or Ephesus, perhaps. Perhaps."

"Do these people know enough to preach the Way?" Matthias asked, raking up the earlier debate. "They have never seen the Master or heard him speak."

"One of them knew how to die for the Way, asking forgiveness for his killers," Simon Peter replied. "That's enough. It's settled then, Philip. You go wherever you can, but as missionaries, not fugitives. We'll turn this defeat into a victory and spread the Master's message to Jews wherever they live."

Simon Peter's decision, though hasty, was wise, and it was to be far more momentous than any of us realized. Some effects were immediately apparent. The very next noon, Temple guards trooped up to the house where Philip had lived with a summons for him to appear before the Great Sanhedrin to answer charges of blasphemy. The guards ransacked the entire house. It wasn't a large place but its rat's maze of tiny cubicles had housed six of our Greek Jews and their families. Now there were only women and children, but enough of them to fill a house several times the size. It was clear, the women believed, that had any males been present, they would have been arrested.

Armed with this information, we were able to persuade Simon Peter to forbid any of the disciples to go to the Temple except to offer sacrifice. I doubt we could have persuaded him had he or the sons of Zebedee been able to resume their activities, but it was several days before any of the three could do more than hobble around the inn and two more weeks before they were back to normal. During that time we developed the access many of the brethren had gained to the smaller synagogues.

That was the pattern of our activities during the next three years. Simon Peter and the others attended synagogues and made some converts and also managed to antagonize many people. Our problems of housing and feeding also continued. Without Josef of Arimathea, I am not sure what would have happened to us. Sharing does not come easily to adults, and there were days when we—at least most of us—went hungry.

Of no small importance for the long run was Simon Peter's continuing lessons in Greek. After two years, he could speak quite well; with the practice of three more years he became not merely fluent but practically bilingual. He never learned to write and only to read occasional words, but he had the illiterate's memory for sound as well as the ear and tongue of a mimic that enabled him to affect, in all innocence, the accent and syntax of an educated man.

Simon Peter insisted, with no success, that the rest of the Twelve learn proper Greek. Only John ben Zebedee and Matthias persisted. The latter was an apt pupil. The other ten managed to create a never-ending chain of excuses.

Of that period from the sixth through the eighth year after the crucifixion, four facts stand out in my notes: The brothers stayed away from the Temple except to offer sacrifice at the great feasts; the chief priests left us alone; the community continued to grow, slowly but grow it did; and some of the Hellenists energetically engaged in missionary activity.

In all, thirty Greek-speaking brothers left for fear of persecution. Four went to the lake with Mary and were safe there. After a few months, another ten quietly returned to Jerusalem to resume life within the community and with their families. A few drifted from the Way and disappeared from our lives. Most, however, remained faithful. And over the months, reports dribbled back of missionary activity, nearby in Joppa and Caesarea and even beyond.

Philip, we heard, was spreading the message in Samaria, which lies between Judea and Galilee, a million theological miles from either. In the eyes of Galilean and Judean Jews, Samaritans are at best apostates, at worst traitors to Judaism. A larger portion of the earlier gentile inhabitants had survived in Samaria than in Judea or Galilee; and, so Judeans and Galileans claimed, Samaritan Jews had contaminated themselves by intermarrying with these gentiles before, during, and after the Babylonian exile. In addition, there were important cultic differences, the most aggravating one being that the Samaritans rejected Jerusalem as the proper site for the Temple and had built their own on Mount Gerizim, which one of the Maccabees' successors destroyed a century and a quarter before the Master was born. The Samaritans, however, still worshiped on that mountain, and it was there that they expected the Messiah to appear.

The upshot was at best armed truce and occasional open hostility between these two groups of Jews. Judeans and Galileans who took their religion seriously would never associate with Samaritans. (Earlier I expressed my own views of Samaritans as an untrustworthy lot.) Some of the Twelve had been vexed when on a trip across Samaria to Jerusalem the Master had conversed at length with a Samaritan woman at Jacob's Well. Worse, at her urging, he had lingered for several days in the nearby town of Shechem and preached to any Samaritan who would listen. That precedent lent some legitimacy to Philip's mission, but only some.

We also heard rumors that several of the brothers had pushed on both north and south along the Mediterranean. One report said someone was preaching the Way in Alexandria. Another put Barnabas in Damascus, but the brothers chose to think that false for two reasons. First, the report also said he was preaching to gentiles, to Syrians who called themselves Greeks and had been worshiping in pagan temples and, for all the brethren in Jerusalem knew, were still doing so. The disciples could not yet believe the Master had been serious when he spoke of every man as a neighbor.

The second reason for disbelief was that the rumor added that Saul of Tarsus, Stephen's one-time friend who had provoked the argument that led to his death, had changed his name to Paul, converted to the Way, and was working with Barnabas in Damascus. That this fanatical Pharisee would embrace the Way was incomprehensible to the Galileans.

Those years were quiet, but they were not dull. They could hardly be so with the community's increasing, even with defections, to 250 adults. I shall not discuss again the difficulties we had coping with that large number. At times, I even prayed that my theory of the Master's return was wrong and that he make his physical reappearance soon. More practically, for the first time in my life, I worked like an ordinary person, giving lessons in Greek and Latin to adults and teenaged children of wealthy Jewish families and in Aramaic to families of two Roman officials.

This, as I shall describe soon, was also the period in which Paul made his first visit to Jerusalem as a member of the Way. But more dramatic changes were sweeping through the Land of Israel outside the movement. Lucius Vitellius, who had earlier twice been a consul at Rome, became governor of Syria in the fifth year after the crucifixion. My father knew his family and spoke of him as an able and energetic man. Certainly events in Jerusalem were to prove him so.

He came to the Holy City for Booths in the sixth year and conducted himself with great respect for the Jewish faith, requiring, for instance, his guards to leave outside the city all banners and symbols that might offend the Jewish proscription of graven images. He found time to meet with a range of Jews—Pharisees, Sadducees, merchants, including Josef of Arimathea, and Annas as well as Caiaphas. Further, Vitellius showed great sensitivity to Jewish reluctance to enter a gentile's house by arranging to meet them in the open at the agora in the Upper City.

On the day he left, three days after the feast had ended, he called at the house of Jonathan, Annas's son, and talked with him briefly in the courtyard. Then Vitellius went to Herod's palace, where he was staying as Pilate's guest, and announced he had deposed Caiaphas as High Priest and appointed Jonathan in his place. It was that simple.

Caiaphas was not a popular man; no High Priest would be unless he were of the family of Zaddok, and I doubt if such a man could still be found. Nevertheless, there was considerable mumbling among the Jews of Jerusalem, for the removal emphasized that they were a conquered people, subject to an idol worshiper's will. On the other hand, at our prayers that night there was neither rumbling nor weeping. Simon Peter led us in a hymn of thanksgiving.

In private, however, John the priest was more restrained. "My cousin Caiaphas is intelligent and cautious, hard but not vicious. My cousin Jonathan is a decent sort, but he's not intelligent. If you must have an enemy, it is better that he be intelligent, for then you can predict his course. Jonathan may turn out to be far crueler than Caiaphas—and out of the best of intentions, for he will be weak and conciliatory at first. When he sees that he is being used . . . who knows?"

I questioned my uncles the next time I saw them to see what they knew—and I also asked that they talk to my father to get his views. The gist of the responses was that Pontius Pilate was Vitellius's principal target. He distrusted the prefect's judgment and feared Caiaphas was becoming Pilate's man, an estimate that both John the priest and I thought incorrect.

Meanwhile, Simon Peter, over John the priest's objections, immediately put the new High Priest to the test by resuming preaching in the Temple. The guards and most of the worshipers ignored him. Soon, he and the sons of Zebedee were putting in almost daily appearances at the Portico of Solomon.

That winter another dramatic episode ensued. A Samaritan "prophet" suddenly announced he knew where Moses had buried certain sacred vessels on Mount Gerizim and offered to lead the people there. Most Jews, of course, recognized the claim as fradulent because, according to Deuteronomy, Moses never entered the Promised Land but died across the Jordan in the land of Moab. Nevertheless, a mob gathered to follow the prophet up the holy mountain.

Pilate, aware that turbulence was brewing, intervened in his usual bloody way, attacking the mob and slaughtering several hundred of them. Some of the survivors and families of the dead sent a delegation to Vitellius, charging Pilate with brutal murder and claiming the victims had not been disloyal toward Rome; their only resistance had been in self-defense against Pilate's savagery. The governor promptly sent an officer named Marcellus to investigate the charges. The man was speedy, thorough, and decisive. Within three weeks, he had heard the evidence, dismissed Pilate, and ordered him to Rome to stand trial before Caesar himself on charges of oppressing the Samaritans.

Once again our community was filled with joy. And again joy triggered hopeful but false predictions about the imminence of the Master's return. James ben Zebedee, stretching his mind to its outmost limits, pompously stated: "Beelzebub's house is now divided against itself; the Romans have deposed both murderers. If a house divided against itself cannot stand, then the kingdom of this world must be collapsing and the Master's kingdom is being born." I could think of no response, but then none was necessary.

There were more surprises in store for us. Vitellius, on his way to attack Arabia, came back to Jerusalem during Passover. The governor was a shrewd diplomat who understood the perils of going to war thousands of miles from home with a tough and discontented people at his back. Thus he continued to act in a conciliatory manner, directing his commanders to avoid all Jewish cities lest the presence of Roman standards give offense.

Nor was that all. Showing typical Roman respect for the jurisdiction of the local deity, he came with only a small guard to the Holy City to offer sacrifice to the Jewish God for the success of his campaign. One of his first acts was to release Jerusalem from taxes on all the fruits bought and sold at the festival. His next was to announce that Tiberius had granted the Jews' request to regain control of the High Priest's vestments, which the Romans had kept locked in the Antonia and released only for use on the three great feasts and the Day of Atonement.

Jonathan, however, managed to muck things up. He assured Vitellius the priests would offer sacrifices in his name at the Temple, but the Roman asked to attend the ceremony. By definition, a pagan could enter the Court of the Gentiles; though, of course, he could not go into the inner court where sacrifices were offered. Rather than think of some gracious accommodation, such as constructing a temporary altar in the Court of the Gentiles and offering sacrifice there, Jonathan merely told the governor he could not go into the Temple. Still the consummate diplomat, Vitellius accepted Jonathan's dictum with a smile. But, when the festival was over, as he was getting ready to leave, Vitellius deposed Jonathan and appointed Theophilus—whose name, I note, could hardly have been more Greek—High Priest, the third in six months. There was one interesting constant in these raisings up and castings down: Annas's influence. For the changes had all been within his family.

Before Vitellius could rejoin his army, another change occurred. News reached Jerusalem that Tiberius had died and had been succeeded by Gaius. Tiberius was not the equal of Augustus, and much of the Empire suffered badly during his morose reign. But he had both a sense of his inadequacies and deep respect for Judaism, neither of which Gaius, nicknamed Caligula—"Little Boots" —possessed. The relative peace we had enjoyed—and seemed destined under Vitellius to enjoy even more—was coming to an end, though that would not become clear for another year or two.

14

✦ Late in the summer after Tiberius's death, seven years and some months after the Master's crucifixion, we received the first of two dramatic visits. It was getting toward evening of the first day of the week, when Simon Peter and the sons of Zebedee were finishing preaching the word. I had entered the Temple that afternoon to observe once more. It seemed safe enough. During his short reign as High Priest, Jonathan had taken no interest in us, and

Theophilus seemed equally unconcerned, though since he was Annas's son and Caiaphas's brother-in-law he undoubtedly knew about us. In any event, I stood deep in the shadows of the portico around the edges of the group and did not participate in the discussion.

I did not join the three disciples until they started to leave. Then, as we were walking toward the Hulda Gates, a slightly high-pitched voice called out: "Cephas, Cephas." It was a red-haired man about my age, slightly taller though with short legs. He seemed vaguely familiar. He came toward us and grasped Simon Peter by the arms and planted the kiss of peace full on his lips. "I am now called Paul," he said in Greek. "You remember me as Saul of Tarsus."

Simon Peter stared at the man with the wary watch a wrestler fixes on his foe at the opening of a match, waiting for him to commit himself. The sons of Zebedee quickly glanced around to see if guards were closing in. I confess I did the same thing.

Saul—or Paul—smiled. "I understand your concern, my friends; but I come in peace."

"So did Stephen," James ben Zebedee noted.

"So he did, and so do I now in the name of Jesus, the risen Lord." From the very first, Paul used the Greek "Jesus" rather than the Aramaic "Joshua"; and for a title he always used "Christos" —the anointed, the Messiah—rather than the disciples' more familiar "Master." Another of his affectations was to call Simon Peter by the Aramaic "Cephas."

"Even in death," Paul went on, "Stephen has been my friend, for his help in my finding the Way has not been inconsiderable."

"If you come in peace," John ben Zebedee said, "leave in peace. We are well rid of you."

"Perhaps. My rhetoric played a role in Stephen's death, but I shall not grovel in guilt. I believe the Most High, Whose mercy is eternal, has forgiven me. Now I come to you at Barnabas's suggestion."

"And when did you last see Barnabas?" Simon Peter asked as he began walking toward the gate again.

Paul fell in step alongside. "At Caesarea, not a week ago. We traveled from Damascus together. He stayed a few days with relatives, and I came on to Jerusalem. He will arrive tomorrow. We are to meet in the evening in the Essene Quarter at an inn run by a man named Matthias."

"It wouldn't be wise for you to go there," Simon Peter said. "People remember Stephen—and his friend Saul."

"The Lord chose me from my mother's womb to teach His word. I must answer that call regardless of the danger. Besides, I have nothing to fear from followers of the Way. Jesus the Christ taught that we should love our enemies, *especially* our enemies."

Simon Peter shrugged his shoulders. "The Master also prayed 'lead us not into temptation,' and some of the brothers're weak." There was silence as we walked through the gates past the priests and down the steps. Then Simon Peter aked, "Why is Barnabas taking you to the inn?"

"To introduce me to the people who knew Jesus, especially you, Cephas, and assure them that since accepting the Way my life has been blameless."

"Why do you want to know us?"

"Barnabas has taught me a great deal, but I must learn much more if I am to spread the good news."

Simon Peter stopped abruptly. "You? You spread the Master's good news?"

"I am the last of the apostles and no doubt the least; yet Jesus has appointed me 'a prophet to the nations.' "

"The Pharisee is drunk!" John ben Zebedee guffawed, "crazy drunk!"

"Or else he has a demon," James ben Zebedee said, chuckling.

Simon Peter may have recognized Paul's quotation from Jeremiah, but if so he ignored it to focus on the heart of the matter. "Who 'appointed' you to preach the Way?"

"Jesus the Christ. He appeared to me and let me know what I must do. I have been preparing myself to do it."

"You saw him?" Simon Peter reached out and clamped Paul's shoulder in a powerful grip. "When? Where?"

"I saw him." Paul stepped back to untangle himself from Simon Peter's grasp. "It was shortly after Stephen's death. My uncle wrote me from Damascus that several Jews from Galilee were preaching in the local synagogue about a certain Jesus whom the Romans crucified. I immediately started out for Damascus to engage them in debate and have them thrown out of the synagogue."

"And lynched like Stephen?" James cut in.

"Shut up!" Simon Peter snapped. "Let the man tell his story."

"It was on the road to Damascus. Without any warning whatsoever, I suddenly saw a light so dazzling I was struck down as if by a blow. It was then I saw him."

"What did he say? Quick!"

"Say? His words were few. 'Saul, why do you persecute me?' I knew the answer but I couldn't help asking: 'Who are you?' He looked at me, laid his hand on my shoulder, and said, 'I have touched you. Come, follow me.'"

"And then? Then what?"

"And then he was gone and I was blind. The other people in the caravan took care of me for several days, until my sight returned. Then I left them and went off for almost three years to the kingdom of the Nabataean Arabs, where they let me live in peace. I practiced my trade of tentmaking to earn bread, but mostly I prayed to the Most High for wisdom to understand what had happened to me."

"When did the Master tell vou to preach the Way?"

"In so many words, never. But when he touched me I knew exactly what I was to do. I did not need words to grasp the message."

"Why do you think it was the Master? You never saw him before his death."

"You're right. I never saw him *before* his death, only *after*." He hesitated a second. "I knew. I knew it was Jesus, just as I knew what he was telling me even though he did not speak the words. My problem was to understand why he was calling me, a man who had had a significant role in executing one of his followers and was on his way to have others driven from the synagogue and perhaps even flogged as well."

"Has he come to you again?" Simon Peter asked.

"No, only that once."

"Why did you leave Arabia?"

"Because I began to understand my mission, why I had been chosen to be an apostle."

"Why?"

"I knew a great deal about the Way. I could debate Stephen because I knew almost as much as he did about the good news. I tried teaching some of it to the Arabs and some were receptive. My mission became clear to me: To bring the good news to the uncircumcised."

"That sounds like a waste of time," James put in. "The Master warned us not to throw pearls before swine."

"Be quiet! No one's a swine," Simon Peter said gruffly. Then to Paul: "Your story rings right. We'll talk to the brothers and see what they say. Do you remember the synagogue you and Stephen attended?"

"Of course."

"When Barnabas comes to the inn tomorrow, we'll talk to him. If he supports you, I'll send him to fetch you. If he doesn't come for you, return each morning for a few days. He may be late. I mean it when I say it's unwise for you to come to the inn alone. 'The flesh is weak.' "

As we walked away, Simon Peter looked at me. "Well, you're Greek and close to half of him. What do you think?"

Before I could respond, James spoke. "I say he's the ugliest man I ever saw, uglier even than those jug-eared Celtic legionnaires. I say forgive him for murdering Stephen but stone him for beauty's sake. It would be a kindness to the world—and to him, too."

"James, you're a fool. What do you think, Quintus?"

"He's pompous, self-righteous, and arrogant. I don't like him, but I think he's telling the truth."

"So do I. We'll see what Barnabas has to say." Not many years earlier Simon Peter would have brashly followed his own instincts and convoyed Paul straight to the inn; but he had learned to wait for evidence—and for someone to share any blame that might flow from error.

Barnabas did arrive the next evening. Simon Peter thought it prudent to postpone discussion until after dinner and to limit the participants to Matthias, John the priest, the Galileans, and three of the returned Hellenes who had known Stephen well, though none would have called himself friend—but then no one except Paul would have done so. I was neither invited nor disinvited, so I attended.

The debate turned out to be long and bitter and to involve two separate problems. Acceptance of Paul as a follower of the Way posed no issue of principle: He was a Jew who professed to believe. The sole question was whether he truly believed or was a spy of some sort. Barnabas supported him totally. "For a year in Damascus, we have worked together. He is always tireless and often, tiresome. But he is fully committed. Twice he has been thrown out of the synagogue, the second time with a threat of scourging if he ever returned; gentiles have threatened his life for the zeal with which he preaches. To me his actions prove his conversion to the Way is genuine."

"But can he become a member of this community?" one of the Hellenes asked. "His very presence might provoke some of the brothers to violence—to sin."

"He doesn't want to join this community," Barnabas answered. "He needs our forgiveness and would like our approval of his work, but his basic reason for coming is to learn more about the Master. I have told him—a dozen times over—all you taught me, but he needs more than I know."

"For what purpose?" Matthias inquired.

"To preach the Master's good news."

"I don't like that," Matthias said, "not at all." The man was consistent.

"Did you baptize him?" James ben Zebedee asked.

"Yes."

"Did he receive the Holy Spirit?"

"I believe so, yes."

"Did he show it by speaking in tongues?" James continued.

"He spoke in tongues, if that is a sign of the Holy Spirit, just as have some of the gentiles."

"Gentiles?" John ben Zebedee asked. "Then the rumors are true that you have been preaching to gentiles in Damascus?"

"Yes, I have. When I arrived I found a small community of believers, a half-dozen gentile and three or four Jewish families. People from Dalmanutha had been there, preaching and baptizing; some men from Gadara had also come through, though they had not baptized. I built on the base they started. Many gentiles are as hungry for the good news as are Jews."

I need not repeat all the arguments for and against expanding our mission to include gentiles. I note only that we heard every reasonable argument for and against and almost as many unreasonable arguments on each side.

After several hours of wrangling—with Paul's case not mentioned again—Simon Peter, recognizing that a majority was against him, finally said: "You're right. Bringing in gentiles'd make our community very different. We could have terrible problems with our rules about food and sexual purity. But if the Master helped the child of the Syrian woman and offered the Samaritan woman the water of eternal life, who're we to refuse to allow gentiles to hear the good news and participate in the Way?"

There was some rumbling. As I have said, even at the time those actions of the Master had not met with the Galileans' approval. James put one of his typical questions: "What would that mean about the Master's return? When he comes, wouldn't we have to share the kingdom with more people?"

"I don't know what it means," Simon Peter replied. "But sharing isn't something we can reject. Isn't the Master's message that through love we share all good things with others?"

"Perhaps," John ben Zebedee cut in, "we must spread the good news among the gentiles before he'll come again."

"Perhaps, but I don't think his coming depends on what we do any more than on what we want."

It was at that point I made my speech. I explained the idea that John the priest and I shared—the idea that the second coming had occurred and how it was linked both to the notion of the kingdom's being within us and how our mission would be a long and continuous one that would include all people of all time. Barnabas nodded in general agreement, and Simon Peter, for the first time, seemed to weigh my words carefully. The others, however, were openly impatient with foolish foreign logic.

As soon as I had finished, Matthias returned to Simon Peter's argument. "I do not suggest we refuse to admit anyone to the Way. I say the path is open. Anyone who wishes to join us can convert to Judaism."

"But that is an immense barrier," Barnabas replied.

"A barrier? Are you a Jew? Are we not all Jews?" Matthias asked, ignoring the obvious fact that I was a gentile. Perhaps I should have felt complimented. "Has that been a barrier to our following the Way? Why should it be a barrier to others?"

"Because we were born Jews," Barnabas answered. "We drank the Law of Moses with our mother's milk; but the Law is alien to these people. They're not asking to become Jews but to follow the Master's Way of love."

"And how does the Master's message differ from the Law?" Matthias asked. "I'm no scholar, but Stephen claimed his rabbi said the gist of the Law was the same as the Master's rule of treating others as we wanted to be treated. How can someone accept the one and not the other?"

"It's not," Barnabas responded, "the gist of the Law these people don't want, but all the details; the changes in life that'd be necessary—their food and, most important, circumcision. They look on it as mutilation. We can't spread the good news to gentiles if we make them convert to Judaism to follow the Way."

"What we are facing, whether we realize it or not," John the priest said with great perception and equally great lack of prudence, "is a fundamental question: Do we form a Jewish sect like the Essenes or are we something different?"

"We are first and foremost Jews," Matthias insisted, "as are the Essenes. And," he added, "even the Sadducees."

"*We* are Jews," Simon Peter put in, "but must *all* followers of the Way be Jews?"

"Yes!" Bartholomew shouted out. "Yes, they must!"

"But the Master told us to go to *all* people, teaching them what he had taught us," Simon Peter retorted. "He did not say to make them accept the Law of Moses."

"When the Master sent us on our mission he told us to go only to the children of Israel. We all heard that command. We have only your word for this business about 'all peoples.' " Bartholomew's mouth turned up in a sneer.

The light was poor, but even so I could see Simon Peter's face change color as anger welled up. Before he could speak, however, John the priest stepped in: "Simon Peter's word would be enough, but we also have my word and that of Andrew and Thomas. The four of us heard the Master speak that command. It was clear beyond doubt."

"You heard the words," Matthias acknowledged. "No one doubts that [though clearly some did] but we are questioning your interpretation of those words. We don't believe the Master wanted us to bring gentiles into our community, only to spread his message to Jews outside Israel. We should not deny gentiles the good news about the kingdom. They may hear it and follow it. But to share fully, they must commit themselves fully to what the Master was—is—and what we are, Jews, sons of the Most High, heirs of the Covenant, and subjects of the Law."

"This man is right," a voice called out from the darkness at the back of the room. "We can never accept gentiles in our community. They can follow the Way if they wish, but we can never eat with them or sleep in the same house with them. We are a holy people consecrated to the Eternal One, blessed be His name. Gentiles eat contaminated food, worship idols, and fornicate with their own relatives. We must keep apart from such foul people."

"Who are you?" Simon Peter asked.

The man strode forward into the lamp's dim circle of light. He wore tassels on his cloak and phylacteries strapped to both arms. In the middle of his forehead there was an impression that could have been made by the phylactery a Pharisee would wear when outside the house. I thought I recognized the man, but I couldn't be certain. The person I remembered was tall and slender, this one was tall and gaunt, almost skeletal. His eyes were different. Even in the dim light, they were black and powerful, reflecting the same sort of fervor as had John the Baptizer. "I am James, the brother of Joshua, whom you call Master."

Simon Peter stared at him. "The last time we saw you, you and your brothers were trying to have the Master put away as a madman. Why've you come here? Who let you in?"

"I let myself in. I heard that the community met at the inn of Matthias in the Essene Quarter. I came."

"Why?"

"Because my brother has appeared to me and told me to follow his Way."

"When? Where did you see him?"

"Three years ago. I was living in Hebron."

"Tell us what happened!"

"It was at night, late; I had worked all day and was tired. My stepmother had gone to bed. I got a loaf of bread and a cup of wine and sat down. Then he was there. First he placed his hand on my shoulder and smiled. Then he took the bread, blessed it, broke it, and gave it to me."

"His exact words!" Simon Peter demanded.

" 'My brother, eat your bread, for the Son of Man has been raised from the dead. Follow me.' "

"Why did you wait three years to come to us?"

"I needed to pray and to think. You know how I felt about my brother. I was convinced he was mad. I could not follow him when he was alive; how could I when he was dead? Even if I could, how? Or better, why? I left my stepmother with friends and went to a monastery above the Asphalt Sea. I have prayed and the Most High has given me the answer: I am come to serve this community."

"Why not the community at Dalmanutha or Damascus or the new one we hear about in Joppa?" Simon Peter asked.

"Jerusalem is the city holy to the Lord; it is here I must serve."

"The Most High, blessed be His name, has said this?"

"Not directly. He did not speak to me in dreams. But through my prayers that answer has come to me."

"This seems to be the season for sinners to join the fold," Simon Peter commented, for once in his life wry. "You'll find much company. Each of us has done his share of sinning."

"I know that. Any one who would defile Judaism by mixing our holy people with pagans is no stranger to sin."

"We appreciate your thoughts," Simon Peter replied, "even

though they're uninvited. We welcome you to our community. The kitchen will see that you have something to eat; when we're done here one of us will find you a place to sleep. Now we ask you to leave so we can finish our discussion."

"I have a right to speak in this place."

"What right?"

"The right of blood. I am my brother's brother and he speaks in me."

"Speaks in you? You rejected him during his life."

"Even as you did, Simon, even as you did."

"Let the man speak," Thaddaeus spoke out. "We want to learn what he has to say." Hearing an echo of approval around the room, Simon Peter waved his hand in resignation.

"The man who spoke last has it almost exactly right. If gentiles wish to follow the Way, it is open to them. But they are unclean, and we cannot contaminate ourselves by table fellowship. If they wish to become our brothers, they must convert to our Law, not we to their immorality. I see yet another danger: Intermarriage will soon follow in any community. If we allow these pagans to enter without accepting the Law, we'll soon be no better than Samaritans—mongrels, an abomination in the sight of the Most High."

"We have all had," John the priest said, "an opportunity to speak our minds. This problem is complex, far-reaching, and vexing; it goes to the heart of what we are all about. We should not try to resolve it in one night. I propose we follow the example of our new brother James when the Master appeared to him and pray over it—and see what happens when the Holy Spirit moves us and others."

"I would rather settle it now," James said, aware, I am sure, he was inserting himself into a position of leadership, "for I do not believe the issue is complex, though I concede it is far-reaching and vexing. However, I would be willing to wait awhile and pray for guidance."

I could see the choler rise again in Simon Peter's neck, but once more he restrained himself and merely said that the meeting was over. Under the circumstances, it was the best we could have

gotten. Faced with the stark choice John had presented, that between being Jews and "something else," Jewish followers of the
Way would naturally choose to be Jews. But that, I think Simon
Peter was trying to argue, however incoherently, was not the real
question. The real question was whether one had to be Jewish to
follow the Way.

I saw James the next day at the morning prayer. He stayed in the
upper room with the Galileans when the others left for breakfast,
as if his admission to the inner circle of leadership was self-
evident. He drank no wine, only water, and took only a few bites
of bread. Darkness had not concealed his shape; he was as gaunt as
I had thought; he could not have weighed much more than a
hundred pounds, yet he stood about five feet, eight inches tall. His
clothes were well made, not the usual peasant stuff, though very
plain; he wore no jewelry. A faint hint of perfume provided another, though enigmatic, clue to the man.

He remembered me, though he pretended not to. Admitting he
knew I was a gentile would have required him to challenge my
membership in the community, something he was not prepared to
do, at least not yet. I was offering some instructions that morning
to two new families and could not resist asking him if he would
like to join us. Anger flashed from those black eyes. "Joshua's
brother does not need instructions in his Way, especially. . . ."
Then he caught himself, turned, and marched away. "I am going
to the Temple to offer sacrifice," he announced and pointed
toward James ben Zebedee. "You may accompany me." James duti-
fully fell in step.

I stood next to Andrew, with whom I seldom felt close. "I
sense much trouble there," I said.

He nodded. "My brother can handle it—with our help. Watch
him, Greek. Don't let him lose his temper." He paused, then
spoke again: "Or become melancholy."

Those were tasks even the Lord God might hesitate to set for
Himself, but I resolved to do my best. And for a time doing my
best was quite easy. James was content to pray and talk quietly

with members of the community. Most of the Galileans were more taken with him than I would have expected, since they could not have forgotten his treatment of the Master. But, I concede, James had an aura of authority; and, to people who wished to be orthodox, his style engendered trust, his manner encouraged obedience.

He was an imposing man, not in spite of his slightness but because of it. His lack of physical stature somehow accentuated the moral force that flowed from his eyes. And his piety soon became legendary. It was no sham. His resemblance to John the Baptizer was more than physical. James, too, could threaten to bring down the wrath of the Most High, and he also stressed repentance and good deeds, emphases that pleased Matthias and many of the others as did his rigorous self-denial of almost every bodily pleasure.

James got up an hour before the rest of the community and prayed most of that time, swaying to and fro in the rhythmic fashion of the Jews, his lips moving with the words. At night he retired well after the others, again spending the intervening time in prayer. Some of the brothers reported that during the middle of the night he arose and prayed for another hour. I construed this obsessive behavior as evidence of a guilty conscience, but to a man the disciples deemed it evidence of profound piety.

His attention to the minutiae of the Law was as great as any Pharisee's; his devotion to the Temple and its rituals exceeded, so John the Priest remarked, that of most Levites. That fact did not please Matthias, who always maintained the Essenes' disdain for the Temple and its rulers.

Simon Peter was acutely aware that another crisis in leadership was brewing, yet there was little he could do. One cannot attack a man for prayer or piety. And during those first weeks, James made no overt challenge. The closest specific act had been during the debate over admission of gentiles, and there he had merely stated his views, as all the others had been doing. Of course, his reference to "blood" was no more lost on his hearers than his presumption that he would be in the inner circle. And a suspicious person might view his asceticism and meticulous adherence to the letter

of the Law as tacit rebukes to Simon Peter's laxity in such matters, though no one doubted James would have followed these
rigid patterns of behavior wherever he found himself.

15

✤ The press of other problems kept us from paying as much
attention to Paul as we should have during the first days of his
visit. We all agreed he should not come into the Essene Quarter,
which meant we had to make arrangements to meet with him
that were sometimes awkward and never as frequent or as long as
he wished. I am afraid we piqued his pride, with Paul not a
difficult sin to commit. He, however, was, as he put it, "not
unpersistent" and tried early one afternoon to visit us at the inn.
It was an unwise and almost disastrous decision, for two of our
Hellene brothers recognized him. Unfortunately, having just finished off a flagon of wine, they were in no mood to put the
Master's teachings into practice and immediately attacked.

Prudently, Paul turned and fled into the Lower City's maze of
streets. The two brothers took off in hot, if not altogether steady,
pursuit. As he passed the synagogue of Greek speakers he and
Stephen had attended years before, Paul decided to take refuge
inside. Our brothers' dimmed vision caused them to miss his turn
into the building, and they continued down the nose of the hill,
shouting obscenities and bumping into pedestrians and merchants,
sending most of them sprawling onto the cobblestoned streets.

The speed with which Paul entered the synagogue and his
panting, sweating condition drew the annoyed attention of the
worshipers. Paul, being Paul and confronting an audience, could
not resist the opportunity to talk, even as he was trying to catch

his breath. "Are you not Saul, who helped execute some blasphemer a few years ago?" one of the people interrupted.

"I am he, an unworthy servant who through ignorance helped murder an innocent man. But the scales have been lifted from my eyes and now I see clearly. The man of whom Stephen spoke so eloquently, Jesus the Nazarene, was indeed sent from the Most High to save Israel and the gentiles from sin. Listen to his words. . . ."

A debate followed that was not unlike some in which Stephen had engaged. In the middle of it, the door burst open and our two brothers came rushing in, still shouting obscenities. Mistaking themselves for the prey and identifying Paul with his assailants, the members of the synagogue began to beat up all three, then threw them out the front door.

Bloody and very bruised, the two brothers returned to the Essene Quarter, and several hours later their news trickled down to us in Matthias's inn. Because Simon Peter and the sons of Zebedee were at the Temple and John the priest and Andrew were off somewhere, Barnabas and I went to look for Paul. Eventually we found him in an alley. He looked worse than either of the brethren. Both eyes were swollen and already purpling and there was some dried blood in the corner of his mouth. When we helped him up, he walked with a distinct limp. "I think," Barnabas said, "it is time you and I left."

"I have come to learn and to preach the word; I shall not leave unsuccessful."

"You may not leave alive," I put in.

"I accept death, if that be the will of the Most High. I, Paul, am His servant. For this purpose the Eternal One placed me in my mother's womb."

"Let's accept life," Barnabas suggested, "and sow the good news in more fertile ground."

Barnabas's good sense won out, but Paul asked Simon Peter to accompany them as far as Joppa. He could visit the new community that had apparently been started there, though by whom we did not know. And on the way, Paul and Barnabas could learn even more about the Master's life and words.

It would have been greatly to Paul's advantage to have Simon Peter alone for a few days, but I did not want him away from the community until he had established a clear—and superior—relationship with James, so I made the countersuggestion that Barnabas investigate the community in Joppa and send us back a letter. I gave him the name of a Jewish merchant who did business with my family and would be happy to carry the letter. Simon Peter, however, felt that spreading the words of the Way was of such importance that he should see for himself what was happening. I suspect he was also bored. I did not protest strongly because I concluded the damage a fit of melancholia might do was greater than what James might wreak if left alone.

In the small hours of the night before the four of us were scheduled to set out, I awoke with a fever, a splitting headache, nausea, and a touch of diarrhea. With considerable difficulty, I managed to ride to the inn and tell Simon Peter. I knew I was not physically able to endure the two-day walk to the coast. I urged him to take Levi in my place. He would need someone who could read and write if he wanted to use my uncles' colleague to deliver a letter. Levi was also moderately in favor of admission of gentiles, and that issue might present itself in a seaport town like Joppa.

A few days earlier, when Paul and I were waiting for Simon Peter outside the Temple, I had suggested that on his return to Syria he stop off at Caesarea and walk inland to visit Dalmanutha. Mary could tell him many things about the Master that Simon Peter and the rest of us had forgotten. After all, she had been the first person to claim to have seen the risen Master. Paul agreed it was a good idea, and we discussed it again for a few minutes that morning. While Levi was putting his few belongings in a knapsack, I wrote a brief letter for Paul to give Mary.

Once the four had set out for Joppa, I returned to my uncles' villa and went directly to bed. It was a full week before I was well enough to visit the inn again, and even then my legs were wobbly. The changes I saw in the community were subtle but real. It was James, not Matthias or Andrew or John the priest, who opened the morning prayer. James even pronounced the words at the sharing of the bread.

And the prayers themselves were different. They were not in Aramaic but Hebrew, a language in which most members of the community could pray but not otherwise use. Furthermore, James went on for almost a half hour, whereas earlier the ceremony had lasted only minutes except in the evening when we sang a psalm or two and listened to recollections about the Master. The difference in time was spent mostly on James's editorializing on Scripture or the Master's message, not in formal prayers.

When the meal was over, I walked over to Andrew. He shrugged his shoulders. "It's what the brothers want," he said before I could speak.

"And the sisters?"

He arched his eyebrows. "How should I know? James agrees with most of us that women should not have an equal role. They lack the Master's nature."

I muttered something vulgar—though mild compared to what Mary of Magdala might have said. More civilly I asked about James's leading the prayer.

"We have a compromise: James leads us at the morning meal; at the evening meal the rest of the Eleven take turns. People thought it fair."

"Yes, one half for him and ten share the other half. That sounds eminently fair."

"What can we do? He is the Master's brother."

Several weeks went by. During that period, the community became more Pharisaic in its habits. There were now three rather than a single water jug at the entry to the inn, and the members washed themselves before eating and praying. Matthias approved of that practice, but then Essenes wash themselves more frequently than cats. He appreciated much less James's inquiries—at times rather sharp—before each meal about whether the food had been tithed. On one occasion, I heard the innkeeper snap back, "We are the people who're supposed to benefit from tithes, not those fat priests in the Temple; we are the poor. Look on this as somebody else's tithe and don't deny our rich brothers the right to obey the Law."

James also began to urge all the members to go to Temple each weekday and pray, and to insist we allocate some of our meager capital to buy doves to sacrifice. On the Sabbath, he and the Galileans went off as a group to the Galilean synagogue. Matthias, however, refused to go up to the Temple and, on the Sabbath, joined the Essene community. I also noticed I was no longer being consulted on financial matters. And on one occasion Bartholomew asked when—not whether—I intended to complete my conversion to Judaism.

Then late one afternoon, just before the evening meal, the Jewish merchant with whom my uncles dealt stopped at the inn and left a letter for us. Levi had written in Aramaic. His grammar and syntax were abominable, though my translation erases that fact from history. The script, however, was done with precision, as one would expect from someone accustomed to keeping accounts.

> To my brother Andrew, the others of the Twelve, John the priest, and all the brothers and sisters of the community of the Way at Jerusalem, Greetings. It is I, Simon Peter, who speaks to Levi.
>
> We made our way to Lydda and there found five followers of the Way, all observant Jews of Judea who had only two months ago received the good news from a Greek-speaking brother from Joppa. We baptized them in the Holy Spirit and spent three days with them, strengthening them in the Way. We ask you to send several brethren to continue our instruction. The people are more open there than in Jerusalem. The man to contact is Aeneas, an elder of the synagogue.
>
> We were called to Joppa by several brethren from that community. They had heard we were only a few hours away and wished us to come and help pray for the recovery of a saintly woman. Afterward, we accepted the hospitality of Simon, a leather tanner, who is firm in the Way. His house is near the harbor and through him we have met the brothers and sisters. There are thirty-eight of them, not including children. They, too, are newly brought to the faith. Parmenaus, one of our Hellenes who fled the persecution under Caiaphas, was returning from Antioch and

spent some time preaching here before going to Samaria to help Philip. Parmenaus spread the word to Jews and gentiles alike.

This bothered me, not because I myself disapprove, as you all remember, but because we weren't of one heart and mind on the matter. I prayed on the question, and it has come to pass that I've received an answer. About ten days after we arrived in Joppa, I became very tired at noon. We'd been talking to the people since early morning, and I felt weak. Simon, our host, suggested I rest on the roof and catch the sea breezes while his wife prepared something to eat. I thought I would only pray, but I fell into a sleep—or a trance. When we meet I'll relate the details to you. To summarize, the Holy Spirit ordered me, a Jew, to eat unclean food. I was confused, even angry.

The trance ended when the Spirit told me to awake, that the retired centurion Cornelius, an honest God Fearer, was waiting to hear what I would say. I awoke and found three young men from Caesarea, who had traveled through the night with the news that Cornelius awaited my words. I left Levi with Simon and brought a group of brothers from Joppa. Because the men from Caesarea were exhausted, we took a ship back, arriving there the next day. Cornelius was in fact waiting, with his whole household and some close friends. He came running out to greet us and fell at my feet. I helped him up and told him it was wrong to treat another man in such a manner. Without realizing why, I blurted out: "We Jews have been forbidden to mix with people of other races, but the Lord has told me I must not call any human being profane or unclean." Only then did I ask why he had sent for me.

His response sent a chill up my spine: "Three days ago, while I was praying, I had a vision. A man in shining robes told me to send to Joppa for Simon Peter, who was at the house of Simon the Tanner. This person had something important to say to us. So now my family, friends, and servants are gathered to hear your message."

It was then I fully realized the meaning of my own vision: The Lord does not have favorites. Anyone of any nationality who fears the Lord and does justice is acceptable to Him. Thus I began to teach these people about the Master and the Way. We discussed the good news for more than two hours and I was becoming weary, when suddenly two of Cornelius's servants began speaking in tongues. Soon all the rest joined in. Afterward, they assured me they had been taken over by the Spirit and had been thanking the Most High, blessed be His name. He had given these people what he gave us. Who was I to bar them from the Way?

I have returned to Joppa and am more at ease preaching to gentiles as well as to the children of Israel. It has not been easy, as some of you predicted, for the two groups to meet; but we have managed.

The community at Joppa had not been so close as ours at Dalmanutha or Jerusalem. The brothers and sisters live in their own houses and do not share their goods, though we have reminded them of their duty to see to the needs of the poorest. As many as can meet each evening and all come together on the Sabbath to share the bread and wine and join in prayer. That loose fellowship has, so far, kept friction among Judean and Greek-speaking Jews and gentiles small. They all worship the one, true God and accept the teachings of the Master. To avoid the problems of contamination, they do not take a common meal beyond the sharing of the bread and wine, though my vision shows this is an unnecessary precaution.

When we first arrived here, Barnabas and Paul took ship for Caesarea to travel to Galilee to visit the community at Dalmanutha. I shall remain here longer, perhaps several weeks. When I return to Jerusalem, we must send someone to take my place here.

In the belief of the risen Master and his return,

Simon Peter

There was also a postscript:

From Levi: Simon Peter has not told you but he has performed several wondrous healings. The brethren recognize that the spirit of the Lord is upon him and even the gentiles say he is a magician.

For me, and I hoped for the Way, Simon Peter's accepting gentiles was good news. Most of the others did not approve, but they faced an accomplished fact that could not be easily undone. Moreover, the report of gentiles speaking in tongues—which John the priest and I interpreted as no more than a primitive form of ecstasy—greatly impressed the others as a sign of the Holy Spirit, and thus a warning that they should be cautious in trying to undo Simon Peter's work. Truly the Lord moves in mysterious ways.

I hoped Simon Peter's bold assertion of leadership would out-flank James's campaign to install himself as head of the community; but the immediate effects on the group were mixed. James suggested that Andrew and Thomas, along with Malachai, a recent Judean convert who had taken a liking to James, meet Simon Peter's request by going to Lydda to preach the good news "to our brothers in circumcision." And not being sophisticated, Andrew was delighted at the suggestion that he help his brother. When he left, so did Simon Peter's main support among the Galileans; Thomas's departure was less serious, but he was among the more intelligent.

Incidentally, I read Simon Peter's letter to any who wished to hear about it, but at the evening service James, a man of good education by Galilean standards, claimed the privilege of reading it to the whole community. At the end, he offered a comment masked as a prayer: "We of this mother community beseech the Most High, blessed be His name forever, to continue to bless Cephas's work now that he has left us to minister to others."

Had Andrew been present, he might have objected, but within the hour of James's suggestion, he, Thomas, and Malachai had been on their way to Lydda.

During the next few weeks, I noticed James remained circum-spect in his behavior. Simon Peter's shadow still hovered over him, and he was not yet ready for a direct challenge. I was satis-fied, though hardly elated, at the turn of events. The news of "cures" had raised Simon Peter's prestige, even more than his acceptance of Cornelius had troubled the ruling group.

I was satisfied until late one evening at my uncles' villa when a servant said a visitor waited in the atrium. He apologized for the lateness of the hour but explained that my friend Levi had said the message was of the utmost urgency—and secrecy. He was to bring it to my home and deliver it personally into my hand. I thanked the man and offered him the hospitality of the house, knowing that as an observant Jew he would not accept.

As soon as he left, I tore open the letter:

Quintus, it is I, Levi, who writes. Come quickly. Do not say anything to the brothers, especially James. Bring Andrew if you can, but only if you can do so in secrecy. Come to the house of Simon the Tanner, near the harbor on the south side of the jetty the Romans have built. Ask for me, not Simon Peter. It is urgent.

Levi was not among my favorite people. He had the mind of a tax collector: mean, suspicious, and neither very smart nor scrupulously honest. And, like many men of his weight, he was rather lazy. Yet the Master had chosen him—in keeping, I reasoned, with his mission to save sinners rather than to celebrate saints. Moreover, Levi was not a man to write me, a Greek, and ask for help if the matter were not powerfully urgent.

The next morning I borrowed one of my uncles' horses (I was not about to walk more than thirty miles to the sea), left a message for a servant to take to the inn, saying I had to go off on business and would return in a few weeks, then started for Joppa. My leaving would be looked on as a normal event. Further, I suspected there would be some relief, for during the past weeks I had felt my status changing from that of ethnic eccentric to gentile misfit.

I made it to Lydda before dark and spent the night with Aeneas, the elder of the synagogue of whom Levi had written. Andrew and Thomas were staying there as well. We spent much of the evening in conversation about the Master and the Way. These new converts were starved for information.

I managed a few minutes alone with Andrew and told him about the letter. His first reaction was to come with me, but I told him flat out I didn't fully trust Malachai. Andrew was shocked by my statement. "He's a devout man, devoted to the Way." I explained that I did not doubt his devotion, only that he might confuse loyalty to James with loyalty to the Way. If Andrew suddenly left with me, James would probably soon hear of it and guess, if not discover, the reason for the departure. Reluctantly Andrew agreed, and I promised to stop at Lydda on my return to Jerusalem and give him a complete report.

I slept a bit late the next morning but was still able to complete the short ride to Joppa by noon. My first task was to locate the merchant with whom my uncles did business and stable my horse with him. The beast was valuable and would not last a night in a seaport town if left in an unguarded stall.

Then I set out to find the house of Simon the Tanner. Levi's vague directions had led me to suspect I would have trouble finding it. I did. Still, I had been tiring of living in a small, walled city, and Joppa was so different from land-locked Jerusalem that I enjoyed wandering about for an hour.

The sea was scrubbing the sand and rocks with dark green waves, the foam retreating as if frightened by the touch of those solid objects. Several times I stopped walking and stood on the shore, watching the wind shift and cut an inch of spray off the top of the waves. The air smelled of sea and salt, of exotic cargoes being unloaded, of treated wood and wet canvas bleached white by sun and salt, as well as of fish, some only minutes from the sea, some several days out of water. The sounds were good, too: Surf pounding against the jetties and wharfs or lapping against the sand, voices jabbering in Greek, Aramaic, Latin, and harsh Celtic gutturals that merged with Semitic dialects.

Simon's house was small but dignified, situated, fortunately, at the other end of town from his tannery and the local slaughter-house. He did a small business out of his home, but his principal clients were merchants who brought large numbers of animals to the slaughterhouse, had them skinned after being butchered, the hides tanned, then resold them to other merchants. Simon had inherited the business from his father-in-law and clearly had no interest in it, leaving its operation to an overseer.

The Way was an obsession with him (I suspected it was not his first, nor would it be his last), and he bombarded me with questions. Still, I sensed something was deeply troubling him. I thought it was Simon Peter, but I did not want to know yet, at least not from a stranger.

Simon himself was short, rather heavy, much like Levi, a very bubbly man of about forty. From the name I had guessed Greek influence; and, indeed, though his mother was Judean, his father was a Jew from Cyprus.

As one would expect of a merchant in a seaport town, he was fluent in Greek and Aramaic as well as Latin. I had to spend several hours at his home, while his wife—who looked and talked very much like her husband—served us wine, bread, and a delicate white fish which she called "wolf of the sea." As I tried to eat, Simon's questions about the Master never slowed, even when his mouth was full of food. Crumbs, pieces of fish, and droplets of wine went spewing about the table.

Finally, he led me to the harbor to search for Levi. We found him, standing on the sand watching fishermen repair their nets for the next morning's catch. I would never have thought of Levi as being homesick for fishing, but the years at Dalmanutha—when he had been impressed onto the Galileans' boats—were probably as deeply etched in his memory as mine. The peace of the community, the presence of his family, and the expectation of the Master's imminent return must have made those days sweet.

Simon showed some tact in leaving us, though not before informing Levi that I had agreed to stay at his house during my visit, a pledge that came as a surprise to me. Levi had embraced me and given me the kiss of peace full on the lips, as had been the Master's fashion, a strong indication that he needed help badly. "Come," he said as soon as Simon had left, "and see for yourself. I'll give you only two words: a woman and melancholia."

Actually he had given me four words, but it was close enough for a tax collector. He led me along the beach to a section near a small mole, where a tavern was set back barely beyond the sand. Inside, it was dark, with the dank smell of stale, cheap wine and a strange odor of other fermented spirits, both mixed with the all-too-familiar musk of sweat from bodies of men who did manual labor in the sun. Once my eyes adjusted from the bright sunlight of the beach to the twilight of the tavern, I made out several clumps of sailors gulping wine and talking boisterously in Syrian-accented Greek.

At the back in almost pitch darkness, Simon Peter sat alone, a flagon of wine on the table in front of him. (I didn't ask where he got the money.) He was already drunk. I sat down beside him. He gave me a look that showed scarcely more intelligence than the gaze I'd seen in several hundred fish for sale on the beach. It took a full minute for him to recognize me, then he put his huge arms around me and gave me a slobbery hug that sent his flagon of wine emptying onto the sandy floor. "Innkeeper!" he bellowed. "Innkeeper! My clumsy friend has spilled my wine. Bring us another flagon. And be quick about it!"

The innkeeper, a fat, unkempt man, gave a surly nod but continued talking to several of the sailors. Simon Peter focused his eyes more or less on me. "Filthy scum in this place," he muttered in Greek. "Syrians, Egyptians, reprobate Jews, Samaritans, whores—male and female—of every size, color, and nationality. Name your slime and this little piece of Eden has it. We've even got drunken, adulterating—is that the fancy word?—followers of the Way. The Lord doesn't have favorite fornicators." He grinned triumphantly at his semiblasphemous paraphrase of himself.

The tavern owner slapped another flagon and a pair of cups in front of us. "One obol for this one and the last," he snarled.

"Pay the man, Quintus. You like to show off you're rich. Pay him."

I gave the man a coin. He bit it, then stuck it in his purse. There were no thanks.

"Have some wine." Simon Peter shoved the flagon toward me. It was a command, not an invitation. I obeyed, then almost threw up. The liquid, whatever it was, was red, sweet and would have sickened a camel. "See?" Simon Peter stammered, "even the wine is slime, red slime. Donkeys make water with better smell."

"Then why drink it?"

"Because it gets me drunk; and if I'm drunk maybe I'll forget."

"Forget what?"

"Forget who, not what. I don't know who or what. I'm not sure. Maybe I want to forget the Master, or maybe I want to forget her—this woman, Ishtar, not Naomi, but I'd like to forget Naomi, too." He paused and stared off somewhere. I expected that when he spoke again he would ramble off on another subject, but he kept to the topic. "I'm lying. I know what I want to forget. I want to forget Simon Peter, that viper who's betrayed his wife and his Master, both in the same bed."

I said nothing, only watched him inhale the wine.

"I love her, Quintus. I never knew what that word meant before, just something you gentiles talked about. A wife is sometimes a pleasure, often a pain, and always a duty. But I love this woman. I love her. She's not a promise or some sort of vision, gone into a cloud as soon as it appears. She's real, alive, warm. She loves me. More than anybody else in the world, she loves me, not John the priest or Mary of Magdala, just me, Simon Peter the rube, Simon Peter the oaf. Me, just me."

"And Naomi? What about her?"

"Naomi?" He stopped for a moment. "That's different. She's a good woman, but it isn't the same. Ishtar is different. We looked at each other, a middle-aged Jew and a young gentile, and all the evil pagan gods couldn't keep us apart."

I stared at the vile red liquid in my cup. "And?"

"And I've left her, Quintus. Left her. The only woman I've ever loved. Two short weeks like Adam and Eve and I'm abandoning her to go back to Jerusalem. Why've I done it? Why? Why, because Simon Peter's more than a rube, he's an idiot. What's this control a dead man has over me?"

He took another gulp of "wine." "To hell with 'em all," he said. "All of them, Caiaphas, Annas, and their whole family of bastards; Pilate and all the Romans who've ever raped or stolen— and that means every Roman ever born; and good old 'beloved' John the priest, the rest of the Eleven, that sweet smelling hypocritical Brother James, and I'm-better-and-holier-than-the-world Mary of Magdala. To hell with them, all of them!"

"And Quintus?" It was a silly question.

Simon Peter put his arms around me, tears welled up in his eyes, and he kissed me on the mouth. Like a good drunk, he could instantly shift from being angry to being maudlin. "Quintus, my friend Quintus. I love you, Quintus—not like one of your Greek queers, but like a man. You're my friend, my brains, my tongue. Good old Quintus."

And like a good old drunk, Simon Peter could instantly regain his former mood. "Good old know-it-all Quintus. Does any Greek know who his father is?" He laughed loudly. "Does any Greek care who his father is?"

I started to get up to leave. Simon Peter switched moods again;

this time he skipped over sorrow and went to deep remorse. "I'm sorry, Quintus, you're my friend. The only one except Andrew I can trust. I'm sorry, I'm sorry." Tears were running down his cheeks, still hot from his anger only a few seconds old, and he put his arms around me again.

I disentangled myself from the wet embrace and stood up. Alas, as I did so, I bumped the arm of one of the Syrian sailors and sent his wine spilling down his front. "You clumsy Jew bastard!" he shouted and pushed me back into the chair. He must have been drunker than he looked to mistake me for a Hebrew. In any case, ethnic misidentification was not the man's major error.

Simon Peter roared up in a drunken rage. A flick of his wrist sent a cup full of wine into the sailor's eyes, and a quick lunge brought his fist slamming into the man's mouth. As the Syrian reeled in shock, Simon Peter caught him—much as he had the banker in the Temple years before—spun him around and threw him out the door. The Galilean turned and faced the others, grabbed a bottle with one hand and a chair with the other. "Does anyone object to the way this clumsy Jew bastard threw that pagan pig out?"

There was angry silence. I ran behind Simon Peter and steered him out the door. His victim was sitting on the sand, groping for missing teeth. I pushed Simon Peter back up the beach toward the tanner's house. Neither of us was up to a drunken brawl. On the way, I stopped at another shop and bought a skin of wine. I knew Simon Peter well enough to realize he was at his worst stage, too drunk to think, not drunk enough to pass out. The sooner he went to sleep, the better off we'd all be.

"He has been a scandal," Simon the Tanner said that night after we had half-carried, half-rolled Simon Peter's bulk onto a pallet on the floor. "It all began so wonderfully. He came to us and taught about the Master. We heard his words and our belief grew stronger. Others heard, and they believed, too. And he had the gift of healing. Twice, once here and once in Lydda, he prayed over the dying, and they recovered. Were those not miracles?"

I ignored the question, and he continued: "Then a woman, now drunkenness. There're no secrets in a town this size. We've lost several people, and the faith of others has been weakened."

"He is a human being, and like the rest of us he sins."

"No, he isn't like the rest of us," Simon responded. "Not if we're serious about the Way. From all we've been told, the Master chose him; he's the head of the Jerusalem community. He's been touched with grace. He's worked several cures of sick people here that some people think are miraculous. He can't be like the rest of us. He must be a stranger to sin."

"No man can be a stranger to sin. To sin is part of our condition."

"Then how are we different from the rest, if we're sinners like the others?"

It was not a simple question, though I suspected he wanted a simple answer. "Well, we hope we sin less, although we can never be perfect. More important, when we sin we know it and ask the Lord's and our neighbor's forgiveness. We pick ourselves up, knowing a loving Father holds out His hand of love, which we can take by renouncing evil and trying once again to do justice to our fellow man. When others fail, we freely give our forgiveness."

His eyes said I'd explained too much, so I switched the subject. "This woman, do you know her?"

"I've talked to her once or twice, but I don't really know her. She's a widow, a gentile. She says her family was from Babylon, but she looks Egyptian to me. Her husband was a Greek from Alexandria, a merchant who worked for a richer merchant. He died a year ago. She stayed on here with her two sons. I think she still has connections with her husband's employer. Anyway, she buys and sells ships' cargoes. Not work fit for a woman."

"How did Simon Peter meet her?"

"She heard him talking about the Way. She came to a meeting or two in my house." He buried his head in his hands. "Am I responsible for this?"

"No," I reassured him. "Simon Peter and the Lord have personal problems; the rest of us can't share them."

*   *   *

I slept well that night; the sound of the surf was like a drug. It was past dawn when I awoke to find Simon standing over me. "He's gone," were the tanner's opening words.

I struggled to reach consciousness. My first problem was where I was and who was standing over me; my next was who "he" was and why I should care where he'd gone. Simon handed me a cup of cinnamon-flavored water. I rinsed my mouth and used the moment to orient myself. It all came back with rapid—and painful—clarity. "When?" I asked.

"Long before dawn. No one saw or heard him leave."

"Do you know where this woman lives?"

Simon gave me breakfast along with directions. I took my time eating and then walked slowly along the beach. I didn't relish breaking into a tryst at the critical moment. I also needed time to think what I would say when I arrived.

Her house was larger and more graciously designed and carefully constructed than Simon's. Obviously, a person of some means lived here. A servant ushered me inside the atrium, gestured toward the well cushioned benches, and said his mistress would see me presently. I looked about the garden. The plants were from the desert; the fountain was circular with three turtles spouting water into the air. I was not sure how one could make a fountain run in this flat terrain, further evidence I was not dealing with a flea merchant.

Any remaining doubts were shattered ten minutes later when Ishtar walked into the atrium. I had expected a flighty young girl who had been swept away in some sort of childish dream by an older man. Instead, I faced a mature woman in her thirties, not much younger than Simon Peter himself. There were other immediately apparent attractions. She was tall and lithe, her coal-black hair pulled severely back from her forehead and fixed in place by combs studded with small gems—the only jewelry she wore. Her nose was long and slender—Egyptian—her complexion as fair and smooth as a Greek's. Her lips were thin, with just a touch of henna to bring out their redness. Grace and beauty were the two words that leaped into my mind, though there was also intelligence in those large, dark brown eyes. She seemed as out of place in the world of Galilee as did Jephthania. I could easily have become his rival for this woman's affections; indeed, it would take some self-restraint not to try to do so. Her combination of fragility and strength along with beauty acted like an aphrodisiac.

She might have been Babylonian. The name certainly was. But from her delicate features I knew there was a Greek among her ancestors. And Simon may have been right: Probably she also had Egyptian blood. The Ptolemys, trying to keep the Egyptians as semi-slaves, had forbidden their troops to fraternize; but such orders seldom work even in the short run and never over as many centuries as the descendants of Alexander's generals had ruled Egypt. Her eyes had a slight slant, like some Orientals I had seen, and her accent in Greek was faint but evident—and seductive.

She walked across the garden and extended her hand, much as Mary of Magdala, but few other women in the Land of Israel, would have done. "I apologize for keeping you waiting, but I was in the midst of some urgent calculations; we're bidding on a cargo this afternoon, and I want to know exactly what the costs are. I am called Ishtar. You must be Quintus. My husband dealt with your uncles and I continue that association." She smiled. "And, of course, Simon Peter has often spoken of you."

I tried to smile back, but it was probably more of a clumsy grin. I felt awkward, as if I had eight fingers on each of my three hands.

"I assume you have not come to negotiate for your uncles." Her voice was a rich contralto.

I shook my head, still afraid to speak lest my voice betray an adolescent crack.

"He's here, asleep. That should answer your first question. Undoubtedly you have others." She snapped her fingers and ordered a servant to fetch wine and cakes. I asked for cool water instead of wine. I felt heady enough. When the man left, she said: "I am at your disposal."

I was unsure if the double entendre was deliberate, but it did not put me at ease. "I, I don't, I don't know where to start."

"You start with a lecture about the importance of Simon Peter to this movement of his, this 'Way,' and how he's a married man, a Jew, who has been committing the terrible sin of adultery with a pagan woman and has just twice more committed that sin with her this morning."

I could feel blood rushing to my face, partially out of embarrassment and partially out of jealousy.

"You remind me that he has a daughter, and you end with an eloquent plea to give him up, to let Simon Peter the man die so that Simon Peter the prophet can live and make goodness and justice flourish in the world." There was irony rather than venom in her tone, which is not to say there was no passion.

I nodded. "Those are the sorts of words I was hoping to find."

She stood up, walked over to the fountain, and made little waves in the water with her hand. "Neither of us is a child, and we love each other very much."

"I know. He told me so."

"He spoke the truth."

"He always speaks the truth." I laughed. "It is among his biggest faults."

"He must have been a terrible businessman and an unbearable husband." Her smile was genuine.

Neither of us said anything for a few minutes. She took her hand out of the fountain and picked up a small cake, looking at me with a steady, strange gaze. I was totally disconcerted. "You're very clever, Quintus. Simon Peter warned me about your mind and your tongue, but not your silence. You're letting my conscience and my desire fight to the death."

"I'm anything but clever," I protested. "And I don't mean to torture you."

"But you are, exquisitely. Still, it's not your fault—or mine or Simon Peter's." She started pacing around the garden. Her voice became sharper. "You've lived with these Jews like a Jew. Why can't they accept fate or the will of the gods or something like that? Why must they blame somebody for anything that happens? Why do they have to judge everyone by those silly, rigid rules Moses or somebody claimed to get from their god a million years ago?"

"They think they have free will to choose good or evil and that the Lord God has told them which is which."

She said something under her breath I didn't hear. I did not ask her to repeat it.

It was at that point Simon Peter came in. His bloodshot eyes gave a full report on his previous day. Where he had found the energy for early morning sin was not apparent. He said nothing to either of us, just took the cup from my hand and filled it with water—twice—stuffed a piece of cake in his mouth, then flopped down on one of the cushioned benches.

I looked at him closely. He was suffering from yesterday's— and probably the day before's—wine, but more than a bundle of much deserved pain was sitting there. This was not the panicked oaf I had chased seven years ago, fleeing from the gore of Golgotha. There were obvious physical changes: He had lost about twenty pounds, leaving him big but lean. His beard was neater, not yet what a genteel Greek would sport but not that disheveled imitation of John the Baptizer. There was also a different odor, though the aroma of stale wine made that less evident. He bathed more often and changed his clothes frequently, a fact for which Matthias's Essene obsession could claim more credit than I.

More important than physical appearance, he had, no less than James the Master's brother, an aura of authority about him. Now he was used to making decisions—albeit not always correct decisions—and to defending them with intellectual argument. His bass voice had developed good modulation; that is, he understood one need not shout to be heard. His Greek was now excellent. His speech was often earthy and sometimes vulgar, even profane; but as I have mentioned, he had the illiterate's ability to mimic, in this instance my style of grammar and syntax, so that he sounded like a man of substantial education.

As I sat there I realized for the first time that he might be sexually attractive to women, and his presence, not merely the content of his message, could move men and women to listen to him. I confess to twinges of envy, not only because of his impact on teaching the Way but also because of his effect on a woman like Ishtar.

No one said anything for perhaps ten minutes. Our silence was interrupted by a clerk's entering the atrium and whispering something in Ishtar's ear. She excused herself and left. As soon as she had gone, Simon Peter walked over to the fountain and dipped his head in the water, shook like a big dog, then quaffed two more cups of water. "I've changed my mind, Quintus. I'm not leaving, and that's final. Go back to Jerusalem, tell them what's happened. Let Andrew lead the community."

"Andrew is at Lydda; and even if he were at Jerusalem, you know who would take over the community."

"If that's the will of the Most High, so be it."

"And the gentiles to whom you've been preaching? What happens to them?"

"My words speak love and repentance, my actions speak love and adultery. Maybe James and the others are right. Their feet stand in the path of righteousness, not mine. I preached to the gentiles, and now I'm in bed with one of them and I have no desire to leave that bed—ever. It's my mattressed tomb."

"So you're abandoning the Way?"

"I can live the Way without the community."

"Absurd. To do justice, you need others."

"Quintus, you don't know what a burden those people are. They drive me to rage."

"Naomi and Jephthania, what justice will you do for them?" It was not a fair, or even a decent, question.

"You know the Law. I can divorce Naomi."

"I know the Law. I know something of justice, too; and I remember the Master's comment."

"Quintus, you're a son of a bitch."

I did not respond; he was absolutely correct.

After a few more minutes of silence, he said very softly, "There's nothing more to say. I love you like my own brother, probably more than I love Andrew. He's a clod, well meaning but a clod, just like I was before I met the Master. I'm not going to spend my life waiting for some second coming to found a kingdom. If he were coming, he'd have been here years ago. Somehow we got it wrong, but then we got most things wrong."

"You know my belief: He has come again, if he ever left us; the kingdom is within us—now."

Simon Peter waved his hand. "No more arguments about such things, not ever again."

I still didn't have the sense to give up. "What about the people you've 'healed'? The beggar at the Hulda Gates in Jerusalem, the two people here? You once said the Master had touched you. Don't these cures prove it?"

He looked away from me. When he spoke, his voice sounded distant, detached. "I don't know. Maybe I don't even care. I'm tired—tired of being a wet nurse to a community and waiting for a dead man to make good on a promise to come back to life and make me a prince. All I really know is that I love her, Quintus, I love her and I won't give her up. I want some *now*; I'm tired of hoping for a *then*. Go back to Jerusalem. Be gentle but be truthful."

I left.

III
ANTIOCH
(38–64 C.E.)

1

❧ My stay in Jerusalem was brief. Despite Simon Peter's request, I did not say anything to the others about his difficulties at Joppa, except to John the priest and, when I had stopped at Lydda on my way back, to Andrew. He was beside himself with grief and anger; it took a great deal of persuasion for me to convince him not to confront his brother. The priest reacted more intelligently. Having endured two years at Dalmanutha without his wife and children, he said, he understood loneliness; and having seen how close to dirt peasants lived, he understood how a man might grasp a chance, even an immoral chance, for love and beauty.

I hoped Simon Peter would rejoin us quickly. Sooner or later he would. Of that I was sure, and John the priest agreed. But in this case, "later" came very late.

It was ironic that we had had no real news of the new communities at Lydda and Joppa until they had existed for some months, while stories of Simon Peter's sins flew back to Jerusalem within a week of my return. James the brother of the Lord—or James the Just, as people were beginning to call him—was visibly and, I believe, genuinely disturbed. At first, he said nothing; he did not even question me. Indeed, most of the time he continued to pretend that I, a mere God Fearer, was not really in "his" community. Others, however, were after me like wild dogs on a stray cat. "Wait and ask Simon Peter," was my standard response. No one found that satisfactory. To ease pressure, I spent a great deal of time at my family's villa.

In the early afternoon, about ten days after the gossip had first reached us, Malachai arrived at the inn. He closeted himself with James the Just for several hours. That night at evening prayer, James, rather than one of the Galileans, presided. At the conclusion of the ritual of bread and wine, he said sadly: "My brothers"—I suddenly noticed no women were in the room—"we have confirmation of very grave news. Our brother Malachai would speak to you."

325

His story was essentially accurate, though more florid in some details than strict adherence to the truth would allow. When he was done, Matthias asked me how Malachai's report squared with what I had seen. I spoke the truth, but ended with a plea to be forgiving toward Simon Peter, not only because of the Master's general principles, but also because Simon Peter's faith had created our community and kept it together and his devotion had borne our burdens for many years. Now, near exhaustion, he had fallen under the weight that we, his brothers and sisters, had laid on his shoulders. Our duty was to help him back to his feet when—not if—he asked for aid.

Then James the Just stood up again. "My brothers, we measure obedience to the Most High, blessed be His name through all eternity, by obedience to the Law. We measure devotion to Joshua, the Master, by adherence to his principles. No one questions the power of the faith Cephas once had. Yet at it strongest, faith without good works is dead. And here we do not see good works, only scandal surrounding the former head"—I carefully noted the term—"of this community. He has broken the Law of Moses by openly committing adultery and, worse, with a pagan. In so doing, he has also violated our ideals—Joshua's ideals—of holy purity."

James looked around the room, allowing his words a few moments to register. "The roots of Cephas's sin run less in lust than pride. He would not listen to the voice of this community. He insisted on some private revelation and felt obliged to preach to gentiles. That practice is dangerous though acceptable. But he went further. He tried to mix Jews and gentiles in one community. He is the first victim of his own tragic decision."

I waited for the old saw. I was not disappointed. "If a man lies down with dogs," James continued, "he will get up with fleas. Cephas has been contaminated by pagan lust because he thought he was immune to the temptations to which all flesh is heir." He cleared his throat, a warning to pay special attention to his next words. "I rule [I record his exact words] that Cephas is expelled from this community. To rejoin us he must first renounce this gentile woman and do public penance."

I started to protest, but John the priest was quicker and more eloquent: "To expel is not the Master's Way nor can it be ours. He chose Simon Peter to lead us, fully knowing his weaknesses as well as his strengths. We have benefited from those strengths; this community exists because of them. We cannot, consistent with the Way, expel him when he displays weakness. The Master has commanded us to love one another and to forgive one another, for we, too, are sinners who need forgiveness. We must act with compassion, not anger; our goal must be reconciliation, not rejection. We hope to become saints, but we know we are now sinners, every one of us, whether our sins be those of lust, pride, greed, or . . . ambition."

There was a stirring among the brothers. Simon Peter had been their hero. They probably knew more of his weaknesses than he—or I—had realized; but most of them also recognized his power. And he had been specially touched by the Master; to that all the Galileans had publicly attested.

James sensed the change in mood. The tone of his reply was less authoritarian than his initial pronouncement, though not quite forgiving. "John is correct. We must keep love before us, love of the Most High, of Joshua, and of Cephas—but also of other brothers who are now with us in the Way and of those who might otherwise be moved to join us. What will these people think if they see one of our leaders living an adulterous life with a pagan? Scandal will drive people from the Way. Out of love for our fellow man as well as for the commandments of the Most High and Joshua's words, we must put a distance between ourselves and this sort of conduct. We must act severely, not from anger, but from rejection of sin, compassion for others, and in hope of reconciliation."

"How does expelling Simon Peter reconcile anything?" James ben Zebedee asked the question James the Just had probably been praying someone would be foolish enough to pose.

"In two ways. First, to others we say those who stand in the Way cannot do such evil deeds. Good works, not sins, are the fruits of Joshua's teachings. Second, we remind Cephas that we are not pagans living outside the Law. We hope our action will tell him that it is he who has cut himself off from us—and from the

Most High. He may return to us, be reconciled to us, just as he may return and be reconciled with the Most High, whenever he wishes. We would receive him with open arms and open hearts. He need only renounce this woman and do some form of public penance to acknowledge he understands his sin and to tell those scandalized by his conduct that he has become a new man. Love, forgiveness, reconciliation, these must be our goals."

He looked around the room and could see he had scored points, though he may not have won the game. Seizing the opportunity presiding gave him, he led us in a recital of a psalm and then sent the brothers to their various houses to eat.

After that night, I knew my association with the community in Jerusalem was nearing an end. James had become the leader; and, day by day, he was making his position more secure. The Galileans had been upset by his "ruling" on Simon Peter. Not being men of quick intelligence, they had been outthought and outmaneuvered. But most of them were not stupid and they realized they had been led where they would not go.

Their brooding resentment threatened James's status, but he cleverly dissipated that danger by edging the Galileans out of Jerusalem. He said he agreed that spreading the good news, as Simon Peter had done with the Hellenes during the time of persecution, was imperative; and, during the next few months, he persuaded most of the remaining Eleven to carry the word to "brothers of the circumcision" around the Diaspora. Andrew and Bartholomew stayed in Lydda, though James asked them to take care of the brothers in Joppa as well—and to preach only to Jews or those willing to convert to Judaism. Matthias and James ben Zebedee remained in Jerusalem, but John ben Zebedee went off with Simon the Zealot to Tarsus; Thomas and James ben Alpheus set off to the east, for Persia; Thaddaeus for Cyprus; and Philip and Levi to Alexandria.

My own status as a God Fearer became more tenuous each day. Not once but a dozen times, brothers I barely knew asked when I intended a full conversion. At first, I offered a witty retort: "To what? Do you wish me to leave the Way?" For a period it put people off, but I realized I was facing a choice I was not yet prepared to make. For me full conversion to Judaism posed no personal theological problems, but I thought, perhaps more because I was a Greek than because I was a follower of the Way, it would betray the universalism I saw in the Master's message. I confess, too, that it would have involved a commitment; and I was still unable to make full commitments; I was yet a Greek, as Simon Peter would remind me, in that the Lord God was more in my mind than my heart.

I took advantage of the mission of Philip and Levi to accompany them to Alexandria. I wanted to get away from Jerusalem, and I also wanted to see Alexandria again, visit my teacher Philo, and find out what had happened to a dozen friends. In turn, Philip and Levi needed my help. They knew nothing of the city or of Egypt; indeed, they hadn't the foggiest notion of where that nation was located, only that it was far from Galilee and Jerusalem. Finally, both men also realized they needed help with their Greek. Levi's was passable though vulgar and ungrammatical. Despite his name, Philip's was primitive. I lost many hours tutoring them.

We walked to Joppa to find a ship. I left Levi and Philip with Andrew and then went alone to Ishtar's house. I didn't want to embarrass Levi or Simon Peter—or Ishtar.

The same servant let me in and swiftly brought Simon Peter. He looked younger and happier than I had ever seen him. He had also taken more steps toward culture. Rather than the usual colobium, he was dressed in a toga. It was simple, but the cloth was of a very fine weave. His hair and beard had been cut and shaped by a professional barber, making him a very handsome man. Indeed, given his Greek, he could have passed for a dark, well-to-do Hellene, perhaps a Macedonian. I also noticed, and with some exertion of will power refrained from commenting on it, a hint of perfume.

For a few minutes, we sparred with questions about our friends, both avoiding serious issues. I fumbled ahead by asking how he occupied himself. "I've been helping Ishtar by wandering around the wharfs and beaches, listening to sailors' gossip and getting a different view of cargoes than the captains give buyers. A woman can't do those things. I've gone out a few times on fishing boats. The water's different, but seamanship's seamanship. Ishtar and I are thinking of buying a couple of boats and hiring crews to run them. She has a man who knows how to cure fish with salt, like your relatives do at the lake. She's a real woman, Quintus, smart and tough like Mary of Magdala, but with a warm, soft side."

I finally got to the point and asked if he knew about the decision at Jerusalem. "James's decision, you mean?"

I nodded. He did not need to say anything more, and he didn't. We embraced and I went to find a ship.

Alexandria was not as I remembered it. The streets were more crowded, the people less friendly, the prices higher, and the heat more oppressive. More disappointing, my visit with Philo was brief, for he was consumed not only by students and his own writings but also negotiations with Roman officials about troubled relations between Jews and gentiles in the city.

My close friends had long since parted. I had, after all, been away sixteen years. I found only one person whom I knew well, a fellow visitor named Sotion, a good Greek I had first met in Athens when we were lads. Later we had sat together at Philo's feet here in Egypt. Now Sotion was living in Rome, earning good fees by tutoring sons of the rich. As two middle-aged pilgrims trying to recapture their less mature years in the educational process, we enjoyed each other's company.

He was a decent sort, too verbose and pompous for a truly close relationship, but quick and smart. Although a bit thick around the middle, he still showed some of the athletic build that, in his youth, had allowed him to be a superb wrestler. (I also noted with considerable envy that he had retained far more hair than I.)

Sotion showed some curiosity about the Way, though he predicted it would disintegrate soon. "How many times," he asked, "have we seen these millenarian sects emerge from the dark holes of Asia or Africa, predicting the imminence of some miraculous event that will end or radically change the world? I can recall a half dozen. Most died very swiftly, the others swiftly. Thus history contraindicates success for your movement, even if the Romans leave you alone—which is less than probable."

Given what Pilate had done to the Master, I could offer no rebuttal.

"This 'second coming' your people expect is intriguing: The schedule is indefinite and the parameters of your man's theologizing present some interesting permutations on the standard scenario. Are you certain he wasn't a Stoic? Well, whatever he was, you must soon redeem your promise, and we both know you can't. So there you are."

Once again, I tried to explain my own theory. "Fascinating," Sotion commented. "In a nutshell, your theory substitutes multiguity for ambiguity. It deactivates the problematics of an exact schedule, but at the price of increasing the probability of Roman counteraction. Having everyone love his neighbor, my dear Quintus, is something no government with imperial ambitions can tolerate."

Again I did not try to convince Sotion. To do that I would have had to have convinced myself; and, so far, that goal eluded me. In any event, we spent pleasant evenings at his inn, drinking and talking, and drinking.

During the day, I was less of a help to Levi and Philip than I had hoped. As James the Just had ordered, they restricted their missionary activity to fellow Jews. Alexandria boasted an ancient, large, and prosperous Hebrew community; thus targets abounded and we made a few converts. More unpleasant, however, were the increased tensions between Jews and gentiles. In fact, shortly before we came there had been serious rioting against the community, due in part to the special privileges the Empire accorded Jews and to the perennial pagan objection that they endangered the safety of others by not respecting local deities. These gods, so the reasoning went, would surely take offense and seek revenge against the entire area, not merely against particular offenders.

As a God Fearer, I was allowed into the synagogues with Levi and Philip, but I was not trusted, a radical change from my youth—or the way I recalled my youth. Soon, seeing some of the distrust of me rubbing off on the Galileans, I stopped going out with them. I continued, of course, to instruct them about living in a gentile city and to help them with their Greek. Levi, already having had the rudiments of the language, progressed nicely. Philip, however, was close to a complete loss. He was as slow of tongue as of mind; and, while he managed to understand much of what was said, he always sounded like a peasant trying to speak an aristocrat's language.

Six weeks after we met, Sotion returned to Rome, and I soon began to get edgy—and lonely. I had come to appreciate Philip and Levi more. They were good men, completely dedicated to the Way. Truly, something remarkable had happened to them and the rest of the rabble who had abandoned the Master that Passover night. Even through their bumbling and ignorance, one could see their faith, a faith I could only partly feel in my own mind. Thus I could envy them.

Alexandria was changing Philip and Levi, at least their outward appearances. Both now bathed regularly and, with my money, had purchased some inexpensive but presentable clothes, which they kept reasonably clean. Moreover, seeing how the Jews of the city lived, they had trimmed their hair and beards. Each had served as the other's barber, so the handiwork was hardly artistic, but no longer did they look like vegetation blown in from the desert.

I was surprised to find that beneath all that dirt and hair, neither was ugly. Philip was slender, almost girl-like in stature, more Arab than Jew in appearance had the clothes been right. Levi was the shorter and, of course, heavy, with close-set black eyes that moved like those of a hungry and not very trustworthy ferret, a scar from his tax-collecting days, no doubt. Philip was only an inch or two taller than I, but he had the loping stride of a man many inches taller.

I was also pleased to learn that neither man was stupid, though it is always difficult to sort out ignorance and stupidity. The Greek culture of the Alexandrian Jews was rubbing off on them, improving not only Levi's tongue but both their minds. Still, with all their improvements, neither was stimulating company. Besides, I needed at least the occasional companionship of a woman.

I seriously considered making a discreet visit to a temple of Isis. One could, I found myself rationalizing, partake of the women's joyful sexual rituals without accepting their theology. In the end, however, I took long walks in the early morning and late afternoon, when the African sun was not baking down. The streets gave me a strange sensation; they were both familiar and, at the same time, alien.

One afternoon, about an hour before sunset, while I was walking near the docks, my name was called. I had heard that voice only once before, but I immediately recognized it. Ishtar was sitting in a large litter next to a sea captain who looked like a Scythian. The two had been arguing. As I walked toward them, the captain got out of the litter and said curtly, "Very well, madam, if that is your highest price, I have to take it. I hope you'll sleep well tonight knowing you've stolen from fifty people."

She was wearing a scarf across her face, but I could tell from her eyes she was smiling. A Scythian should have known better than to expect to get the better of a Babylonian, or an Egyptian, or a Greek, in bargaining. She let the scarf fall from her face and motioned for me to come inside the litter. "What are you doing here?" I asked.

"I live here now. My husband's employer has agreed to let me try to do here what I was doing for him in Joppa. He is a brave man to hire a woman."

I hesitated, then started to speak, but she was quicker and considerate. "I left Simon Peter in Joppa, about three weeks after you last saw him. I should hate you, Quintus."

In my puzzlement, "Why?" was all I could think to say. That Simon Peter would eventually return to the Way I had always believed, never that Ishtar would leave him. And I could think of no plausible reason for her to hate me.

She took my hand and held it gently between hers. "Because you took him from me. Just before you saw him, he was my wild, Hebrew prophet. He might have looked like a big, handsome Greek but underneath he was an untamed Hebrew barbarian. Then the night you saw him, he became impotent—full of guilt and despair and soon wine. I'd thought that once he'd left me and gone on that binge when you first came to Joffa to 'save' him and yet came back to me—I thought then I'd won my battle against that cruel Jew-god and his angel Joshua. Between your two visits, we had two months that could have lasted forever. And I don't just mean passion, but tenderness and understanding. He's much more intelligent than he—or you—believes and much more vulnerable."

I agreed but I thought it best to be quiet.

"Then you came again, a reminder of his 'sin,' of his 'duty' —and of his wife and child and his precious community in Jerusalem and his joyless, judging god—and that crucified apparition that haunts his guilt-ridden soul."

One of the litter bearers approached us; she snapped her fingers and motioned for him to back off. "We could have compromised on religion," she went on. "I don't care about it. It's all shit." [I blushed at hearing a respectable woman say such a word in Greek. Servant women often use that word in one of the Aramaic dialects; but, in a foreign tongue, vulgarities do not shock.] "I'll pay to burn a sheep to whatever Jews worship, or to Astarte or Baal or Isis. I don't believe in any of them, but I'll do my civic duty by supporting local gods and buying off provincial demons."

"Simon Peter would not be Simon Peter were he anything but a Jew and a prophet."

She let go of my hand. Immediately, I missed the warmth of her touch. "I know that now," she said. "And you set off all sorts of memories that left him a eunuch. I couldn't fight those memories. I loved him in bed and I loved him out of bed. But he couldn't live with those memories, and I couldn't live with his guilt and his wine."

"Those sorts of things come and go," I ventured weakly.

"The impotence? I know that; he probably did, too. Sex drew us together, but it wasn't what kept us lovers. And I could understand an occasional binge. I feel like one myself on occasion. For months after my husband died, I drank too much wine. But we both knew what was wrong with Simon Peter—that avalanche of guilt you set off."

"Forgive me," I said. "I wouldn't have deliberately hurt him—or you. I didn't ask him to leave you."

"You didn't have to. Your eyes, Quintus—you have very expressive eyes, and you judge people. Simon Peter says you think like a Greek, but you judge like a Jew. You convicted him of sin, my Jew-Greek. I know"—she put a finger softly on my lips when I tried to respond—"you didn't condemn him with your tongue. Your eyes delivered the verdict and the death sentence. Andrew told us about what that pious buffoon James and the people at Jerusalem had done. It angered Simon Peter that people to whom he'd given so much would have such short memories. But it only angered him. You shamed him, Quintus. He read it all in your eyes."

"I'm sorry," I muttered. And I was, genuinely, profoundly, desperately.

"I know, and that's why I forgive you. I've learned that much from Simon Peter." She leaned over and kissed me on the mouth. As a reflex, my hand moved to her shoulder and pulled her body toward me. Her mouth opened softly and her arms went around my neck. We kissed passionately for a few moments, then I slowly pulled away.

"Now you have something else for me to ask forgiveness for," I said, trying to hide my embarrassment.

Ishtar was instantly and irrationally furious. She clapped her hands for her bearers. "Home!" she snapped and pushed me out of the litter.

I took the next available ship to the Land of Israel. We sailed along the coast, never out of sight of land. At night we dropped anchor, setting out again at first light. The winds were fair, the seas calm, and the vessel rather large; thus I experienced only some queasiness, not my usual misery. The trip gave me the opportunity to sort out my mixture of emotions about Ishtar, Mary of Magdala, and, of course, Simon Peter. Unfortunately, one cannot always make good use even of the finest of opportunities, and when we docked at Caesarea, having bypassed Joppa, I was as confused as when we left Alexandria.

Before deciding whether to walk back down to Joppa or find another boat, I took time to visit Cornelius, the catalyst for Simon Peter's disaster. I had not known what to expect, so I introduced myself merely as my father's son. I met a formal, polite Roman officer, now retired. He had known my father—I inferred their relations had been less than cordial—but he offered me the hospitality if not the warmth of his house.

It was not until after dinner that I identified myself more fully. As a result, I spent a week with Cornelius and his entourage. Like the Jews at Lydda, these gentiles were hungry for information about the Master and the Way. I couldn't leave them without a promise, though I didn't know how I could keep it, to send someone to teach them more.

I took a small ship to Joppa and quickly went to the house of Simon the Tanner. After we had embraced and exchanged the kiss of peace, he immediately began to tell me of the progress the Way was making among both Jews and gentiles.

Despite what they had heard was the wish of the brothers in Jerusalem, here the people still lived in the sort of loose association Levi had written us about. Bartholomew came out from Lydda several days a week to offer instructions and join them in the sharing of bread and wine. Andrew had initially done so and probably would visit again when he returned from Galilee.

At Simon Peter's suggestion soon after he had first made converts, the community had chosen Simon as its leader and was still meeting in his house for prayers and sharings. It was, however, a practice that might have to stop because there were now too many people—seventy-five he estimated, including women and children—to accommodate when all showed up. It was, he concluded, not the worst of problems.

I waited a full hour before broaching the critical questions, the whereabouts and status of Simon Peter. The tanner looked surprised that I didn't know and proceeded to give me a terse but full report. "It was about a month after you, Levi, and Philip sailed for Alexandria that one of the brothers came to my house and told me that Ishtar had left Simon Peter and had gone to Egypt. Nobody saw him for at least another week. I tried twice, but the house was locked and guarded. Then one morning some fishermen brought him in, more dead than alive. They had found him swimming more than a mile from shore. He was angry and kept asking why they hadn't left him to drown."

At first it was difficult to imagine Simon Peter trying to take his own life, but not when I recalled the depths of despair to which he could plummet. I wanted to ask Simon several questions, but I waited.

"My wife nursed him for a few days. He barely spoke, just stared out toward the sea. I was afraid he'd try again. I think he might have, but then Andrew and their cousin from Bethsaida arrived with the tragic news."

"What tragic news?"

"I guess if you hadn't heard about Simon Peter you hadn't heard about his daughter."

Images of that beautiful child Jephthania flashed into my mind, though she was no longer a child; at fourteen she was a woman. "What happened? Was she killed?"

"Worse." His voice dropped to a whisper: "An attempted rape, at least the message said only 'attempted.' She became palsied, probably the Lord's punishment for tempting some poor man."

I was aghast. That beautiful child, humiliated, abused, turned into a thing, wounded physically and psychologically, then paralyzed for life. I badly needed to hear the Master reassure me that the Lord God was a loving Father who cared for his children, not a cruel demon who was indifferent to their suffering.

I didn't hear the rest of the conversation; if I did, I have no recollection of it. Once more I found the merchant with whom my family did business, borrowed a horse, and set off for Jerusalem, to get additional transportation to Dalmanutha, even a camel, if need be.

When I arrived in the Holy City, I decided to visit the community, but only after stabling the horse at our villa. At the inn, James the Just acknowledged my presence with only a curt nod. Matthias, James ben Zebedee, and a few others were glad to see me, the rest were distant. I tried to keep in mind that the Galileans were gone as were most of the Hellenes. The people here were largely Judeans, at least a dozen of whom had joined since James the Just had arrived. Those newcomers knew Simon Peter by name and reputation only, and the latter was indeed an Oriental stew.

It took an hour to get Matthias alone, but even that told me little I hadn't suspected. He spent the first twenty minutes delivering a monologue about the way the community was nearing economic disaster. Apparently James was a worse administrator than Simon Peter, who at least had had the sense to cultivate good relations with Josef of Arimathea and me. But James had no time for Josef. The Just One was too busy praying in the Temple, which to Matthias was, of course, an abomination before the Lord.

We'd recruited few additional Hellenes; but the new members, mostly Judeans, were as poor as the Galileans. James himself had brought a large sum to the community, but he was insisting all the men put tassels on their cloaks and buy phylacteries. The community had to bear much of the cost, since most were too poor or too lax to have fulfilled those particular religious obligations. The main burden of all of this was falling on Matthias; and with Levi gone, there was no one even to help with the accounts.

I understood the severity of these problems, but I needed to know other things about Simon Peter. "Yes," Matthias said, finally stopping his talk about money, "he came through here. It was doubly sad business. He loved his daughter very much."

"And?"

"And he publicly confessed his sins. James the Just gave him the kiss of peace, we all embraced him, and he left."

"Left?"

"Yes, he went down to Galilee."

"When?"

"Almost four weeks ago."

"Will he be back?"

Matthias shrugged. "I doubt it. He understands his position and he accepts it. He's out. In disgrace. James says what happened to Simon Peter's daughter was the Lord's punishment for his sins."

"Ridiculous!" I blurted out.

"I'd say something more direct," Matthias smiled. "But James believes it and a lot of others believe it. Worse, Simon Peter believes it; deep in his heart, he truly believes it."

"And James is now completely in command?"

Matthias nodded. "Completely. He has the Master's blood in his veins; he's educated; he's like a Pharisee; the people in the

Temple, not the priests, but the scribes and pilgrims, love him. He competes with the priests for holiness; and he wins. We're a different group, Quintus. We say the same words, but we're not the same. We tithe—the poor, we tithe! And we fast, too."

"We always fasted."

He smiled again. "Yes, but now because it's a holy thing to do—as if it pleased the Most High to hear our bellies growl. At least it saves us some money. And we keep the Sabbath like we were fanatic Temple priests. When the trumpet in the Temple tower blasts on Friday, we're near death from preparing to rest on the Sabbath. And we say the Shema every morning and evening, alone but out loud. At meals we even recite the Pharisees' thanksgiving: 'Blessed are you, O Lord, for not having made me a gentile; blessed are you, O Lord, for not having made me a woman; blessed are you, O Lord, for not having made me one of the lax people of the land.' That's funny. The Master was a lax man of the land and so were all the Galileans. By James's standards just about every Jew in Jerusalem is lax, but we thank the Most High because we aren't what the Master was or what we still are. It's crazy."

Matthias shook his head and ran a hand through his thick hair. "I don't know. I don't like some things about the Essenes; they've got too many trivial regulations and act like a clan rather than a people. Now this community is getting that way. Hell, we are that way. James is a good man, a holy man, but I wonder if he understands what the Master was all about. We still love each other, but we don't love outsiders."

He stopped and looked at me, then put a huge paw on my shoulder. "And you're an outsider, Quintus; worse, a gentile. You know how we Essenes feel about strangers. I accepted you because the Master loved you. At first, his word was enough for me, then I realized he was right, and not just about you. You and Simon Peter have made me realize the Master really meant it when he said all men were brothers. But James. . . . Well, we have to love him because he's the Master's brother. I only wish he understood more."

I embraced Matthias and said good-bye, troubled by a premonition I would never see him again. He must have felt that same shiver of death for his embrace threatened my ribs, and he kissed me on both cheeks. As I was walking out the door, he said softly, "Prepare yourself for when you see Simon Peter. He's a different man, if he's still a man."

I went down to Galilee as quickly as I could. It meant borrowing a camel and riding alone, the first distasteful, the second dangerous, to Jericho and then up the Jordan. I didn't even stop at Scythopolis; I could leave the camel to the salting factory at the lake. I rode straight into Dalmanutha, pushed away the curious brothers and sisters who swarmed around me—or the camel— gave my sister Theodora a cursory hug and kiss, then entered Mary's hut. She was working at a table. I thought I saw a message of welcome in her eyes, but her words were curt: "I wondered when you'd be back. He isn't here. He's not a member of the community."

"Why?" I was confused and, I confess, angry at the coldness of her greeting. "Have you no pity?"

"Pity? What has pity to do with it? I grieved with Naomi for weeks when she had no husband to comfort her. The women here have nursed Jephthania. But Simon Peter chose not to join us. He did not come here on his way to Capernaum, nor has he come here since he has returned. And, speaking of pity, I notice you asked only about Simon Peter, not about his wife or daughter, the victims of his neglect—and adultery."

I did not argue. I wanted to see Simon Peter—and Naomi. Besides, Mary had a point: I had been insensitive. I knew the way to Capernaum and the house that had belonged to Simon Peter's mother-in-law, just opposite the synagogue. What I found there was heartbreaking. Jephthania was sitting in the small courtyard. When she saw me, her eyes filled with terror; she tried to cry out but only a guttural, half-choking sound, something like "Help!" came out. I stood still, unsure whether to run to her or away from her. Fortunately Naomi came out of the house and put her arms around her daughter and let her weep in safety.

After a few minutes Naomi looked at me. "Sit down. Don't take a step toward her, and don't try smiling at her. A man's smile terrifies her. It isn't hard to guess how that blood-drinking, pig-eating, son of a camel-loving whore got close to her."

"How is she?" It was not an intelligent question.

"See for yourself. She's palsied. Her right arm is useless. She can move her right leg a little, but it's too weak to hold her weight. We can only hope it'll grow stronger."

"Her speech?"

"You've heard every word she remembers—a cry for help." I had read that people palsied on the right side quickly regained their speech, but Jephthania seemed to be an exception.

"What can I do?"

"Never come near her unless I'm with her, or Simon Peter is."

"I'm sorry; I didn't know."

"You do now." She hesitated, as if she hadn't meant to be quite so sharp. "Life is hard," she said in a half-apology. "If you want to talk to Simon Peter, he's probably down by the water—what's left of him."

Capernaum has no harbor, but just south of the town there was a sandy beach of sorts. I took the camel—dragged him more than led him—there and found Simon Peter sitting in the shade of a willow, staring out at the mountains of Gadara across the lake. He must have heard me, camels are not quiet beasts; but he did not look up. I tethered the animal and sat down beside him. "You're back," he said after several minutes. "I saw you go by a little while ago."

I didn't know quite how to respond. I thought a bit and said, "I saw her."

"You saw the punishment for my sin."

"What's this foolishness? What happened to Jephthania had nothing to do with your sin, only the sin of that bastard who assaulted her."

He shrugged his shoulders, as if his case were too obvious to argue, and stared out at the lake. I looked at him. He was not the handsome Simon Peter I had left in Joppa, but an aging image of the man I had first met. His hair and beard were again unbarbered and uncombed; he was once more wearing an old and dirty colobium. It could have been the one from a decade earlier. Worse, he was much thinner than I had ever seen him, less Simon Peter the muscular fisherman than the reedlike John the Baptizer, but without John's fire in his eye, indeed, without any fire at all.

I tried again: "What did the Master teach us about the Lord?"

I got no response, but I continued anyway. "Did he not teach us about a loving Father? Would such a God punish Jephthania for *your* sin? He might well punish you; perhaps He did in sending Ishtar away from you and in having the community at Jerusalem expel you. But this. . . ."

"Yes, this," he suddenly blurted out. "This. How do you explain what happened to Jephthania? How do you explain a father's love and that poor child? Why would He punish her? She has no sin."

"I don't, I can't explain it, any more than Job could."

"I'm not a slobbering, pious jackass like Job. But if it would help Jephthania I would be. I'd be anything. I prayed; I begged. 'Whatever you ask in my name,' the Master told us, 'the Father will give you.' Well, as soon as my cousin brought the news, I started praying. I prayed and I prayed and I asked in the Master's name, I asked in my name, I asked in Jephthania's name. People say I have some of the Master's healing power. I touched that beggar at the Temple gate and told him in the Master's name to walk, and he did. Caiaphas was probably right: The beggar was a fake. I don't know. But there was a woman at Lydda and a man at Joppa I laid hands on and prayed over; both got better. When I came back to the lake, I laid my hands on Jephthania and prayed over her. And she screamed in terror—terror at me, her father."

He picked up a stone and skipped it expertly along the lake's surface, as he had been able to do when he was blind. "I 'purified' myself," he went on. "I went to Jerusalem and 'confessed' my sin to those hypocrites, to that pompous, holier-than-the-Lord-God-Himself James. I crawled to those sheep. But the Lord didn't help Jephthania. So much for the Master's promise, no better than the one that he'd return. The Lord must be punishing me by crippling her. Why else? Why else would a loving Father strike down an innocent child? Answer me! Answer me!"

I shook my head.

"If the God of Israel is quiet, can't the philosopher of Greece say anything?"

"No one can explain evil. We have to bear it. There is no other choice."

"Yes, there is. I found it at Joppa, but those meddling fishermen stopped me."

"A choice for you, but for Naomi and Jephthania?"

"I could take them with me to the middle of the lake, capsize the boat, and it would all be over."

"That might be your choice, but would it be theirs? Do you have a right to decide they will die because it's what you want?"

He put his hand to his head. "I don't want to argue, Quintus, I don't want to think. I don't want to live. Have you got some wine on that stinking beast?"

"No, no wine, and if I did I wouldn't give it to you to drown in self-pity." I stood up, and he got up with me, though much more slowly, as if it were expected of him. I decided to take a wild chance. "Simon Peter, the attack on Jephthania was a tragic blow. You have to hate it, and you have to mourn what she—and you—have lost; but you also have to live with it. You've got a different problem, another one of forgiveness and love. You look for a reason to hate. You need hate, you feed on it. Deep down you can't forgive the Master. Now you've got a reason to hate the Lord God; that's why you can sit here all day. You're not mourning for Jephthania; you're enjoying feeling superior to the Lord. He's wronged you and you feel superior to Him just like you feel superior to the Master because he wronged you. Now you've got an excuse to sit here and rot. You enjoy that sick pleasure."

Probably his hitting me was a good sign, though at the time it didn't seem so. When I came to, he was wiping my forehead with a wet cloth. My jaw ached, and I thought several teeth were loose. I sat up slowly, and when I did Simon Peter put his arms around me, laid his head on my chest, and wept, sobbing as pitifully as had Jephthania.

The years slipped quickly by. In many ways they were good. I rejoined the community at Dalmanutha, went to see my family at Scythopolis regularly, and managed to finish the final draft of my book. There were still tensions in my relations with Mary, but my encounter with Ishtar had taught me to cope with that particular pain—outwardly at least.

During this period, I got to know Theodora more closely. Despite my father's protests, she had remained with the community and claimed to have known happiness for the first time in her life. She became a full-fledged member of the group, baptized in the Way without embracing Judaism. When I discussed that problem with Mary, she merely shrugged her shoulders. "In Jerusalem, one behaves like a priest. In Galilee, one acts sensibly. We are 'people of land.' [It was the term that Pharisees—and James the Just—used to disparage the religiously lax.] One should not expect us to know any better than to follow the Master's command to share with others."

The Master's word was, indeed, taking on the character of mustard seed. The Way was spreading across the Land of Israel, even Samaria; and it was also being heard—and listened to—by foreigners. Theodora and I were not the only gentiles at Dalmanutha. Others, mostly from Gadara, though also a couple from Pella, were baptized. And in turn some of them spread the good news in the Dekapolis. Seeing Mary's openness to gentiles, I asked her to send people to Caesarea to help Cornelius and his entourage. Within a few months, we had a small but prospering community there.

From passing travelers we heard more news about communities at Damascus, Tarsus, and Antioch. Most of these missions were probably the fruit of the Hellenes of Jerusalem whom Simon Peter had commissioned; but some also, we hoped, were the fruit of Dalmanutha.

Jephthania got no better, not physically. She never learned to walk again; her right leg did not regain enough power. A stick or a crutch was of no help because her right arm was also paralyzed. The best she could do was to lean on another person and half hop, half walk for short distances. Nor did her speech return. Psychologically, however, her improvement was vast. Gradually, the terror receded from her eyes; and, over time, she ceased to panic when a male came near.

Despite her infirmity, she was still beautiful. Naomi washed and dressed her, carefully combed her long red hair and helped her with all the human tasks, some of them embarrassingly personal for an adult. But more than anything else, Jephthania developed an aura of love and, no less, of courage, which in a strange fashion comforted all of us who knew her. She could smile—not a full smile, for the right side of her mouth sagged, but a smile that revealed acceptance of her own suffering and warm understanding of others'. In looking back, I recall that, after the first few months, I never felt sorry for her. She had lost an immeasurable amount in physical capacity, but she had turned that loss into a spiritual gift to aid others.

Jephthania and Naomi remained fully participating members of the community at Dalmanutha, though they continued to live in Capernaum. One of the men built a small cart in which Jephthania could sit and Naomi or Simon Peter could pull. Occasionally he joined us at Dalmanutha, but only occasionally. He never presided at the sharing of the bread and wine or instructed the people in the Way. Nor, during those years, did I ever hear him reminisce about the Master. When at the community, he sat quietly alone or with me or with Naomi and Jephthania, never with Mary or any of the others. The members respected his privacy and his pain.

At first, with my help and Naomi's, he fished like the poorest fishermen. He and I held nets outside the reeds, while Naomi ran through them making as much noise as she could. The small fish that came scooting into our nets we gave to Mary for our communal meals.

A few other members had boats. In fact, Simon Peter's old vessel was still in use, but Mary made no offer to return it. Justice surely did not require her to do so. She had taken care of Naomi and Jephthania during all the years Simon Peter had been in Jerusalem; and the community needed fish to survive, just as its new captain deserved to retain his status. He was good at his work.

After two years, however, Mary asked Simon Peter's advice about buying a boat for sale at Gennesaret. The three of us looked at it, and he decided it was basically in good shape. She bought it and appointed him captain. That made life somewhat better for him, though he still did not join the community.

Nor did he fully rejoin his own family. As I explained, they had lived in a house owned by Naomi's mother. Andrew was married to Naomi's sister, and lived in another section of the house. Naomi's mother died long before the assault on Jephthania, and Andrew's older children moved into their grandmother's section. When Simon Peter returned to the lake, he slept there too, apart from Naomi and Jephthania.

He was most tender and loving with his daughter, helping her to regain strength, then being her right leg as she leaned on him. Gradually, he took over from Naomi much of Jephthania's care; and, better than anyone, even Naomi, he could decode the sounds from her throat into words and ideas. Never did I see him lose patience with her. She was, indeed, his hair shirt, the mirror of his sin, and yet the cause of what little joy he had left. She, Naomi, and I were the only three people at whom he looked. He tried to avoid close contact, especially eye contact, with others; I noticed that, when he was obliged to talk, he kept his eyes focused on the ground and the conversation as short as the rough manners of Galilee allowed, which was short indeed.

What was said between Simon Peter and Naomi about Ishtar, I have no idea. She must have known there was another woman, everyone else in the community did. In any event, their marriage had become much more serene, though, with Simon Peter's sleeping in another section of the house, less intimate.

The world around us changed in those years. Death visited my family several times. My mother died quietly, its gentle coming while she was asleep altogether appropriate to the sweetness and passive suffering of her life. My elder uncle, Myron, was stricken by palsy as he rode from Pella back to Scythopolis and passed from us several days later. Theophilus, his brother, retired, leaving the family's far-flung interests to his sons and nephews—my cousins. We saw each other seldom, the essence of good relations with blood kin. He asked if I wanted a share, but was pleased when I declined. He gave me, instead, a sum of money that would allow me to live in some comfort for the rest of my life. And, since I got along well with my cousins, I could still utilize my family's contacts around the empire.

Rome, too, felt the hand of death. As I have mentioned, Tiberius had died about seven years after the crucifixion, replaced by Gaius Caligula, who soon became absolutely mad and reigned only about five years before his own troops murdered him. Still, he lived long enough to have a profound effect on Judaism and the teaching of the Way. He almost forced a revolt against Rome by insisting that statues of himself—he had by then declared himself a god—be worshiped in Jerusalem. I need not rehearse the details of that conflict beyond noting that had provincial Roman officials not been sensitive to Jewish taboos, the land might have run with blood; and I am certain the Romans would not have distinguished among followers of the Way and other Hebrew sects.

Caligula also became enmeshed in the bloody internal politics of the Herods. Agrippa, grandson of Herod the Great and half-nephew to Antipas, had been living in Syria and Rome, putting distance between himself and family feuds while cultivating the favor of the imperial clan and regional Roman officials. Since Herod the Great had murdered assorted wives and children, including Agrippa's father, and since Antipas possessed no higher sense of morals than his own father and despised his half nephew to boot, one cannot justly accuse Agrippa of paranoia, though he, too, possessed in full measure his family's penchant for ruthlessness.

Agrippa's problems with money and looseness of tongue had caused Tiberius to imprison him, but the young Herod had managed to cultivate both Gaius Caligula and the family of Caligula's own successor, Claudius. When Tiberius died, Caligula released Agrippa, gave him a gold chain of the same weight as the irons that had shackled him, and appointed him to the tetrarchy of Philip, which ran on the other side of the lake from us. Furthermore, Gaius styled Agrippa "king," a title Antipas had vainly sought from Tiberius. Antipas was foolish enough to let his vanity—or his current wife's vanity—move him to try to use his own Roman influence against his half-nephew; but Agrippa was far more adept at Roman intrigue, and Caligula soon deposed and exiled Antipas, giving his tetrarchy to Agrippa. Rumor has it "the Fox" died in Iberia.

A few years later, Claudius changed the status of Judea and Samaria from provinces under direct Roman rule to a dependent kingdom, and appointed Agrippa monarch, giving him jurisdiction over much of what had been his grandfather's domain. For Jewish nationalism, this was a step forward; and, after Caligula's sacrilege, appointing a king who could both pretend to be Jewish and to rule in Jerusalem was a wise decision for Rome's policy of firm but peaceful control of the world.

For us, it was less happy. Agrippa attacked our community in Jerusalem. His excuse was that we were betraying the Law of Moses: By admitting unconverted, uncircumcised gentiles to our ranks and sharing food and housing with them, we were breaking the Covenant the Lord God made with Abraham, Isaac, and Moses. Why, if that excuse were genuine, he attacked the brothers in Jerusalem, where James the Just kept out gentiles, and not in Samaria, Joppa, or Dalmanutha, where the alleged sins were in fact being committed, I do not pretend to know.

Having been away from Jerusalem for some years, I can only speculate about whose favor Agrippa was trying to win. Without doubt, his general policy was to appear to Jews as a true Jew, though to the Romans he put himself forward as a cultured Hellene. The Sadducees in the Temple elite would have been pleased, since they always feared our group, even as they feared the Pharisees, the Essenes, and everybody else. Some Pharisees might have been concerned over what they heard about our communities outside the city. But, given James the Just's reputation as a Pharisee's Pharisee, I doubted that sect wanted to see us wiped out. The Romans were a third possible audience; but their troops were no longer in Jerusalem and news that Agrippa had executed a few followers of a Jew crucified more than a dozen years earlier would hardly have elated them.

My only explanation, only feebly supported by evidence, is that, as a Jewish nationalist and a manipulator, Agrippa could well have been upset by the prospect of his people closely associating with foreigners. (That he himself did so was, of course, a different matter.) His moving only against the community at Jerusalem might have been due to his inefficiency, to his desire not to start widespread blood-letting that would make the Romans nervous about his rule, or to his belief that if the community at Jerusalem were erased the movement would collapse.

Among the first casualties were James ben Zebedee and Matthias. Agrippa had them arrested, brought to the Antonia Fortress overlooking the northwest corner of the Temple, and had their heads cut off. It was all done swiftly and matter of factly: quick arrests, no trials, and bloody death. No time for heroic deeds or words beyond speedy and silent prayers; just murder, plain and simple. It was the same fate Agrippa's half uncle Antipas has bestowed on John the Baptizer.

James ben Zebedee was not among the more intelligent men I have ever met; he misunderstood the Master's message about what the kingdom of God entailed. He was not a man of iron will or saintly disposition; yet, if he often wavered and sometimes ran, he had remained faithful to the Way over the hard years, expecting in vain the Master's imminent return.

Matthias—I wept when I heard the news. Essenes are bundles of contradictions, I had been told, people who love and hate with fierce intensity. That description was apt. And no one had worked harder for the Way or given more of his hairy hide than this big bear. Without him, we could not have long existed as a community; without his openness to change, we would have foundered in other ways. The Holy Spirit had made the correct choice to fill the vacant place among the Twelve that Judas's betrayal and suicide had created.

It was almost noon, ten days before Passover, when the soldiers arrived to arrest Simon Peter. It had been six years since I left him at Joppa and thirteen years since the crucifixion. I was sitting under the willows along the lake at Dalmanutha, thinking about what I would do now that I had finished my work on the Master's life. The book closed with the empty tomb and reports—I still could not call them "facts"—of various appearances. The work had taken me longer than I had expected and I was tired. I most certainly did not want to write about the movement's course since that fateful Passover, not yet at least.

I was curious but not concerned about the troop of Herodian cavalry trotting up the road. As soon as they were out of earshot, I closed my eyes and reflected on my own life. I was now in middle age and, I suspect, suffering from the post-partum depression writers always experience after completing a project. But my self-indulgent indolence had no effect on Simon Peter's fate, for I could not have outrun the soldiers to Capernaum had they been on foot, much less on horse.

Barely more than an hour later, I saw the cavalry returning at a brisk canter. In the center of the formation was a big civilian who looked very much like Simon Peter. The soldiers were long gone before I could make it to the road to get a better look. As quickly as I could, I walked to Capernaum and learned the troops had indeed arrested Simon Peter and were taking him to Jerusalem for trial. I was frightened—for him and also for myself, for I knew I would have to follow him.

2

✣ On my way to Jerusalem I made a brief stop at Scythopolis. My ostensible purpose was to pay my respects to my father, though he had been at the lake not three weeks earlier to enjoy Theodora's company and to go through the motions of a visit with me. He was aging rapidly. Since my mother's death, it had become more and more plausible that he had truly loved her. He had acted as he thought, in that wanton Roman way of possessing and dominating rather than sharing and cherishing. But his grief, and his efforts to conceal that grief, made his attachment seem less shallow than it had during her life. My heart softened.

Our relations, however, were only barely easier. Yet that in itself was positive, for I had no doubt—though he never spoke the words—he blamed me for Theodora's decision to remain at Dalmanutha. And she was the one person in the world whom he both loved and could act toward as if he loved.

I confess my real reason for stopping was to consult my Uncle Theophilus. He, however, was in Jericho, visiting old friends and colleagues, an excuse to follow the caravan trails once more. I found him there without difficulty, except for that involved in riding a camel.

As usual, he gave me his wisdom honestly and fully. "If you want my advice, go back to Scythopolis or go on to Philadelphia. I hear they've got a new school of philosophy there. If that doesn't please you, go over to Athens or Alexandria. Forget what you've been doing the past dozen years. Agrippa likes to pretend he's a wenching, drinking, gambling libertine. And he is all of those things, but he's also a clever bastard, utterly without regard for money or decency. And he twists the Romans around his little finger like no Jew since his grandfather has been able to do."

"But what if I can't leave these people? What if I must get Simon Peter away from Agrippa before he's murdered?"

Theophilus sighed. "My sons and nephews are all soft. Your uncle and I—and your father, too—grew up in a harder world. We understood the enormous role fate plays in our lives and knew better than to oppose it. Every man's days are numbered; some have fewer than others. A wise man accepts that fact and does not try to extend his own—or another's—beyond what is set." He sighed again. "But, because I am partially responsible for your upbringing, I must share responsibility for this fault, though I lay it more to your Hebrew associations than to your Greek education."

He sat back and took a sip of wine and smiled at me. "What," he asked, "does one do whenever public officials choose to follow hurtful policies?" He paused, but before I could speak he answered his own question: "One reaches for one's purse. The only problems are whom to bribe and how much. 'How much' because bribery is a fine art. Too little creates enmity; too much, greed. 'Whom' because every man does not have a price. There are honest men, just as there are double cheats who will take a bribe and then act honestly. Well, I'll make a few inquiries. Jericho is under Agrippa's jurisdiction, so these people do a great deal of business—of various sorts—in Jerusalem."

My uncle's solution was as good as his sources, and his purse as open as his heart. He gave me the name of an Idumean captain who was stationed in the Antonia, part of which Agrippa used as his prison, and the tavern the captain frequented during the hours he set aside for private business. "What you want is expensive," Theophilus warned. "It will take at least several people to cooperate, and there's a real risk—which they will all understand—that Agrippa will execute them in place of an escaped prisoner. It's a cruel but not unusual punishment; and it does tend to keep the troops on their best behavior."

He handed me a letter made out to a silver trader in Jerusalem, instructing him that I was on my way to Alexandria and to give me whatever sums I required as an advance against my inheritance, which unfortunately was invested in another enterprise at the moment. Theophilus waved my thanks aside, saying he'd deduct the amount, whatever it was, from my money on deposit in Scytholopolis. "Now," he went on, "I suspect the best way will be to have a warrant ordering your friend's release to someone else's custody. For that you'll need a true artist. Here's the name and address of a man in the Lower City. Memorize it and destroy it. Give him seventy-two hours and he could produce a copy of Caesar's will that would convince the Roman Senate. Alas, he, too, will be expensive. Your uncle and I have used him on occasion." Theophilus actually blushed. "Business affairs, you understand."

I nodded.

"One final point: Don't trust the Idumean very far. He's a professional, with a reputation to maintain as a 'facilitator,' but the executioner's ax can be a powerful temptation to betrayal. Give him an incentive to stay bought. Put up no more than half his price when you strike the bargain, the rest when you're certain your friend is free—really free."

It was all sage advice. I had not known my uncle was quite so at home in such matters, but then I realized that for forty years he had managed to turn a profit dealing in a dozen Oriental countries under a wide variety of regimes that shared only oppression, greed, and corruption.

Finding the Idumean in Jerusalem turned out to be more difficult than I had imagined. I arrived in the Holy City five days before the beginning of Passover, and the place was already filling up. The crowds meant the soldiers—supposedly now Jews instead of Romans, but in fact more often than not half-Jews or gentile mercenaries—were busy. During my third night's vigil in the captain's tavern, I made contact. We talked, circuitously that first night over wine, more directly the next morning over fruit and cheese. Then we bargained. Next we haggled. The sum he first demanded was outrageous; after hours of negotiating, he reduced it to mere exorbitance. His excuse was precisely as Theophilus had noted, the number of people who would have to be bought and the mortal risk they ran.

Eventually, we came to terms and I agreed to half the payment in advance. One point, however, I found irksome. "You must be involved in the escape," the captain insisted.

"Why me? I'm an amateur."

"Perhaps, but your presence will give the guards a chance. As a Greek of obvious importance—Agrippa likes to think of himself as a Greek and he likes to be with important people—you'll be credible when you present the warrant. A Jew would not be, unless he were from the High Priest's family. [Why not John the priest, I couldn't help asking myself.] The officer of the watch will keep the warrant and show it to whoever investigates the escape—and he'll describe you. So will the guards. It will be their pass to freedom. You'll need Agrippa's seal and at least four armed guards to make the release plausible."

"Where can I get Agrippa's seal?"

"You could forge one, or. . . ." From under his cloak, he produced an official looking document with a wax seal at the bottom. "Or you can buy this one and have it transferred. A good forger might be able to do that, or at least make a close duplicate."

We haggled again before arriving at a price.

The plan was similar to what Theophilus had suggested. I would show up at the Antonia at the time the Idumean would specify, enter, present the warrant, take custody of Simon Peter, and march him away with my guards. All very simple, but also all very dangerous. I did not like entering the Antonia. If anything went wrong, I would already be imprisoned. Beyond that risk, my family was sufficiently well known that there was a possibility of my being recognized or the guards later giving a description that would enable others to recognize me, especially if it were essential I be identified as an important Greek.

That latter danger meant I could involve my family no further. It also meant that, like Simon Peter, I would have to flee the Land of Israel, for Agrippa's jurisdiction included Galilee as well as Judea. And Scythopolis would be barred, too; for Agrippa was a wily negotiator who would want my head for thwarting his plans.

The forger was expensive, though open to negotiation. Still, when we were done, much of my inheritance was gone.

The next problem was getting guards. I could not use my family's people, and the brothers, if I could find any, wouldn't fool anyone if they pretended to be soldiers.

The only answer was Cornelius from the community at Caesarea. He had an entourage of guards and as a God Fearer would have a perfect excuse to go up to Jerusalem for Passover. Timing was the great difficulty. Given the possibility of having to wait for a ship between Caesarea and Joppa, it would take him at least two days and probably longer to travel to Jerusalem and as long to get him a message, even if I could find a horse—and a messenger.

Clearly I needed a fellow conspirator I could trust. With my family excluded, only the brothers were left. But where were they? Matthias's execution undoubtedly meant that the inn had been raided and might still be watched. I decided to risk wandering around the Essene Quarter, but with the precaution of wearing an Arab burnoose and a kaffiyeh on my head to hide my blondness— though each passing year made it plainer I was also concealing the approach of baldness.

I walked by the inn. It was in full use, but I saw no evidence of any of the brothers. Indeed, in the entire Quarter, I saw no one whom I recognized except a few Essene sympathizers. Since I had been away six years, I could not be sure whether the brothers were gone or just different people now. I stopped at several inns—not at Matthias's, I could not bear that—paid scandalous prices for watered rot-gut wine, and listened to conversations. I learned nothing except that it was unlikely I was being followed.

My courage fortified with that probability, I decided to take a further chance and go to one of the houses we had used. I chose the farthest from Matthias's inn, a rather decent-sized place on the edge of the Lower City. It had been owned by an elderly woman named Ruth. She was the mother of a newer Hellene, John Mark, younger cousin of Barnabas, our initial convert on that first Pentecost. Ruth had not joined the movement, but she had been sympathetic to the Way and during my time in the community had allowed us to put people up in her house. She also had a bit of money in addition to her house. I am afraid we thoroughly exploited her hospitality and her purse.

I stood by the wall, making sure I was at the right place. Cities change in six years. I was reasonably sure and rapped on the gate in the wall. There was no response to my first set of knocks, so I tried again. A few more minutes went by. As I was about to try a third time, a peephole opened in the gate and a male voice asked: "Who are you and what do you want?"

"I'm an old friend of Ruth's family. I have come up to the city for Passover and am here to pay my respects."

"I'll give them to the family." With that the peephole slammed shut.

I assaulted the door again, this time with my foot. The peephole opened again. "I have your message. Now go!"

I took a chance and removed my kaffiyeh. "Mark, John Mark," I whispered.

I could see the eyes behind the gate staring at me more curiously. "Who are you?"

"Mark, it is Quintus."

"Who is Quintus?"

"The man who instructed you in the Way, nitwit," I hissed.

The gate opened and Mark greeted me with the kiss of peace, then took me through the atrium and into the house. It turned out that the place was bulging. No less than six of the brothers, four of them with their wives and children, were hiding there. Agrippa's "persecution" had been erratic. Of the dozen or so brothers arrested, only James ben Zebedee and Matthias had been executed. The others had been flogged as badly as Simon Peter had been, but then released.

Soldiers had seized the inn, and one of Agrippa's friends had taken it over as his own property. John the priest had fled, taking his family with him. No one knew where, though I heard guesses that ranged from Bethany to Samaria to Ephesus. James the Just was holed up in the Temple. The Sadducees didn't like it, but the Pharisees in the Sanhedrin had insisted; and Agrippa, always the sly diplomat, had respected the notion of sanctuary. Many of the other brothers were hiding in the Lower City or in Bethany and Bethpage. We at Dalmanutha, of course, had been untouched except for Simon Peter's arrest, and none of the others in Ruth's house knew of attacks on the communities in Lydda, Joppa, or Samaria. In all, it seemed that casualties had been few, but fear great.

In a perfect world, John Mark would not have been among my first choices as a messenger. My real reason may have been that I could not put much confidence in a Hellenistic Jew who wrote Greek as poorly as he did. But it was not his skills as an author I needed, only his body. I got him alone as quickly as I could and put the problem to him. He was reluctant to go. Courage was not among his greater virtues; I sympathized and searched for a compromise. He need go only to Lydda and give the message to Andrew, who would get to Joppa, take a boat to Caesarea, and bring Cornelius and his men back. It took some persuasion, but Mark agreed. Getting him to leave immediately required an additional investment of time.

Fortunately he could ride a horse, though not very well. I purchased a beast for him for an enormous price and sent him on his way. With luck he would find Andrew that night; and, if there were a boat available, Andrew could be in Caesarea by the next afternoon. (I also gave John Mark enough money for his own expenses and Andrew's.)

I spent a miserable five days. It was the morning of the last day of Passover when Andrew arrived at Ruth's house. Cornelius, he said, was at the Temple, in the Court of the Gentiles. We could meet there in an hour. He thought it was better to meet in public, where there would be no aura of conspiracy. Andrew had suggested Solomon's Portico. It had a nice ring to it.

Our meeting was brief. Cornelius fully grasped the situation and suggested he take my place. I protested, but he insisted. His clinching argument was that he could carry it off. I might find pretending to be a powerful official more difficult than playing the role of an important Greek. Years of imperial service had conditioned him to command. He would have had a good chance of obtaining the release even without the warrant. "But if you are recognized?" I asked.

"I'll be recognized as a Roman officer; I'll be in full uniform and so will my soldiers. No one will question my word in the Antonia. The Jewish people may think Agrippa is king, but he and his men know he rules only at our sufferance. And Romans, I am ashamed to say, have a reputation for suffering very little."

"And after?"

"After? I won't announce myself as Cornelius, and there's no reason why my face should be known to any of the Herodians. But if it is . . . I'll take my chances. I am a soldier. I've spent my life taking chances, and for the first time I'll be doing so for a truly worthy cause."

I shall not pretend not to have been relieved by Cornelius's decision, but I like to think I gave in for reasons of efficiency rather than timidity.

The Idumean had offered two options, that night or the next. Cornelius thought it wiser to move immediately. On the last night of Passover week, the guards might have eaten and drunk too much and would be less likely to be fully alert than the next night.

My account of the escape is secondhand, but both Cornelius and Simon Peter were reliable witnesses. I waited at Ruth's house with the other brothers. We prayed while Cornelius and his four guards rode up on horseback to the Antonia shortly before midnight. They had a pair of extra horses. There were troops on duty not only at the entrance but also patrolling the street outside. Evidently, Agrippa was worried about a rescue attempt, for this was not what one would expect outside such a formidable fortress.

As protection for the conspirators, the Idumean had explained, we would not know which guards had and which had not been bought. Thus Cornelius put on his most imperialistically haughty air and treated all of Agrippa's soldiers and officer of the watch as the scurvy scum they undoubtedly were. He tossed his reins to a sentry and ordered in Greek, "Take care of these animals. We are on Caesar's business." Only the commander of the watch dared ask a question: "What do you plan to do with this prisoner?"

"As a Roman soldier, I plan to carry out my orders. I recommend you follow the same course—and promptly. His friends plan a rescue."

"They could never get through my troops."

Cornelius arched his eyebrows and sneered as if nothing could be easier. "Be that as it may, my good man, we want to be sure this seditionist is nailed to a cross."

Not unnaturally, the commander was angry at the insult, and he seemed reluctant to cooperate. It was not clear whether he had not been bribed and was genuinely honest or had been bribed and was playing a skeptic's role to which his men could later testify. But he scrutinized the warrant with special care—twice. Cornelius stood there, hands on hips, staring all the while, saying nothing but communicating utter contempt through his facial expression. Finally, the commander said, "Follow me."

"You do mean '*Please* follow me, sir,' do you not?"

The commander glared at Cornelius, then, meeting the Roman's cold stare, lowered his eyes. "Yes, sir."

The two officers and Cornelius's guards followed a jailer down into the prison itself and walked along a narrow stone corridor. At the end, there was a cell lit by a small lamp. The jailer turned the key and opened the door. Inside Simon Peter sat on the floor dead asleep. Two sets of chains, one attached to each side wall, prevented him from lying down. On duty in the cell were a pair of soldiers. "Unchain the prisoner," the commander ordered. The jailer did as he was told, but Simon Peter managed to sleep through the process.

The jailer shook him. "Get up! Put on your belt and sandals!" Simon Peter tried to stand, but fatigue and long confinement in one position made it difficult. Cornelius leaned over and slapped him hard across the face. "Get up, pig!" Two guards grabbed Simon Peter's arms and jerked him to his feet. Another threw him his belt. He still looked half-asleep as he tied the rope around his waist and awkwardly stuck his feet in the sandals. He was not so groggy, however, as to betray any recognition of Cornelius.

"Get your cloak!" the Roman ordered. One of the guards slipped a noose around Simon Peter's neck and pushed him out of the door.

"Would you prefer a chain for the prisoner?" the commander asked.

"No, thank you," Cornelius replied. "The noose and this"—he pulled his sword half out its scabbard—"should keep him in line. He has a long ride ahead and he'll need his hands on the horse. We wouldn't want him to break his neck and cheat the gibbet."

With that, Cornelius and the guards marched out of the prison, climbed on their horses, and with Simon Peter in tow went off into the Passover night.

It was well after midnight when the knock came at the outer gate. Rhoda, one of Ruth's servants, ran through the atrium and opened the peephole. "Who is it?" she asked.

"It's me, Simon Peter."

Rhoda let out a squeal of delight and came running back into the house. "He's free! He's here! He's here!"

"Where is he?" Mark asked.

"Outside the gate."

"Outside the gate?" Andrew bellowed. "Let him in, you stupid twit. Don't leave him standing there."

Simon Peter entered. He was even dirtier and more unkempt than he had been at the lake—and thinner. But there was light in his eyes. He kissed Andrew first, then me, and finally Mark, then embraced the other brothers—only one of whom he knew. "Where are the rest?" I asked.

"A few streets away. Horses would attract attention here. They have a horse for me and one for you," he said to me. "Neither of us can stay."

I knew he was right. Cornelius was in as much danger as Simon Peter and I would be also if the Idumean were put to the torture. I doubted he would speak on his own, at least not soon. My arrangements with the silver dealer for the second half of the bribe required a wait of several more days.

"Where will you go?" Mark asked.

"To another place," Simon Peter replied.

In three minutes we were back on the street where Cornelius and his men waited. The horses jogged off, their bulk forcing people still carousing in the streets to give way or be trampled. At the gate guarded by Herod's three magnificent towers, the sentries ordered us to halt; but, as soon as he saw the Roman uniforms, the soldier in charge waved us through, and we were off at a canter. I was not comfortable in the saddle, but Simon Peter was miserable.

We rode for the better part of an hour before Cornelius stopped to rest the horses—and Simon Peter and me. "We probably have until dawn. The Herodians change the watch then. I'm hoping our leaving by the road to Joppa will make them think we're going north to Galilee or east to Jericho or even south to Beer-sheba and Egypt. Agrippa is too wily himself to believe we'd leave by the gate to the road we're really taking. That might buy us more time."

Fifteen minutes later we were cantering again. After forty-five minutes, we rested the horses for a full half hour and got them water at a cistern. Then for the rest of the night we alternated walking at a brisk pace and cantering. At dawn, we were at the outskirts of Lydda. There Cornelius and his men left us, and Simon Peter and I set off to walk. Our behinds were blistered and our legs cramped, but it felt good to move under our own power.

At Lydda, the brothers fed and bathed us, gave us fresh clothes, and walked with us to Joppa. There we took a ship bound for Caesarea, Berytus, and Antioch on the Orontes, the largest city in the Orient. Later we learned the Idumean captain never claimed the other half of his money. Agrippa, who probably had some knowledge of the man's second career as a "facilitator," put him to the torture, then killed him, along with the commander of the guard and the guards who had been stationed in Simon Peter's cell. Fortunately for Cornelius, the Idumean identified me, not the Roman, as the one who engineered the escape. It was fame that I was glad to accept. The pain was slight, for Agrippa was dead within two years and the Romans took over all of Israel as a province under their direct rule.

3

✥ When our ship stopped at Caesarea, we thought it prudent to stay on board. While we were not sure what fate had befallen Cornelius, we knew that, even had he returned safely, Simon Peter's coming to his house would heighten any suspicion Agrippa's soldiers might then or later have about him. And we were also concerned about our own safety. Although a detachment of Roman auxiliary troops was garrisoned in the town—it had been and soon would again become the seat of the Roman governor of Judea—Caesarea was then within Agrippa's jurisdiction; and his people might well have been alerted to Simon Peter's escape.

Not until we docked at that lovely city Berytus did we feel free to stroll about on dry land. Up to this point, Simon Peter had said nothing to me beyond what had been necessary for our escape. But he was looking at people when he spoke and his voice was full again, without the self-pity of recent years. I was with a new person, one more like the Simon Peter who, on that Pentecost Sunday so many years earlier, had set out to convert Jerusalem with a tongue of fire. More like, yet different. The fire of Pentecost was again burning, more steadily if not so brightly.

The most obvious changes were in maturity, confidence, and humility. At Pentecost, he had been been driven by raw courage energized by a powerful, if inconstant, faith. For a time, that courage had overwhelmed his natural fear and feelings of incompetence. His activity had been propelled more by frenetic energy, which he and the others diagnosed as divine inspiration, than by cool calculation, for, with good reason, he had been unsure of his faith as well as of his capacity to recruit, organize, and lead a community. As a result he had been full of both arrogance and self-doubt, of power and indecision.

Now, however, his faith was again strong but it was not overwhelming his intellect—an instrument he had learned how to use. He accepted his own fear and sinfulness as impediments to be overcome, not as causes for panic and despair. Somehow, the trauma of his arrest, imprisonment, impending execution, and escape had erased much of the self-condemnation of the previous half dozen years. I did not understand the process, but I was nonetheless grateful.

We sat down on the beach, reluctant to return to the cramped, smelly quarters of that bouncing hollow splinter. "I've sinned, Quintus," Simon Peter said matter-of-factly. "I realize that; and I, only I, know how deeply I've sinned. My flesh was weak; my human desires overpowering. Ishtar is a beautiful woman and a warm, intelligent, loving human being. Part of me will ache for her as long as I live. I wept from the pain of it when she left me; that pain would make me weep right this minute if I let it. She was part of my bone and my soul. Do you know what it is to have to give up a woman you love with all your being?"

I avoided his question by asking one of my own. "How can a philosopher know anything about the human heart?"

He looked at me and laughed. "Maybe you do understand. I've seen you look at Mary—and she look at you." He laid his big hand on my shoulder. "It hurts, old friend, it hurts."

He was silent for several minutes as we watched a pair of terns chase after a darting sand crab that zigzagged back to its hole a bare millimeter ahead of an open beak. "We've been together since we followed the Master around the lake towns. I tell you my life story and you teach me intransitive Greek verbs and try to teach me about philosophy. You're better with verbs."

"They're easier for peasants to grasp," I countered.

He smiled. "We both lose the Master; you lose Mary; and I lose Ishtar and see my daughter palsied. It hasn't been easy."

"No, but sometimes it's been good."

"Sometimes—when I remember what he meant to us and forget how much I resent him. The Lord tempted me to despair, and I fell. I cursed the Most High because He dared to test me beyond my power. I was weak, not only in the flesh but in my faith. Like the brothers who deserted us in Jerusalem, I was doubting that the Master would return. I saw my 'new heaven and new earth' as so much drivel. As long as I could keep in my mind the vision of his coming, I could blot out most of the usual temptations. But I couldn't always. You know that."

I nodded. Who knew better than I?

"More and more I lost it, until my faith was only a fleeting thing. Then the rest got unbearable. I was relieved when James showed up. It had gotten to be too much. Without faith, with memories of the Master's hurtful love of John, and my own loneliness. . . . You know the rest."

"We have discussed this before," I said, "but it may be that the Master has returned, that he meant it when he said the kingdom is within us. Could it be that as long as the Holy Spirit is with us, the Master is with us?"

Simon Peter waved his hand, but not so dismissively as in the past. "There is something in what you and John claim, Quintus. [Actually, it had been my idea before it had been John's, and I had suggested, not claimed.] I have thought about this more than you know. Even at the lake when I was busy rejecting the Lord and the Master, I was remembering the Master's words, playing with them, trying to make sense of them."

All I said was, "And?"

"And, I'm not sure, but I think you're at least partly right. The Master rebuked the sons of Zebedee—and me—for worrying about who'd be first. He did say the kingdom was within us, but I don't see how we can have that kingdom within us if he doesn't come again."

"I'm not sure what you mean."

"I'm not either." He picked up a clump of damp sand, squeezed it into a ball and threw it at one of the terns that was poking its beak down the crab's hole. "I think I mean we can only have peace and love both inside and outside if he comes to rule. We can act toward one another that way in small communities like Dalmanutha or Jerusalem. But if we act that way toward the outside world and they notice us, we'll be stamped on, maybe enslaved. His coming would stop others from hurting us."

"So we need his return so we can live the Way without any cost?"

"Yes."

"And if people could see they didn't have to suffer for being good, they would repent and reform their lives?"

"Something like that, I guess. But it doesn't sound very convincing, does it?"

I nodded. I thought of several responses that would have exposed the contradictions in his reasoning, but, frail as it was, it represented a step in the right direction. First, he was using his mind rather than his reflexes. And, second, he had rejected that perverted view of the kingdom as the Roman Empire with himself a prince. Besides, we were off on what Simon Peter thought— mistakenly—was a tangent. He wanted and needed to talk about the current state of his soul much more than about the future of the kingdom. "And right now," I asked. "Why the change?"

"I don't know. Maybe I came to realize that I'd sinned through pride, even blasphemy. I dared to judge the Holy One. You know that. You told me so yourself, and James may've been trying to say it when he threw me out of Jerusalem until I did public penance."

We had to get up and move a few feet so a crew of Numidian slaves could carry several huge cedar logs across the beach to the ship. Then Simon Peter went on: "I don't know if the Lord hurt Jephthania to punish me for my sins. I thought so at the time—I was sure of it. You said not, John the priest said not, my heart said not, the Master would've said not, but my guilt said yes."

"And now?" I asked.

"Now I'm no longer sure; but even if I believed the Lord God was testing me, it wouldn't change my anger." He picked up a small branch that had broken off one of the cedars, snapped it in his hand, and began using the stub end to draw aimlessly in the sand. "You know how hard forgiveness is for me," he muttered. "The Lord God let the Romans crucify the Master; He took Ishtar from me; and then He crippled my child. The Master said the Father marks the sparrow's fall, but I'd treat any bird, fish, or animal with more consideration than He's shown to me—or my Jephthania. Jephthania. If she hadn't fought to keep her purity she probably wouldn't have become palsied. Because she was virtuous, He took away her speech and her use of her right arm and leg. I don't understand it; I loathe it; and I can't forgive it. The anger I felt toward the Master was nothing compared to what I felt—still feel—toward the Lord. That's why my sin is so deep. I know it's blasphemous to judge the Most High, but I do it anyway."

"Then what are you planning to do with your life?" I had thought I knew the answer, but now I was uncertain.

"I can't spend it living off anger with the Lord, any more than I could spend it living off love with Ishtar. If I could make Him pay, I would; but I can't. He pushes my face into a bucket of slime and says, 'Love Me.' What kind of idiocy is that? I'm caught, trapped. I can't escape Him. He grabs me, takes me away from my lake and my family, changes me, punishes me, and still expects me to serve Him."

"Yet you seem more at peace with yourself than I've ever seen you. Why?"

"The Master touched me, Quintus. Maybe that's what I should really be angry about. He touched me; and, when he touched me, somehow—I don't pretend to understand what I'm trying to say— somehow, the Most High touched me. I've never been the same since and can never be the same again. I've been set apart; blessed or cursed, or both. I've tried to run away. By leaving Jerusalem, I gave James the . . . Just a chance to take over the community. I was tired of carrying other people's burdens every day of my life, having nothing for myself but a few shards of time and never the warmth or love of a woman. 'It is not good for man to be alone,' the Torah says. As much as I love Ishtar, she was, in a way, another escape. She made me cursed among pious Jews, yet at the same time she freed me from them."

"I'm not sure what you're saying," I put in.

"I may be just babbling, but I'm trying to explain why I died and why I've come back from the dead and what it is I must do. Why did Agrippa arrest me? Was I worth something, dead if not alive? Was he the instrument of the Lord raising me back up from the dead by telling me I was worth something alive? Why were you able to rescue me so easily?"

Out of pique, I didn't respond to his question. "Easy" was hardly the word for his escape: It had risked the lives of Cornelius and his men, endangered my family, cost me half my inheritance, sent me into exile, and frightened the color out of what hair I had left.

"It was the hand of the Lord, Quintus, acting through that bastard Agrippa and through you. He has called me again. I don't understand Him; I'm angry with Him; I can't love anyone who treated Jephthania like He has. But He is the Most High, the All Powerful, the Eternal One. How does a man resist Him? He can't, at least I can't. But I may be able to teach Him that He, too, should be bound by the Master's commands to love. Perhaps a miserable, ignorant peasant can touch *Him* and teach *Him* about decency and love. By doing His will, by spreading the Master's good news despite the evil He has inflicted, maybe I can teach Him something about love and justice."

We stood up and started toward the boat. "Let me reverse the Pharisees' prayer," I said, "I thank God I was born a gentile and not a Jew." And I meant it. For these Jews, God walked the land with them, learned which ewe would have trouble in birthing, knew when their pots were empty, cared how their bones ached. He would join in the rejoicing when a child was born and in the mourning when a loved one died. And one could get angry, even furious, at Him. To them, He was a real person, not an abstract idea.

This vision of God did not fit a style my learning could accommodate. For me, God was the Unmoved Mover, the Uncaused Cause, an abstraction, not a person. He ruled the universe through general and uniform laws of physics, not through direct intervention on an individual basis. My philosophic soul wanted no such personal connections with the Deity as Simon Peter experienced. Still, part of me envied these people. For all the fright a personal God engenders, there must also be comfort in thinking one not only has the attention of an omnipotent, omniscient being but can also convince and convert Him as well.

After a day's unloading and reloading, we set sail for Antioch—or rather its port, Seleucia Pieria. From there we walked upstream toward the city called by such titles as "The Fair Crown of the Orient" and "Queen of the East." It is huge as well as beautiful, smaller only than Rome and Alexandria. And it is preeminently a Greek city, founded a little more than 300 years ago by one of Alexander's generals, Seleucus I, "the Conqueror," who named it, as he did fifteen other cities he founded, for his father or his son, both of whom were named Antiochus.

There is much folklore surrounding the area. I thought it best not to mention to Simon Peter the legend that Io, the daughter of the river god Inachus, died here in grief after Zeus raped her. Jewish traditions list the valley as the ancient Riblah in the land of Hamath, where Pharaoh Necho captured the Jewish king Jehoahaz, who "had done evil in the sight of the Lord." Two centuries later Nebuchadnezzar took another Jewish king, Zedekiah, to Riblah to witness the execution of his sons, then to be blinded and led to captivity in Babylon. Yet another and, of course, gentile story claims Alexander himself stopped at this site on his march east and, after drinking from one of its many springs and proclaiming the water to be mother's milk, announced his intention to build a city there.

Whatever the truth of such legends, Antioch's location is nearly ideal. It lies along the Orontes River, which divides the Taurus Mountains from those of the Lebanon by a valley whose rich soil combines with forty-six inches of yearly rainfall to provide wheat, barley, vegetables, and excellent grapes as well as the usual olive trees. The valley opens to the east and serves as an avenue for trade between the Mediterranean world and the upper reaches of the Euphrates River. Moreover, a mile or so east of town is the main north-south caravan artery linking Damascus and Arabia to the provinces between Syria and the Black Sea.

Antioch's sole shortcoming is that it is virtually indefensible. Seleucus nestled the original settlement between the south bank of the river and the northern slope of Mount Silpius, which steeply rises almost 1,300 feet above the valley floor. On its southern side, however, Silpius offers no natural defense. Children easily manage its long, gradual slope. Indeed, historians tell of no unsuccessful siege of Antioch. Thus its security had depended on the Seleucids' ability to keep hostile armies far from their capital, a feat they usually accomplished. The coming of the Romans a hundred years ago merged the defense of Antioch into the larger strategy of the Empire; in that century, the region has not been seriously threatened.

Unlike most modern cities that have sprawled out willy-nilly from nests of existing villages, this one began from careful planning. To design his city, the Conqueror had had the sense and taste to engage Xenarius, the great architect, who designated an oblong area of about a square mile, fixed so as best to catch the breezes sweeping up from the sea and still avoid the landslides from Mount Silpius. According to tradition, he borrowed elephants from Seleucus's army to mark the towers, then laid out the streets with straw. Those streets are straight and cross each other at right angles instead of coiling around in serpentine fashion as they so often do in Jerusalem and even in Rome itself. Thus in Antioch, one can find one's way and direct others by using such concepts as "blocks."

The city has grown, of course, but again by plan. Various Seleucid rulers extended the boundaries so that it now consists of four sectors. In addition to Xenarius's original town, there is another to the east toward the north-south caravan route, a third occupies the large island in the middle of the river, and the newest, and now main, quarter called the Tetrapolis, or Fourth City, has taken over a good part of the slope of Mount Silpius.

For Seleucus, Antioch represented a careful and deliberate choice; for us it was pure chance. Our sole consideration had been to get as far from Agrippa's power as quickly as we could, and the first ship we found leaving Joppa was going to Antioch. That we believed there was a community of brothers and sisters there was a bonus. We would have happily sailed for Cyrene, Iberia, or even Rome.

We knew little of what to expect or even whom to look for. Nicolaus of Antioch, one of the seven leaders the Hellenes in Jerusalem had chosen, had returned home after Simon Peter had sent all the Greek-speaking males away to avoid persecution. Once in his own town, he had begun to preach the Way. Later, we heard from travelers who passed through Dalmanutha, Barnabas had joined him in preaching the good news. That report was probably true, because I had a letter from Paul saying he hoped to join Barnabas there; and again, travelers had told us Paul was preaching in Antioch. Still, that news was several years old; we had no idea where either was now or where a community of believers might be located.

I knew Antioch, but only a bit. I had stopped here twice, on my way to and from Athens, and spent several weeks each time. But those visits had occurred almost twenty years earlier. I did, however, recall a few useful items. One was a lovely small town called Daphne, about five miles south of the city, situated on a plateau overlooking the river. It was older and even more beautiful than Antioch. Indeed, the ancients had initially distinguished this Antioch from the others by calling it "Antioch near Daphne." But long since, Daphne had become a suburb in which wealthy Antiochenes lived. There was a synagogue there. I also recalled good-sized Jewish neighborhoods in Antioch proper and to the northeast, by the north-south caravan route.

Indeed, Antioch had a larger Jewish population than any city in the Land of Israel itself, and the city's Jewish roots ran deep. As his first settlers, Seleucid had mostly put in retired Macedonian soldiers, but he also included a group of Jewish mercenaries who had fought for him. On my first visit, I had heard estimates of the Jewish population at about 65,000, or about one of every seven or eight inhabitants; this figure was probably too large, but the number was still considerable. Throughout the Diaspora, there were always strains and friction between Jews and gentiles. Just a few years earlier, violence had erupted at Antioch, bloody riots that tore up the city's peace and snuffed out many lives. But it had been in the interest of all sides to end the conflict, for there were too many Jews to drive out without civil war and the Romans would not tolerate that. The following year, Claudius had sealed the truce with a letter to the city reconfirming Jewish rights. Despite this outbreak, when compared to relations in most other cities, Antioch was an oasis of mutual toleration.

As was typically the case in the Empire, members of the Hebrew community were exempt from public rituals involving pagan gods and even from some taxes. Furthermore, the community, headed by a council of elders, the *gerousia*, could practice its religion freely, run its own market so that Hebrews could purchase proper food, buy or erect buildings for communal use, operate courts to settle disputes if all the people involved were Jews, collect some taxes, and send the half-shekel Temple tax to Jerusalem.

On the other hand, Jews could not, as long as they remained part of their own community, become full-fledged citizens of the city. Here, as everywhere in the Diaspora, Hebrews were always aliens and strangers. This mix of special privilege and second-class status generated constant tension, but in Antioch it was as much within the Jewish community as between it and gentiles. Jews with secular ambitions were often severely tempted to leave their own community and gain not only full rights of citizenship but also social acceptance within a larger and more cosmopolitan community. The temptation was all the stronger because the Antiochenes' generally tolerant culture infected many Jewish inhabitants and loosened the tight ethnocentric bonds that so constricted Jerusalem.

To the more orthodox Jews, however, all of the gentiles' principal forms of social intercourse were taboo: eating at table where the menu might not only include forbidden food such as pork but also meat that had been offered to false gods, the civic-religious rituals themselves, and participation in public games, gymnasia, and baths—the last because nakedness was an abomination. Defections were frequent, and one could see evidence of cultural assimilation. For example, Jews in Antioch, as in some other cities of the Diaspora, had their own gymnasium, a scandal to Jerusalem and one of the excuses for Judean discrimination against Hellenes. That the Hasmoneans had built gymnasia in the Holy City itself was irrelevant.

My brief acquaintance with Paul gave me one clue as to where we might begin our search. I had detected more than a hint of class snobbery in him. I thus suspected that he would have spent much time at the synagogue in Daphne, for the richest Jews in the region were likely to live there. Since Daphne was located between the port and Antioch, we decided to begin our search there.

We crossed Paul's spoor quickly enough, though it was seasoned with red pepper. The synagogue at Daphne was easy to locate. Everyone knew its location, and well they should have, for it was a large and lovely marble building, more elegant than any I had seen outside of Leontopolis in Egypt. The elder to whom we spoke stroked his beard thoughtfully before he responded to our inquiry. "Yes, yes, it's been five years, but how could I forget that arrogant, overbearing, self-righteous young man who claimed to have been born again?" The elder paused, then went on: "If true, it must have been quite hard on his mother."

The synagogue had offered Paul its hospitality, but after a month the elders had asked him to leave because his preaching of "the Way" offended many of them. He, however, had continued to attend the synagogue. He insisted on constantly speaking out on the Sabbath, sharply contradicting any and all who tried to comment on the Scriptures. And he also tried to persuade individual members and small groups who came to the center for prayer, meditation, or socializing. As a result, the elders had forcibly expelled him, after having bestowed the forty blows less one with the rod that Antioch, like most cities around the empire, allowed the Jewish community to inflict on its own members.

Simon Peter nodded without comment. One could wish Paul every success in his mission and still sympathize with those who had to listen to him. In that respect he was Stephen writ large.

As unfortunate as all that was, Paul's stripes had brought positive results, for at least four members of the community at Daphne, including one of the elders of this synagogue who was also a *gerousiarch* of the entire Hebrew community in and around Antioch, had been very taken with "this grotesque person," as our informant described our fellow disciple. "We told them they would have to choose between this new Way and the Law of Moses, but that our doors were always open when they wished to return.

"We, of course," he continued, "quietly kept after them to abandon this new sect and return to the faith of their fathers. We are, after all, neighbors and Jews in a gentile world. We have the Lord, the Law, and each other, no person and no thing else. Only our *gerousiarch* has remained hard of heart. He has companions in Antioch itself. There the new sect has made some substantial inroads into the congregations of our synagogues. And," his voice dropped to a whisper, "I hear that they encourage Jews to sit at table with idol-worshipers."

"Who is this *gerousiarch* who is so stubborn?" Simon Peter asked.

"Manaen—Menahem in Aramaic, though he prefers the Greek. He is a goldsmith, or was; he's mostly retired now. His family is Judean and wealthy, which explains why he was educated in Rome. There he was a companion of Antipas, the son of Herod the Great. Perhaps you have heard of him."

Simon Peter allowed as how the name Antipas was familiar, but Manaen or Menahem didn't register. "Where might we find him?" I asked, not wanting to leave all the deviousness to Simon Peter, who was not yet good at it, though he was learning. "It might not hurt were two men from the Land of Israel to talk to him."

With the elder's directions we easily located Manaen. His home, somewhat smaller but much more opulently appointed than my family's villa at Scythopolis, looked like he had maintained indecently intimate relations with Antipas's treasury, but then few goldsmiths have been paupers. Despite our dusty appearance, the servant—a Syrian, not a Jew or a real Greek—who answered our knock treated us with respect, offering us water to wash our hands and feet, and to drink. Manaen himself greeted us with courtesy:

" 'Blessed is he who comes in the name of the Lord,' " he said and offered us wine. We refused and instead took fruit juice, for we were both tired and thirsty, even after several cups of water.

Manaen was a man in his mid-sixties, but his eyes were bright and alert, darting from one to the other of us and around the atrium. No doubt a broad field of vision had been essential to survival in youth if one counted a Herod among one's companions.

Having identified ourselves only as a Jew and a God Fearer from the Land of Israel, we sparred with Manaen for almost half an hour. We spoke of the marvels of the sweet springs that bubbled up all over Daphne, he about the weather during our voyage. We asked about the climate in Antioch, he about our reaction to Daphne's magnificent cypress forests. We admired some of the art in his salon, he our flawless Greek. As we were finishing our third cup of fruit juice, Simon Peter casually mentioned that we were fleeing political oppression. A man accustomed to Oriental bargaining, Manaen only raised an eyebrow quizzically. "There is much of that in our world," he noted.

"Indeed," I put in, "and religious persecution as well." I knew that only a Jew was likely to grasp the difference between the two.

"And that, too." He nodded, but his expression remained blank. He did, however, pass us a tray of bread and cakes.

"I understand," Simon Peter said, "we have a mutual acquaintance, a man of Tarsus who was once named Saul but now calls himself Paul."

For the first time, Manaen betrayed interest. His expression did not change but his eyes crinkled at the corners. "The name is familiar, but it is not uncommon."

"May I have wine now?" Simon Peter asked.

"Of course." Manaen snapped his fingers and a servant—this one a Jew—entered and poured each of us a large goblet of dry, sandy red wine.

Simon Peter took a piece of bread, broke it, and whispered, "The Master has died, the Master has been raised, the Master will come again." He took the goblet, repeated those words, and passed the bread and wine to Manaen, who smiled, ate a bite and took a long swallow, then passed both to me. *"Maranatha,"* he said in Aramaic: "Come, Lord."

After I had eaten some of the bread and drunk at least half of Simon Peter's wine—I saw no point in leaving temptation in his way—Manaen asked: "Who are you?"

"I am called Simon Peter and this is Quintus."

"Simon Peter? The one whom the Master chose to lead his people? The Most High, eternal be His glory, has doubly blessed my home. You are well known here."

"I fear so. My sins have been great. I haven't been true to the trust the Master left me. You may have heard."

"We have heard fragments, but enough. Communication with Dalmanutha is difficult, easier with Jerusalem since so many people go up on Passover. Barnabas has spoken of the power of your faith. He said we should pray for you but not be troubled. Your faith would triumph over your demon. The timing was in the hands of the Lord." Manaen waved his hand. "One of the few advantages of old age is that one is expected to be sententious. Thus I tell you no one can be a great saint without first also being a great sinner."

"Paul, what does he say?" I should not have asked but I could not resist.

"Paul?" For an instant a look of panic flashed across Manaen's face. "Paul, of course, agreed with Barnabas. Simon Peter is the first among the disciples. Now, let us put the past aside. Have you come to lead us?"

"I have come to try to help you—and to help myself—find the Way and stay in it."

Manaen got up with surprising agility and gave us each both a warm embrace and the kiss of peace full on the lips. "You are both welcome. There is much work for you in Antioch. You, no doubt, know Antioch's connections to our people's history. [I did, but I doubted that Simon Peter did.] They knew it as Hamath. And Isaiah had a prophecy I have hoped we might fulfill:

> But a shoot shall sprout from the stump of Jesse,
> And from his roots a bud shall blossom.

The spirit of the LORD shall rest upon him: a spirit
   of wisdom and understanding,
A spirit of counsel and of strength. . . .

On that day,
The root of Jesse, set up as a signal for the nations,
The Gentiles shall seek out, for his dwelling shall
   be glorious.
On that day,
The LORD shall again take it in hand to reclaim the
   remnant of his people that is left from Assyria and
   Egypt,
Pathros, Ethiopia, and Elam, Shinar, Hamath, and the
   isles of the sea.
He shall raise a signal to the nations and gather the
   outcasts of Israel;
The dispersed of Judah he shall assemble from the four
   corners of the earth.

"The 'spirit of the Lord' surely rested on the Master, and it rests on you, too, Simon Peter. And we, the remnant of his people of Hamath, outcasts in our own city, 'the dispersed of Judah,' may yet have a great role to play in uniting the peoples of Israel—and the gentiles as well—bringing them all home to the Most High, blessed be His name forever."

It seemed that Antioch had already begun to play a major role in spreading the way. Nicolaus, who had first brought the good news here, had died several years ago, but Barnabas and Paul had carried on his work. They had been effective among gentiles as well as Jews. The followers were not organized in a single community as in Jerusalem. What organization there was was loose, looser even than in Joppa. There were three different groups of from twenty to twenty-five adults, a total of sixty-eight adults and possibly forty children. Each group came together regularly at the home of a brother who had enough space for a meeting, read from Scripture, recounted some of the stories about the Master that Paul or Barnabas had given them, and then, as part of a meal, performed the ritual sharing of the bread and wine.

These assemblies met at Manaen's villa in Daphne, in Antioch itself at Simon Niger's house in the large Jewish quarter on the south bank of the river, and in the house of Lucius of Cyrene, located just to the east of the city, near the north-south caravan route. The first two were composed of a large majority of Jews with a few God Fearers. Lucius's group, however, included only nine Jews. Of the rest, eight were pagans (or former pagans) and nine God Fearers. It was a practice that would raise hackles in Jerusalem, but it had had, first Nicolaus's, then Barnabas's, and finally Paul's blessing.

"Where is Paul now?" I asked Manaen.

"Who knows? He spreads the good news wherever the Spirit blows him. He could be in Galatia, Corinth, Athens—or here tomorrow."

"He built well here," Simon Peter said.

"Nicolaus and Barnabas built well here," Manaen corrected. "Paul added in important ways, but they came first. And it was they who drew not only Jews but also God Fearers and gentiles. In any event, much remains to be done. The brothers are growing anxious about when the kingdom will come."

I heard Simon Peter's sigh and knew he was thinking it was Jerusalem all over again. But whatever else it was, Antioch was not Jerusalem. The differences were vast, and Simon Peter had learned a great deal.

We spent the night with Manaen and the next afternoon he brought Simon and Lucius, the other two leaders, to meet us. There was much embracing and kissing. If Manaen knew of Simon Peter's fall, the others must have, too; but it seemed to have had no effect on the adulation they heaped on him. Being the Master's chosen one had stamped him with an indelible charisma. The discussion went on into the evening and so late in the night that Lucius and Simon also slept at Manaen's house.

The result of all that talking was that we would, unless prevented by forces beyond our control, make Antioch and its environs our chief responsibility for at least the next few years. Simon

Peter asked that the three men remain leaders of their communities. Since the groups met in their houses, it was little enough to grant. Indeed, there was no feasible alternative. "Elders" was the title we agreed to give them, with a definition of authority much like that of the *gerousiarchs* of a Diaspora synagogue.

The next morning we left with Simon and joined his people that night. Once again Simon Peter was treated like a man sent directly by God. He led the sharing of the bread and wine and spoke briefly. It was a familiar message:

I bring you good news: The kingdom of God is at hand.

I am not an eloquent man. I lack the words to tell you what the Master was like—soft as gentle rain, sweet as black earth in early spring, hard as iron, devoted as an Essene, totally, absolutely devoted to the Most High and the coming of his kingdom, a reign of peace, freedom, and love in which life will triumph over sin.

But I can tell you of his message, of the good news: The Most High, Our Father, is with us, walking in our midst. As Jews, we always knew something of this. Now we know it as Jews, God Fearers, and gentiles, and we know it in a different, fuller way. His kingdom will come. It is a kingdom in which loving others and accepting our obligations toward all mankind come before being loved and making others respect our rights. For it is only in freely loving the Lord God with our whole hearts and souls and loving our neighbor as we love ourselves that we can, in turn, receive a full measure of love. For those who have little love cannot understand what it is to be loved.

When the Master returns, he will create for us a new heaven and a new earth. We wait in joyful and prayerful hope for that return.

"Simon Peter," a Jew asked, "the Master was crucified many years ago. Some of us have faithfully followed the Way since Nicolaus's time. We have suffered much: the riots of a few years ago, the ostracism of our fellow Jews, and we are no less strangers to the gentiles around us. When will the Master come again?"

"We have all suffered, my brother, and all the more because no one knows the answer to your question. What we do know is that the Lord in His mysterious, loving fashion has chosen us, has allowed the seed of faith to grow within us. That growth has not been steady. At times we doubt, perhaps even despair. I know. I like to think of my faith as a trumpeting elephant, but often it has been like a quivering cat, as unsteady as land shaken by an earthquake. The Holy Spirit, whom you have received, will strengthen your will. Scripture reminds us that the Lord our God is a patient God. With Him a thousand years are like a day."

Simon Peter hesitated, then seeing the people wanted more, continued: "Our ancestors in Egypt and Babylon must have thought His day would never come. But it did. Their wait seems short to us now; I doubt it did to them then, any more than ours does to us. 'Come, Lord!' is our constant prayer. And we must be ready for that coming, by living holy lives. My brother, if there is a way to sin, I have found it. I have been a victim of the flesh, and worse, of despair. Learn from my failings."

It was hardly the direct, concise, or even logically coherent response of a philosopher. Yet even its wanderings showed a deeper understanding than what Simon Peter had been saying a decade earlier.

After the meeting, a God Fearing physician named Theophilus, a true Greek whose family had a century earlier escaped the Romans' destruction of Corinth and settled in Antioch, offered Simon Peter and me a small house he owned in the center of the city. He said he had a larger and more comfortable villa near Daphne and would prefer to live there, nearer to his clients. We, of course, refused, but he insisted and in the end we gratefully gave in.

The following day we walked to town and saw our new house. It was not as small as Theophilus had implied. Its furnishings were modest by my standards, luxurious by those that Simon Peter had enjoyed before living with Ishtar.

We left our few miserable belongings there and went to see Lucius. He was a completely Hellenized Jew, more Hellene than Hebrew except in his worship of the one, true God. He was a big man, almost the same size and build as Simon Peter, at fifty beginning to show more fat than was healthy, though he frequented the gymnasium, a practice that had met with the disapproval of most local Jews. His beard and hair were neatly barbered, his quiet but elegant dress that of a wealthy Greek. Widowed for more than five years, he seemed content to live out his life alone. Like Simon the Tanner, our man in Joppa, his business bored him and the Way devoured his attention.

His villa was situated just at the eastern edge of the city, close enough to the north-south caravan route to be accessible without the obstacle of city traffic but far enough away not to be an obvious target for itinerant thieves. (Still, I noticed as many guards here as at my family's villa outside of Jerusalem.) Lucius's place was typical of the large Oriental household; with minor changes it would have fit nicely into our neighborhood in Scythopolis.

The sprawling courtyard was jammed with people, women and children as well as men, hoping to see, hear, and even touch Simon Peter, the Master's anointed. Lucius had them form a line and file by Simon Peter so that each might take his hand—and the more brave embrace him and kiss his cheeks. His talk was short and different from any I had heard him give to Jews:

> Because we drank different notions of God from our mothers' breasts, we once looked at heaven and earth in very different ways. But now, Jew or gentile, we share a vision of a new heaven and a new earth. We have received the Master's good news that the Lord God is with us and within us, that His kingdom is at hand. The one true God walks among his people; and his people are all those who acknowledge His fatherhood, repent their sins, and follow the Master's precept to share with their fellow human beings, their brothers and sisters, the burdens and joys of this short life. The kingdom will be a reign of peace, joy, and love. We must prepare for it, for the Master's return, by living that future life *now*, by living it as best we can in holiness and hope.

Again the first question was, "We have waited now for many years, Simon Peter. When will the Master come again?" Again Simon Peter gave his response and again as at Simon's house it had inched toward my position.

After the talking, we sat on the stone floor and shared bread and wine, with Simon Peter giving the blessing. The response,

"*Maranatha*," was so loud that Lucius looked worried. There had been no trouble with the local community, except that during the riots the gentiles had not distinguished among different groups of Jews. Still, he was not anxious to call attention to our existence by seeming to disturb the peace.

4

✤ Simon Peter spent a few weeks with each of the three communities in Antioch. He would go to Lucius's or Simon's or Manaen's house in late morning and wait there. If no one had come to see him by the time the heat of the day began to break, he would visit the brothers where they lived, worked, or slaved. He would offer advice or consolation and sometimes reminisce about the Master and recount his teachings. In essence, Simon Peter acted much like a Jewish scribe, interpreting the Master's message and to some extent the Torah. He would not have liked the analogy; but, as a Jew, he was familiar with the model and followed it without thinking.

I spent much of those first weeks in the suqs, taverns, and even synagogues, listening and talking, getting a feel for Antioch and its people. Simon Peter operated through instinct and personal communication with the Holy Spirit. I needed evidence and analysis to function comfortably. I do not say this to criticize. The two of us operated well together, probably better here than in Jerusalem.

Simon Peter's calm reassurance that *the day* was truly coming helped hold these people together in a time of great stress, for discontent about the Master's delayed return was quite real. Like Simon Peter and the rest of the disciples after Pentecost, Nicolaus, Barnabas, and later Paul had preached that the end was imminent.

The bill for that error had come due, and Simon Peter had been able to negotiate a postponement—no mean feat—but he could not bring himself to try to quit the debt.

Despite his calming effect and tangible success in tightening the bonds within and among the three communities, he was not pleased. He was, of course, no longer the listless, depressed man from Capernaum; but his energy was more disciplined than it had been at Pentecost. Still, the monotony of daily service was grinding on him. "It is Barnabas's community that I am holding together," he complained one rainy Sabbath as we sat in the house Theophilus had loaned us. "Barnabas's and Paul's, not mine."

"Is it not God's community?" I could not help asking.

"You know what I mean. I have not led them to the Way, only helped keep them there. If I were to bring more people in, do you think we could take care of them?"

I winced, not out of surprise but because, even though I knew Simon Peter would inevitably begin proselytizing, I dreaded the problems that would create with the synagogues, the local civil authorities, and with our very meager resources. My only consolation was that, so far, in Antioch, the communities had not shared their material goods and taken over complete economic responsibility for the poor. It was a fact that bothered Simon Peter. Several times he had brought it up with the elders, but they had managed to evade a head-on confrontation. Clearly, they wanted to separate their spiritual lives from much of their material lives, something Simon Peter thought impossible. Our task, he had said, was not merely to catch men but to live with them according to the Master's message of love and sharing.

"You haven't answered me," he said, "and I can guess why. You're concerned I'll fall again."

In fact, I hadn't thought of that; but it was a good point, so I was silent.

"I might. I can't deny it. But I've got to take the chance. The Master told me to preach, and preach I must, however badly."

I nodded. When Simon Peter quoted what he thought the Master had told him in that vision at the lake, it was futile to argue with him. "I've been thinking about the people here who're following the Way—who they are and why they're with us."

"What is there to understand? They're with us because of the Holy Spirit."

"True," I conceded, "but She seems to be giving Her grace pretty selectively, mostly to those who are marginal."

"Marginal?"

"To people who are on the edges of society, like Galilean peasants are to the Sadducees in the Temple."

"If you mean to the downtrodden and oppressed, why not say it plainly?"

"Because it's not just the poor or the oppressed who've joined us. Manaen is rich, just like Nicodemus and Josef of Arimathea; Simon and Lucius are pretty well off, like Mary of Magdala and I was . . . at least before I bribed your guards in the Antonia." It was an honest slip. I had never meant to tell Simon Peter about that.

"Quintus, I didn't know." His hand closed heavily on my shoulder.

I pulled away. "It was nothing. The Master said to ransom prisoners, even thick-headed ones." I went on quickly to prevent any further dysfunctional display of emotion: "No doubt some of the brothers are oppressed. In Lucius's group, four of the God Fearers and three of the other gentiles are slaves. The other gentiles are freedmen, no longer slaves but not yet accepted by society. Among the Jews, most are poor. But some of our people are not poor and we're not attracting all the poor. If we were, two-thirds of Antioch would be following the Way. A man can be marginal for many reasons."

"Not Manaen or Lucius or Simon. They're rich, pillars of society."

"They don't have problems with money, but they're not pillars of society now and they hadn't been for some years. Manaen was a *gerousiarch* because of his wealth, not his popularity. His daughter married a gentile, and he didn't disown her. Some people say he didn't even try to stop her. You know how pious Jews feel about that."

Simon Peter shrugged. He knew what some *pious* Jews felt,

but, as a Galilean, he, like his neighbors, was more practical—and humane. "People forget about such things," he muttered.

"Perhaps, perhaps not. At one time, Simon had a gentile mistress."

"People don't forget about that," Simon Peter agreed, "but they can live with it."

"I hope. But each of the three has a strong religious urge. I would guess they feel guilty for not following the rules at the same time they resent what they think is gossiping criticism behind their backs."

"You didn't mention Lucius."

"Before he found the Way, he was a very unhappy man."

"All men are unhappy; only animals are happy—and usually just before they're eaten. Why is Lucius, what's your fancy word, 'marginal'?"

"He's had differences with the synagogue. The specifics of each case are not my point. My point is more general, it's. . . ."

"I know what your point is. Why is Lucius marginal?"

"Because he's homoerotic."

"He's what?"

"Men arouse him, not women."

Simon Peter leaped up. "How long've you known? We've had an abomination in our midst, a man cursed by the Most High Himself for the filth of his body and mind, and you haven't told me?"

Having had ten days to think about the problem, I had my defense prepared. It was short on reason but long on barbs. " 'I came to save sinners, not the just man,' is what the Master said. 'The Holy Spirit blows where She will, not where we will,' is what Simon Peter said."

"If we tolerate those kinds of sinners, people will say we're sodomites too."

"The Master preached to whores, tax collectors, winebibbers, and other kinds of sinners, and people said he was all of those things and worse. Did he turn away anyone who wanted to hear the word of God? You and I are in no position to judge who is worthy to receive the Master's message. Do you want to play James the Just in Antioch?"

"I don't know." He got up and walked into the courtyard. The rain had pretty much stopped, but there was still a drizzle. I don't think he felt it. "I just don't know. To a Greek, it may not be much; but to a Jew. . . . How is it that Jews meet in his house? Are they . . . like him?"

"How do I know? Maybe they accept him for what he is, a decent man who's trying to be more decent. Maybe they take the Master's message seriously. Lucius believes in the Way; he tries to follow the Way by repenting his sins, by treating others with respect and dignity. He shares. Is that not enough?"

"The Law. . . . The Law—if we catch him in the act, how will I apply the Law?"

"Exactly as the Master said: 'If you are without sin, cast the first stone. If not, forgive, just as you want to be forgiven.' "

"Forgive. . . . Why did you bring this whole business up, Quintus? To torture me?"

"I was trying to explain to you who was most likely to hear our message. I tried to avoid talking about Lucius specifically. My only point was that he's marginal like most of the others."

"I'll preach to the poor, to slaves, to anyone who wants to repent his sins, even the rich, but I won't seek out sodomites."

"You needn't seek them out; just don't reject them."

After that exchange, things were never the same between Simon Peter and Lucius. A relationship that had begun as warm and trusting turned cold and formal. Lucius understood that Simon Peter knew, though Simon Peter—to my knowledge—never said a word. Yet the relationship continued. Simon Peter made no effort to exclude Lucius from the movement or remove him as head of his group. It was not a full victory, but neither was it a full defeat.

And so we began proselytizing again. As in Jerusalem, we went first to the synagogues, beginning with that in Daphne, an expedition that was momentous for the movement. For in the dialogue there, Simon Peter gave the definitive explanation of the movement's relationship to the more traditional forms of Judaism. "How can you be a Jew and give full membership to gentiles?" the elder who had first directed us to Manaen asked. "You accept them, even eat with them at table, before requiring them to renounce their pagan gods and accept the Law."

"It cannot be wrong to invite gentiles to join us. You in Antioch try to persuade them to join you, even as we do. You even allow God Fearers into your synagogues, even as we do. And we are both right, for the prophet Isaiah has told us that the Most High 'will prepare for all peoples a feast of rich foods, a banquet of fine wines. . . . He will take away the veil of mourning that covers all people, and the shroud that enwraps all nations. He will destroy death forever.' The Most High has fulfilled that promise. By raising the Master from the dead, after the Romans crucified him, He has destroyed death for those who repent and accept His kingdom, which is at hand."

"We accept converts, but they must renounce their gentile customs and accept the Law," the elder insisted.

"And so with us, they must renounce their gentile customs."

"There is doubt about that. We have heard many stories to the contrary, stories about lewd behavior, drunkenness, orgies. Further, you do not require them to accept the Law, to abstain from forbidden foods or to accept circumcision, the sign of the Covenant. That's why you cannot control their behavior."

"Put those foolish stories out of your mind. I've never seen or heard of any such conduct among our people. We don't require gentiles to repent *before* hearing the Master's message, only if they wish to follow in his Way. But you're partly right, though only partly. We don't require them to accept the *details* of the Law, only its essence: to repent their sins, to love the Lord with their whole hearts, and to love and share with their neighbors. We're Jews, just as you're Jews. We differ among ourselves on some things, just as the Essenes in the desert, the Sadducees, and the Pharisees may differ on some things with each other, with us, and with you. But we're Jews nonetheless, for we join in the great Shema and pronounce that the Lord our God is One."

"But how can you be Jews and reject the Law of Moses?"

"We do not reject the Law," Simon Peter reiterated. "We believe the Master has fulfilled the Law, and the Eternal One has made a new Covenant through the Master. All people of the world may join this Covenant. Its sign is not circumcision, but baptism, being cleansed of sin and born again. We are the New Israel, faithful to the commands of the Most High, awaiting the new heaven and new earth He will create when the Master returns. It was about this the Master spoke the night before the Romans took him. He said, when he shared the cup of wine with us, that it was his blood, the blood of 'the new Covenant.' Just as the animals that Abraham slew made the blood of the old Covenant, so the Master's death, signified in that wine, became the blood of the new."

"The New Israel": It was the most sophisticated concept I had ever heard Simon Peter use. I could imagine Paul or Stephen, since they had studied under the great Gamaliel, saying something like that, but hardly Simon Peter. Yet I heard it with my own ears. It was a message he repeated in varying forms in each synagogue. Sometimes, he came on the Sabbath and participated in the reading and discussion of Scripture; sometimes he came in the late afternoon and engaged two or three men in conversation. (I went along on Sabbath but separately, so his being in the company of a God Fearer would not reduce the Jewishness of his message.)

Simon Peter had some effect here and elsewhere. For within two months, we had another fifteen Jewish families in the movement. Our success among the gentiles was even greater. Like Nicolaus, Barnabas, and Paul before him, Simon Peter took to the streets. Here my ethnicity was a positive factor, so I was always in close company with him. Once or twice I even spoke on my own, though I am no orator and my message was too complex to attract ordinary people.

Our favorite posts were in front of the large statue of Romulus and Remus in the piazza at the northeast end of the great colonnaded street that runs the length of the city, and in Jawbone Street, where Barnabas and Paul had preached. Here over the first six months, we gathered fifty-two Syrians, most of whom, of course, fancied themselves Greeks. About a third of them were slaves and most of the rest had families.

Simon Peter assumed I would handle the logistical problems. At least they were somewhat less difficult here because the communities were organized around "house churches," rather than fully sharing groups as in Jerusalem. But that only eased problems, for none of the new people was wealthy, and no synagogue was about to allow us to use its facilities for meeting and eating together. We grasped the obvious solution and used the house that Theophilus had loaned us. It was, however, large enough for only twenty people, so we had to schedule a ceremony each evening and ask our people to attend no more than twice a week so that all might participate.

Those nightly gatherings drained Simon Peter's energy and mine even more so. Almost as important, they also nearly emptied our fisc. Simon Peter, as I have mentioned, was troubled by the lack of sharing that the house churches allowed, and he insisted that at our meetings we provide a full meal for the brothers and their families, not merely a half cup of wine and a hunk of bread.

That generosity required money. Simon Peter had no time to work; the only marketable skill I had was to tutor children of the rich, and I was not anxious to engage in such demeaning labor again. Thus we had to depend on contributions from the less poor among the brethren and, even more so, on gifts from the other house churches. Simon Peter took responsibility for keeping a flow of cash and food coming from Manaen and Simon, but left it to me to solicit help from Lucius.

In this fashion we limped along for some years.

We lost some people and added even more, including several who allowed us to use their homes for meetings. The outside news was mixed. We did not weep when we heard of Agrippa's death, but neither were we cheered when we learned the Romans were directly ruling the entire Land of Israel through a prefect subordinate to the governor of Syria.

In the fifteenth year after the crucifixion, we received a visit from several of the brothers from Jerusalem. Simon Peter and I knew none of them, not even Agabus, the group's leader. We were suspicious of them, and they of us. Clearly, James the Just had sent them to give him firsthand information about what we were doing. We allowed them to stay in our house and took them to all the communities. They asked various kinds of questions but always they inquired of gentiles whether they were God Fearers or intended to convert and accept circumcision and the Law. I do not think they were pleased by most of the answers.

Agabus was an interesting man. He had moved from Alexandria to Jerusalem for religious reasons. Unlike most Hellenistic Jews I had known, he thought of the Temple as the place where the Lord God actually lived. Physically, he was unimpressive, a little on the short side, a bit bowlegged, with a peculiar combination of the barbered hair of a Greek and the shaggy beard of a Judean. Only if one got close could he see the prophet's fire that burned in his eyes. But it was his voice that set him off, a deep bass that resonated syllables in Greek when he conversed and in Hebrew when he read the Scriptures to us. And he was as meticulous about the Law as James or any other Pharisee I'd ever met, which also meant that even our Jewish brethren gave him little to be happy with. There were many Pharisees in Antioch, but few in our communities.

Most curious, one night at Manaen's house—so I was told—Agabus went into a trance and began speaking in those strange tongues that some of our people took as a sign of the Holy Spirit. Afterward, when he recovered consciousness, he said that the Lord had appeared to him and told him that a famine would come on Israel. And the next year, just such a disaster occurred. For some reason, the winter rains were scant, and even in Galilee the crops were poor. At Simon Peter's urging—and it did require urging for, as I have said, we were not rich—our people at Antioch dug deep into their purses and sent money to help Jerusalem. The delegation stopped at Dalmanutha but reported on their return that, while food was scarce, Mary's community was not threatened. The lake's fish made up for the land's limited yield.

The returning Antiochenes brought thanks and greetings from Jerusalem. More welcome to us, they also brought word that Mary of Magdala, Naomi, Jephthania, and Theodora were all well and sent love. That news affected Simon Peter and me in much the same way, leaving us with happiness that all was well, but also with great sadness in reminding us how far we were from those we loved.

5

❖ Malachai, officious as ever, came straight to the point: "We at Jerusalem have heard that you have not only been preaching to gentiles but that you encourage Jews of Antioch to eat at table with them. You know that is against our rules. And you," he looked straight at Simon Peter, "of all people, should realize the dangers to holy purity that kind of contact brings."

It was a wet, dreary day in late spring of the nineteenth year after the crucifixion. The two groups arrived almost simultaneously. First, Paul, Barnabas, and a gentile named Titus came back from Iconium, where after some initial success they had been run out of town and barely escaped stones thrown by both Jews and gentiles. Only a day later, Manaen brought three Judeans, led by Malachai, who had come down from Jerusalem. It was fortunate that Paul and his party had arrived first; otherwise I'm sure he would have claimed we were part of a conspiracy against him.

Before Simon Peter could reply to Malachai, Paul leaped in, his face flushed with an anger that made his voice tremble: "By what authority do you give orders to us? Standing before you is Paul, a Pharisee more learned in the Law than you semiliterate Judeans, and, most important, one directly chosen by the risen Christ himself, not by James or even Simon Peter, and certainly not by you."

"We speak for the community of Jerusalem," Malachai said proudly.

"The Most High has no favorites among men. Why should He have favorites among cities? Insofar as Jerusalem has an honored place it is because Simon Peter and the other apostles founded its community."

"It was there the Master first appeared," Malachai retorted, "and it is there he shall first come again when he returns."

Simon Peter's voice was calmer than Paul's, though there was still an edge to it. "When the Master was raised, he first appeared not to James or to me, but to Mary of Magdala, and she led us back to Galilee. If there is honor in being the Master's first community, then it belongs to Dalmanutha, not Jerusalem. Where the Master will appear when he comes again is something no man knows, and no sensible man pretends to know. We will hear what news you have of our brothers in Jerusalem and what fraternal counsel you wish to offer; but you mistake your authority—and ours—if you presume to command."

There seemed to be no more to be said, but Paul was determined to say it. "I have walked my ankles off up to my knees preaching Christ crucified in every town between Antioch and Athens. I have been whipped and imprisoned. I wear my stripes with pride and I do not acknowledge that James or Jerusalem or any other man or city controls my mission to spread the message of Jesus the Christ."

Paul stripped off his toga, turned, and showed the ugly welts that crisscrossed his back. "Look at these scars!"

Simon Peter had an equal number, as Paul well knew; but Paul was the focus of Paul's oration.

"Look at this! And this!" Paul pointed to his thigh and then to his shoulder, which were still brown, yellow, and purple from the stoning at Iconium. "Show us your credentials! What have you suffered to prove your faith?"

Malachai was shaken. He had expected to find only Simon Peter, still contrite over Ishtar and easily manipulable through guilt. He had not anticipated Paul's moral outrage or Simon Peter's calmer assertion of authority.

Manaen took up some of the slack. "Let us not speak in anger, my brothers. Jerusalem is doubly a holy city, and James is our brother. The blood of the Christ flows in his veins, and he is the head of the community in Jerusalem. I think we must pay close attention to what our brother Malachai asks. [I had not heard him *ask* anything, only accuse.] I have heard persistent, ugly rumors of evil practices among gentiles claiming to follow the Way."

"What evil practices?" Simon Peter asked.

"I prefer not to say anything specific, only vague mutterings about licentious conduct. Sexual orgies, to be more precise. My sources are members of the synagogue where I was *gerousiarch*. I consider them reliable, though I realize they have an interest in painting as black a picture as the truth allows."

Malachai and the two Judeans gloated at the surprise that registered on Simon Peter's and Paul's faces.

"Would it not be prudent," Manaen went on, "to compromise with our brothers at Jerusalem?"

"I cannot compromise the command the risen Christ gave me!" Paul said angrily.

"Let's hear what Manaen has in mind," Simon Peter suggested.

"We continue to preach to all who would hear the good news, but we insist that, before baptism, gentiles become at least God Fearers." Manaen glanced nervously toward me.

"And first be instructed at synagogue?" Paul asked.

"No. They can receive from us instruction in the essence of the Mosaic Law and what it means for moral human behavior. When they understand and accept that much, they can be baptized and become full members of one of our house churches. That would put a stop to these rumors, this scandal brewing in our midst."

"You, Manaen? You who were among the first in Antioch to stand up for the Way, you would join the cutters?" Paul's tone was as sneering as the curl of his lips. "You call it a compromise to make these Greeks accept circumcision. That is not compromise, that is surrender to the Judaizers. Your 'compromise' would betray what I have preached—and you have received. In Christ Jesus we are neither Jew nor Greek."

"Enough!" Simon Peter spat out the word. "We are quarreling like enemies, not loving one another like brothers as the Master commanded." He looked at Malachai. "When you entered this house, we offered you food and drink. You refused this hospitality. As Pharisees, you were right. We Galileans are people of the land. Among our many faults, we eat food that hasn't been tithed or washed according to your priestly rituals, and we don't say the proper number of prayers. But we are Jews no less than you *or* James. We are the New Israel, not the old."

Malachai grunted as if he wanted to speak, but Simon Peter was not about to yield: "We have a new Covenant with the Most High, one which all men may join. Our sign is baptism not circumcision. If there's a scandal brewing in our midst, we must snuff it out like a dirty wick. Acceptance of the Way is not a license for revelry. But we cannot impose the detailed obligations of the Law of Moses on these people, only its essence, the Ten Commandments and the obligations to love the Most High and all his children."

"You would have us, then," Malachai asked, "return to Jerusalem and say that once again you reject the brothers' counsel and will go your own bullheaded way?"

Paul's face reddened again, but this time Simon Peter was able to speak first. "No, not at all. As followers of the Way, we owe you, James, and the brothers at Jerusalem a full explanation of our position. I gave it once, many years ago; but much has happened since then. We need to make the case again, not out of an obligation to have Jerusalem's permission but out of love and respect for our brothers. Paul and I shall go up to Jerusalem with you."

Malachai nodded stiffly.

"Manaen," Simon Peter went on, "would you take our Judean brothers to your house and show them your hospitality? They'll be more comfortable with you. We'll try to be ready to sail within a week. Please see if your people can find a ship bound for Caesarea or Joppa."

As soon as the others had left, Paul spoke in an icy tone. "You have spoken only for yourself, Simon Peter. My commission is from the risen Christ. I am not without respect for James as the brother of Jesus, but I am without need of any man's permission to preach the good news to Jew and Greek alike, not even your permission."

There was silence in the house. Five of us stood facing one another, Simon Peter, the Galilean Jew; Barnabas and Paul, the two Hellenistic Jews; Titus, a former idol worshiper; and I, an uncircumcised, God-Fearing Greek. After several minutes, Simon Peter sighed audibly. "I cannot stand much longer." He kicked a cushion into the corner of the room and sat on it, leaning back against the wall. "Well, my brothers, where are we?"

I thought a bit of dispassionate analysis might give us some strategic perspective. "We are experiencing a problem from which all organizations suffer," I began. "We are feeling tension caused not only by differences of opinion about specific questions but also about who shall decide such differences. We face a problem of legitimacy, in our case of inheritance of authority. The Master led us not because of his parents, or any office he held, or any tradition that makes people like him leaders, but by the force of his personality and our recognition and acceptance of that authority. We Greeks call that kind of rule charismatic, touched with grace. It is a wonderful source of authority, but it carries a huge price: How can one transmit charisma to others? James claims authority over the Way by virtue of blood and a vision. You, Simon Peter, claim it through the Master's words during his lifetime and words he spoke to you in a vision. So far we have a conflict of who is at the center, Simon Peter or James."

"And where do I fit into your scheme?" Paul asked.

"Your authority is based on a vision alone, but you do not claim authority over others, only independence from others. The conflict between Simon Peter and James for the center is irrelevant for your perception of your mission. Your conflict with James is closer to classic clashes between center and periphery." I did not add that just as his conflict with James was now real, so conflict between him and Simon Peter was quite possible, even probable, in the future.

Barnabas and Paul both appeared interested in my analysis, but Simon Peter interrupted. "Paul, we need unity and love. Please go up to Jerusalem with me."

"You have your own ghosts to appease," Paul responded, "and I am not unsympathetic. But I have no one in Jerusalem to justify myself to."

"Not even Stephen's ghost?" I could not help asking. It was a serious mistake. A slap across Paul's face could not have triggered sharper outrage.

For a very brief moment he was silent, then he exploded at me: "Have you been threatened? Paul has been threatened. Have you been persecuted? Paul has been persecuted. Have you suffered? Paul has suffered, and no man has suffered more. Examine your own consciences. Mine is clear. I preach Christ Jesus crucified and raised from the dead. That is conscience enough for me!" With that he stalked out of the house.

Simon Peter looked at Titus. "Go with him. Don't let his anger take him from us."

"He will go to our friends in Jawbone Street," Barnabas added. "You can find him pouting there."

I tried to avoid the reproach in Simon Peter's eyes. "My remark was unnecessary," I confessed, "but the man is so boorish."

"And so touched by the Holy Spirit," Simon Peter said.

"Perhaps. I was wrong to mention Stephen, but my analysis was correct. With Paul we have a classic case of conflict between center and periphery. For him, you, Simon Peter, are the real center. The Master chose you first and he picked you to lead the others. You're the one Paul's worried about; you're the one he's claiming to be independent of, not James or Jerusalem. He sees James as wrong and without authority. You're another matter."

"Quintus is probably right," Barnabas put in. "I know Paul better than anyone. He is difficult to live with, but. . . ."

"But," Simon Peter completed the sentence, "it may be impossible for the Way to survive without him. He is truly the instrument of the Most High." He paused for a few seconds. "And the Lord our God is not above making us pay a price for what blessings He chooses to give us."

I was not sure whether Simon Peter did not comprehend or did not care about my analyses, or whether he came to the same understanding through some sort of intuition rather than logical analysis and did not need my verbalizations. I offered them, however, if for no other reason than to reinforce his own conclusions, for if Paul had his weaknesses, so did Simon Peter.

It was two days later. We were busy making arrangements to go up to Jerusalem. Simon Peter had had several long conversations with five young men who left in a rush. I could pay no attention to those discussions for I was trying to persuade a banker to arrange a loan, with my family's reputation as my only collateral. I was also trying to write down some notes for a future work. As I have said, I thought that in creating the concept "the New Israel" Simon Peter had provided the formula to resolve our crisis of Jewish-gentile relations. I also sought out Paul and apologized. There was no need to mention for what, which was just as well, for I could think of no actual wrong I had done, except to upset Simon Peter. Happily, Paul's ego was large and tender enough to have perceived a dozen slights, and he forgave me—magisterially—with compassionate remarks about my having to live with such guilt.

The next day, I came back in the house from a haggling session with the banker to hear Paul's voice: "I have had a revelation. The Most High has told me to put out of my mind the injustices I have suffered for faithfully carrying out my holy mission. I must go up to Jerusalem with you and justify myself among men, however perfectly I am already justified before the Eternal One."

"I am happy," Simon Peter said.

"Yes, I am not insensitive to your wishes for unity, and I am willing to degrade myself to serve the Most High, for I am nothing. I do not seek glory from men. What matters is that through me others will have new life in Christ Jesus."

Paul's humility was truly impressive.

Eight days after Simon Peter's decision, we sailed from Antioch's port, Seleucia Pieria. There were eight of us, Simon Peter, Barnabas, Paul, and Titus, Malachai and his two Judean companions, and, of course, I was with them. The ship stopped first at Berytus and then Caesarea. Since its next port was Alexandria, we got off and spent two days with Cornelius and his household and the two brethren from Dalmanutha. We wanted to leave immediately, but Cornelius had been insistent. Only Antioch had had the privilege of having the three great apostles, Simon Peter, Barnabas, and Paul, at one visit. It was good for the community, and good for us to see a thriving group of gentiles so firm in the Way. It was also good for Malachai and his friends to see it, though the Judeans were uneasy in the company of gentiles, even God Fearers like Cornelius, and, I assume, me. Thus after a brief and formal greeting, the trio set off for Jerusalem, though not before giving us directions to James's house.

When we left it was with a map that Cornelius had prepared. Communications among the communities had improved, so that letters were being exchanged every few months among Dalmanutha, Caesarea, and three villages in Samaria. Jerusalem remained outside this network.

Our route was not the most direct. Following Cornelius's map, we doglegged across Samaria and stopped at each of the three villages. Simon Peter had spoken of visits of a few hours, but again the local communities persuaded us to share their food and homes and spend the night with them. I am sure that we all expected the lion to lie down with the lamb before Jews and Samaritans would meet as brothers in the fellowship of common table and common worship. Surprisingly, Simon Peter, usually impatient, seemed in no hurry to push on.

At each evening's meal, the people asked him to say the blessing over the breaking of the bread. As at Caesarea, he invited Barnabas and Paul to share the ceremony with him, testimony to the prudence he had developed.

At Caesarea, Cornelius, Roman officer that he was, had assumed command of the community. Indeed, many of its members were his family, soldiers, servants, and slaves. In the Samaritan villages, however, there seemed to be no organization. In each of them, Simon Peter brought the men together, asking them to pray and then nominate three of their number as elders. We then cast lots, with the winner receiving a position similar to that of *gerousiarch* of a synagogue and the other two serving as elders with him.

The eight of us slipped quietly into Jerusalem. Pilate had been deposed more than a decade earlier and Agrippa was now dead. But all of the Land of Israel was under direct Roman rule, and Roman memories are long—as are those of the Temple hierarchy. Thus we thought it best not to attract attention. Passover would begin in another few weeks, and we tried to blend in with a few hundred other tired and dusty early arrivals.

With only moderate difficulty, we found James's house in the Valley of the Cheesemakers. Inside, he and five of the brothers were finishing the evening meal. I recognized only James and two others.

Simon Peter threw open his arms and caught James in a tight embrace that clearly embarrassed the man. Simon Peter's kiss of peace, aimed at James's lips, met a slight turn of the head and James's heavily bearded cheek. His greeting was correct but firm: "Blessed is he who comes in the name of the Lord." His tone was that of a disciplinarian, not a host. To Barnabas and Paul he merely bowed. He did not acknowledge either Titus or me.

"We have come up to the city to discuss problems of gentiles and the Way."

"Malachai has brought that news," James replied flatly. "We are always open to discussion, but the Law is clear."

"Anyone who looks to the Law for salvation has separated himself from the Christ," Paul responded.

"My brothers," Simon Peter put in before James could reply in kind, "let's not haggle like camel dealers. Two evenings from now, after we've rested, we will present our cases and discuss the matter with the brethren."

"There is no place in our community large enough to hold more than twenty people." James's tone discouraged further exploration.

"On our way," Simon Peter said, "we stopped to visit Josef of Arimathea. He's old and infirm now, but he said we could use his house for our meeting. Meanwhile, we'd be beholden to you for hospitality."

James looked both pained and nervous. Before he could speak, I said: "We are five. That is a heavy burden. Titus and I can stay at my family's house."

After the long trek from Caesarea around Samaria and across Judea, the few miles to our villa brought additional aches to my sore legs. Only after a long, hot bath and a brisk massage, several goblets of fruit juice followed by one of red wine, did I feel human again.

And only then did I have my first real conversation with Titus. He was a Gaul—the first of those barbarians I had ever met—a few years younger than I with considerably more energy and hair, not so shaggy as Judeans or Galileans but still full and black. His eyebrows were thick and equally tar in color, but he was clean shaven, like a Roman, emphasizing the paleness of his skin and the light hazel color of his eyes.

In the town of Lyon in his own country, he had taken a job with a Roman merchant, who later had decided to move east and had taken Titus with him, for he had a flair for languages. Indeed, I had assumed he was from one of the islands in the eastern Mediterranean where somewhat corrupt forms of Greek were the native languages. At Cyprus he had met Barnabas and later Paul, abandoned his merchant, and was now firm in the Way, though, like many others, without fully comprehending what the Way entailed.

Titus enjoyed the villa even more than I. Not only was this his first such luxury, but while I was tired he was physically and emotionally exhausted. When he came to Antioch, he, Barnabas, and Paul had already had a long and harrowing trip in which they narrowly escaped death. I found myself fascinated by their adventures. If Paul was an egotist, he had good reason, for he was a ball of kinetic energy, constantly preaching, arguing, wheedling, cajoling, intimidating people into accepting the Way. And he had suffered all the painful consequences of which he had boasted—and more of which he had not.

Titus was bright, not a philosopher or even a potential philosopher, but naturally quick. I found myself enjoying his company. "Rome," he said as we sat in the courtyard, wrapped in towels and sipping our wine, "Rome. That's where we must go."

I was in a languid half stupor. "Rome? Rome? Why ever Rome? Don't we have problems enough in Jerusalem and Antioch?"

"Because once we spread the good news there, once the Romans become Christians, the empire will be ours. Jesus the Christ will come again and found his kingdom."

"And we'll be masters of that empire?"

He smiled. "It's a thought, one that Paul won't accept, and you don't seem to either. What about Simon Peter?"

"He did once—at least something like it. Most of the disciples did, but so did Pontius Pilate. Now Simon Peter knows he was wrong, but he isn't sure what's right. Pilate didn't care whether he was right or wrong."

villa,
The
lked
eans
ve of
Paul
pt us
"My
mpor-
f the

ut in,
under-
alked.
ed, he
e used
ss—to
Spirit,
to the

time.
n Peter
hon the
ckering
nger
nt
ts
p

r thought it was right. Why?"

lain. Titus listened carefully. Only Theodora, and John the priest had done me that courtesy, ning to get through to Simon Peter.

," Titus said slowly. "It makes sense with what though I don't think he's thought it out yet. or the Christ to return at any moment, and s are getting anxious."

smile. "They're getting anxious? Simon Peter been waiting for almost twenty years. I only understand before they become cynical and

"

at James believes. Maybe that we're a sect the Essenes. Until recently Simon Peter ; now I think he's worked it out. But James? spect, though, he'd look on a second coming

t of a bother to the Romans, too," Titus s tend to make us seditionists."

tandards. The Lord God does it all. We just h while the angel of death passes over us."

n't understand the difference."

Then why do you think we should go to

s a soldier," he said. "He was captured by the into slavery; he bought his way out with the . He taught me a great deal about strategy. His Always go for the heart.' "

ded. It was inappropriate to note that his father ated soldier. Still, there was something in what he m, we had a foothold in the holy city of the Jews; Alexandria we had communities in the two most es in the Orient. Why not Rome itself? Why not the It was worth thinking about.

* * *

Shortly after dark, the brothers began slipping into Josef's
two, three, and four at a time so as not to attract attention.
house was not far from my family's villa, so Titus and I wa
over in daylight. James brought Malachai and the two Jud
who had gone down to Antioch. Eventually another twenty-fi
his community showed up. I recognized perhaps ten of them.
and Barnabas were a few minutes late, but Simon Peter ke
waiting for more than an hour. James was impatient to begin.
brothers," he said, "Simon Peter seems to have other, more i
tant, things to do, and we must move on with the work
Holy Spirit."

"I am not without knowledge of the Holy Spirit," Paul
"and She is not hasty. Like love itself the Spirit is patient,
standing." And then he began to talk; and he talked and t
He was, as he himself would have put it, not unclever. Ind
was brilliant if self-righteous and verbose. And that night h
his reputation for verbosity to force us to listen—more or l
how he, with minor assistance from Barnabas and the Holy
had spread the good news through the provinces and or
mainland of Greece itself.

It was enough—not to persuade but to gain the neede
For as Paul was savoring retelling events in Iconium, Simc
entered with Andrew, Bartholomew, John ben Zebedee, Sir
Zealot, and John the priest. Even in the courtyard's fli
shadows, I could read the look, first of surprise, then of a
James's face. Simon Peter would not be making his argum
before James's Judeans but also before Galileans—membe
Twelve—and John the priest, who, unlike any of James's su
or even James himself, could claim direct, personal know
the Master's teaching.

I suddenly understood the eight days between our de
leave Antioch and beginning the journey, Simon Pete
conversations with the young men in Antioch, and our
on the way. He had been playing for time for the young n
to Tarsus, Ephesus, and the Land of Israel to rally supp
surprised not only at Simon Peter's cunning, but also th
said nothing to me.

"Quintus never thought it was right. Why?"

I tried to explain. Titus listened carefully. Only Theodora, Mary of Magdala, and John the priest had done me that courtesy, though I was beginning to get through to Simon Peter.

"It makes sense," Titus said slowly. "It makes sense with what Paul is preaching, though I don't think he's thought it out yet. He's still waiting for the Christ to return at any moment, and some of the brothers are getting anxious."

It was my turn to smile. "They're getting anxious? Simon Peter and his friends have been waiting for almost twenty years. I only hope they come to understand before they become cynical and despair."

"And this James?"

"I don't know what James believes. Maybe that we're a sect like the Pharisees or the Essenes. Until recently Simon Peter wasn't sure about that; now I think he's worked it out. But James? I'm just not sure. I suspect, though, he'd look on a second coming as a nuisance."

"It would be a bit of a bother to the Romans, too," Titus chuckled. "And it does tend to make us seditionists."

"Not by Jewish standards. The Lord God does it all. We just stand back and watch while the angel of death passes over us."

"The Romans won't understand the difference."

"Probably not. Then why do you think we should go to Rome?"

"My father was a soldier," he said. "He was captured by the Romans and sold into slavery; he bought his way out with the money he earned. He taught me a great deal about strategy. His prime rule was, 'Always go for the heart.' "

I merely nodded. It was inappropriate to note that his father had been a defeated soldier. Still, there was something in what he said. In Jerusalem, we had a foothold in the holy city of the Jews; in Antioch and Alexandria we had communities in the two most important cities in the Orient. Why not Rome itself? Why not the Eternal City? It was worth thinking about.

*   *   *

Shortly after dark, the brothers began slipping into Josef's villa, two, three, and four at a time so as not to attract attention. The house was not far from my family's villa, so Titus and I walked over in daylight. James brought Malachai and the two Judeans who had gone down to Antioch. Eventually another twenty-five of his community showed up. I recognized perhaps ten of them. Paul and Barnabas were a few minutes late, but Simon Peter kept us waiting for more than an hour. James was impatient to begin. "My brothers," he said, "Simon Peter seems to have other, more important, things to do, and we must move on with the work of the Holy Spirit."

"I am not without knowledge of the Holy Spirit," Paul put in, "and She is not hasty. Like love itself the Spirit is patient, understanding." And then he began to talk; and he talked and talked. He was, as he himself would have put it, not unclever. Indeed, he was brilliant if self-righteous and verbose. And that night he used his reputation for verbosity to force us to listen—more or less—to how he, with minor assistance from Barnabas and the Holy Spirit, had spread the good news through the provinces and onto the mainland of Greece itself.

It was enough—not to persuade but to gain the needed time. For as Paul was savoring retelling events in Iconium, Simon Peter entered with Andrew, Bartholomew, John ben Zebedee, Simon the Zealot, and John the priest. Even in the courtyard's flickering shadows, I could read the look, first of surprise, then of anger on James's face. Simon Peter would not be making his argument only before James's Judeans but also before Galileans—members of the Twelve—and John the priest, who, unlike any of James's supporters or even James himself, could claim direct, personal knowledge of the Master's teaching.

I suddenly understood the eight days between our deciding to leave Antioch and beginning the journey, Simon Peter's quiet conversations with the young men in Antioch, and our dawdling on the way. He had been playing for time for the young men to go to Tarsus, Ephesus, and the Land of Israel to rally support. I was surprised not only at Simon Peter's cunning, but also that he had said nothing to me.

Seeing the arrival, Paul quickly recapped: "Throughout our missions, we saw marvelous deeds—gentiles' accepting the good news. They embrace it as much as, perhaps even more than, our Jewish cousins. My brothers, the Law was fulfilled in Christ Jesus. It is through faith in him and his message that we are now reconciled to the Most High, not in the Law but in faith. Those who have faith in Christ Jesus, a gift of the Holy Spirit, will be saved without the Law, without circumcision. Those who lack faith in Christ Jesus will not save themselves through the Law. Otherwise how do you explain the crucifixion and resurrection? If the Law were sufficient, why do we have the Christ?"

"Blasphemy!" Malachai shouted. "What you are proposing is a new religion, that we break with the faith of our fathers, renounce the heritage handed down to us through the promises of the Most High Himself, blessed be His name through all eternity, made to us through Abraham, Moses, and the prophets. You would renounce the Lord our God, the Holy One Himself!"

" 'Hear, O Israel,' " Simon Peter broke in, " 'the Lord our God, the Lord is one!' My brothers, we are Jews even as you are Jews. Our parents were Jews and their parents before them as long as memory runs. We are heirs to the Covenant of Abraham, and we do not renounce that gift. How could we? But do you not see that through the Master we have yet another gift? The Holy One, acting through the Master, has made a new Covenant, one open to all people of the world, not because of blood but because of faith. We are the New Israel. Since the Master's coming we live on a new earth and we await a new heaven. The kingdom of the Lord is at hand, and it is open to all people. We tempt the Lord our God if we dare to put a yoke on this New Israel. Whoever fears the Lord and acts righteously is acceptable to the Most High."

"We do not doubt the kingdom is open to all men," James responded. "But more than faith is required. Faith without good works is dead. The Law gives us the only guide for good conduct. Malachai is right. In rejecting the Law, you separate us from the faith of our fathers."

"The Antiochenes call you Christians," Malachai added. "And they're right. In rejecting the Law you reject Judaism. Worse still, in rejecting the Law you reject all behavior pleasing to the Most High. You allow your people to engage in lewd and systematic revelry in the name of the Master. They say they embrace the Way, but they behave like gentiles worshiping their filthy, orgiastic gods like Astarte and Dionysus."

"No!" Simon Peter shouted. "We do not allow our people to engage in any sort of lewdness. Do you have any facts that show otherwise?"

"Not facts," Malachai admitted, "but we have heard stories."

"As children we heard stories and believed them," Simon Peter said, "but as adults we've learned to test them against our experience. Now you all know Simon Peter fell victim to sins of the flesh and lay with a gentile outside of marriage. But you also know that Simon Peter confessed those sins and humbly begged forgiveness from the Eternal One. Those of you who knew me from the time I walked with the Master or from the time my brothers and I founded this community—you all know I am weak. But you also know I am truthful. May my right hand wither and drop away if I know anything of lewdness in our communities. Is it likely that some of our gentile brothers have sinned? Yes, just as some of our Jewish brothers have sinned, just as I've sinned, and perhaps just as some of you here tonight have sinned."

"You all know my brother speaks the truth," Andrew yelled out. There were loud yesses from the other Galileans.

"It is not Simon Peter's truthfulness we question," James said, "but his judgment. We would not exclude gentiles. We would preach to them and encourage them to follow the Master; but we would insist that they reject their pasts by embracing the Law of Moses. Then their faith in the Master's good news will have firm root in practice."

"My brothers," Barnabas spoke up, his voice quiet but his words clear. "Some of you know me. Most of you do not. I am a Jew, but I did not see the Master. My name was once Josef, and my family was from Cyprus, though I had come to live in Jerusalem. I heard Simon Peter speak at Pentecost many years ago. His words led me to the light and the truth. When I accepted the Way, Simon Peter gave me a new name, Barnabas, Son of Encouragement. With other Hellenistic Jews who believed in the Master's message, I had to leave Jerusalem during the persecution after Stephen's execution. It was then—how many years ago, fifteen?—that Simon Peter commissioned us to preach the Way to others, even as the Twelve were missionaries. I have preached in Damascus, in Antioch, across the Asian provinces, and in Greece. As Paul says, gentiles have accepted the good news as wholeheartedly as have Jews, and in far greater numbers. We cannot impose on them the burdens of circumcision and the details of the Law."

"Why not circumcision?" a Judean asked.

"For one thing," Barnabas explained, "it's painful for an adult. There's also danger of infection. Most important, many gentiles consider it a form of mutilation. It is, I am told, a crime under Roman law for a non-Jew to be circumcised."

"Then the solution is simple," James put in. "Let them become Jews and reject lewd practices."

"My experience is that they do reject lewd practices," Barnabas rejoined.

"In proclaiming ourselves the New Israel," Simon Peter said, "we reject neither Judaism nor the Law. Rather, we say that accepting the Way means accepting obligations that transcend the Law, and even justice itself. We reject imposing all the Law's details on gentiles because those details get in the way of the basic purposes of love and service. Like us, gentiles must accept the Law's core, the Ten Commandments, the Torah's injunction to love the Most High above all others and to love our neighbor as ourselves. 'All the rest is but a gloss,' I have heard that scholars say. That core is a necessary part of the Master's message. I believe that, Barnabas believes that, Paul believes that, and so do we all who come to you. More critical for this discussion, our gentile members believe that."

Before James or Malachai could respond, John the priest stood up and spoke in a hoarse whisper: "You all know me by name if not by sight. I am a Jerusalemite priest of the High Priest's own family. During the Master's life, I followed him, but, to my shame, only secretly. Only at the end did I do so openly. But I was allowed to share Simon Peter's vision of the risen Master.

And, I remind you, as a priest I am sensitive to matters of the Law."

John began coughing—a worrisome sign—and had to take a cup of water. "At the lake the Master appeared to Simon Peter, Thomas, Andrew, and to me as well. He told us to go and teach what he had taught us. He did not say to impose the details of the Law, but what he had taught us. And what he taught us was that the Most High was a loving Father Who walked with His people, and that we must love Him and our neighbors. Barnabas says more gentiles accept the Way than our own people. He is right. At Ephesus, our brother Jews have hardened their hearts against us. I go further than Barnabas. I conclude that our true mission is with gentiles. It is within them that the Holy Spirit is working."

"I cannot believe that!" Malachai started to say.

Andrew interrupted, speaking before he stood up: "I have wrestled with this question of gentiles long and hard. Like some of you, I thought the good news was only for us or for those who would become Jews. I have come to see that I was wrong, that my brother Simon Peter was right."

"And I, too," Bartholomew added. "And as far as I know all the others of the Twelve who are still alive."

"I, too," John ben Zebedee shouted. "Simon Peter speaks for me. Simon and I have been at Tarsus for some years now. Barnabas could be describing our experiences as well as his own. We would differ with John the priest only in noting that the Holy Spirit has also been active among the Jews of Tarsus."

Simon the Zealot stood up and cleared his throat for attention. He was not, as I have noted, an impressive man. Skinny and sallow in complexion, with a furtive look in his eye, he was also reticent. Friends called him meek; others thought him merely slow and timid. His Greek, once atrocious, was now only bad. Happily for comprehension he spoke in Aramaic. "My brothers, I align myself with Simon Peter, Barnabas, Paul, John the priest, and the others of the original disciples who are here. But we forget the most convincing argument for continuing our policy of admitting gentiles without requiring them to adhere to the Law, a live argument, alive in this room."

Even the Galileans looked at Simon with curiosity. When my eyes turned back to him, I saw his finger pointing at me. "There. Quintus the Greek. He followed the Master, for . . . for how long, Quintus?"

"Two years."

"Did the Master ever ask you to be circumcised?"

"No, but then he never paid attention to the Pharisees' rules about ritual purity either."

"If the Master could accept a Greek as a disciple and not ask him to be circumcised, then I don't know how we can." With that, Simon sat down.

It was a powerful array of forces, Paul's self-righteousness, Barnabas's quiet testimony about the facts of the gentile missions, Simon Peter's continuation of Judaism as the New Israel, John the priest's evidence, Andrew's and Bartholomew's confessions of changes of heart, John's vocal support, and Simon's live example.

Wisely, James did not care to pit the authority of his blood against the united word of those who had followed the Master and the Master's own practice. He stood up and looked around, his face at its most solemn, which was solemn indeed. "My brothers, I see grave dangers in the course you have taken, dangers that Simon Peter's own history shows are real. But. . . ." He paused. "We accept, as we always do and must do, the teachings of the Master, my brother. His will must be mine just as his blood is mine. Thus, I rule that this assembly and the Holy Spirit [Simon Peter's back stiffened at the words 'I rule,' and Barnabas laid his hand on Paul's shoulder] approve the mission to the gentiles, that they may be admitted to the Way without circumcision or requirements to obey the details of the Law, only its core as Simon Peter and others have characterized it."

There was silence.

After a few moments, James went on: "I also rule that gentiles, while exempt from circumcision and the details of the Law, must, to avoid scandal, not consume blood, eat food sacrificed to idols, or engage in incest, sodomy, adultery, or other sins of sexual lewdness."

James's second dictum was an obvious and feeble effort to save face, and Simon Peter let him do so. The matters of blood and food were trivial, and sexual license was something that neither Simon Peter, Barnabas, Paul, nor the others would have allowed, if they knew about it. Thus, at the time, it seemed prudent to accept the conditions, though we could not know what the future held. James's regal "I rule" was what bothered me, though I agree that Simon Peter's letting the claim pass was wiser than extending or worsening disagreement. Besides, in the wake of his resounding defeat, James's claim had a hollow ring.

Simon Peter suggested that he and James collaborate on a letter to be sent to Antioch telling the people there of the decision. Barnabas proposed sending it to all the communities we knew about, a suggestion we quickly accepted. It was a good idea. If the document were clearly written, James—or some other—would not be able to undo our work. Of course, it fell to me to do the drafting for Simon Peter. James took his burden on himself.

I must report that, though I never liked James or approved of his narrow, Pharisaical view of the Way, once the decision was made, his attitude toward me changed markedly. He did not become warm and friendly; neither trait was in his nature. But I had become a person. He talked with me frankly and haggled over words as cunningly as a Bedouin, but he accepted me, perhaps as an evil yet as a necessary one. He was, as I had thought, ambitious, manipulative, exploitive, hard, cold, and pettily legalistic. Still, however narrow his view of the Way, he was sincerely and totally committed to it.

It was repentance James stressed, and a blameless life through which men would earn the privilege of entering into the kingdom. He was deeply suspicious of proclamations of faith and contemptuous of speaking in tongues, indications of some good sense. He wanted us to follow a rigid, detailed moral code that would legislate what the Master had said must come through love. But the Master had also said that in his Father's kingdom there were many mansions. I only hoped I would never be lodged in James's.

Yet with that much noted, I must report our conversation as we completed the letter. "There," he said, "it's done. That should satisfy them."

"Simon Peter will be pleased; Paul will find it acceptable," I replied.

"I was not thinking of them."

I was quite surprised. "Who then?"

"Some of the people within and outside the movement."

My expression must have been one of incredulity, for that, indeed, was my reaction. James looked me directly in the eye and began talking very matter-of-factly. "I know you think me a hard man. I am. And I know Simon Peter can never forgive me for rejecting my brother during his lifetime. But Simon Peter is weak. His record shows it, and he admits it. If he had continued to lead that ramshackle collection of peasants, drifters, layabouts, parasites, and saints who were here when I first came, the Romans and the Temple officials would have wiped them out in three more years."

"They didn't for many years before you came."

"Yes," he conceded, "but there are limits to the Holy Spirit's tolerance. James ben Zebedee and Matthias were killed because Agrippa thought the people would approve his executing heretics. And many did. But by being more Pharisee than the Pharisees, I have eased the pressure on us. And this business of gentiles threatens to overturn our good work. There's change in the wind in the Land of Israel. I smell a revolt, and only the Most High knows what will happen. But if our people oust the Romans—even for a day—it will only be by the work of religious zealots. And they are not apt to share the tolerance we Jews have historically shown one another."

"And if the Romans win?"

"Then we'll need to have a hole to hide in, a Jewish hole. With this letter I can show our friends and opponents that we are as Jewish as they; for they, too, are trying to make converts. They understand that one can make small, temporary compromises to spread the word of the Most High."

"You spoke of people within the movement."

"Yes. I suspect you recognized few friends among the brothers in Jerusalem. Many of the older people left in despair at the slowness of the Master's return; others out of fear of Agrippa.

Some of them died; new members joined. We now have a substantial element of Pharisees. Malachai is the leader of that faction. He
doesn't represent a majority, but he has the largest minority. My
brother's message does not contradict the Law, it only goes beyond
the Law; and that's what Pharisees love to do. So they find us
attractive. And they make intelligent and sincere followers of the
Way. More reliable people than what we had."

"And the women?"

"That was arrant nonsense. Simon Peter had guilt about that
woman Mary of Magdala who followed my brother, so he wanted
to treat women as equal to men. But we know that a woman lacks
a man's nature." He paused for a moment. "Besides being foolish,
it was making people outside the movement angry. I heard rumbling before I even came back to Jerusalem, real fear that we were
setting a dangerous example by starting to treat women as equal
to men. People were saying we were threatening the natural order
of life."

I listened without making a critical comment. Much of what
James said was true; some of it was no more than a rationalization
for usurping Simon Peter's place; and some was flatly wrong. For
during his leadership, we had suffered only one bout of persecution, and we had weathered that. As for the loss of many of the
brothers, he did not mention their leaving during his leadership,
only during Simon Peter's.

From talking to Matthias I had no doubt that, whatever the
effect of hardship, James's turn toward Pharisaism was partly
responsible for the exodus of many older members, though, I had
to admit to myself, the delay in the promised second coming was
no small factor. On women, James spoke the truth; Simon Peter's
policy had angered even most of the Twelve. But it was the Master
who had begun the practice, not Simon Peter.

I made mental notes of the conversation to pass on to Simon
Peter, for I had no doubt that James was confiding to a Greek for
very practical reasons relating to the diplomacy of unity, not out
of a new-found sense of universalism.

6

❖ James and his people left after the meeting. I went back to my family's villa, and the rest of our faction spent the night at Josef's, where I rejoined them for breakfast. As we were getting ready to go into the city, John ben Zebedee asked us to wait a few moments. "There's something I must tell you. I spoke the truth last night, Simon Peter. You were right and we were wrong about gentiles. But James has a point."

"A point? What point?"

"Some of our gentiles in Tarsus haven't given up their old ways. Some of them are still worshiping idols." Paul's face crinkled at the mention of Tarsus, but John ben Zebedee continued talking. "They've just added the Lord God to their stable of deities; and some of them are talking about the Master as if he were a god, too."

"Jesus' relationship to the Father is not uncomplicated," Paul put in.

"The Master's relation to the Father was certainly very special, far beyond what any of us has experienced," John the priest added. "It's something we have to think through. I haven't yet been able to do so."

"Nor have I," John ben Zebedee said, which was likely to be true enough. He was a bit brighter than his brother had been, but neither could have boasted of great intelligence. "And I leave that to another day. I mention it because it's part of a larger problem."

"Which is?" Simon Peter asked.

"I keep hearing stories," John ben Zebedee went on, "that some gentile members of the Way are also having orgies, just like James and Malachai claimed. I can't prove it, but they're taking Paul's teaching that we're saved through faith and that the Law is dead to mean they're free of moral reins—not that they had many as idol worshipers to begin with, but some were God Fearers and knew better."

"Of what are you accusing me? What do you charge me with teaching?" Paul interrupted. "I have always spoken and written against fornication and worshiping false gods. Whatever blame there is, none attaches to me; my stripes attest to that."

"I was not looking for anyone to blame," John ben Zebedee said quietly. "I only thought we should all be aware of what I hear and be careful of what we say."

"I am never uncareful of what I say."

Simon Peter waved his hand impatiently, but his voice was soothing. "We're trying to find an explanation, Paul, not place blame. We all admire your intelligence and devotion. This is grave news and we must wrestle with it. Give Quintus a place where we can send a letter. Manaen the goldsmith in Daphne can always find us."

"My family has contacts with merchants across the Orient," I added. "Find someone who does business with us, and he'll see to it that a letter reaches me."

"You will find," Paul insisted, "that I am blameless."

Three days later, when we left Jerusalem, Barnabas, Paul, Titus with John Mark as their companion, Andrew and Bartholomew, John ben Zebedee and Simon the Zealot, and John the priest walked west to Lydda and Joppa, where all but Andrew and Bartholomew would look for ships going to Antioch, Ephesus, or Tarsus.

Simon Peter and I headed north for Dalmanutha. Actually, it was I who had first said he was going down to Galilee. Initially, Simon Peter had planned to return to Antioch to deliver the letter himself; but the next morning he told me he had changed his mind and would accompany me.

I had mixed feelings about his coming along, and not until later did I understand his decision. Company on the road was always welcome, and it was comforting to see someone who detested camels as much as I; but I would have preferred to be alone. I had important decisions to make about my own life. The crucifixion was almost twenty years in the past, and I was forty-five years old, getting a little paunchy, and quite bald—the latter concealed by a kaffiyeh, in the Arab style my uncle Theophilus had affected. Theodora and my father were financially secure, my cousins would see to that. My father's health was poor, but he had moved to Dalmanutha to be near Theodora. She was more than competent to care for him.

I had a few productive years left. How should I spend them? During our years at Antioch, Simon Peter had only once fallen into one of his black fits of despair. True, I had helped avert a few crises that might have pushed him into wine and depression; but he had, I thought, fundamentally changed. Assured, fluent, at times even eloquent, in Greek, with a much firmer judgment and even, as the recent council had shown, a real measure of political acumen, Simon Peter had little need of my help, certainly not as he had at Dalmanutha, in Jerusalem, or during the opening months at Antioch. What Paul called faith was hard in Simon Peter. At last, he seemed to have become the rock on which the communities could build.

Thus, whither Quintus? My first role, chronicler of the Master's life, had been filled; my second, the shepherd's shepherd, seemed no longer necessary. I remained, of course, deeply committed to the Way, though in my own fashion of hope rather than faith, of seeking rather than comprehending, analyzing rather than accepting, questioning rather than believing. I had long ago come to terms with the fact that, if I had faith, it was thin and brittle. I had adopted Theodora's rationalization that, if the Lord God had wanted me otherwise, He would have made me so.

With that much said, the emptiness in my heart torn open by the nails on the cross two decades earlier was still there. My relationship with the Master had never been fulfilled. My book was, I realized, a partial and ultimately unsuccessful effort to complete that relation, to re-create him in my memory's image. And I had other unfulfilled relations among the living, principally Mary of Magdala. (I had written my father off as a lost cause, and I still tried not to think of Ishtar.)

*   *   *

We arrived at Dalmanutha at dusk. Simon Peter handed me Mary's copy of the letter and told me to give it to her, while he went on to Capernaum.

I found her getting ready for the evening meal. She had aged in the last few years but nobly, I thought. Her once jet black hair was now flecked with gray; lines ran out from the corners of her eyes; and she was perhaps ten pounds heavier. Yet to me she was still lovely. The calm I had practiced during my last extended stay at the lake had left.

When Mary saw me, she looked surprised and, for a fleeting moment, pleased, as she brushed a few strands of hair from her forehead and straightened her robe. I accepted a gourd of cold water from her hands, now thick and calloused, no longer those of the only daughter of a wealthy family. I did not give her the kiss of peace, but merely handed her the letter. "Simon Peter and some of the others have met with James and his people in Jerusalem. We gave in on trivia, but I think you'll be satisfied."

She took it from me, motioned for me to sit on the cushions, and read the letter over quickly once, then more carefully a second time. "It's good," she said simply. "Here we seldom get red meat of any sort; Galileans don't drink blood, and there haven't been idols on this side of the lake for centuries. I'm content with this." She laid it on the table, then added: "But we would have continued to practice the Way as the Master taught us no matter what people at Jerusalem—or Antioch—said."

It was the response I had expected, indeed, so close that I knew Mary was playing a role she had written for herself in the play of life, one that minimized risks to the Way—and to her own heart.

I spent the next week visiting with Theodora and even a bit with my father. He had failed badly. I doubted I would ever see him again, and so did he. Still, neither of us could break down the old barriers. We were more than civil; but, as much as we tried, we could not coax caring into warmth.

Occasionally I went up to Capernaum to visit Simon Peter and his family. Naomi and Jephthania were still very much members of Dalmanutha, and most evenings Simon Peter joined them in the walk to and from the community. He felt, I could tell, a bit awkward treading on Mary's territory, but she was punctilious in her courtesy toward him, reading the letter from Jerusalem to the group, lauding Simon Peter's role in the decision, and several times inviting him to lead the ceremony of the breaking of the bread.

During the second week, I could detect that Simon Peter was becoming nervous, anxious to return to Antioch and learn how widespread was the problem John ben Zebedee had warned him about. He told me of his decision on a Sabbath, as we walked back the few yards from the small synagogue to his house. "We are leaving in two days," he said matter-of-factly, leaving me to argue about the wrong topic.

"I'm not quite ready," I protested. "And don't you think you owe Naomi and Jephthania a little more time?"

"Yes. That's why I'm taking them with me."

A hundred thoughts and a dozen explanations flashed across my mind, but I thought it better to say nothing.

"I've neglected them. I've not only left father and mother but also wife and daughter. To be honest...." He paused for a moment. "To be honest, when we started out for Jerusalem at that Pentecost I had no idea what would happen to us."

"I know."

"I expected the Master to come soon. To take my family would not only have been a burden, it would've been an act of unfaith; and my faith was weak enough."

"And now? Is your faith stronger or do you think the Master will not return? Or both?"

"Now, I've come to realize a lot of things." He smiled. "You might have guessed that, too." He didn't wait for me to offer a smart reply. "Your idea about the Master's having already come again—I don't know; I just don't know. It isn't how I first understood it, but then very little's turned out to be how I first understood it. I'm not sure, but I've learned some other things."

"Such as?"

"Such as what the Master meant by repentance, forgiveness, and love. Most of us don't commit huge sins. If we steal, it's not much; and if it is much it's only from the governments; and

Roman or Herodian, they're nothing but thieves themselves. We may get in an occasional fight, but we aren't likely to hurt anyone badly. Our lies are usually petty. Most of us don't see enough food to commit gluttony, though we might like to."

"Adultery?"

He smiled again. "Yes, adultery. The flesh is more complicated. The Torah forbids only adultery, which may be why we Jews get married so young. But those are usually sins of weakness, not of deliberate hurtfulness. Our sins are most likely to be sins of not thinking about others, not caring enough, not being considerate enough. That's what's so hard to forgive in others and so easy to commit ourselves—slights, unintended wrongs, selfishness, thoughtlessness. When the Master told us to repent our sins, he was telling us much the same thing as in commanding us to love each other, to worry about others' feelings, not to be concerned only with ourselves or our personal goals."

"So?"

"So, while I've been teaching others about the Way and having my own problems with the Master's slighting me, I've been ignoring, slighting, hurting my wife and my daughter. I've been inconsiderate and selfish. I thought I was acting for the good of the Way, and that's partly true. But maybe there's more. Maybe I believed that, if I suffered, I was more worthy. I might have been trying to earn the Master's love as I hadn't when he was alive. I didn't stop to think how I was making Naomi and Jephthania suffer. That they can forgive me shows they've followed closer in the Way than I have. At least now if Naomi and Jephthania go with me, we suffer together."

I agreed and told him I was genuinely pleased, for I had grown fond of Naomi, and no one in his right mind could help but love Jephthania and admire her courage. I added, however, that I would not be accompanying him, at least not yet. "I have a decision to make about my own life," I said.

"I know," he replied. "I'm not sure what that right answer is either."

*   *   *

As one might expect, it was Theodora who helped me toward a decision. She put to me my own question of whither Quintus. I had no answer, but she did. "Why not here in Dalmanutha? There is work to be done with people from the Dekapolis. We see more and more of them every year. And you have always loved Mary."

"I have always loved Mary? Why do you say that?"

"Because of the way you look at her, follow her with your eyes, seem hurt when she pretends not to notice you. If you don't know that you love her, you're the only one."

"What do I do about it? What are my choices?"

"Quintus." Her tone was one of exasperation. "You can be an ass. Why must you analyze everything? What do you feel?"

"I feel I should analyze the situation."

"Shit," she said, though in Aramaic not Greek, so it sounded less vulgar, and walked away, leaving me to try to skip stones across the lake.

It was right after breakfast. I came into the building that Mary used as her home and office. I had decided to go directly to the point, not out of any sort of strategy, for I was painfully aware that I was ignorant of the rules of the game I was playing, but out of fear that, were I to use time in indirection, I would lose courage and run away without saying my carefully rehearsed speech.

"Yes?" she asked curtly.

It was not a propitious cue, but I began: "We have known each other for many years."

"That's true."

I was not sure whether her tone evidenced boredom or irony, but I pressed on. "We are alike in many respects."

"That's true as well."

I did not let her interruption divert me. "We are growing old without the companionship and love we both need. I have been attracted to you since we first met, but each of us has had other obligations."

"And another love has consumed us," she said softly.

"What I am trying to say . . ."

"What you are trying to say is not possible, Quintus." Now there was real warmth in her voice and in her dark brown eyes. "I have felt the same sort of attraction to you. And I've known you felt it to me. But. . . ." She paused.

"Why 'but'?"

"Because we're both fully committed to something else."

"What else? The Master's return?" My ego was already smarting, and I'm afraid there was an edge to my voice.

"No, the more I have thought of it, the more I am convinced you are right and the others wrong. The Master has come again, and he will never leave us. The kingdom is within us. The Most High and so the Master's teaching will walk among His people forever. They need only repent their sins and love one another and share with one another to enjoy that kingdom."

"Then why can't we marry and share the love we have? Paul and some of the others say it isn't sensible to marry because the end is near. But if you don't believe the Master's coming on a white stallion to slaughter Romans, then follow what your own Scripture says: 'It is not good for man to live alone.' "

"But I am not alone, nor are you. He is with us, always, just as is the Holy Spirit. You've said so yourself."

"I didn't mean he was with us in the way you imply. Besides, wouldn't he want us to have our share of happiness?"

"I have a plentiful share, Quintus, except when I realize I am hurting you."

"You've forgotten he snatched leadership away from you and gave it back to Simon Peter?" It was a nasty, cruel, selfish, even vile thing to ask, but I was hurt.

Mary didn't answer immediately, but waited until some of the flush drained from her cheeks. "I have had much time to think and to pray. I am at peace with myself now, Quintus. Who leads is unimportant. In fact, it is the wrong question to ask. What matters is that the Master is with us always."

"You do not worry about others *mis*leading us?"

"I have faith in the Master's promise of the Holy Spirit who will guide us. The letter you brought from Jerusalem is evidence of that guidance."

It was also, I thought, evidence that the Holy Spirit had enjoyed considerable human help in guiding Her people. But the work of the Holy Spirit was not my central concern that day. All that mattered was that I had failed. I could think of no additional argument.

The nonrational act of taking Mary in my arms was not something I had planned. I merely did it, as much surprised as she. She returned my embrace and my kiss for several long, but too short, moments. Then she moved her head against my shoulder without releasing her arms from around me. Indeed, as she spoke her embrace tightened. "No, Quintus, no. There's nothing left for me to share with others."

I pushed away and looked at her eyes. She was not sobbing, but tears were running down her cheeks. "No," she repeated, then kissed me again lightly on the lips and walked away.

I left Mary and Dalmanutha. Now I was the one angry with the Master. By keeping her bound to him even in death he was depriving me of the love and comfort of the woman I wanted since my youth. For the first time I felt true empathy with Simon Peter. I was full of hurt and resentment, but together these forces could grapple only temporarily with something else that welled up inside me, something that, like Simon Peter, I could neither explain nor even understand.

I went back to Scythopolis, mended fences with my cousins, and, refusing offers of transportation, walked up the Valley of the Jezreel and across the Great Plain of Galilee to the coast, then south to Caesarea and spent a few weeks with Cornelius. As a gift before his death my uncle Theophilus had had three copies made of my book on the Master's life. I had sent one copy on to Antioch with Simon Peter, another to James at Jerusalem, and the third to Cornelius.

Then I went walking again, this time south and east, stopping at one of our communities in a Samaritan village, next at Jerusalem, then Jericho, and finally, with the help of Neriah, the priest at Jericho who had followed John the Baptizer, at an Essene monastery in the cliffs above the Asphalt Sea.

With Neriah to vouch for me, the monks took me in without question. Life there was hard, yet it was good, though I washed more than I needed and ate less than I wanted. For six months, I stayed in the huts on top of the cliffs, sharing the monks' existence, living like a lizard among the rocks, trying to pray for divine guidance. But my soul remained as dry as the hot air we breathed. I got no answer, but then I am not sure how much I truly prayed. Mysticism and asceticism are alien to my philosophy.

When I left, it was with a better understanding of John the Baptizer, the Master, and Matthias, though I knew little more of Quintus.

I went first to Scythopolis, where I learned my father had died. In the Jewish fashion, Theodora had buried him immediately in a tomb in the Valley of the Doves, west of the lake. Then she had come home with the news. I arrived while she was still at my family's villa, so we were able to visit, eliminating any reason whatever for my going back to Dalmanutha. I waited for a small caravan heading west and spent a few more days with Cornelius and his people. Then I took a ship to Antioch, tired and cleansed but still unsure of my life and my faith.

I found the life of the Antiochene communities basically unchanged. A few of the followers had left us, mostly, I heard, because of impatience at the Master's failure to return. On the other hand, we had recruited new members. On balance, we had had a net gain of four adults and six children.

Since Simon Peter now had his family with him, I thought it best to find new lodgings, but he insisted I stay on with them in Theophilus's house. Naomi was polite though hardly enthusiastic. Although I had grown fond of her, we had never been close. Perhaps in some way of which we were not conscious, each looked on the other as a rival for Simon Peter's love. In any event, we had long ago sealed a tacit truce, and it remained in force at Antioch.

I could have refused Simon Peter's hospitality, but not the pleading invitation in Jephthania's eyes. When I had visited them in Capernaum, whenever I had been in Dalmanutha, I read to her from my manuscript, from the copy of the Torah that I found in Mary's villa, and from a few of the plays of Sophocles I had brought from Scythopolis. When Theodora joined the community, she took over the task. Being read to was Jephthania's greatest pleasure, though she always cheerfully looked for things she could do to help others.

John Mark was a minor addition to our entourage. He had had a falling out with Paul and Barnabas (mostly Paul, I gathered) and had returned to Antioch, where he had fastened himself onto Simon Peter. As in my case, Naomi insisted that John Mark share Theophilus's house, but unlike my case, John Mark accepted without protest.

A tall, thin young man, he was a bit vain, best evidenced by the careful barbering of his thick black curls and constant trimming of the small, Greek-like beard he affected. He fancied himself both an orator and a writer. There was some justification for the first; his voice was as deeply resonant as Simon Peter's. Indeed, I suspect he practiced mimicking Simon Peter's style. As for the second claim, his Greek was, at best, primitive. And diminishing both claims was the fact that never did I hear from his lips or read from his scribblings an original thought. Still, he was basically a good, if not overly intelligent, young man. I put him to work by allowing him to copy my life of the Master.

The most significant difference I found at Antioch was in Simon Peter's personal life. I never understood his relationship with Naomi, but, obviously, I never understood how one should, or even could, relate to women. She mothered him, bossed him, advised him, deferred to him, served him, ordered him about. If those things add up to love, then she loved him and he her. I think, though I can neither document nor explain it, she joined iron to the rock of his faith.

And Naomi goaded Simon Peter to push for a larger role for women. Her model was Dalmanutha, where the sexes were close to equal despite sharp divisions of labor. He tried as best he could, but his success was limited. Centuries of culture had left a deep cleft in conscience. Eventually, however, we did have two churches that met in widows' houses, and they exercised, quite capably, I might add, the functions of leader. Occasionally in the other communities, a woman would lead the ritual of the sharing of the bread, but only occasionally. To break the grip of tradition, one needs a person like Mary of Magdala who combines intelligence, practical judgment, beauty, money, crushing will power, and the fact of having been singled out as special by a revered male leader. It is not a combination that frequently occurs among men or women.

With Jephthania the emanations of love were so tangible one could almost touch the rays that went out from her eyes and returned from Simon Peter's. Whenever he was not with the communities, he was her nurse, her companion, friend. He seldom spoke to her and she, of course, never to him, but one sensed complete communication between the two. And, at Antioch as at Dalmanutha, she was able to communicate her love and understanding to others as well. Thus she was again a source of strength for us all.

I could not help reflecting on our lives, especially Simon Peter's. Above the Asphalt Sea, I had had firsthand acquaintance with ascetic, mystic men who spent much of their lives in prayer and fasting. In their way they were very holy, very close to the Lord God in a relation that seemed marvelously peaceful and left them wonderfully serene about the affairs of man.

Simon Peter was not like them at all. He was passionately, often angrily, involved in the tedious business of living in this grubby world. He was no recluse who communed in solitary prayer with his God. If he did so commune, he did it quickly, for most of his life was spent in action. That he prayed, I am sure; but what he said I would not presume to know. And while Simon Peter spoke to the Lord God, I believe the Lord basically listened. His grace came silently, indirectly, and, as events had shown, when we least expected it.

I am trying to say, however badly, that Simon Peter expressed his ambiguous feelings toward the Lord God through action rather than contemplative prayer, and the Lord reciprocated in kind. The New Israel was a well chosen title, for Israel means "he who wrestles with God," and Simon Peter did that. I hoped some day there might be forgiveness as well as obedience in his attitude toward the Most High and that the Lord might learn from that experience to be a little kinder toward all His children. Perhaps the Master, who called Him Father, might fully convert Him to the Way. I remembered the story I had heard from Philo that once the Lord God prayed, and the prayer was: "Let My justice be tempered by My mercy."

During the intervening months, Simon Peter, I quickly found, had made little progress in discovering whether there were systematic abuses of the doctrines of the Way among our gentile members. It was not, I suspect, something that he wanted to discover. I didn't either, but I thought we had little choice in the matter. Thus I went to my usual sources, suqs and taverns. I learned enough to be suspicious, but not enough to identify particular individuals or to pinpoint where they were meeting or even what they were— exactly—doing.

7

✤ Balsides was a slave, a Greek-speaking Parthian whom the Romans had taken, along with his wife and two small daughters, during an incursion to retaliate for a Parthian raid. The captured soldiers had been carted off to Patmos to work the mines, a brief and painful postponement of the death they might have suffered in battle. At the slave mart in Antioch, Glaucon, an Antiochene banker, was attracted to Balsides because he could read and write three languages.

The banker bought the Parthian, along with his family, reason-ing he would get more work out of a slave emotionally as well as

legally tied to his household than from a man who constantly
sought to escape. As Glaucon had hoped, Balsides's post as a
minor government official had taught him much about the trade
between the Mediterranean and the Tigris-Euphrates Valley. And
for six years, he served his master well. In return, like some
educated slaves, he had more freedom than many citizens because
he had economic security.

Then, when Balsides was thirty-four and his children twelve
and fourteen, Glaucon died. His closest relative, a brother living in
Tarsus, put the entire estate, including the slaves, up for sale. This
time Balsides and his family were less fortunate. He was purchased by a caravan master from Pontus on the Black Sea who
needed Balsides's skills but not his entourage. A merchant from
Cyrene bought his wife as a concubine, and a wholesaler in slaves
won the auction for their daughters. Balsides twice tried to escape
and was caught, branded, whipped to within a few millimeters of
death, then sold to an Antiochene family. By that time it was
much too late to trace his wife or children.

A year after returning to Antioch he heard Paul speak in Jawbone Street: "Those of you who have been baptized have clothed
yourself in Jesus, God's anointed one. In him there is neither Jew
nor Greek, slave or free, male nor female; but all are one." The
next afternoon Balsides returned to the neighborhood, listened
again, and followed Paul back to the steps of a synagogue in the
eastern sector of the city and heard him argue with a group of Jews
that the coming of Jesus meant that faith had replaced the Law.

The following day Balsides asked to be baptized and, with four
other slaves, became a member of the group that met at Lucius's
villa. What Lucius did not know was that Balsides soon began
preaching a version of the good news to other slaves and even to
his owner, the widow of the man who had bought him from the
Pontian. Within a few months, Balsides dropped out of Lucius's
group, but not from his own version of the Way, which he continued to preach and practice. This man was to have momentous
effects on all the communities.

*   *   *

I did not expect it to happen, then or probably ever again. My love for Mary, broken by only a brief and almost incestuous attraction to Ishtar, had led to a deep pain that I had no desire to repeat. I had left the Essenes reconciled to a celibate life, a condition easier to accept on their diet than on the rich food of Scythopolis or Antioch.

Then, she came in alone, her face modestly covered with a shawl; but no veil could conceal the milk-pale skin of her hands and forehead or the startling blue of her eyes. Even less could a veil disguise the quiet assurance and independence of her walk. I had never seen her before, of that I was absolutely certain. She was a slightly taller version of Ishtar; and I rationalized staring at her by telling myself that I was concerned about Simon Peter.

I watched her until she was at the edge of the courtyard, a few paces from anyone else. I realized I was violating the social rules, but it was as if I was watching myself cross the stones and approach her. "I am called Quintus," I said half-apologetically. "You are new to our group."

I think she smiled; it was difficult to tell what was going on behind that shawl, but her eyes—on a level with mine—looked like she was smiling. "I am Merope. Do you recognize all the women who follow the Way?" Her Greek was exact, with only the slightest trace of an accent I couldn't place.

I felt the blood rushing to my cheeks. "No, not really. I . . . people with blue eyes are rare here."

"But your eyes are blue."

"I am Greek, a real Greek," I added defensively—and stupidly.

"A real Greek! And one with a Roman name."

"My mother's family is from Athens." I did not tell her how far back.

"And the man who gave the name Quintus to his son?"

"A Roman officer," I responded. Then seeing her eyebrows arch, I quickly added: "I grew up with my mother's family in Scythopolis."

"Scythopolis, Scythopolis. I have heard of it. You have a magnificent statue of Bacchus there, don't you?"

"We call him Dionysus. The Romans call him Bacchus."

"Dionysus, Bacchus, the name doesn't matter. Does that mean you revel a great deal?"

I laughed rather than spoke. The truth was, of course, no; but I didn't think it would hurt to appear more sophisticated about such things than I was. "Revelry is out of favor with all Jewish sects," I said.

"Are followers of the Way members of a Jewish sect?"

"Perhaps we're new Jews."

"Well, with *agape*, our love feast, we can't be old Jews. They're such a stolid, joyless people, so full of 'thou shall nots'; but I like their idea of a single god. One gets so confused around here. There must be just hundreds of gods. I never know who I'm supposed to offer incense to or kill a chicken for."

I could not tell how much she was making fun of me and how much she was trying to provoke a serious conversation, so I shifted the topic. "And you, are you Greek?"

"Don't you know that all of us in the Orient are now Greeks or Romans or even both?"

"What were you born?"

"A woman, at least so I have been told."

"I meant where?"

"In Galatia. I am a Celt."

"Why are you in Antioch?"

She blinked. "I married an Antiochene." She must have seen my expression change, for she quickly added: "He died ten months ago."

"I'm sorry."

"Don't be, unless for him; not for me." Her tone became less frivolous. "The marriage was arranged; that is to say, I was bartered. My parents weren't poor, but neither were they as rich or important as their ambitions. A wealthy son-in-law, even if he was their own age, made a nice addition to their prestige."

"And for you?"

She shook her head. "Eight years of a comfortable, rich life that could hardly have been more dull. My husband was a decent man; but, because we had no children, I lost his . . . favor."

"And tonight? Why have you come?"

"Curiosity, of a sort. I wanted to meet Simon Peter. I heard him speak once, near the statue of Romulus and Remus. I didn't expect a fisherman to speak such educated Greek. [I suspect I grinned at that observation.] He promises 'a new heaven and a new earth' and Paul says this kingdom will come without the no-no's of that dreary Jewish Law. Is Simon Peter such a saint as everyone says?"

"At least."

"I hope so. Balsides, one of my slaves, is a follower of the Way. He talked to me several times about it, but it was Simon Peter's talk that made me decide to become a Christian."

"A what?" I had only heard that term once before, during our recent debate with James in Jerusalem.

"A Christian. That's what the Antiochenes call us to distinguish us from the Jews."

"Oh. I don't think Simon Peter will like that."

"Why?"

"I told you, we're Jews—of a sort."

Her brows knit together in what I guessed was a frown. "I thought we'd settled that we weren't."

"We are the New Israel, Simon Peter says. The Master's death has made a new Covenant with God, one open to all people of the world, not just to the sons of Abraham."

"How fortunate for us. I've always wondered how it would be to run around saying no to everything that seems interesting or fun." There was a slight lilt to her voice, not enough to tell me whether she was bantering or really being ironic.

"Balsides," I asked, "the name means nothing to me; is he a member of Lucius's community?"

"No, not really. He's come to Lucius's house and once to yours, but he is a member of his own group. There're only a half dozen of us."

It was my turn to arch my eyebrows. "Oh?"

"You seem surprised. Israel old or new doesn't have a monopoly of the Way. There are eight or ten gentile groups scattered around the city."

"Your people have been baptized?"

She nodded. "Of course. Some by old Nicolaus, some by Barnabas and his friend Paul, some by Manaen or Lucius; and these people baptized others. We eat together, share bread and wine at our love feast in the Master's name, and wait in joy for his return."

I was totally smitten, as I probably need not add; and she seemed at least mildly interested in me. In fact, it was her suggestion, not mine, that we slip out of the meeting after Simon Peter had finished his brief talk. Leaving a dark, crowded courtyard with attention fixed on a charismatic figure was not difficult. We stood by her litter and looked at the sky and talked and looked at the buildings and talked and looked at the sky again and talked more about trivia. The message, I have concluded in my old age, is in the movement of the lips, not the sounds that come from them.

She left with a squeeze of my hand and a promise I would call at her house in two nights. It was only six "blocks" from Lucius's villa and scarcely more than twenty from the house that Theophilus had loaned us. I confess I thought of little else in the intervening time. I even forgot to dun Lucius for money.

I tried to explain to Simon Peter that I would talk to "a friend" who seemed to know something about some groups we didn't, and these might help us in our search. Without grasping the similarity to Ishtar or the other subtleties of the situation, Naomi and Simon Peter understood I was going courting more than I was protecting the Way and were supportive, though teasingly so.

I rented a litter. In my naïveté I thought it would make a better impression than walking. Simon Peter frowned on the extravagance, but his protest was mild. It was, after all, my money.

Merope's house was not large, but it was stately. The outside wall circled a garden that in turn encircled the house itself, built not unlike Simon Peter's in Capernaum, though vastly different in size and elegance. The house itself formed three sides of a square, with a smaller garden in the center, complete with a pair of olive trees, a mimosa tree, a small fountain, and three benches. The walls of the two wings of the house had no opening to this center courtyard. One had to go straight ahead through a narrow door into the heart of the house. As I passed through that door, I noticed that the walls of the living area were movable, mounted on tracks. In winter they closed off the house from the courtyard; in the summer they would roll back to allow free entry to the breeze and the smell of flowers.

A pair of handsome young Scythian slaves, both in their late teens, had opened the outer door in the wall and led me through the courtyards into the house itself. There, a pair of lovely young Scythian girls, a matched set with each other and the two boys, took off my sandals, washed my feet with warm water, dried them carefully with a fluffy towel, and helped me put on fur-lined slippers. Then one offered me a small goblet of wine, thickened with syrup in the Roman fashion. I could not help admiring the girls' beauty. It was a tribute to Merope's self-esteem that she could tolerate such rivals for masculine attention—as well as evidence of the size of her purse that she could have outbid dozens of lechers for such a gracefully proportioned pair of blond slaves.

When they left, I took time to admire the room's architecture, inhaling the odor of sandalwood chips scattered among the wood burning in the open fireplace. The quiet taste of the house was impressive; but neither that nor my veiled glimpses of Merope two evenings earlier prepared me for the stunning woman who greeted me.

Her long black hair hung loose about her shoulders, kept in place by a thin silver band around her head, her only jewelry other than matching silver bracelets around her wrists and ankles. The rest of her face was as striking as her eyes: a full mouth, with lips slightly dyed to accentuate their redness, a long thin nose, and high cheekbones.

Her body was draped rather than covered by a plain white wraparound dress of silk that left one shoulder bare and reached only to her knees, revealing ample cleavage at the top and lovely legs at the bottom. No Jewish woman and few Greeks would have dared to wear such a gown. I was reduced to a gawking youngster.

She smiled as she came across the room, took the wine from me, sipped it, and gave it back. "Welcome," she whispered in a voice that was huskier than I remembered. Then placing her hand gently on my arm, she guided me into the dining area. The heat from my slippers, four charcoal braziers, the fireplace, and perhaps from my own interior furnace made the room seem very warm.

There were two dining couches, set close to each other, separated by a long table on which the servants could place food and wine. The two Scythian boys helped us to recline, facing each other. Our feet were toward the open fireplace; at our heads, a pair of lamps. In the flickering shadows next to the fireplace another young man began strumming a lyre. Behind him a woman began to sing softly. From the timbre of her voice, I guessed the singer was older than the Scythians. I could not understand the language; it was not Semitic; perhaps one of the Celtic dialects. But my attention focused on linguistics for only a moment.

A steward appeared wearing fur slippers like mine and white pantaloons, without a top. "This is Balsides," Merope said, "the man who introduced me to the Way." He bowed but did not smile. Even in the half-light, I could clearly see the ugly brand burned into his cheek and forehead, his mutilated right ear, and, when he turned away, his back, scarred like Paul's and Simon Peter's. He took my goblet, replaced it with a larger one that he set on the table between us with a small loaf of bread.

He smiled for the first time and tore the bread into three chunks, took one himself, and gave us the the rest. As we finished chewing he said, "Jesus has died, Jesus has been raised, Jesus will come again." Then he lifted the goblet, took a long swallow, and said, "*Maranatha.*"

Merope sipped the wine and handed the goblet to me.

As silently as he had come in, Balsides was gone. Then the Scythian girls, dressed like him, though with blouse-like tops that left their navels bare, brought in trays of small pieces of meat—I guessed pork—marinated in an exotic sauce, and, I judged from the smoky flavor, roasted on an open fire. Next came a tray of large shrimp, with the same smoky flavor, though without the sauce, then trays of mussels, and small pieces of lobster. Each tray came with two slabs of bread so we could clean our fingers and palates.

Despite the variety, the meal was light. I am not sure, however, how much wine I drank. Not only were we sharing the same goblet, but each time it decreased by more than two inches, Balsides would swiftly refill it. Several times as I reached for the wine my fingers met Merope's. Not only did she make no effort to retreat, she stroked the back of my hand.

At the end of the second course, Balsides removed the center table, and the two Scythian boys pushed my couch next to Merope's. At that point, the woman stopped singing and the music changed: The beat quickened and the soft chords became discordant, even jarring. The two blonde girls returned to the room. Sliding between us and the open fire, they shed their clothes and began a rhythmic dance, emulating two young lovers. Merope began to moan softly.

I should have left then, of course, but my physical reactions were drowning my reason and urging me to stay.

I shall not describe what followed or the various partners we both enjoyed. When it was done—for the time—I heard Merope's voice: "The slaves will prepare a hot bath for us. It will restore our strength for the rest of the evening."

I pulled myself up wearily. The room was empty, except for the two of us, and the dark singer, who was sitting on the other side of the couch, languidly running her hands over Merope's body. I tried not to look at them, partially out of shame for what I had done and even greater shame at what I would happily do again under the temptation of those lovely bodies.

Merope read something in my face, but the wrong thoughts. "We can thank Paul for this and your friend Simon Peter for bringing us together."

I sat up. "What?"

"Paul taught us that we can have the protection of the great Jewish god and keep our own customs. The Hebrew Law does not bind us. We are saved by faith in Jesus the Christ. All we need do is believe in his return and in love share everything we are and have with all our brothers and sisters."

A true missionary would have explained, even argued; but I picked up my clothes and began walking—probably staggering—out into the courtyards and through the gate to the waiting litter. I assume it was only in my imagination that the bearers snickered.

*   *   *

At home, I washed myself thoroughly—twice—then went to bed. I could hear Simon Peter breathing heavily in the next room, but I could not slip off. After an hour of tossing and turning, I got up and paced around the cold courtyard.

Of course, I felt deep disappointment. I had been enormously infatuated with Merope. Indeed, I had fantasized about marrying this beautiful, intelligent woman. That I had lain next to her while she had heterosexual intercourse with three other men and homosexual intercourse with three women left me sickened and angry. But more than disappointment in Merope, I felt disgust with myself. I had been a willing—no, hyperactive—participant in the orgy—with her and her female slaves, but, at least I could say, not with her male slaves. I had to admit that, at the physical level, I had completely enjoyed the experiences; and even now flashing recollections aroused erotic physical twinges along with shame. Still, my conscience ached, painful testimony to the route I had so slowly traveled and down which I had so suddenly returned.

By the standards of Scythopolis, the evening had been, up to my leaving, spectacular. Among my people, sex was something to be enjoyed, savored, and on occasion even overdone. That one's partner was equally ecstatic only promised greater pleasure the next time. (As nonpersons, slaves didn't count; as long as they were doing their master's or mistress's bidding, they were mere instruments like the dildoes some women used.) Romans were more straitlaced about such matters; but, where no adultery was involved, especially no adultery with the wife of a powerful man, they took their sexual gratification wherever and whenever it was freely offered—and when going a-conquering, even where it was not. Only Jews would hurl condemning thunderbolts at Merope or me. In many ways I had become, I suddenly realized, more Jew than Greek—a very disquieting thought.

I tried, without great success, to put the issue of my personal corruption out of my mind, for tonight had the gravest of implications for the movement. There could now be no doubt of some factual grounding for the rumors and innuendos we had so often heard about our gentile converts. I had seen a nightmare of how some people envisioned the Way: the promise of a new heaven right here and now on this old earth, in which all one had to do to gain citizenship was to believe in the command of the Master to love and share without limit. No law, moral or man-made, blocked the path of a continuous love feast. It was a terrifying image, one that made me more understanding of James and even of that pious ass Malachai.

I waited a few days before I said anything to Simon Peter. Indeed, I might never have told him had we not been graced by another visit from Malachai. He was accompanied by the same two Judeans as on the first trip; and again Manaen, Lucius, and Simon had joined us at Simon Peter's invitation. Paul and Barnabas, back from another of their missionary sallies, also attended.

Pontifically solemn as ever, Malachai made a great show of delivering a letter (in Aramaic) from James to Simon Peter, who handed it to me. I read it aloud:

> From James, the brother of the Master, and all the followers of the Way at Jerusalem, to Simon Peter and our brothers at Antioch, peace in the name of the Most High, blessed be His name for all eternity.
>
> We commend to you our brother Malachai, who is well known to you and to us. He has more specific information of the matter we discussed at Jerusalem some nine months ago. This information comes from Jews in your city, some of whom have given it directly to us, others of whom have sent it to the family of the High Priest. I need not tell you the pressures that are being exerted on us in this affair. We rely on your loyalty to the Master's teaching to rid us of this terrible scandal.
>
> We bid you a holy farewell as we await in joyful hope the Master's return.

Malachai was, I noticed, gloating as I read the document. When I was done, he wrinkled his nose and arched his eyebrows. "Do you want my specific information?" he asked.

"Yes," Simon Peter, "but first, what is this 'pressure' James speaks of?"

"You may recall"—now Malachai was smirking—"we suffered a scandal a few years ago when the then leader of the Way in Jerusalem was committing adultery with a gentile woman. That scandal not only caused some members to desert us, it also once again brought the movement to the attention of the priests in the Temple, who were angered to see a Jew behave in such a manner. No doubt the deaths of James ben Zebedee and Matthias the Essene were an indirect result of that anger. This news—and this time, it is hard testimony, not merely vague stories—has reached those same people. We fear that, at the very least, we shall be barred from the Temple, perhaps even from synagogues in the Land of Israel. There is also the risk of more serious action. The Romans, you may have heard, have never been fond of us."

Simon Peter did not deign to respond to the false imputation of guilt in the deaths of the saints, nor even to the final piece of pompous cuteness. "And your specific information?" he asked.

Malachai proceded to tick off the names and locations of five households in which orgies were being regularly conducted under the guise of our *agape*, the breaking and sharing of bread and wine in memory of the Master. Merope's name was second. "You see what happens," Malachai, mustering every ounce of his wit, concluded, "when you lie down with dogs."

Lucius nodded his head sadly. "I have talked to some of my people. No, I confronted them. Only one admits directly participating in such vileness himself, but all said they knew about such practices. Their information is incomplete, but it confirms what Malachai has told us."

The veins in Simon Peter's forehead were bulging, but his voice was calm. "We thank you for the trouble you have taken to make this long journey to help us. If you can stay with us a few days, we'll have a response for you to take to James." Then he turned. "Manaen, could one of your people escort our brothers back to your house in Daphne so they may rest in comfort?"

As soon as our esteemed visitors had left, we tried to get down to business; but Naomi had other plans. She helped Jephthania

into the room and edged her onto a chair Simon Peter had built
for her. We, of course, could only gather round her and talk to her,
while Naomi served us wine. (I should say that all of us but Paul
did so; he stood sulking in a far corner of the room.) I have no
doubt that Naomi had overheard everything and was deliberately
delaying so that Simon Peter's temper would cool. After fifteen
minutes, the two women left us alone.

The reprieve may have saved Simon Peter from apoplexy, but
not from all his temper. As soon as the women had left, I said,
"At least some of this is true. I can bear witness." I then told the
story of what had happened at Merope's house, not in full, lurid
detail, but enough so the picture would be clear without being
pornographic.

Simon Peter roared: "This, this is . . . ." He switched to
Aramaic: "This is vile sacrilege. We break the bread in memory of
the Master, a symbol of the pure love we must share, not lewd
lust. How dare they? They're nothing but pig-eating, blood-drinking
whores and whoremongers."

We let him vent his rage for several minutes. The epithets he
created would have amazed even a citizen of Fescennia, a town
whose sole claim to fame is the high level to which it had brought
the art of scurrilous imagery. Eventually he quieted, and we all sat
in silence for a full ten minutes. Not even Paul ventured a comment. Finally, Simon Peter said, "We must do what Malachai
wants, which, Quintus has told me, may be more than even James
wants."

"What do you mean?" Barnabas asked.

"I mean we must not allow gentiles and Jews to eat at table
together; we must not baptize any more gentiles until they have
at least become God Fearers, until they've taken instruction in the
Law and followed it for six months or more. Perhaps we should
even require circumcision before baptism. I'm not sure about
that."

"But I am!" Paul spoke, his voice now reaching a high, strident
pitch. "I am sure you're wrong. You have eaten with gentiles for
years. You have never required Quintus to be circumcised. I am
not without direct evidence of your true position. This is Paul,

who heard you speak at Jerusalem; this is the apostle called by Jesus the Christ himself. You are playing the coward!"

"I am playing the good shepherd," Simon Peter replied evenly. "My sheep are in serious trouble. I am trying to isolate the cause of trouble and cure it, not only for the sake of this flock, but also for the flock at Jerusalem."

"Simon Peter is right," Manaen said. "We have tried and failed."

"I agree." I was surprised to hear Barnabas say those words. "I was the first in this room to preach to gentiles. It was I who brought you on my mission, Paul. We have worked hard and the Holy Spirit has rewarded our work. But we have not built as well as we thought. Simon Peter is right. We have to go more slowly. This . . . this lewdness is sacrilegious. It makes a mockery of all that we believe. They have used your words about the Law to justify their lust—and in the Master's name."

"They have twisted my words, not used them," Paul insisted. "Did the Law ever bind these people? Did Moses speak to them or only to heirs of the Covenant?"

"Of course Moses spoke to Jews," Barnabas responded, "but in its broad reach the Law speaks to all men."

"The *core* of the Law, yes!" Paul shouted. "The core! Because the Ten Commandments are written in the hearts of men, at least all men of goodwill. And we preach that core. We have had this argument out many times before, and you, Barnabas, and you, Cephas"—Paul pointed his finger at each, in turn, his voice so filled with emotion as to crackle like old leather—"you were always on the side of the angels. But now you have abandoned the truth, the Master's truth, for the sake of peace with Jerusalem. In the face of a scandal, serious but not disastrous, you run away. You renounce the New Israel to slip back into the Old, your tails between your legs like whipped curs. You lack judgment and you lack courage."

Then he spun and glared at Barnabas. "And you, you who helped instruct me in the Way! Joining Cephas against me, as if his authority transcended mine—and the truth besides! You have become as tinkling brass, betraying all we preached. I leave you to your spineless compromises. Paul goes to preach Christ crucified to Jew and gentile alike!"

With that he stalked out of the room.

No one said anything for several minutes. Then Lucius spoke: "Paul is a powerful advocate. But, if we follow his way, we cut ourselves off from Judaism. We will truly become what the Antiochenes are calling us, 'Christians.' "

"Christians. I have heard that word, and I don't like it." Simon Peter's voice was quiet, but I could tell he was angry. What I could not tell was how much that anger was directed at Paul and how much at himself.

"Perhaps not," I said, trying to play for time again, "but it's yours. You remember what you said at Caesarea Philippi? We had been running away from Antipas and were heading back. The Master asked us who men said he was."

"I said the anointed one, the Messiah. But I said it in Aramaic. How was I to know that it translated into Greek as 'Christ' and we'd be called 'Christians'? Enough trivia. Lucius presents us with a choice. I hope it isn't real. As long as we do not forget the great Shema, that the Lord our God is One, how can we be other than Jews, the Jews of the New Israel?"

"How we see ourselves and how others see us are different things," Manean noted sadly. "I consider myself a true Jew, yet I have been excluded from the synagogue for years now."

"You're right," Simon Peter conceded. "How others see us is something we can't control. But ... but, damn it, Paul, self-righteous, arrogant bastard that he is—Paul is right. I have been a coward—again. It's something I'm good at. Well, if he's right, we can't change our rules. But we must root out this scandal. We—and Paul—will have to go to every one of our communities and warn them about this vileness.

"He'll prefer to write a letter," Barnabas observed, "and he may be wise. If John ben Zebedee is correct, we face the same problem in Tarsus."

"In my work," Manaen said, "such as it still is, I hear things from travelers. Corinth and Ephesus may well suffer from the same disease."

"Whatever he does, he'll have to make it clear what we teach. I'll have to do that, too," Simon Peter said. Then he shook his head and said softly to me: "Perhaps this is my punishment for

Ishtar, not Jephthania's palsy. I have to save people who're as sinful as I am. What hotter hell could there be?"

Barnabas and I went as emissaries to Paul. Our mission was to convey the fact that Simon Peter had changed his mind and wished to talk with him. We found him in a house on Jawbone Street that belonged to one of the brothers. Titus, who was also staying there, brought back a message: Paul would see me, but not Barnabas. Barnabas shrugged his shoulders and suggested I go in. I did. My audience was brief.

"I am glad that Cephas has seen the truth. I have not been unaware of his many weaknesses, and I regret having to reprove him before you and the others; but I was filled with the Holy Spirit and could do no less than speak the truth. You may tell him I shall write to all the churches, reminding them the body is the Temple of the Lord. To defile it is to defile the Eternal One. I have always made that clear in my teaching, but in light of what has happened I shall make it even more clear, if such is possible."

"Simon Peter will be pleased. Why not come with me and tell him?"

"Charity is the greatest of the virtues, but even my patience has limits. I am not sure how much more weakness my charity can tolerate in one day."

"And Barnabas? Don't you want to be reconciled to him? Harsh words were spoken." I thought the passive voice diplomatically appropriate here.

"You may tell him he has my complete forgiveness for his betrayal. Under the circumstances, however, I do not think we should travel further together. Loyalty to the good news of Christ Jesus is essential if we are to spread his word, and Barnabas obviously lacks that loyalty. Now, if you will forgive me, I would begin the letter. I shall have a copy made and sent to you."

Paul called me back as I was leaving. "Has Cephas imposed a public penance on you for your sins?"

I blushed. "No. I . . . I don't think he'll bring the matter up again."

"No, *he* couldn't very well," Paul mused. "Nor shall I, though for very different reasons. Still, I think for your own sake, you should undertake some private penance."

I did.

8

✣ Paul and Titus left the day after our visit, without delivering a copy of the promised letter to the communities. That omission was worrisome. Paul's departure also thrust the full burden of replying to James on Simon Peter, which is to say, on me. My letter was short and to the point:

> To James, the Brother of the Master, and the entire community at Jerusalem, peace, love, and blessings from Simon Peter, Barnabas, Paul, the elders, and all the communities at Antioch and Daphne.
>
> We have received your letter in sorrow and make haste to assure you that its contents and the information conveyed by Malachai will allow us to stamp out any scandal. We shall proceed to do so forthwith, in accordance with the terms of the letter we and all the brothers at Jerusalem agreed would govern our mission to the gentiles.
>
> We reluctantly cut short this letter, but we must begin the cleansing work, even as we wait in joyful hope for the Master's return.

I had the additional hope that we could make good on our promise to erase the scandal. Knowing the earthy, hedonistic culture of the Mediterranean world made me less optimistic than Simon Peter was.

Barnabas and John Mark remained with us in Antioch. And it was fortunate for us that they did, for we needed help in following up on the leads Malachai had given us. It was tedious, emotionally draining work. We sought out the people, at least those we thought to be in charge of the house churches, and asked to be present at their next *agape*. The first time that worked reasonably well. Simon Peter delivered a scorching talk that evoked memories of John the Baptizer's accusing that generation's Jews of corruption. Fifteen people had been present. Four had been God Fearers and we kept them in the Way. I am afraid we lost all except one of the others, including the man in whose house they had met; but the message got through. Simon Peter insisted that those who wished to remain with us should join one of the "regular" communities.

The second time, at Merope's house, there was even less success. I stayed away from that visit, of course; but Barnabas reported that no one outside of Merope's household appeared. I took that to mean news of the purge was spreading and our message was being evaded—a much more difficult tactic to cope with than blunt confrontation. We found much the same reaction at the other communities. It is impossible to preach to those who will not attend. At least our message had been etched in fire and brimstone on the memories of those present.

Equally important, Barnabas, John Mark, and Simon Peter attended rituals at each of the three orthodox communities and spoke at length about the vileness of what was being done in the name of the Way. Simon and Manean wanted us to order our people not to have any dealings whatsoever with those who had been in the secret groups, but Simon Peter refused. His argument was that no one should be denied the good news of the kingdom. Any of those who asked should be fully accepted on confession of error and promise of amendment. Indeed, he urged the brothers and sisters to seek out people in the secret groups and try to bring them back to righteousness. Manaen's approach was more prudent, but Simon Peter's more in keeping with the Master's.

About two months later, a young man from Pontus brought a letter from Paul, written in Galatia. It was addressed to the communities at Antioch. Other copies had gone out, so the young man

told us, to Corinth, Ephesus, and Galatia. The contents were
vintage Paul:

> From Paul, an apostle who does not owe his authority to any
> human being but has been chosen by Jesus the Christ and the
> Father Who raised him from the dead, to his beloved brothers and
> sisters in the communities at Antioch.
>
> Blessed be the Father of Jesus, the God of consolation. I can
> never stop thanking Him for all He has done to you through me.
> My sufferings are well known to you, my stripes, my hunger, my
> imprisonment; but I count all these for nothing if they have led
> you to salvation through the good news of Jesus the Christ. My
> pride is that my work with you has not been ineffectual. If there
> are those who would supplant Paul, pay no attention to that, for
> of myself I am nothing. I was born to be the Lord's instrument, to
> be used and cast away when one better than I appears. It matters
> not to me or to the Father that your faith is strengthened by Paul
> or some other. It is to Christ Jesus and his Father we owe
> gratitude, not to Paul.
>
> But I urge you to pay close attention to what others preach if
> their message is different from mine, for I have given you the
> message of the crucified Christ, whose Father offers you love and
> salvation. It is the true gospel, of love but also of purity. I have
> warned you against greed, envy, sloth, idolatry, and also against
> lust. My most beloved brothers and sisters, I have heard things
> about some of you that have made the stripes on my back burn
> again in agony, causing me to rue the day I came to your city. I
> have heard stories of drunkenness and, worse, of wild, adulterous
> fornication, done in the name of the Christ. Have you listened to
> false prophets, or have you thought of this filthy madness on
> your own?
>
> When we spoke to you of being free of the Law, we did not
> mean all deeds were good. Jesus's first call was to repentance of
> our sins. The Lord wants us to be holy, to be faithful to wives
> and husbands, to be sober, to wait in prayerful hope for the
> return of the Christ. Our God is a holy God, and we are a holy
> people. Our bodies are His temple. If we defile that body with
> drunkenness and lust we defile the place where He dwells. We
> make a mockery of the love we proclaim for Him and for each

other. We turn the suffering of Jesus into a charade, into a vile plea for debauchery.

The wages of sin are death; when we are free of sin, we are free from death. We have been called to be children of life and light, not of darkness and death. For we have been born again in faith, in justice, and love. And love is not lust. Conduct yourself in righteousness, as I did when I was with you. Avoid adultery, drunkenness, gluttony, and all other forms of revelry. Wait and work in prayerful hope, for we know not the day nor the hour when the Christ will return.

If your neighbor yields to corruption of the flesh, warn him in charity of his error, counsel him. If he persists in his evil ways, have no more to do with him, for he has rejected the saving grace of the Holy Spirit. If he continues to speak in tongues after surrendering his soul to the flesh, it is Satan not the Holy Spirit who comes out of his mouth.

I write to you in love. I write to you in anger. Do not think that, when I return to you, I shall be less angry if these foul, disgraceful deeds continue. And do not think the Christ, when he returns, or the Father on the Last Day will be more gentle than I.

The grace of the Holy Spirit and the grace of Jesus be with you. They are enough for you, even in temptation. *Maranatha.*

One could hardly have asked for a more explicit, more clear, more damning rejection. For all his problems of ego, Paul had a massive talent for writing. And, like Simon Peter, I had come to accept his being touched with grace—and other, less attractive, elements as well.

Of course, neither Paul's letter nor his and our preaching could make our problem disappear, any more than could the letter we had agreed on in Jerusalem remove tensions between Jew and gentile. Greeks and pseudo-Greeks have as full a share of human failings as do Jews.

The next years slipped by quickly. I was getting older, and even Simon Peter showed signs of age—in the gray that streaked his beard and temples, then in the white that began to take over his hair. There were dark circles under his eyes that refused to leave, even after a few days' rest. It may have been my imagination, but I even thought he became a bit less tall. His voice remained deep and firm, his step long and sure.

Only on rare occasions did he speak to me of the dark mixture of emotions that fueled him. It is possible that Naomi had taken over my role of confidant, but I doubt it. I think he had learned to live with himself, for I noted a serenity developing. I say "developing," not developed, for, at least to my eye, while resentment of the Master had receded, his anger toward the Lord God still churned along with his love and devotion. The combination continued to pulse through his personality. Neither Simon Peter's love nor his resentment could conquer the other, but they seemed to be able to co-exist for long periods in armed truce if not friendship. He could preach love and forgiveness, but the latter always came hard to him, for, like Paul, his ego was immense. The surprising difference was that this sometime peasant fisherman from the backcountry of Galilee had achieved greater self-discipline than the educated, Hellenistic Pharisee.

Days, weeks, months, even years went by. I kept a diary, but looking over its contents does little to unravel the sameness I recall. I say sameness, not dullness, for those days were mostly good and fully rewarding. If Simon Peter had a truce between his conflicting emotions, Naomi and I had a similar arrangement with each other. She tolerated me, I suspect, because she knew I loved both Simon Peter and Jephthania; I tolerated her for the same reason.

More important, I felt my work was of use to the Way. I persuaded John Mark to make several copies of my book on the Master's life, and I began this account of Simon Peter's argosy. I was also helpful in advising Simon Peter about conditions in the Greek world. His experience, after all, had been limited to Galilee, a brief stint in the Golan with a ragtag guerrilla band, travels with the Master, Jerusalem, and then a brief and nearly disastrous foray into Lydda and Joppa. And most of this small experience had been with Jews, not Romans, Greeks, and would-be Greeks.

I also found time for philosophic reflection, not only in the abstract but about the Master's message and its long-range implications. That reflection only confirmed my conclusion that he had come again and that the kingdom was within us—now. To be honest, I made little progress in strengthening my faith. But that was not a matter of great concern, for, with Theodora's help, I had long ago reconciled myself to analyzing rather than believing.

Simon Peter was pastor to the flocks at Antioch and Daphne, but he was also a fisher of men there and elsewhere. On occasion, he spoke in the city's streets and also undertook missions to nearby towns, to Corinth, Galatia, Pontus on the Black Sea, and islands between us and the Greek mainland. His initial targets were always Jews; but he preached to gentiles as well and baptized anyone who wished to follow the Way, though his explanations of what was required and forbidden had become much more explicit.

His trip to Corinth, his first outside Antioch's environs, brought results that were both unifying and disruptive. A pair of Jewish Christians—I now accepted the word, and even Simon Peter tolerated it, though he never used it himself—brought us news.

They were a rather well-to-do couple, Aquila and Priscilla. Originally born in Pontus, they had migrated to Rome, where a sizable Jewish community has resided for many decades, perhaps for a century or two. Aquila and Priscilla had heard about the Way on a pilgrimage to Jerusalem, then later listened to another Roman Jew named Alexander the Coppersmith and had been baptized. Later, they had been among the Jews Claudius had expelled from Rome and had gone to Corinth, where they had met and helped Paul both in that city and in Asia. They had come to Antioch to meet the great Simon Peter.

Priscilla was obviously the dominant partner. A tall, dark woman, she walked as if she had a Roman lance for a backbone. Her face was handsome rather than pretty and her manner direct, not abrupt or rude, merely direct, more like that of a Galilean woman than a Judean or even Antiochene. It was her family, I later learned, who had the money, and her father had hired a lawyer who had made arrangements so that her husband never knew the full amount of her wealth, much less how to control it.

Actually, I doubt that Aquila would have dared to try to run his wife's affairs. He was a humble man. I use that word in its best sense, for I found him a most agreeable person. Physically, he was not much more impressive than I, short, balding with a slight paunch, but with much heavier arms than mine. I would not have wanted to wrestle with him in a gymnasium, but it was a delight to wrestle with him intellectually. He had spent years studying the Torah, much like a scribe; later he had become interested in philosophy. Thus when he learned I had studied under Philo, we became immediate friends.

Their news of Corinth was upsetting but familiar, very like the story we had heard at Antioch. Paul's letter had arrived, but even its fiery words had failed to sear the consciences of some of the brethren. That was as I would have expected. Even in Greek culture, Corinth was known as a bawdy city. During their conquest of Greece, the Romans had razed it and sold its survivors into slavery. The site, however, is too good to lie fallow, for not only does it sit on a skinny isthmus astraddle the sole land route between mainland Greece and the Peloponnesian peninsula, it has two ports: Lechaeum, opening to Italy and the West; and, only five miles away, Cenchreae, opening to Alexandria, Ephesus, Antioch, and the Orient.

Thus Julius Caesar had rebuilt it as a colony, and eventually it had become the capital for the entire province of Achaia, the seat of the Roman proconsul for the southern and central Greek mainland. The colonists the Romans sent were freedmen, retired soldiers, and assorted riffraff. These sorts of classes may eventually become respectable, but with Corinth's huge volume of trade and its two ports, sailors abounded. And where sailors gather, whores of both sexes, pimps, thugs, gamblers, and taverns flourish.

Since we had no idea where Paul was, Simon Peter decided he would go to Corinth and cleanse the community. At our first discussion of the matter, I had been opposed, largely on the ground that Corinth, for reasons I did not understand, was very dear to Paul and he might well be upset were another to plough his field. "All fields are the Lord's, not Paul's, not mine," was Simon Peter's response.

I would have argued, but I was not feeling well that evening. Indeed, the next day I was quite ill and remained so for several months, with a fever, severe pain in my lower back, and general lack of energy. Getting out of bed in the morning was an ordeal. I consulted Theophilus, the physician, who assured me that if I took his potions, drank a great deal of water and stayed in bed for a few weeks, all would be well. I followed his directions, but his estimate of the period of recovery was only a fraction of the real cost in time.

I worried about Simon Peter's going alone, but he had no such intention. As his amanuensis he took John Mark, who had a delicate handwriting but primitive syntax and inadequate vocabulary in Greek. Simon Peter also took Naomi and Jephthania, another mistake, but, I confess, I was too ill to offer more than suggestions. And Simon Peter said he would not be separated from his family again if he could help it.

They were gone four months. John Mark had promised to write, and he did, as best he could. His letter arrived after two months. I reproduce it here with only minor stylistic editing to make subjects and predicates agree in number and adjectives conform in gender to the nouns they modify, subtleties beyond John Mark's grasp.

> Quintus, it is I John Mark who writes. Simon Peter, Naomi, Jephthania, and I have now been in Corinth for several weeks. The crossing was hard on us all, especially Naomi, because the water was rough and the boat bounced a lot. We sailed to Cyprus, then Rhodes, Patmos, and then to Cenchreae. We got off the ship there and walked the last six or seven miles. It was mostly uphill and hard with Jephthania and took us all day.
>
> We found the house of Crispus. He had been head of the synagogue, and he let us stay at his house. The trouble was just as we feared, but not as bad as at Antioch. Simon Peter preached

against it in the house churches and even went to the great South
Stoa, a huge colonnaded pavilion in the city's upper agora. The
local government has its offices there. We preached there and
brought a few new people to the Way before some officials arrested Simon Peter and kept him in prison overnight for disturbing the peace. They let him go the next morning with a warning.
That afternoon he preached again in the lower agora and got a
few more new people. They did not arrest him there.

Paul is well known here. He was the first of us to preach here.
People here say they love him. I think they are afraid of him, too.
Some of them are afraid of us also because, like you, they think
Paul will be angry if they are nice to us. Simon Peter thinks that
is wrong. I am not sure. We will stay a little longer and then
come back to Antioch. We may stop at one of the islands on the
way and preach there.

You asked that I tell you about the colors and smells. The
ship smelled like a privy. The port of Cenchreae smells like fish
and salt marsh and rotting wood and rope. There was a grove of
cyprus trees between Cenchreae and Corinth that smelled very
nice and was cool because the trees gave us some shade. But
mostly the road is hot and dusty. The country is very brown like
Judea in the summer. The sky is very blue and so is the sea, but
much darker, sometimes almost black, especially when the
wind blows.

So much for local color.

I put the letter with my other material and made a mental note
to find time to instruct John Mark on how to write. As it turned
out, however, his remarks about Paul were absolutely accurate. I
was present at the confrontation two years later, when we—Simon
Peter, Naomi, Jephthania, John Mark, and I—met him quite by
accident in the beautiful city of Nauplia on the Argolic Gulf,
south of Corinth. It is a small but magnificent place. Never have I
seen the sky and water so blue, and so alike in shade. The city had
once been proud and important, but, unlike Corinth, had faded
under Roman rule. We arrived, as did Paul, because of a storm that
blew us up the gulf.

Paul's temper made the gale seem a mere breeze. I shall not
repeat his harsh words. In essence, he charged that Simon Peter

had betrayed him, gone behind his back, tried to make him look inadequate, first at Antioch, then at Corinth. Once more we heard about the authenticity of Paul's vision of and commission from the risen Master.

We were also again instructed that Paul was the equal of any apostle in authority and superior to any in suffering as well as virtue. Simon Peter, he insisted, should tend to his drinking and idol-worshiping women and leave Paul's communities alone. They had no need either to hear Simon Peter's preaching or to support his family. In all, it was not Paul's finest hour.

Simon Peter tried to explain, but with no success. Yet he took that failure with remarkable serenity. Naomi shared my feeling. I could hear her mutter a few very choice words in Aramaic that made me feel warmer toward her. Jephthania, of course, was terribly distressed at the outburst, as she always was at any emotional explosion.

As I have said, the years drifted by. We got older, the number of followers decreased and increased, though on the whole increases were larger than decreases. Crises came and went: between Jews and gentiles, libertines and pious, about the reality of the Master's return, and clashes of personality. The last were the most persistent, but the least serious. We lost many converts during the years we used Antioch as our base; and, from what we heard, other communities suffered similarly. On the other hand, they, like us, also brought fresh brothers and sisters to the Way.

During the last fifteen of those years, we received letters regularly, at least once a year, from Athens, Caesarea, Corinth, Dalmanutha, Galatia, Joppa, Pontus, Thessalonica, and, after Aquila and Priscilla returned, from Rome itself.

We heard on six occasions from Jerusalem, once to give us the sad news that James the Just had been murdered. We lacked details, but it seemed that, like Stephen but for far less reason, he had been accused of blasphemy. In the quarrel that followed, he had been thrown off the Temple wall near Solomon's Portico into the Kidron Valley. The fall had probably killed him, but our report said that some of his accusers went down and threw stones to crush what was left of his body. The brothers placed him in the Master's tomb in Josef's garden.

While Simon Peter and his family were in Corinth and after I had recovered from my illness, I found myself a small house of my own. On his return, John Mark wanted to move in with me. While I preferred to be alone, I felt I owed Naomi that much. Besides, I hoped that if John Mark and I shared a house, I might better instruct him in the art of writing. I made a mistake in judgment. The man was tone deaf to rules of grammar and of syntactical structures.

The great change in our lives came with a letter from Priscilla. It was longer and more candid than the other two we had received from the man called Alexander the Coppersmith. There were, she said, several Christian communities in the Eternal City. Outwardly they seemed to be flourishing, but she was deeply concerned. They had the typical problems of the movement. First, Jews and gentiles—and Christians there were mostly Jewish—were enemies, not brothers and sisters. Secondly, people in both groups were muttering about the long wait for the Master's return. Thirdly, the problem of licentiousness was very much present among the gentiles, at least so the Jews believed.

Priscilla closed with a plea that we visit Rome and try to cure the communities' diseases and heal the breaches between them. She reinforced her plea by mentioning that Paul was living in Rome. He had come to the Empire's capital to assert his right to appeal to Caesar against charges brought by enemies of the Way in the Land of Israel. While he awaited an audience, the Romans were keeping him only under a form of light arrest, which allowed him some freedom to preach.

Simon Peter was much taken with the idea of going to Rome. I could tell that from what he said and what he did not say. I encouraged the idea, not enthusiastically but rationally, trying to point out to him the costs, risks, and potential payoffs. Not least of the problems was Paul's presence. He would probably resent Simon Peter's arrival, indeed view it as an effort to check his own authority. And that interpretation would not be wholly inaccurate, for we all knew that, although Paul was invariably eloquent, he was also often eloquently divisive rather than uniting.

The decision wasn't easy for Simon Peter, for he also knew that were he to go to Caesar's own city, the odds were against his leaving. In all probability, he would stay, whether in victory or defeat. And, as I have noted, he seemed more than ever at peace with himself, his family, and his work, though not with his God. But then, I found, few Jews were. One of the many costs of believing in such a personal deity is the sometimes overpowering temptation to hold Him directly accountable for evil events and demand He repent *His* sins.

Still, Rome was *the* city, the center of the world. The Way's triumph there, as Titus had said many years ago in my family's villa outside of Jerusalem, would surely mean its triumph across the Empire. On the other hand, defeat in the form of denunciation by the imperial government would have the gravest consequences for the movement everywhere.

As I calculated the costs and benefits, it seemed we should go, though my analysis came to that conclusion by only a small margin. Simon Peter's decision was less self-consciously reflective, which is not to say irrational. As always, he seemed to operate by intuition, a process religious people are apt to confuse with the breath of the Holy Spirit.

We sent John Mark ahead as a messenger. I gave him a letter for Sotion, my old friend and fellow student whom I had met again in Alexandria when I was there with Philip and Levi—how many years ago? Sotion, I was certain, would know much Roman gossip and his curiosity would drive him to be helpful to us. As a neutral and a scholar, if a self-centered one, his analyses were not likely to be biased by prejudices for various factions—though, as with all gentiles, I would have to discount a certain amount of anti-Semitism.

IV

ROME

(64 C.E.)

1

❧ And so we came to Rome. It was in early spring of the thirty-fourth year after the crucifixion and during the eleventh year of Nero's reign. The handsome young prince had begun his reign as a welcome change to Claudius's imbecility. Generous, open to advice from wise men like Seneca, a talented charioteer, a patron of the arts as well as a poet, actor, and musician, for a time Nero had been forgiving of enemies, openhanded toward friends, and fair toward the people of his empire. But for the last few years, his dark side had been becoming more and more dominant. Ugly rumors of intrigue, incest, exile, and even murder were circulating around the capital and beyond.

In Rome itself, there were rumblings among the patricians against the prince's plans to erect a massive palace whose buildings and gardens would appropriate at least a square mile of the richest section of the center of the city, including part of the Forum Romanum as well as the palaces of a bevy of noble families. Nero was not taking this grumbling kindly. Paranoids seldom appreciate criticism from those who have the wealth, power, and opportunity for revenge.

Fear mixes with ambition to form an unstable political compound, making that spring's omens inauspicious for visiting Rome; but the forces that drove Simon Peter never respected such petty human considerations. The Holy Spirit blows where She wishes, and the power of Her breath usually, though not always, pushed Simon Peter ahead.

We had anchored off Ostia the previous night and at first light put into the harbor. There, while slaves unloaded the boat, we transferred to a barge that was about to make the trip upriver. Simon Peter had climbed ashore with the galley slaves who had served us, coming as close as their chains would allow to carrying one of them. The Syrian captain had permitted Simon Peter to talk to the slaves during the voyage, but only when a stiff wind was blowing that made their sweat unnecessary. Now he shook his head at this latest kindness and muttered to me in rather good Greek, "That bastard will be dead within the week, probably by tomorrow. Helping him is a waste of time." I did not try to explain. Simon Peter had tried, twice, in fact, with only harsh laughter for his efforts.

When we came aboard the barge, its galley slaves had their oars at the ready, for the captain did not want to lose the force of the incoming tide to help push us upstream against the current. The river was swollen with spring rains, and we could see garbage, branches, and an occasional full-sized tree riding down to the sea. Even with the tide and fresh muscles, the trip up the twisting river consumed a large part of the day.

In its initial stages, the Eternal City sprang up close to the southeast bank of the Tiber, to our right as we came upstream, on three hills: the Palatine, the Aventine, and the Capitoline. Rome had spread over the centuries, but more than three-quarters of it—all that was critical to the Empire—was still located on that right bank. Those three hills and the shallow, twisting valley they shared contained the very heart of the Empire: the major temples of Rome's panoply of divinities, the great forums, and the Senate itself. The left bank, Transtiberinum, was thinly populated. For hundreds of years it had been farm land, then the Romans had built a shanty town there to house prisoners from the Carthaginian wars. Now, between the river and the Janiculum Hill to the northwest, the emperors had put up dozens of huge warehouses to hold the grain that was periodically distributed to the plebs. A mishmash of people—dubbed Transtiberini—marginal to Roman society made their homes in that district: poor freedmen, struggling artisans, small shopkeepers who could not afford to rent on the right bank, peasants recently migrated from the countryside, petty thieves, retired soldiers, and, of course, Jews.

Farther up the river on Transtiberinum's bank was the Vatican Hill, where Nero had built a huge circus to amuse his own and the Roman mobs' baser instincts. Fortunately the Janiculum Hill draped that part of the city from our eyes.

Despite the river's breadth and the force of its current, the

Romans had bridged it in a half-dozen places. Our target was any empty dock at the main commercial center, located on both banks, on the right near the Forum Boarium, the place where cattle were butchered and sold, between the Capitoline and Aventine hills, and on the left directly across the Tiber.

Near the edge of the city, the river made a swinging turn to our right and much of Rome swept into view: the Capitoline crowned with the massive marble Temple of Jupiter, Juno, and Minerva, the huge theatre of Marcellus, a sea of smaller temples and public buildings, the Aventine and Palatine hills with palaces spackled amid the blood-red clay of their soil.

Simon Peter tried to conceal his excitement, but Naomi and Jephthania made no effort to hide their awe. This was the Eternal City, the center of the world, indeed, the ruler of the world; it was Babylon, the perpetually whoring mother goddess of modern paganism. But to conquer Rome and its evil lust for power was to conquer the world. Simon Peter understood that, just as he understood that death and defeat were more likely than victory in his lifetime.

As soon as we were close enough to the wharf to take a line on board, the galley slaves shipped their oars and stored them inboard, while the crew and dockhands used the rope to crab the vessel in a doglegged course against the current until both bow and stern rested full against the pilings and were securely fastened. At that point, John Mark and an immense, swarthy, bowlegged man of about forty leaped from the wharf onto the deck with a thump that caused the timbers to quiver. John Mark ran toward us. "Simon Peter, Simon Peter!" he called out and began to embrace him. But the big man pushed him aside and planted the kiss of peace on Simon Peter's cheek. "Peace be to you, brother," he said.

"Peace to you also, my brother," Simon Peter replied and returned the kiss.

"Yes. I am Alexander the Coppersmith." The man grasped Simon Peter's arm in the Roman handshake, then threw his thick arms about the Galilean and gave him a tight hug. Alexander was as tall as Simon Peter and perhaps fifty pounds heavier, but from what I saw of the bulges in his shoulders much of that bulk was muscle. His beard was as heavy and inky black, though not quite as wild, as Simon Peter's had been when I first met him.

Alexander's dark eyes were never at rest; they constantly flickered, like Manaen's, taking in everything within their range. "Some of the brothers have come to welcome you." He gestured toward a clump of twenty or so people at the base of the wharf. "We guessed you would dock here rather than at the Boarium. There would be more of us, but we've been taking turns meeting every barge for a week."

"You're kind to greet us, brother," Simon Peter said flatly. "My family and I accept your hospitality with thanks, as does our friend and brother Quintus."

Alexander looked me over with his darting but thorough glance. Much less quickly he extended his hand. "Quintus, yes, of course, Quintus. Yes, John Mark said you'd come."

"He knew the Master and has followed the Way since the earliest days." Simon Peter had caught Alexander's slight hesitation.

"Yes, yes. Quintus. We have heard of you even here in Rome." The sentence was dragged out, punctuated by several smiles. "Now we must go. We have arranged for you and your family to stay in my house in the Transtiberinum. John Mark has been with us these weeks." He glanced at me again. "You'd probably be more comfortable with your own people, Quintus."

"We are Quintus's people," Simon Peter said softly, "and we are not comfortable without him." It was obvious "we" included only Simon Peter, John Mark, Naomi, and Jephthania.

"Yes, of course, of course," Alexander said swiftly. "We have room, but we were afraid that a wealthy Greek would not find our humble Jewish accommodations suitable."

"I am honored by your hospitality," I lied as smoothly as a merchant in a suq.

"Now then," Alexander beamed, "the gangplank is down and the brothers are anxious to meet Simon Peter. Yes, I'll have someone take your baggage."

"We have very little," Naomi noted. "In his declining years my husband has given up his concern for baggage." Simon Peter winced but made no response.

As we went down the gangplank—I helped Jephthania so that Simon Peter could walk ahead with Alexander—and across the wharf, the brothers stared open-mouthed at us, more in awe of Simon Peter than he of Rome. Two of them rushed forward; each grabbed one of his hands and began to kiss it. Simon Peter pulled them up and embraced them. The others swiftly thronged around him, sharing hugs, handclasps, and kisses of peace.

A pair of litters awaited Jephthania and Naomi and a third was for Simon Peter, but he chose to walk with the rest. "Yes, we're all good Jews here," Alexander confided, "good Jews and"—he looked at me—"a few trustworthy God Fearers. But there are others in this city. . . ." His voice trailed off ominously. "John Mark can tell you."

We walked through the greasy, cobblestoned back alleys of the Transtiberinum, with the air rancid from garbage and other human waste. Rome's system of sewers on the right bank was a model for the Empire's urban planning; but Transtiberinum, having sprung up rather than grown up, was more primitive. There was only an occasional open sewer to carry the neighborhood's effluence into the Tiber.

It was dark before we reached our destination, but the night was pleasant, not unlike Jerusalem in another month. Alexander's house was hidden behind a crumbling stone wall. The thick timbers of the door to the street had once been a dark green, but now were a mass of peeling paint. From my previous visit, which had lasted eight weeks, I knew enough of Rome to realize that once one moves beyond the ostentation of the Aventine and Palatine palaces, one must be careful about judging houses, or the wealth of those who live in them, by their exteriors, which were often left in semishambles to deceive tax assessors.

Once inside the wall, no one could doubt he was in a rich man's home. There was ample room in the courtyard for all of us, at least two dozen people. The place was well lit by torches—I assumed their cases were copper—anchored into the outside wall and the stone of the side of the house. Six or seven slaves flitted about offering, more in the Jewish than Roman fashion, water for us to wash ourselves, then, when that ritual was done, wine and cakes. The wine, I noticed, was served in gold, not copper, goblets, the cakes on small silver plates. I also noticed that Naomi and Jephthania were the only women present. I'm sure they made the same observation, as did Simon Peter. But they stayed with us.

Alexander tapped his goblet with a small dagger. "Yes, Simon Peter, we, the Jews of Rome who follow the Way, welcome you to our midst. We, the true believers, have great need of your wisdom and your power to convince others to accept the Law and the Master's teachings. We thank the Eternal One, blessed be His name forever, for giving you a safe voyage to us."

"Hear, O Israel," Simon Peter began in Aramaic, "the Lord our God, the Lord is One. That we, too, may be one, let us pray together as the Master taught." Then in Greek, we recited the prayer that opens with "Our Father," as I exactly recorded it in my earlier work. That done, Simon Peter reached out and took a plate of cakes from one slave and a ewer of wine from another and set them on a small table at his side. "On the night the Master was betrayed and abandoned, he took bread, blessed it, broke it, and gave it to us, saying 'This is my body.' Then he took wine, blessed it, and passed the cup among us, saying, 'This is my blood, the symbol of a new Covenant.' And because he told us to repeat that sharing in his memory, we now take this bread and wine together."

Simon Peter passed the cup and plate among us. We each took a few crumbs and a sip of the wine, then recited together: "The Master has died, the Master has been raised, the Master will come again. *Maranatha.*"

While the others were engaging in a few minutes of prayerful meditation, I took the opportunity to look around the courtyard at the people Alexander had invited. From their demeanor as well as their clothing, I judged most to be of rather humble means. Four had the cropped ear by which some owners marked their slaves, though that fact alone did not mean either that they were still slaves or that others present were not slaves. In fact, my guess was that all were free. Jewish communities everywhere had a reputation for buying their people out of bondage.

I picked out only two of the group as men of means. I later identified them as Nereus, an elderly physician whose family had migrated to Ephesus after the Babylonian captivity, and Jacobus, a middle-aged man skilled in both Roman and Jewish law, and well connected to some of Seneca's friends. Except for a brief period of Jewish exile under Claudius, Jacobus had lived all his life in Rome. His family had been merchants who amassed enough capital to enable him to loan money to patrician families whose reputations exceeded their tangible assets.

My sociological analysis was interrupted by Simon Peter's speaking again. "My brothers, one of the reasons I have come to Rome is to try to heal the breach within the community. News of your divisions has spread among the brothers and sisters in Greece, Asia, Syria, and even Jerusalem. It is a source of scandal. I have heard much but know little of the causes of this factionalism. I shall spend time learning before speaking, but my heart is heavy that all of the brothers do not love one another. Loving each other is not only the Law of Moses; it is the essence of the Master's message. More than anything else, it *is* the Way."

I noticed glances exchanged among the guests. Knowing little about the community, I did not attempt a fine translation, but the message I received was not one of agreement.

Most of the group left within an hour, all, that is, except for Nereus and Jacobus. They joined us for the evening meal—feast would have been a more accurate description. We reclined in the Greek fashion and were served at least six courses by relays of slaves who made certain that our goblets were always full of sweet red wine. Several times I glanced at Simon Peter, but he neither ate nor drank very much. The years had changed him in many ways.

The meal had begun on an embarrassing note. Clearly Alexander had expected Naomi and Jephthania to go to another part of the house with his wife, a thin, very attractive woman a full fifteen years younger than he. Naomi, however, stayed next to Simon Peter, who affected not to notice Alexander's ordering two additional couches.

Simon Peter had the place of honor, with Alexander and Nereus, the physician, closest to him. I noted that I was the buffer, separating the women from the men. I spent much of the time conversing with Jacobus, whom I found fascinating in a rather strange way. He reminded me of my uncles in that he was wealthy and obviously managed his business affairs skillfully, yet was more interested in ideas than in money.

Later, as we were about to retire, Alexander asked Simon Peter if the two might talk privately. He agreed and, to Alexander's annoyance, immediately asked if I would join them. "Yes, about our divisions," the Roman began as soon as we reached his garden, "love is a divine command, but we must separate ourselves from these gentiles, not only because of love of the Law of Moses but because of love of the Master's teachings as well. They have listened to Paul the apostate. He tells them the Law has no meaning for them. It was made for children of darkness, and they are children of light. The Master has fulfilled the Law; it has no more use to us. As a result we have moral anarchy."

"Paul," Simon Peter cut in, "is a most moral man. In fact, he's a prig."

Alexander held up his hand. "Yes, I am willing to believe that Paul's own life is blameless; but he allows his zeal for converting people to the Way to lead them astray. And these pig-eaters will go astray on any excuse. They take him literally. Because they believe they are saved through faith not good works, they believe that good works don't count for them or orgies against them. 'We believe in Jesus,' they say. 'We are justified by faith apart from the Law. We are at peace with the Lord.' And there is drunkenness and revelry and sexual excess among these 'brethren' that is a scandal even to Romans."

Simon Peter looked weary. He was hearing an ofttold tale. "There is more?"

"Yes, there is more. It has to do with the Romans. I hesitate to speak about it."

"Speak, please," Simon Peter almost begged. "It's late and I am exhausted."

"Yes, there is a group—we hear only rumors—among the gentile converts who are said to teach that the Master will come only when we rise up against Rome. He will lead us in battle if we revolt. We want no part of that foolishness. It goes against what we know of the Way, besides being suicidal."

Simon Peter bowed his head in pain and anger. "You are sure of this?"

"No, not sure. But in the markets we hear things. And if we hear things the Roman officials will hear them, too. These gentiles put us in fear of our lives as well as our souls."

"Do you have a solution?"

"Yes, a solution, though not an easy one. First, we must go to the magistrate and speak for the Jewish community of Rome; dissociate ourselves from these hypocrites; and tell him the rumors we have heard. Second, we must require that all future followers fully accept the Law of Moses as part of the Way. The Master was a Jew. You and all the disciples are Jews; Paul is a Jew. The burdens can be heavy, but they are necessary."

"Like circumcision?" Simon Peter asked.

"Yes, yes," Alexander nodded, "like circumcision and all the other parts of the Law."

"I have heard similar proposals before. In Jerusalem, we, together with James the Just, the elders, and all of the Twelve we could gather, decided against such requirements."

"Yes? You did? Yes, but if you did, you did it in the abstract. Now you see the problems, what it means to let gentiles live on faith alone."

"That's not what we teach, and it's not what Paul teaches."

"Perhaps, but it's what the gentiles believe Paul teaches. Simon Peter, you must think about this problem. Those people were lost before they heard of the Way. They are still lost; and if they provoke the Romans' wrath, they will not only kill us but also prevent us from bringing the good news to others."

Simon Peter looked up at the sky. "I shall think about it as I talk and listen over the next few days. Now I am very tired."

"Yes, I understand that, but there is much you must know."

Simon Peter sighed loudly, but that did nothing to stop Alexander. "Paul is staying here in Rome at the house of Aristobulus. The Roman authorities trust him; he's also one of the leaders of the gentile hypocrites who claim to follow the Way. Do you know him?"

"I've heard of him—vaguely," Simon Peter said. His voice was weak.

"Yes, well, he's a half-Edomite, half-Greek. His father was an Edomite slave who came here with Herod the Great on one of his visits to Augustus Caesar and stayed on to oversee Herod's political and economic interests in the capital. The old man was shrewd enough to keep Herod's fortune prospering and make one for himself. He bought his freedom and bought and married a Greek slave woman. His son bought Roman citizenship. He'd like social status, but he'll settle for money and power."

"Why do the Roman authorities trust him?" I asked.

"Like a lot of these parvenus, he's more Roman than the Romans. He wears his citizenship on his forehead like a phylactery. Besides, he earns his fortune as an expediter, so he knows all the government officials."

"Expediter? What's that?" Simon Peter asked wearily.

"Yes," Alexander smiled condescendingly. "Each month hundreds of people come from the provinces to get action from the government—whether an old soldier who hasn't received his pension, or a rich merchant who wants a license of some sort or maybe just to buy citizenship, or a delegation from a community to protest against a provincial administrator who's taking bribes from the wrong people. They haven't any idea about where to start. There are literally thousands of government offices here. Most of the officials who run them are honest, some aren't. A few are very efficient; most aren't. Aristobulus can tell you whom to see, where his office is, if he's corrupt and what's his price, what documents you'll need, when the political climate is ripe and when it's sour. He keeps in touch with many people." Alexander smiled sourly. "Yes, by that I mean he pays a great deal for information, both in cash and in kissing rear ends. He's a man without dignity or scruples."

"So?" Simon Peter asked.

"So? So that's the type of person with whom we're dealing. I've heard it said that, if a client wants, he'll go along to a pagan temple and offer sacrifice. Yes, and he hates Jews. When Herod the Great was on his way here, the ship got caught in a bad storm. He bargained with the Most High, blessed be His name. If he made it to Rome safely he would force all the gentiles in his entire household to convert. He survived—showing, after that blasphemy that the Lord's mercy is without limit—and kept his promise. But Aristobulus's father renounced Judaism as soon as Herod died. And Aristobulus himself despises Jews. He helped persuade Claudius to exile some of us, fifteen years ago."

"Perhaps he's changed since he's accepted the Way," Simon Peter suggested.

"A few years ago, long after he said he was following the Way, a delegation from the Jewish community at Alexandria came here to file a grievance with Caesar. Yes, they'd heard about him and sought his help—for a fee, of course. He threw them out of his house. He said he'd sooner deal with a Samaritan whore than a Jewish prophet."

"What do you want me to do, find some Sicarii and have them stick daggers in the man? He's my brother, Alexander; and he's your brother, too. He shares with both of us in the fellowship of the risen Master and the Holy Spirit."

Now it was Alexander's turn to try to end the conversation. "You do look tired, Simon Peter. Perhaps we should retire and speak again in the morning when we're all fresh."

After we adjourned, I woke John Mark and, as soon as he came out of his fog and stopped complaining, we conversed in whispers. He knew little more than what Alexander had said. Indeed, he had not yet met any gentile Christians, having confined himself to meeting Transtiberini. His only positive contribution was that he had found Sotion's house, no mean feat in a city Rome's size, I had to admit.

2

✦ At dawn the next morning, under a thick gray sky that threatened to soak us at any moment, Simon Peter and I left the house. Wisely, we did not bring John Mark. Alexander had insisted on accompanying us so that we could continue the previous evening's conversation as we walked. Even more insistently Simon Peter had declined the offer, just as he refused to be accompanied by a slave who could lead us through Rome's labyrinths. I reassured Alexander that once across the Tiber I could function as an adequate guide.

We crossed the river and went straight toward the Campus Martius on the eastern edge of the city. The most direct route led through the Portico of Pompey and its adjoining cluster of large temples, public baths, and government buildings. We stopped there while I pointed out the place where Brutus, Cassius, and their friends had murdered Julius Caesar. The names meant little to Simon Peter so I gave him a brief lecture on recent Roman history. I chose my words carefully because I knew he would remember each one in its exact order.

I took that route not only to save time but, more important, to give Simon Peter a sense of the grandeur of the Eternal City. Augustus had boasted that he found Rome brick and left it marble. How it was before him, I do not know; but fifty years after his death the city was a veritable forest of magnificent marble. Antioch was almost as noisy, but it was not as large or nearly so rich in monuments—probably not even Athens at her peak was except perhaps on the Acropolis, and that was much smaller in area.

Simon Peter was impressed as much by the atmosphere as the architecture. He sensed the haughtiness that hung in the Roman air. The very walk of the citizens proclaimed not only that they were the masters of the world but also that they deserved that role. They believed the words that Virgil put in Jupiter's mouth: "No limits do I set to Romans' fortune or time. To them I give empire forever."

We continued through this complex, past the Pantheon, the temple to all the gods, that Agrippa had built almost a century earlier. It was circular and, though small, beautifully proportioned, one of the loveliest buildings in Rome. Alas, the architect's eye for beauty had not translated into craftsmanship in construction. Cracks were appearing in its walls and, worse, in the foundation. The building would soon have to be torn down before it fell down.

We turned to our right again, to the Via Flaminia, then went east past the Mausoleum of Augustus and climbed up the hill to the Pincian gardens. We knew from Alexander and from John Mark that Aristobulus's house was in that area, but not precisely where.

It took not much more than an hour to reach the gardens, but we needed almost as long to locate the house. Romans call that kind of place a *domus*, distinguishing it from an *insula*, or block of apartments. In fact, it was a mansion. Its fresh, high walls proclaimed new wealth as obviously as Alexander's crumbling stones proclaimed genteel poverty. Inside, its grounds were large, its own gardens manicured. A servant led us to the small villa that Aristobulus had provided for Paul's use. We stood in the atrium, where three stone turtles spouted water into a pond. Benches had been moved about in an effort to capture some sun, a waste of energy on days like today. The man offered us some wine while we waited. It was a bit early in the morning for alcohol, but the damp chill demanded wine and warm cloaks.

After a few minutes we heard the clop of sandals on a stone floor. The man who appeared in the doorway was much older than the Paul of my memory, though I suppose Simon Peter and I were also more weathered than Paul's picture of us. His once red hair, what there was of it—he had little more than I—was pure white; his shoulders stooped; black sacks of flesh bulged beneath his eyes; and he had sprouted a belly, not huge, but a palpable paunch. Deterioration, however, was not the most dramatic change in his appearance, but rather ennoblement.

Paul's intellect had always been powerful, his will indomitable, his courage indefatigable. From that day on the road to Damascus, he had always been a true believer who never wavered, always a faithful follower of the Way, always a loyal instrument of the Holy Spirit. Nevertheless, as I have reported, when he had been young he was homelier than even the ugliest Celt I had ever encountered. What had brought about the change, I was not sure. The loss of red hair, perhaps, or his shaving his beard, or possibly the suffering he had undergone had carved dignity in his face. His teeth were still irregular, and his large ears still protruded like a Celt's; now, however, these defects reflected character. One thing had not changed a whit: His eyes were still those of a lion, flashing pride, ambition, and ferocity.

Paul rushed into the atrium and gave first Simon Peter and then me the kiss of peace. In the same motion, he snapped his fingers at the servant. "Onesimus, cushions for the benches!" The man hurriedly complied. Then Paul gestured for us to sit. His demeanor eloquently conveyed the message that we were being granted an audience. "I see you have wine," he said to Simon Peter. His tone was lavish in its concern, and the manner in which his eyes focused on the cup rather than on his guest let us both know that Paul remembered Simon Peter's difficulty, and, of course, was himself far above that or any other of the Galilean's many weaknesses.

"I am well."

"And your daughter. She must be forty now. Can she speak yet?"

"No."

"Pity. She was such a beautiful child. 'Who knows the mind of the Lord?' All we can be certain of is that the Eternal One, blessed be His name, loves us." He paused for a few seconds. "And your very charming wife. Does she still feel it necessary to accompany you?"

"Naomi is with me in Rome. And how are things with you?"

"I have fought the good fight, Cephas. I have run the race. What few laurels I have won are withering. Now I must pass the baton to others. But I have the satisfaction of knowing that my legs have always run after the risen Jesus, never away from him."

It was a virtuoso performance, a masterful, though quite unconscious, parody of the self-righteous Pharisee, parading most of Simon Peter's flaws and problems before him and doing it behind a façade of concern and humility. Thirty-five years ago, Simon

Peter would not even have recognized such consummate acting; twenty-five years ago, he would have recognized it and probably responded with angry invective. That day in Rome, however, he could recognize it, appreciate its artistic integrity, and even understand and sympathize with the reasons motivating it. Most important, he could ignore it. "Don't pass the baton yet, Paul. There is still work for old men in Rome."

"Rome, yes, in Rome." Paul paused theatrically. "We *are* in Rome, Cephas. And if we win here, we win everywhere. It is at the Tiber that we must gather, not at the Jordan or at the Plain of Megiddo, but at the Tiber, from whose water earthly power flows, power that we may channel into divine service. Mark my words, Cephas, mark them well: Some day Jesus the Christ will rule in Rome."

Simon Peter nodded in full agreement. "First, however, we must keep our people together. There shall be one fold and one shepherd, the Master said."

"And you, of course, are that shepherd."

"The Master told me to feed his sheep."

"So I've heard you and your brother say." Then Paul smiled condescendingly. "Yes, as I have written, and with some elegance, you must concede, 'all were made to drink in one spirit.' But why come to me? Many among your circle doubt I am a legitimate apostle."

Simon Peter sighed audibly. "Paul, I am not responsible for what others think. I have never belittled the great deeds you have done or doubted the Holy Spirit was operating through you, not in Jerusalem when we first met, nor in Antioch, where we first disputed, not even in Corinth, where we fought so bitterly. I come to you because you are a fellow laborer in the Master's vineyard. You've been in Rome for more than a year now. You know the disease that's eating at our people."

Paul looked at us sideways, then moved his chair next to the fountain, took off his sandals, and let his feet dangle in the cold running water. The sight made me take another gulp of wine and pull my cloak tighter about my shoulders. When he began to talk again, Paul's tone was much less sharp, much less defensive, his pitch lower. (I suddenly realized I had not heard the whistle that had once punctuated his speech. Undoubtedly he had consulted a Greek teacher of oratory to correct that defect.) "I know the disease and I know its source. The disease is called Judaizing and its source is Jerusalem. The Way came to Rome through two separate paths. To the gentiles it came from Aquila and, even more importantly, from Priscilla, those two people from Pontus you know so well. The Holy Spirit brought them to me in Greece and again in Asia. I sent them back here to spread the good news. The Eternal One, blessed be His name, has made their work fruitful."

"And the other path?"

"The other path leads directly from Jerusalem, from James, may he sleep in peace until the Master comes again, from Passover pilgrims who met him and the brethren in the Temple or the Essene Quarter or the synagogues. These disciples of James will have nothing to do with gentile followers of the Way unless they first fully convert to Judaism and accept every jot and tittle of the Law of Moses. There is a certain congruence here. James would not acknowledge his brother during his lifetime; now that James is gone his disciples will not acknowledge most of his brother's followers."

"We have been over this ground many times before,"

"We have, we have, indeed. Cephas," Paul sighed. "We are both Jews. You have been lax, but I have always meticulously kept the Law. When I am in the Land of Israel or with a Jewish community in the Diaspora I live—and eat—like a good Pharisee. When I am in the gentile world, I keep the basic tenets of the Law. But I cannot insist that my gentiles accept all the ritual rules we have built up. The core, yes, that goes without saying. The Ten Commandments are, after all, written in the hearts of men."

"Your friend Stephen used to say that."

"Stephen, my friend Stephen—a name from my youth. I'm glad you remember him, Cephas. I can never forget him. I recall the day he said it to me. We were much alike then and would be more alike today had I not baited him and abetted his murderers."

Paul waited and then waited some more for Simon Peter to say something to absolve him of guilt, but Simon Peter was silent. It was a tactical error. Again Paul's voice tightened and began to rise in pitch. I thought I detected a slight whistle. "You're right, we have had this matter out before. You and I and James and all the brethren at Jerusalem. We won for the gentiles freedom from the details of the Law. But later in Antioch you waffled, but I stood firm and led you back to the truth. Will you stand firm this time, Cephas our rock?"

Simon Peter ignored the insult. "When did our community start here in Rome?"

"At least fifteen years ago, perhaps as many as twenty, but what they think is 'faith' has been renewed by frequent pilgrimages to Jerusalem."

"Then they may not have understood the decision that the Holy Spirit inspired us in Jerusalem to make about gentiles not having to follow the details of the Law."

"You tell them, Cephas. I have tried, but to me they will not listen. They've heard lies about me from synagogues in Antioch, Asia, and Greece. And I'm sure the Jerusalem crowd gave the Roman Jews an earful. James envied me; his friends still envy me; and because they envy me, they hate me—me, Paul. Are they servants of Jesus? Yes, but I have been better. I've been imprisoned, three times scourged with the whip, twice with rods, stoned once, starved; I almost died of thirst, almost drowned after shipwreck, was almost killed by poisonous snakes; now I await trial before Caesar—all for the sake of Jesus' name."

Paul stopped for a moment, lifted his feet from the fountain, then thought better of it and resubmerged them. I took another long swallow of wine and, out of the corner of my eye, saw Simon Peter do the same thing.

"I do not complain about these sufferings. I glory in them. I have thanked the Lord that He has seen fit to put my faith to the test and that I have met and overcome each test. But these people, my own brothers according to the flesh through Abraham, even those who join in proclaiming the crucified and risen Christ, brand me apostate, false prophet, libertine. You, my dear Cephas, you, the disciple who denied and abandoned the Christ, you, the drunkard, the adulterer, the waffler, you they revere and listen to. There is small justice in this world, small justice."

Once again Simon Peter held his temper. "If justice were plentiful in this world, the Master's message would be of little significance. Are your gentiles faithful to the Way in their behavior as well as in claiming faith? Have they put lewdness behind them?"

"As you said in Jerusalem, they are human beings. They sin: Some steal, some go back to temple rituals, some even commit adultery. I have warned all people, Jew and gentile alike, that fornicators will not have eternal life; I have warned them that idol worshipers, whether of flesh or clay, choose death by choosing sin; and they will suffer eternal death. Time and again I have preached this; time and again I have written it."

Paul paused and in a loud voice offered us a paragraph from what was obviously a well rehearsed sermon:

> For this is the will of the Lord, your sanctification; that you abstain from immoral sexual acts; that each of you know how to take a wife for himself in holiness and honor, not in the grip of lust like a heathen who does not know the Lord; that no man wrong his brother in this matter, because the Lord is an avenger in all of these things. For He has not called us to uncleanness, but to holiness.

He lowered his voice again. "Most who accept the Way listen and obey, some listen but do not obey. Even among those who do not obey, many continue to listen. We must be patient with human beings, Cephas. Rome cannot be converted in a day."

"Is it like the problem in Antioch and Corinth?"

Paul snapped his head and looked away from us. He spoke to the turtles in the fountain: "Why do you bring up those cities? You like to recall my defeats, not my triumphs. Are you, too, envious of me, Cephas? Envious like James and his friends? Even though I am nothing, in no respect have I fallen short of the most superlative of apostles. If you wish to talk about me, let us talk of the gentiles of Corinth and Antioch whose faith flourished, of the church that meets at the house of Lucius, whose soul I won. Let us talk of my coming to Antioch before you and conquering the

Greeks' hearts so that you could come and reap my harvest. For how many years did you reap the harvest I sowed?"

"The Master and the Holy Spirit reaped that harvest, Paul. We are the Master's men, not our own. You told the Corinthians they were not Paul's or Appollos's or Cephas's, but the Master's. You were right—for Corinth, for Antioch, for Ephesus, and for everywhere else, including Rome."

Paul swung his legs out of the fountain and snapped his fingers. Onesimus appeared with a towel to dry his master's feet. Then Paul held out his cup for it to be filled with wine. He took it down in one long quaff that would have done a Galilean proud. "Yes, Cephas; you're right, I did say it well, did I not? Sometimes . . . Sometimes the Lord tests us with defeat as well as suffering, does He not?"

"Who knows that better than I?"

"Who indeed? You've had enough personal failures to fill seven lifetimes, yet you are still with us."

"*He* is still with us, and that is all that matters."

"Do you experience his presence, Cephas? Do you truly feel him with you?" For a time, all play-acting vanished.

Simon Peter hesitated. "Not always. Sometimes I feel only anger and despair—frustration and rage at years of loneliness, devoured by trying to convince the hard-hearted of the Master's message of repentance and love, years spent on dusty highways and leaky ships that threaten to choke away my life and the lives of my wife and daughter. Sometimes I look at Jephthania, withered since adolescence, and I curse the deity who afflicted her. Sometimes I call out at night and hear only frightening silence. But at other times, at other times I feel the Master's hand. I know he has touched me."

"Yes, the Eternal One's grace is sufficient, but we are deficient. There is something to what James and his friends want. These gentiles, my dear Cephas, would make splendid Jews. They are stiff-necked, opinionated, vulnerable to every form of sin; yet they are touched by divine grace."

Simon Peter smiled. "I have one other question, Paul. We have heard talk of revolution among the brotherhood. Are these only rumors?"

"Rumor, according to the Latin poet, is a bird-like monster with as many tongues as feathers." Paul hesitated. "I hope so, Cephas, with all my heart I hope so. I, too, have heard rumors, but no one will confide such evil to me. The whole world knows that I have always preached that 'no authority exists except from God, and all authority that exists is established by God. Therefore, he who resists authority rebels against the ordinance of God; those who do so condemn themselves.' No man can speak more plainly."

"The question is not what Paul has taught, but what others are teaching in the Master's name."

"I can only repeat that I hear rumors, but no more."

Simon Peter nodded. "Could you get us an appointment with Aristobulus?"

Paul thought for a moment. "It is difficult. He is a very busy man. But . . . if anyone could arrange it, I could. Yes, Cephas, for you I'll arrange it. Tomorrow, here, at sundown. We'll take supper together."

Paul was immediately putting Simon Peter to a double test. Sabbath began tomorrow at sundown and the three of us knew the Christian Jews of Rome would be offended if Simon Peter did not celebrate it with them. Worse, they would be angered, perhaps outraged, if they learned we were eating with Aristobulus, whom they considered a pagan hypocrite. If, however, Simon Peter refused Paul's invitation he would be repeating what Paul considered a shameful, however transitory, retreat in Antioch and would risk alienating the gentile Christians. Simon Peter responded immediately: "Quintus and I shall be here tomorrow to wish you good Sabbath."

Simon Peter and I were planning to walk; but, at the completion of our audience, the rain began and Paul insisted that we use a pair of Aristobulus's litters to carry us back to the Transtiberinum. We agreed without much protest. Once back on the Via Flaminia, however, I instructed my bearers to carry me to Sotion's lodgings on the Quirinal Hill. As at Antioch, I thought I could help Simon Peter by learning about the social structure of the Christian com-

munities of Rome and perhaps about the existence of a revolutionary group in our midst.

As I have noted, I had known Sotion since our youth, when I
first pursued philosophy in Athens. Later I met him again in
Alexandria when I was studying under Philo and once more on my
visit with Levi and Philip. Even as a young man, Sotion had had a
pompous streak. I first noted it in an Athenian bordello when he
insisted on instructing a buxom barbarian about metaphysics,
when she had been eager only to earn her fee. But pomposity well
fits men who dedicate their lives to teaching the young.

We had corresponded over the years, and in Alexandria Sotion
had shown an interest—coolly academic—in the Way. As soon as
Simon Peter had begun to talk seriously of coming to Rome, I
wrote Sotion and asked him to find out all he could about our
brothers there. I could trust him to be both thorough and discreet,
to remember everything, and to explain everything.

He had an apartment in a rather small and modest—after
Aristobulus's *domus*, humble—*insula*. The building was densely
inhabited by rather poor people, a typical Roman *insula*. The first
floor, which Sotion rented, was stone and had once been a small
shop. The upper stories, in the usual Roman fashion, were of
wood. They looked like firetraps, but that is not an especially
astute observation after the fact. Among the drawbacks of living
on the first floor was the noise of wooden-sandaled feet pounding
on the floors above and the terrible din from street traffic; the
bonus was exclusive use of a garden of adequate size. Inside, the
apartment consisted of one large room where Sotion could meet as
many as ten of his students at a time, a kitchen, a lavatory, and
a small bedroom. There was no view and the garden did not have a
fountain; but it did have a small yet lovely bronze statue of
a stallion, rearing up on its hind legs.

"Dear, dear Quintus, this is an unexpected surprise. I had
expected you every day last week; I feared you'd been lost at sea.
Well, we must be grateful for these chance encounters of a schol-
arly kind."

He gave me a warm embrace, then held me at arm's length and
looked me over carefully. He was a short man, shorter than I, but,

as I mentioned earlier, he had been an excellent wrestler in his youth. Now he was quite fat. Even his lips and earlobes were padded with extra flesh. His head sat on his body like a large plate on the rim of a huge platter. His arms and legs now seemed made for a man much shorter than he. "The years have been kinder to you than to me. I see too many lines in your face and too few hairs on your head, but I also see great peace in your eyes. You must serve a kind master. But come, come inside, out of this rain. The gods have forgotten that Rome's weather in June is hot and dry. I have mulled wine to warm our bones, and some adequate olive oil and good brown Roman bread."

He waddled ahead of me into his kitchen, where we sipped wine and gossiped about the missing years while he toasted chunks of bread on hot coals, then rubbed them with olive oil and garlic. The result was as hard as stone on the outside but rich and mellow on the inside. I ate four pieces, though I knew I would smell like a Galilean.

After that meal, we sat in comfortable chairs in front of the fire and dozed for an hour or so. Then we got down to work. Sotion spoke in a rapid, almost staccato style. "You asked that I explore the dimensions and structure of your Jewish sect's followers here. Needless to say, I am more fascinated now than I was at Alexandria—was it really a quarter of a century ago?— by the problematics of your friends' theologizing and linking this messiah myth to what the Romans can only consider a threat to their Empire."

"That's precisely what Pontius Pilate thought."

"To be sure. Your Master twisted the tail of the imperial tiger, and the tiger twisted back. Empires do that sort of thing. But that's another matter. I am trying to overcome my propensity to dilate. Let us focus on your gentile converts. I don't know them all. I've had opportunity to study only three groups closely. They have no temples but meet in private homes to hold their . . . what do you call it?"

"Commemoration. The breaking of the bread."

"Yes, to be sure. An odd ceremony, smacking of magic and cannibalism with someone reciting a formula over food and having it turn into a dead man's body. Couldn't you at least have made it a live woman's body?"

I did not smile, a fact he noticed.

"Forgive me, old friend. All religion seems odd to the true philosopher. To business: I've had several trusted students infiltrate. First demographics. Your believers come from varied backgrounds—slaves, former slaves, *nouveaux riches*, a very few people of status, even an occasional philosopher." His smile forgave my belief's sin against philosophy. Had he known how tenuous that belief could be, his forgiveness would have been even fuller.

"The leaders of the gentiles?"

"In sum, members of the abler, if not better, classes, but their career configurations differ. Rufus—the name may mean little to you, but it connotes a great deal to old Romans—is of a noble but no longer wealthy family. He's a decent sort. Aristobulus, a sly government finagler, is the richest and certainly has the most obvious political connections. He probably knows everything that's happening or about to happen in Rome. He should, he pays enough— and charges enough—for his information. He was my student many years ago. Obviously I taught the rogue too much and charged him too little."

Sotion paused to emphasize that charity was not costless.

"Then there's a woman—Priscilla, a Jew. She doesn't live in the Transtiberinum with her cousins; and neither she nor her husband, whom she runs like an eager but stupid puppy, attend synagogue. They have money—foreign trade, I think—but they're pariahs among their own people. Still, I'd trust them much more than Aristobulus. Clear so far?"

I nodded. It sounded much like Antioch.

"There're a half-dozen others. I mention only two. One is a Greek slave named Onesimus—'Useful,' a nice touch. He's closely connected to your friend Paul and that's important in your sect's gentile community."

"I've met him."

"Interesting. The other is called Chrestus, a common enough Roman name, but it provides another nice touch in being close both to your Christus and to the word 'good' in Greek. He's honest, high on energy, and low on brains—always a dangerous combination, in this case volatile. He's a freedman and has money. Somehow all freedmen have, unless they've been doing something useful like tutoring. But I digress. The dozen or so people who meet at night in his house are poorer than he and even less intelligent. These people are true believers. That worries me. If no one deeply believed in anything, the world would be a more peaceful place."

I smiled but said nothing.

"You wrote of a messiah myth and how, curiously, the sect's leaders don't believe they or their followers should do anything to speed or retard your Master's magical return. Well, my dear Quintus, I do not pretend to know anything about chthonic forces, but Chrestus and his friends are much more logical than you and your friends. They think that if the Messiah is coming, they have a duty to help bring about that event soon, perhaps now."

I nodded. That intelligence confirmed what Alexander had said, and it was bad news indeed. I wanted to ask questions, but if my memory was correct there would be no need. Sotion would provide a full explanation. My memory was exact.

"Now, let us disambiguate these data and probe the parameters of our uncertainty. If we can fit the data into a coherent pattern, we can understand the problem we're confronting. While my knowledge of the Jews of Rome is only general, they are aliens and strangers here and everywhere except in their homeland. But they have a sense of history, a sense of a personal god, and they have one another. Always they live in communities, reinforcing their sense of personal, cultural, and communal identity, no matter how alien to and alienated from our Greco-Roman world they are."

"I think that's right."

Sotion went on. The possibility that he might be wrong had not occurred to him. "There are exceptions. This Alexander, who started out running a coppersmith's shop—he's tried for years to get himself elected president of the synagogue. But most of the other Jews don't like him. He has money and awesome size, but no status. I'd guess his people know something in his past, and it's not to his credit. It's easy to see why your sect appeals to him."

"Interesting," I said.

"To be sure. Now, your gentile followers tend to be radically different from the Jews. A few people like Rufus have both a family name and secure social status, but very few. Most live on the margins of society. Not just slaves like Onesimus, but *nouveaux riches* like Aristobulus and Chrestus, or less affluent freedmen, or even pariahs like Priscilla. Like the Jews, most of these people are outsiders; but, unlike the Jews, they are isolated outsiders. There is no 'community of slaves,' and if one came into existence the Romans would immediately hang its members on crosses from here to Brundisium. The memory of Spartacus can still freeze the Tiber solid in August. There isn't even a society of freedmen, no tradition of tribe and religion, no personal or group sense of identity to knit them together, to comfort them. They may have shared the same suffering, but there is no society of people who've bought their freedom. And almost by definition there is no society of pariahs."

Sotion got up to mull some more wine. He continued to talk as he mixed and warmed our drinks. "Aliens and strangers: aliens and strangers to society at large and to each other, plus a small group of fanatics—not that a rational man might not judge the whole sect fanatical. Well, that's the problem with which you're dealing."

"Most have no cultural identity?"

He pursed his lips together and arched his eyebrows indicating some ambivalance. "If they're Greeks, real Greeks, of course they think of themselves as Greek. It's only natural that products of a superior culture should recognize that fact. And many of them, Greeks as well as barbarians, also identify with Rome in a twisted but significant way. They live in the Eternal City. Many are even citizens. Rome is an important symbol to them, all of them, slaves, too. Even though part of their souls may passionately hate the Empire, another part knows that Rome's power, its cosmic preeminence, gives them something to cling to. The rest of the world looks up to them because they live along the Tiber. Like language, geography can confer status and prestige, if only at long range."

"So?"

"So, my old friend, you must prioritize. First, if you want your sect to survive, you must eliminate Chrestus and his friends. The

Romans are tolerant about religion, but within limits. They're suspicious of people who meet at night or of sects that allow men and women to attend the same gathering. They'll kill a witch or a soothsayer and try to stamp out a religion that practices magic or any form of cannibalism. Even without Chrestus you're vulnerable. Let the Romans get wind of what he's saying, and you're doomed, all of you, Jew and gentile alike."

"How do we get rid of him?"

"I am a philosopher, Quintus, not a soldier. Now, secondly, if you want your sect to grow, rely on gentiles for recruits. There are lots more of them than Jews. Besides, the gentiles need you. They have no alternatives, the Jews do. To convert many of them you'd have to convince them intellectually, and one can't make an intelligent argument about religion. Your sect's demand for total participation may put Jews off, but it has immense appeal to gentiles. Your notion of community offers most of these poor devils something their miserable souls have been crying out for. If you told them that your god is a great mushroom, they'd still be interested, providing they understood the fellowship you're offering."

Sotion brought me the fresh cup of wine. "Third, Chrestus aside, do not try to incite disaffection toward the Empire among your gentiles. That would be suicidal. Rejection impacts negatively on Roman officialdom. It would also be dysfunctional in attracting and retaining gentiles. Rome may be a mixed symbol in their lives, but on balance it's positive. Perhaps it's the only positive social bond they have other than your sect. Don't make them choose between the two. Clear?"

"Quite clear."

"Good. My final point is my most general. Here we enter the vortex of cruciality: You get rid of this foolishness of a messiah and a new kingdom. On the one hand, it encourages fanatics like Chrestus; on the other, it will cause mass desertion when your people realize the millennium is never coming."

3

❖ I had dismissed Aristobulus's litter bearers when I found Sotion's apartment; thus I had to walk back to the Transtiberinum. The rain had stopped, but the streets were greasier than usual. Horse manure is soluble in water, and the rain had mixed with a heavy residue of animal droppings to coat the cobblestones with a thick, slippery gravy one traversed at considerable peril to limb, laundry, and dignity.

When I arrived at Alexander's house, it was almost dark. Our host, along with Nereus, Jacobus, and Simon Peter, was conversing in the atrium. A charcoal brazier was fighting the dampness, but the four men were putting out far more heat. Simon Peter was finishing his explanation of what the brothers at Jerusalem, with James the Just himself presiding, had decided fourteen years earlier about admission of gentiles to the Way. Then the Roman Jews developed the case that Alexander had outlined the previous evening. He nodded to me as I came in, but did not break his sentence. Apparently, the rules of Oriental courtesy had not survived Roman demands for efficient allocation of time.

"Like you, Simon Peter, we are Jews; and the Master was a Jew."

"The Master *is* a Jew," Simon Peter corrected.

I listened as the argument went on. I had heard much of it before, at Jerusalem, at Antioch, everywhere. Even brethren plotting revolution was not new. I admired Simon Peter's patience in going over the same ground so many times without losing his temper.

At the end of an hour, he finally said: "When he was in Samaria, the Master didn't ask the Samaritans to purify their corrupt form of Judaism. He didn't even insist that the adulteress whom we met at Jacob's Well renounce her lovers. The Master offered the water of eternal life as a free gift to all who would receive it. As his followers, we can do no less. There must be one fold and one shepherd. Our sharing isn't complete unless it's open to all. We must remember we're not merely sharing with one another. The Master is also present, sharing with us. In Galilee he told us, 'As I have freely given so must you freely give.' I can't refuse any person the right to share with the Master, a gift he freely gave me. Think on it, my brothers, and pray on it."

"But," one of our guests answered, "the conduct of the gentiles shows they need a specific code to follow, something to measure their actions by. We have to lace them up straight."

"I think that reasoning misses the point of the Master's message," Simon Peter replied. "It is a command to love with a love that can't be measured. The Law can't be our measure of action because our love must transcend the Law. It must even transcend justice. We must love one another as we do ourselves. Just as there's no limit to self-love, there can be no limit to our love for others. Our duties are thus unlimited. It is in giving that we become whole, not in receiving or in obeying a code. Pray on it, I beg you."

How much the three Romans prayed on the problem, I do not know; but think about it they did—and talk about it they did as well. The next morning, Friday, more Jewish Christians joined the discussion. Other people might have called it a loud and bitter argument, but to Jews it was merely a discussion, a bit more extended and vociferous than most, but still only a discussion.

Shortly after noon, all the visitors left so that we might eat in peace. The rich ate three meals a day, rather than the two the poor managed—when they had the food to eat at all. Alexander's household observed the civilized Mediterranean custom of a nap after the midday meal. As we were awakening, yet another delegation of Jews appeared and "discussion" began anew. I stayed long enough to be polite, but soon slipped away. I was bored to tears by the issue of gentiles and the Law, and I suspected that I knew as much about Chrestus as anyone present. I took the opportunity to walk around the Transtiberinum and learn more about the area. It did not take me long to decide that it was not my favorite part of Rome.

I returned in ample time to refresh myself before going to Aristobulus's for dinner. Out of prudence, Simon Peter had only told Alexander that we had important plans for the evening without offering details or inviting inquiry. Alexander was miffed, but there was little he could say to such a distinguished guest, though he did remark that some of the brothers had planned to escort Simon Peter to their synagogue and show him off to the rest of the community. Simon Peter reassured him that we would both go to the synagogue the next day.

Alas, this incomplete explanation turned out to be an error. As I was putting on fresh clothes after my walk, I heard a loud banging at the gate in the wall, feet shuffling, and muffled voices disputing. When I went down into the reception room, I heard Alexander speaking to Simon Peter. There was ice in his voice. "Rab' Simon, Aristobulus, the noted gentile and hater of Jews, has sent litters to fetch you and your Greek friend to his house for dinner tonight."

Simon Peter could only mutter thanks, but he stopped as we were leaving and laid his hand on Alexander's shoulder. "I'm sorry, my friend. I must try to heal this illness in the community, and to do that I must see these people. I should have told you, but I feared it would offend."

"It does, the more because you did not trust me to understand."

"For that I am doubly sorry—for your pride and for my stupidity."

Aristobulus was a rascal, but he hid it cleverly. His disguise was not to conceal it at all, but to talk about his work as a comedian might describe the life of some exotic tribe from the eastern steppes or the African jungles. He was a small man, probably about forty-five though it is difficult to tell with Orientals, dark-skinned as one would expect an Edomite to be, clean-shaven, neat, and precise in appearance if not speech. His having been a student of Sotion explained his perfect Greek as well as his mistaking pomposity for learned discourse. His black eyes exuded such sincerity that I swiftly concluded he had to be a rogue.

He greeted us effusively with the holy kiss on the lips and a warm embrace. "Paul had planned that we dine in his apartment, but I insisted we come into the main house. His man Onesimus is a terrible cook," Aristobulus said in a stage whisper. More softly he added: "Not that mine is much better. How is it that Empire manipulation comes easier to me than getting a decent supper in my own house?"

Paul was already inside, and the four of us reclined on couches set in a square. Service quickly began, and Aristobulus immediately began to eat. Simon Peter, however, pretended not to notice and took the bread and wine in his hands and began the commemoration.

Afterward, when I had taken my first few bites, I realized that Aristobulus had not been guilty of false modesty about his kitchen. There were huge amounts of food, most of it poorly selected and all of it badly prepared. I am not fond of Roman cooking, but it can be made fit for human consumption, Aristobulus's cook notwithstanding. The first course was simple and the only one palatable: large, ripe olives and lettuce with slices of hard boiled peacocks' eggs and tuna. The wine—the same one throughout—was a well aged Falernian. It might have been delicious, but someone had added, in the Roman fashion, so much honey that it had become viscous.

The second course was a long barrage of meats. Initially the servants brought in a large roast goose (underdone and overpeppered) immersed in a cold sauce of celery seed, coriander, mint, and rosemary. The goose should be well done and blotted to absorb as much of the fat as possible, then served piping hot under the cold sauce. This bird had not been blotted and had sat too long before having the sauce poured over it. As a result it was cold and greasy, with the color of dark lard and much the same consistency.

Five minutes later came platters of venison marinated in a vinegary sauce that burned even in the esophagus, chicken livers cooked to the point where they had the consistency and flavor of the basalt rock around the Lake of Galilee, and a white fish of some sort, smothered in an oregano plum sauce, with so much vinegar and olive oil that it tasted much like the gooey mess on the venison—and charred only slightly less. The vegetables were overboiled leeks and beets (which my father had taken on occasion as a laxative), liberally flavored with cumin and pepper, on which the cook had poured too much olive oil.

Throughout the meal our host was charming and witty. He told amusing stories about the foibles of the people around the imperial personage, even about Nero himself and his fear when, a few years earlier, a star had fallen across the sky over Rome, a sure omen, local superstition had it, of a change in dynasty. The young prince's fear had turned to panic when a bolt of lightning struck the dinner table at his villa near Subiaco and tossed dishes about the room. He was so upset, Aristobulus assured us, that he exiled a nobleman named Plautus, whom Nero fancied to be his successor because his ancestral home was near Subiaco.

Paul seemed to find the conversation—it was more a comic monologue—entertaining, though he was genuinely grieved by news of Seneca's fall from imperial grace. "A few years ago," he noted, "Gallio, Seneca's brother who was then proconsul in Achaia, treated me with justice. Ever since, I have prayed for him and his family."

On the other hand, Simon Peter was bored. Most of the names Aristobulus dropped meant nothing to him, even Seneca's. And, despite all my efforts, he never learned to take pleasure in banter. Where humor and intellectual play were concerned, Simon Peter remained a Galilean on whose peasant character had been stitched some trappings of Greek culture.

As the servants were clearing away the plates from what I prayed was the final course, Simon Peter cut into one of our host's stories: "Tell us about Chrestus."

"Chrestus?" Aristobulus slowly wiped his lips with his napkin, then took a sip of the sweet, thickened wine. "Which one? There are hundreds by that name in Rome." Except for that instant between the question and the napkin's going to his lips, Aristobulus's expression had remained that of an innocent, if slightly mischievous, child. Then, as the servants left the room, he rolled his eyes and pointed to his ears and the pantry.

"Paul, I recall your saying that Onesimus has prepared a honey cake." Aristobulus's tone was deliberately hypocritical, but it seemed to suggest only that his solicitude was a mask for his appetite. "He will be offended if we do not at least sample it. I suggest we adjourn to your quarters."

Once in Paul's villa, Aristobulus returned to the story that Simon Peter had interrupted. After only a few seconds the Galilean broke in again. "Chrestus." It was a command, not a statement, and certainly not a question.

"Chrestus. Chrestus." Aristobulus put his hands together lightly so that only the fingertips were touching. He spent a few minutes admiring the framework he had created. Finally: "Chrestus, yes, our Christian Chrestus. What information do you require?"

"We know the basic facts. Give us details," Simon Peter said.

"Wait," Paul put in. "Some of us do not know the basic facts, only the name and that it means trouble."

I thought it wiser to let Aristobulus do the explaining than to tell him how much we knew—and did not know. "A difficult case," Aristobulus began, "but we can manage it."

"Unless," I said, "the Romans take a hand first."

With that nudge Aristobulus gave us a detailed account of Chrestus that fit most of what Sotion had told me. The new information was that he was a man of about thirty-five, lived on the Viminal Hill, was extraordinarily good with figures, and was indeed well off. Like Aristobulus's own father, Chrestus had managed his master's finances, though he had begun earlier and by his twenty-fourth birthday had been able to purchase his freedom and still have enough capital to buy a house, several slaves of his own, and start a service counseling the rich on how to invest their money. More to our point, the group who met regularly in his house numbered exactly twelve plus Chrestus himself. And alone of the gentile groups of Christians in Rome, this one did not include women, not even wives of its male members.

"How smart is this man?" I asked.

Aristobulus inhaled slowly. "That is difficult to say. With numbers, no one is better. [I was sure that was not faint praise. Aristobulus, I had no doubt, could instantly compute costs and benefits to the tiniest copper coin.] But with people and events, he has no judgment. He's insane. He has persuaded his followers to move into his villa. He has bought the freedom of three who were slaves and promised to share his goods with them and the other nine. That is a very persuasive argument. Even by Roman standards he lives like a rich man—though the wealth may actually belong to his clients." That, too, was something about which Aristobulus undoubtedly knew a great deal.

"All of which makes him more dangerous," Paul said, shaking his head sadly. "I wrote so clearly, so eloquently about being subject to authority. So many have ears but do not hear. I do not like this at all."

"What do Roman officials know about him?" I asked.

"I have kept my ear close to the wheel on this situation," Aristobulus assured us. "And I can tell you unequivocally that they suspect nothing."

"But that could change as we are talking," I noted.

"Such situations are always fluid," he admitted.

"We four have much to talk about tonight, but tomorrow I must see this Chrestus. Can you arrange it?" Simon Peter looked directly at Aristobulus.

"I'll do my best to help you access him. I'll send a messenger to you when I have time and place data." Aristobulus nodded to Paul. "I'd like to use Onesimus. He knows where Chrestus lives, and he's one of us. I'm wary of the other slaves."

Aristobulus cleared his throat. "I have not been totally forthcoming with outsiders about my Way affiliation. I do not see how it would do good, and it might do harm. At this point in time, Nero seems a bit, a bit, let us say, maladjusted. That's why I've used my influence to delay Paul's trial. Since the prince's unfortunate affair, I use the term advisedly, with his mother, he thinks Rome is seething with plots. We wouldn't want Paul to be sacrificed to a wild fantasy, nor my information sources to defructify."

"A few minutes ago Chrestus did not seem a problem to you," Paul observed tartly.

"No, my dear friend, I have always viewed Chrestus as a serious problem. But I did not want to trouble you with him. I was about to deactivate it myself, but now Simon Peter has translated it into his business." Aristobulus's smile did not change.

"It *is* my business. The Master put the care of those who follow the Way in my hands." Simon Peter spat more than he spoke the words. Then more softly: "Paul, I would take it as a kindness if you would join me tomorrow when I see Chrestus. I shall need your eloquence."

"What are our options if Simon Peter fails?" I asked. We needed to know, but Paul was too angry to think clearly and Simon Peter's mind never functioned that way.

"I have surveyed the entire gamut of options. I have concluded that our options are limited. For one . . ." Aristobulus paused and chuckled. "Chrestus could always meet with an accident fatality." I doubted he was joking. Indeed, I had mixed feelings about having learned about Chrestus. Had Aristobulus been left alone, Chrestus might have had too much to drink, fallen in the Tiber, and drowned. That would have solved the problem, though at the price of a terrible sin.

"Or," Aristobulus continued, "concerned friends might spirit him away somewhere to a well guarded house in the mountains until he recovered his health or slept in peace, to be waked when the Master comes again."

"Any others?" I persisted.

"One of the more prominent brothers, perhaps someone like Rufus, who is well known in Rome, might speak on behalf of the community to a magistrate and have Chrestus's freedom discontinued. But we should look at the risks of that option carefully. While we might earn some official goodwill by turning in a madman, we might also focus government attention on ourselves."

"Murder, kidnapping, betrayal? Those are our choices?" Simon Peter asked in a hoarse whisper.

"You have a fourth?" Aristobulus's voice was silken.

"And a fifth and a sixth and seventh: prayer, love, reason, and faith."

Aristobulus gave us his puckish smile again. "Perhaps we should table this matter until after Simon Peter's visit."

"Very well," Simon Peter agreed. "We have other business—the split between the Jewish and gentile communities. Chrestus is part of the difficulty, but so is concern about the morals of some gentiles."

"And the Judaizing of some people across the river," Paul added sharply.

"Yes," Aristobulus agreed. "I'd like to agenda that."

"Judaizing is part of it," Simon Peter admitted, "but I'll take that up with Alexander and his friends. Why aren't our people one here in Rome?"

"I think," Aristobulus said, "that, too, is a matter for Alexander, though I doubt that big eel will give you an honest reply. We are completely open to our Jewish brothers. It is they who reject us."

"Why?"

"Because we listen to Paul. It isn't necessary for our salvation for us to become Jews."

"Do you personally hate Jews?" Simon Peter asked.

"I can easily defense myself there. As a follower of the Way," Aristobulus punctuated his reply with another of his innocent smiles, "I do not 'hate' anyone. I admit that I do not like *Jews*, but listen to how I pronounce the word. I speak with underlining. I do not care if a man is born a Jew or a gentile. My helping Paul and you, too, Simon Peter, testifies to that. But I do not like *Jews*—people whose minds are narrow, clannish, self-righteously certain that they and they alone have God's ear. Those *Jews* may be born Jews or gentiles—Greeks, Romans, Arabs, or even Edomites. Alexander and his friends are not just Jews, they are *Jews*. They show that toward us. Either we become just like them or we do not follow the Way."

"If, then," Simon Peter said, "the Jewish community accepts you on the terms that we in Jerusalem agreed on, the gentile Christians of Rome would form with them one fully sharing, fully participating community?"

"Hopefully. I could relate to that, but at this point in time I can speak only for myself. If Judaizing stopped, and you and Paul worked hard with our people, I see a chance for unity. It would be growth experience for entire faith communities, but it will not happen as a matter of course. We have political as well as religious differences with the Jews. They are not popular anywhere in the Empire, certainly not here in Rome. Whatever our other problems, most of us gentiles think of ourselves as Romans. I don't mean we're citizens; most of us aren't. I mean heartwise. Few Jews think of themselves as Roman. They despise Rome and the Empire. Most of us detest many things the Empire does and represents—

slavery for example—but we are Romans from Rome, and we are proud of it."

"Very well," Simon Peter said solemnly. "I shall work and pray with our Jewish brethren. One final point: Rumors of immorality, of orgies and all sorts of sexual things, have reached us."

"Cephas," Paul began, "you and I . . . ."

"Please," Simon Peter put his hand up. "I would like to hear Aristobulus speak."

"Let me background you," Aristobulus began.

"We have 'background' already. We need facts and solutions."

"Well, I would not defense all that goes on among our people. No doubt about it, some take our good Greek word *agape*—love feast—literally. The kiss of peace can become the ploy of passion. Despite all that Paul has said, some people argue that, if they are saved through faith, they may do whatever they wish—whatever gives them pleasure. But they are a minority, a small minority."

"I hope so." Simon Peter looked at Paul. "I assume this is work for you, Priscilla, and your other helpers. The Jews will never accept gentiles who foul the Way with such filthy practices."

I suddenly realized that Simon Peter was half dead with fatigue, as well he should have been after a long day of debate. "I think we have accomplished a great deal," I put in. "We see Chrestus tomorrow; Simon Peter will work with the Jews, Aristobulus with the gentile community to prepare them for unity, and Paul with the gentile minority who are perverting the Way. We are not likely to accomplish more tonight except to kill ourselves from exhaustion. Aristobulus, could you be good enough to have your litters take us back to the Transtiberinum?"

The next morning's visit to the synagogue began uneventfully. Alexander was cool but polite, as far as I was concerned an entirely satisfactory demeanor. As a God Fearer, I was allowed to enter—unlike the Temple in Jerusalem, a synagogue was a center for many phases of the community's life, including prayer, not simply a holy place reserved for special cultic worship. In addition to individual prayers, one of the members read a passage from

Scripture and commented on it. Several men questioned him—sharply—on his commentary. In sum, it was much like Sabbath in Alexandria, Capernaum, or even Jerusalem. At least it was until the men were beginning to file out.

Then a loud voice called out: "Alexander, why have you defiled our community by bringing an idolater into our midst?" That shout halted the exodus. I assumed I was the offending person and started to explain that I was a God Fearer. "I don't mean you, Greek," the man interrupted. "I mean that apostate Jew with you who sets another alongside the Most High." The man's long, bony finger pointed directly at Simon Peter.

"You slander our guest, Philip," Alexander said, pushing the two of us ahead of him toward the exit. Clearly he wanted to avoid a confrontation. Followers of the Way were well represented in this synagogue, he had told us, but they were a definite minority.

"Do not run away from the truth, Alexander. Answer my question. If I slander your guest, let us hear him speak in his own defense. Let us hear him deny that he believes that this Joshua"—the man Philip had been speaking Greek, but he used the Aramaic form of the Master's name—"is divine."

"You know many of us in this synagogue follow the Way, and we do not teach that the Master was divine," Alexander retorted.

"I did not accuse you, but your guest. I have heard your gentile friends speak of this Joshua as having been with the Most High, blessed be His name, from all eternity; Saul of Tarsus, your other apostate Jew, says that Joshua 'drained himself' of divinity and came down to earth to save mankind. Is that what you believe?" Philip continued to point his finger at Simon Peter.

"Hear, O Israel, the Lord our God, the Lord is one," Simon Peter replied.

"That's not good enough. We all know the great Shema; and Satan can recite the Torah. Who is this Joshua whom the Romans crucified and you claim rose from the dead?"

"Once, when we were fleeing from the wrath of Herod Antipas, the Master asked me who I thought he was. I replied, 'You are the Messiah, the son of the living God.' I'm not a scholar. I can't tell you precisely what I meant by those words, for they came from my heart not my mind. But they express my faith. His message is that of love, caring for one another as for ourselves. It is in this selfless love that we achieve unity with one another and ultimately with the Most High, just as the Master achieved unity with Him."

"I ask you a simple question and you give me a mystic answer about love and unity. I repeat: Do you claim this Joshua was a god and not a man?"

"I don't completely understand the Master's relation to the Father and what little I understand I can't express clearly. All I can say is that the Most High, blessed be His name, revealed Himself and His love for us through the Master. The two are united in that love, and through the Master, the Most High offers all mankind that same love, just as He reveals His wisdom and care of us through the Holy Spirit."

"You have not given me a yes or a no."

"I'm sorry, but that's the best I can do. I see the Most High as all-powerful Creator, the Most High as Love, the Most High as Wisdom, but still the Most High is One. I know that isn't well stated, yet it's all I can do. Still, however poor my expression, it's not idolatry."

"Do not our sacred Scriptures speak of Holy Wisdom as being with the Most High?" another man asked.

"That is not the same thing," Philip retorted.

"And why not?"

As the circle of debate widened, Alexander pushed us out the door and marched us back toward his house. "I am sorry. Some of the community accept us for the good Jews we are, but some resent us. Your friend Paul is largely to blame. He can be lavish with his praise of the Master, so lavish he sometimes seems to be turning him into a god, just like the pagan pigs make their rulers."

"No, it is I who am sorry," Simon Peter said. "I'm sure that Paul could've explained himself with total clarity. But I am not very good with such complex ideas. The Master's message is a command to do justice, not to do theology—to do charity, to love the Lord and one another. It is not a call to debate the nature of the Most High or other things we can never understand. It is a call to spread the good news that the kingdom of God, the kingdom of love and justice, is at hand, not the kingdom of the scribes of Jerusalem."

4

❧ I went with Simon Peter and Paul to see Chrestus. We took litters—Onesimus ran alongside—only as far as the foot of Viminal and walked from there. We thought it prudent to share Aristobulus's worry about his servants. That day was more typical of late Roman June, and the first few hundred yards made for steep, sweaty climbing. Chrestus's *domus* was set off by itself in a garden plot. It was not up to Aristobulus's standard, but neither was it modest.

Not a servant but the man himself greeted us at the door. He placed the kiss of peace full on our lips, just as the Master had done. I had been expecting an imposing figure, but the most accurate description of Chrestus's appearance was that it was forgettable. He was neither tall nor short, fat nor thin. His hair was a darkish brown, cut rather short in the Roman fashion. He wore no beard or jewelry and his toga was plain. I looked into his eyes expecting to find John the Baptizer's revolutionary fire dancing there. Instead I saw only hazel calm. One could have walked by the man fifty times in the marketplace without noticing him at all.

His courtesy was exact, properly respectful of the two great men of the Way, yet not fawning or obsequious. He gave us wine and exchanged small talk. Soon, true to form, Simon Peter came directly to the point. "We are concerned about your teaching."

Chrestus arched his eyebrows, but said nothing.

"We hear," Paul put in, "you are telling the brothers they must be prepared to rise up, to rebel against Rome. Surely, you cannot be teaching such sheer madness. It contradicts all that is in the Master's message."

Chrestus half closed his eyes. His reply was so soft I almost missed it. "Does it?"

"I have carefully explained to you," Paul said with patronizing patience, "that because all authority comes from the Lord, we must be subject to authority."

"If all authority comes from the Lord, from whence does mine come?" Chrestus asked.

"Your authority?" Paul and Simon Peter spoke simultaneously.

"Simon, Simon, do you not recognize me? It is I." Chrestus's voice grew more animated, but his facial features and body language showed no emotion. It was as if he were an actor auditioning by merely reading the lines of a play.

Simon Peter was completely confused. Paul saw what I saw and was equally appalled.

"Do you not recognize me? I have come again, as I promised you. The kingdom of God is at hand, Simon! Your coming here with Paul is the signal. The day of glory is near. Where is your sword? We must rise up! The sword of Jerusalem shall slay the born-again whore of Babylon!"

Neither Paul nor Simon Peter could yet say anything, so I questioned the man. "You cannot have forgotten the instruction to turn the other cheek, to love every man as your neighbor. You do not wish us to violate those holy words, do you?"

"Those were for a different time and a different place. After I spoke those words the Romans hanged me on a tree to die. But I rose again, and I promised to return. I have returned, to rally my people. The kingdom of God is at hand! These idolaters will drink the wine of God's fury. Their blood shall run out as mine did and that of my brother James in Jerusalem. Thus speaks the Lord our God: 'I shall squeeze them on the winepress of My anger!' "

Like a good Jew confronting blasphemy, Paul tore his clothes. Simon Peter stood up as if to leave.

"You desert me again, Simon?" Chrestus's voice took on a mocking lilt. "Once more you refuse to stand and risk all with me? Must I always depend on others?" Then he lifted his arms and showed them to Simon Peter. At each wrist was a big, ugly scar that could have been made by nails. "Do these mean nothing to you?"

Simon Peter's olive complexion turned as white as goat's milk. Giant beads of sweat popped out across his forehead. He opened his mouth to speak, but only guttural sounds of agony escaped. He whirled and bolted out of the house. Paul and I tried to follow, but he ran to the street and began furiously pushing his way through the crowds. We managed to keep him in sight until, at the foot of the hill near the scaffolding for Nero's Golden House, Paul had to stop to catch his breath. I could not have kept up the pace much longer. Like Simon Peter, we were old men; but we were not driven by demons. I motioned for Onesimus to continue after him, while Paul and I sat on some large stones and pretended to watch the builders work.

"Well," I said after a few minutes' rest, "we cannot claim that Aristobulus didn't warn us. The man is absolutely insane."

Paul shook his head. "How dare he pervert my words? If authority comes from the Lord, whence does his come? From Beelzebub, where else?"

"The question is," I said, "what to do about him."

"Perhaps I should not say it," Paul noted, "but Aristobulus's option of an accident now seems less bizarre."

"Simon Peter would never take on the curse of Cain."

"Nor would I, but killing that man would be more like insecticide than homicide. He even maimed his own wrists!"

"If we checked his feet and side, we'd find other scars. And he's probably had himself circumcised."

"I would not care to test that." Then after a moment: "I am concerned, but Cephas is panicked. Why?"

I shook my head as if I did not know. It was not quite a lie; but neither was it quite the truth. About ten minutes later, Onesimus returned and said that Simon Peter was on the Tiber Island, sitting on a bench outside the Temple of Aesculapius. I wanted to see him alone, but Paul insisted on coming along. I think he was genuinely concerned. We compromised. He would follow behind, but would not join us until I signaled him. With that agreement and some foreboding, I went to Simon Peter.

The Tiber Island had once been only a sandbar in the middle of the river, but Roman engineering had built it up with huge stones into a boat-shaped oasis of serenity in the blaring cacophony of a wild city. In the peace of the island's western tip was a small but graceful temple to the Roman god of healing. Simon Peter was sitting there staring downstream. I sat beside him.

At least a quarter of an hour passed before either of us spoke. I was afraid that Paul would soon lose patience and join us. "There are many things I cannot fathom," Simon Peter finally said, his voice betraying a familiar lack of self-confidence. "Has he come again and have I failed to recognize him?"

"We saw a madman, a dangerous man, one who is absolutely insane."

"They said that about the Master, too. The scars?"

"More evidence of insanity. He had someone hammer nails into his wrists—or he's crazy enough to have done it himself."

"Is it all a farce then, Quintus? Have we spent our lives for a farce that can be played out by a madman? Has Satan beaten us by infecting our people with his demons? Or has the Master really come again?"

"None of these."

"Quintus, I have envied your ability always to keep back a part of yourself. To give your whole heart and soul to something is to choke a part of yourself. I cannot breathe and neither can I escape. And I know I am not worthy to do what I try to do. I should be able to handle such problems. Most of all—before all and before everyone else—I should know who the Master is. I don't. Yesterday in the synagogue, I didn't give a good answer to that question about the Master and idolatry because I don't understand who the Master is. Worse, I couldn't recognize him if he appeared here in this filthy temple. A few moments ago, I half mistook a crazy man for the Master."

He stood up, walked to the edge of the island, and put his hand on a huge boulder. "Mary was right, James was right: I am an ignorant, frightened peasant, reeking of stale sweat and dead fish. I have been a drunkard and an adulterer; I have run away from danger and from truth. I have denied the Master through my pride and self-love; I have waffled, as Paul puts it. I am not Simon the Rock, I am Simon the Millstone."

"Yet the Master was crucified more than thirty-four years ago," I said. "And this millstone has rolled from Jerusalem through Asia and Greece to Rome itself, preaching the gospel the Master taught."

"Preaching out of love or out of pride? Many years ago at the lake you asked if I had forgiven the Master. I told you then that I wasn't certain. Now, three decades later, I can see myself as vain, childish, more like an immature girl than a man. The Master touched me, that is enough. I am absolutely certain I will see him again."

He stopped and gave me a half-smile. "I said I'd been childishly vain, but have I worked so hard out of love for him and his word, or to prove to him he was wrong to love John more than me? Have I fallen so often because I have loved only myself?"

"Then why have you picked yourself up so often?"

"Pride is a powerful engine; perhaps it's no more than that."

"Yet you've seemed more at peace in recent years."

Simon Peter nodded and half-smiled again. Then his tone changed, his voice became hard. "At peace? With whom? I have come to terms with the Master's love for John, but I'm still not certain I've forgiven the Most High for what He did to Jephthania."

Once again we lapsed into silence. Minutes, perhaps more, passed until Simon Peter spoke again. "I despair, Quintus, I despair. Have I followed a dream, a fantasy? Sometimes at night I cry out to him, but all I hear is silence, cold, shattering silence. He touched me once. I just said that is enough. Sometimes, when I can remember that touch, it is enough; at other times I feel nothing. Nothing but emptiness and loneliness. When will he come again?"

Paul had joined us. I did not hear him come up, but he had apparently caught the last part of our conversation, for he embraced Simon Peter. "I can understand and share, my brother," he said. "I, too, have felt that bleak despair. The Lord is truly the tester of our hearts." It was a Paul I had heard about but had never seen.

We rejoined Onesimus and walked back together to Aristobulus's house. The noise, crowds, and jostling prevented conversation, which was all to the good. Fortunately, too, our gentile patron was about his business in the Senate, and we were able to go straight to the garden of Paul's little villa, where Onesimus fetched us cushions, a large flagon of wine, and some bread and cold meats. Half an hour later he brought us another flagon, and Simon Peter insisted the slave sit with us. Paul raised his eyebrows but said nothing. Talk quickly petered out, as each of us, encouraged by the wine, succumbed to the custom of siesta.

We awoke to a different mood. Paul's compassion had moved Simon Peter and prevented what I had dreaded, another extended period of black despair. He was grave and subdued, but his mind was active. Paul's mood had also changed. His compassion, having played, retreated.

As I drifted back up to consciousness, I heard Simon Peter speaking. His voice was again firm. "We must struggle with this problem, but we must also remember it isn't ours alone. The Master is always with us. The Holy Spirit may be telling us something, something we don't wish to hear. Chrestus and the dilemma he presents may be partially our fault. By refusing to accept a hard truth, we may have encouraged this sort of madness. Let us pray on this problem."

"No man prays more zealously or more often than I," Paul— the Paul I knew—replied, "or has greater faith in the Master's capacity to intervene to help us. But I do not know what fault you allude to, Cephas. My life has been upright, just, and irreproachable; and I can think of no hard truth I've not honestly confronted."

"No one doubts that," Simon Peter said. "The fault is entirely mine. It concerns the Master's return. I pray that the Holy Spirit will give us the wisdom to understand this mystery. It was thirty-four years ago this spring that the Master was crucified and rose again. He came first to Mary, then to the brothers on the road to Emmaus, then to others in Jerusalem, and much later to me at the lake."

"And to me on the road to Damascus," Paul put in.

"And to you," Simon Peter added, "and also to James. Like us, Paul, you expected the Master to return soon and found his kingdom."

"I did. I got that promise directly from you, Cephas, when I came to Jerusalem to learn all I could of the Master. I taught and I wrote that the day was near at hand, but it was from your lips, Cephas, I got that message. I did not make it up any more than I made up any part of the gospel I have preached and kept."

"Of course not. That is why I said 'like us.' Quintus, you've always had doubts about the sort of return that we expected, a return to found an earthly kingdom."

"Yes," I said. "I never thought the promises the Master made before his execution were the ones you and the sons of Zebedee heard. Forgive me, but I thought that all of you were so consumed by ambition to be princes that you missed what he was saying. Of course, I never had a vision of the risen Master nor heard any later promises."

"I doubt those words would have changed your mind. His promise at the lake was that he would be with us all days. I remember once [it had been several times] you said perhaps the Master had come again and that the fulfillment of the promise was that he was with us always."

I nodded.

"I finally see you were right. At the Day of Judgment the Master will come with the Father to judge the world, but that wasn't what he meant by his return. His return has happened. The appearances were only—how do you philosophers put it?—symbols of that return. He is with us, just as the wisdom of the Holy Spirit is with us, though we so seldom recognize either."

Simon Peter stopped and looked at Paul, but it was Onesimus who spoke. "Were slaves not to have the hope of release from their bondage, how many would follow the Way?"

"Do we bribe them with promises of an end to their earthly suffering?" Paul asked.

"You do not mean to, but you do," Onesimus responded. "Worse, you haven't fulfilled those promises. Chrestus fills the void between your promise and reality. Silence him and another will take his place—here or in Athens or Alexandria, Ephesus, or elsewhere. But if we say the promises were mistaken, people will ask what else is mistaken."

"To persist in error lest we scandalize others by confessing our error," I mused. "Or to lead a revolt ourselves and be wiped out. Or to admit error and lose our credibility. Those are not happy options."

"Our error was not happy," Simon Peter conceded.

"Yes," Paul said, "you have led your sheep astray, Cephas. You failed to listen to the Holy Spirit, but I think you now hear Her voice. I, too, have been slowly coming to just this sort of position, though I, of course, would state it in a more nuanced way."

"We must face Onesimus's question about what is to be done," I said.

"I could," Paul offered, "I could write a letter to all the churches explaining what the Master's return really implies and noting that Cephas agrees with what I am saying. That would cut the ground out from Chrestus present and all Chrestuses future."

"If a letter is to be written," I injected, "would it not be better that it come from Simon Peter, the one whom the Master chose?"

"The Master also chose me!" Paul retorted. "I, too, am an apostle. My authority is equal to that of any apostle, for the risen Christ appeared directly to me. He did not reveal himself through others but directly to my face."

"Most communities," Onesimus countered, "pay great honor to the name of Paul but others, like that in Rome, deny his legitimacy. A letter from Paul on so delicate a problem might divide; a letter from Simon Peter would unify the brethren to understand with one heart and mind."

Paul turned in surprise at this objection from his own slave. He said nothing for a few moments. "Very well." He waved his hand as if the matter were of no importance. "I take no pride in my talents; they are free gifts of the Holy Spirit."

"If I dictate a letter," Simon Peter said, "I will of course let you see it first so that you might edit it. But . . . I am not sure anyone should write quite yet. Except for you, Quintus, none of us has held this idea in his heart for very long. We should pray on it for a time and discuss it with others, perhaps John the priest."

"That is sensible," Paul agreed. "We must consider the vast implications this decision has for our work."

"It means we must be founding institutions that will last until the end of time, not merely spreading a gospel to this generation and keeping these people in the fold. And we have been doing precisely that," Simon Peter noted, "though I confess I did not understand why. Since the first, like Mary at the lake and the other disciples, once we have spread the word, we have chosen people to help us and to lead when we moved on."

"That," Paul humbly agreed, "has always been my policy. I assume you have followed my lead."

Lest Simon Peter correct the claim about leadership and divert us from our immediate problem, I remarked: "It also means that John ben Zebedee will never become a prince."

Paul and Onesimus looked blank, but Simon Peter gave a belly laugh.

"We are still left," I reminded them, "with the problem of Chrestus. If we cannot have him killed, kidnapped, or betrayed, what then?"

"Prayer, love. If we meet again I hope to show less fear and more love." Simon Peter spoke almost wistfully. He paused for a few moments. "Quintus, do you recall what John the priest said Rab' Gamaliel told the Sanhedrin when the sons of Zebedee and I were arrested the second time?"

"Yes, almost the exact words: 'Leave these men alone. If their work is of human origin, it will fail. If it comes from the Lord, you cannot fight them without fighting the Most High Himself.' "

"We should take that advice to heart and do nothing. Chrestus is the Lord's affair, not ours."

"He may be the Lord's affair," Onesimus commented dryly, "but it'll be our necks if the Romans hear about him."

"If the Most High wills it thus, then thus it will be," Simon Peter responded. "If He, the Lord of History, chooses to intervene, it will not be. We can pray for His help, but we can't use violence to spread a gospel of love."

Paul was silent, and for Paul that was strange indeed.

5

❧ Neither Simon Peter nor Paul ever dictated a letter explaining the development of their views on what the Master's "return" really meant. During the next few weeks our time was consumed by talking—and talking and talking and talking—at first separately and then together with groups of Jewish and gentile followers of the Way.

We made some progress. Paul's sarcasm did not help, nor did Simon Peter's reasoning move mountains. But the force of his integrity and the power of his will were always impressive and often effective. At one point on a hot July afternoon in Priscilla's apartment after the gentiles and Jews had exchanged recriminations, Alexander, Nereus, and Jacobus stood up and prepared to stalk out. Simon Peter, however, moved between them and the door. "There are only two exits," he said. "One leads through loving one another as brothers; the other leads through my fists. The Master commanded me to hold his people in my hand. And I *will* hold you." The two groups may not have loved each another, but they continued to talk and agreed to talk again.

It was exhausting work, for emotions ran at a high pitch and some grievances on both sides were just. Most of the Jews were reluctant to accept gentiles on any terms at all. Even gentiles who completed the conversion from God Fearers to Judaism could never become fully equal.

It logically followed that Jews found the minimal conditions set by the agreement at Jerusalem profoundly disturbing. Not only did they require accepting despised idol worshipers into the intimacy of one's family; these rules would have also drastically weakened, if indeed they would not have severed, Christian Jews' connections with the larger Jewish community of Rome—and perhaps Judaism everywhere. And it was from this community, its long history of faith and kinship, that these people had received and been able to maintain their identity.

The gentiles, in turn, were only slightly less hostile to Jewish Christians. When they had been pagans, they had shared the Greco-Roman world's antipathy toward Hebrews not only as strangers but also as privileged aliens whose atheism could anger the gods and provoke divine wrath. In addition, despite repeated assurances by Paul, Aristobulus, and some of the others, gentile attitudes toward sexual matters were basically different from Jewish.

Further, most of the gentiles could see no harm in attending pagan festivals, which they said were as much social as religious functions, or even eating food offered at these affairs. After all, they argued, the poor must eat when and what they can; choice in food was a privilege reserved to the rich. It was only at such festivals that many of the poor got to eat meat at all or to drink more than a cup of wine. From my own limited observations, the most frequent sins these ceremonies encouraged were gluttony and drunkenness.

Aristobulus had another and more special reason for attending heathen rituals. He said that one simply could not deal effectively with the Roman government without doing so. Indeed, distinguishing between the religious and secular aspects of the Roman system was impossible. Not only were public officials typically in attendance, priests were often influential political actors.

Throughout, Chrestus remained a demon who constantly threatened to break out of his box and spread the plague of persecution. Simon Peter and Paul warned all the faithful to whom they talked, Jews as well as gentiles, of Chrestus's dangerously lunatic apostasy. I also suspect, though a smirk is not hard evidence, that Aristobulus was planting a few seeds in Roman ears. He had both the incentive and opportunity to do so.

I can establish what happened next but not the exact order of events, nor do I pretend to understand fully the causes of the series of catastrophes I am about to describe. If, however, the Lord God is the Author of History and nothing happens without His knowledge and consent, if not without His positive intervention, then we must believe that what unfolded was part of a divine plan. I hope some day at least to glimpse its purpose.

This chapter in our lives began on a late afternoon in mid-July. It was a typical summer day in Rome. The sirocco, the wind that comes from the Sahara Desert across the Mediterranean into central Italy, was blowing hot, sand-laden air across the city. The heat of the crowded streets was made more oppressive by the wild medley of noises—people shouting over the cries of vendors hawking their wares, construction crews tearing down old buildings and erecting new ones, the clop of animals' hooves, and the clanging of an unending stream of carriage wheels beating against cobblestone pavements.

Simon Peter and I had just left Priscilla's apartment in an *insula* in a modest section southeast of the Aventine Hill. As we came toward the river near the Circus Maximus, we heard loud shouts of "Fire! Fire!" That was a dread cry in any city, for modern science, with all its miracles, has not yet perfected effective instruments with which to combat flames. Thus arson is a heinous crime in urban areas, and convicted arsonists are often executed by being tied in animal skins and thrown before wild, starving dogs.

In Rome, the dangers were worse than I remembered them in Alexandria, Athens, Antioch, or Jerusalem, for in the city's central sector the streets were narrow and several hundred thousand people were packed into *insulae*—rabbit warrens—that, like Sotion's, were stone only on the first floor, with the other three or four or even five storeys constructed of wood—tinderboxes. A famous architect had remarked that Rome had grown vertically rather than horizontally. The city had suffered several disastrous fires in the last half century, the most recent being scarcely fifteen years earlier under Claudius.

By the time we heard the shout, we were on the northern side of the Circus, down in the valley. At first, because of the size of the buildings around the Circus—it was 2,000 feet long and 300 feet wide, with a three-tiered grandstand—we could see only a pillar of thick, black smoke rising from somewhere around the base of the Caelian Hill. No doubt oil in one of the rows of shops there had ignited. We ran a bit up the slope of the Palatine and from that height could see the actual flames. Within minutes the whole area was a mass of flame and smoke, fanned by the sirocco. We could see people running willy-nilly in panic.

Simon Peter's first instinct was to help the fire fighting, but I persuaded him that we would be more a hindrance than a help. The capital of the Empire, I reasoned—as it turned out, incorrectly— could cope with fire. The city had seven cohorts of *vigiles*, all freedmen, not slaves, trained for this sort of emergency, and every Roman building was required to have water to fight fire. Moreover, the aqueducts and sewers were full. I also argued that he must conserve his strength for problems he could solve; and the split in Rome within the fellowship of the Way demanded his full energy.

Reluctantly, he acquiesced, even if he did not agree; and we crossed the Tiber below the island. Once on the other side, we stopped to get another perspective of what was happening. Black smoke was billowing up from the areas south and east of the Circus Maximus, but the fire did not seem likely to spread very far. The wind was driving it southwest toward the wide streets and gardens of the villas on the Aventine, rather than toward the thickly populated tenements to the east. We could see a great deal of confused as well as apparently coordinated movement, no doubt a cohort of *vigiles* going into action.

After dinner, Alexander, Simon Peter, and I walked back to the river to check on progress in arresting the fire. Even from Alexander's courtyard we could see a red glow in the sky to the southeast. At the river's edge, we could look straight into the Aventine area, but the darkness made it difficult to pick out the exact boundaries of the fire. Still, I was convinced that the flames had moved considerably to the west since we had left. That was a good sign, unless, of course, one owned one of the magnificent villas on the slopes of the Aventine.

We went to bed reasonably sure that, while the damage to the city and its people was going to be severe, it would be of less than catastrophic proportions. Several hours before dawn, however, we were awakened by banging at the gates and shouting in the streets. The wind had backed around, pushing the flames east. And refugees were pouring across the bridges to the Transtiberinum, some begging for food and lodging. Fortunately the weather was warm; in winter many would have died of exposure.

For the next five days all we could do was watch in horror. The government tried to direct people to the Campus Martius, because from time to time the fire would swing around and threaten to seal off the area of the Aventine and Palatine hills from the river. The heat became so intense and the wind so strong that fire leaped across the wide streets and gardens on those two hills that Romans thought would act as natural firebreaks. Even Nero's palace was gutted. Worse, the wind's frequent shifting spread the fire in several directions. It swung east, then north, then west again, then northeast, roaring like a fiery cyclone gobbling up everything in its scorching path.

As the smoke got thicker, the refugees became more numerous and the rumors wilder. Stories abounded of a people who refused to leave the area until they located their loved ones, only to be burned alive. There were persistent assertions that a group of men with torches had attacked the *vigiles* and set additional fires, claiming to be following "orders." Another popular account had the emperor himself in the tower at the Gardens of Maecenas singing the ancient song of the sacking of Troy. That Nero was at Antium when the fire began and that the tower and gardens had been consumed did nothing to make the tale less credible.

Simon Peter and I, of course, were distraught, for most of the gentile Christians, as well as Priscilla and Aquila, lived in the areas that were being destroyed. We were also concerned about Chrestus and what role, if any, he had played in this tragedy. But we could find out nothing. To keep down looting and prevent additional confusion, soldiers were on all the bridges, allowing people to escape but not to enter the city.

Finally, after six horrible days, the *vigiles* checked the flames by razing blocks of *insulae* on the Esquiline Hill and so depriving the fire of fuel. But the embers in central Rome continued to glow, and on the seventh day fire broke out once more, this time in the Campus Martius where most of the refugees were huddled. Panic, chaos, and fiery death ran riot again. Several more days of terror

ensued, until finally rain and the muscle power of the *vigiles*
checked the flames.

I have no idea how many people were trapped in burning
buildings, crushed by falling timbers, or trampled by panicked
fellow citizens. But the number had to be huge. The physical
damage was immense. Houses, apartment building, shops, government offices, temples, and art—most of it Greek—were lost. Three
of Rome's fourteen regions were almost obliterated, and seven of
the others severely damaged. We in the Transtiberinum suffered
no physical harm. Curiously, among the other areas least damaged
was the First Region, which lies immediately to the southeast of
where the fire began.

Needless to say, during the ten days of the fire, most of our
work of reconciliation ceased. Simon Peter continued to talk to
Jewish Christians and even returned to the synagogue to debate
Jews who would not accept the Way. Still, the pall of smoke, the
stench of burning oil, wood, animals, and human flesh, and the
dangerous rumors floating in the air focused our minds much
more on problems of this world than the next. We prayed that our
cousins would be rescued as well as that we ourselves would be
spared their ordeal.

Ten days after the first blaze had started, the last of the fires on
the Campus Martius was extinguished. But human suffering continued. As many as 150,000 homeless were gathered in the gardens, open fields, and public buildings of the Campus Martius.
The usual free distribution of grain continued and was augmented,
but slowly and with difficulty. The warehouses on the southeast
bank of the Tiber had incinerated, forcing the government to order
emergency shipments of grain up the Tiber from Ostia. As a
further measure, Nero was sending units of Praetorian Guards to
confiscate foodstuffs in the nearby countryside and towns. He had
also ordered grain that was sold to be offered for no more than
three sesterces a peck, a drastic reduction.

Despite all the government was doing, anger, hunger and fear
stalked the city. People whose entire possessions had been burned
could not afford cheap grain, and free grain was of little use to
urban folk when mills had been destroyed and ovens lost. My

own dread was the outbreak of some sort of plague. Rome's system of public sanitation was the most modern and efficient in the world. Almost every building of any size had a privy opening onto a sewer that was full of running water, and hundreds of public latrines were located in the more densely inhabited areas to serve the poor. But now people were using the fields, even the streets and recesses of buildings, for their waste. Hordes of flies appeared almost instantly, and rats became bold. I suggested to Simon Peter that the four of us retire to Pompeii for a few months; but, alas, he would not listen.

I confess I was also deeply troubled by the mood of Rome. I felt an undercurrent of latent rage. Looting had broken out in several quarters, and there were reports of a dozen lynchings of people caught stealing and, even more ominously, several riots over distribution of grain. Alexander was even more concerned than I. Not only did he hire several private guards and have his slaves reinforce the decrepit gate in his wall; he came close to forbidding us to leave the grounds of his house. "I have lived in the world long enough," he said, "to know that Jews will be blamed for every disaster. When it floods, we have brought the rain; when there is drought, we have stopped the rain. Where there is foul play of any sort, gentiles automatically suspect Jews. It is a fact of life we must live with."

"How will these few guards help?" I asked. "They won't fight soldiers, and even if they would they'd be killed in a minute."

"I fear soldiers far less than Roman citizens or freedmen," he answered.

On the twelfth day after the fire had broken out, Onesimus came to Alexander's door and asked that we go with him to Aristobulus's villa. Alexander strongly urged us not to do so, but we thought it essential to find out what had been happening to our gentile brothers and sisters and also to learn how we could ease their suffering.

Onesimus apologized for the absence of litters and explained that, with the breakdown in law and order, we would be safer if we were inconspicuous. We stayed on the Transtiberinum side and crossed the river to the Campus Martius near the Vatican Hill.

Immediately, we entered a different world. It was not so much the physical damage, though the second fire had made the area near the river look like it had just been sacked by a hostile army. More striking was the human desolation. Thousands of people were still camped in the charred gardens and ruins of public buildings. Gone were the arrogant, strutting Romans of two weeks ago; in their places were lost souls, dirty, hungry, bewildered, and benumbed. It tore at one's heart. More ominously, however, was another look that was also often apparent, one of sullen anger seeking revenge.

We stopped many times as Simon Peter tried to offer consolation, but I doubt that we did any good. And several times we were cursed at and threatened as foreigners who might, somehow, be responsible for this massive misery.

There had been no damage to Aristobulus's sector. Nevertheless, like Alexander's gates, his were securely bolted and private guards were much in evidence. Onesimus took us directly to Paul's quarters, then went to fetch Aristobulus. We exchanged expressions of grief and pieces of information with both men. From them we learned of the death of many of the followers of the Way. Among them was Aquila, Priscilla's husband. Knowing she had been at home, he had come back from the Capitoline Hill to save her. She had escaped, but he had been trampled in the stampede as he tried to cross the area south of the Circus Maximus. It was one of a thousand similar tragedies.

Paul explained how Aristobulus and other brothers and sisters from the less damaged parts of the city had been helping the homeless Christians with food and money. "But we cannot do enough for so many." Aristobulus added. "Only Nero can dent this problem." Simon Peter suggested an additional recourse: We fell on our knees to implore the mercy of the Most High on all the people of Rome.

"Are the brothers and sisters scattered or have they joined in one section of the Campus?" Simon Peter asked when our prayer was done.

Paul started to answer, but Aristobulus interrupted. "They have now disaggregated. They came out of the fire like everyone else, panicked, no semblance of order. But many of them found each other and clustered together. Paul, Onesimus, Rufus, and I located some of them and were able to give a bit of help. But yesterday I told them to scatter, to leave Rome if they could—instantly."

"Why?"

He looked around as if making sure none of the servants was in Paul's quarters. Then he lowered his voice. "I have intelligenced something very grave. My work, as you know, sometimes requires me to speak on a very high confidentiality level with government officials. In a nutshell, the Emperor is mad, perhaps possessed by a demon. No doubt about it, none at all. He's heard the rumors—all Rome has heard them—that he started the fire to clean out the sector east of the Circus Maximus where he wants to build his great Golden House and, even more grandly, to destroy central Rome so he could rebuild it and rename it in his honor."

"The story is," Paul added, "that he will rename the city 'Neronis.'"

"Exactly," Aristobulus agreed. "To be sure, rumors come and go around Rome like flies, but what we call 'rumor prevalence' and 'rumor persistence' are factors of government concern. And this rumor is both prevalent and persistent. Worse, it is stirring up not only the people, but also many patricians who despise Nero anyway and whose Aventine and Palatine palaces are now only ash pits."

"How does it concern us?" I inquired.

"Let us hope it does not," Aristobulus replied.

"There is a 'but' here somewhere, is there not?" I asked.

"Alas, there is. Nero needs a scapegoat, someone or some group to assume the guilt."

"And?"

"The most obvious scapegoats are the Jews," Aristobulus said. "They're foreigners, the Roman people don't like them, their area was untouched by the fire, and they're too few to fight back effectively and not rich enough to bribe court people. I have heard it suggested by top men that the Jews are ideal."

"What can we do to help our people?" Simon Peter blurted out.

Aristobulus held up his hand. "Our brothers may not need our sympathy and support. The whole court may agree that Jews make ideal sacrificial lambs; but Poppaea, Nero's whorewife, dissents. I hear she is interested in Judaism herself, which made me hope that someday we might persuade her to follow the Way. Her policy influence varies, one never knows from day to day to whom the prince listens. At this moment, however, she has apparently vetoed a condemnation decree against the Jews."

"The mercy of the Most High is without limit," Simon Peter said.

"Who is next in line?" I asked in a trembling voice.

He hesitated, then cleared his throat. "We have that honor. Only last evening I accessed several top men who confided that within the week, Nero will blame us for starting the fire."

"That is monstrous," Paul injected, "absolutely monstrous! No one who knows anything about us could think we pose any threat to the Empire. 'Be subject to authority.' I can show them my letter on the point."

Aristobulus sighed. "Monstrous but plausible, very plausible. The Way is Oriental in origin; the Master was executed as a seditionist. How better to revenge ourselves on his executioners than to burn their capital? We have also been augmenting our numbers from among slaves and the plebs. Such activity is evidence of stirring rebellion."

"But we have not stirred rebellion," Paul insisted. " 'Be subject to authority,' I have repeated time and again."

"Irrelevant, my dear Paul, totally irrelevant. Nero needs scapegoats. We fit. We're new, and you know how the Romans revere tradition and hold the new in contempt. Besides, we don't worship the old gods and so expose the city to their wrath. We're small in number, not more than five hundred adults including Jews and gentiles. And, except for a few people like Rufus and me, we have no policy influence."

"I have encountered Roman justice across the Empire," Paul retorted. "It's been harsh and sometimes even unfair, but it sticks to clear rules of evidence. And the evidence here is overwhelming."

"You're right about the law, Paul; but we're talking about Nero's survival. Reason, evidence, and legal rules won't matter, except as things to manipulate. He will prioritize the factors and, believe me, his survival comes before reason, evidence, and our lives. And there's more. He does have some damning evidence."

"What evidence?" I'm not sure which of us asked first.

"Chrestus. Chrestus is the evidence. When the fire first started, he attacked the *vigiles* with a flaming torch. They cracked him over the head and left him to burn, but somehow he got away—or someone rescued him. When the fire broke out a second time on the Campus Martius, our friend Chrestus was there again. This time he stood on the steps of Pompey's Theatre giving a sermon on the wrath of God, proclaiming himself the Messiah, and shouting that he had come again to punish the Roman swine for nailing him to a cross. The *vigiles* liberated his soul—with axes, I was told. A crowd of people saw and heard him, but there was so much madness during the fire that nothing more would have come of it if Nero hadn't needed scapegoats."

"What do you advise we do?" Simon Peter asked.

"Go. Get out of Rome. All Christians should scatter—as soon as possible. Today if they can. The roads are full of people going back to the countryside. You in particular, Simon Peter, you must get out. When the Roman government gets moving, it can be fearsomely efficient. And yours will be one of the first names they will discover."

"And Paul?" Simon Peter asked.

"I am technically in Aristobulus's custody. If I escape, he will be held responsible. Besides, how can I be thought guilty of arson if I've been under arrest?"

"From what Aristobulus has just said," I put in, "guilt or innocence will have nothing to do with Nero's actions."

"Perhaps. Well, I have run my race. I am ready to take up my cross. [Paul was a Roman citizen, and we all knew he could not be crucified for the crimes of which he was accused.] I have boasted that I have never run except after Jesus; I am too old now to learn how to run away. You have experience here, Cephas. You must use it to stay alive and preserve the Way."

"The Way will survive you and it will survive me," Simon Peter replied. "Each of us will have to make the choice for himself and his family. There is no disgrace in escaping from danger. The Master ran from Herod Antipas, and he hid himself from the priests in Jerusalem. To die serving the Lord is a holy thing; to die serving Nero is quite another." Then to Aristobulus: "We can spread the word among the Jewish families. Do you think you have reached all the gentiles?"

Aristobulus shook his head. "Only some of them. We must pray they will message the others. The worst part, however, is that somehow my credence level is low. But I shall try."

We returned to the Transtiberinum as rapidly as we could and spread the news. Alexander's reaction was dubious. "Yes, the Romans have let this Aristobulus believe they're after Christians, knowing he'd tell Jewish Christians. That would make the other Jews of Rome feel safe. It's the Jews the Romans will punish, and they won't care if they're Christian or not. It's not a distinction gentiles could understand."

"Will you pass the warning on to the others?" Simon Peter asked.

"Of course. They're in danger either way. But I doubt that it will do much good. Thinking ahead is not something most people are good at; they usually just hope for the best."

With Alexander and Aristobulus spreading news of the danger around Rome, we could be reasonably certain that the brothers and sisters would at least be alerted, even if they chose not to act prudently. We had also learned of another community in Italy, located to the south in the port city of Puteoli, not far from Capri, where members of the imperial court liked to relax. To warn our people there, Simon Peter dispatched John Mark. Thus he was able to escape what was to follow.

Aristobulus's information turned out to be accurate. Within a week, Nero issued a decree blaming "an atheistic, Jewish sect called Chrestians, whose founder the Prefect of Judea executed for sedition," for starting the great fire and murdering thousands of innocent Romans. We heard reports that while the decree was being read on the Senate's steps, soldiers were arresting twenty or more of the gentile brothers and sisters and imprisoning them in a building near the Capitoline Hill that somehow had survived the fire. Surprisingly, we heard of no Jewish Christians being arrested, at least not yet.

Other news was even more dire. Onesimus crossed the river one evening to warn us that soldiers had appeared at Aristobulus's villa that afternoon with an order to conduct Paul to the prison near the Capitoline. Aristobulus, however, had known the centurion and had produced documents that he claimed were of higher rank than the soldier's and had agreed to go to the Forum the next morning and straighten the affair out, meanwhile keeping Paul in his custody.

Late that night Onesimus woke us. He had scaled Alexander's wall and told us that Paul and Aristobulus were waiting in the alley outside. We joined Alexander, who had ordered a servant to admit the men into the atrium. He offered them no welcome. "Yes, you endanger the lives of all here," he began. "You can have food, water, and money, but you must leave."

"What is this talk?" Simon Peter asked.

Alexander continued to look directly at the three refugees. "They are wanted men, is that not true?"

Aristobulus nodded. "I have learned that my friend the centurion will be at my house at dawn with a warrant for my arrest as well as Paul's."

"I don't care," Simon Peter said. "You cannot turn out your brothers." His tone had a calmness that the fisherman from Galilee could never have maintained.

"My brothers? Yes, my brothers," Alexander snarled. "A hypocritical, idol-worshiping Roman citizen who hates Jews and earns his living by trading in political influence, an apostate Jew, and a runaway gentile slave? If the Romans find them here, they will take me, my family, and you and your family, and every Christian Jew in the Transtiberinum. Yes, and if they were angry enough, they might take every other Jew as well. We live on the inside slope of a rumbling volcano."

"You prioritize clearly," Aristobulus said very softly.

" 'Greater love has no man . . . .' " Simon Peter started to say.

"We are not talking about laying down my life for another," Alexander broke in, "but the lives of my family and my friends and my whole community."

"But all men are your family," Simon Peter insisted.

"No."

Simon Peter turned away. "How can a man call himself a Jew and not have compassion?"

"Yes, I have compassion," Alexander replied. "And I know the Romans. They will show no pity to any man—or woman. I am protecting those closest to me first. I am also protecting you and those closest to you."

"At what cost to our brothers and to your conscience?"

"They are dead men, Simon Peter. We can keep them alive for a day or a week or perhaps a month; but, if the Romans want them, they are dead men. The cost of keeping them alive for whatever brief period is the death of dozens, perhaps hundreds of others. What do you think Aristobulus would have said if I had shown up at his door? Yes, as he would put it, he would 'prioritize,' just as I have. Only a fool would do otherwise."

"Then count me a fool of the Most High," Simon Peter said. "We stand or fall as a band of brothers and sisters, as a family. The whole message of the Way, Alexander, is that we love one another as we love ourselves. We do not 'prioritize' where human beings are concerned."

"Yes, but we cannot save everyone. If we refuse to make choices we kill all."

"The Romans kill; we refuse to make their choices for them. If it is the will of the Lord of History that all the followers of the Way in Rome die for their faith in the Master, so shall it be."

"We'd better leave while it's still dark," Aristobulus said very quietly.

Alexander went back in the house, and Simon Peter and I embraced the other three, giving them the kiss of peace. "We shall not stay in this house another hour," Simon Peter said to us.

Paul, curiously, had spoken hardly a word during the argument. Now he said: "Stay, Cephas. Where else can you go?"

"I don't know. I cannot stay here. Priscilla may be able to take us."

"No, it would increase her danger," Paul protested. "If the Romans don't know who you are, they soon will. Jephthania will be obvious to any soldier—or any slave, freedman, or citizen who believes Nero's lies. Live, Simon Peter, for the Way, for all the brothers and sisters who need you. And forgive Alexander; he is not a great man."

As Paul and his companions left, I thought of Stephen, who had been almost as disagreeable a person, yet who had also staged an heroic exit.

6

✣ We left Alexander's house two days later, but not because of our own decision. At dawn, a centurion and a unit of troops smashed through the door in the wall and seized all of us they could find, including the slaves. As we stood in the atrium, the centurion read an order in badly accented Latin for the arrest of " 'Simon Peter, a Galilean fisherman who leads the followers of one Jesus the Nazarene, a notorious seditionist executed for claiming to be the King of the Jews.' Are you this man?"

Simon Peter hesitated, whether because of his difficulty with Latin or because of fear, I do not know. "I am called Simon Peter."

"Very well. I also have an order for the arrest of your family, friends, followers, and any person who has given you aid or comfort. Since you are staying in this Jew's house, all here fall under my order."

"What possible charge is there against us?" I asked.

"The charge is arson—setting fire to the city of Rome."

"You know that is false!" I half shouted.

"I know I have an order for your arrest. That is all I need to know."

At that point two soldiers came out of the house. One was half carrying, half dragging Jephthania, still a beautiful woman, though she was forty. The other was pushing Naomi roughly ahead. The soldier with Jephthania was obviously fondling her breasts as he dragged her along. Her face was contorted in terror. She was trying desperately to scream, but the only sounds that came out were guttural animal noises, the sort a small prey makes in the seconds before the wolf sinks its teeth into its flesh. I have no doubt she was reliving the earlier sexual assault.

The grin on the soldier's face reflected his enjoyment. Simon Peter let out a roar like a maddened bull and, in a single long step grabbed the soldier, spun him around, and smashed a big fist squarely on his chin. The man screamed in pain and surprise and fell heavily onto the stone floor of the atrium. Quickly, two other soldiers tackled Simon Peter and a third cracked him across the back of the head with a sword hilt.

The centurion looked Greek to me so I spoke to him in that language. "It would not be wrong to use kindness. The woman is paralyzed because of an attempted rape when she was a child. She is a virgin."

The centurion's face was blank. I repeated my message in Latin, which brought a slight smile. "Really? Rome has perfected an instant cure for virginity. If she's lucky, one of my men will make her well."

There was, however, no further sexual assault, unless one counts leering and a bit more groping. We were taken to Nero's Circus on the Vatican Hill, about a mile upstream from Alexander's house on the same side of the Tiber. All of us were led, hobbled by chains, except for Jephthania. The centurion allowed two of Alexander's slaves to carry her and two others to help Simon Peter, who was a bit groggy and bleeding profusely, as one typically but not dangerously does from a blow to the skull. It was just as well we did not have to cross the river, for we later learned that angry mobs had attacked and stomped several groups of brothers and sisters to death when they were taken through the central city. Evidently, many Romans believed Nero's accusations, not a happy omen for our future.

Our chains were removed and we were taken down to rooms below ground level, where the Romans usually kept the animals and gladiators for games. The heavy stench of lion dung permeated the dank atmosphere. Perhaps another 150 people were cooped up there, an appallingly large share of the gentile Christians in Rome. We knew most of them and exchanged greetings. The light was poor, but we could see that Paul, Aristobulus, and Onesimus were not among the prisoners; nor was Priscilla.

Naomi immediately began comforting the women. To my surprise, she was quite good at it, offering not sympathy but cheer and what little physical help she could. Jephthania limped slowly on her mother's arm, unable to speak, only to smile and to touch with her left hand. Still, the silent courage with which she faced life was contagious.

For a few hours Simon Peter was too weak to do anything except rest. But, as soon as he was able, he took command, dividing us into groups of ten and instructing each group to choose members for special duties—one to be in overall charge, another to be responsible for gathering and distributing food, one to help mothers with small children, another to help take care of the sick, and another to coordinate with his opposite numbers in other groups on how to cope with problems of sanitation.

The last was more serious than one might think. There was no privy in the big chamber, no slop buckets, and no reason to expect the soldiers would let us out to relieve ourselves in the public facilities around the circus. The early arrivals had been using the floor, and that seemed to be what the Romans intended. The ground sloped slightly eastward, toward the river, and twice a day, according to our brothers, attendants opened a valve that sent about an inch of water flushing across the stone floor and out a crack between the floor and the eastern wall, carrying some but not all of the human waste along with it.

Toward evening the big iron gates swung open again, and about twenty more people were shoved through. All were Jewish Christians from the Transtiberinum. We were achieving unity at last.

Shortly afterward, the evening meal arrived. It was the same as every other meal we got at the circus, bread and water. When the servers had distributed the food to their groups, Simon Peter stood up, broke off a corner of his bread for each person in our group, and in a loud voice pronounced the blessing in Greek: "The Master has died, the Master has been raised, the Master is with us now and always." I translated it into Latin, then we drank water instead of wine.

After a few minutes—that's all it took to dispose of our supper—Simon Peter stood up again and began to address us, still in Greek:

People of God, tonight at the breaking of the bread, you heard me use different words, different because I have come to realize—and Paul with me—what some others have recognized from the beginning. At the Lake of Galilee, when the risen Master restored my sight, he told us in so many words what we have been groping toward during these past three decades. He had risen as he promised; he had come back to us; and he promised never to abandon us. That is the good news: He has come again; and he will never leave us. His kingdom has come! That kingdom, the kingdom of God, the Master's kingdom, is within us. He tried to tell us that a thousand times, but we never heard, never understood, that his kingdom is within the hearts of all people who acknowledge and repent their sins and love the Lord and their fellow humans with all their minds.

Simon Peter paused while I translated. Then he began again:

Thus we are not alone, never, not ever, not even now in this rotting hole of a prison. Where we are, he is, sharing our joy, our pain, always renewing the wisdom and courage that are the gifts of the Holy Spirit. Today we are suffering—and worse, we are terrified of what we may suffer tomorrow, just as he suffered and feared more suffering. We shall all pass from this life that we know and cherish, if not today or tomorrow or next week, yet too soon for our mortal minds.

But the Master's promise is not one of mortal life and glory. "My kingdom is not of this world," he said. That kingdom, the kingdom of God, is within us now and for all eternity. If we believe in the Way and follow the Way, we shall never die to eternal life, though we may lose—with brief but real pain—this mortal life. "He who wants to save his life will lose it," the Master told us, "but anyone who loses his life for my sake will find it."

Our bodies fear mortal death, but our souls do not. Our souls welcome it, for we have the grace of eternal life.

As I listened and translated, I noted Simon Peter's usual traits of simple directness and painful honesty. Yet there was more here, a touch not only of eloquence but also a vision that was a cosmos removed from the grubby, selfish almost to the point of venality, hopes of Galilean fishermen to become princes in a realm in which they would crush their former oppressors.

Afterwards we talked in our groups about what Simon Peter had said. People came over to discuss it further with him. All whom I heard found his words, whether out of faith or merely hope, utterly convincing.

For two more days we were kept in our makeshift prison. It was not a pleasant experience. The only changes consisted of our being joined by fresh groups of brothers and sisters, mostly Jews. There were now more than two hundred of us, including children. I doubted if there were that many of us left in central Italy. Naomi and Jephthania continued their work, Simon Peter his.

On the third day, a porthole opened in the gate, and a soldier called out: "The man called Simon Peter, the Galilean, come to the gate immediately." Simon Peter and I looked at each other quizzically, then walked slowly across the chamber. As we made our way through the mass of prisoners, people called out blessings and tried to touch Simon Peter. At the gate, the guards held me back until I explained that Simon Peter's Latin was poor and I was his translator. It was not a total lie.

We were led up to the ground level to one of the rooms used as an office by officials who ran the games. As a precaution, the guards had clapped light chains on our wrists and ankles. Thus we hobbled rather than walked. It was a gait to which I was becoming accustomed. Waiting for us were three officials; two wore simple togas, the third was in military uniform. I could recall enough of my childhood to recognize the soldier's insignia as those of a legate, a very high rank. The civilians were of even more impressive status—*praetores*, professional judges of the highest status. I recognized the one who was in charge of the inquiry as Fabius Marcus, a strikingly handsome young patrician who had the clearest blue eyes I had seen outside of Galatia. Unlike most Roman aristocrats, he approved of Nero, even considered himself a friend.

The officials were comfortably seated; we stood, with a guard at each side. For Simon Peter it must have been a familiar scenario.

Fabius Marcus spoke: "You, you are the man called Simon Peter, the Galilean?"

In translating to Simon Peter, I used Aramaic so that we would have some means of private communication. In translating to Marcus, I spoke as rapidly as I could and, wherever possible, used difficult constructions and unusual words to mask from Simon Peter how I was conveying his responses.

"I am," Simon Peter answered.

"Directing your attention to events some thirty-four years ago in the, the Province of Judea, were you then a follower of a man called Jesus the, the Nazarene, whom the Prefect Pontius Pilate executed for sedition?" Marcus's intonation caused my mind to leap back across those years. Except for his slight stammer, the tone was identical to that Pilate had used in interrogating the Master.

"Unjustly executed."

"Answer my question without, without comment. You shall not receive a second warning. Still directing your attention to those events, did this executed criminal place you second in command of his, his forces?"

"He did."

"Directing your attention now to events of recent weeks, why did you order your people to, to burn Rome?"

"My people did not set fire to this city or any other. They could not use any form of violence without denying everything the Master and his gospel stand for."

"Let us not waste time. What did you hope to gain by this vicious arson and murder?"

"We did not start the fire. We believe that we must love everyone as we love ourselves."

Marcus raised his eyebrows, then continued: "Directing your attention to the, the events of the last few weeks, do you know a freedman called Chrestus? Was he not a member of your vile, atheistic cult?"

"I know Chrestus. He claimed to be a follower of the Way, but he was not. He was possessed by a demon." I translated that last sentence: "He was a lunatic."

"You disown this Chrestus?"

I translated Simon Peter's reply as: "He was a lunatic. I wanted to help him, but I could not."

"You are an obstinate man," Marcus said. Then to one of the soldiers: "Bring in the other prisoner."

A few moments later a pair of guards led Aristobulus into the room. He was naked, except for chains around his ankles. He was drooling and his remaining eye was staring straight ahead. His face was dirty but, except for the empty, bloodcaked left eyesocket, unmarked. The rest of his body, however, was a mass of black welts; his genitals were raw meat. Someone had poured boiling tar on him.

"What is your name and why are you here?" Marcus asked.

"I am called Aristobulus," he answered in a hollow voice. "I am here to do my duty as a loyal subject and testify against my fellow Christians who are plotting against the Empire and our divine prince."

"Directing your attention to this Christian plot, in what does or did it consist?"

"In a foul conspiracy to burn the Eternal City."

"Directing your attention to the people in this room, do you see the leader of this, this conspiracy?"

"I do." He raised a trembling hand and pointed at Simon Peter. "He is there, Simon Peter. He is the leader. He ordered Chrestus and all other Christians to set fires around Rome and to attack the *vigiles* when they tried to save the city. He ordered me to take part in this revolution, but I refused."

Simon Peter broke in: "Why this farce? You've tortured this poor man to the point where he'll say anything to stop the pain."

Marcus smiled. His demeanor changed from that of harsh interrogator to patient negotiator. I did not immediately understand why. "Or it may be that the pain has cleared the lies from his mind and he now speaks the truth. Of course, I wouldn't expect a barbarian Jew to realize how important the law is to us. When we have the games—and your trial and execution will be a central, a central feature of those games—we want people to know that you are guilty."

"Hypocrisy!"

"Law, order, and Empire are worth a bit of, of hypocrisy."

"But why this farce now? Why not save it for your 'games'?"

"Because I wanted you to know our plans. That way you can weigh my offer with greater, shall we say precision?" Marcus looked at me. "Can you teach him to say a few sentences in clear Latin?"

I nodded.

"Very well. You will confess at these games that you ordered Chrestians to start the, the fires—both of them. We have Aristobulus, but too many people know he's a rascal. He poses a problem of credibility. Just among ourselves, 'questioning him severely' wasted time. We could have bribed him more quickly. Within an hour of his arrest, he offered us your, your hiding place in exchange for his freedom. But some of our people are cynical. They didn't trust such an easy admission. And there it is." He gestured toward Aristobulus as one would toward a lamed pack mule. "In any event, you, the leader of the Chrestians, will make a wonderfully credible witness. Everyone will believe your confession, especially if afterward you grovel a bit and beg for mercy. Perhaps you might oblige us by acknowledging the prince as an, an immortal god."

Simon Peter's response began with critical comments about pagan idols and ended with specific references to Nero's mother's notorious sexual adventures with her son and assorted large dogs. I thought it best to let these remarks remain in Aramaic and translated his answer as: "You know the charge is false; I know the charge is false; and each of us knows the other knows. Why should I do this?"

"Because you, you want to live. Life is sweet, is it not, Simon

Peter? It would be sweet to get out of this stinkhole and on a ship headed back to the Orient, with your wife and daughter and your Greek friend safe and sound and this, this unpleasantness all behind you, would it not?"

Simon Peter said nothing.

"Before you make up your mind, you should know the entertainment our benign, benign prince has planned. Some will suffer the traditional arsonist's fate: tied up in animal skins, and wild dogs—we use well trained and quite hungry killer dogs—will be let out. Arms will be tied but, but legs will be free. That way one can buy a few more moments of life by trying to run away. It amuses the crowds to see the dogs chase frightened men and women around the, the arena."

The other praetor spoke for the first and only time during the scene: "Of course, the prince wants a bit of variety. People tire of watching dogs eating criminals. He plans to do to you what you did to Rome: to nail you on crosses, put pitch on you, and set you on fire. He's been working out the pattern of the crosses to provide some very special effects. Well, Jew, how would you prefer to see that crippled daughter of yours die, eaten alive or burned alive? Either way, we'd get rid of a piece of garbage."

Simon Peter suddenly twisted his body around and threw his weight against the guard on his right, sending the man crashing into the chair of the second praetor. It happened just as I was finishing my translation. Almost as quickly the guard on the left kicked Simon Peter in the back of his knee, dropping him to the floor. Another soldier put a hammerlock on the Gaililean that threatened to break his neck.

Marcus smiled as his colleague slowly got up and dusted himself off. "Love everyone? No, no violence? And you talk to me about, about hypocrisy?" Marcus gestured to the guards. "Instruct him we don't play games, then let him up."

One guard kept the hammerlock on Simon Peter while another kicked him three times in the ribs; then they jerked him to his feet. "Go back to the others," Marcus said softly. "Look at your wife and daughter—and your baldheaded Greek friend. Picture them roasting on a cross or being the main course for some, some animal's supper."

I asked the question that Simon Peter could not or would not: "And if he does what you ask?"

"Ahh, one can always count on a Greek to be sensible. No doubt that's why you make such good slaves. If your friend does what we suggest, he and his family—and you—will be allowed to, to 'escape.' We shall give you a head start. If, after a week, we find you in Italy we shall crucify you on the spot. There, you have the alternatives: a bit of hypocrisy and freedom or a bit of, of truth and a slow, horrible death for you all."

"And the other Christians?" I asked.

"The others? Well, they'll have to be sacrificed, won't they? As our legate here would remind us, soldiers must always be ready to die for their fatherland. We can't disappoint the people of Rome. After all they've been through, they deserve some, some diversion. Personally, I would give them Jews for amusement, but Poppaea likes them. Oriental religions seem to have a special appeal to, to women. That's why Antioch's Orontes has been able to dump its effluvia in the Tiber, I suppose."

He gave us his smile again. "Do think hard. This is an ideal case for rational choice—costs and benefits and all that sort of thing."

"How long do we have?" I asked.

"Not long. The prince plans to open the, the ceremonies to-morrow evening." Marcus snapped his fingers. "Take them away!"

I did not think about it. The choice was not mine, and I was glad of it. Simon Peter did not talk to me about the issue, and I was glad of that, too. He was thinking, of course. His moroseness provided ineluctable evidence of moral wrestling. Being locked up had the small advantage of denying him the escape of wine, though it was an advantage I would have happily traded for a wineskin of my own.

We made it through the rest of the day and the night and the next morning without hearing more than an occasional grunt from Simon Peter. Not only did he refuse to talk to us; he waved away any of the brothers who tried to approach him for solace. Alexander led us in prayer that night. Simon Peter sat silently in a corner.

If he was not a source of comfort to the others, neither was he a source of scandal. Respect for the Master's messenger led the others to read his black mood as one of prayerful meditation, which was at least half correct.

Early that afternoon it became obvious that something was about to happen. The skeleton work force of a few dozen men we had seen as we were led into prison must have grown several times, for we could hear hammering and sawing and many human voices and footsteps above us. Then came another set of sounds, far more dreadful for those of us who knew the traditional Roman punishment for arson—the howling and snarling of big dogs being brought into the next chamber.

In mid-afternoon, a guard opened the peephole and called again for Simon Peter, his family, and for me to come to the gate. Once more as we crossed the prison room, people reached out to touch Simon Peter's robe or kiss his hand. As the guards pulled us roughly through the gate, Alexander led the people in singing a hymn based on Psalm 103. The Jewish Christians, of course, knew it by heart, and the gentiles quickly picked it up.

> Bless the Lord, O my soul,
> Bless the Lord, O my soul,
>
> He forgives our sins
> And redeems our lives.
> Bless the Lord, O my soul
> Bless the Lord.
>
> Merciful and gracious is the Lord,
> Slow to anger and plenteous is His Mercy.
> Bless the Lord, O my soul
> Bless the Lord.
>
> His mercy is from ever to ever
> And His justice is full of love.
> Bless the Lord, O my soul,
> Bless the Lord.

We could hear the words over the growls of the dogs as we were shackled, then pushed and shoved back up to the room where we had been interrogated. To our left we could also see some early arrivals among the spectators filing in. They were obviously wealthy people, for the men and women were well dressed and slaves trailed behind, carrying picnic baskets and flasks of wine.

The same three men awaited us; Fabius Marcus again presided. He came directly to the point: "Well, Jew, have you made up your, your mind?"

"Where is Paul?"

"Paul?" Marcus looked genuinely confused. "Who or what is this Paul?"

The legate leaned over and whispered in Marcus's ear. "Oh, yes," the praetor said, "you mean this, this other Jew who's been awaiting the prince's judgment on his case from Judea. Nero has decided to spare him the embarrassment of a hearing. My friend," he motioned toward the legate, "has a warrant for your friend's execution."

"You do not have him then?"

"Not at this, this moment, but we soon shall. We have his slave. The legate's men are questioning him now. He'll soon be happy to tell us all he knows—and much more."

The legate whispered something else into Marcus's ear. The praetor looked up at us. "My last statement is no longer valid. It, it seems that the slave is at this very moment negotiating with Charon to cross the River Styx. His, his interrogation was not— how shall we put it?—successful. But never fear, your friend Paul is a dead man. Our legate would never let a Jew escape—not and remain a legate. But come now, my good fellow, the, the sand is running out. Here, let me push things along."

Marcus snapped his fingers and two guards came in, each carrying a couple of goat skins sewn together so that they would pretty much cover a human being. The guards draped the skins around Naomi and Jephthania. "There, now," Marcus purred, "not quite the fit you get from a tailor on the Vicus Tuscus, but they'll be good enough for the, the dogs. The brutes don't seem to care much for fashion anyway. It's meat they fancy."

"What assurance do we have," Simon Peter asked, "that if I do what you want, you will let us all go?"

Marcus curled his lips in what was more a sneer than a smile. "You have the, the word of a Roman praetor. There is no bond more sacred."

"Other than sheep manure," Simon Peter said in Aramaic, which I translated as "I need some time."

"Your answer, Jew!" Marcus demanded.

Simon Peter's voice was flat: "You have won. Tell me exactly what I must do. But first take those filthy skins off my family."

Marcus's instructions were exactly as he had outlined them the previous day: a confession to having planned and conducted arson on a massive scale against the city, a plea for mercy, and an acknowledgment of Nero's divinity. "The prince considered having you also acknowledge the, the divinity of his horse, but some of us believed that might undermine the, the credibility of the rest of your statement." Marcus graced us with another of his clear-eyed smiles. "We persuaded the prince to drop it for artistic reasons: People might think of the horse instead of him. What we have will do very nicely. Instruct him in the, the proper Latin," Marcus commanded me.

We were taken to the adjoining room and locked securely in. My task was not difficult. In our years of traveling, Simon Peter had picked up an elementary knowledge of the language. In a pitiful effort to protect his reputation, I chose a florid literary style which anyone who knew him would immediately realize he would never use.

With Simon Peter's memory, the instruction took less than half an hour. Naomi and Jephthania sat silent during the coaching session. Then the four of us sat silent for another two hours, as the shuffling of feet above us turned into the massive tromping of 30,000 people filing into the circus. At about seven, when there was still plenty of light, we heard the clomp of soldiers' sandals. The door swung open and our legate with a squad of a dozen guards stood in the entry. He pointed a finger at Simon Peter. "You, come with us now. The noble people of Rome will want the dogs to enjoy their supper while there's still enough light to watch the feast."

I started to move alongside Simon Peter, but the legate pushed me back. "Not you, Greek; we only need one for this performance." He motioned to one of the guards. "Here, give them their things." The soldier tossed us the knapsacks and small handbags we had left at Alexander's. "Repack," the legate said, not unkindly. "Take only what you absolutely need. You'll be on the run. Don't be caught in Italy."

Simon Peter waited while the soldiers fixed shackles to his legs and hands. As he stood there, Naomi recited in her mocking tone, " 'He who wants to save his life will lose it.' " Then she walked up close to him and put her arms on his shoulders. "Rab' Simon, from the bottom of my heart—" She spat full in his face. He hobbled out without a word, spittle running down his beard. It was not the first time a woman had so decorated him.

We could only guess at what happened. We heard the shuffling feet of brothers and sisters—I estimated about fifty—being led up above, then the roar of the crowd as our people entered the arena, then faintly a set of speeches. At one point, I thought—probably imagined—I could make out Simon Peter's voice. It may have been he, for immediately afterward the crowd's noise became a jumble of angry screams.

Then we could hear the yapping and snarling of the dogs as they were being let out, and another roar came from the crowd, this one of excited expectation. I feared that Marcus had broken his "sacred" word; but just then the door opened again, and the legate stood there with Simon Peter. "Out now," the officer told us. "My advice is get to Ostia and take the first ship—anywhere. Do you have money?" He answered his own foolish question by handing me a purse. "I'm releasing three young men from the other group to help you with the cripple. They'll have some wine and food."

"Thank you," Simon Peter said. "Do the others know?"

The legate shook his head. "The ones who're being eaten know; perhaps the ones who're about to be crucified and burned heard something, but not the ones still in the holding pen. The three young men know only that when they've taken you to Ostia they'd better not come back to Rome—ever."

"They will all know soon enough," Naomi said in halting Greek. "The world will soon know about Simon Peter."

The legate scowled at Naomi. "Do not judge your husband, woman. He is saving your life and the life of your daughter."

"'He who wants to save his life will lose it,'" she repeated.

I supported Jephthania until we were outside the circus and the three young men took over the task. They seemed even more eager than we to escape from Vatican Hill and the smoldering ruins of Nero's Rome and Rome's justice.

Epilogue
You Will Stretch Out
Your Hands
(64 C.E.)

I awoke slowly. It was shortly after dawn and my aging muscles were aching from yet another night spent on damp dirt. I was uncertain where I was. It was a problem from which I often suffered in the days when we moved around so much. When I saw the wounded structure of the old farmhouse, I remembered our "escape" from Rome, last night's storm, and today's long walk. In the background I could hear loud breathing I recognized as Simon Peter's. I closed my eyes for a few more moments to allow my muscles to muster energy to pull me up. It was then I realized I felt no one else's presence.

I sat up quickly and looked around. Naomi, Jephthania, and the three brothers from Rome were gone, and Simon Peter was sleeping outside, propped up against the shattered wall. I could see a piece of papyrus sticking out of my pack. I snatched it and, holding it as far as I could from my face so I could focus my eyes, tried to read what Jephthania—the only other one of us who could write—had scrawled with a piece of charred wood in left-handed Aramaic letters: "We go to Rome to meet the Master. Peace."

I went over and shook Simon Peter. The wineskin beside him was empty, an eloquent explanation of why he was hard to rouse. It took several minutes for him to bring himself to a sitting position, and even so the blurry look in his eyes promised little immediate comprehension. Quickly, he lay back again, holding his head in obvious pain. "Quintus, why is it that you must shake me whenever my head aches?"

While he was recovering, I walked over to a tiny stream that was slightly downhill from the house, rinsed the empty wineskin, and filled it with water. When I returned, Simon Peter was standing up, not steadily but upright nonetheless. He grabbed the skin and drained half its contents before asking: "Where are the others?"

"They've gone back to Rome." I showed him the note. He couldn't read it, but its existence confirmed my words.

He nodded but did not speak.

I waited for an explosion, but there was none, not even an exclamation of surprise. After a few minutes of silence, he said simply: "It had to be. I knew that; they knew that; but they had courage . . . . I need to be alone, Quintus. I need to pray, to beg for forgiveness and guidance. Give me an hour. Then come back."

I already knew what he would do. The brothers would make slow time carrying Jephthania. Thus, if Simon Peter wanted, he could have left immediately and overtaken them before they reached Rome. To delay was to decide. Part of me was relieved by his decision, but only the better part.

I tried to put it all out of my mind as I walked off into the field. The farmland seemed rich. The moist earth had a good smell to it. Last night's rain and this morning's sun were turning the brown grass back to green. It was easy to see why the house had been abandoned but not why the land was lying unused. Perhaps some wealthy Roman had bought it and was planning to build a villa here. The site was excellent, only a few hours' horseback ride along the Appian Way back into Rome, but still far enough away to be free of the city's noise and even some of its scandal.

When I returned, Simon Peter was draining the last of the water from the wineskin. He slipped his pack on his back. His eyes were still bloodshot, but his jaw was firmly set. "Well?" I asked.

"I return to Rome."

"Why?" I was not sure I wanted to know, but I had to ask.

"Because the Master has told me I must."

"The Master has come to you again?" It was not an intelligent question, but my heart was in command, not my mind.

Simon Peter looked at me gently, as if I were his dearest friend, not his perpetual goad. "He has never left me, Quintus. You have always known that; I was the slow one."

I nodded.

"That may be why the Master loved John and Mary more than he loved me. They understood."

(I knew Simon Peter was wrong: Since I was the first to understand, by his logic the Master would have loved me the most.)

"I should have dictated that letter to the churches of Asia and

Greece, and even Jerusalem," he went on, "telling them the Master has come again, that is what 'I am with you all days' means."

"You could still dictate the letter as we walk back to Rome. I could find a business associate of my cousins who would send it on to Corinth or Antioch for me."

I am not sure Simon Peter heard what I said. He shrugged his heavy shoulders, shivering as if shaking off his sins like a big dog shaking off water. "The first time I denied the Master I did so mostly out of spite. I was frightened, I admit that; but even more I was resentful. This time, this time there was still spite. The Master spared John in Jerusalem and promised him long life at the lake. In Rome the Father has let Paul escape and left me to be taken and tortured to death. Most of all He crippled my beautiful Jephthania."

"The Master himself was tortured to death."

I don't think Simon Peter heard those words either, for he continued without a break: "Forgiving still comes hard to me, even forgiving those I love most. You of all people know that. You first told me that, and I've since told it to myself often. Spite pushed me to decide to accept the offer to escape."

He was silent for a few moments as he adjusted the straps of his pack. "I confess to you, Quintus, my old friend and teacher, that it was fear, too—for myself, but more for Naomi and Jephthania. I love them both. I've given them nothing, yet they have followed me across the world, sharing my danger and my suffering. I can lay down my life for my faith in the Master. I managed to forgive him years ago—I think. But the Father . . . . The Father, the Eternal, the All Powerful One, the One who palsied Jephthania—that was another matter."

"How can you judge what is ineffable?"

"Because I am a man, Quintus, a man who thinks and feels and prays and tries to understand. That's why I can judge. But I judge differently today from how I judged yesterday. Then I asked, why should I choose to sacrifice Naomi's life and Jephthania's to amuse a foul mob? If the Lord wants our lives, let Him take them. He is all-powerful. Do you remember that day at the lake when I spoke of ending all our lives together? You told me I had no right to choose for my family. When we sat in prison, I asked myself if I had a right to choose death for them. I couldn't answer it, not then."

"Naomi and Jephthania have answered it for you. They have chosen to lay down their lives. The decision is theirs, not yours."

"Yes, they've answered it for me. More. In a strange way, they have taken away my anger at the Father. Without their courage . . . . Sometimes my faith has been strong enough to move mountains, Quintus. And at other times every passing breeze has threatened to blow it away. I've got that wrong. I've always believed, just as I've always doubted—and envied, and resented, and lusted, even while I prayed. I've never been free from sin."

"That may be the only way. To think is to doubt; and no intelligent human being can stop thinking. If you didn't doubt, why would you need faith?" As one who had little faith, I spoke presumptuously.

"But I have acted on my doubts, not just on my faith. Mary, now Naomi and Jephthania—they may have had doubts, but they fought them down and acted on faith. They have been the rocks; I have been mere shifting sand."

I grunted something unintelligible.

"And, I know it sounds stupid now, after my desertion, I feared for something else, the movement, the brothers and sisters in all the communities. Without me to lead them, what would happen to them? John is no leader, he's smart but he's weak; Mary has the courage, but she is a woman. Few men, even among those who follow the Way, accept her for what she is. Paul won't do; he's running."

Simon Peter stopped and snorted. "Besides, even though he loves the Lord with all his contentious soul, he's better at founding than at leading, at dividing than at uniting. As for the others, James is dead, though many of his faults live on among some of the others at Jerusalem. They cannot share; they would close the Master's doors to the gentiles, keep alive ancient hatreds of gentiles. They cannot grasp that the new Covenant has been given to them to share, not to monopolize. The Lord's grace is infinite. We lose none of it when we share it."

I nodded.

Simon Peter went on: "And your Greek friends, Quintus, many of them are worse. They don't believe Jews are good enough to be their brothers, and they think the good news is that they're free of all moral obligations to each other and even to the Eternal One, whom they confuse with Zeus or Jupiter or some other pagan demon. And some of them would rebel just as violently against Rome as those Jews who now called themselves Zealots would; and if they won, they'd spend their days in taverns and their nights in whorehouses."

There was a great deal to his exaggeration. Who in the civilized world does not resent the Roman sword at his throat? And the cult of Dionysus, as the huge statue in the central plaza of my beloved Scythopolis testifies, grapples itself onto the Hellene's soul.

"Without me, Quintus, without me, what would happen? Our *brothers* in Jerusalem would create a new Sanhedrin and make the Master's words a yoke to hang petty rules around people's necks. They'd forget all about the commandment to love with all your heart. Some of your Greek cousins would turn the Master's words into licenses for debauchery. The whole movement would shatter and fester in its own rot. All of them, Jews and Greeks, would betray the Master and one another, just as Alexander betrayed Paul and Aristobulus, me. My faith has been weak, Quintus; you've seen my doubt parade in public like the troops of a Roman garrison. But I have come to know the truth and to accept it, and I can lead. Without me, what would happen? It was a fair question."

I put my hand on his shoulder. "It is more than a fair question. You have given us leadership. Without you—"

He pushed my hand away. "Don't patronize me, old friend. I was speaking of my fear, of my pride. That fear and that pride almost drove me to mistake Chrestus for the Master. I was wrong. I see that. 'Behold I am with you always,' the Master told us at the lake. He did not say 'I am with you until Simon Peter dies.' Once again I was weak; once again I heard but did not hear. As Paul argued, by dying the Master conquered death. 'As long as two or three of you gather in my name, I shall be there among you.' It is hard to accept that everything important does not end with my own death, but I must accept it: He will be with us even when I am gone."

He looked up at the sun; it was two hours past dawn. "I must hurry. I wouldn't want the others to meet Nero—or the Master— without me."

"*We* must hurry," I said, though I was not sure that my feet would willingly carry me to my death.

"No, Quintus, you must return to Scythopolis—better yet, to Dalmanutha. Work with Mary. She's strong and her mind is open. Write the letter for me and write the truth about us who've tried to follow the Master. There's the true miracle, that clods like me could pray and fall and get up to pray again, that ignorant country bumpkins could spread the Master's message across the world. Simon Peter must die to give witness to the present; Quintus must live to give witness to the future."

I began to protest, undoubtedly more feebly than I wish to remember, but he mercifully cut me off: "I order it, Quintus, by the Master's commission to bind and loose, I bind you to obey me. Here, take the legate's purse. I won't need it."

I nodded. "Let me try to take Naomi and Jephthania with me."

"It would please me, but we both know it won't work. The Romans will have them soon enough. Even if we overtook them, they'd never agree to run away again; and they would never forgive us if we forced them. The Book of Wisdom tells us there's a proper time for everything. Now is the time for Simon Peter and his family to bear witness to the Master by their deaths. We've run away for the last time."

I embraced him. For once the heavy smell of Galilean sweat was welcome. He held me for a moment. "We both go to serve the Master, I in Rome, you in Galilee. He waits for both of us."

As he pulled away, he continued to hold my arms in his powerful hands and looked directly into my eyes. "Quintus, my old, old friend, stop philosophizing about the Lord. Criticize Him, accuse Him, rant at Him, call on Him to repent, but accept Him. Naomi and Jephthania have taught me to do that. Let me pass it on to you as my final gift. In that respect at least, be a Jew and not a Greek."

With that, he pushed me away, turned, and strode toward Rome, his back straight, his pace steady.

I waited a few more hours and walked back to Rome. As an aging philosopher, a citizen of Rome, a member of a wealthy family with a small but decent purse at his belt, a few relatives of good repute in the Eternal City, and the names of several wealthy merchants who, even in the wake of the great fires, would advance any reasonable sum on my cousins' account, I felt safe, as long, that is, as I met neither of the *praetores* or any of the soldiers who had arrested us. (I felt no fear of the legate.) I found lodgings with one of the sons of my father's youngest brother, who lived near Aristobulus's villa, in the area untouched by fire. He didn't seem happy to have me as his guest, but he could think of no proper way of turning out a homeless relative.

I listened to the news—Greek slaves were fertile sources of information—that it would be on the final night of the games that Simon Peter, the great Christian leader, would be executed. Two evenings later, I crossed to the other side of the Tiber near Vatican Hill and joined the crowd entering Nero's Circus. For almost an hour I sat there staring at the big, oval-shaped arena, almost 200 yards long and seventy-five yards wide. Around its edges ran a track perhaps fifteen yards wide. The center plot was decorated with twenty-five T-shaped crosses, shorter than the usual gibbets and with the crossbar already in place. They were arranged so that together they formed a huge T, no doubt Nero's personal touch of artistry.

Soon the first bevy of Christians staggered into the arena. As Marcus had said, their legs were free but their arms were bound. They were trying to sing; but they were wrapped in animal skins, and the muffled sound of their voices was drowned out by the noise from 30,000 Romans stamping their feet and chanting, "Bring on the dog meat! Bring on the dog meat! Dog meat! Dog meat! Bring on the dog meat!"

I kept my eyes tightly closed for the next half an hour, but I could not shut my ears to the savage snarls, the pitiful cries of agony from the children, or the even more horrible cracking of bones being torn from living bodies. The noise ebbed, then stopped, to be replaced by the sound of trainers recalling their dogs and sweepers piling the gory remains into one heap at the top of the great T.

Then the last group of Christians came in. Simon Peter was in the lead, carrying Jephthania on his arm for the final time. Naomi was by his side.

They were greeted by catcalls, but the dignity of Simon Peter and his people hushed the crowd as they awaited the hideous ritual of darkness, fire, and light. The brothers and sisters were singing a Greek variation on the Ninety-eighth psalm. It was a hymn of great joy, not mournful sorrow:

> Sing a new song unto the Lord; let your song be sung
>   from mountains high.
> Sing a new song unto the Lord, singing Alleluia.
>
> Rise, O children, from your sleep, your savior now has
>   come.
> He has turned your sorrow to joy and filled your soul
>   with song.
>
> Sing a new song unto the Lord; let your song be sung
>   from mountains high.
> Sing a new song unto the Lord, singing Alleluia.
>
> Glad my soul for I have seen the glory of the Lord.
> The trumpet sounds; the dead shall be raised;
>   I know my savior lives.

Once all were in the center of the arena, Nero's henchmen moved with efficiency honed by much recent practice. Starting at the rear ranks, soldiers began grabbing Christians and pulling them to crosses. The shortness of the posts meant the people had to be propped up rather than hanged, no doubt a compromise to keep the crowds from getting bored and the soldiers exhausted by the long process it took to hoist a human being onto a tall gibbet. The soldiers then roped the hands of each person to the crossbar and nailed the feet to the post.

The crowd remained silent, so that I could hear Simon Peter's voice ring out in perfect Greek: "The Master has died, the Master has been raised, the Master is with us all days."

A weak but clear "Amen" came from the others.

Then I saw a soldier try to pull Jephthania from Simon Peter's arms. For a moment I feared we would see the Simon Peter of old, but he merely kissed Jephthania and handed her to the Roman. Three other soldiers grabbed Simon Peter. He offered no resistance, but stretched out his hands for two of them to tie in front of him, while the third slipped a rope around him like a belt and pulled him toward the central cross at the head of the T. Naomi was weeping, but she followed behind alongside the soldier carrying Jephthania, meekly accepting death.

When all the crosses were full, soldiers carefully drove chariots through that evil forest of crooked trees and doused the victims with thick tar. For the last time, I heard Simon Peter's voice, now neither in Greek nor Aramaic, but Hebrew, chant the Shema: "Hear, O Israel, the Lord our God, the Lord is one!"

I could stand it no longer. I pushed my way through the crowd and came as close to running as I could, moving down the street that led from Vatican Hill to the Tiber. Although I did not look back, in a few moments the night became deep black. I had heard about the gruesome ritual. The soldiers had extinguished the torches around the arena. Then my way was suddenly illuminated by the reflection from a cruel flash of light that only slowly faded.

I hurried on, tears running down my cheeks. For a few moments I felt the same cold despair that had gripped me thirty-four years earlier on yet another hill of Roman slaughter. And I wanted to run again—away from Romans, away from Jews, away from Christians, away from Greeks, away from the world, even away from the Lord God Himself, to find a dark hole in which to bury my anguish, indeed, my very soul.

Then at last I, too, saw the risen Master. He did not dance like a ghost in the glow reflected from the walls along the river's banks or appear as a shining light in the sky. It was a real man I saw, the man I had followed around Galilee, young, as if the years had never come upon him. He placed his hand on my shoulder, his voice soft yet firm: "I have touched you," he said, and then he was gone.

There was nothing else. No praise for past deeds, no exhortation to future good works, no marching orders, not even a promise of eventual victory or reward; only a simple statement of a simple truth.

It was enough.

> As the Holy Spirit is my witness,
> given by my hand at Dalmanutha in
> Galilee, during the thirty-fifth
> year after the Resurrection,
>
> Q.

The Mediterranean World